Black Art of
Java
Game
Programming

Joel Fan, Eric Ries, Calin Tenitchi

WAITE GROUP PRESS™
A Division of Sams Publishing
CORTE MADERA, CA

Publisher: Mitchell Waite
Associate Publisher: Charles Drucker

Acquisitions Manager: Jill Pisoni
Acquisitions Editor: Joanne Miller

Editorial Director: John Crudo
Project Editor: Kurt Stephan
Content Editor: David Davis
Software Specialist: Dan Scherf
Copy Editor: Merilee Eggleston/Creative Solutions

Production Director: Julianne Ososke
Production Manager: Cecile Kaufman
Production Editor: K.D. Sullivan/Creative Solutions
Senior Designer: Sestina Quarequio
Designers: Karen Johnston, Jil Weil
Production: Ginny Bess, Carol Bowers, Bruce Clingaman, Cheryl Dietsch, Michael Henry, Lisa Pletka, Andrew Stone, Tim Tate
Illustrations: Larry Wilson
Cover Illustration: Greg Winters

Technical Review: Digital Connection™, New York, NY
                       Joachim Kim, General Manager
Reviewers: Michael St. Hippolyte, Joachim Kim, Mark Nichols,
                       R. Scott Schmitt

For more information regarding Digital Connection, see ad in back of book.

Printed in the United States of America
96 97 98 99 • 10 9 8 7 6 5 4 3 2 1

Library of Congress Cataloging-in-Publication Data
Fan, Joel, 1969-
    Black art of Java game programming / Joel Fan, Eric Ries, Calin Tenitchi.
        p.   cm.
    Includes index.
    ISBN 1-57169-043-3
    1. Java (Computer program language) 2. Video games. 3. World Wide Web (Information retrieval system)
I. Ries, Eric, 1978-   .   II. Tenitchi, Calin.   III. Title.
QA76.73.J38F36   1996
006.6'7--dc20
                                                                    96-33455
                                                                    CIP

Dedication

To all my friends everywhere.

—Joel Fan

To Mom, Dad, Nicole, Amanda, Nana, Brooke, Erica, Tony, Jessica, Clare, Ivy, Brendan, Keshia, Beth, Irene, and everyone else who has helped and put up with me.

—Eric Ries

I dedicate this book to my parents for their unquestioning support.

—Calin Tenitchi

Message from the
Publisher

WELCOME TO OUR NERVOUS SYSTEM

Some people say that the World Wide Web is a graphical extension of the information superhighway, just a network of humans and machines sending each other long lists of the equivalent of digital junk mail.

I think it is much more than that. To me, the Web is nothing less than the nervous system of the entire planet—not just a collection of computer brains connected together, but more like a billion silicon neurons entangled and recirculating electro-chemical signals of information and data, each contributing to the birth of another CPU and another Web site.

Think of each person's hard disk connected at once to every other hard disk on earth, driven by human navigators searching like Columbus for the New World. Seen this way the Web is more of a super entity, a growing, living thing, controlled by the universal human will to expand, to be more. Yet, unlike a purposeful business plan with rigid rules, the Web expands in a nonlinear, unpredictable, creative way that echoes natural evolution.

We created our Web site not just to extend the reach of our computer book products but to be part of this synaptic neural network, to experience, like a nerve in the body, the flow of ideas and then to pass those ideas up the food chain of the mind. Your mind. Even more, we wanted to pump some of our own creative juices into this rich wine of technology.

TASTE OUR DIGITAL WINE

And so we ask you to taste our wine by visiting the body of our business. Begin by understanding the metaphor we have created for our Web site—a universal learning center, situated in outer space in the form of a space station. A place where you can journey to study any topic from the convenience of your own screen. Right now we are focusing on computer topics, but the stars are the limit on the Web.

If you are interested in discussing this Web site or finding out more about the Waite Group, please send me e-mail with your comments, and I will be happy to respond. Being a programmer myself, I love to talk about technology and find out what our readers are looking for.

200 Tamal Plaza
Corte Madera, CA 94925
415-924-2575
415-924-2576 fax

Website:
http://www.waite.com/waite

Sincerely,

Mitchell Waite

CREATING THE HIGHEST QUALITY COMPUTER BOOKS IN THE INDUSTRY

Waite Group Press

Come Visit
WAITE.COM
Waite Group Press
World Wide Web Site

Now find all the latest information on Waite Group books at our new Web site, **http://www.waite.com/waite.** You'll find an online catalog where you can examine and order any title, review upcoming books, and send e-mail to our authors and editors. Our FTP site has all you need to update your book: the latest program listings, errata sheets, most recent versions of Fractint, POV Ray, Polyray, DMorph, and all the programs featured in our books. So download, talk to us, ask questions, on **http://www.waite.com/waite.**

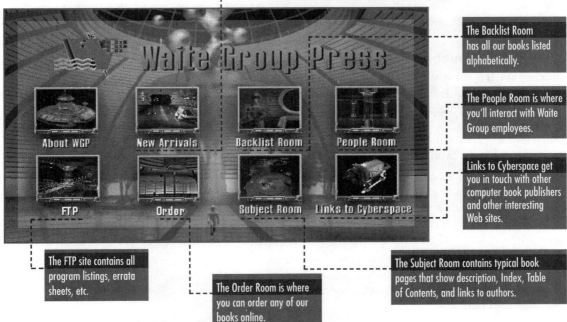

The New Arrivals Room has all our new books listed by month. Just click for a description, Index, Table of Contents, and links to authors.

The Backlist Room has all our books listed alphabetically.

The People Room is where you'll interact with Waite Group employees.

Links to Cyberspace get you in touch with other computer book publishers and other interesting Web sites.

The FTP site contains all program listings, errata sheets, etc.

The Order Room is where you can order any of our books online.

The Subject Room contains typical book pages that show description, Index, Table of Contents, and links to authors.

World Wide Web:

COME SURF OUR TURF—THE WAITE GROUP WEB

http://www.waite.com/waite
Gopher: gopher.waite.com
FTP: ftp.waite.com

About the Authors

Joel Fan is an expert programmer and multimedia developer in Java, C/C++, and Macromedia Director. He has worked as a programmer, analyst, and developer for many years on the PC/UNIX/Macintosh platforms, on projects ranging from the cosmic (the Hopkins Ultraviolet Telescope) to the comic (an animation teaching toolkit) to the downright serious (currently, cryptographic and security development using the SSLava SSL/Java toolkit). He has published papers in the field of computer vision, and holds degrees in computer science from Harvard University and The Johns Hopkins University.

Eric Ries, an undergraduate at Yale University and freelance technical writer, has been developing Java applets since the very early days of Java's alpha release. He enjoys all manifestations of computer programming, as well as writing, which he does in his spare time. In addition to this project, he has recently completed work for Sybex and the *Java Developer's Journal*. He is a founding member of TeamJava (http://teamjava.com) and a member of the Southern California Web Programmers' Forum (scwpf).

Calin Tenitchi is currently pursuing his M.S. degree in computer sciences at Lunds Institute of Technology in Sweden. He also runs a successful consulting firm with his business partner Mathias Lagerwall that specializes in Java applications and intranet solutions. Calin always likes to be on the cutting edge of new and exciting technologies like Java, and is happy to be living in an age in which technology evolves at an amazing pace.

Game Gallery Contributors:

Roman Mach is currently designing and managing engineering projects for Web applications at Saltmine Creative, Inc., a Seattle-based Web design and engineering company. Roman has written C and assembly applications in performance-critical areas such as remote radio-telephony software, server-side search engines, and mobile robotics. He has a Masters in electrical engineering from the University of Washington. Roman's interests include mountain biking, bass playing, and road tripping. His work can be explored at his Web site: http://www.halcyon.com/mach.

Ethan Koehler is presently studying for a Masters in business administration at Marquette University, as well as doing consulting for companies interested in the Web. Much of his technical background comes from his management computer systems degree from the University of Wisconsin-Whitewater and far too many years of staring at computer screens. Like many of his fellow programmers, Ethan enjoys quiet, romantic nights and long walks on the beach, as well as industrial music.

Kyle Palmer is a student at the University of Alberta studying computing science at the Bachelors level. His computing-related interests include algorithm design and World Wide Web technologies, including VRML and Java. Kyle is also an enthusiastic member of the University of Alberta Juggling Club and performs in the Edmonton area.

Steve Green is a self-employed computer consultant. He is married to Adrienne; they have two wonderful daughters, Nikki and Alix. In his spare time, Steve enjoys cycling and Tae Kwon Do.

Zuwei Thomas Feng is a Ph.D. student in the math department at Princeton University, specializing in algebraic geometry. He loves to write computer programs for fun. More examples of his work can be found on his home page: http://www.math.princeton.edu/~ztfeng/.

Table of Contents

Contents

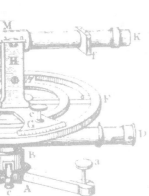

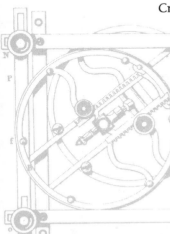

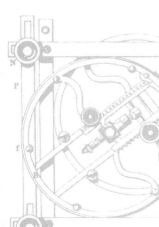

Acknowledgments

First of all, thanks to the entire Waite Group Press team, especially Jill Pisoni, who shepherded me through the acquisitions process; Kurt Stephan, who has been a wonderful, understanding project editor; and Mitchell Waite for providing the vision behind this book. Many thanks to Dave Davis for his helpful suggestions and edits, K.D. Sullivan for her masterful handling of production editing, and the team of tech reviewers at Digital Connection.

Finally, I'd like to thank my parents, my brother Brian, and my sister Grace for their encouragement and support; Victor Boyko for his comments, criticisms, and suggestions; and Irina Srubshchik, who has been a part of this project from the beginning to the end.

—Joel Fan

Thanks to Tony Long for providing figures and graphics for Chapters 8, 9, 15, and 16; to Jessica Rubles-English for help with graphics and animation in Chapter 15; and to Erica Maxion, Clare Long, and Marie Long for artistic consulting.

—Eric Ries

I'd like to thank Mathias Lagerwall for helping me complete this project, and my girlfriend Jenny for putting up with my lifestyle. Thanks, as well, to my parents and, of course, all my friends. I would also like to thank LTH for being an outstanding educational facility, and the creators of the ancient '80s game Cholo for lighting up my interest in 3D graphics as a kid.

—Calin Tenitchi

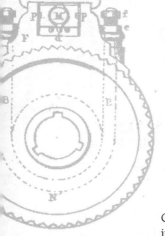

Introduction

Gaming on the Web is the next blockbuster business. Have any doubts? The video game industry, which already eclipses Hollywood in terms of revenue, targets the Web as the next huge growth area. Software developers are busily porting games to the online environment, or developing entirely new ones. And numerous popular Web sites, many of which charge fees, are devoted to game entertainment.

With *Black Art of Java Game Programming*, you'll learn how to create your own dynamic online entertainment using the Java programming language. Java heralds a revolutionary shift in gaming, away from the desktop and into the network. Using Java, you'll create games that people can download through the Web and play. Using Java, you'll enable players from around the world to compete against one another. As Java enters its maturity, the possibilities of creating innovative entertainment are endless, and the potential for profit unbounded.

This book provides you with the foundations for creating Java games of all types, such as board games, video games, and networked/multiplayer games. We recommend that you have some basic knowledge of C, C++, or Java before diving in. The underlying thread of this book is that good object-oriented design and good Java games go hand in hand, so we devote the early chapters of the book to covering and applying object-oriented principles to graphics and games. Once the foundations have been laid, we build a wide variety of games. As you will see, game programming is almost a game in itself, and once you learn the basics, you'll be well equipped to write innovative games on your own.

Organization

Black Art of Java Game Programming is divided into three parts:

Part I, Fundamentals of Java Game Development
Part II, Advanced Game and Graphics Techniques
Part III, Game Gallery

Part I, Fundamentals

Part I takes you on a whirlwind tour of Java, graphics, and object-oriented game programming. This section is for you if you're learning Java, if you're new to object-oriented design, or if you want to see how to build a game step by step.

This is what's covered in the Fundamentals section:

Chapter 1, "Fundamental Java," delivers a turbocharged introduction to the Java language, the API, and object-oriented design. By the end, you'll create graphics applets.

Chapter 2, "Using Objects for Animation," shows you how classes, inheritance, and dynamic method binding help you animate objects. You'll also learn about clipping and double-buffering, two basic graphics techniques.

Chapter 3, "Animating Sprites," teaches you to create a simple abstract class for representing graphics objects called sprites. In addition, you'll learn about interfaces, bitmap animation, and sound.

Chapter 4, "Adding Interactivity," shows you how to create applets that respond in real time to player input.

Chapter 5, "Building a Video Game," shows you how to apply what you've learned in the first four chapters to create a shoot-'em-up video game. What you learn here can be applied to creating many other types of games.

Chapter 6, "Extending Your Video Game," shows you how to take a game that you've developed and add new features to it without starting from scratch.

Chapter 7, "Creating Customizable Games with the AWT," demonstrates how Java's Abstract Windowing Toolkit allows players to change parameters in your games. What you learn here about the AWT will be applied throughout the rest of the book.

Part II, Advanced Game and Graphics Techniques

In Part II, you'll learn the skills necessary to bring your games into the next dimension, such as multithreading, networking and multiplayer techniques, and 3D.

Chapter 8, "Implementing a High Score Server on a Network," takes you through Java's networking and GUI facilities, and teaches you to build a high score server for your games.

Chapter 9, "Advanced Networking and Multiplayer Gaming Concepts," illustrates techniques for enabling multiuser game play over the Web. In addition, you'll deepen your understanding of Java's networking capabilities by implementing a chat room.

Chapter 10, "Advanced Techniques," covers features of Java and the Java API that are useful in writing games and organizing programs.

Chapter 11, "Into the Third Dimension," demonstrates the process of defining, transforming, projecting, and painting three-dimensional models, and builds classes that can be used to make a simple 3D engine.

Chapter 12, "Building 3D Applets with App3Dcore," shows how the App3Dcore (a set of classes) works and how it can be used to develop some simple 3D applets and an advanced 3D game.

Part III, Game Gallery

In Part III, you'll apply the skills you've learned in earlier chapters as leading Java game designers take you step by step through the creation of a wide spectrum of cool games.

Chapter 13, "Building the JAVAroids Game," shows you how to create a Java version of the video game classic Asteroids.

Chapter 14, "Daleks!," takes you through the creation of an enhanced Java version of a classic computer game.

Chapter 15, "NetOthello," builds on your networking skills learned in earlier chapters to create a networked implementation of the classic game Othello.

Chapter 16, "WordQuest," takes you through the creation of a Java game specifically designed to teach vocabulary, but which could easily be extended to teach a plethora of other concepts, demonstrating Java's potential as a learning tool.

Chapter 17, "The Magic Squares Puzzle," is an example of a deceptively simple, yet challenging puzzle game that will delight Rubik's Cube enthusiasts (and many others).

Chapter 18, "The Internet MahJong Server," demonstrates a software package that allows people to play the classic Chinese strategy game MahJong with each other online.

Chapter 19, "Slider Puzzle," shows you how to write a Java applet for a simple slider puzzle enhanced with animation and sound.

Chapter 20, "The Game of Worm," develops a game in which you control the direction of a virtual worm on a rectangular playing surface, collecting treats while avoiding collision with solid objects.

What's on the CD-ROM?

The CD-ROM included with *Black Art of Java Game Programming* contains the project files and source code for examples in Parts I and II of the book, as well as all applets and source code for all the games included in Part III, Game Gallery.

How the CD Is Structured

Source code, examples, and projects for the tutorial chapters of *Black Art of Java Game Programming* (Parts I and II) are found in a directory called BOOK at the root of the CD-ROM. Within this BOOK directory are subdirectories for Chapters 1 through 12, which contain all code and examples for their accompanying chapters. Games from the Game Gallery section of the book (Part III) are included in subdirectories for Chapters 13 through 20 in a directory at the root of the CD called GAMES. The Java Developer's Kit (JDK) version 1.0.2 for Macintosh, Solaris, Windows 95, and Windows NT is included in the root directory JDK. All the materials on the CD-ROM in ZIP or TAR format are included in the root directory ARCHIVES. Please refer to the Read Me on the CD for complete information about the contents of the directories.

Installation

Please refer to the Read Me file at the root level of the CD-ROM for detailed instructions on installation of the included files, JDK, games, bonus items, and any late-breaking updates.

We hope you'll enjoy *Black Art of Java Game Programming* and will tell us about the games that you've created!

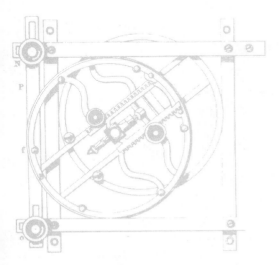

Part I

Fundamentals of Java Game Development

1

Fundamental Java

Joel Fan

ome tutti fioni le manovelle el lequali produono ellalsa
e grape si muove lementa di igonesso sategrano tibone
gare nellamodo elsa permanrtosta alsa manovella pegi qua u
forga o più i somo possibili.

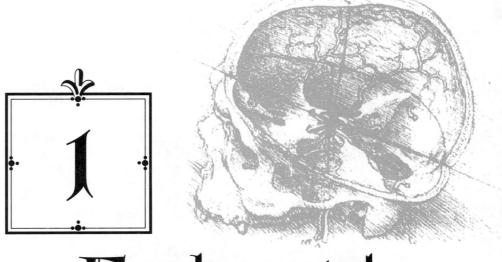

1

Fundamental Java

Goals:

Understand the fundamentals of Java

Understand basics of object-oriented design

Create simple Java graphics applets

You've heard about Java, and you've seen what it does for the World Wide Web. Imagine what *you* can do with it. In this chapter, you'll get a quick jump on learning Java and creating graphics with Java. You'll also learn about object-oriented programming, which is necessary for unleashing the full power of Java. By the end of this chapter, you'll know how to use Java to create a graphics applet that will spice up any Web page. So hold on to your mouse for an exciting ride!

But first, *what exactly is Java?*

What Is Java?

Java is a programming language that's engineered for the demands of the Internet. Although Java is a relatively new language (the 1.0 release appeared early in 1996), it has received intense media coverage and even engendered speculation about seismic shifts in the software industry! Let's see why Java has created such excitement, and why it's an innovative platform for creating games. First of all, you should understand how Java dramatically changes the nature of the World Wide Web.

The World Wide Web

The World Wide Web, simply put, is a collection of hyperlinked documents that reside on computers throughout the world. Figure 1-1 shows a diagram of the Web.

The Web achieves its wide reach by allowing computers connected to the Internet to request and transmit documents using the Web protocol. This protocol, called HTTP (HyperText Transfer Protocol), is based on the *client-server* paradigm: a *client* requests a service, and a *server* fulfills this request. Thus, a Web client requests a document from

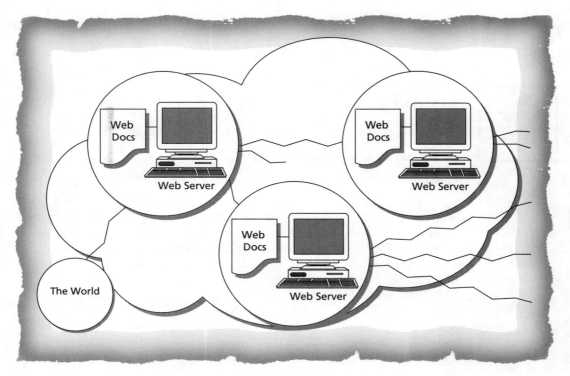

Figure 1-1 ◉ *The World Wide Web*

a Web server, and the server returns the desired document. The interaction that occurs between a Web client and server is illustrated in Figure 1-2.

The most common type of Web client is a *browser*, such as Netscape's Navigator or Microsoft's Internet Explorer. Browsers allow you to request documents by pointing and clicking, and they display Web documents in an attractive format.

The appearance of the document on your screen is suggested by the HTML (HyperText Markup Language) tags embedded in the document. HTML controls such things as the formatting of text or the alignment of an image, but it doesn't provide facilities for creating dynamic multimedia, such as animations or video games. In other words, once an HTML document is loaded and displayed, it doesn't do anything (unless it contains an animated GIF). As a result, the HTML documents found on most Web pages are static and unchanging. For example, Figure 1-3 shows an HTML document as displayed by a Web browser. The actual Web page is as passive as the figure in this book.

Now let's see how a Java applet can liven up an HTML document.

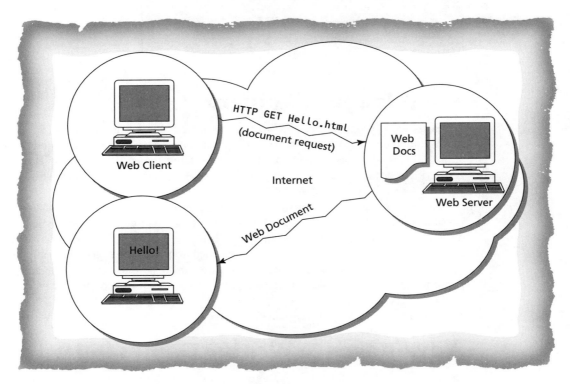

Figure 1-2 ◉ *Interaction between a Web client and server*

FIGURE 1-3

◉ ◉ ◉ ◉ ◉ ◉

*Web page
and HTML
document*

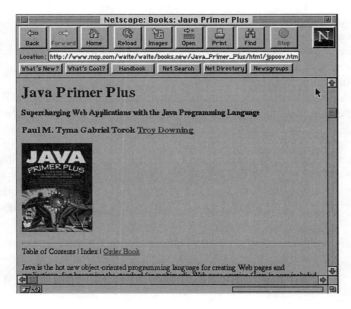

What Is a Java Applet?

A Java *applet* is a program that a browser can download and execute. To add an applet to a Web document, you insert an HTML tag that tells the browser where to find the applet. The browser loads the HTML document and the applet. When the applet finishes loading, it runs on the client computer. Figure 1-4 illustrates the interaction between the Web server, browser, and applet.

Since Java is a full-fledged programming language, applets can do things that aren't possible with HTML. For example, you can create animations and other dynamic multimedia presentations with Java applets, such as games. Applets can open a network connection back to the server they were downloaded from, which enables you to implement chat rooms and multiplayer games. Since applets run on the local computer, interactive performance is relatively quick and stable. Thus, you can create a video game applet and include it on a Web page.

Now that you know what Java can do, let's see why you should write games with it.

Advantages to Writing Games in Java

Here are five reasons that make Java a great environment for writing games:

 It allows you to distribute your games on the Web. The Web is a revolutionary medium for the distribution of information, such as news, music, intergalactic pictures, and—software! With Java, you can create games that

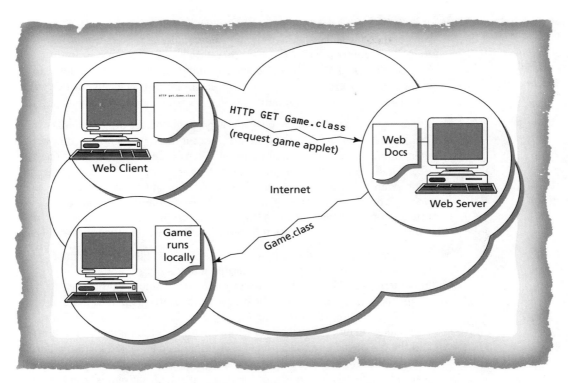

Figure 1-4 ◉ *Interaction between Web server, browser, and applet*

anybody with a Web browser can access. This means an instant worldwide audience, and it's a vast improvement over writing games that only your kids have access to.

 It supports multiple platforms. In many programming environments, programs are compiled and linked to create executable code that is specific to a particular platform. In contrast, a Java program compiles to *bytecode*, which is executed by the Java virtual machine (JVM). The JVM isn't a real computer, but an abstract machine that can be simulated on many computers, regardless of CPU or OS. Thus, any platform that implements the JVM will be able to run your bytecode. In addition, by using Java's Abstract Windowing Toolkit (AWT), your game can have the appropriate look and feel regardless of the underlying window system. In concrete terms, this means you can compile a Java game once, and it will run on any computer that has a Java-enabled browser, such as the Netscape Navigator. The combination of multiplatform support and worldwide distribution over the Web gives Java games the widest possible audience.

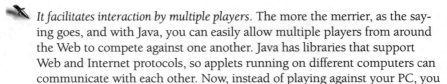 *It facilitates interaction by multiple players.* The more the merrier, as the saying goes, and with Java, you can easily allow multiple players from around the Web to compete against one another. Java has libraries that support Web and Internet protocols, so applets running on different computers can communicate with each other. Now, instead of playing against your PC, you can challenge Joe from Denmark.

It is an object-oriented programming language. Being object-oriented makes Java a great language to write games in, since it helps you manage complexity and reuse your code, thereby cutting down on development time. The object metaphor is ideal for creating graphics and games. Although diehard C programmers may scoff at the additional overhead used by object-oriented programs at runtime, some benchmarks show that an object-oriented program may even run faster than a comparable program written in a procedural style! (Of course, it depends on who's writing the program...)

It is simple. Java is a simple language in several ways. First, Java's syntax resembles that of C and C++, so it is simple to learn for C and C++ programmers. Second, Java eliminates features from C and C++ that the designers of Java felt were redundant or led to poorly written or insecure code. The result is a smaller, simpler language than either C or C++. Third, Java makes memory management simple, with the elimination of pointers and the use of garbage collection to reclaim unused allocated memory. This removes a common source of bugs and frustration. The simplicity of Java makes games easier to understand and debug, which simplifies your task as a programmer.

Other Benefits

The benefits of Java go far beyond its use on the Web. Java's blend of multiplatform, multithreaded, and networking capabilities bring the promise of a universal OS closer to reality. For example, you can compile stand-alone applications once and execute the code on a diverse set of architectures, eliminating the need for porting your code. You can make use of Java's communication and multithreaded capabilities to create applications that incorporate the decision-making powers of a heterogeneous network of computers. Java heralds a new age in computing, with you at the helm!

Current Limitations to Writing Games in Java

Since this all sounds like an advertisement for using Java, let's mention two disadvantages to writing games in Java:

Interpreted Java code is 10 to 20 times slower than comparable compiled C++ code. Although this seems like a huge gap, Java's performance is adequate for many types of games. In addition, the promised release of the Java "just-in-time" compiler and specialized Java chips will bring the speed of Java to C++ levels. The performance gap between Java and C++ will be less of a concern in the near future.

The abstraction provided by the Java virtual machine and Abstract Windowing Toolkit makes platform-specific optimizations and tricks difficult. For example, you won't be able to rely on a really cool feature of a particular video board without eliminating the multiplatform nature of your applet. So the tradeoff here is between specialized performance and wide distribution.

Now it's time for an advanced introduction to Java. We're going to start with object-oriented fundamentals.

Object-Oriented Fundamentals

Java is an *object-oriented* language, and to use Java effectively, you need to build your programs and games in an object-oriented manner. While traditional languages such as C treat data as passive entities that are manipulated by procedures, object-oriented languages bundle data together with the procedures that operate on the data. This bundle is called an *object*. When writing Java games, you need to think in terms of the states and behaviors of the objects involved.

Thinking with States and Behaviors

Look at the room around you. You'll see lots of things, such as lamps, computers, a piano, and a pet dog, if your room looks anything like mine. How might you represent these things in a computer program? One way is to model the *states* that the thing can be in, and the *behaviors* that the thing exhibits. States are usually described by nouns and adjectives (speed, energy, color, rich, happy), whereas behaviors correspond to verbs (attacking, firing, driving, flipping, vomiting). An object, with its bundle of data and procedures, allows you to represent the functionality of real-world (and imaginary-world) things with their states and behaviors. Here are some examples.

Let's start with a lamp. A lamp exists in two states: on or off. By turning the knob on the lamp, you change the lamp state. So the behavior of a lamp is flipping from on to off, or off to on. State is essentially a passive concept—a thing exists in various states. Behavior is action and doing—the transition from state to state, for example.

The only way to turn a lamp on or off is by turning the knob. Put another way, you can't alter the lamp's state without using the knob. The lamp's state is shielded, or *encapsulated*, from the outside world. The knob is the lamp's *interface* to the world—the point at which another object can send a *message* to the lamp to switch states.

Figure 1-5 shows one way of representing a lamp object. The lamp's state, shown as the inner circle of the diagram, is protected by the knob, which is the lamp's interface.

Here's another example of an object—an alien UFO in a shoot-'em-up video game. The UFO states and behaviors will depend on the actual game, of course, but let's see what they might be. The UFO object is either dead or alive, so being dead or alive is one aspect of the UFO's state. Other aspects might include direction, speed, or energy left. UFO behaviors could include updating position, changing direction, or dying. When does a UFO interact with other objects? Perhaps when you've fired a missile at it, and the missile scores a direct hit. The missile object sends a message to the UFO object— you've been hit!—and the UFO blows up. The UFO has an interface so other objects can notify it when a collision has occurred. A diagram of the UFO object we've described is shown in Figure 1-6. Of course, the actual state and behaviors will depend on the particular game.

Now that you've defined the states and behaviors of an object, you can define the *class* that it belongs to. Let's see how to do this.

Defining a Class

By defining a class, you construct a new type from which you can create actual objects. A Java class resembles a struct in C, except that it can hold *methods* as well. (A method is an object-oriented term for a function or procedure.) As an example, let's create a Lamp class, based on our discussion in the preceding section. Here it is:

FIGURE 1-5

Diagram of lamp object

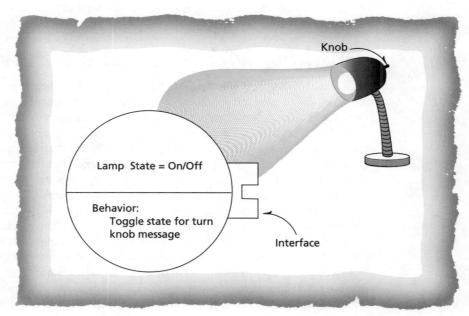

FIGURE 1-6
◎ ◎ ◎ ◎ ◎ ◎
Diagram of UFO object

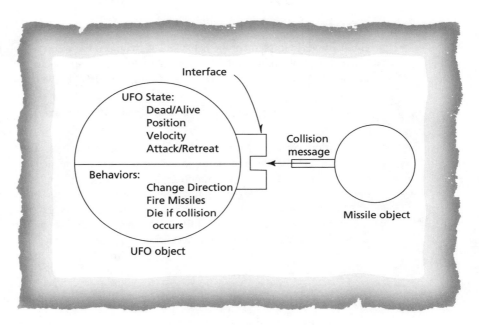

```
class Lamp {
   private boolean lampIsOn;   // instance variable
   public void turnKnob() {    // method
     lampIsOn = !lampIsOn;
   }
   public Lamp() {             // constructor
     lampIsOn = false;
   }
}
```

This tiny class illustrates the three elements found in most class definitions: variables, methods, and constructors. Let's discuss them in turn.

Variables

Use variables to represent the state of an object. For example, the state of a Lamp object is on or off, so a boolean variable, which takes on the values *true* or *false*, will suffice:

```
private boolean lampIsOn;
```

lampIsOn is an example of an *instance variable*, which means that each Lamp object will have its own copy of *lampIsOn*. Declare variables in the same manner as you would in C.

Methods

Use methods to implement the behaviors of an object. For example, when another object "turns the knob" of a Lamp object, its state flips between on and off. The turnKnob() method implements this behavior by toggling *lampIsOn* between *true* and *false*.

```
public void turnKnob() {
  lampIsOn = !lampIsOn; // ! is unary negation operator
}
```

Other objects will call turnKnob() to alter the state of the lamp. The turnKnob() method is the interface between the Lamp object and external objects.

A Java method looks like a function definition in C, except that it occurs within the declaration of a class. Methods are called "member functions" in C++ terminology.

The keywords *public* and *private* are access modifiers—they specify the visibility of the variables or methods that follow. A *public* variable or method can be directly accessed by all other objects; a *private* variable or method can only be accessed by a method in a class where the *private* member is defined. You'll learn about two other access levels—*protected* and *default*—in the following chapters.

Constructors

A constructor method is called to initialize an object. Constructors have the same name as the class, and they do not specify a return type. For example, the Lamp() method is a constructor that initializes the value of *lampIsOn* to *false*.

```
public Lamp() {
   lampIsOn = false;
}
```

As you see, the aspects of objects that we've discussed—state, behavior, and interface—have a direct mapping into Java. The state of an object is stored in one or more variables defined in the class. Similarly, behaviors correspond to methods that are defined within the class of the object. These methods are able to access and manipulate the object variables. Finally, the interface of the object is the set of methods that external objects can invoke. Thus, the functionality of an object, as expressed by its variables and methods, is defined in the class of the object.

Creating an Object

Creating an object of a particular class is also known as creating an *instance* of the class, or *instantiating* an object. For example, let's create an instance of the Lamp class.

First, declare a variable that refers to a Lamp object:

```
Lamp lamp;
```

To allocate a new Lamp object that the *lamp* variable refers to, use

```
lamp = new Lamp();
```

The *new* keyword dynamically allocates memory for a Lamp object, and calls the Lamp()
constructor for initialization.

Of course, you can instantiate many Lamp objects:

```
Lamp lamp1 = new Lamp();
Lamp lamp2 = new Lamp();
...
Lamp lamp17 = new Lamp();
```

This creates 17 Lamp instances, each with its own copy of instance variable
lampIsOn.

Accessing Object Variables and Methods

To refer to a variable of a given object, use the following construction (the same notation is used in C to select struct members):

```
objectName.variable
```

Similarly, to invoke a method of an object, use

```
objectName.method();
```

Here's an example.

Each lamp's turnKnob() method can be used by other objects to send a message to
that particular lamp. If any object wants to send turnKnob() messages to *lamp1* and *lamp13*,
it would use the following statements:

```
lamp1.turnKnob();  // turn lamp1's knob
lamp13.turnKnob(); // turn lamp13's knob
```

A *public* method like turnKnob(), or a *public* variable, is visible from methods of any
object.

On the other hand, access to *private* variables and methods is restricted to the class
that defines the *private* members. For example, the *private* variable *lampIsOn* can be modified by the turnKnob() method, as both are members of the Lamp class. A non-Lamp
object can't access *lampIsOn* directly, as in

```
lamp7.lampIsOn = true; // violates private visibility
```

Now, let's talk briefly about *inheritance*, which is another key to object-oriented design.

Inheritance

You've inherited physical characteristics from your parents, such as hair or eye color.
Similarly, a class can inherit the states and behaviors of another class. By using inheritance, you can structure relationships between classes of objects, which makes the code
for your games easier to understand.

One relationship that occurs often is when one class is a specialization, or refinement, of another. For example, a strobe lamp is a lamp that alternates automatically between on and off. A colored lamp is a lamp that gives light with a particular color. And all three—lamp, strobe lamp, and colored lamp—are objects.

Inheritance allows you to reuse code that's been written for the Lamp class in the definitions of StrobeLamp and ColoredLamp. In particular, the StrobeLamp class can *inherit* the public variables and methods of Lamp. Put another way, the StrobeLamp class *extends* the definition of Lamp by providing additional variables and methods to the public members of Lamp. The keyword *extends* indicates inheritance in Java. Here are the definitions of Lamp and StrobeLamp:

```java
class Lamp {
   private boolean lampIsOn;  // instance variable
   public void turnKnob() {   // method
     lampIsOn = !lampIsOn;
   }
   public Lamp() {            // constructor
     lampIsOn = false;
   }
}

// StrobeLamp inherits public members from Lamp

class StrobeLamp extends Lamp {
  private int strobeRate;       // instance variable
  public setStrobeRate(int s) { // method
    strobeRate = s;
  }
}
```

The public method turnKnob(), defined in the Lamp class, is inherited by StrobeLamp. It's as if StrobeLamp had copied the code for turnKnob() directly in its declaration. Thus, an instance of StrobeLamp understands the message turnKnob(), even though this method isn't defined in the interior of StrobeLamp.

Similarly, ColoredLamp can inherit from Lamp. The Lamp class is called the *parent* or *superclass*, and StrobeLamp and ColoredLamp are both *subclasses*. Furthermore, the Object class (defined in the Java API) is the parent of the Lamp class. Every class in Java automatically inherits from the Object class.

The *inheritance* (or *class*) *hierarchy* we've described is shown in Figure 1-7.

Using objects and inheritance effectively is really important to writing games in Java, and we'll flesh out these concepts in the next few chapters. This section introduced many new terms (and there are a few more coming!), so here's a glossary to help you out.

FIGURE 1-7
◎ ◎ ◎ ◎ ◎ ◎
*Inheritance
hierarchy*

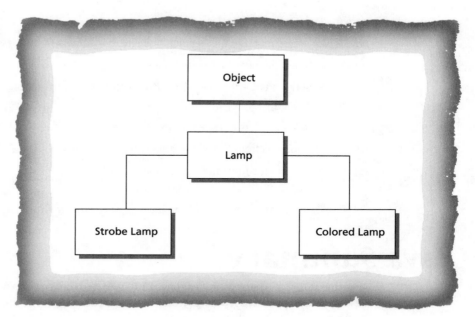

▦ Object-Oriented Terminology

behavior   What an object does. Usually corresponds to a verb (driving, attacking, laughing).

class   A template for creating objects. Consists of a collection of variable and method definitions.

class hierarchy   The inheritance relationships between classes.

constructor   A method that has the same name as the class. It initializes a new object.

encapsulation   Hiding information (data and methods) from the outside.

extends   A Java keyword that indicates inheritance.

inheritance   Creating new classes by reusing code from existing classes.

instance   An object.

instance variable/method   A variable/method associated with an object.

interface   The members of an object accessible from the outside.

message   An invocation of a method.

method   A function that occurs in a class declaration.

object   A bundle of data and methods.

continued on next page

continued from previous page

parent class Same as superclass.

private An access modifier that restricts visibility to members of the class.

public An access modifier that permits all access.

state The modes an object can exist in. Usually corresponds to a noun or adjective (hungry, sad, energy level).

static variable/method A variable/method associated with a class.

subclass If X inherits from Y, X is a subclass of Y.

superclass If X inherits from Y, Y is the superclass of X.

Now it's time for a summary of the Java language and environment.

Java Summary

Let's summarize the basic aspects of Java. This is a brief, bird's-eye view to get you started as quickly as possible, so don't worry if you don't catch everything. The details will be fleshed out in the following chapters.

The Java system can be divided into three major components:

The Java core. This consists of the base language and fundamental classes you'll use in your programs.

The Java API. These are the standard libraries of classes that you may use with your programs.

The Java interpreter. This loads, verifies, and executes your program.

The interplay of these components gives Java many of its benefits. Let's examine each component in turn.

The Java Core

Java's syntax resembles C and C++. However, the syntactic similarities belie some important semantic differences. In the following, we'll briefly cover

Data types. We'll discuss primitive types, arrays, classes, and objects.

Instance, static, and final variables and methods.

Memory management. Java's garbage collector frees unused memory for you.

Packages. These are groups of classes.

Operators. Java uses most of the operators found in C.

Control flow. Java's control flow constructs are practically the same as C's.

Advanced features. Java includes support for threads and exceptions.

Major differences between Java, C, and C++.

Primitive Data Types

In addition to the basic types found in C, Java supports *boolean* and *byte* types. Listing 1-1 shows the syntax of the primitive types, which looks reassuringly like C.

Listing 1-1 *Primitive types in Java*

```
/* this is a comment */
// this is also a comment

class PrimitiveTypes {
  /* integer types */
  byte b = 37;        // signed 8 bits
  short s = 7;        // signed 16 bits
  int i = 2013;       // signed 32 bit
  long l = 200213L;   // signed 64 bits; trailing 'l' or
                      //    'L' indicates a long literal

  /* floating point types */
  float f = 232.42f; // 32 bits; trailing 'f' or 'F'
                     //    indicates a float literal

  double d = 177.77; // 64 bits; without a 'f' means
                     //             a double literal

  /* boolean type */
  boolean t = true;  // true and false are the only allowable
  boolean f = false; //    values allowed for a boolean.
                     // Casts between booleans and numeric types
                        are not allowed.

  /* character type */
  char c = 'J';        // unsigned 16 bit Unicode character
}
```

These primitive data types are *passed by value* to Java methods. In other words, when a variable of a primitive type is passed to a method, its value is copied to the formal parameter. This is illustrated in a sample program (Listing 1-4).

Arrays

To create an array, you need to declare a variable that refers to the array, and then allocate space for the array using the *new* keyword.

For example, here's how to declare a variable that refers to an array of int:

```
int intArray[];
```

or

```
int[] intArray;
```

intArray is a *reference* to an array of integers. The default value for an array variable such as *intArray* is *null*, which indicates an absence of reference. Figure 1-8 shows what an unallocated array looks like.

To allocate space for an array, use the *new* keyword:

```
intArray = new int[17]; // array of 17 integers
```

Now the *intArray* variable refers to the allocated memory, as shown in Figure 1-9.

Another way of creating an array is by explicitly initializing it, using the usual C syntax:

```
char charArray[] = { 'r', 'n', 'a', 'I', 'I'};
```

Arrays are 0-indexed, and individual array elements are accessed using subscript notation:

```
intArray[7] = 13;  // assign 13 to the 8th element of intArray
```

Array accesses are checked for legality at runtime; attempting to access array elements that are out of bounds throws an *exception*.

FIGURE 1-8
◎ ◎ ◎ ◎ ◎ ◎
Unallocated array

intArray   null

FIGURE 1-9
◎ ◎ ◎ ◎ ◎ ◎
Allocated array

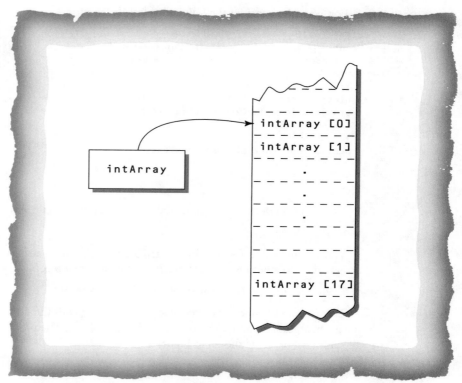

Every array has a *length* field, which stores the size of the array. For example, the length of *intArray* is

```
intArray.length
```

Since an array variable is a reference to array contents, these contents can be modified when the array is passed to a Java method. For example, in the following method call:

```
myclass.method(intArray);
```

the contents of *intArray* can be modified in the body of myclass.method(). You'll see an example of this in Listing 1-4.

Classes and Objects

As you've seen above, the concepts of class and object go hand in hand. A class declares a bundle of data and methods that are associated with the class name; an object is an instance of a class. When you declare a class, you're creating a new type that can be used in variable declarations. To create an object of a given class, declare a variable that refers to the object, and then allocate space for the object using the *new* keyword. (This process is analogous to creating a Java array.)

For example, consider the following class declaration:

```
class Foo {
  int x = 0;            // instance variable
  int add(int a) {      // instance method
    x += a;
  }
  static float y;       // class variable
  static void minus() { // class method
    x -= 1;
  }
  public Foo(float z) { // constructor
    y = z;
  }
}
```

Now you can declare a variable that refers to a Foo object:

```
Foo f;
```

The default value for an object variable is *null*, which means that the variable doesn't refer to anything (yet). Here's how to create the object:

```
f = new Foo(13.0); // allocation and initialization
```

This statement allocates memory for a Foo object, calls the Foo() constructor with the given argument, and sets *f* to refer to the new object. The process of declaring and allocating an object is shown in Figure 1-10.

FIGURE 1-10
◎ ◎ ◎ ◎ ◎ ◎
Declaring and allocating an object

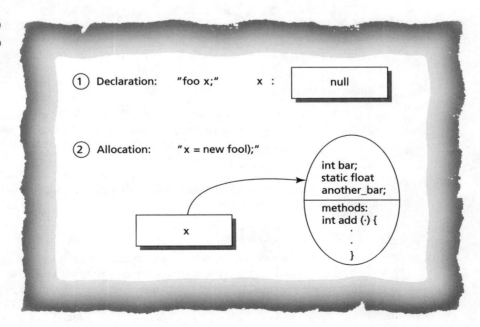

As with array variables, object variables are actually reference handles to the allocated object. Thus, a method can alter the contents of an object that is passed to it.

Instance, Static, and Final Variables and Methods

Look at the definition of the Foo class again. The variable *x* is an *instance variable*, which means that each object of type Foo has its own copy of *x*. The *static* keyword in the declaration of *y* makes it a *class* or *static variable*. A static variable exists whether or not the class has been instantiated. Furthermore, there is only one copy of a static variable, regardless of how many instances of the class you create. This distinction is mirrored in the way you access these variables:

```
f.x = 13;        // objectName.instanceVariable
Foo.y = 17.0f;   // className.staticVariable
```

In other words, to access an instance variable, you need an instance of the class. To access a class variable, prefix the variable with the class name. Figure 1-11 illustrates the distinction between an instance and a class variable in the Foo class.

FIGURE 1-11

◎ ◎ ◎ ◎ ◎ ◎

Comparing instance and class variables of Foo

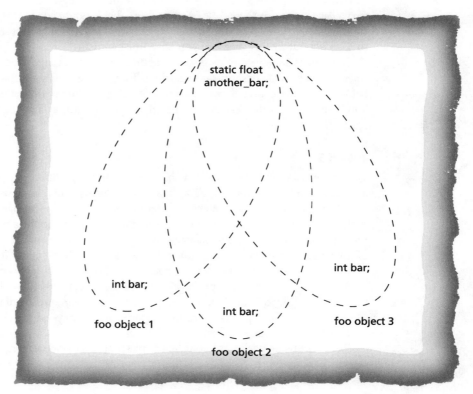

Methods can also be declared static; in this case, they are known as *class* or *static methods*, and can be invoked even if there aren't any instances of the class around. Instance methods, on the other hand, require the presence of an object to be invoked. Again, the syntax is illustrative:

```
f.add(3);        // objectName.instanceMethod();
Foo.minus();     // className.staticMethod();
```

A variable that is declared *final* is a constant. A variable declared both *static* and *final* (a static, final variable) is a constant that is a static variable. In the following:

```
class Constants {
  static final double PI = 3.14159;
}
```

Constants.PI is a static final variable. Methods and classes can also be declared *final*; you'll learn about this in the next chapter.

Memory Management

In Java, memory is dynamically allocated with the *new* keyword. But unlike C++, there isn't a *delete* operator to free allocated memory that is not needed. This is because Java's runtime system automatically garbage-collects memory no longer in use. You don't need to worry about freeing memory you have finished using.

Sometimes an object holds system resources that the garbage collector doesn't keep track of, such as file descriptors or sockets. In this case, you should *finalize* the object before it's garbage collected, by providing a finalize() method in the definition of the class. You'll see how to do this in Chapter 8, Implementing a High Score Server on a Network.

Packages

A package is a group of classes that share related functionality or purpose. Each package has a name that identifies it. A package name consists of one or more names separated by periods, such as java.awt.image. To refer to a given class in a package, prefix the name of the class with the package name, and separate the two names by a period. For example, the Graphics class in the package java.awt is java.awt.Graphics. The combination of the package name and class name is known as the *fully qualified name* of the class.

All classes in Java belong to some package. Within a class definition, you can refer to another class in the same package by using the class name alone. However, a class must use the fully qualified name when referring to a class outside of its own package. Otherwise, you can *import* the class in your program. By importing a class, you can refer to it with the class name alone.

We'll start using packages in our first applet, and Chapter 10, Advanced Techniques, covers them in depth.

Operators

Java uses most of the C operators you're familiar with, but eliminates

✦ Dereferencing operators: * and ->

✦ Address operator: &

✦ *sizeof*

✦ Comma operator: ,

However, Java adds a few operators as well. The most notable additions:

✦ *instanceof* tests to see if an object is an instance of a class. More precisely,

```
object instanceof class
```

returns *true* if *object* is an instance of *class*, and *false* otherwise. If *object* is null, *false* is returned.

✦ >>> is an additional operator that denotes logical right shift. In other words, the vacated bits are filled with zeroes. >>>= performs an assignment along with the shift. The >> and >>= operators perform arithmetic right shifts (i.e., the vacated bits are filled with the sign bit).

✦ + and += are overloaded to perform String concatenation. You'll learn about Strings in Chapter 4, Adding Interactivity.

Appendix A, Java Reference Tables, contains a complete listing of Java operators.

Control Flow

Java supports the control structures found in C: *if...else*, *for*, *while*, *do...while*, and *switch*. Listing 1-2 gives an illustration of each of these.

Listing 1-2 *Java control structures*

```
class ControlFlow {
  public static void main(String argv[]) {

    /* for loop */
    /* prints numbers from 0 to 17 */

    for (int i=0; i<17; i++) {
      System.out.println(i);
    }

    /* while loop */
    /* steps through charArray elements */
    char charArray[] = {'r','i','a','I','n'};
    int j = 0;
```

continued on next page

continued from previous page

```
      while (j < charArray.length) {
        System.out.println(charArray[j++]);
      }

      /* do...while loop */
      /* prints 3
                2
                1 */
      int k = 3;
      do {
        System.out.println(k);
        k--;
      }
      while (k != 0);

      /* switch */
      /* prints "case 13" */
      int s = 13;
      switch (s) {
        case 3:
          System.out.println("case 3");
          break;
        case 13:
          System.out.println("case 13");
          break;
        default:
          System.out.println("default case");
          break;
      }

      /* if...else */
      /* prints "Bye" */
      if (j - s == 17) {
        System.out.println("Hello");
      }
      else {
        System.out.println("Bye");
      }
    }
  }
```

As you see, the control structures in Java are practically identical to the ones in C!

Java also eliminates *goto*, and adds labeled *break* and *continue* statements that allow you to get out of nested blocks. Here's an example of the use of a labeled break statement:

```
find:                   // this is a label that
                        //   refers to the following
                        //   statement
  for (int i=0; i<13; i++) {
    for (int j=0; j<17; j++) {
      if (i*j == 1713)
```

```
        break find;      // exit out of statement
                         //    labelled 'find'
    }
  }

// execution resumes here if break is executed
```

Threads

In the real world, many different things happen at the same time; similarly, there are many programming situations where it's necessary to simulate multiple, concurrent processes. This is done in Java with *threads*. Think of threads as subprograms that execute independently of one another, and yet can work together as well. Threads are a powerful tool for creating simulations. We'll cover threads in detail in Chapters 8, Implementing a High Score Server on a Network, and 10, Advanced Techniques.

Exceptions

An *exception* indicates a condition that is out of the ordinary, such as an error. When a method detects an error, it can *throw* an exception. An exception handler can *catch* the thrown exception. Here's a quick example:

```
try {
  // execute the code in here.
  // if exception occurs, flow of control
  //     jumps to catch block
  // else finish executing try block
}
catch (Exception e) {
  // code in here is executed if exception occurs
}
finally {
  // code in here is ALWAYS executed, after try block
  //     and/or catch block are executed
}
```

Java's powerful exception handling mechanism is based on the *try-catch* construct found in C++. You'll see exception handling at work starting with the next chapter; Chapter 8, Implementing a High Score Server on a Network, will cover it in depth.

Major Differences Between Java, C, and C++

Here are some of the major differences between Java, C, and C++:

 Java has no pointers. However, this doesn't prevent you from implementing data structures that use pointers, such as linked lists, because an object (or array) variable is a reference handle to object (or array) contents. You'll see an illustration of this program in Listing 1-5. Also, remember that objects and arrays are passed by reference.

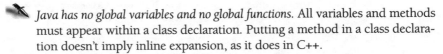

Java has no global variables and no global functions. All variables and methods must appear within a class declaration. Putting a method in a class declaration doesn't imply inline expansion, as it does in C++.

Java supports method overloading. The same method name may be used multiple times in a class declaration to denote distinct methods, as long as the argument lists or return types are different. You can define many methods named foo() in the same class, as long as each one has a different method signature.

Java has no preprocessor. Thus, there are no macros (*#define*) or built-in facilities for conditional compilation (*#if* and *#ifdef*) as provided in C. In addition, Java doesn't use function prototypes or header files, so it doesn't need *#include*.

In Java, instance (nonstatic) methods are bound dynamically by default. In other words, Java methods behave like virtual functions in C++.

In Java, a String is an object, and not an array of char. In addition, a String object is *immutable*, which means that you can't change its contents. Strings are discussed in Chapter 4, Adding Interactivity.

The designers of Java wanted to create a simpler, more orthogonal language than either C or C++, so they eliminated several features. Table 1-1 enumerates some features that have been eliminated, and their Java substitutes.

C/C++ Feature	Java Substitute
#*define* for constants	Static final variables
#*define* for macros and other preprocessor directives (e.g., #, ##, #*ifdef*)	None
Enumerated types	Static final variables
Function not defined in a class	Static method
Multiple inheritance	Multiple interfaces
Operator overloading	None
Struct or union or typedef	Class
Templates	None

Table 1-1 ⊙ *C/C++ features eliminated from Java*

The Java API

An API, or Application Programming Interface, is the boundary between your application and the underlying programming environment. The Java API consists of standard, predefined classes that implement functionality ranging from graphics, networking, and I/O to trigonometric functions and basic data structures. As with the C/C++ libraries, the Java API provides support for features that are found beyond the core language. And since Java is an object-oriented language, you can directly extend the functionality of API classes.

The classes that make up the API are grouped into packages. Below are the packages in the API.

java.applet

This package contains the classes necessary for creating applets. As applets, your games can be distributed over the Web and executed in a Web page. We'll create applets at the end of this chapter.

java.awt

The extension *awt* stands for Abstract Windowing Toolkit. The java.awt package consists of classes that allow a Java application to use the underlying window environment. Here you'll find declarations of standard GUI widgets, such as checkboxes and scrollbars, as well as classes for handling events and graphics. You're going to be spending a lot of time in this package, because it's crucial to writing video games.

The java.awt class that handles graphics is called java.awt.Graphics, and you'll be using it by the end of this chapter.

java.awt.image

This package provides classes for performing image processing. You'll use it in Chapter 10, Advanced Techniques.

java.awt.peer

This is a package that's used to port the AWT to different platforms. You won't need to use it at all.

java.io

The java.io package is the Java version of stdio.h (if you use C) or stream.h (C++). In other words, here are the classes for performing input and output. You will use this package in Chapter 8, Implementing a High Score Server on a Network.

java.lang

This package is automatically imported by the Java compiler. It contains the fundamental classes used in Java development, such as Object, Class, Thread, and Exception, as well as classes that provide access to system resources, such as System and Runtime. You will also find a Math class that handles mathematical functions, and lots of other frequently used classes.

java.net

The java.net package contains classes for interfacing with the Internet and the World Wide Web. You'll be using it to create multiplayer games, and you'll start exploring it in Chapter 8, Implementing a High Score Server on a Network.

java.util

In this package you'll find declarations of basic data structures that come in really handy, such as a stack and a hashtable. You'll learn about these classes in Chapter 10. Now let's see how Java programs are executed.

The Java Interpreter

Once you've written a Java program, you'll want to run it! There are few steps involved. First, compile the source file with the Java compiler. The compiler produces *bytecode,* which is stored in a class file. Then, invoke the Java interpreter for this class file. You can explicitly invoke the Java interpreter from a command-line prompt, or let a Web browser do it for you. (You'll see how this works by the end of the chapter.)

Then, the Java interpreter takes over. It does a few things:

1. The appropriate class file is loaded by the *bytecode loader*. The class file can come from the local file system or from the Internet.

2. Since the bytecode may be of unknown origin, it is checked by the *bytecode verifier*. Code that passes the tests of the verifier can be safely executed. In effect, the bytecode verifier acts as a gatekeeper, which prevents nasty, damaging programs from being executed.

3. The successfully verified bytecode is executed by the implementation of the Java virtual machine.

These components—loader, verifier, and virtual machine—work in conjunction so that classes are dynamically loaded and linked as needed. The components of the Java interpreter are diagrammed in Figure 1-12.

Now let's apply your knowledge of Java to understanding three sample programs.

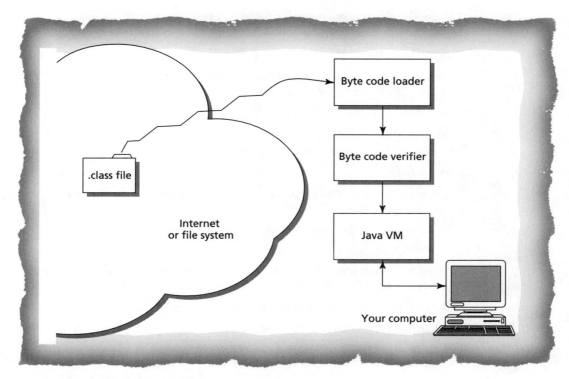

FIGURE 1-12 ◉ *The Java interpreter*

Three Sample Applications

In this section, you'll examine three programs more closely to see how Java is used. These programs are *applications*, which means they can be run directly by the Java interpreter. All applications must define a method called main(), which is where execution starts.

Program 1: Your First Java Program

Here it is, shown in Listing 1-3:

Listing 1-3 *Fun.java*

```java
// Your First Java Program

class Fun {
public static void main(String argv[]) {
  System.out.println("Java is FUN!");
  }
}
```

Store this short program in a file called Fun.java. The name of the file must match the name of the class. Now, compile it by typing

```
% javac Fun.java
```

The Java compiler, javac, produces a file that's called Fun.class, which contains the bytecode. To run your program, type

```
% java Fun
```

Now java, the Java interpreter, locates the file Fun.class, and starts execution from the main() method. The result is

```
Java is FUN!
```

The class Fun defines a method called main(). What meaning do the three keywords in front of main() have?

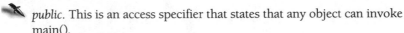 *public*. This is an access specifier that states that any object can invoke main().

static. This means that main() is a class method, and can be invoked even if an instance of the class isn't allocated.

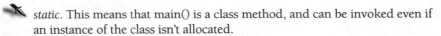 *void*. This means that main() doesn't return anything.

Inside main() is the line

```
System.out.println("Java is FUN!");
```

System is a class that's part of the java.lang package, and thus automatically included by the Java compiler. System has a variable *out*; *out* is an object with a method println(). This method, as its name implies, takes an argument (in this case, a String) and prints it to standard output. So the result of running this program is a reminder that you are having fun!

Let's go on to the next example.

Program 2: Parameter Passing

In the language overview, we touched a little on passing parameters to methods. Now you'll see a concrete example of how this affects your programs.

In Java, variables of primitive types (numeric, character, and boolean types) are *passed by value*. In other words, the value of the variable, and not the address of the variable, is passed to methods. When you pass a variable of primitive type to a method, you can be sure that the value of the variable won't be changed by the method.

Arrays and objects behave differently. An array or object variable actually stores a reference to array or object contents. When you pass an array or object variable to a method, the array or object contents can be modified by the method. In effect, arrays and objects are *passed by reference*. The equivalent behavior in C is achieved by passing a pointer to the data, and dereferencing the pointer in the function body.

Here's a demonstration. The program shown in Listing 1-4 illustrates the difference between passing a primitive type and passing an array.

Listing 1-4 *Parameter passing (ParamTest.java)*

```java
// Parameter Passing Comparison

class ParamTest {

  // method foo illustrates passing a variable of primitive type
  static void foo (int bar) {
    bar++;
  }

  // method foo2 illustrates passing an array
  static void foo2 (int a[]) {
    a[0] = 1;
  }

  // this method does the test
  static public void main(String argv[]) {
    int x;                      // x is int;
    x = 3;                      // x is assigned 2
    foo(x);                // pass x to foo()
    System.out.println("x = " + x);
                                // x is unchanged!!!!

    int y[];                     // y refers to array
    y = new int[2];              // y is allocated 2 ints
    y[0] = 17;              // y[0] is assigned 17
    foo2(y);                // pass array variable y to foo2()
    System.out.println("y[0] = " + y[0]);
                            // y[0] is changed!!!!
  }
}
```

After compiling and running this class, the output will be

```
x = 3

y[0] = 1
```

Thus, *x* hasn't been modified, as the *value* of *x* is passed to method foo(). On the other hand, *y* is an array, so the contents of *y* can be modified by method foo2().

Now for our final example.

Program 3: A Linked List

Java, unlike C and C++, has no explicit pointers. This not only has an effect on the way parameters are passed, as you saw in the previous example, but also on the declaration of data structures that use pointers, such as *linked lists* or *binary trees*.

For example, consider the problem of defining a linked list of integers. A linked list is a data structure that stores a sequence of elements that can grow or shrink dynamically. Each *node* in the list contains an integer and a pointer to the next node. The diagram in Figure 1-13 illustrates a circular linked list, where the end of the list points to the front.

In Java, a node of a linked list may be defined like this:

```java
class Node {
  private int value; // stores int
  private Node next; // refers to the next Node
  ...
}
```

A node variable is a reference handle to the contents of the node, so this definition works. Now, let's define, in Listing 1-5, the circular linked list that's shown in Figure 1-13:

FIGURE 1-13

⊚ ⊚ ⊚ ⊚ ⊚ ⊚

Circular linked list

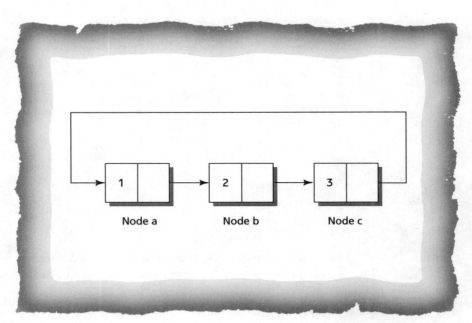

Node a   Node b   Node c

Listing 1-5 Circular linked list (CircularList.java)

```java
// a single node of the list
class Node {
  private int value;
  private Node next;

  // Node constructor
  public Node(int i) {
    value = i;        // initialize value
    next = null;      // no next node
  }

  // print value stored in this node
  public void print() {
    System.out.println(value);
  }

  // get handle to next node
  public Node next() {
    return next;
  }

  // set the next node
  public void setNext(Node n) {
    next = n;
  }
}


// define the circular list in Figure 1-12
class CircularList {
  public static void main(String argv[]) {
    Node a;              // declare nodes
    Node b;
    Node c;
    a = new Node(1);     // allocate nodes
    b = new Node(2);
    c = new Node(3);
    a.setNext(b);        // create circular list
    b.setNext(c);
    c.setNext(a);
    Node i;
    i = a;
    while (i != null) {  // print circular list
      i.print();         // print value in node i
      i = i.next();      // set i to next node
    }
  }
}
```

Upon compiling and running CircularList.java, the output will be an infinite sequence 1, 2, 3, 1, 2, 3, 1, and so on, which means there's a circular list. We'll stay away from using linked lists in writing games, since arrays are simpler and faster. But the point of this program is to show that the elimination of pointers from Java doesn't prevent you from coding data structures that use them.

Now that you've seen Java in action, it's time write a graphics applet. For this, you'll need to use the class java.awt.Graphics.

Understanding Applets

In this section you will learn all about applets: executing an applet, creating graphics in an applet, and the applet life cycle. At the end, you'll write your own graphics applet!

Executing an Applet

An *applet*, as you'll recall, is a Java program that executes in conjunction with a Web browser, or *appletviewer* (a program that runs applets). Here are the steps needed to execute an applet you've written:

1. Compile the applet source file with javac, the Java compiler. The result is a class file.

2. Create an HTML file with an applet tag that refers to the class file.

3. Invoke appletviewer (or the browser) on the HTML file.

For example, the minimal HTML document shown in Listing 1-6 refers to applet code found in Example.class.

Listing 1-6 *Sample HTML file for an applet*

```
<html>
<body>

<applet code="Example.class" width=113 height=117>
</applet>

</body>
</html>
```

The applet tag tells the Web browser (or appletviewer) the dimensions, in pixels, required by the applet. After the browser loads the HTML file, it fetches the applet, places the applet on the screen with the desired dimensions, and executes the applet. In this particular case, the browser will set aside a 113x117 swatch of screen real estate.

Creating Graphics

Graphics operations are performed by a Graphics object (also known as a Graphics context). Graphics is a class that's defined in the package java.awt. Every applet has a Graphics object associated with it that addresses the screen real estate allocated for the applet. For example, the Graphics object of the applet from the preceding section paints to a rectangle that's 113 pixels wide and 117 pixels high. Figure 1-14 illustrates the coordinate system that's used by the Graphics object.

Now let's look at some instance methods that java.awt.Graphics provides.

Drawing

 drawLine(int x1, int y1, int x2, int y2) draws a line between (x1,y1) and (x2,y2). To draw a single point, use *drawLine(x,y,x,y)*.

 drawRect(int x,int y,int w,int h) draws a rectangle at (x,y) with width *w* and height *h*.

drawOval(int x, int y,int w,int h) draws an oval inside the rectangle at (x,y) with width *w* and height *h*.

Filling

fillRect(int x,int y,int w,int h) fills a rectangle with the specified dimensions.

 fillOval(int x,int y,int w,int h) fills an oval with the specified dimensions.

FIGURE 1-14

◎ ◎ ◎ ◎ ◎ ◎

Coordinate system of Graphics object

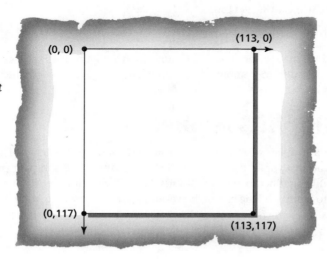

Color

 setColor(Color c) sets the current Color of the Graphics object. Subsequent graphics operations, such as drawing or filling, will use the given Color object. The sidebar shows a list of static constants that are defined in the Color class. To set the color to green, for example, use

```
g.setColor(Color.green);  // g is a Graphics object
```

▣ java.awt.Color

Predefined colors: (These are static constants.)

Grayscale: white, lightGray, gray, darkGray, black

Other colors: red, green, blue, yellow, magenta, cyan, pink, orange

Here's a little example of how to use these Graphics methods. Assume that the Graphics object g is passed into the paint() method:

```
void paint(Graphics g) {
  g.setColor(Color.green);
  g.drawLine(17,17,273,273);
  g.drawLine(17,18,273,274);

  g.setColor(Color.red);
  g.fillRect(30,130,130,130);

  g.setColor(Color.yellow);
  g.fillOval(100,50,130,130);
}
```

This little masterwork is called Composition 2. Figure 1-15 shows what it looks like. Now it's time to combine your knowledge of Java and graphics into your first graphics applet!

A Graphics Applet

To write an applet, you must create a subclass of the Applet class. The Applet class is part of the java.applet package. To refer to the Applet class in your program, you can use its fully qualified name, java.applet.Applet, when it's needed. It gets pretty inconvenient to type such long names, however, so Java allows you to *import* a class or package. The *import* statement

```
import java.applet.Applet;
```

FIGURE 1-15

◎ ◎ ◎ ◎ ◎ ◎

Composition 2

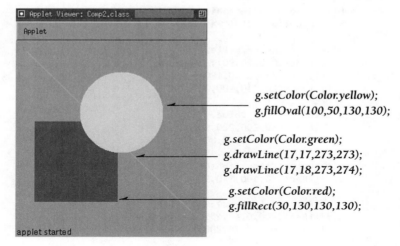

g.setColor(Color.yellow);
g.fillOval(100,50,130,130);

g.setColor(Color.green);
g.drawLine(17,17,273,273);
g.drawLine(17,18,273,274);

g.setColor(Color.red);
g.fillRect(30,130,130,130);

at the start of the source file allows you to use "Applet" as a shorthand for the fully qualified name. Another form of the *import* statement,

```
import java.applet.*;
```

allows you to use the unqualified class names for all the classes in the package java.applet.

Let's jump right in. This applet, shown in Listing 1-7, is called Mondrian.java, and you'll soon see why.

Listing 1-7 *Mondrian applet*

```
import java.applet.*;
import java.awt.*;

public class Mondrian extends Applet {

  public void init() {

    System.out.println(">> init <<");
    setBackground(Color.black);

  }


  public void start() {

    System.out.println(">> start <<");

  }
  // paint squares of varying colors
```

continued on next page

continued from previous page

```
        public void paint(Graphics g) {
          System.out.println(">> paint <<");

          g.setColor(Color.yellow);
          g.fillRect(0,0,90,90);
          g.fillRect(250,0,40,190);
          g.fillRect(80,110,100,20);

          g.setColor(Color.blue);
          g.fillRect(80,200,220,90);
          g.fillRect(100,10,90,80);

          g.setColor(Color.lightGray);
          g.fillRect(80,100,110,90);

          g.setColor(Color.red);
          g.fillRect(200,0,45,45);
          g.fillRect(0,100,70,200);

          g.setColor(Color.magenta);
          g.fillRect(200,55,60,135);
        }

      public void stop() {

        System.out.println(">> stop <<");

      }

      public void destroy() {

        System.out.println(">> destroy <<");

      }

    }
```

The associated HTML file is shown in Listing 1-8.

Listing 1-8 *Mondrian applet HTML code*

```
<html>

<body>

<title> Mondrian </title>

<applet code="Mondrian.class" width=300 height=300>

</applet>
```

```
</body>

</html>
```

Since Mondrian is a subclass of Applet, it inherits all of Applet's public methods. Mondrian redefines, or *overrides*, some of Applet's methods—init( ), start( ), paint( ), stop( ), and destroy( )—to provide the appropriate behavior. You'll learn what these particular methods do in the following section. For now, let's run the applet.

First, compile Mondrian.java with javac (as before):

```
%javac Mondrian.java
```

Now use appletviewer to see it:

```
%appletviewer Mondrian.html
```

Appletviewer finds the applet tag in the HTML file, loads the Mondrian class file, and starts executing it. The result is depicted in Figure 1-16. Hmmm...maybe Mondrian *was* a genius! (In case you were wondering, Mondrian was a 20th-century artist who specialized in arranging rectangles.)

Now let's explore the execution of a Java applet in more detail.

The Applet Life Cycle

What happens when Joe from Denmark accesses the HTML file Mondrian.html with his Web browser? First, the bytecode contained in Mondrian.class is loaded by the Java runtime environment in Joe's browser. Then, after ensuring that the bytecode won't harm Joe's computer, the methods in Mondrian.java are invoked in the following order:

FIGURE 1-16

◎ ◎ ◎ ◎ ◎ ◎

Mondrian applet

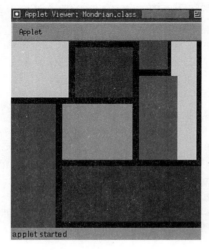

1. init(). This method is called to initialize the applet.

2. start(). This method starts the execution of the applet.

3. paint(Graphics g). paint() controls what the applet looks like. The browser automatically passes in the Graphics context.

4. stop(). This method is called when the Web page that the applet is running on is hidden, as when Joe clicks on another site. It stops execution of the applet.

5. destroy(). This method releases the resources held by the applet.

Figure 1-17 illustrates the short, happy life of an applet that occurs when Joe enters the Mondrian HTML page.

Congratulations! You're now a Java artist!

Suggestion Box

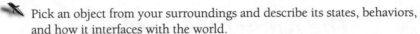 Pick an object from your surroundings and describe its states, behaviors, and how it interfaces with the world.

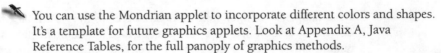 You can use the Mondrian applet to incorporate different colors and shapes. It's a template for future graphics applets. Look at Appendix A, Java Reference Tables, for the full panoply of graphics methods.

You can also use standard C/C++ control structures to create more complex patterns. For example, you could use a for loop to draw overlapping rings across the graphics context. You can alternate colors in a loop as well.

The best way to understand how Java graphics applets work is to experiment. Don't hesitate to have fun. Who knows, you might even create a great work of art. The journey of a thousand miles begins with one step, as they say.

Summary

This chapter has covered a lot of ground: Java basics, object-oriented fundamentals, some simple Java programs, and a graphics applet. In many ways, you are already over the hump of learning Java. Now you can begin learning the art of writing Java games.

In the next chapter, you'll create simple animations with your applets!

FIGURE 1-17

◎ ◎ ◎ ◎ ◎ ◎

The Applet life cycle

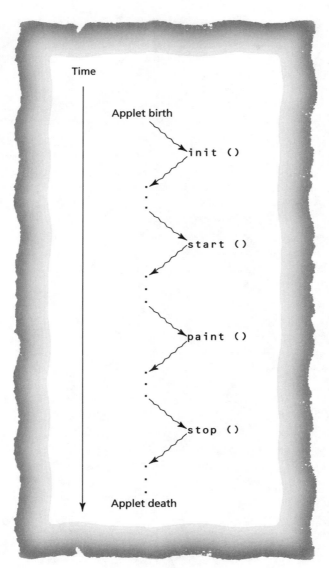

2

Using Objects
for Animation

Joel Fan

ome trible fiore e manouelle .... le quali jimoderno e llalza

e grap. si e mette le mente di .. genti o la go yano di bo no

gare nella mano e sa per ma gista alla manouella pegi quo ti

forga. o più i somo peb. bal.

nel pro . ... ui e .. meg ... di ....

... ie .. tra s o ... us .. di ... met

mu me .. a y ome s. ... ys

c ... . met ... m . n ... ... alfacro

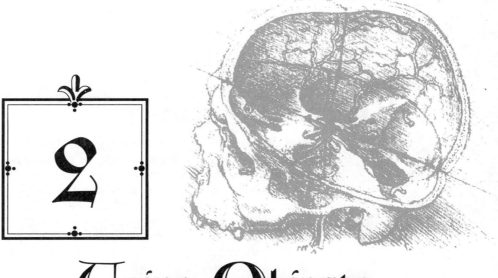

2

Using Objects for Animation

Goals:

Understand animation

Use objects, inheritance, and dynamic method binding to design Java programs

Create animation applets

You've already seen how to paint masterpieces of art using Java. Now it's time to make objects that move and shake on the screen. The process of breathing movement into art and graphics is called *animation*. Along with learning about animation in this chapter, you'll also get a better grasp of the major features of object-oriented programming: objects, inheritance, and dynamic method binding.

Here's the plan for this chapter. First, you will get a general overview of animation. Then you'll create an animation applet named Broadway Boogie Woogie, and learn about techniques that allow you to improve the appearance and performance of your animations. After that, you'll see how to redesign the applet in an object-oriented way that makes it easy to understand, manage, and extend.

Let's talk first about animation.

47

What Is Animation?

Back in the olden days, movies were called *moving pictures*. This quaint term is contradictory, since a single picture can't move, but it points to the technique that's used to create the illusion of movement: single pictures, shown in rapid succession. If the difference between consecutive pictures is small enough, your eye is tricked into believing that smooth motion is taking place.

Animation relies on the same technique, except that the pictures are hand-drawn, or computer-drawn, instead of being snapshots of reality. For example, Figure 2-1 shows a sequence of frames that might be used to animate a walking figure, if the frames were cycled one at a time, at a rate of twelve per second.

And though it still takes a team of experts to make the highest-caliber Disney animations, computers make animation easy, since you can easily control what appears on the screen. In fact, the loop shown in Listing 2-1, which we'll call the Universal Animation Loop, will create animations on any computer.

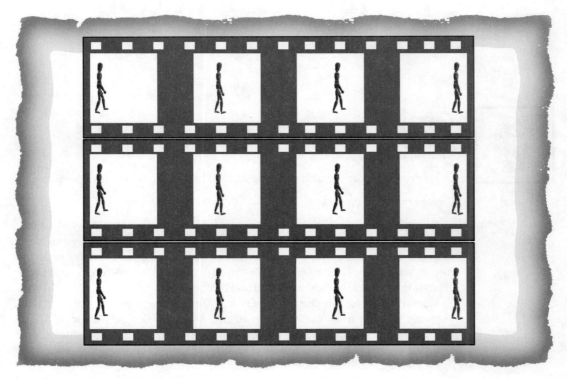

FIGURE 2-1 ◉ *Animating a walking figure*

Listing 2-1 Universal Animation Loop

```
while (
    1. Draw the Current Frame f.
    2. Set f = the Next Frame.
    3. Pause for an interval of time.
}
```

Of course, this isn't Java code, but it captures the essence of computer animation in three steps! You'll flesh out this loop in the following sections. For now, let's discuss step 3. As the pausing interval gets shorter, the animation appears smoother, for a given sequence of frames. Equivalently, the greater the number of frames per second, or fps, the better the animation looks. Of course, there's a natural limit to how many frames per second you can perceive. If the frame rate is too fast, things become a blur. Accordingly, movies display at 24 fps, and that rate would be ideal for computer animation. Unfortunately we're limited by the speed of computing resources. A rate of 10–15 fps (equivalent to a pausing interval of around 60–100 milliseconds) gives an adequate illusion of motion, and it's attainable with Java on most computers. So that's the frame rate we'll shoot for in our applets.

With these concepts in mind, let's create an animation applet.

Creating Our First Animation Applet

This applet's called Broadway Boogie Woogie, with apologies to Mr. Mondrian again! It's an extended version of the applet at the end of Chapter 1, Fundamental Java, except that now the center rectangle boogies about. Figure 2-2 illustrates the boogie action.

This boogie action is implemented with a simple *state machine* in updateRectangle(). The rectangle has four states of motion—up, down, left, and right—and when a threshold is crossed, the rectangle enters the next state. We'll use state machines again for defining the behavior of alien ships in your first game.

Let's jump right into the code, shown in Listing 2-2. Try to pick out all the places where this applet is different from its predecessor.

Listing 2-2 Broadway.java

```java
import java.applet.*;
import java.awt.*;

public class Broadway extends Applet implements Runnable {

    Thread animation;
    int locx,locy;        // location of rectangle
    int width, height;    // dimensions of rectangle
```

continued on next page

FIGURE 2-2

◎ ◎ ◎ ◎ ◎ ◎

Rectangle boogie

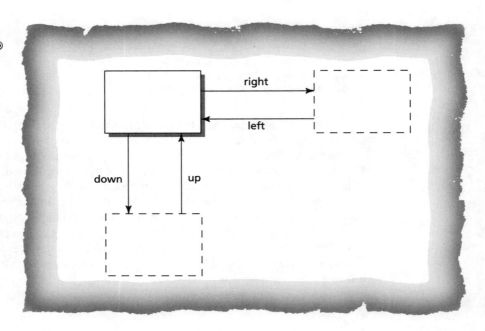

continued from previous page

```
static final byte UP = 0; // direction of motion
static final byte DOWN = 1;
static final byte LEFT = 2;
static final byte RIGHT = 3;

byte state;                 // state the rect is in
                            // length of pausing interval
static final int REFRESH_RATE = 100;    // in ms

// applet methods:

public void init() {

  System.out.println(">> init <<");
  setBackground(Color.black);
  locx = 80;                // parameters of center rect
  locy = 100;
  width = 110;
  height = 90;
  state = UP;
}


public void start() {

  System.out.println(">> start <<");
```

```
      animation = new Thread(this);
       if (animation != null) {
         animation.start();
       }
    }

    public void paint(Graphics g) {
      System.out.println(">> paint <<");

      g.setColor(Color.yellow);
      g.fillRect(0,0,90,90);
      g.fillRect(250,0,40,190);
      g.fillRect(80,110,100,20); // hidden rectangle

      g.setColor(Color.blue);
      g.fillRect(80,200,220,90);
      g.fillRect(100,10,90,80);

      g.setColor(Color.lightGray);
      g.fillRect(locx,locy,width,height);

      g.setColor(Color.red);
      g.fillRect(200,0,45,45);
      g.fillRect(0,100,70,200);

      g.setColor(Color.magenta);
      g.fillRect(200,55,60,135);
    }

    // update the center rectangle
    void updateRectangle() {
      switch (state) {
      case DOWN:
        locy += 2;
        if (locy >= 110) {
        state = UP;
        }
        break;
      case UP:
        locy -= 2;
        if (locy <= 90) {
        state = RIGHT;
        }
        break;
      case RIGHT:
        locx += 2;
        if (locx >= 90) {
        state = LEFT;
        }
        break;
      case LEFT:
```

continued on next page

continued from previous page

```
            locx -= 2;
            if (locx <= 70) {
            state = DOWN;
            }
            break;

        }


    }

    public void run() {
      while (true) {
        repaint();
        updateRectangle();
        try {
         Thread.sleep (REFRESH_RATE);
        } catch (Exception exc) { };
      }
    }


    public void stop() {

      System.out.println(">> stop <<");
      if (animation != null) {
        animation.stop();
        animation = null;
      }
    }

}
```

To run this applet, update the Mondrian.html file from Chapter 1 with the following applet tag. (In future applets, we'll assume that you know how to create the applet tag in the HTML file.)

```
<applet code="Broadway.class" width=300 height=300>
```

Compile the source and run it with appletviewer or a Web browser.

Although this applet is a bit more complex than its predecessor, it has methods that you learned about in Chapter 1—init(), start(), paint(), and stop()—that are called at various stages in the applet's lifetime. Broadway.java has one extra method, run(). Can you guess what it does before reading on?

Using the Universal Animation Loop

The run() method should look familiar. It is a Java version of the Universal Animation Loop, so it draws the current frame, updates the center rectangle for the next frame, and pauses before looping back to the top. Let's examine the loop in more detail.

The first line of run() is a call to repaint(), which is defined in the Applet class. Remember that Broadway is a subclass of Applet, so it inherits all of Applet's methods. The method repaint() is one of these, and calling it has two effects:

1. It clears the screen.

2. It draws the current frame of the animation, by calling paint().

Thus, paint() is the Applet method that actually draws to the screen; repaint() redraws the screen by calling paint().

The second method of run() is called updateRectangle(), which computes the newest location of the center rectangle and stores it in the variables *locx* and *locy*, which mark the rectangle's upper-left corner. This has the effect of moving the rectangle for the next animation frame.

The last line of run() causes a delay of 100 milliseconds (.1 seconds) before looping back to the top and repeating the entire process, for a frame rate of around 10 fps. *Thread.sleep()* refers to the static method of the Thread class named sleep(); recall that static methods are invoked by prefixing the method name with the class name and a dot.

The run() method has its name for a particular reason. Take a look at the first line of Broadway:

```
public class Broadway extends Applet implements Runnable {
...
```

Not only does Broadway extend Applet (meaning that it's a subclass of Applet), but it *implements* Runnable as well. Runnable is an *interface*, which means that it specifies a set of methods that must be implemented by Broadway. run() is an example of such a method. You'll learn more about interfaces in the next chapter; for now, remember that a class that *implements* an interface supplies the needed methods, whereas a class that *inherits* a method gets it for free!

Now let's trace the execution of Broadway to see how it reaches the run() method.

Tracing the Applet's Execution Path

The execution path of Broadway is a bit complex. As you will recall, init() is called to initialize the applet, and then start() is called:

```
public void start() {

  System.out.println(">> start <<");
  animation = new Thread(this);
  if (animation != null) {
    animation.start();
  }
}
```

FIGURE 2-3

◎ ◎ ◎ ◎ ◎ ◎

Broadway execution path

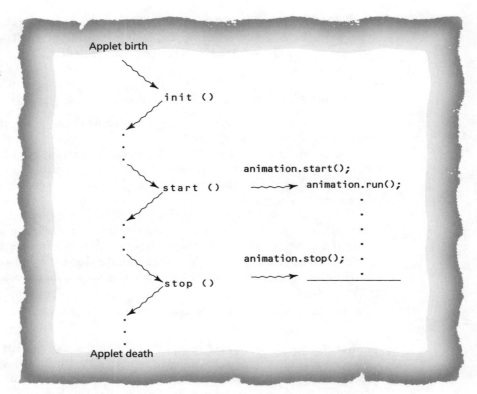

start() does two things:

1. It creates a new thread called *animation*. (You'll learn what the *this* keyword is, in the Using Objects section below.)

2. It tells the *animation* thread to start executing the code in run(), by calling animation.start().

In effect, another thread of execution is created to execute the animation loop in run(). Figure 2-3 shows how the execution path of Broadway splits into two separate paths once the new thread is started.

The *animation* thread operates independently once its start() method is called, and stops executing in response to stop(). And while the *animation* thread is running, it causes the rectangle to jiggle around.

Why is all this code needed to create a simple animation? For example, why could you not just put the animation loop in the start() method, like this:

```
public void start() {
  while (true) {
    repaint();
```

```
    updateRectangle();
    try {
     Thread.sleep (REFRESH_RATE);
    } catch (Exception exc) { };
}
```

As an experiment, try running Broadway with this rogue start() method. It won't work, and the screen will stay blank! The reason is that the code you write in an applet works in conjunction with a lot of other code that you've inherited. If your start() method loops forever, instructions after the start() method are never executed. The result is that the screen stays blank! Figure 2-4 makes this clear. It shows what happens when you use the infinitely looping start() method, instead of the start() method that creates another thread of execution.

This should illustrate another point of creating graphics with Java: when paint() is called, the painting doesn't occur simultaneously, but usually a short while later. If you call paint() too many times per second, Java can't keep up, and it executes the most recent paint() to catch up (ignoring the previous paint() requests). As a result, there's a limit on how fast a frame rate you can achieve; beyond that, the quality of the animation suffers. You can test the limits of your particular machine by setting the frame rate to a really high number and seeing what happens. (Try a pausing interval of less than 5 milliseconds.)

Even with the frame rate at a reasonable number, say 10–15 fps, you'll notice an annoying flicker that mars the animation. Let's find out how to get rid of it and improve animation performance by using two techniques: double-buffering and clipping.

FIGURE 2-4

◎ ◎ ◎ ◎ ◎ ◎

Broadway execution path with infinitely looping start() method

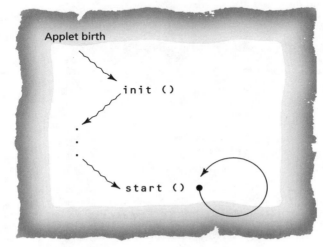

Improving Animation Quality

In this section, you'll learn the cause of animation flicker and how to use double-buffering and clipping to improve the quality of your animations. We will use the Broadway Boogie Woogie applet as our example.

First, let's find out what's causing flicker in the animation.

Understanding Animation Flicker

Why does the screen flicker when Broadway is running? The answer is in a method, update(), that Broadway inherits from the Applet class. Every time you use repaint(), it actually calls update() to do the dirty work of clearing the screen and calling paint(). Here is the update() method that your applet inherits:

```
public void update(Graphics g) {
  g.setColor(getBackground());
  g.fillRect(0, 0, width, height);
  g.setColor(getForeground());
  paint(g)
}
```

The net result of a repaint() call is that the screen is filled with the background color before the foreground is painted. When repaint() is called quickly, the rapid alternation between background and foreground colors causes the flickering effect. Figure 2-5 clarifies the relationship between repaint(), update(), and paint(), which you should understand.

FIGURE 2-5

◉ ◉ ◉ ◉ ◉ ◉

Relationship between repaint(), update(), and paint()

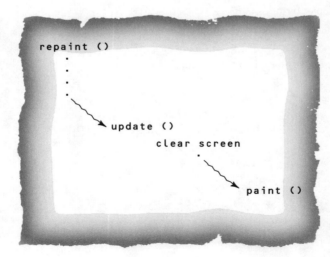

```
repaint ()
   .
   .
   .
   .
         update ()
              clear screen
                   .
                        paint ()
```

An obvious way of curing flicker is by overriding update() so it no longer clears the screen:

```
public void update(Graphics g) {
  paint(g)
}
```

The problem with this cure is that there will be a "trail" behind any animated object (or *sprite*) that moves, since the previous frame is no longer erased. You can use this trail to make some cool effects, but there's a more general solution to flickering, called *double-buffering*.

Using Double-Buffering to Eliminate Flicker

Double-buffering, as the name implies, makes use of two buffers: the original graphics context and an *offscreen* graphics context. Each frame of the animation is rendered on the offscreen buffer, starting with the splash of background color. When the offscreen buffer is ready, its contents are drawn to the original graphics context. The net result: There isn't any flicker, because all of the elements of each frame of the animation are drawn to the screen at once, instead of one by one. Figure 2-6 illustrates the action of double-buffering.

Let's translate this into Java. First, you must declare an offscreen buffer, using the following syntax:

```
Graphics offscreen;    // Declaration of offscreen buffer
Image image;
```

Think of an Image as a complete picture that can be blasted to the screen. (You'll learn more about images in Chapter 3, Animating Sprites.)

The actual allocation of the offscreen buffer should take place in the init() method of the applet:

```
public void init() {
  ... other initializations ...
  image = createImage(width,height); // allocation of offscreen
  offscreen = image.getGraphics();   //                buffer
}
```

The Image method getGraphics() returns the graphics context associated with the image.

Now modify paint() so that it draws to the offscreen buffer, instead of to the original graphics context. You must clear the offscreen buffer now to prevent getting trails. When the offscreen buffer is ready, dump it to the screen by using drawImage(). For example, here's how Broadway's paint() would be changed to implement double-buffering.

FIGURE 2-6

◉ ◉ ◉ ◉ ◉ ◉

*Double-
buffering in
action*

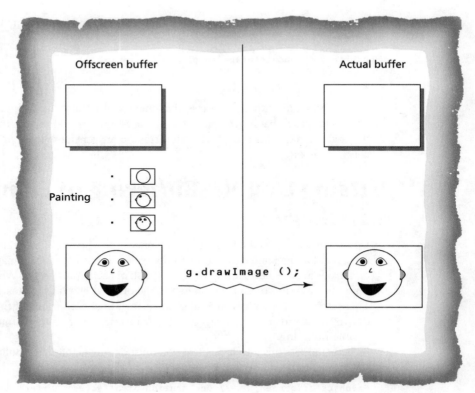

Note that the Graphics method drawImage() paints *image* to the screen at coordinates
(0,0) of the applet's graphics context.

```
public void paint(Graphics g) {

    offscreen.setColor(Color.black);
    offscreen.fillRect(0,0,300,300);  // clear buffer
    offscreen.setColor(Color.yellow);
    offscreen.fillRect(0,0,90,90);
    offscreen.fillRect(250,0,40,190);

    ...
    offscreen.setColor(Color.magenta);
    offscreen.fillRect(200,55,60,135);
    g.drawImage(image,0,0,this);       // draw offscreen buffer
                                       //   to screen
}
```

To use double-buffering in your own applets, paste in the declarations of the image
and offscreen buffer, and modify init() and paint() as has just been discussed. You'll also
need to override update() so it doesn't clear the screen:

```
public void update(Graphics g) {
    paint(g)
}
```

Voilà—flicker-free animation! Next, let's discuss a simple way of improving the performance of the animation.

Using Clipping to Improve Performance

If you look carefully at the Broadway applet again, you'll notice that the animation takes place in the center of the screen, and the surrounding portions remain unchanged. As a result, dumping the entire offscreen buffer to the screen seems to be a waste. Ideally, only the part of the offscreen buffer that changed should be copied. Java makes it easy to specify the portion of the graphics buffer that needs to be modified by subsequent graphics operations. Defining a *clipping rectangle* for a graphics context limits future changes to the interior and edges of that rectangle. In the case of Broadway, the clipping rectangle

FIGURE 2-7

◎ ◎ ◎ ◎ ◎ ◎

Clipping rectangle for Broadway

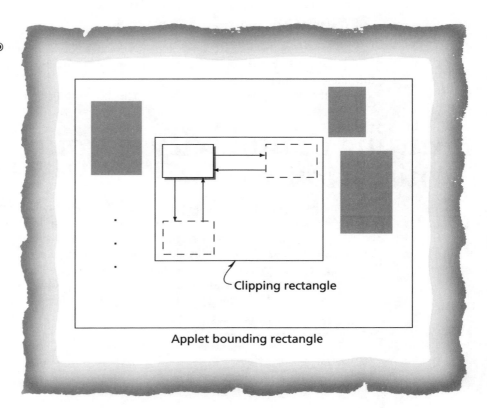

Clipping rectangle

Applet bounding rectangle

might be the maximum region that the moving rectangle traverses, as shown in Figure 2-7.

To define a clipping region, use the Graphics method clipRect():

```
// sets clipRect to rectangle at (x,y) with the
//    specified width and height
  g.clipRect(int x, int y, int width,int height);
```

Now Broadway's update() can be modified in the following way:

```
public void update(Graphics g) {
  g.clipRect(70,90,130,110);
  paint(g);
}
```

You might be wondering why the call to g.clipRect() occurs in update(), instead of in the paint() method. Remember that paint() is called to draw the applet when it first appears on the screen. By clipping in the paint() method, you've restricted painting to the clipping rectangle, and the region outside the clipping rectangle will always stay blank. The proper moment to clip in our applet is when a repaint() takes place, and the call to clipRect() fits nicely in update().

Another way to restrict painting to a given rectangle is by using the following form of the repaint() method in the run() method of the applet:

```
repaint(70,90,130,110);
```

This version of the repaint() method paints the area bounded by the arguments.

Compile and run the double-buffered, clipped version of Broadway, and you'll see the difference immediately.

Now, the next step is turning this solo boogie into a group dance!

Adding Complexity to Your Animation

Let's consider the problem of making all the rectangles jiggle on the screen. This is easy, you say. Just add arrays of ints to track each rectangle's location (location arrays), another array to track the state of every rectangle, and bounds arrays that store how far each rectangle can move. Then modify the updateRectangle() method so that it cycles through every rectangle, updating the position and state of each. Finally, paint() will draw each rectangle at its new location by using the updated location arrays. In other words, the code might look something like the following pseudocode. What's wrong with it?

```
// add this code to Broadway for multiple
//      moving rectangles

// arrays for location
```

```
int locx[NUM_RECTS] = new int[NUM_RECTS];
int locy[NUM_RECTS] = new int[NUM_RECTS];

// arrays for bounding rectangle movement
int bounds_left[NUM_RECTS] = {90,100,...};
int bounds_right[NUM_RECTS] = {110,120,...};
int bounds_up[NUM_RECTS] = {90,100,...};
int bounds_down[NUM_RECTS] = {170,130,...};

// array for rectangle state
byte state[NUM_RECTS];

...
// routine for updating rectangles
void updateRectangles() {
  for (int i = 0; i < NUM_RECTS; i++) {
    switch (state[i]) {
    case UP:

  ...

}

// paint all rectangles
void paint(Graphics g) {
  for (int i = 0; i < NUM_RECTS; i++) {
    g.fillRect(locx[i],locy[i],width[i],height[i]);
  }
}
```

Actually, this code would work fine if you filled in all the blanks. The problem is that it's not a good foundation for a more complex animation applet. Let's say you wanted to devise new dance patterns for the rectangles, and add new shapes, such as ovals or triangles. Placing all this new information into the definition of Broadway would quickly lead to a complex program that's both difficult to understand and to extend.

Programming languages were devised to help programmers manage complexity. Object-oriented languages like Java encourage you to use objects to design and manage complex programs, such as games. Writing a program in an object-oriented language doesn't mean that it's designed in an object-oriented manner; the Broadway applet is a case in point. Let's use objects to build a version of Broadway that's easily extensible and understandable. We will build Broadway in three steps, using

1. Objects

2. Inheritance

3. Dynamic method binding

As it turns out, these are the three keys to object-oriented programming. Let's get to work!

Using Objects

Sometimes it's necessary to tear down what has already been written in order to construct a better infrastructure that allows you to move ahead. That's what we're doing right now. Our immediate goal is to build an applet that will support multiple rectangles dancing in various ways. The key is defining a class that implements the desired states and behaviors.

Defining the Class

Let's identify the candidates for objecthood in this new applet. Since there are multiple dancing rectangles, and each has a different state, such as its position and its current dance step, each dancing rectangle should be an object. Its instance variables will track the state. What behaviors will a dancing rectangle have? That depends on the actual dance steps the rectangles will implement. For now, we'll delay making a decision on the particular dances, and provide a default method, danceStep(), which does the simplest dance step—standing still. In addition, each dancing rectangle will also be responsible for drawing itself to the screen. Figure 2-8 shows a schematic of what a DancingRect object looks like.

The danceStep() and paint() methods provide the public interface to a DancingRect object. All other objects can access these methods. By contrast, the data inside a

FIGURE 2-8
◉ ◉ ◉ ◉ ◉ ◉
DancingRect object

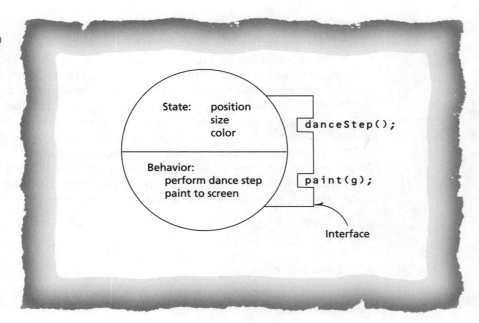

DancingRect, such as its location, is shielded from the outside, or *encapsulated*. Encapsulation means that data inside an object is not visible from the outside. By hiding information inside objects and providing interfaces to these objects, you protect yourself when you decide to make modifications to an object's internal structure. For example, if you decide to change the variable name of the location from *locx* to *XPosition*, you want to be sure that any changes are isolated in the definition of DancingRect. By doing this, code outside DancingRect won't be affected. This makes it easier for you to manage complex programs.

Let's provide the class definition, in Listing 2-3, for DancingRect.

Listing 2-3 *DancingRect class*

```
///////////////////////////////////////////////////////////////////
class DancingRect {
  // instance variables:
  int locx, locy;       // (locx,locy) are coordinates of upper
                        //     left corner of rectangle
  int width, height;    // width and height of rectangle
  Color myColor;        // color of rectangle


///////////////////////////////////////////////////////////////////
  // constructor
  public DancingRect(int locx,int locy,
                     int width,int height,
                     Color myColor) {
    this.locx = locx;
    this.locy = locy;
    this.width = width;
    this.height = height;
    this.myColor = myColor;
  }

  // methods:
  public void danceStep() {

    // does nothing

  }

  public void paint(Graphics g) {
    g.setColor(myColor);
    g.fillRect(locx,locy,width,height);
  }

}
```

The this Keyword

Let's look inside the constructor method of DancingRect. (Remember that a constructor is a method with the same name as the class, with no return type.) What is *this*?

```
public DancingRect(int locx,int locy,
                   int width,int height,
                   Color myColor) {
  this.locx = locx;
  this.locy = locy;
  ...
}
```

An object encapsulates variables and methods, and *this* is a reference to "this particular object that the variable or method belongs to." Each variable in a method definition is preceded by an implied *this* (unless it's a member of an explicitly stated object). Thus, the paint() method defined above is shorthand for

```
public void paint(Graphics g) {
  g.setColor(this.myColor);
  g.fillRect(this.locx,this.locy,this.width,this.height);
}
```

The keyword *this* is necessary in the constructor for DancingRect to distinguish the local variables (which are temporary) from instance variables *of the same name* (which provide storage for the object).

Here's another example of *this*, taken from the Broadway animation applet above.

```
animation = new Thread(this);
```

The *Thread* constructor takes an object as its argument. By passing *this*, the Broadway applet object passes a reference to itself as the argument.

Using this in Constructors

There's one more way that *this* is used. Methods, and constructors in particular, can be overloaded. In other words, a class can have several constructors, as long as each one has a distinct signature (i.e., argument list). When *this*, followed by an argument list, is the first statement in a constructor, the appropriate constructor is called. For example, look at the following class, which has two constructors that invoke each other:

```
class A {
  // constructor #1
  public A(int x, float y) {
    this(y);                 // invoke constructor #2
    ...
  }

  // constructor #2
  public A(float x) {
```

```
    this((int)x, x);        // invoke constructor #1
    ...
  }
}
```

As you see, the *this* statement must occur at the beginning of each constructor. this() (*this* with no arguments) calls the constructor with no arguments.

Being able to invoke another constructor can save you a bit of typing, if you've written one constructor that does all the work and you want another way of calling it.

Using the DancingRect Class

Now let's go back to the DancingRect class. We can create an instance of DancingRect by calling the constructor in the following manner:

```
// create an instance of DancingRect at (80,80)
//    with width 40 and height 40
DancingRect r = new DancingRect(80,80,40,40);
```

To tell *r* to perform a dance step and paint itself, use the following syntax:

```
r.danceStep();  // make a dance step
r.paint();      // paint r to screen
```

Let's use the DancingRect class to implement a new version of the Mondrian class from Chapter 1. In Listing 2-4 you can immediately see how information is now distributed, handled, and encapsulated by the objects that need it, instead of being accessible to all.

Listing 2-4 Rebuilt Mondrian.java

```
import java.applet.*;
import java.awt.*;

// rebuilt Mondrian with objects

public class Mondrian2 extends Applet  {

  static final int NUM_RECTS = 9;

  DancingRect r[];            // array of dancing rectangles

  public void init() {
    System.out.println(">> init <<");
    setBackground(Color.black);
    initRectangles();
  }

  public void initRectangles() {

    // allocate dancing rectangles
```

continued on next page

continued from previous page

```
        // now the data is encapsulated by the objects!
        r = new DancingRect[NUM_RECTS];
        r[0] = new DancingRect(0,0,90,90,Color.yellow);
        r[1] = new DancingRect(250,0,40,190,Color.yellow);
        r[2] = new DancingRect(200,55,60,135,Color.yellow);
        r[3] = new DancingRect(80,200,220,90,Color.blue);
        r[4] = new DancingRect(100,10,90,80,Color.blue);
        r[5] = new DancingRect(80,100,110,90,Color.lightGray);
        r[6] = new DancingRect(200,0,45,45,Color.red);
        r[7] = new DancingRect(0,100,70,200,Color.red);
        r[8] = new DancingRect(200,55,60,135,Color.magenta);

    }

    public void start() {

        System.out.println(">> start <<");

    }



    public void paint(Graphics g) {

        for (int i=0; i<NUM_RECTS; i++) {
            r[i].paint(g);            // paint each rectangle
        }
    }


    public void stop() {

        System.out.println(">> stop <<");

    }

}
```

This new Mondrian is not only cleaner and easier to understand, it is also easily extensible, as you'll see soon. To extend Mondrian, you're going to define dancing rectangles that *actually* dance, using inheritance.

Using Inheritance

In Chapter 1, Fundamental Java, you learned some of the basics of inheritance, and you've been using inheritance to create applets. Now we will explore inheritance in greater detail.

Inheritance allows you to reuse class definitions for creating new classes. Inheritance is signified by the *extends* keyword, as in the following:

```
class foo extends bar {
...
}
```

In this case, the foo class inherits bar's public variables and methods. An instance of foo will be able to use a public method or variable defined in the bar class, as if it were actually defined by foo. (Protected variables and methods are also inherited, and you'll learn about *protected* access in the next chapter.)

The foo class is said to be the *subclass* or *derived class*; the bar class is the *parent class*, *base class*, or *superclass*. Look at Figure 2-9 for a diagram of what happens in the inheritance.

As you can imagine, being able to reuse code in this manner can be a huge time-saver. Another advantage of inheritance is that changes to the behavior of a superclass are automatically propagated to its subclasses, which can cut down on code development time. But for inheritance to be a time-saver that makes code extensible and manageable, it must be used in the proper way. There are situations when it is needed, and times when it is inappropriate.

FIGURE 2-9

⊚ ⊚ ⊚ ⊚ ⊚ ⊚

foo inherits public variables and methods from bar

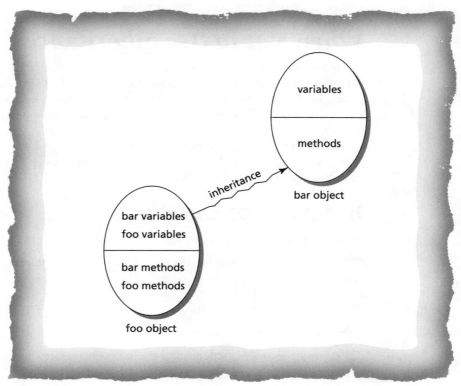

When to Use Inheritance

Inheritance is appropriate when there is an "is-a" relationship between two classes. To determine if such a relationship exists between two classes A and B, create the sentence, "A is a B." If this sentence makes sense, then inheritance is called for, with A as the subclass, and B as the superclass.

For example, a human is a mammal, so a Human class would properly inherit from a Mammal class. Similarly, a Computer is an ElectricPoweredDevice, so the first class would inherit from the second one. These are examples of *extension* relationships, since the subclass adds extra characteristics to the parent class. In other words, a human has all the characteristics of a mammal, plus intelligence, speaking ability, and a few other noteworthy features.

The second kind of is-a relationship is called *specialization*. In this case, the subclass usually refines or specializes methods found in the base class. For example, musicians play instruments of one kind or another, and a Musician class would have a method play() to produce this behavior. Now, a pianist is a type of musician, as is a violinist, or a conductor, but each has different methods of playing music, and so as subclasses, each denotes a different specialization of the Musician class.

When Not to Use Inheritance

Inheritance is not appropriate for "has-a" relationships. A boat, for example, has a rudder; however, inheriting a Boat class from a Rudder class isn't the proper way of reusing the Rudder code. Instead, the Boat class should have an instance of a Rudder object, to capture the has-a relationship. Boat is called a *container* class, since it contains Rudder.

Sometimes the relationship between classes isn't so easy to define, and it might have elements of extension and specialization, as well as containership. In this case, you must experiment to find out what works.

Inheritance Details

In this section, we'll cover further details of using inheritance in Java:

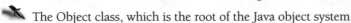 The Object class, which is the root of the Java object system

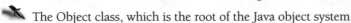 Method overriding

 Using the super keyword

 Final classes and methods

Feel free to skim this section and come back when needed.

The Object Class

The Object class defined in package java.lang is the root of Java's class hierarchy; all other classes are subclasses of Object. If a superclass isn't specified by a class declaration (with the *extends* keyword), the class extends Object by default. This means that the public and protected methods of Object are inherited for all objects.

For example, even the "empty" class

```
// class A automatically extends java.lang.Object

class A {
(c)  // nothing here!
}
```

inherits the public and protected methods defined in Object. Since an instance of any class "is an" object, this implicit inheritance makes sense, and it serves to unify Java's object system. To implement a collection of generic objects, for example, you can use an array of Object.

The Object methods, which we won't use in this chapter, contain facilities for comparing equality of objects, cloning objects, synchronizing threads, and more.

Method Overriding

Sometimes it makes sense for one class to inherit behaviors from another, but you'd like to redefine, or *override*, some of the inherited behaviors. This situation comes up often in specialization relationships. For example, a Pianist class inherits the play() method from a Musician class, but it can override play() to provide the specific behavior desired.

To override an inherited method, simply redefine it in the subclass. The overriding method must have the same method signature as the original version. In the following, Pianist overrides the play(int) method from its superclass, but doesn't override starve().

```
class Musician {
  public int yearsOfStruggle;
  public void play(int howLong) {
    ...
  }
  public void starve() {
    ...
  }
}

class Pianist extends Musician {
  // override play(int) method from Musician class
  public void play(int howLong) {
    ...
  }
}
```

Thus, an instance of Pianist will use the play(int) method defined in Pianist, and the starve() method from Musician. Any class that inherits from Pianist (say a VirtuosoPianist) will inherit the play(int) method defined in Pianist.

Sometimes you've overridden a method, but you still need to invoke the version from the superclass. This is possible with the *super* keyword.

The super Keyword

The keyword *super*, used within the definition of a class, allows you to reference the variables and methods available to the superclass. As an illustration, let's subclass a VirtuosoPianist from the Pianist class defined in the preceding section:

```
class VirtuosoPianist extends Pianist {
  public long yearsOfStruggle = 21L;

  // override play(int) method from Pianist class
  public void play(int howLong) {
    ...

    // call play(int) method defined in superclass
    super.play(howLong * 137);

    // refer to variable defined in this class
    long i = yearsOfStruggle;

    // refer to variable from superclass
    int j = super.yearsOfStruggle;
  }
}
```

The play(int) method of the class (VirtuosoPianist) invokes the play(int) method that's available to the superclass (Pianist) by using *super*.

Furthermore, using *super*, you can reference variables available to the superclass, but hidden by the class. For example, the variable *yearsOfStruggle* defined in VirtuosoPianist (a long) hides the variable of the same name. The *super* keyword allows you to access the *yearsOfStruggle* (an int) inherited through the superclass Pianist.

Using super in Constructors

You can also use *super* in a constructor to invoke a superclass constructor. In the following, the constructor of B calls a constructor of its superclass A by using *super* followed by the appropriate argument list.

```
class A {

  // constructor #1
  public A(int x) {
    // implicit super() here
    x++;
    ...
```

```
  }

  // constructor #2
  public A(float x,int y) {
    // NO implicit super() here
    this(y);                  // call constructor #1
    y++;
    ...
  }

}

class B extends A {

  public B() {
    super((float)13, 17);  // call A's constructor #2
    ...
  }
}
```

If there's a call to a superclass constructor, it must occur at the beginning of the constructor. And if you don't invoke a superclass constructor yourself, Java does it for you! There are three rules involved:

1. Constructors that don't explicitly invoke a superclass constructor *automatically* invoke the superclass constructor with no arguments. In effect, Java inserts super() at the beginning of constructors that don't call a superclass constructor. For example, constructor #1 of class A has an implicit super() at its beginning. (super() in this case invokes the constructor of Object.)

2. An exception to the previous rule occurs when the first statement of the constructor invokes another constructor, using *this*. For example, constructor #2 of class A does not have an implicit call to super().

3. If you don't define a constructor with no arguments in a class, Java inserts one for you. This default constructor simply calls super(). For example, class A has the implicit constructor

```
// implicit constructor
public A() {
  super();
}
```

The upshot of these rules? Each time you create an instance of an object, a sequence of constructors gets executed, from the Object class, through the inheritance hierarchy, and to the class that's instantiated.

Final Classes and Methods

A *final* class is a class that can't be extended. Thus, you can't create a subclass of the following:

```
final class Infertile {
  ...
}
```

A *final* method can't be overridden. For example, no subclass of Sandwich can override the applyMayonnaise() method:

```
class Sandwich {
  final public method applyMayonnaise() {
    ...
  }
}
```

Now let's apply inheritance to our dancing rectangle applet!

Using Inheritance in Our Example Applet

Inheritance is appropriate for creating subclasses of DancingRect that actually know some dance steps! For example, a BoogieRect is a DancingRect; similarly, a WaltzRect is a DancingRect as well. By inheriting DancingRect's members, you'll save yourself from defining those methods and variables again for the subclasses. However, BoogieRect and WaltzRect are specializations of DancingRect, and they'll need to override the danceStep() method that they inherit in order to provide the right behavior.

By overriding danceStep(), an instance of BoogieRect can perform a boogie step instead of standing still. Figure 2-10 diagrams the relationship between the three classes, and their danceStep() methods.

Let's look at the code to get a better idea of how method overriding is implemented. To refresh your memory, here's the definition of DancingRect again:

```
class DancingRect {

  int locx, locy;      // (locx,locy) are coordinates of upper
                       //    left corner of rectangle
  int width, height;   // width and height of rectangle
  Color myColor;       // color of rectangle


  //////////////////////////////////////////////////////////////////
  public DancingRect(int locx,int locy,
                     int width,int height,
                     Color myColor) {
```

```
      this.locx = locx;
      this.locy = locy;
      this.width = width;
      this.height = height;
      this.myColor = myColor;
   }


   public void danceStep() {

      // does nothing

   }

   public void paint(Graphics g) {
      g.setColor(myColor);
      g.fillRect(locx,locy,width,height);
   }

}
```

BoogieRect will use the "dance algorithm" from Broadway in its danceStep(). The full class definition of BoogieRect is shown in Listing 2-5.

FIGURE 2-10

◎ ◎ ◎ ◎ ◎ ◎

DancingRect, BoogieRect, and WaltzRect classes

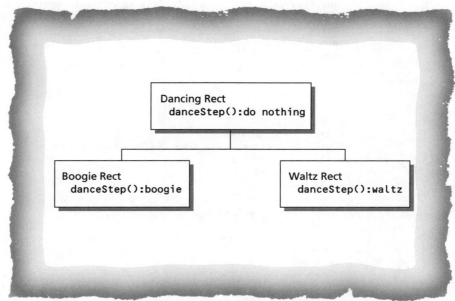

Listing 2-5 BoogieRect.java

```
/////////////////////////////////////////////////////////////////
/////////////////////////////////////////////////////////////////

class BoogieRect extends DancingRect {

  // BoogieRect inherits all instance variables and
  // methods from DancingRect

  static final byte UP = 0;    // direction of motion
  static final byte DOWN = 1;
  static final byte LEFT = 2;
  static final byte RIGHT = 3;

  byte state;                // state of rectangle

  int max_x;                 // max x value
  int min_x;                 // min x value
  int max_y;                 // max y value
  int min_y;                 // min y value

/////////////////////////////////////////////////////////////////

  public BoogieRect(int x,int y,int w,int h,Color c) {
    super(x,y,w,h,c);          // call superclass constructor

    max_x = locx + 13;
    min_x = locx - 13;
    max_y = locy + 13;
    min_y = locy - 13;

  }


  // override danceStep()
  // use the state machine from the Broadway applet
  public void danceStep() {
    switch (state) {
    case DOWN:
      locy += 2;
      if (locy >= max_y) {
       state = UP;
      }
      break;
    case UP:
      locy -= 2;
      if (locy <= min_y) {
       state = RIGHT;
      }
      break;
    case RIGHT:
      locx += 2;
```

```
      if (locx >= max_x) {
       state = LEFT;
       }
      break;
     case LEFT:
      locx -= 2;
      if (locx <= min_x) {
       state = DOWN;
       }
      break;
    }
  }
}
```

To see exactly how method overriding works, consider the following rectangles:

```
DancingRect d = new DancingRect(  );
BoogieRect b = new BoogieRect(...);
```

As you might expect,

```
d.danceStep();
```

produces a call to DancingRect's danceStep() routine, whereas

```
b.danceStep();
```

invokes BoogieRect's version. By contrast,

```
b.paint();
```

uses the paint() defined in DancingRect, since this method hasn't been overridden by BoogieRect.

Now, let's give the definition of a WaltzRect. The dance motion of WaltzRect is shown in Figure 2-11.

The dance motion is also implemented by overriding the danceStep() method inherited from the superclass, as you will see in Listing 2-6.

Listing 2-6 *WaltzRect.java*

```
///////////////////////////////////////////////////////////////
///////////////////////////////////////////////////////////////
// WaltzRect also inherits from DancingRect

class WaltzRect extends DancingRect {
  byte state;
  static final byte SE = 0; // going southeast
  static final byte NE = 1; // going northeast
  static final byte W = 2;  // going west

  int bottom_x;            // the x coordinate of
```

continued on next page

continued from previous page

```
                              //      bottom pt of the waltz
    int right_x;              // the x coordinate of
                              //    right pt of the waltz
    int left_x;               // the x coordinate of
                              //    left pt of the waltz

///////////////////////////////////////////////////////////////////

public WaltzRect(int x,int y,int w,int h,Color c) {
   super(x,y,w,h,c);          // call superclass constructor
   bottom_x = locx + 17;
   right_x = bottom_x + 17;
   left_x = locx;
}

// override danceStep()
 public void danceStep() {
   switch (state) {
   case SE:
     locx++;
     locy++;
     if (locx == bottom_x) {
      state = NE;
     }
     break;
   case NE:
     locx++;
     locy--;
     if (locx == right_x) {
      state = W;
     }
     break;
   case W:
     locx-- ;
     if (locx == left_x) {
      state = SE;
     }
     break;
   }
 }
}
```

The WaltzRect and BoogieRect constructors illustrate the use of *super* to invoke the superclass constructor. For example, the first line of WaltzRect's constructor is

```
super(x,y,w,h,c);          // call superclass constructor
```

which calls the constructor of DancingRect.

You are almost ready to put the dancing rectangle classes on stage! Before you do, there's one more feature of object-oriented programming left to discuss, called *dynamic method binding*.

FIGURE 2-11

◎ ◎ ◎ ◎ ◎ ◎

*Dance motion
of WaltzRect*

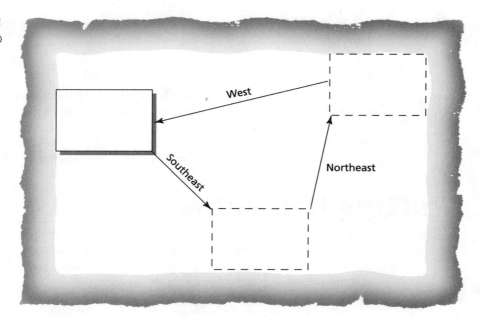

Using Dynamic Method Binding

Dynamic method binding is the last key to object-oriented programming that we'll discuss. It corresponds to using virtual functions in C++, and it is best illustrated by an example. This example serves simply as an introduction to dynamic method binding. In the following section, you will see how it is applied in greater detail.

Consider two classes, A and B, where A is a subclass of B. Class A is also a *subtype* of B. This means that any variable of type B can be assigned a value of type A. For example:

```
B x;            // x is a variable of type B
A a = new A();  // a refers to an object of type A
x = a;          // Assigns x to a
```

The last line assigns variable *x*, which is of type B, to *a*, which is type A. This assignment is legal because A is a subtype of B.

Now let's say that A overrides the method foo() in B, so that instances of A have a different foo() than instances of B, as you saw in the section on inheritance. Consider the following code:

```
B x;            // x is a variable of type B
A a = new A();  // a refers to an object of type A
B b = new B();  // b refers to an object of type B
x = b;          // assign b to x
x.foo();        // which foo() method is called?
```

x.foo() calls the foo() method of B, as you would expect. However, this code produces a different result:

```
x = a;         // assign a to x
x.foo();       // which foo() method is called?
```

In the last line, x.foo() calls the foo() method in A! So the method foo() isn't bound until runtime, which is why this feature is called "dynamic" method binding. In Java, instance methods are bound dynamically *by default*. Final and static methods are not bound dynamically.

This is all pretty abstract, and the next section shows how it's used in practice.

Putting It Together

Let's create an applet called Woogie that will extend the rebuilt Mondrian applet to animate multiple dancing rectangles. Woogie sets all three types of dancing rectangles on the screen. You'll see how the investment that we made in the last few sections pays off in terms of clean, understandable, extensible code.

Let's discuss some highlights of Woogie.

First, all the dancing rectangles are allocated in initRectangles():

```
public void initRectangles() {

    // allocate dancing rectangles

    r = new DancingRect[NUM_RECTS];
    r[0] = new DancingRect(0,0,90,90,Color.yellow);
    r[1] = new BoogieRect(250,0,40,190,Color.yellow);
    r[2] = new WaltzRect(200,55,60,135,Color.yellow);
    r[3] = new BoogieRect(80,200,220,90,Color.blue);
    r[4] = new WaltzRect(100,10,90,80,Color.blue);
    r[5] = new BoogieRect(80,100,110,90,Color.lightGray);
    r[6] = new WaltzRect(200,0,45,45,Color.red);
    r[7] = new WaltzRect(0,100,70,200,Color.red);
    r[8] = new BoogieRect(200,55,60,135,Color.magenta);

}
```

The array *r* points to each rectangle. Since WaltzRect and BoogieRect are subtypes of DancingRect, the assignments don't cause type errors.

Next, the loop in run() is modified slightly, but it still resembles the Universal Animation Loop:

```
public void run() {
    while (true) {
      repaint();
```

```
      updateRectangles();
      try {                          // pause for REFRESH_RATE ms
       Thread.sleep (REFRESH_RATE);
      } catch (Exception exc) { };
    }
  }
```

run() calls updateRectangles(), which tells each rectangle to dance. This is where dynamic method binding is used to provide the desired behavior for each rectangle:

```
public void updateRectangles() {
   for (int i=0; i<NUM_RECTS; i++) {
    r[i].danceStep();      // each rectangles dance step

   }
}
```

Finally, the paint() method cycles through all the rectangles, telling each to draw itself. Double-buffering is implemented by passing the offscreen buffer to the paint() method of each rectangle.

```
public void paint(Graphics g) {

   offscreen.setColor(Color.black);
   offscreen.fillRect(0,0,300,300);  // clear buffer

   for (int i=0; i<NUM_RECTS; i++) {
    r[i].paint(offscreen);            // paint each rectangle
   }

   g.drawImage(image,0,0,this);
}
```

Now take a look at the full listing of Woogie.java, shown in Listing 2-7. You'll agree that it's quite easy to understand and modify, which will be your homework assignment for tonight!

Listing 2-7 *Woogie.java*

```
import java.applet.*;
import java.awt.*;

// run this applet with width=300 height=300
public class Woogie extends Applet implements Runnable {

  Thread animation;

  Graphics offscreen;
  Image image;

  static final int NUM_RECTS = 9;      // in ms
```

continued on next page

continued from previous page

```
              static final int REFRESH_RATE = 100;        // in ms

              DancingRect r[];

              public void init() {
                System.out.println(">> init <<");
                setBackground(Color.black);
                initRectangles();
                image = createImage(300,300);
                offscreen = image.getGraphics();
              }

              public void initRectangles() {

                // allocate dancing rectangles

                r = new DancingRect[NUM_RECTS];
                r[0] = new DancingRect(0,0,90,90,Color.yellow);
                r[1] = new BoogieRect(250,0,40,190,Color.yellow);
                r[2] = new WaltzRect(200,55,60,135,Color.yellow);
                r[3] = new BoogieRect(80,200,220,90,Color.blue);
                r[4] = new WaltzRect(100,10,90,80,Color.blue);
                r[5] = new BoogieRect(80,100,110,90,Color.lightGray);
                r[6] = new WaltzRect(200,0,45,45,Color.red);
                r[7] = new WaltzRect(0,100,70,200,Color.red);
                r[8] = new BoogieRect(200,55,60,135,Color.magenta);

              }

              public void start() {

                System.out.println(">> start <<");
                animation = new Thread(this);
                 if (animation != null) {
                   animation.start();
                 }
              }

              // update each rectangle's position.
              // DYNAMIC METHOD BINDING OCCURS HERE!
              public void updateRectangles() {
                for (int i=0; i<NUM_RECTS; i++) {
                  r[i].danceStep();       // each rectangles dance step

                }
              }


              // override update so it doesn't erase screen
              public void update(Graphics g) {
                paint(g);
              }
```

```
public void paint(Graphics g) {

  offscreen.setColor(Color.black);
  offscreen.fillRect(0,0,300,300);  // clear buffer

  for (int i=0; i<NUM_RECTS; i++) {
    r[i].paint(offscreen);            // paint each rectangle
  }

  g.drawImage(image,0,0,this);
}

public void run() {
  while (true) {
    repaint();
    updateRectangles();
    try {
     Thread.sleep (REFRESH_RATE);
    } catch (Exception exc) { };
  }
}


public void stop() {

  System.out.println(">> stop <<");
  if (animation != null) {
    animation.stop();
    animation = null;
  }
 }
}
```

Suggestion Box

🗡 Create new types of dancing rectangles, and add them to the Woogie applet. Try a ChaChaChaRect. How would you implement the delay between the dance steps? One solution is to bump an internal counter each time danceStep() is called; when the counter reaches a certain value, update the rectangle's position.

🗡 Change the width and height of the rectangles as part of the danceStep().

🗡 Add new shapes to Woogie, such as Ovals or Arcs. Can you think of a good way to alter the inheritance hierarchy to easily allow new shapes? The answer is in the next chapter, but here's a hint: You might want to create a superclass of DancingRect, and move some functionality of DancingRect to the superclass.

 Make a gravity simulation of bouncing rectangles. This will look cool, and it just takes a new formula in the danceStep() routine!

 Right now, the coordinates used to define new rectangles are hardcoded into Woogie. Use the Applet method bounds() (which returns the dimensions of the applet) to compute the coordinates of the rectangles, so that they adjust automatically to the applet size.

Summary

As usual, this chapter's chock-full of information that you're going to need in writing a video game. You've learned how to create animations in Java by using the Universal Animation Loop, and that the applet methods you override execute in conjunction with the surrounding environment. You've seen how to use double-buffering to improve the quality and performance of your animations.

Finally, you learned about three cornerstones of an object-oriented language such as Java:

 Objects

 Inheritance

 Subtyping with dynamic method binding

These are important keys to creating animations, games, and other applications in Java.

In the following chapter, you're going to learn about sprite and bitmap animation.

3

Animating Sprites

Joel Fan

ome trible fare le manoue le la ... le quale pio obano el la fia
igra pe fi i nure la mine ne di agonio o la te prano de bo ne
h a ré nella ma de rfa per ma resta ac fa mano bella peg quo r
orga o pio i fomo pib bal.

nel pio ... ...
... ...
... ...

3

Animating Sprites

Goals:

Understand sprites

Use abstract classes and interfaces to design sprite hierarchy

Use sound

Create bitmap animation

In this chapter, you will be introduced to sprites and begin constructing classes that you can reuse for your own graphics applications and games. You'll learn how abstract classes and interfaces allow you to build understandable, modular Sprite classes, and how they work to give your objects conceptual unity. You will also see how to create all kinds of sprites—from rectangle sprites to bitmap sprites—that can animate at will. Finally, you will create an applet that bounces these sprites around!

Let's get started.

What Are Sprites?

Sprites are figures or elements on the screen that have the capability of moving independently of one another. These elements could be text, graphics, or bitmaps, which you might think of as preformed images that can be pasted on the screen. You've already seen an example of a sprite—the dancing rectangles from the last chapter.

Sprites are commonly used in classic video games to provide screen representations for objects in the game world—for example, the classic game Galaxians, in which enemy ships fly toward you while unleashing a barrage of missiles. The elements of this game, such as the enemies, the missiles, and your ship, are represented by distinct sprites.

In specialized game machines, like the ones you'll find at arcades, the sprites are implemented by hardware to provide the best performance. Because we are programming for a multiplatform environment, we can't rely on specialized hardware, so we will have to translate the functionality of the hardware sprites into Java code. To do this, let's identify the fundamental properties that our Java sprites will have. These properties can be divided into two categories, states and behaviors.

Sprite States

- Internal representation of screen appearance. Sprites will be responsible for drawing themselves to the screen, which means they need an internal representation for how they should appear.

- Screen location. In the case of a sprite that displays a rectangle, as you saw in the previous chapter, it might be sufficient to track the current screen location, as well as the width, height, and color. For a bitmap sprite, it's necessary to store the current location, as well as the Image that makes up the bitmap. (You'll learn all about bitmaps soon!)

- Visibility. Sprites are either visible or invisible. For example, if you fire at an enemy ship and score a hit, it disappears. In other words, the sprite that displays the enemy changes from visible to invisible.

- Priority. Sprites often have priority in relation to other sprites. A sprite of a certain priority appears in front of those sprites with lower priority.

- Updateability. Some sprites need to be updateable. For example, one sprite may be moving to a new location on the screen, another sprite might change colors as time passes, and a third sprite may be expanding in size. Each sprite's behavior might be different, but what unifies them is that their appearance on the screen changes with time. You've already seen an example of an update operation: danceStep() from the dancing rectangle classes of the previous chapter, which jiggles the rectangle in accordance with the rules of the particular dance. An updating sprite can be told to stop and stay frozen. In this case, we'll say that the sprite moves from an active state to an inactive one.

Sprite Behaviors

 Painting. The sprite paints itself to the screen. The way it does this depends on its internal representation. If the sprite is invisible, painting does nothing.

 Updating. The sprite computes how it will appear next, possibly depending on other sprites. A sprite that is inactive doesn't update.

Later in this chapter, you will learn to implement sprites with Java. By constructing sprite classes with these properties, you'll have a layer on which you can write games and graphics applets. But first, let's discuss *abstract classes*, which will provide a way of expressing essential sprite behaviors.

Using Abstract Classes

A class stores information about state and behavior. The classes that you have seen are templates from which you can create, or *instantiate*, actual objects. By contrast, an *abstract class* is a class in which no instantiation is allowed. Let's see why abstract classes are useful.

Consider the problem of creating classes that describe physical features of dinosaurs, for use in a Dinosaur battle game. Particular dinosaur types, such as the Triceratops, Stegosaurus, and the infamous Tyrannosaurus Rex, are all deserving of their own classes, since each has distinct physical characteristics that distinguish it and make it dangerous or vulnerable to attack. A Triceratops, for example, is a powerful foe, armed with three horns and a shield on its head. On the other hand, in a battle game, a Brontosaurus is a definite liability, with a long, humped body, a long neck, and a preference for leafy greens. Moreover, each class has features common to all dinosaurs, such as tough, reptilian skin, cold blood, and intelligence worthy of an earthworm. These essential dinosaur features properly belong to a parent class called Dinosaur.

Let's briefly sketch what the Triceratops, Brontosaurus, and Dinosaur classes might look like in our game:

```
public class Dinosaur {
  byte brainMass;    // in milligrams
  short weight;      // in kilograms
  int scalySkinStrength;
  boolean plantEater;
  boolean meatEater;
...
}
```

continued on next page

continued from previous page

```
public class Triceratops extends Dinosaur {
  short hornLength[] = new int[3]; // array of horn lengths
  short shieldStrength;
...
}

public class BrontosaurusStegaosauraus extends Dinosaur {
  short humpSize;
  short neckLength;
...
}
```

Figure 3-1 illustrates the relationship between the three classes.

Now, here's the dilemma. It is possible to create Triceratops and Brontosaurus objects with these definitions for use in the game. But you can also instantiate a Dinosaur object. This should *not* be possible, since the Dinosaur class doesn't specify an actual object in our game, but the characteristics common to all dinosaur objects.

The solution is simple. Declare Dinosaur to be an *abstract class*, by using the *abstract* keyword as follows:

```
public abstract class Dinosaur {
...
}
```

FIGURE 3-1

◎ ◎ ◎ ◎ ◎ ◎

Dinosaur hierarchy

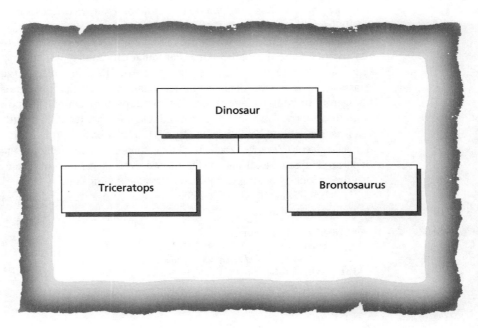

Now no instantiation of Dinosaur is possible:

```
Dinosaur d = new Dinosaur(); // illegal for abstract class
```

Abstract classes usually sit at the top of class hierarchies and often correspond to categories of objects that are so broad, in the scope of the problem, that further refinement is needed before instantiation is possible. For example, classes such as Mammal, Musician, and ElectricPoweredDevice, discussed in the previous chapter, might best be represented by abstract classes.

Methods can be abstract as well. Abstract methods serve as placeholders for behaviors that subclasses can implement. For example, behaviors common to all dinosaurs are eating and sleeping. This could be specified in the Dinosaur class in our game as follows:

```
public abstract class Dinosaur {
...
// methods:
  public abstract void eat();
  public abstract void sleep();
...
}
```

Now the abstract methods can be brought to life by the Triceratops class, for example:

```
public class Triceratops extends Dinosaur {
...
// methods:
  public void eat() {
    System.out.println("Triceratops eating");
    ...
  }
 public void sleep() {
    System.out.println("Triceratops sleeping");
    ...
 }
}
```

If a subclass of Dinosaur doesn't implement these abstract methods, it must be declared abstract. Put another way, any class that defines or inherits abstract methods (which remain unimplemented) must be declared abstract, or else an error results. Abstract methods correspond to pure virtual functions in C++, and they are called *deferred methods* in other object-oriented languages.

Now let's see how abstract classes can help us in defining the root of our sprite hierarchy.

Defining the Sprite Class

Let's define the Sprite class that will be at the top of the Sprite hierarchy. To do this, let's recap the essential features of our sprites:

 State: internal representation of onscreen appearance, location on screen, visibility, priority, updateability

 Behavior: painting, updating

The root of the Sprite hierarchy should specify and implement as many of these elements as possible, to promote a common interface and functionality among all sprites. However, most of the implementation will be deferred to the subclasses. For example, the sprites we will define have a variety of internal representations (some of which we don't even know yet), and it makes sense to leave their implementation to subclasses. Behaviors such as painting and updating rely on the internal representation of the sprite, and they'll also be given concrete form by the appropriate subclass. Thus, the paint() and update() methods, and the Sprite class itself, will be declared abstract.

The definition of Sprite is shown in Listing 3-1.

Listing 3-1 *Sprite class*

```
abstract class Sprite {
  protected boolean visible;        // is sprite visible
  protected boolean active;         // is sprite updateable

  // abstract methods:
  abstract void paint (Graphics g);
  abstract void update();

  // accessor methods:
  public boolean isVisible() {
    return visible;
  }

  public void setVisible(boolean b) {
    visible = b;
  }

  public boolean isActive() {
    return active;
  }

  public void setActive(boolean b) {
    active = b;
  }

  // suspend the sprite
  public void suspend() {
```

```
    setVisible(false);
    setActive(false);
}

// restore the sprite
public void restore() {
    setVisible(true);
    setActive(true);
}

}
```

Let's examine this class. The booleans *visible* and *active* keep track of whether the sprite can be seen and updated. The notions of suspending a sprite (resetting both *visible* and *active*) and restoring a sprite (setting both booleans) are so common that they are implemented as distinct methods. Finally, the paint() and update() methods are declared abstract, as we have discussed earlier, since they depend on how the appearance of the sprite is represented internally.

You might be wondering what the *protected* keyword (in front of the boolean declarations) refers to. This is an example of an *access specifier*, and since these come up rather often, let's discuss what they are.

Using Access Specifiers

As you know, one of the key features of objects is *encapsulation*, which means that an object's variables and methods are bundled inside it, and shielded from the outside world. Encapsulation makes building complex software easier, because it limits the interdependencies between various sections of code. The degree of encapsulation can be modified by *access specifiers—private, public,* and *protected*—which allow you to specify the access level allowed. Java supports four levels of access:

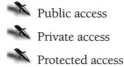 Public access

Private access

Protected access

Package/default access

Now let's find out what these mean. Consider the following class definition:

```
public class Foo {
  public float publicNumber = 13.17f;
  public void publicMethod() {
...
  }

  private double privateNumber = -4.4;
```

continued on next page

continued from previous page

```
  private int privateMethod() {
...
 }

 protected float protectedNumber = 17.13f;
 protected void protectedMethod() {
...
 }

 int defaultAccessLevelNumber;
 void defaultAccessLevelMethod() {
...
 }
}
```

Let's discuss the four different access levels that are present in class Foo.

Public Access

The public access level is the most liberal level in Java. Variables or methods declared public are accessible to arbitrary classes. Furthermore, the public variables and methods of a class are inherited by its subclasses.

Here's an example of public access. Any class that instantiates a Foo object f can modify its public variables and call its public methods. The following code could appear in the method of any class:

```
f.publicNumber = 4.4f + 4.9f; // access allowed
f.publicMethod();             // access allowed
```

A class uses public methods to allow arbitrary clients to access its functionality. On the other hand, you should be really careful when using public variables. Any object can change the value of a public variable, and computations that depend on this value will change as well. This can lead to code that's bug prone and hard to understand. Thus, most instance variables should not be public unless absolutely necessary.

Private Access

The private access level stands at the opposite end of the spectrum from public access. It is the most restrictive level. Unlike public members, private variables or methods are *only* accessible within the class itself.

Thus, if another class (even a subclass) tried the following, the compiler would not accept it.

```
                  // f is a Foo object
f.privateNumber = 7.3 - 4.4; // access NOT allowed
f.privateMethod();           // access NOT allowed
```

Use private methods as often as necessary in your games. First of all, they don't incur the performance penalty associated with dynamic method binding, so they're slightly more efficient than regular instance methods. Furthermore, they hide the implementation of the class, which eliminates the possibility of another class calling a method it's not supposed to.

Private variables keep external objects from accidentally or malignantly modifying the object's state, so they're "safer" to use than public variables.

Protected Access

The protected access level lies somewhere between public and private. Protected variables and methods are inherited, just like public members. However, protected members are visible only within a class and its subclasses.

Let's contrast protected access with its counterparts. In the following class definition, Bar is a subclass of Foo, so the protected and public members of Foo are visible within Bar. However, the private members of Foo aren't visible in Bar.

```
public class Bar extends Foo {
  ...
  public void barMethod() {
    publicNumber = 17.17f;      // access allowed
    publicMethod();             // access allowed

    protectedNumber = 13.13f;   // access allowed
    protectedMethod();          // access allowed

    privateNumber = 9.1;        // access NOT allowed
    int x = privateMethod();    // access NOT allowed

    Foo f = new Foo();          // instance of superclass
    f.protectedNumber = 4.4f;   // this is fine also
  }
}
```

Here's another way of contrasting public, protected, and private. Protected access allows a programmer to *extend* the functionality of your class; public access allows others to *use* your class. Private access is for variables and methods used within the class.

In our Sprite class, the booleans *active* and *visible* are declared *protected* so that they'll be visible in future subclasses of Sprite.

Package/Default Access

The *package* access level takes effect when no access modifier is used (which is why it's the default level of access). Variables and methods at the default access level are accessible to all code throughout the package, but aren't visible outside the package. Furthermore, the nonprivate members in a package are also visible throughout the package. Packages and package access are useful in constructing libraries of classes, and we'll cover packages in greater detail in Chapter 10, Advanced Techniques.

Figure 3-2 contains a summary of the access levels that Java provides.

FIGURE 3-2

◎ ◎ ◎ ◎ ◎ ◎

Java access levels

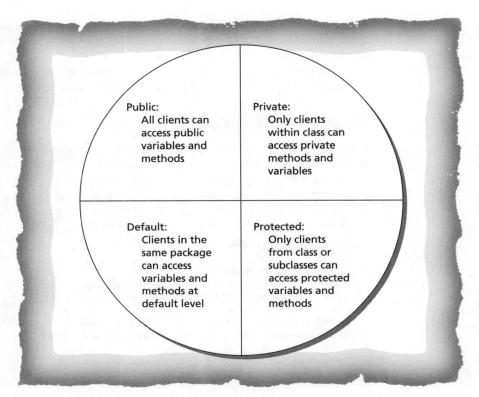

Before moving on, let's discuss one technique that's used in conjunction with private and protected variables.

Accessor Methods

Sometimes it's necessary for an outside class to access a protected (or private) variable. Instead of making such a variable public and exposing it to the world, you can provide an *accessor method*. The methods isVisible() and setVisible(), defined in the Sprite class, are examples of accessor methods that allow other classes to test and set a protected variable.

```
// accessor methods:
public boolean isVisible() {
  return visible;
}

public void setVisible(boolean b) {
  visible = b;
}
```

In a way, accessor methods allow you to have your encapsulation cake and eat it too. By providing accessor methods, you allow external clients to access a protected or private variable. At the same time, clients cannot alter such a variable directly, which preserves the benefits of encapsulation. The penalty is the additional overhead of a method call. Often, accessor methods will be declared *final* to eliminate the runtime cost of dynamic method binding.

Accessor methods are a common technique in object-oriented programming, and you'll see them again and again.

Now you should understand what's happening in the Sprite class. To see how this class is used, let's rewrite the Mondrian applet we created in Chapter 1, Fundamental Java, using the Sprite class.

Applying the Sprite Class to an Example Applet

Let's look once again at the Mondrian applet we created in Chapter 1 and modified in Chapter 2. The first version was quick and dirty, the secondversion used objects, and this version will use the Sprite class. As you'll see, the abstraction provided by Sprites enables you to reuse the applet code for sprites of any kind.

The first step is to create a subclass of Sprite that displays a rectangle. This sounds like a trivial problem, but you need to create subclasses with future extensibility in mind. For example, you'll want to derive a BitmapSprite as well as a TextSprite pretty soon. These Sprite subclasses have internal representations different from subclasses that will rely on primitives provided by java.awt.Graphics, such as RectSprite.

To unify the sprites based on the Graphics class primitives (like RectSprite), let's derive another abstract class called Sprite2D, shown in Listing 3-2.

Listing 3-2 *Sprite2D class*

```
abstract class Sprite2D extends Sprite {

  protected int locx;
  protected int locy;

  Color color;
  boolean fill;

  public boolean getFill() {
    return fill;
  }

  public void setFill(boolean b) {
```

continued on next page

continued from previous page

```
        fill = b;
    }

    public void setColor(Color c) {
      color = c;
    }

    public Color getColor() {
      return color;
    }

}
```

This class introduces instance variables that track the screen location of the sprite (*locx* and *locy*), the sprite's color, and whether it is filled or an outline. All these variables are declared *protected*, so they are directly accessible by all subclasses, but not to other clients. Sprite2D provides accessor methods to test and modify *color* and *fill*. Methods to modify *locx* and *locy* are provided in the lower subclasses.

RectSprite will derive from Sprite2D. Figure 3-3 shows what this class hierarchy will look like.

Since you'll want to instantiate RectSprite objects, the RectSprite class must have no abstract methods. In particular, it must implement paint() and update(), which are declared by RectSprite's grandparent, the Sprite class. Look for these methods in the definition of RectSprite, shown in Listing 3-3.

FIGURE 3-3

◎ ◎ ◎ ◎ ◎ ◎

Current Sprite hierarchy

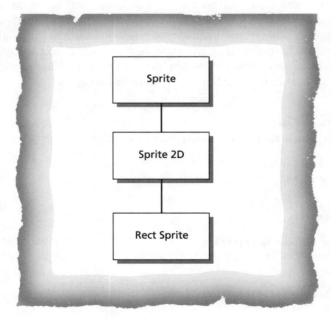

Listing 3-3 *RectSprite class*

```
class RectSprite extends Sprite2D {

  protected int width, height;    // dimensions of rectangle

  public RectSprite(int x,int y,int w,int h,Color c) {
    locx = x;
    locy = y;
    width = w;
    height = h;
    color = c;
    fill = false;                  // default: don't fill
    restore();                     // restore the sprite
  }

  // provide implementation of abstract methods:

  public void update() {

    // does nothing

  }

  // check if sprite's visible before painting
  public void paint(Graphics g) {
    if (visible) {
      g.setColor(color);

      if (fiil) {
       g.fillRect(locx,locy,width,height);
      }

      else {
       g.drawRect(locx,locy,width,height);
      }

    }

  }

}
```

RectSprite's update() method is empty, but it is no longer abstract. RectSprite's paint() method checks the values of the inherited booleans *visible* and *fill* before displaying the rectangle. By allowing instance variables defined in the Sprite and Sprite2D superclasses to control painting and other behaviors, you lay the groundwork for consistent, predictable semantics across the entire Sprite hierarchy. For example, if r is a RectSprite instance, then invoking

```
r.setVisible(false);  // Sprite method
```

prevents r from painting, and calling

```
r.setFill(true);      // Sprite2D method
```

causes r to paint as a solid rectangle. Other Sprite2D subclasses that implement paint() in a similar way will also function in a predictable way that is controllable by methods defined in Sprite and Sprite2D.

Now let's discuss the new Mondrian class. We are not going to actually implement it here, since it is practically the same as Listing 2-3 of the previous chapter. Instead, here is a summary of the three modifications needed to use Sprite classes.

First, instead of an array of DancingRect, declare an array of Sprite:

```
Sprite sprites[];                    // sprite array
```

Now modify the initRectangles() method. You might want to rename it initSprites() to initialize the *sprites* array, and instantiate the RectSprite objects. For example:

```
public void initSprites() {

  sprites = new Sprite[NUM_SPRITES]; // init sprite array

  // create RectSprite objects
  sprites[0] = new RectSprite(0,0,90,90,Color.yellow);
  ...
}
```

Finally, you will need to use the *sprites* array in all of the new methods used in Mondrian. For example, let's examine the loop in Mondrian's paint() method:

```
for (int i=0; i<sprites.length; i++) {
  sprites[i].paint(offscreen);      // paint each rectangle
}
```

This loop enforces a notion of priority among the sprites by painting the *sprites* array from the lowest index to the highest. Thus, a sprite of a given index will be painted later than sprites of lower indices, occluding those that occupy the same spot on the screen. The priority feature of sprites is implemented in this simple manner. For example, a sprite with index 0 will appear behind every other sprite.

This applet is only a simple demonstration of our Sprite classes, so here's an easy assignment for you. Derive a BoogieRectSprite (as defined in Chapter 2, Using Objects for Animation) from RectSprite. You will only need to rename the danceStep() method of BoogieRect to update(), and the BoogieRectSprite will be ready to dance.

Now let's create a fancier applet, with moving sprites, by using another abstraction that Java provides—*interfaces*.

Using Interfaces

You've already seen an informal definition of an interface. Now you'll see how Java lets you create interfaces to highlight relationships and similarities among classes. In this section, you will learn about Java interfaces and how they help in designing programs. Then, you will apply your knowledge in creating a Moveable interface for Sprite subclasses.

What Is an Interface?

Interfaces form a bridge between the internals of an object and external objects. More precisely, an interface is the set of method specifications that external objects can use to send messages to an object. In the nonabstract classes that you've seen, the set of public methods provide the public interface to objects of that class. For example, Figure 3-4 illustrates the interplay between a RectSprite's internals, its interface, and the outside world.

Interfaces highlight a key principle of software engineering: the separation of specification from implementation. The public interface, or specification, is all the outside world must know to interact with the object. No knowledge of the implementation is needed, or even desired. By separating specification from implementation, you can write code that relies on classes that have not yet been implemented. This is a powerful paradigm for creating programs, because classes can be implemented independently of one another (for example, by different programmers) once the design of the classes is settled.

FIGURE 3-4

◎ ◎ ◎ ◎ ◎ ◎

RectSprite internals, interface, and external environment

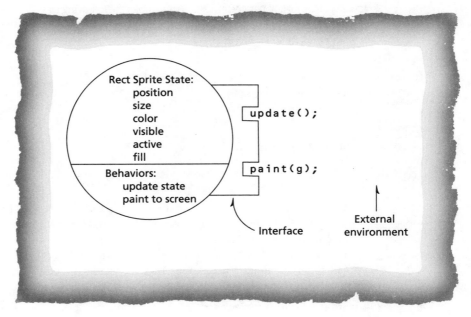

Java Interfaces

Java provides a way of declaring an interface that is completely free of implementational detail. For example, the following declares an interface called myInterface:

```
public interface myInterface {
  void method1();
  int method2(int i);
  float method3(float i, int j);
}
```

Each method declared in an interface is implicitly *public* and *abstract*. In other words, the above declaration is equivalent to

```
public interface myInterface {
  public abstract void method1();
  public abstract int method2(int i);
  publc abstract float method3(float i, int j);
}
```

No method bodies are permitted in an interface declaration, because all methods are abstract.

Now, a class *implements* an interface by providing the definitions of the methods specified by the interface. To implement myInterface, for example, the implementing class needs to provide definitions of method1(), method(), and method3() that match the return types and the formal parameter lists. For example, the following class implements myInterface:

```
public class myClass implements myInterface {
  public void method1() {
    // do nothing
  }

  public int method2(int f) {
    return f * 17 + 13;
  }

  public float method3(float s, int f) {
    return s * f;
  }
}
```

As you see, the variable names in the parameter lists don't need to match; only the types do. Another interface you've used several times is the Runnable interface, which is implemented by providing a run() method.

Interfaces may also declare constants (i.e., static final variables). Then, a class that implements such an interface can use these constants directly, without having to prefix them with the class name, as is the case with static variables. Here's an example:

```
interface FavoriteNumbers {
  static final int IRA = 13;
```

```
  static final int JO = 17;
}

class Us implements FavoriteNumbers {
  int minus(int x) {
    return JO - IRA * x;
  }
}
```

Multiple Interfaces

A class can implement multiple interfaces, as in the following:

```
public class MyLife extends HardLife
implements Birth,School,Work,Death {
...
}
```

MyLife must provide the definitions of the methods specified in Birth, School, Work, and Death to compile without error. Some of these methods might be inherited from the superclass HardLife.

An interface may inherit from other interfaces, as in the following example:

```
public interface Work extends WakeUp,Daydream,GoToSleep {
...
}
```

Work inherits the abstract methods and constants declared in its parent interfaces. A class that implements Work must define the methods specified in WakeUp, Daydream, GoToSleep, and in Work itself.

Be sure to distinguish inheritance from using an interface. A class can inherit elements of state and behavior from a superclass, but a class that implements an interface must supply the specified methods. Furthermore, a class inherits from only one class, while there is no restriction on the number of interfaces a class can implement.

Abstract Classes vs. Interfaces

You might be wondering when it's better to use an abstract class or an interface. An abstract class can provide instance variables, and nonabstract (i.e., implemented) methods, as well as abstract methods. If you have a purely abstract class that consists of only abstract methods, you will achieve greater flexibility by defining it as an interface. Neither an abstract class nor an interface can be instantiated; however, you can create variables that refer to objects that implement the interface or the abstract class. You will see examples of this below.

Now let's apply interfaces to Sprites.

Creating a Moveable Interface

One of the most important things that sprites can do is *move*. For example, in the BoogieRectSprite class (your exercise), the update() method causes movement by modifying the values of *locx* and *locy*. This movement remains internal to the BoogieRectSprite object. Once the object is instantiated, the pattern of motion is fixed and unalterable by external objects.

However, some sprites need to be able to respond to external requests to move. Consider a video game where you control a ship that can move left or right. A sprite represents the ship, and this sprite must alter its motion based on your input. The sprite needs an interface to bridge the gap between its internal state and requests from the outside to move.

There are two solutions, and the one you'll choose depends on the particular nature of the application.

✎ One solution is to incorporate the movement methods into the Sprite class. In this case, all subclasses will respond to messages from the outside to move, unless these methods are overridden.

✎ The other solution is to use a Moveable interface. This is the one we will adopt. This solution allows you to explicitly state which Sprite subclasses will obey requests to move. In addition, it allows you to address other classes that implement the Moveable interface in a uniform manner.

Here's a short list of movement methods that we'll use in the next few chapters:

✎ setPosition(int x, int y). This method moves the sprite to the screen location (x,y).

✎ setVelocity(int x, int y). Velocity is the rate of change in the position, and it will be represented by two new instance variables, vx and vy. This method sets the values of vx and vy.

✎ updatePosition(). This method updates the sprite's location, based on its velocity.

Let's translate this interface into Java. The definition of the Moveable interface is shown in Listing 3-4.

Listing 3-4 *Moveable interface*

```
interface Moveable {
  public abstract void setPosition(int x, int y);
  public abstract void setVelocity(int x, int y);
  public abstract void updatePosition();
}
```

Next, let's see how a Sprite subclass could implement this interface. We're going to create an applet that bounces sprites off walls.

Creating an Applet with Bouncing Sprites

Here's the plan for this applet. First, we will derive a BouncingRect from RectSprite. Then, the applet will instantiate a few BouncingRects and run with the standard animation driver. You will see how the Moveable interface is used to set the BouncingRects in motion!

Take a look at the BouncingRect class, shown in Listing 3-5.

Listing 3-5 *BouncingRect class*

```
class BouncingRect extends RectSprite implements Moveable {

    // the coords at which
    //  the rectangle bounces
    protected int max_width;
    protected int max_height;

    // sprite velocity. used to implement Moveable interface
    protected int vx;
    protected int vy;

    public BouncingRect(int x,int y,int w,int h,Color c,
                    int max_w,int max_h) {
      super(x,y,w,h,c);
      max_width = max_w;
      max_height = max_h;
    }

    // implements Moveable interface //
    public void setPosition(int x,int y) {
      locx = x;
      locy = y;
    }

    // implements Moveable interface //
    public void setVelocity(int x,int y) {
      vx = x;
      vy = y;
    }

    // implements Moveable interface //
    // update position according to velocity
```

continued on next page

continued from previous page

```
public void updatePosition() {
  locx += vx;
  locy += vy;
}

// move and bounce rectangle if it hits borders
public void update() {


  // flip x velocity if it hits left or right bound
  if ((locx + width > max_width) ||
    locx < 0) {
    vx = -vx;
    }

  // flip y velocity if it hits top or bottom bound
  if ((locy + height > max_height) ||
    locy < 0) {
    vy = -vy;
    }
  updatePosition();
}

}
```

As promised, BouncingRect provides implementations for the methods specified by Moveable. By calling setPosition() or setVelocity(), you can alter the location or velocity of a BouncingRect object.

The update() method calculates the new position of the BouncingRect for each frame of the animation. If one of the edges of the rectangle goes beyond the borders, the rectangle bounces by negating the proper component of the velocity. For example, Figure 3-5 illustrates how the rectangle bounces off the right border by flipping the sign of *vx*.

Now let's create an applet called Bounce. The initSprites() method of the Bounce applet creates each BouncingRect and sets it in motion by using the Moveable interface. Pay particular attention to the last three lines.

```
public void initSprites() {

  sprites = new Sprite[NUM_SPRITES]; // init sprite array

  // define sprite for border
  sprites[0] = new RectSprite(0,0,width-1,height-1,Color.green);

  sprites[1] = new BouncingRect(0,0,30,30,Color.yellow,
                            width-1,height-1);

  sprites[2] = new BouncingRect(17,17,13,13,Color.red,
                            width-1,height-1);


  ((Moveable)sprites[1]).setVelocity(4,3);
```

FIGURE 3-5

◎ ◎ ◎ ◎ ◎ ◎

Rectangle bounce

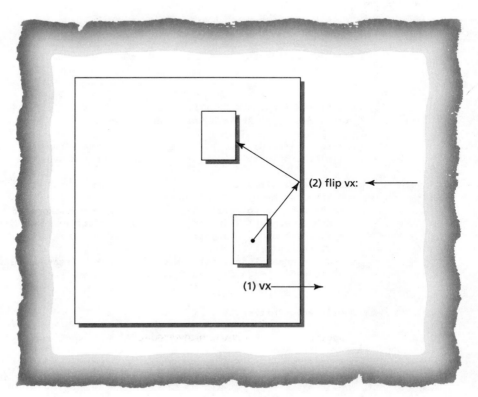

```
((Moveable)sprites[2]).setVelocity(1,2);
((Sprite2D)sprites[2]).setFill(true);  // fill this sprite
}
```

The last three lines demonstrate how to access interface and subclass methods that aren't declared in the base abstract class. By casting elements of the *sprites* array to the appropriate subclass, such as Sprite2D, or interface, such as Moveable, you can access the methods declared there. You will get a compile-time error if you don't perform these casts, since methods such as setFill() and setVelocity() are not declared in Sprite.

The complete Bounce applet class is shown in Listing 3-6.

Listing 3-6 Bounce class

```
import java.applet.*;
import java.awt.*;

/////////////////////////////////////////////////////////////////////
public class Bounce extends Applet implements Runnable {
```

continued on next page

continued from previous page

```java
    Thread animation;

    Graphics offscreen;
    Image image;


    static final int NUM_SPRITES = 3;
    static final int REFRESH_RATE = 80; // in ms

    Sprite sprites[];                    // sprite array
    int width, height;                   // applet dimensions

    public void init() {
      System.out.println(">> init <<");
      setBackground(Color.black);        // applet background
      width = bounds().width;            // set applet dimensions
      height = bounds().height;
      initSprites();
      image = createImage(width,height); // make offscreen buffer
      offscreen = image.getGraphics();
    }

    public void initSprites() {

      sprites = new Sprite[NUM_SPRITES]; // init sprite array

      // define sprite for border
      sprites[0] = new RectSprite(0,0,width-1,height-1,Color.green);

      sprites[1] = new BouncingRect(0,0,30,30,Color.yellow,
                          width-1,height-1);

      sprites[2] = new BouncingRect(17,17,13,13,Color.red,
                          width-1,height-1);


      ((Moveable)sprites[1]).setVelocity(4,3);
      ((Moveable)sprites[2]).setVelocity(1,2);
      ((Sprite2D)sprites[2]).setFill(true);  // fill this sprite
    }

    public void start() {

      System.out.println(">> start <<");
      animation = new Thread(this);
       if (animation != null) {
         animation.start();
        }
    }

    // CALL EACH SPRITE'S update() METHOD
```

```java
// DYNAMIC METHOD BINDING OCCURS HERE!
public void updateSprites() {
  for (int i=0; i<sprites.length; i++) {
    sprites[i].update();            // call each sprite's
                                    //    update() method
  }
}



// override update so it doesn't erase screen
public void update(Graphics g) {
  paint(g);
}

//
public void paint(Graphics g) {

  offscreen.setColor(Color.black);
  offscreen.fillRect(0,0,width,height);  // clear buffer

  for (int i=0; i<sprites.length; i++) {
    sprites[i].paint(offscreen);     // paint each rectangle
  }

  g.drawImage(image,0,0,this);
}

public void run() {
  while (true) {
    repaint();
    updateSprites();
    try {
     Thread.sleep (REFRESH_RATE);
    } catch (Exception exc) { };
  }
}


public void stop() {

  System.out.println(">> stop <<");
  if (animation != null) {
    animation.stop();
    animation = null;
  }
}

}
```

This should look familiar, since it's basically the same animation driver you have seen before. It's easy to incorporate new sprite types into this animation. First, define

Sprite2D subclasses for any of the graphics elements supported by java.awt.Graphics, such as lines, ovals, or polygons, by following what we have done for rectangles. Then, instantiate and initialize the sprites in initSprites(), and you have your own animation!

You are not limited to the drawing primitives in Java's Graphics class, of course. In the next section, you will see how you can incorporate *bitmaps* into the same animation.

Using Bitmaps

In this section, you will learn about bitmaps and how they are handled in Java. Then you will create bitmap sprites that you can plug right into our standard animation applet!

Bitmaps in Java

A bitmap is an image that you can paint directly to the screen. Figure 3-6 shows a bitmap that you will use in the next video game to represent your ship.

You can create bitmaps by using the many paint programs that are written for your computer. For example, Macintosh users can use MacPaint, UNIX users might try xpaint, PC users can use the Paint tool that comes with Windows. When you are creating bitmaps to use in Java applets, save them as GIF files, since installations of Java will definitely use this format. Other common formats, such as BMP or TIFF, might not be understandable to the particular system.

Loading and Drawing a Bitmap Image

There are only three steps needed to load and draw a bitmap, or Image, as Java calls it.

1. First, import the java.awt.Image class, by using one of the following:

```
import java.awt.Image;
```

or

```
import java.awt.*;
```

FIGURE 3-6

◎ ◎ ◎ ◎ ◎ ◎

Ship bitmap

2. Load and create an Image object with the Applet method getImage(). The following section will explain how to specify the correct location of the image.

3. Now you're ready to draw the image. Use the drawImage() method defined in the Graphics class:

```
public void paint(Graphics g) {
    g.drawImage(alien,13,17,this); // draw alien image at screen
                                   //  location (13,17)
}
```

If this looks familiar, it should! The offscreen image used in double-buffering is drawn to the screen in the same way. The upper-left-hand corner of the bitmap is placed at the x and y coordinates specified in drawImage().

Another version of the drawImage() method allows you to scale the bitmap to the desired proportions:

```
// scale image to the specified width and height,
//   and draw it at (x,y)
g.drawImage(image,x,y,width,height,this);
```

Specifying the Location of a Bitmap Image

Since your applet could be running anywhere across the Internet, you need to tell the applet where to find the right image. There are three ways:

 Use the URL of the image file. If the bitmap is located at a URL, such as http://www.somewhere.com/images/alien.gif, you can load the image into your applet by using the following syntax:

```
Image alien = getImage(
    new URL("http://www.somewhere.com/images/alien.gif"));
```

This works by creating a URL object with the desired location, and loading the image found there. In general, however, you should avoid hardcoding URLs, because your applets will break if you move the image to a different location. As a result, the next options are preferable.

 Find the Image relative to the HTML document. Let's say, for instance, that the HTML document that includes your game applet is at http://www.somewhere.com/game/game.html. Then, if the image is in the same directory as game.html, use the following syntax:

```
Image alien = getImage(getDocumentBase(),"alien.gif");
```

If the subdirectory "bitmaps" is in the same place as game.html, and alien.gif is found in "bitmaps," use

```
Image alien = getImage(getDocumentBase(),"bitmaps/alien.gif");
```

The last option is similar.

 Find the Image relative to the applet class. If the image is in the same directory as the applet class, then use

```
Image alien = getImage(getCodeBase(),"alien.gif");
```

 You can find images in subdirectories, as in the previous case.

Now you're ready to create bitmap sprites.

Creating Bitmap Sprites

Bitmap sprites are completely different from the sprites you have already seen, which are subclassed from Sprite2D, so let's derive, in Listing 3-7, BitmapSprite from the root Sprite class.

Listing 3-7 *BitmapSprite class*

```
class BitmapSprite extends Sprite {
  protected int locx;
  protected int locy;

  // image dimensions
  protected int width,height;

  Image image;                    // the bitmap
  Applet applet;                  // the parent applet

  public BitmapSprite(int x,int y,Image i,Applet a) {
    locx = x;
    locy = y;
    image = i;
    applet = a;
    restore();
  }

  // set the size of the bitmap
  public void setSize(int w,int h) {
    width = w;
    height = h;
```

```
    }

    public void update() {

      // do nothing

    }

    public void paint(Graphics g) {
      if (visible) {
        g.drawImage(image,locx,locy,applet);
      }
    }
  }
```

This follows the basic outline used for RectSprite. The instance variables *locx* and *locy* track where the bitmap should be painted, and *image* points to the bitmap itself. The variable *applet* is needed to call the drawImage() method, and it refers to the applet that the BitmapSprite object is in.

Now let's create a BouncingBitmap sprite. This class derives from BitmapSprite, and implements the Moveable interface. It resembles the BouncingRect class you saw earlier. The definition of the BouncingBitmap is shown in Listing 3-8.

Listing 3-8 *BouncingBitmap class*

```
class BouncingBitmap extends BitmapSprite implements Moveable {

  // the coords at which
  //   the bitmap bounces
  protected int max_width;
  protected int max_height;

  // sprite velocity. used to implement Moveable interface
  protected int vx;
  protected int vy;

  public BouncingBitmap(int x,int y,Image i,Applet a,
                        int max_w,int max_h) {
    super(x,y,i,a);
    max_width = max_w;
    max_height = max_h;
  }

  public void setPosition(int x,int y) {
```

continued on next page

continued from previous page

```
        locx = x;
        locy = y;
}

public void setVelocity(int x,int y) {
  vx = x;
  vy = y;
}

// update position according to velocity
public void updatePosition() {
  locx += vx;
  locy += vy;
}

// move and bounce bitmap if it hits borders
public void update() {


  // flip x velocity if it hits left or right bound
  if ((locx + width > max_width) ||
    locx < 0) {
    vx = -vx;
    }

  // flip y velocity if it hits top or bottom bound
  if ((locy + height > max_height) ||
    locy < 0) {
    vy = -vy;
    }
  updatePosition();
}

}
```

The implementation of the Moveable interface and the update() method are identical to those in BouncingRect. Thus, a BouncingBitmap behaves just like a BouncingRect, except it paints a bitmap! Figure 3-7 shows a Sprite hierarchy of everything we've constructed in this chapter.

FIGURE 3-7

◉ ◉ ◉ ◉ ◉ ◉

Sprite class hierarchy

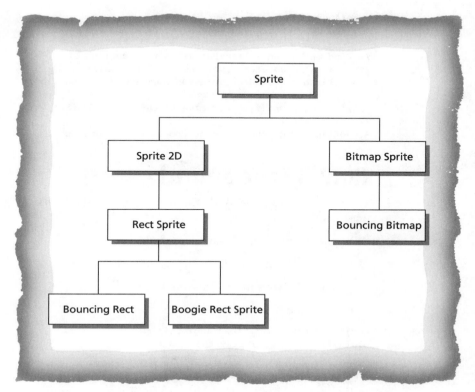

Using Sound

Sound is an integral part of a full multimedia experience, and Java makes it easy for you to put sounds into your applets. Java represents sounds with AudioClip objects. AudioClip is an interface that's defined in the java.applet package. There are two steps involved in using an AudioClip: loading an AudioClip, and playing the AudioClip.

Loading an AudioClip

To load an AudioClip, use the getAudioClip() method, defined in the java.applet.Applet class. Here's an example of the three ways you can use this method, which are analogous to the ways of loading an Image:

```
// need this at the start of the code
import java.applet.*;
...
// Use the absolute URL of the sound file
AudioClip a =
```

continued on next page

continued from previous page

```
getAudioClip(
  new URL("http://www.somewhere.com/sounds/sound.au"));

// Find the sound file relative to the location of
//   the HTML document that contains the applet
AudioClip b = getAudioClip(getDocumentBase(),"sound.au");

// Find the sound file relative to the location of
//   the applet
AudioClip c = getAudioClip(getCodeBase(),"sound.au");
```

Playing the Sound

The interface java.applet.AudioClip defines the methods that an AudioClip object must have. They are

✎ play(). This method plays the sound.

✎ loop(). This method loops the sound over and over.

✎ stop(). Use this method to stop the sound.

For example:

```
AudioClip a = ... // load AudioClip
a.play();          // play the sound
a.loop();          //loop the sound
a.stop();          // stop the sound
```

Let's use sound along with our new classes in the last applet of this chapter.

Four Rectangles and a Sushi Chef

This applet (shown in Figure 3-8) is a straightforward extension of what we have already built. By using the abstract Sprite class, you can plug a sprite in with a completely new representation, such as a bitmap, without making any changes to the animation driver. By creating an environment of plug-n-play sprites, you make game and graphics programming more understandable and extensible.

In fact, Listing 3-9 shows the only change from Listing 3-6.

Listing 3-9 *New initSprites() method*

```
public void initSprites() {

  sprites = new Sprite[NUM_SPRITES]; // init sprite array


  sprites[0] = new BouncingBitmap(37,37,
                           getImage(getCodeBase(),
```

```
                                                    "sushi.gif"),
                                        this,
                                        width-1,height-1);
            sprites[1] = new BouncingRect(0,0,30,30,Color.yellow,
                                        width-1,height-1);

            sprites[2] = new BouncingRect(17,17,13,13,Color.red,
                                        width-1,height-1);

            // border of the smaller box
            sprites[3] = new RectSprite(0,0,114,114,Color.green);

            // this rect bounces in a smaller box!
            sprites[4] = new BouncingRect(13,13,17,17,Color.green,
                                        114,114);

    // define sprite for border
            sprites[5] = new RectSprite(0,0,width-1,height-1,Color.green);


            ((Moveable)sprites[1]).setVelocity(4,3);
            ((Moveable)sprites[2]).setVelocity(1,2);
            ((Moveable)sprites[4]).setVelocity(3,1);
            ((Sprite2D)sprites[4]).setFill(true);  // fill this sprite
            ((Moveable)sprites[0]).setVelocity(1,3);
            ((BitmapSprite)sprites[0]).setSize(144,113);
        }
```

As you see, the sushi bitmap is defined as sprite 0, which is the lowest priority, so it will appear behind everything else. Put this method into the Bounce applet, and be sure to redefine

```
static final int NUM_SPRITES = 6;
```

so the applet knows how many sprites there are!

FIGURE 3-8

◉ ◉ ◉ ◉ ◉ ◉

Four rectangles and a sushi chef

A final point. Notice how the abstraction provided by the Moveable interface allows you to request behavior from relatively distant classes in a clear, uniform manner. This is illustrated by the last six lines of initSprites(). You'll be using more interfaces in future chapters.

Suggestion Box

Here are three ideas that you should think about (for fun!). We will cover the solutions in the following chapters.

- Create Sprite2D subclasses for the other primitives in java.awt.Graphics. Follow the model of the RectSprite to make an ArcSprite, OvalSprite, or PolygonSprite.

- Right now, the BitmapSprite only displays one bitmap. Subclass a BitmapLoop, which will display a sequence of bitmaps in a single sprite. You will want to define an array of Images to do this, and a counter that tracks the current frame.

- In the bouncing applets, the sprites don't interact with each other. Consider creating an interface to allow sprites to determine if an intersection has occurred. Then you can create an animation where all sprites bounce off each other!

Summary

In this chapter, you've learned about abstract classes and interfaces, and how they permit the clean, modular design of applets. In particular, you've created Sprite classes that you'll use in your first Java game (which is coming up really soon!). And you now know how to use bitmaps, which are important in creating customized looks for your graphics applets.

Next, you will see how to take control of your sprites!

4

Adding Interactivity

Joel Fan

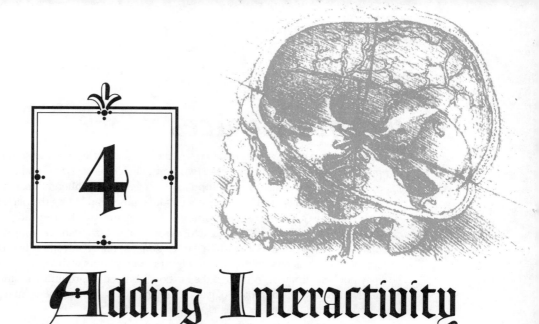

4

Adding Interactivity

Goals:

Understand input devices and Java's event handling

Learn more about bitmaps

Create interactive applets

Interactivity is a critical element in games. Your users must be able to act and react within the game world. (Otherwise, it's a simulation, not a game!) In this chapter, you will learn how to add interactivity to your applets by allowing players to manipulate *input devices*, primarily the mouse and the keyboard. The key is understanding how the Java Abstract Windowing Toolkit (AWT) structures and handles *events*.

So far, you have learned how to animate sprites that operate on their own after they have been created. Now, you'll see how applets and sprites can respond to external input. You'll also learn how to display text and use bitmaps in a variety of ways. The final applet of the chapter uses event handling and bitmap animation so you can fly a UFO in space! To begin, let's talk about input devices.

How Input Devices Work

An input device allows information from the outside world to be transmitted to the computer. The Java AWT supports the two input devices—keyboard and mouse—that are available on practically every computer. Each device has different uses in game design.

The keyboard is ideal for inputting text, of course, and letting the player control multiple activities concurrently. Anytime an arcade game uses buttons, for example, it can be adapted to a keyboard. There's an obvious limit to how many buttons you can manipulate at once—humans usually have ten fingers, and controlling five or six buttons simultaneously is probably at the limit for (human) players with average dexterity. (Aliens may not be as limited!) Although the keyboard is good for inputting multiple binary values, which is sufficient for lots of games, it's not the best device when you need to navigate a two-dimensional space. This is a job for a mouse.

There are two basic ways of mapping mouse motion into a 2D playing field:

One method treats the mouse as an absolute pointer into 2D space, in the same way as windowing systems, such as Windows 95 or the MacOS. This approach is well suited for games where the playing field is limited to the size of a particular window, like card games, or board games such as chess and Monopoly.

The second method interprets the mouse move or location as an indicator of relative motion. This way, the mouse can navigate a game world that exists beyond the confines of the window. For example, DOOM, which has a 2D playing field (although the graphics are 3D), uses the mouse in this way. When you pull the mouse toward you, your character appears to move forward.

Figure 4-1 illustrates these two ways of using the mouse in games.

A mouse also has one or more buttons that might trigger actions such as firing a gun, jumping into hyperspace, or betting all your money.

Sometimes, it's not obvious which input device—keyboard or mouse—is better for the game you're writing. One solution is to permit both forms of input and let the player decide. But try to stay away from requiring your players to manipulate both mouse and keyboard rapidly and simultaneously—it's like asking some people to rub their heads while patting their stomachs!

Now, let's see how mouse and keyboard input gets transmitted to an applet. Such input is an example of an *event*.

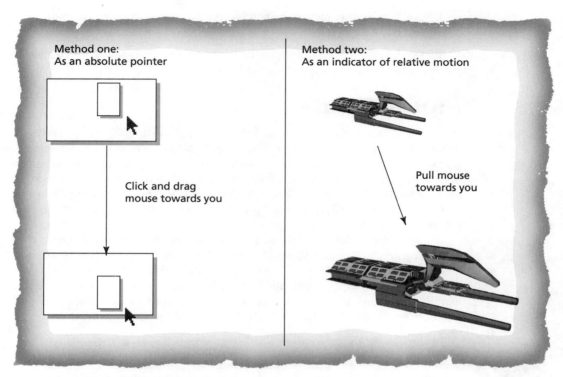

FIGURE 4-1 ◉ *Using the mouse in games*

What Is an Event?

An event is an action such as a keypress or a mouse move. When you manipulate an input device, such as the mouse or keyboard, you trigger an event. And by providing the appropriate event *handlers*, you can determine what actions a program will take when an event occurs. An event handler is simply a method that you provide in an applet class. As you can guess, events and event handling are crucial in creating games that respond to people.

As a Java game designer, your task of handling events is considerably simplified by the AWT, which does the dirty work of encapsulating events as objects and passing these event objects to the appropriate handlers. The following is a high-level view of what happens:

1. The player triggers an event through the mouse or keyboard.

2. The event is wrapped as an object and passed to the appropriate event handler. This step happens automatically. (Sometimes, associated parameters, such as the location of the event, are passed as well.)

3. The event handler method, which you provide, takes action based on the contents of the event object.

Before we go any further, let's distinguish between events triggered through the mouse and events initiated from the keyboard.

Mouse Events

Here's an illustration of a mouse event. Let's say an applet is running, and you press the mouse button inside the applet's bounding rectangle. You've triggered a *mouseDown* event. An Event object is created and passed, along with the mouse's location, to the appropriate event handler. This handler is the mouseDown() method, which is inherited by your applet class. The default mouseDown() does nothing, but by overriding it in your applet, you can specify what happens. Figure 4-2 summarizes how the mouseDown event gets passed to your applet.

Of course, mouseDown isn't the only mouse input event. Some others that the AWT also recognizes are *mouseUp*, which occurs when the mouse button is released, *mouseMove*, triggered if the mouse changes location, and *mouseDrag*, which is a combination of depressing the button and moving the mouse (i.e., dragging the mouse). To handle these events, all you need to do is override the appropriate method. Table 4-1 is a list of mouse events and the methods that get called when they occur.

Event	Method
mouseDown (mouse button pressed)	public boolean mouseDown(Event e,int x,int y)
mouseDrag (mouse moves while button down)	public boolean mouseDrag(Event e,int x,int y)
mouseEnter (mouse enters applet region)	public boolean mouseEnter(Event e,int x,int y)
mouseExit (mouse exits applet region)	public boolean mouseExit(Event e,int x,int y)
mouseMove (mouse moves while button up)	public boolean mouseMove(Event e,int x,int y)
mouseUp (mouse button up)	public boolean mouseUp(Event e,int x,int y)

TABLE 4-1 ◈ *Mouse events*

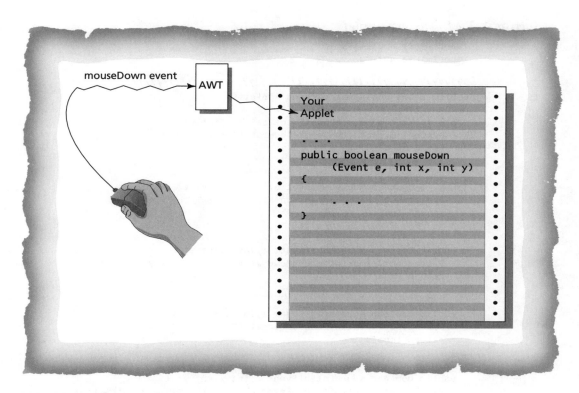

FIGURE 4-2 ◎ *mouseDown event*

Each of these methods is called with the actual Event object, and the screen position of the mouse (relative to the upper-left corner of the applet's bounding rectangle). This way, you can customize behavior depending on where the mouse is or how much it moves, as you'll soon see.

Let's start with a simple example. If you want to intercept a mouseDown event, you'll need to override the default mouseDown() by putting the following in the applet definition:

```
public boolean mouseDown(Event e,int x,int y) {
  // Your mouseDown handler here
  ...
  return true;                        // or return false
}
```

Listing 4-1 shows an applet that responds to mouse events by echoing the event that's occurred. Try it now. It really illustrates how mouse events work!

Listing 4-1 *MouseTest applet*

```
import java.applet.*;
import java.awt.*;

//////////////////////////////////////////////////////////////////
public class MouseTest extends Applet {

  public boolean mouseDown(Event e,int x,int y) {
    System.out.println("mouseDown at (" + x + "," + y + ")" );
    return true;
  }

  public boolean mouseUp(Event e,int x,int y) {
    System.out.println("mouseUp at (" + x + "," + y + ")" );
    return true;
  }

  public boolean mouseMove(Event e,int x,int y) {
    System.out.println("mouseMove at (" + x + "," + y + ")" );
    return true;
  }

  public boolean mouseDrag(Event e,int x,int y) {
    System.out.println("mouseDrag at (" + x + "," + y + ")" );
    return true;
  }

  public boolean mouseEnter(Event e,int x,int y) {
    System.out.println("mouseEnter at (" + x + "," + y + ")" );
    return true;
  }

  public boolean mouseExit(Event e,int x,int y) {
    System.out.println("mouseExit at (" + x + "," + y + ")" );
    return true;
  }
}
```

Two points should be made here:

First, each event handler returns a boolean. When the handler returns *true*, this tells the AWT that the Event has been handled and doesn't need to be passed to another AWT object. If the handler returns *false*, the Event is propagated by the AWT. You'll understand the reason for this when we discuss the AWT below.

Second, you might be wondering what all the + signs are doing. They are performing String concatenation, and the text delimited by double quotes are String objects. Strings are explained later in this chapter.

Keyboard Events

Keyboard events work in the same way as mouse events. For example, if you press a key, the keyDown() method inherited by the Applet class gets invoked. Unlike mouseDown, a keyDown event triggers again and again while the key is depressed, due to the repeating nature of the keyboard. keyUp happens when the key's released. Table 4-2 shows these keyboard events, and the event handlers that are called in response.

Event	Method
keyDown (key is pressed)	public boolean keyDown(Event e, int key)
keyUp (key is released)	public boolean keyUp(Event e, int key)

TABLE 4-2 ◈ *Keyboard events*

You can examine the key passed into the keyUp() or keyDown() methods to take the appropriate action. For example, you might compare the variable *key* with character literals:

```
public boolean keyDown(Event e, int key) {
  if (key == 'S') {      // if S pressed
  ...                    // do something
  }
  else if (key == 'F') { // if F pressed
  ...                    // do something else
  }
  return true;
}
```

To test for function keys, you'll need to use constants defined in the Event class. Let's examine this class and some of the functionality it provides.

The Event Class

The Event class is defined in the java.awt package, and it's used to wrap and pass events among the various components of the AWT. For example, the object that is passed into event handlers is an instance of the Event class. To decipher some Event objects, you need to use constants and methods defined within Event. Let's see how this is done.

Handling Function Keys

Event defines static constants that represent the special keys you will find on your keyboard—function keys, arrow keys, and the <HOME>, <END>, <PAGE UP>, and <PAGE DOWN> keys. You can use these constants in your key handlers. For example:

```
public boolean keyDown(Event e, int key) {
  if (key == Event.UP) {    // if up arrow pressed
  ...                       // do something
  }
  else if (key == Event.F7) { // if F7 pressed
  ...                         // do something else
  }
  return true;
}
```

Table 4-3 lists the static constants defined for keys in the Event class.

Keys	Static constants defined in Event
Arrow keys	UP, DOWN, LEFT, RIGHT
Function keys	F1, F2, F3, F4, F5, F6, F7, F8, F9, F10, F11, F12
Movement keys	HOME, END, PGUP, PGDN

TABLE 4-3　◈　*Constants for function keys in the Event class*

Handling Modifier Keys

The Event class provides a way of testing for the presence of modifier keys, such as <CTRL>, <SHIFT>, or <META>, during an event. For example, you can use the Event methods controlDown(), metaDown(), or shiftDown() to provide three types of mouse clicks:

```
public boolean mouseDown(Event e,int x,int y) {
  if (e.shiftDown()) {
  // handle shift-click
  ...
  }
  else if (e.controlDown()) {
  // handle control-click
  ...
  }
  else if (e.metaDown()) {
  // handle meta-click
  ...
  }
```

```
   ...
   return true;                    // or return false
}
```

Another way of checking if a modifier key is pressed is to examine the *modifiers* instance variable of the Event object. You'll need to bitwise-AND the appropriate bitmask defined in Event with the *modifiers* variable. If the result is not equal to 0, the associated modifier key is down. Table 4-4 lists the modifier keys, along with their bitmasks defined in the Event class.

Modifier Key	Static bitmask defined in Event
<ALT>	ALT_MASK
<CTRL>	CTRL_MASK
<META>	META_MASK
<SHIFT>	SHIFT_MASK

TABLE 4-4 ◈ *Bitmasks for modifier keys defined in the Event class*

For example, here's how you could test if a mouse click occurred with the <SHIFT> and <ALT> keys down:

```
public boolean mouseDown(Event e,int x,int y) {
  if ((e.modifiers & Event.ALT_MASK) != 0 &&
      (e.modifiers & Event.SHIFT_MASK) != 0) {

    // handle shift-alt-click
    ...
}
```

On a mouse with multiple buttons, depressing the right button is equivalent to a mouseDown event with the <META> key down, and clicking the middle button corresponds to a mouseDown event with the <ALT> key down. Thus, you can write a game that utilizes the input from a multiple button mouse, and works with a single button mouse as well.

The Event class is a crucial part of Java's AWT. In the next section, you'll get the big picture of the AWT, and how the AWT passes Event objects around.

Event Handling in the AWT

The java.awt package in the API provides GUI functionality—windows and scrollbars, list boxes and menu bars—so that users can interact with Java applications in an eye-pleasing way. In this section, we'll focus on how the AWT handles events. In Chapter

7, Creating Customizable Games with the AWT, you'll see how to create graphical user interfaces with the AWT.

Overview of Component classes

The heart of the AWT derives from the abstract class Component. Figure 4-3 shows some of the classes that have Component as a superclass.

The Component class defines many methods—paint(), repaint(), update(), setBackground(); event handlers such as mouseUp() and keyDown(), and so on—that the other AWT classes inherit or override. You've used or overridden some of these methods before, since the Applet class, which is part of the java.applet package, also derives from Component.

Right below Component is Container, which is another abstract class. A Container, as its name implies, can contain other Components. For example, an Applet could contain a Button object and a Checkbox object. The Applet is known as the *parent container* of the button and checkbox. A Frame (another Container class) could contain this Applet and another Button object. Figure 4-4 depicts the containment hierarchy for the components we've just described.

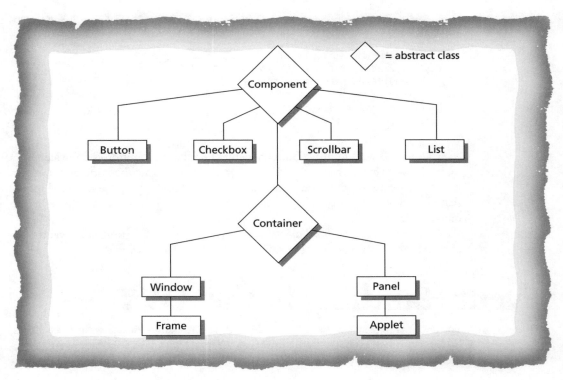

FIGURE 4-3 ◉ *Classes derived from Component*

FIGURE 4-4
FIGURE 4-4

◎ ◎ ◎ ◎ ◎ ◎

Example of a containment hierarchy

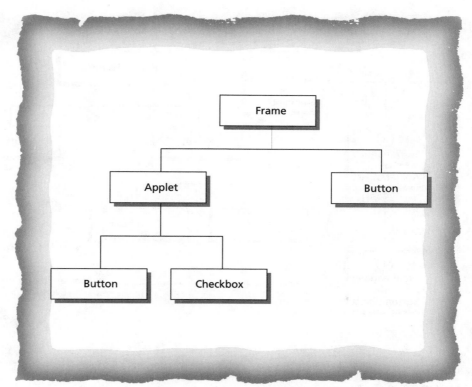

How the AWT Handles Events

When an event such as a mouseDown occurs in a Container, there might be several AWT objects that could possibly handle the event. For example, a click that occurs in an applet might be of use to the window that contains it; the applet's event handler needs to pass the mouseDown event to the event handler for the window. Java uses the following convention to achieve this. When the event handler of a Component, such as an Applet, returns *false*, the event is passed to the handler in the parent Container. A return value of *true* indicates that the event should not be propagated. Thus, events are passed from the event handler of the "innermost" component (the component that triggered the event), up the containment hierarchy, to the handler of the "outermost" component (the root of the containment hierarchy). Figure 4-5 illustrates how an event is passed from component to component.

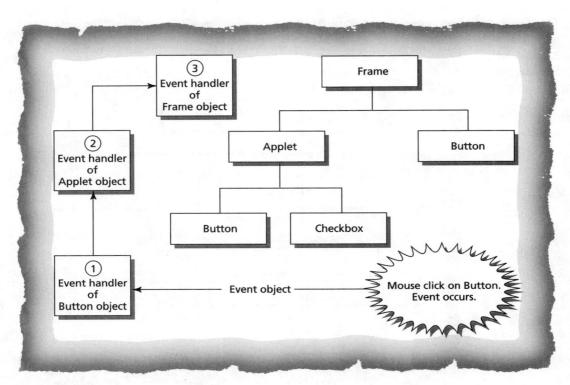

FIGURE 4-5 ◉ *Event propagation*

All components, including Applet, use the method handleEvent() as the default event handler. handleEvent(), in turn, dispatches events to the "helper" handlers you've seen above, such as keyDown(), mouseDrag(), and mouseMove(). By overriding handleEvent(), you can test for GUI events that don't have helper methods. Although this isn't necessary until Chapter 7, Creating Customizable Games with the AWT, which describes GUIs, let's see how it's done.

The handleEvent() method is called with an argument of class Event. The Event instance variable *id* stores the type of event that has occurred; you'll compare *id* with static constants defined in the Event class. (A complete list of these constants appears in Chapter 7.) The Event instance variables *x* and *y* store the coordinates of the event.

Here's an example of using the handleEvent() method:

```
// this code appears in a subclass of Component
public boolean handleEvent(Event e) {
  switch (e.id) {
  case Event.MOUSE_UP:
    // handle mouse up. Now, mouseUp() is NOT called
    if (e.x == e.y)        // compare x and y coords of event
```

```
        ...
      break;
    case Event.WINDOW_DEICONIFY:
      // no helper method for this event, so this is
      //   the only way to check for it
      break;
    case Event.WINDOW_MOVED:
      // no helper method for this event, so this is
      //   the only way to check for it
        ...
}
```

When you override handleEvent(), helper methods such as mouseUp() and keyDown() aren't called, unless you pass events to these methods explicitly. Another way of resuming the default event handling, even when you've overridden handleEvent(), is to call the superclass handleEvent() at some point in the overriding method:

```
super.handleEvent(e);
```

Now that you understand how Java handles events, you're ready to create interactive applets. First, we'll take a brief digression and show how to display text, which we'll need for applets later on in this chapter.

Displaying Text

An easy way to show text is by using the static method System.out.println(), which is in the class java.lang.System. This method is overloaded, so it works with many different types of arguments, such as numeric types or Strings. If you use it, the output appears on the standard output stream, or on the "Java console" if you're running a Web browser.

Another way of displaying text is to use the method showStatus(String), defined in the class java.applet.Applet. This Applet method shows the String on the status line of the applet. (If you run appletviewer, the status line appears at the bottom of the applet window.)

To display text within the applet, there are three steps involved: defining the text string, choosing a font, and drawing the text to the screen. Let's cover each part in turn.

Defining Strings

A String in Java is an object, and not an array of char. In addition, a String object is immutable, which means that you can't change its contents. If you want a string of characters that can be modified, create a StringBuffer object.

The easiest way of creating a String object is actually shorthand for invoking the String constructor:

```
String helloString = "hello";
```

As a String object, *helloString* can use all the methods defined in java.lang.String. The String class provides a lot of the functionality found in the C library strings.h, such as length(), which returns the length of the String, and substr(), which pulls out a substring. Furthermore, the + operator concatenates String arguments, as you have seen. Look in Appendix A, Java Reference Tables, for a list of String methods.

Choosing Fonts

The font determines how the String will appear on the screen. To specify a certain font, point size, and font style (plain, bold, italic, bold + italic) you must create a Font object. For example, the following defines a Font object of Courier, 14-point bold and italic:

```
Font courierFont =
  new Font("Courier",Font.BOLD+Font.ITALIC,14);
```

Fonts and Font Styles Supported by Java:

Fonts: Courier, Dialog, DialogInput, Helvetica, TimesRoman, ZapfDingbats.
Font styles: These are static constants defined in the java.awt.Font class: Font.PLAIN, Font.ITALIC, Font.BOLD. If you need both bold and italic, use Font.ITALIC + Font.BOLD.

If your applet picks a font that is not supported by the platform, Java uses a default font.

Drawing Strings

There are two steps here. First, you should set the font of the graphics context, like this:

```
g.setFont(courierFont);
```

Then you can draw *helloString* at the given width and height:

```
g.drawString(helloString,width,height);
```

A lot of times, you'll want to justify the text. To do this, use the class java.awt.FontMetrics. A FontMetrics object can tell you how much space a String will take, for a given Font. For example:

```
g.setFont(myFavoriteFont);
FontMetrics m = g.getFontMetrics();
int stringWidth = m.stringWidth(helloString);
```

stringWidth now contains the width, in pixels, of *helloString*.
Let's illustrate all this in an applet.

Inserting a Text String into an Applet

If you ran the MouseTest applet, you noticed that the applet was completely blank. Now we will display a little reminder of what the applet is supposed to do at the center of the applet.

The new version of the MouseTest applet is shown in Listing 4-2. It also uses the Applet method showStatus() to display the mouse event at the bottom of the applet window.

Listing 4-2 *Revised MouseTest applet*

```java
import java.applet.*;
import java.awt.*;

public class MouseTest2 extends Applet {
  Font courierFont;
  String testString = "Test the mouse in here!";

  public void init() {
    courierFont = new Font("Courier",Font.BOLD+Font.ITALIC,24);
  }

  public void paint(Graphics g) {
    g.setFont(courierFont);

    // center the string
    FontMetrics m = g.getFontMetrics();
    int stringWidth = m.stringWidth(testString);
    int width = (bounds().width - stringWidth )/2;
    int height = bounds().height / 2;

    // draw the string
    g.setColor(Color.green);
    g.drawString(testString,width,height);
  }

  public boolean mouseDown(Event e,int x,int y) {
    showStatus("mouseDown at (" + x + "," + y + ")" );
    return true;
  }


  public boolean mouseUp(Event e,int x,int y) {
    showStatus("mouseUp at (" + x + "," + y + ")" );
    return true;
  }

  public boolean mouseMove(Event e,int x,int y) {
    showStatus("mouseMove at (" + x + "," + y + ")" );
```

continued on next page

continued from previous page

```
      return true;
   }


   public boolean mouseDrag(Event e,int x,int y) {
      showStatus("mouseDrag at (" + x + "," + y + ")" );
      return true;
   }

   public boolean mouseEnter(Event e,int x,int y) {
      showStatus("mouseEnter at (" + x + "," + y + ")" );
      return true;
   }

   public boolean mouseExit(Event e,int x,int y) {
      showStatus("mouseExit at (" + x + "," + y + ")" );
      return true;
   }
}
```

The message

```
Test the mouse in here!
```

will display in the center of the applet, as Figure 4-6 shows.

Now let's see how you can control sprites with the mouse. In the next section, we will build an applet that lets you drag and move a rectangle.

FIGURE 4-6

◉ ◉ ◉ ◉ ◉ ◉

Revised
MouseTest
applet

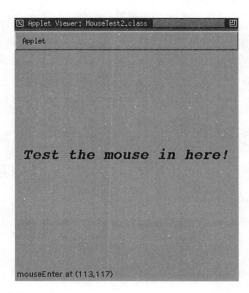

Clicking and Dragging Sprites

Clicking and dragging an icon is a common activity in any GUI. First, the user selects the icon by clicking the mouse on it. Then, the icon moves with the mouse, as long as the button stays down. Figure 4-7 illustrates the steps involved.

Now you'll see one way of doing this in Java.

First, let's define, in Listing 4-3, a DragRect class, which will be used as the "icon" in this applet. The DragRect inherits from RectSprite, which was defined in the previous chapter. It defines an additional boolean called *draggable*, which records if the DragRect can be moved or not. Since *draggable* is *protected*, we will include the usual accessor methods.

FIGURE 4-7

◎ ◎ ◎ ◎ ◎ ◎

Clicking and dragging

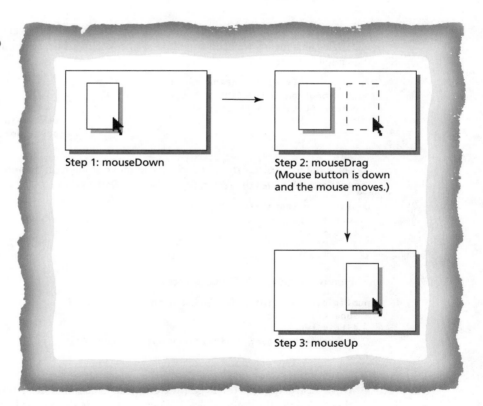

Step 1: mouseDown

Step 2: mouseDrag
(Mouse button is down and the mouse moves.)

Step 3: mouseUp

Listing 4-3 DragRect class

```
//////////////////////////////////////////////////////////////////
class DragRect extends RectSprite {

  protected boolean draggable;     // is rectangle draggable?

 // accessor methods: modify draggable
  public void setDraggable(boolean b) {
    draggable = b;
  }

// return draggable
  public boolean isDraggable() {
    return draggable;
  }
```

Now, when does the rectangle become draggable? When the user clicks inside the rectangle. This means we need a method to check if an arbitrary point, (x,y), is inside the DragRect:

```
// check if (x,y) is inside rectangle
public boolean inside(int x,int y) {
  return (locx <= x && locy <= y &&
                                    (locx + width >= x) &&
                                    (locy + height >= y));
}
```

Once the user selects the rectangle, it can move along with the mouse. The following method translates the rectangle by the specified amount:

```
public void translate(int x,int y) {
  locx += x;
  locy += y;

}
```

Finally, DragRect needs a constructor:

```
public DragRect(int x,int y,int w,int h,Color c) {
  super(x,y,w,h,c);
  fill = true;
  draggable = false; // initially not draggable
}
}
```

This constructor calls the RectSprite constructor first, before setting the booleans.

Now let's write the main applet. We need to provide the mouse handling methods. mouseDown() checks if the mouse gets clicked in the rectangle. If so, set *draggable*, and save the old mouse position.

```
// if user clicks in the rectangle, make rectangle draggable

int oldx,oldy;    // stores old mouse location
```

```
public boolean mouseDown(Event e,int x,int y) {
  if (r.inside(x,y)) {
    oldx = x;
    oldy = y;
    r.setDraggable(true);
  }
  return true;
}
```

mouseUp() clears *draggable*:

```
// if mouseUp, rectangle is no longer draggable
public boolean mouseUp(Event e,int x,int y) {
  r.setDraggable(false);
  return true;
}
```

The following method, mouseDrag(), translates the rectangle by the difference between the new mouse position and the old. This makes the rectangle move with the mouse:

```
// translate the rectangle by the difference between
//   the new mouse position and the old one

public boolean mouseDrag(Event e,int x,int y) {
  if (r.isDraggable()) {
    r.translate(x-oldx,y-oldy);  // move rectangle
    oldx = x;                    // store old mouse position
    oldy = y;
    repaint();                   // redraw screen
  }
  return true;
}
```

The code to the applet is shown in Listing 4-4. Note that this applet doesn't implement Runnable, since the actions only occur in response to events. This is an example of *event-driven programming*. Since this applet's not double-buffered, you will get flickering, but you know how to cure that!

Listing 4-4 Draggable Rectangle applet

```
import java.applet.*;
import java.awt.*;

//////////////////////////////////////////////////////////////
public class Drag extends Applet {
  Font courierFont;
  String testString = "Drag the Rectangle!";
  DragRect r = new DragRect(0,0,107,103,Color.red);

  public void init() {
```

continued on next page

continued from previous page

```
            courierFont = new Font("Courier",Font.BOLD+Font.ITALIC,14);
        }

        public void paint(Graphics g) {
          g.setFont(courierFont);

          // center the string
          FontMetrics m = g.getFontMetrics();
          int stringWidth = m.stringWidth(testString);
          int width = (bounds().width - stringWidth )/2;
          int height = bounds().height / 2;

          // draw the string
          g.setColor(Color.green);
          g.drawString(testString,width,height);
          r.paint(g);
        }

        // if user clicks in the rectangle, make rectangle draggable

        int oldx,oldy;    // stores old mouse location
        public boolean mouseDown(Event e,int x,int y) {
          if (r.inside(x,y)) {
            oldx = x;
            oldy = y;
            r.setDraggable(true);
          }
          return true;
        }


        // if mouseUp, rectangle is no longer draggable
        public boolean mouseUp(Event e,int x,int y) {
          r.setDraggable(false);
          return true;
        }

        // translate the rectangle by the difference between
        //   the new mouse position and the old one

        public boolean mouseDrag(Event e,int x,int y) {
          if (r.isDraggable()) {
            r.translate(x-oldx,y-oldy);  // move rectangle
            oldx = x;                    // store old mouse position
            oldy = y;
            repaint();                   // redraw screen
          }
          return true;
        }


        }
```

Finally, let's make the rectangle grow or shrink, depending on input from the keyboard. To do this, you will need to intercept keyboard events.

First, let's modify the Draggable Rectangle applet so that the rectangle grows in response to the right arrow key, and shrinks if the left arrow key is down. Add the methods grow() and shrink(), shown in Listing 4-5, to DragRect.

Listing 4-5 *Revisions to DragRect*

```
// increase size of rectangle. Note there is no
//     maximum size!
public void grow() {
  width++;
  height++;
}

// shrink the rectangle
public void shrink() {
  if (width > 0) {
    width--;
  }
  if (height > 0) {
    height--;
  }
}
```

Now add the following key handler, shown in Listing 4-6, to the Drag applet.

Listing 4-6 *Keyboard event handler for Draggable Rectangle applet*

```
// Resize rectangle:
// if Right arrow key, grow the rectangle
// if Left arrow key, shrink the rectangle

public boolean keyDown(Event e,int key) {
  switch (key) {
  case Event.RIGHT:
    r.grow();
    repaint();
    break;
  case Event.LEFT:
    r.shrink();
    repaint();
    break;
  default:
    break;
  }
  return true;
}
```

Just insert these methods into the previous applet, compile, and run!

Now it's time to lay the groundwork for our final interactive applet of the chapter. This applet allows you to move a sprite that animates a sequence of bitmaps. To do this, we'll create a class called BitmapLoop.

Creating Bitmap Loops

In the previous chapter, you saw how to load, draw, and move a single bitmap. Now let's create animation by looping a sequence of bitmaps. This requires loading several images, and we're going to use the MediaTracker class, which is part of java.awt, to do this. Why use MediaTracker? When you execute the following in an Applet,

```
Image I;
I = getImage(...);
```

the getImage() routine returns immediately with a handle to the Image. However, the requested Image isn't loaded until it is actually needed, as when a drawImage() takes place. In other words, the process of loading the Image happens asynchronously. And if the Image hasn't finished loading, drawImage() displays what's been loaded so far. This is why the bitmap in the Bounce applet looks incomplete at the start of the animation. Clearly, this isn't desirable in a game! The cure for this is in the MediaTracker class.

Using MediaTracker

MediaTracker allows you to wait for the images to finish loading before proceeding with the animation. To use it, first define a MediaTracker object:

```
MediaTracker t;
t = new MediaTracker(this);
```

Now let's tell *t* to track the status of the image sushi.gif. This takes two steps: defining the Image location, and adding the image to the MediaTracker:

```
Image i = getImage(getCodeBase(),"sushi.gif");
t.addImage(i,0);
```

The second argument to addImage() is an ID number. Images of lower ID are loaded first; furthermore, the MediaTracker can wait for images of the same ID to finish loading together.

To tell MediaTracker to wait for all images to load, use

```
try {
  t.waitForAll();
}
catch (InterruptedException e) {
}
```

To wait for images with ID 13, use

```
try {
  t.waitForID(13);
```

```
   }
catch (InterruptedException e) {
   }
```

The *try-catch* construct catches the exception that the MediaTracker object might throw.

A simple example is shown in Listing 4-7 of an applet that loads two images, and displays them only when they're done loading.

Listing 4-7 *Applet to illustrate MediaTracker*

```
// simple MediaTracker demo
///////////////////////////////////////////////////////////////

import java.applet.*;
import java.awt.*;

public class Track extends Applet {
  MediaTracker t;
  Image i,j;

  public void init() {
    setBackground(Color.black);
    t = new MediaTracker(this);
    i = getImage(getCodeBase(),"sushi.gif");
    t.addImage(i,0);
    j = getImage(getCodeBase(),"chef.gif");
    t.addImage(j,0);
    showStatus("loading");

    // wait for all images to finish loading //
    try {
      t.waitForAll();
    }
    catch (InterruptedException e) {
    }

    // check for errors //
    if (t.isErrorAny()) {
      showStatus("error");
    }
    else if (t.checkAll()) {
      showStatus("successfully loaded");
    }

  }

  public void paint(Graphics g) {
    g.drawImage(i,13,17,this);
    g.drawImage(j,203,207,this);

  }
}
```

When you run this, you will have to wait in the beginning for the images to load, but they're displayed completely once loading is done.

Table 4-5 contains a list of some useful MediaTracker methods.

java.awt.MediaTracker Method	Purpose
public MediaTracker(Component comp);	Constructor
public void addImage(Image image,int id);	Loads and tracks the specified image
public boolean checkAll();	Returns *true* if all images are loaded
public boolean checkId(int id)	Returns *true* if images with the given *id* have loaded
public synchronized boolean isErrorAny()	Returns *true* if any errors occurred in loading
public void waitForAll() throws InterruptedException;	Waits for all registered images to load
public void waitForId(int id) throws InterruptedException;	Waits for the image with the given *id* to load

TABLE 4-5 ◈ *MediaTracker methods*

Now let's define the BitmapLoop sprite class.

Defining the BitmapLoop Class

BitmapLoop will derive from BitmapSprite. Here are the definitions of Sprite and BitmapSprite, which we discussed back in Chapter 3, Animating Sprites:

```
abstract class Sprite {
  protected boolean visible;       // is sprite visible
  protected boolean active;        // is sprite updateable

  // abstract methods:
  abstract void paint (Graphics g);
  abstract void update();

  // accessor methods:
  public boolean isVisible() {
    return visible;
  }

  public void setVisible(boolean b) {
    visible = b;
  }
```

```java
    public boolean isActive() {
      return active;
    }

    public void setActive(boolean b) {
      active = b;
    }

    // suspend the sprite
    public void suspend() {
      setVisible(false);
      setActive(false);
    }

    // restore the sprite
    public void restore() {
      setVisible(true);
      setActive(true);
    }

}


class BitmapSprite extends Sprite {
  protected int locx;
  protected int locy;

  // image dimensions
  protected int width,height;

  protected Image image;                    // the bitmap
  protected Applet applet;                  // the parent applet

  public BitmapSprite(int x,int y,Image i,Applet a) {
    locx = x;
    locy = y;
    image = i;
    applet = a;
    restore();
  }

  public void setSize(int w,int h) {
    width = w;
    height = h;
  }

  public void update() {

    // do nothing

  }
```

continued on next page

continued from previous page

```
public void paint(Graphics g) {
  if (visible) {
    g.drawImage(image,locx,locy,applet);
  }
 }
}
```

Let's see how BitmapLoop will extend BitmapSprite. Since BitmapLoop animates a sequence of images, you need to add new instance variables: *images*, which refers to the array of Images, and *currentImage*, which tracks the Image that is currently shown.

```
protected Image images[];      // sequence of bitmaps
protected int currentImage;    // the current bitmap
```

We'll use the inherited *image* variable to store the background bitmap for the animation. This way, a BitmapLoop will behave like a BitmapSprite if it doesn't have foreground images to loop (i.e., *images[]* is empty). Finally, the boolean *foreground* tells if there are any images in the foreground loop.

```
protected boolean foreground;   // are there foreground images?
```

Figure 4-8 illustrates what happens in a *BitmapLoop*.

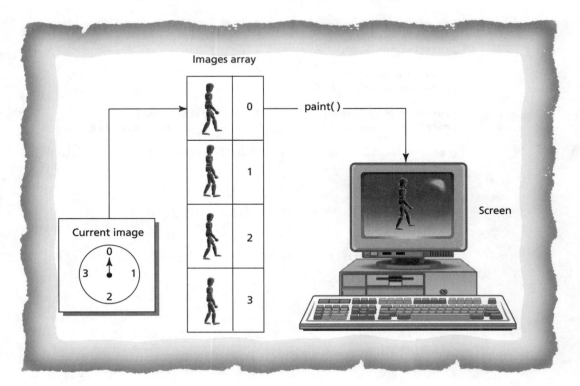

FIGURE 4-8 ◉ *BitmapLoop schematic*

Listing 4-8 shows the definition of the BitmapLoop, which also implements the Moveable interface, so we can plug it into our final applet. Of course, you can redefine the Moveable methods to provide the motion you want.

Listing 4-8 *BitmapLoop class*

```
interface Moveable {
  public abstract void setPosition(int x, int y);
  public abstract void setVelocity(int x, int y);
  public abstract void updatePosition();
}


//////////////////////////////////////////////////////////////////
class BitmapLoop extends BitmapSprite implements Moveable{
  protected Image images[];        // sequence of bitmaps
  protected int currentImage;      // the current bitmap
  protected boolean foreground;    // are there foreground images?

  // constructor. Assumes that background image is already
  // loaded. (use MediaTracker)

  public BitmapLoop(int x,int y,Image b,Image f[],Applet a) {
    super(x,y,b,a);
    width = image.getWidth(a); // get size of background
    height = image.getHeight(a);

    images = f;
    currentImage = 0;
    if (images.length == 0) {
      foreground = false;          // nothing in images[]
    }
    else {
      foreground = true;
    }

  }



  // cycle currentImage if sprite is active, and there
  //   are foreground images
  public void update() {
    if (active && foreground) {
      currentImage = (currentImage + 1) % images.length; ✓ loop
    }
    updatePosition();
  }
```

continued on next page

continued from previous page

```
public void paint(Graphics g) {
  if (visible) {         // draw background first
    g.drawImage(image,locx,locy,applet);
    if (foreground) {  // now draw foreground image

g.drawImage(images[currentImage],locx,locy,applet);
    }
  }
}

// implement moveable interface


public void setPosition(int x,int y) {
  locx = x;
  locy = y;
}
protected int vx;
protected int vy;

public void setVelocity(int x,int y) {
  vx = x;
  vy = y;
}

// update position according to velocity
public void updatePosition() {
  locx += vx;
  locy += vy;
  vx = 0;
  vy = 0;
}

}
```

Let's put together everything we've learned in this chapter. The following applet uses a BitmapLoop to animate a UFO that you can control!

An Interactive Applet Using BitmapLoop Sprites

In our final applet of the chapter, you'll use the BitmapLoop sprite defined above, along with your knowledge of MediaTracker and Java's event handling. You can use this small applet to animate any series of bitmaps that you'd like to control with the arrow keys. We've rigged it up with a sequence of UFO bitmaps, but you can replace them with images of your choice.

This applet adapts the sprite animation driver that you saw at the end of Chapter 3, Animating Sprites, with two differences:

 First, the initSprites() method (which initializes the sprites) now uses MediaTracker to ensure that images are fully loaded before proceeding. The images are stored in the directory image/, which is in the same location as the applet class. The foreground images are named fore0.gif, fore1.gif, ..., fore5.gif, and you can load them with a loop that uses String concatenation:

```
for (int i=0; i<6; i++) {
  foreImage[i] = getImage(getCodeBase(),
                          "image/fore" + i + ".gif");
  t.addImage(foreImage[i],0);   // add to MediaTracker
}
```

 Secondly, this applet overrides the keyDown() method:

```
public boolean keyDown(Event e,int key) {
  switch (key) {
  case Event.RIGHT:
    ((Moveable)sprites[0]).setVelocity(3,0);
    break;
  case Event.LEFT:
    ((Moveable)sprites[0]).setVelocity(-3,0);
    break;
  case Event.UP:
    ((Moveable)sprites[0]).setVelocity(0,-3);
    break;
  case Event.DOWN:
    ((Moveable)sprites[0]).setVelocity(0,3);
    break;
  default:
    break;
  }
  return true;
}
```

This event handler works by comparing *key* to class variables defined in Event that represent the arrow keys. If an arrow key has been pressed, *sprites[0]*, which refers to a BitmapLoop, gets cast to Moveable. In this way, you can access the Moveable methods not defined by the Sprite abstract class.

The complete UFOControl applet class is shown in Listing 4-9. We've used the UFO animation bitmaps from the next chapter, seen in Figure 5-2, as the foreground bitmap loop, which is stored in files fore0.gif, fore1.gif, .., fore5.gif. The background image is a blue circular halo surrounding the UFO, stored in the file back.gif. Of course, feel free to plug in your own bitmaps!

Listing 4-9 UFO applet

```
//////////////////////////////////////////////////////////////
// demo of BitmapLoops and user interaction
//////////////////////////////////////////////////////////////

import java.applet.*;
import java.awt.*;


public class UFOControl extends Applet implements Runnable {

  Thread animation;

  Graphics offscreen;
  Image image;

  static final int NUM_SPRITES = 1;
  static final int REFRESH_RATE = 80; // in ms

  Sprite sprites[];                    // sprite array
  int width, height;                   // applet dimensions

  public void init() {
    System.out.println(">> init <<");
    setBackground(Color.black);        // applet background
    width = bounds().width;            // set applet dimensions
    height = bounds().height;
    initSprites();
    image = createImage(width,height); // make offscreen buffer
    offscreen = image.getGraphics();
  }


  public void initSprites() {
    sprites = new Sprite[NUM_SPRITES];
    Image backImage;                   // background Image
    Image foreImage[] =  new Image[6]; // 6 foreground Images

    MediaTracker t = new MediaTracker(this);
    backImage = getImage(getCodeBase(),"image/back.gif");
    t.addImage(backImage,0);
    for (int i=0; i<6; i++) {
      foreImage[i] = getImage(getCodeBase(),
      "image/fore" + i + ".gif");
      t.addImage(foreImage[i],0);
    }

    System.out.println("loading Images");

    // wait for all images to finish loading //
    try {
```

```
      t.waitForAll();
    } catch (InterruptedException e) {
      return;
    }

    // check for errors //
    if (t.isErrorAny()) {
      System.out.println("error");
    }
    else if (t.checkAll()) {
      System.out.println("successfully loaded");
    }
    // initialize the BitmapLoop
    sprites[0] = new BitmapLoop(13,17,backImage,foreImage,this);

  }


  // Move UFO depending on Arrow Keys

  public boolean keyDown(Event e,int key) {
    switch (key) {
    case Event.RIGHT:
      ((Moveable)sprites[0]).setVelocity(3,0);
      break;
    case Event.LEFT:
      ((Moveable)sprites[0]).setVelocity(-3,0);
      break;
    case Event.UP:
      ((Moveable)sprites[0]).setVelocity(0,-3);
      break;
    case Event.DOWN:
      ((Moveable)sprites[0]).setVelocity(0,3);
      break;
    default:
      break;
    }
    return true;
  }




  public void start() {

    System.out.println(">> start <<");
    animation = new Thread(this);
    if (animation != null) {
      animation.start();
    }
  }
```

continued on next page

continued from previous page

```java
                    // CALL EACH SPRITE'S update() METHOD
                    // DYNAMIC METHOD BINDING OCCURS HERE!
                    public void updateSprites() {
                      for (int i=0; i<sprites.length; i++) {
                        sprites[i].update();          // call each sprite's
                                                      //    update() method
                      }
                    }



                    // override update so it doesn't erase screen
                    public void update(Graphics g) {
                      paint(g);
                    }


                    //
                    public void paint(Graphics g) {

                      offscreen.setColor(Color.black);
                      offscreen.fillRect(0,0,width,height);  // clear buffer

                      for (int i=0; i<sprites.length; i++) {
                        sprites[i].paint(offscreen);     // paint each rectangle
                      }

                      g.drawImage(image,0,0,this);
                    }

                    public void run() {
                      while (true) {
                        repaint();
                        updateSprites();
                        try {
                                                    Thread.sleep (REFRESH_RATE);
                        } catch (Exception exc) { };
                      }
                    }



                    public void stop() {

                      System.out.println(">> stop <<");
                      if (animation != null) {
                        animation.stop();
                        animation = null;
                      }
                    }
                  }
```

Run this applet, and use the arrow keys to maneuver the UFO!

Suggestion Box

Create TextSprite by wrapping the String and Font in a Sprite subclass. Then, you can define a TextLoop sprite, which flashes a sequence of messages, by modeling it from BitmapLoop.

Here are some options you can add to BitmapLoop. Randomly specify how long each particular bitmap should be displayed. This way, you can show certain bitmaps for varying amounts of time to create jerky motions. Also, write the methods addImage() and deleteImage(), which permit you to add and remove images from the loop dynamically. One way of doing this is to allocate a new array of the appropriate size, and use System.arraycopy() to copy the desired elements.

Create new behaviors for the UFO by defining different sprites that are restored or suspended depending on user input. For example, when you press an arrow key, display a BitmapLoop that animates UFO thrusters. Another example is a shield, which you can define as an OvalSprite that overlays the UFO sprite.

Summary

In this chapter, you have learned the intricacies of handling mouse and keyboard events in applets, which you will use in all future games. In addition, you have seen how to display text in an applet, which is necessary to relay information to the player. Another important thing that you have learned is the use of MediaTracker to load images synchronously. Finally, you have learned to create BitmapLoop sprites, which are sprites that are little animations in themselves.

Now you are ready for your first Java video game!

5

Building a Video Game

Joel Fan

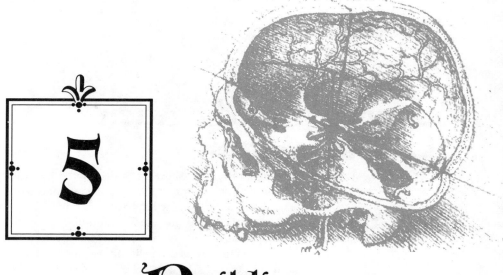

5

Building a Video Game

Goals:

Apply object-oriented principles to designing games

Create the Alien Landing game simulation

In this chapter, you will develop the core of a video game, step by step, with what you have learned about Java, animation, and event handling. This game is called Alien Landing, and you will witness the transformation of the initial concept to a full-fledged game by the next chapter. Along the way, you will learn how to structure games (and other applications) in an object-oriented manner, making them easy to understand, extensible, and cutting down on code development time. By the end of this chapter, you will have a game simulation that implements many of the features found in video games: missiles you can fire, aliens you can kill, and continuous, heart-pounding action.

First, let's describe the video game we will create.

Overview of the Alien Landing Game

The year is 2217, and humans have been discovered by hungry aliens from the Andromeda Galaxy who are seeking a tasty, warm, and nutritious meal. These aliens have decided to stage a final assault on the last bastion of humans—New York City—since the large population there will provide a bountiful harvest for years to come. As humanity's last hope, the player's job is to protect the city from these alien marauders.

The player commands the last remaining weapon: a mouse-controlled missile launcher, shown in Figure 5-1. The launcher moves left and right according to the x coordinate of the mouse. Clicking the mouse fires a single missile.

The aliens will try to land on the planet surface. When they are trying to land, they are defenseless, and any contact with the missile launcher will destroy them. But if three aliens land successfully, the banquet begins, with the player as the first appetizer!

Aliens can also go on kamikaze attacks, with the purpose of destroying the missile launcher. When an alien is in attack mode, it's invulnerable to missiles. If the launcher is hit by an attacking alien, it is destroyed.

Figure 5-2 shows the sequence of bitmaps that animate the alien landers.

Finally, Figure 5-3 shows what the game simulation will look like when you are playing it.

Before we start designing Alien Landing, let's look at the way video games execute at the top level.

FIGURE 5-1

Missile launcher

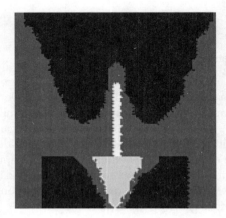

FIGURE 5-2

ⓞ ⓞ ⓞ ⓞ ⓞ ⓞ

Alien lander

FIGURE 5-3

ⓞ ⓞ ⓞ ⓞ ⓞ ⓞ

The game simulation

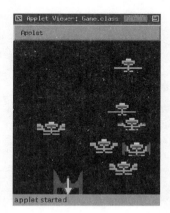

The Video Game Loop

Animation is at the heart of any video arcade game, so it's not surprising that the top-level loop of a video game is similar to the Universal Animation Loop discussed in Chapter 2, Using Objects for Animation:

```
// "Universal Animation Loop"
while there are more Frames {
  1. Draw the Current Frame f.
  2. Set f = the Next Frame.
  3. Pause for an interval of time.
}
```

Since a video game consists of many objects, including sprites, we can modify the Universal Animation Loop to get the pseudocode instructions shown in Listing 5-1, which we will call the Video Game Loop.

Listing 5-1 *Video Game Loop*

```
while playing game {
  1. Paint objects.
  2. Update objects.
  3. Pause for an interval of time.
}
```

FIGURE 5-4

◎ ◎ ◎ ◎ ◎ ◎

*Video Game
Loop*

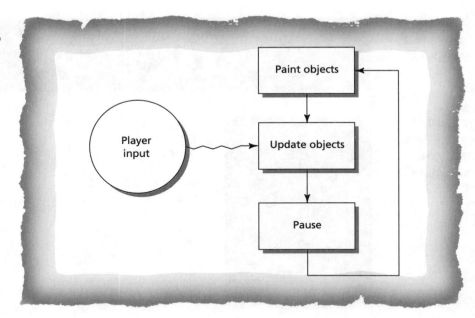

This is pretty straightforward, but let's elaborate on the first two steps. The paint step is only performed for objects with onscreen representations, such as sprites. For example, you would be hard pressed to paint an object that implements a hashtable!

The update step is the "brains" of the game, and it determines the frame-to-frame sequence of action. Update operations might modify the state of the objects, monitor interactions between objects, such as collisions, and track the state of the game, such as the score. Some objects will be updated according to player input, thereby providing the interactivity critical to video games. Figure 5-4 shows how player input fits into the Video Game Loop.

The Video Game Loop is also at the core of Alien Landing, and we're going to implement this loop by the end of the chapter. The first step is to structure the various elements of the game into logical units, each with a well-defined set of responsibilities. Let's see where these logical subdivisions are.

Dividing Responsibility Among Functional Units

One of the first steps in designing an application is deciding where the different functional units are and how responsibilities are allocated among these units. Of course, there are numerous ways of doing this for any nontrivial project, and the art of programming involves choosing a solution that is logical, understandable, and efficient. In the case of Alien Landing, the labor divides in a clear way.

The GunManager Unit

First, the missile gun should be a distinct unit, which we will call the GunManager. This unit needs to receive commands from the player and translate the input into action on the screen, such as moving left or right, or firing a missile. Each missile will keep track of its possible targets, and check to see if it has collided with an alien. Finally, both the missile launcher and the missile will be represented with sprites, GunSprite and MissileSprite, which are responsible for the onscreen appearance of these objects. Figure 5-5 shows a schematic of the GunManager unit.

The UFOManager Unit

The aliens, or UFOs, are part of another functional unit called the UFOManager, which is responsible for initializing the UFOs and telling each UFO sprite to paint and update. Each UFO sprite implements the various behaviors of the particular alien, and also determines if it has collided with the missile launcher. A diagram of the UFOManager is in Figure 5-6.

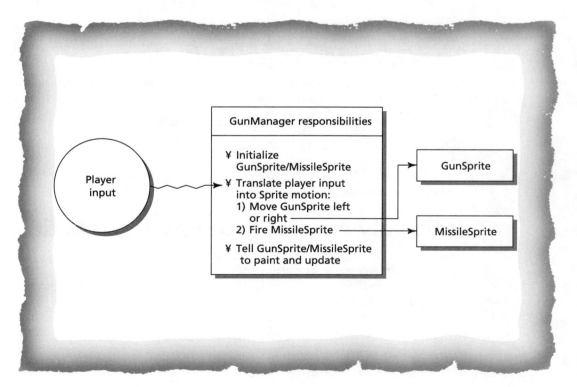

FIGURE 5-5 ◉ *GunManager*

FIGURE 5-6
◎ ◎ ◎ ◎ ◎ ◎
UFOManager

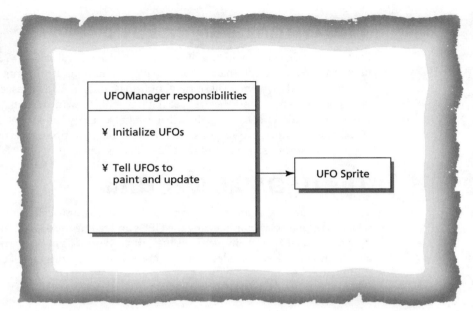

The GameManager Unit

The top-level functional unit is the GameManager, which handles parameters associated with the game as a whole. For example, the GameManager

🗡 Initializes the UFOManager and GunManager classes

🗡 Relays player input to the GunManager

🗡 Implements the Video Game Loop

Figure 5-7 illustrates these functions.

Interplay Among the Functional Units

Finally, Figure 5-8 shows how the three functional units communicate with each other. There is interaction between the GunManager and UFOManager classes. The UFOs need to know if they've been destroyed by missiles. Similarly, the missile launcher can be hit by the UFOs.

Now let's implement these units, one by one, starting with the GunManager.

FIGURE 5-7
◉ ◉ ◉ ◉ ◉ ◉
GameManager

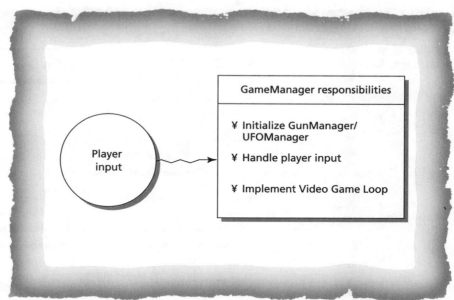

Defining the GunManager

The GunManager communicates with two sprites: one that draws the missile gun, another that paints the missile that has been fired. Let's define these sprites before proceeding to the GunManager. Both the missile and the launcher will derive from the sprite classes that you have created in the previous chapters. Listing 5-2 shows the definitions of Sprite and Sprite2D, which are the two abstract classes that rest at the top of the sprite hierarchy.

FIGURE 5-8

ⓞ ⓞ ⓞ ⓞ ⓞ ⓞ

*Interplay of
functional units*

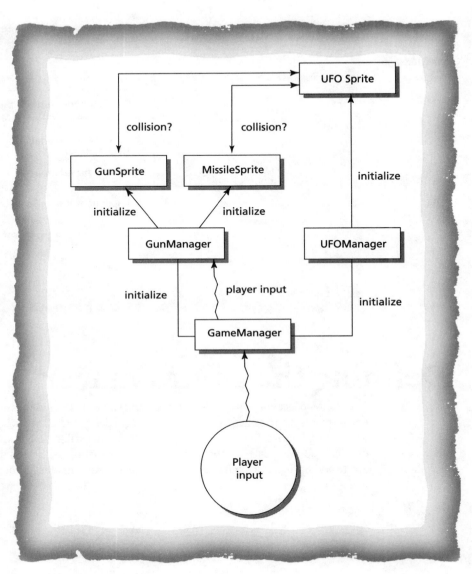

Listing 5-2 *Sprite and Sprite2D classes*

```
abstract class Sprite {
  protected boolean visible;      // is sprite visible
  protected boolean active;       // is sprite updateable
```

```
    // abstract methods:
    abstract void paint (Graphics g);
    abstract void update();

    // accessor methods:
    public boolean isVisible() {
      return visible;
    }

    public void setVisible(boolean b) {
      visible = b;
    }

    public boolean isActive() {
      return active;
    }

    public void setActive(boolean b) {
      active = b;
    }

    // suspend the sprite
    public void suspend() {
      setVisible(false);
      setActive(false);
    }

    // restore the sprite
    public void restore() {
      setVisible(true);
      setActive(true);
    }

  }

  abstract class Sprite2D extends Sprite {

    protected int locx;
    protected int locy;

    Color color;
    boolean fill;

    public boolean getFill() {
      return fill;
    }

    public void setFill(boolean b) {
      fill = b;
    }
```

continued on next page

continued from previous page

```
public void setColor(Color c) {
  color = c;
}

public Color getColor() {
  return color;
}

}
```

Now let's define the GunSprite class.

GunSprite

The GunSprite keeps all information that relates to the appearance of the missile gun onscreen, such as a bitmap for the actual gun (shown in Figure 5-1) and its coordinates in the applet.

The BitmapSprite Class

Let's subclass GunSprite from the BitmapSprite class we created back in Chapter 3, Animating Sprites. The BitmapSprite class is shown in Listing 5-3, with a new constructor added for convenience.

Listing 5-3 *BitmapSprite class*

```
class BitmapSprite extends Sprite {
  protected int locx;
  protected int locy;

  // image dimensions
  protected int width,height;

  protected Image image;          // the bitmap
  protected Applet applet;        // the parent applet

  public BitmapSprite(Image i,Applet a) {
    locx = 0;
    locy = 0;
    image = i;
    applet = a;
    if (image != null) {
      width = image.getWidth(a); // get size of background
      height = image.getHeight(a);
    }
    restore();
  }


  public BitmapSprite(int x,int y,Image i,Applet a) {
```

```
      locx = x;
      locy = y;
      image = i;
      applet = a;
      if (image != null) {
        width = image.getWidth(a); // get size of background
        height = image.getHeight(a);
      }
      restore();
    }

    public void setSize(int w,int h) {
      width = w;
      height = h;
    }

    public void update() {

      // do nothing

    }

    public void paint(Graphics g) {
      if (visible) {
        g.drawImage(image,locx,locy,applet);
      }
    }
  }
}
```

GunSprite will inherit from BitmapSprite, but it also needs other public methods that permit it to interact with the outside world. By specifying these methods in interfaces, you can formalize the interactions they represent and apply them to other objects. The Moveable interface is an example of such an interface.

The Moveable Interface

The Moveable interface, which we initially defined in Chapter 3, Animating Sprites, will enable external objects such as the GunManager to tell GunSprite where to move. Listing 5-4 defines the Moveable interface.

Listing 5-4 *Moveable interface*

```
interface Moveable {
  public abstract void setPosition(int x, int y);
  public abstract void setVelocity(int x, int y);
  public abstract void updatePosition();
}
```

The GunSprite class will implement Moveable.

The Intersect Interface

Another interface you'll need is the Intersect interface, which allows sprites to ask each other if an intersection has occurred. Think of this interface as formalizing the interaction that occurs between a missile sprite and its target, as shown in Figure 5-9.

The missile object passes its position and area on the screen to the target sprite. The target object performs the intersection test and replies *true* or *false* depending on the result.

Finally, the missile sprite can notify the target of the collision. The definition of the Intersect interface is shown in Listing 5-5.

Listing 5-5 Intersect interface

```
interface Intersect {
  public boolean intersect(int x1,int y1,int x2,int y2);
  public void hit();
}
```

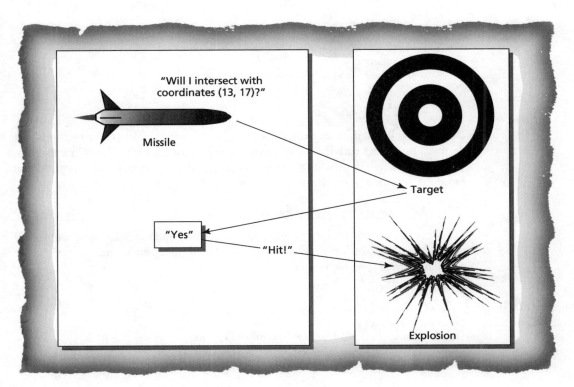

FIGURE 5-9 ◉ *Interaction between missile and target*

The GunSprite will implement Intersect, since aliens need to know if a collision has occurred with the missile launcher. One question you might be having—how do you decide if two sprites collide?

Determining Intersections with Bounding Boxes

The easiest way to determine if two sprites intersect is by comparing their *bounding boxes*. A bounding box is the smallest rectangle, with edges parallel to the x and y coordinates, that contains the entire sprite. For example, Figure 5-10 shows the bounding boxes for the alien bitmap.

Here's a simple formula for determining if two sprites intersect. Let's say that the smallest pair of coordinates of box 1 is (x1,y1), and the largest pair is (x2,y2). Similarly, box 2's smallest coordinates are (x3,y3), and the largest are (x4,y4). Figure 5-11 shows these two boxes in the applet coordinate system. Box 1 intersects with box 2 if and only if the following condition is true:

```
(x2 >= x3) && (x4 >= x1) &&    // x-extents overlap

(y2 >= y3) && (y4 >= y1)       // y-extents overlap
```

Here's another way of describing this equation. The x extent of a box is the range of x coordinates that the box occupies; y extents are defined analogously for y coordinates. The two boxes intersect if both their x extents and their y extents overlap. You can extend this intersection formula to three dimensions by testing whether the z extents also overlap.

This intersection formula trades simplicity and speed for accuracy, since parts of the bounding box are outside the sprite, as you see for the alien in Figure 5-10. For video games, that's a tradeoff that we will make. If you're concerned by the occasional error, shrink the bounding boxes by a few pixels before performing the intersection routine. Now, let's translate this intersection formula into the Java code used by GunSprite:

```
// compare bounding boxes
public boolean intersect(int x1,int y1,int x2,int y2) {

  return visible && (x2 >= locx) && (locx+width >= x1)
    && (y2 >= locy) && (locy+height >= y1);

}
```

FIGURE 5-10

◎ ◎ ◎ ◎ ◎ ◎

Bounding box for alien

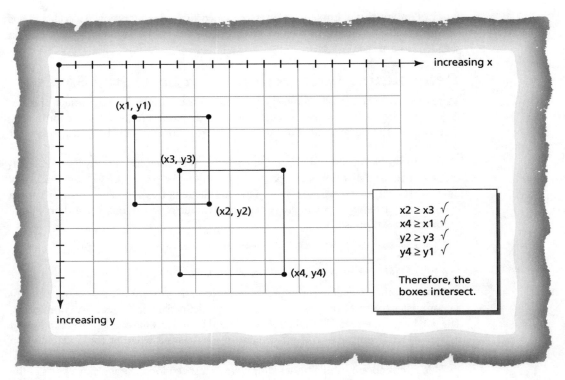

FIGURE 5-11 ◉ *Determining bounding box intersection*

This routine checks if the sprite at *(locx,locy)*, with the given *width* and *height*, intersects the bounding box between the coordinates *(x1,y1)* and *(x2,y2)*. And if the sprite is not visible, it won't overlap another sprite.

Implementing GunSprite

Let's put this together, into the definition of GunSprite, shown in Listing 5-6.

Listing 5-6 *GunSprite class*

```
class GunSprite extends BitmapSprite
  implements Moveable,Intersect {

  public GunSprite(Image i, Applet a) {
    super(i,a);
  }
```

```
// the following methods implement Moveable:

public void setPosition(int x,int y) {
  locx = x;
  locy = y;
}

public void setVelocity(int x,int y) {

}

public void updatePosition() {

}

// the following methods implement Intersect:

// compare bounding boxes
public boolean intersect(int x1,int y1,int x2,int y2) {

  return visible && (x2 >= locx) && (locx+width >= x1)
    && (y2 >= locy) && (locy+height >= y1);

}

// echo to stdout
public void hit() {
  System.out.println("HIT!");
}
}
```

As you see, the hit() method just echoes to the standard output stream, for now. (In the next chapter we will make an explosion.)

Now let's move on to the missile!

MissileSprite

The missile will be a long, thin rectangle that moves vertically. It will derive from the RectSprite class that we first defined back in Chapter 3, Animating Sprites.

The RectSprite Class

This version of RectSprite, shown in Listing 5-7, adds an additional constructor to the Chapter 3 version.

Listing 5-7 *RectSprite class*

```
class RectSprite extends Sprite2D {

  protected int width, height;     // dimensions of rectangle

  public RectSprite(int w,int h,Color c) {
    locx = 0;
    locy = 0;
    width = w;
    height = h;
    color = c;
    restore();
  }

  public RectSprite(int x,int y,int w,int h,Color c) {
    locx = x;
    locy = y;
    width = w;
    height = h;
    color = c;
    fill = false;                 // default: don't fill
    restore();                    // restore the sprite
  }

  // provide implementation of abstract methods:

  public void update() {

    // does nothing

  }


  // check if sprite's visible before painting
  public void paint(Graphics g) {
    if (visible) {
      g.setColor(color);

      if (fill) {
       g.fillRect(locx,locy,width,height);
      }

      else {
       g.drawRect(locx,locy,width,height);
      }
    }
  }
}
```

MissileSprite overrides RectSprite's update() method to provide the missile behavior. First, the missile moves upward by updating *locy* with the y velocity, *vy*. If it passes the top boundary, stored in *stop_y*, the MissileSprite suspends, and the missile disappears from the screen:

```
// move missile
   locy += vy;
   if (locy < stop_y) {
    suspend();

   }
```

Incorporating the Intersect Interface

After moving, the missile checks to see whether it has collided with any targets. By using the Intersect interface, the missile object passes its bounding box to the potential victims, who are in the *target* array. If an intersection happens, the missile notifies the victim using the hit() method, and the missile sprite suspends:

```
Intersect target[];          // array of targets
...
      for (int i=0; i<target.length; i++) {
        if (target[i].intersect(locx,locy,
                               locx+width,locy+height)) {

        target[i].hit();  // tell target it's been hit

        suspend();
        break;
       }
      }
```

As you see, the missile can interact with any object that implements the Intersect interface. If we had hardcoded the class of the target sprite into this code (say UFO), then the missile would only be able to interact with UFOs and their subclasses. By using an interface, the MissileSprite can communicate with all target classes that implement Intersect, and this makes our game more extendable.

Implementing MissileSprite

Finally, the full definition of the MissileSprite is shown in Listing 5-8.

Listing 5-8 MissileSprite class

```
class MissileSprite extends RectSprite  {
  protected int vy;          // velocity in y coordinate
  protected int start_y;     // starting y coord
  protected int stop_y;      // stop at y coord
  Intersect target[];
  public MissileSprite(int w,int h,Color c,int vy,
                    int start_y,int stop_y,
                    Intersect target[]) {
    super(w,h,c);
    setFill(true);           // fill rect sprite
    this.vy = vy;            // initialize speed
    this.start_y = start_y;  // initialize starting point
    this.stop_y = stop_y;    // initialize stopping point
    this.target = target;    // initialize targets
    suspend();
  }

  // start the missile at the given x coordinate
  public void init(int x) {
    locx = x;
    locy = start_y;
    restore();
  }

  public void update() {

    if (active) {

      // move missile
      locy += vy;
      if (locy < stop_y) {
       suspend();

      }
      // else if missile hits target, suspend it
      else {
       for (int i=0; i<target.length; i++) {
         if (target[i].intersect(locx,locy,
                           locx+width,locy+height)) {

           target[i].hit();  // tell target it's been hit

           suspend();
           break;
         }
       }
      }
    }
  }
}
```

MissileSprite also defines a method called init(), which starts the missile at the given x coordinate. The GunManager will use init() to fire the missile, as you will see next.

GunManager

The function of the GunManager class is to communicate the player's commands to the GunSprite and MissileSprite. In other words, it translates the raw input given by the player into arguments to the sprite methods. Let's see how this is done.

Computing Variables

First of all, the constructor of the GunManager initializes the GunSprite and MissileSprite variables, *gun* and *missile*, and also initializes several variables used during game play. By computing these values at initialization, you can cut down on the amount of calculation required when the game is running at full tilt.

In general, you should always try to precompute commonly used values, and use constants (i.e., *final* variables) whenever possible. In keeping with this philosophy, here's the GunManager's constructor:

```
static final int MISSILE_WIDTH = 3;
static final int MISSILE_HEIGHT = 27;
static final int MISSILE_SPEED = -27; // missile flies upward
static final Color MISSILE_COLOR= Color.red;

public GunManager(int width,int height,
                Image gunImage,Intersect target[],Applet a) {
  this.width = width;
  this.height = height;
  gun = new GunSprite(gunImage,a);

  gun_width = gunImage.getWidth(a)/2;
  gun_height = gunImage.getHeight(a);

  gun_y = height - gun_height;
  min_x = gun_width;
  max_x = width - gun_width;
  gun_min_x = 0;
  gun_max_x = width - 2*gun_width;
  mis_min_x = min_x-2;
  mis_max_x = max_x-2;
  gun.setPosition(width/2-gun_width,gun_y); // center gun
  missile = new MissileSprite(MISSILE_WIDTH,MISSILE_HEIGHT
                        MISSILE_COLOR,MISSILE_SPEED,
                        height-gun_height,
                        0,target);
}
```

In case you feel discombobulated, Figure 5-12 illustrates what all these variables mean for the GunSprite.

FIGURE 5-12
◉ ◉ ◉ ◉ ◉ ◉
GunManager
variables

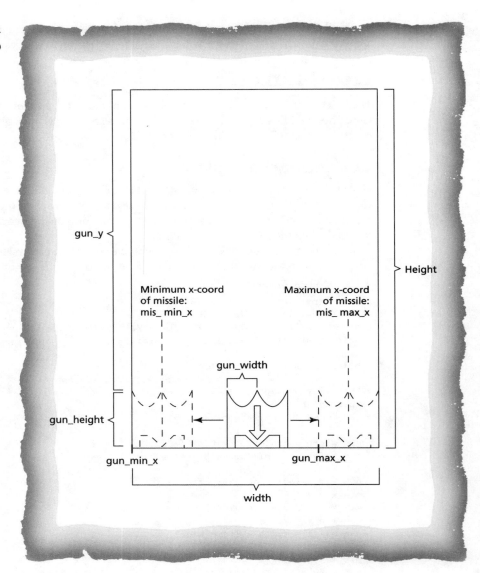

Why all these variables? The gun will be controlled by the x coordinate of the mouse, and we want the center of the gun aligned with the mouse pointer. Thus, GunSprite needs to be drawn at an offset, *gun_width*, from the mouse x coordinate. Furthermore, the missile launcher should stay within the applet's bounding rectangle, regardless of where the mouse goes. If the mouse pointer is less than *min_x*, for example, the gun should be drawn at *gun_min_x*, and the missile fired at *mis_min_x*. The case for *max_x* is similar.

Listing 5-9 shows the GunManager.

Listing 5-9 *GunManager class*

```
public class GunManager {

    private GunSprite gun;              // your gun
    private int gun_width;              // width of gun
    private int gun_height;
    private MissileSprite missile;       // missile
    static int width, height;          // applet dimensions
    private int min_x,max_x;           // min and max x coords
                                       //   for gun movement
    private int gun_min_x,gun_max_x;
    private int mis_min_x,mis_max_x;
    private int gun_y;

    static final int MISSILE_WIDTH = 3;
    static final int MISSILE_HEIGHT = 27;
    static final int MISSILE_SPEED = -27; // missile flies upward
    static final Color MISSILE_COLOR= Color.red;

    public GunManager(int width,int height,
                    Image gunImage,Intersect target[],Applet a) {
      this.width = width;
      this.height = height;
      gun = new GunSprite(gunImage,a);

      gun_width = gunImage.getWidth(a)/2;
      gun_height = gunImage.getHeight(a);

      gun_y = height - gun_height;
      min_x = gun_width;
      max_x = width - gun_width;
      gun_min_x = 0;
      gun_max_x = width - 2*gun_width;
      mis_min_x = min_x-2;
      mis_max_x = max_x-2;
      gun.setPosition(width/2-gun_width,gun_y);
      missile = new MissileSprite(MISSILE_WIDTH,MISSILE_HEIGHT,
                          MISSILE_COLOR,MISSILE_SPEED,
                          height-gun_height,
                          0,target);

    // move gun to the given x coordinate
    public void moveGun(int x) {
```

continued on next page

continued from previous page

```
             if (x <= min_x) {
               gun.setPosition(gun_min_x,gun_y);
               }
             else if (x >= max_x) {
               gun.setPosition(gun_max_x,gun_y);
               }
             else {
               gun.setPosition(x-gun_width,gun_y);
             }
         }

         // fire missile from given x coordinate
         public void fireMissile(int x) {
           if (!missile.isActive()) {       // if missile sprite
                                            //   isn't active

             if (x <= min_x) {
              missile.init(mis_min_x);
             }
             else if (x >= max_x) {
              missile.init(mis_max_x);
             }
             else {
              missile.init(x-2);                 // initialize missile
             }
           }
         }

         // update all the parameters associated with the
         //   gun. In this case, only the missile needs to move
         //   automatically. Also the gun manager checks if the
         //   missile hits anything

         public void update() {
           missile.update();
         }

         // paint all sprites associated with gun
         public void paint(Graphics g) {
           gun.paint(g);
           missile.paint(g);
         }

         // accessor function for gun
         public GunSprite getGun() {
           return gun;
         }

         public int getGunY() {
           return gun_y;
         }
     }
```

Notice that the missile is fired by calling its init() method. This is much faster than creating a new MissileSprite object for each mouse click, and it illustrates another general rule when writing games: *Avoid dynamic allocation of objects during game play.* Try to allocate all the objects you will use at the very beginning, if possible, so the runtime system doesn't need to construct one when the game is running.

Now, let's create the aliens!

Defining the UFOManager

The UFOManager is responsible for initializing the individual UFO sprites, and telling them when to paint and update. Let's create the UFO class first, before defining UFOManager.

The UFO Class

The UFO class will animate the sequence of bitmaps shown in Figure 5-2, so it becomes a subclass derived from the BitmapLoop sprite, which we introduced in Chapter 4, Adding Interactivity.

The BitmapLoop Sprite Class

Listing 5-10 shows the current definition of BitmapLoop.

Listing 5-10 *BitmapLoop class*

```
class BitmapLoop extends BitmapSprite implements Moveable{
  protected Image images[];        // sequence of bitmaps
  protected int currentImage;      // the current bitmap
  protected boolean foreground;    // are there foreground images?
  protected boolean background;    // is there background image?
  // constructor. Assumes that background image is already
  // loaded. (use MediaTracker)

  public BitmapLoop(int x,int y,Image b,Image f[],Applet a) {
    super(x,y,b,a);
    if (image != null) {               // if there's a background image
      background = true;
    }
    else {
      background = false;
    }

    images = f;
    currentImage = 0;
    if (images == null || images.length == 0) {
      foreground = false;              // nothing in images[]
```

continued on next page

continued from previous page

```
      }
      else {
        foreground = true;
        if (!background) {                // if no background
         width = images[0].getWidth(a); // get size of images[0]
         height = images[0].getHeight(a);
        }
      }
    }

    // cycle currentImage if sprite is active, and there
    //   are foreground images
    public void update() {
      if (active && foreground) {
        currentImage = (currentImage + 1) % images.length;
      }
      updatePosition();
    }


    public void paint(Graphics g) {
      if (visible) {
        if (background) {
         g.drawImage(image,locx,locy,applet);
        }
        if (foreground) {
         g.drawImage(images[currentImage],locx,locy,applet);
        }
      }
    }

// implement moveable interface

    public void setPosition(int x,int y) {
      locx = x;
      locy = y;
    }
    protected int vx;
    protected int vy;

    public void setVelocity(int x,int y) {
      vx = x;
      vy = y;
    }

    // update position according to velocity
    public void updatePosition() {
      locx += vx;
      locy += vy;
    }
}
```

The UFO reuses most of the code from the BitmapLoop, but it overrides update() to provide alienlike behaviors. The new update() implements a state machine that permits the alien to switch behavior at random moments. You saw a simple example of state machines in the DancingRect classes of Chapter 2, Using Objects for Animation; the UFO machine is just a bit more complex. By using state machines, you create a simple kind of machine intelligence in your enemies.

The Four UFO Behavioral States

The UFO has four behaviors, each represented by one of the following states :

✈ Standby. When the UFO is in Standby mode, it moves back and forth horizontally.

✈ Attack. An attacking UFO moves quickly downward, toward the missile launcher, and it is invulnerable to your missiles.

✈ Retreat. The UFO can break off the attack at any moment, and retreat, which means that it moves up, toward the top of the screen.

✈ Land. Finally, the alien can try to land, and to do this it descends vertically at a slow rate.

Figure 5-13 illustrates these various UFO behaviors.

Now let's describe how the UFO can make transitions from state to state.

Transitioning Between States

The best way to illustrate how the UFO goes from one state, or behavior, to another is with a transition diagram, in which the circles represent the four possible states, and the arrows indicate allowable transitions, as shown in Figure 5-14.

Now, the UFO moves from state to state depending on random numbers generated by the static random() method in java.lang.Math:

```
double x = Math.random(); // x is assigned a random
                          //   double from 0.0 to 1.0
```

If the random number is higher than these following constants, the UFO exits the corresponding state:

```
// probability of state transitions
static final double STANDBY_EXIT = .95;
static final double ATTACK_EXIT = .95;
static final double RETREAT_EXIT = .95;
static final double LAND_EXIT = .95;
```

Thus, the pattern of UFO behavior is unpredictable, and you can customize it by changing the probabilities.

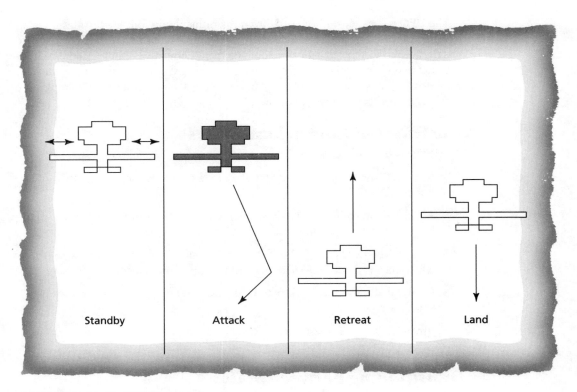

Standby   Attack   Retreat   Land

FIGURE 5-13 ◉ *UFO behaviors*

The UFO's update() method first checks to see if a collision has occurred with the missile gun. GunSprite implements Intersect, so it can be a target of the UFO sprite:

```
// this implements the state machine
public void update() {

    // if alien hits target
    //   gun_y contains the y-coordinate of the top of
    //   the gun. The first test is done to quickly
    //   eliminate those cases with no chance of
    //   intersection with the gun.
    if ((locy + height >= gun_y) &&
        target.intersect(locx,locy,locx+width,locy+height)) {
        target.hit();
        suspend();
        return;
    }
```

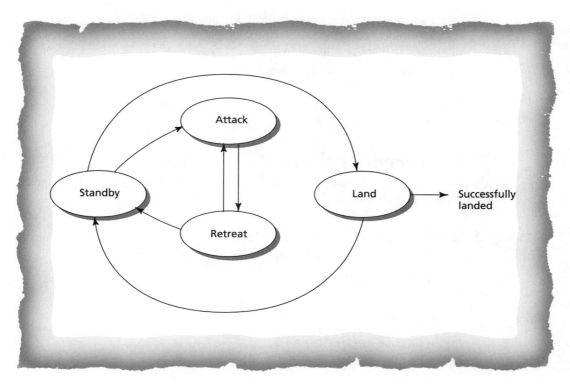

FIGURE 5-14 ◉ *UFO transition diagram*

If no collision occurs with the gun, the UFO executes behaviors according to its state. Let's examine the Standby state:

```
double r1 = Math.random();      // pick random nums
double r2 = Math.random();
switch (state) {
case STANDBY:
  if (r1 > STANDBY_EXIT) {
  if (r2 > 0.5) {
  startAttack();
  }
  else {
  startLand();
  }
  }
```

Depending on the random numbers, the UFO can go to the Attack state or the Land state. The methods startAttack() and startLand() set the UFO's velocity for those states.

If a state transition doesn't occur, the UFO continues with the Standby update, which reverses the UFO's direction if it strays too close to the edges of the screen, or if the random number is above a threshold:

```
else if ((locx < width) || (locx > max_x - width) ||
    (r2 > FLIP_X)) {
  vx = -vx;
  }
  break;
```

Implementing the UFO Sprite Class

Now take a look, in Listing 5-11, at the complete UFO sprite class, and the update() method in particular.

Listing 5-11 UFO class

```
public class UFO extends BitmapLoop implements Intersect {

  byte state;

  // UFO states
  static final byte STANDBY = 0;
  static final byte ATTACK = 1;
  static final byte RETREAT = 2;
  static final byte LAND = 3;

  // probability of state transitions
  static final double STANDBY_EXIT = .95;
  static final double ATTACK_EXIT = .95;
  static final double RETREAT_EXIT = .95;
  static final double LAND_EXIT = .95;
  static final double FLIP_X = 0.9;
  static final int RETREAT_Y = 17;

  int max_x, max_y;               // max coords of this UFO
  static Intersect target;        // refers to the gun
  static int gun_y;               // the y-coord of gun

  public UFO(Image ufoImages[],int max_x,int max_y,
         Applet a) {
    super(0,0,null,ufoImages,a);
    this.max_x = max_x;
    this.max_y = max_y;
    currentImage = getRand(5);  // start at random image
    startStandby();

  }

  // finish initializing info about the player's gun
  static public void initialize(GunManager gm) {
```

```
     target = gm.getGun();              // refers to gun sprite
     gun_y = gm.getGunY();              // get gun y-coordinate
   }

   // implement Intersect interface:

   public boolean intersect(int x1,int y1,int x2,int y2) {

     return visible && (x2 >= locx) && (locx+width >= x1)
       && (y2 >= locy) && (locy+height >= y1);

   }

   public void hit() {
     // alien is invulnerable when it's attacking
     //   otherwise, suspend the sprite
     if (state != ATTACK) {
       suspend();
     }
   }


   // this implements the state machine
   public void update() {

     // if alien hits target

     if ((locy + height >= gun_y) &&
       target.intersect(locx,locy,locx+width,locy+height)) {
       target.hit();
       suspend();
       return;
       }

     // otherwise, update alien state

     double r1 = Math.random();     // pick random nums
     double r2 = Math.random();
     switch (state) {
     case STANDBY:
       if (r1 > STANDBY_EXIT) {
       if (r2 > 0.5) {
       startAttack();
       }
       else {
       startLand();
       }

       }
       // else change the direction by flipping
       //   the x-velocity. Net result: ufo moves
```

continued on next page

continued from previous page

```
//    from side to side. And if the ufo gets close to
//    the left or right side of screen, it always changes
//    direction.
else if ((locx < width) || (locx > max_x - width) ||
 (r2 > FLIP_X)) {
  vx = -vx;
}
break;
case ATTACK:

// retreat if the alien flies too close to
//    the ground
if ((r1 > ATTACK_EXIT) || (locy > gun_y - 17)) {
 startRetreat();
}

// flip x-direction if it gets too close to edges
else if ((locx < width) || (locx > max_x - width) ||
        (r2 > FLIP_X)) {
 vx = -vx;
}

break;
case RETREAT:
  if (r1 > RETREAT_EXIT) {
   if (r2 > 0.5) {
   startAttack();
   }
   else {
   startStandby();
   }
  }
  // stop retreat if ufo goes too close
  //    to top of screen
  else if (locy < RETREAT_Y) {
   startStandby();
  }
  break;
case LAND:

  if (r1 > LAND_EXIT) {
   startStandby();
  }
  // if the ufo is low enough,
  //    start the landing procedure
  else if (locy >= max_y-height) {
   landingRoutine();
  }
  break;
}
```

```
    super.update();    // BitmapLoop update draws the
                       //   appropriate image
}

protected void landingRoutine() {
  System.out.println("ufo landed") ;
  suspend();
}

protected void startStandby() {
  vx = getRand(8)-4 ;
  vy = 0;
  state = STANDBY;

}

protected void startAttack() {
  vx = getRand(10)-5;
  vy = getRand(5)+4;
  state = ATTACK;

}

protected void startRetreat() {
  vx = 0;
  vy = -getRand(3) - 2;
  state = RETREAT;
}

protected void startLand() {
  vx = 0;
  vy = getRand(3) + 2;
  state = LAND;
}

static public int getRand(int x) {
  return (int)(x * Math.random());
}
}
```

The UFO class is the most complex of this entire chapter, and you can use it as a template for enemies in your own games.

Now let's discuss the UFOManager class.

The UFOManager Class

The UFOManager's constructor allocates the UFO sprites that will be used during the course of the game, circumventing the need for dynamic allocation during game play. In addition, the UFOManager sets the initial position of the UFOs, and tells them when to update and paint. If a UFO sprite is hit by a missile, it becomes inactive, so it disappears from the screen.

For this simulation, the UFOManager's update() method simply restores the sprite at a different location, making it appear as if a new UFO has entered the fray, but keeping the number of aliens constant. In the next chapter, you will learn how to create a UFOManager that will increase the number of active UFOs as the game progresses, making it harder to play! Listing 5-12 defines the UFOManager class.

Listing 5-12 *UFOManager class*

```
public class UFOManager {

    static int width, height;              // applet dimensions
    private UFO ufo[];
    static final int NUM_UFOS = 7;

    public UFOManager(int width,int height,
                      Image ufoImages[],Applet a) {
      this.width = width;
      this.height =  height;

      ufo = new UFO[NUM_UFOS];
      for (int i=0; i<ufo.length; i++) {
        ufo[i] = new UFO(ufoImages,width,height,a);
        initializePosition(ufo[i]);
      }
    }

    // This method tells the UFO class where
    //   the gun is (so the UFOs know if they've
    //   collided with it)
    public void initialize(GunManager gm) {
      UFO.initialize(gm);
    }

    private void initializePosition(Moveable m) {
      m.setPosition(UFO.getRand(width - 100)+50,
                UFO.getRand(height - 150)+10);

    }

    // accessor method, so the missile knows where
    //   the targets are!
    public UFO[] getUFO() {
      return ufo;
    }

    public void paint(Graphics g) {
      for (int i=0; i<ufo.length; i++) {
        ufo[i].paint(g);
      }
    }

    public void update() {
```

```
        for (int i=0; i<ufo.length; i++) {
          if (ufo[i].isActive()) {
           ufo[i].update();
          }
          else {                      // restore ufo
                                      //   at different location
           initializePosition(ufo[i]);
           ufo[i].restore();
          }
        }
     }
}
```

Defining the GameManager

The GameManager, the final building block of this chapter, has the following responsibilities, as noted earlier:

◆ Initializes the GunManager and UFOManager

◆ Relays player input to the GunManager (event handling)

◆ Implements the Video Game Loop

As with the animation driver you used at the end of Chapter 4, Adding Interactivity, it uses MediaTracker to load the images.

Two Responsibilities of the GameManager Class

Let's examine two responsibilities of this class.

Passing Mouse Input to the GunManager

First, here's the way the GameManager passes mouse input to the GunManager:

```
public boolean mouseMove(Event e,int x,int y) {
  gm.moveGun(x);
  return true;
}
public boolean mouseDrag(Event e,int x,int y) {
  gm.moveGun(x);
  return true;
}
public boolean mouseDown(Event e,int x,int y) {
  gm.fireMissile(x);
  return true;
}
```

Each event handler passes the x coordinate of the mouse location to the appropriate method of the GunManager. mouseDrag must be handled, so that the player can move the gun even if the mouse button is pressed.

Implementing the Video Game Loop

Next, let's look at how the GameManager implements the Video Game Loop:

```
public void run() {
  while (true) {
    repaint();
    updateManagers();
    Thread.yield();
    try {
     Thread.sleep (REFRESH_RATE);
    } catch (Exception exc) { };
  }
}
```

As you see, this code is pretty general, and you can adapt a loop like this for your own games.

Implementing the GameManager Class

Finally, the definition of the GameManager is shown in Listing 5-13. Compile it along with the other classes defined in this chapter, and run the Alien Landing simulation!

Listing 5-13 *GameManager class*

```
public class GameManager extends Applet implements Runnable {

  Thread animation;

  Graphics offscreen;
  Image image;

  static final int REFRESH_RATE = 80; // in ms

  Image ufoImages[] =  new Image[6]; // 6 ufo Images
  Image gunImage;                    // gun image
  GunManager gm;
  UFOManager um;

  int width, height;                 // applet dimensions

  public void init() {
    showStatus("Loading Images -- WAIT!");
    setBackground(Color.black);      // applet background
```

```
        width = bounds().width;          // set applet dimensions
        height = bounds().height;
        loadImages();
        um = new UFOManager(width,height,ufoImages,this);
        gm = new GunManager(width,height,gunImage,
                       um.getUFO(),
                       this);
        um.initialize(gm);              // initialize gun parameters
        image = createImage(width,height); // make offscreen buffer
        offscreen = image.getGraphics();
    }


    public void loadImages() {

        MediaTracker t = new MediaTracker(this);
        gunImage = getImage(getCodeBase(),"image/gun.gif");
        t.addImage(gunImage,0);
        for (int i=0; i<6; i++) {
            ufoImages[i] = getImage(getCodeBase(),
                         "image/ufo" + i + ".gif");
            t.addImage(ufoImages[i],0);
        }


        // wait for all images to finish loading //
        try {
            t.waitForAll();
        } catch (InterruptedException e) {
        }

        // check for errors //
        if (t.isErrorAny()) {
            showStatus("Error Loading Images!");
        }
        else if (t.checkAll()) {
            showStatus("Images successfully loaded");
        }
        // initialize the BitmapLoop

    }

    public boolean mouseMove(Event e,int x,int y) {
        gm.moveGun(x);
        return true;
    }
    public boolean mouseDrag(Event e,int x,int y) {
        gm.moveGun(x);
        return true;
    }
```

continued on next page

continued from previous page

```java
public boolean mouseDown(Event e,int x,int y) {
    gm.fireMissile(x);
    return true;
}



public void start() {

    showStatus("Starting Game!");
    animation = new Thread(this);
    if (animation != null) {
        animation.start();
    }
}



public void updateManagers() {
    gm.update();
    um.update();
}



// override update so it doesn't erase screen
public void update(Graphics g) {
    paint(g);
}


//
public void paint(Graphics g) {

    offscreen.setColor(Color.black);
    offscreen.fillRect(0,0,width,height);  // clear buffer

    gm.paint(offscreen);
    um.paint(offscreen);

    g.drawImage(image,0,0,this);
}

public void run() {
    while (true) {
        repaint();
        updateManagers();
        Thread.currentThread().yield();
        try {
            Thread.sleep (REFRESH_RATE);
        } catch (Exception exc) { };
    }
}
```

```
public void stop() {

  showStatus("Game Stopped");
  if (animation != null) {
    animation.stop();
    animation = null;
  }
}
}
```

🎮 Recommended Applet Tag to Run the Alien Landing Game

<applet code="GameManager.class" width=240 height=300>

Suggestion Box

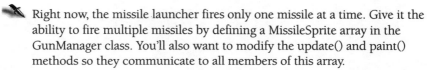

Right now, the missile launcher fires only one missile at a time. Give it the ability to fire multiple missiles by defining a MissileSprite array in the GunManager class. You'll also want to modify the update() and paint() methods so they communicate to all members of this array.

The UFO animation stays the same, regardless of its behavior. How would you modify the UFO class so that the animation loop is different for the attacking state? (We'll cover the answer to this in the next chapter.)

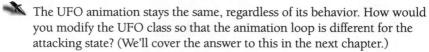

Define another UFO class that has the ability to fire back. You have all the building blocks, such as the Intersect interface and the MissileSprite class, to do this easily.

Add sound to the game simulation. You know how to do this already, and it's really easy. Perhaps you can add a sound when collisions occur, and another sound if an alien lands successfully.

Draw a background image. You might want to use a bitmap of a city, in keeping with the theme of the game.

Summary

There's a lot of code in this chapter, but it is structured into units that have specific responsibilities and consistent behavior. This way, your program is understandable and extensible, which cuts down on the number of bugs, and the amount of time you will need to write a complex game.

In the next chapter, we'll extend the GameManger unit so it also handles the initial and closing sequences of Alien Landing, and keeps track of the score. We'll also modify the UFOManager so the difficulty level increases as time goes on. By the end, you'll have a real video game!

Extending Your Video Game

Joel Fan

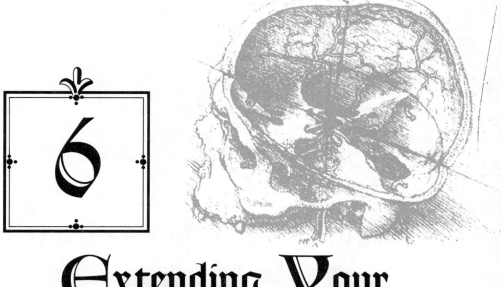

6

Extending Your Video Game

Goals:

Add features to the Alien Landing simulation using incremental development

Complete the Alien Landing video game

In this chapter, you'll extend the Alien Landing simulation of the previous chapter into a complete video game, by adding explosions, a status display, levels of play, scoring, and other features. In addition, you'll create an introductory screen, so that new players understand how to play your game, and a closing sequence, so that they know when the game is over.

There are two types of extensions you will implement on top of the existing Alien Landing simulation:

Extensions that primarily involve a single class

Extensions that require messaging between classes

For example, explosions will be handled within the UFO class, once the bitmaps are loaded and passed in. On the other hand, scoring will require communication between the UFO and the GameManager, and when the UFO sprite is hit, it sends a message to GameManager to update the player's point total.

195

By developing and testing these extensions one at a time, you can build on the game simulation with a minimum of errors. This process is called *incremental development*, and it can cut down on the amount of time you spend tracking down nasty bugs! As you progress through this chapter, feel free to implement and test each extension individually, so you really understand how the pieces fit together.

Let's get started. First, let's extend the UFO class so the animation loop changes, depending on the state of the alien.

Changing the UFO Animations

When the alien gets shot by a missile, it should explode in a ball of fire. But if the alien is in attack mode, it is invulnerable to the player's missiles. Let's see how to signify these alien states—exploding and attacking—by changing the animation loop in the UFO class. The UFOManager and GameManager must also be modified to provide the initializations needed.

Extending the UFO Class

Figures 6-1A and 6-1B show the sequence of bitmaps that animate attacking and exploding aliens.

FIGURE 6-1A
◎ ◎ ◎ ◎ ◎ ◎
Attacking aliens

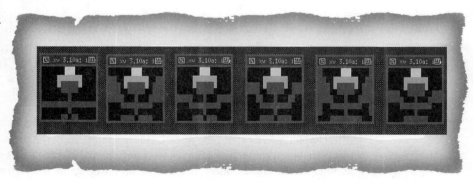

FIGURE 6-1B
◎ ◎ ◎ ◎ ◎ ◎
Exploding aliens

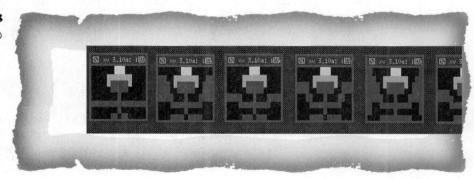

Remember that the UFO class extends the BitmapLoop class, and that it inherits BitmapLoop's paint() method:

```
public void paint(Graphics g) {
  if (visible) {
    if (background) {
      g.drawImage(image,locx,locy,applet);
    }
    if (foreground) {
      g.drawImage(images[currentImage],locx,locy,applet);
    }
  }
}
```

The *images* variable refers to the array of bitmaps that comprise the animation. Right now, *images* refers to the UFO animation, but if we store references to the exploding, attacking, and UFO sequences, we can switch animations by assigning *images* the correct image array. Thus, the first change is in the constructor to the UFO class, which now refers to the various animation sequences in the variables *ufo, attack,* and *explode.*

```
// bitmap animations
protected Image ufo[];          // ufo animation
protected Image attack[];       // attack animation
protected Image explode[];      // explosion sequence
...
// constructor: initialize image references, instance vars
public UFO(Image ufoImages[],
        Image attackImages[],
        Image explodeImages[],
        int max_x,int max_y,
        UFOManager um,
        Applet a) {
  ...
  ufo = ufoImages;
  attack = attackImages;
  explode = explodeImages;
  ...
```

Now *images* will be assigned the appropriate animation sequence, depending on the alien state. As Figure 6-2 shows, the change in the animation loop occurs only when the alien starts or exits the Attack state. Thus, only the methods that implement state transitions to and from the Attack state are modified. These are the UFO methods startAttack() and startRetreat():

```
// start attack state
protected void startAttack() {
  vx = getRand(10)-5;
  vy = getRand(5)+7;
  images = attack;                // change to attack animation loop
  state = ATTACK;
}
```

continued on next page

continued from previous page

```
// start retreating state
protected void startRetreat() {
  vx = 0;
  vy = -getRand(3) - 2;
  images = ufo;               // change to usual animation loop
  state = RETREAT;
}
```

In addition, let's add a new state, Explode, which signifies an exploding alien, and a method, startExplode(), which causes a transition to this state:

```
static final byte EXPLODE = 4;
```

```
// start explosion state
protected void startExplode() {
  images = explode;          // set bitmap to explosion sequence
  currentImage = 0;          // start at beginning of animation
  explosion_counter = 0;     // count the number of frames
  um.playExplosion();        // play explosion sound:
```

FIGURE 6-2

◉ ◉ ◉ ◉ ◉ ◉

UFO transition diagram

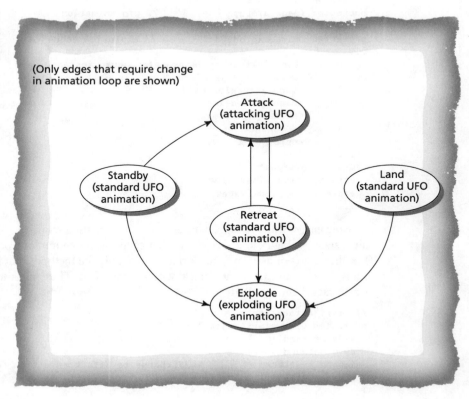

```
                              //   (um is reference to the
                              //    UFOManager class)
          state = EXPLODE;
}
```

The startExplode() method is called when the alien is hit by a missile and the alien is not in the Attack state (so it is vulnerable). startExplode() also calls the UFOManager method playExplosion(), which plays the explosion sound.

Now modify the hit() method of the UFO class so it calls startExplode(). Let's also add a feature so that attacking aliens get repulsed, or pushed upward, by a missile hit. This is accomplished by subtracting a constant from the y coordinate of the attacking alien:

```
// this is called if a missile hits the alien
public void hit() {
  // alien is invulnerable when it's attacking
  //   but it gets "pushed back"
  if (state == ATTACK) {
    locy -= 17;
  }
  // otherwise explode!
  else if (state != EXPLODE) {
    startExplode();              // start explode state
    ...
  }
}
```

Finally, UFO's update() needs to be changed, so that it takes the Explode state into account and suspends the sprite after the explosion animation is complete:

```
    case EXPLODE:
    explosion_counter++;      // bump counter

                              // suspend once animation
                              //   is finished
    if (explosion_counter == explode.length) {
     suspend();
    }
```

You can find these changes to the UFO class in Listing 6-5.

Now let's modify the UFOManager and the GameManager so that they load and pass these new animation sequences to the UFO class.

Modifying GameManager and UFOManager

The GameManager needs to register the attacking and exploding animations with the MediaTracker so that they are loaded prior to the start of the game. This is done by declaring new variables and modifying the loadImages() method in GameManager. In the following code, all the GIFs are assumed to be in a directory image/, which is in the same location as the GameManager applet class.

```
Image ufoImages[] =  new Image[6];    // 6 ufo Images
Image attackImages[] =  new Image[6]; // 6 attack Images
Image explodeImages[] =  new Image[4];// 4 explode Images
// load all images used in game
public void loadImages() {

  MediaTracker t = new MediaTracker(this);
  gunImage = getImage(getCodeBase(),"image/gun.gif");
  t.addImage(gunImage,0);
  for (int i=0; i<ufoImages.length; i++) {
    ufoImages[i] = getImage(getCodeBase(),
                          "image/ufo" + i + ".gif");
    t.addImage(ufoImages[i],0);
    attackImages[i] = getImage(getCodeBase(),
                          "image/attack" + i + ".gif");
    t.addImage(attackImages[i],0);
  }
  for (int i=0; i<explodeImages.length; i++) {
    explodeImages[i] = getImage(getCodeBase(),
                          "image/explode" + i + ".gif");
    t.addImage(explodeImages[i],0);
  }
  ...
}
```

The GameManager also loads the explosion sound, which plays when a UFO blows up:

```
try {
   expsound = getAudioClip(getCodeBase(),"Explosion.au");
}
catch (Exception e) { }
```

Now modify the GameManager's init() and UFOManager's constructor to pass the animations and explosion audio clip to the UFO constructor. You'll find these changes in Listings 6-1 and 6-3.

Compile and run these modifications. You can immediately see how the attacking and exploding animations improve the game simulation. Now, let's add increasing levels of difficulty.

Adding Levels of Difficulty

In video games that pit human players against computer opponents, the strength of the opponents increases as play continues. Usually, the game starts at a level that the novice player can handle, but grows more difficult so that an accomplished player will still feel challenged. And if you're charging money each time the game gets played, as with arcade machines, you'll want to make it almost impossible to play for a very long time!

There are lots of ways to introduce skill levels into a game, and you're limited only by your creativity. For a game such as Alien Landing, in which state machines try to destroy the player, here are four ways you can increase the difficulty:

🗡 Increase the number of UFOs. More aliens will appear on the screen as the game progresses.

🗡 Increase the velocity of the UFOs. This will make them harder to shoot.

🗡 Make the UFOs more intelligent. For example, the attacking aliens could aim for the player's current location, instead of moving randomly.

🗡 Allow the UFOs to gain extra powers. They could start firing back at the player, or perhaps they might gain resistance to the player's missiles.

The possibilities are endless, and they are not difficult to add to the Alien Landing simulation. For example, let's see how you might implement the first option, increasing the number of aliens as the game continues. This change will require communication between the UFO sprite and the UFOManager. Figure 6-3 diagrams the communication channel we'll add between these two classes. First, let's see what changes are needed in the UFOManager.

FIGURE 6-3

◎ ◎ ◎ ◎ ◎ ◎

Communication between UFO sprite and UFOManager

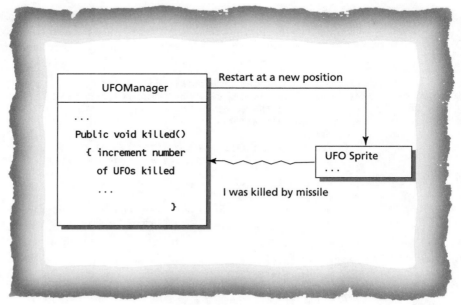

Define a new variable *levels*, which represents the number of UFOs active at a given moment. The player will progress from level to level, after killing a certain number of aliens, defined by the constant KILL_FOR_NEXT_LEVEL. The variable *ufosKilled* tracks the number of UFOs that the player has destroyed during the game. These variables are initialized in the UFOManager method newGame(), which also suspends the UFO sprites that are not needed for the starting level.

```
int ufosKilled;              // count ufos killed
int level;                   // the level
                             //    (i.e. #ufos on screen)


// kill 13 ufos until next level
static final int KILL_FOR_NEXT_LEVEL = 13;

// initialize parameters of new Game
public void newGame() {
  ufosKilled = 0;
  level = 2;                        // start with 2 ufos
                                    //   on the screen
  for (int i=0; i<ufo.length; i++) {
    initializePosition(ufo[i]);
    if (i >= level) {               // suspend ufos
                                    //   above start level
      ufo[i].suspend();
    }
  }
}
```

To move from level to level, the individual UFO sprites need a way of telling the UFOManager that they've been killed. We will add a public method to the UFOManager called killed() that the sprites can call. The killed() method updates *ufosKilled*; it also increases *level* every time *num_killed* is divisible by KILL_FOR_NEXT_LEVEL:

```
// tracks the number of ufos killed. If the
//    num_killed is divisible by  KILL_FOR_NEXT_LEVEL
//    increment the level
public void killed() {
  ufosKilled++;
  if (ufosKilled % KILL_FOR_NEXT_LEVEL == 0) {
    level = (level == NUM_UFOS) ? NUM_UFOS : level+1;
  }
}
```

When a UFO sprite is destroyed, it sends the killed() message to the UFOManager. The UFO class stores a reference to the UFOManager in variable *um*, so it can call killed() after it has been hit(). Here is the change to the UFO's hit() method:

```
// this is called if a missile hits the alien
public void hit() {
  // alien is invulnerable when it's attacking
  //    but it gets "pushed back"
  if (state == ATTACK) {
```

```
      locy -= 17;
    }
    // otherwise explode!
    else if (state != EXPLODE) {
      startExplode();              // start explode state
      um.killed();                 // tell UFOManager
                                   //  another UFO's dead

    }

  }
}
```

Finally, the UFOManager methods update() and paint() will take the number of sprites for each level into account:

```
// paint all ufos in a level
public void paint(Graphics g) {
  for (int i=0; i<level; i++) {
    ufo[i].paint(g);
  }
}

// update all ufos in a level. Otherwise start
//   ufo if it's not on screen
public void update() {
  for (int i=0; i<level; i++) {
    if (ufo[i].isActive()) {
     ufo[i].update();
    }
    else {                     // make new ufo
     initializePosition(ufo[i]);
     ufo[i].init();
    }
  }
}
```

Try out each of these changes. At first, you will see two UFOs on the screen, then three, then four, and so on, and the game gets harder and harder to play!

Now let's modify the GameManager so it will track and display information about the score, and the number of aliens landed.

Tracking Game Status

The GameManager is responsible for handling input from the player and relaying game information back. It will track and display two pieces of information that are vital to the player: the score and the number of aliens landed. This will require messaging from the UFO class to the GameManager. Figure 6-4 diagrams the messaging between the two classes.

FIGURE 6-4
◎ ◎ ◎ ◎ ◎ ◎
*Communication
between UFO
sprite and
GameManager*

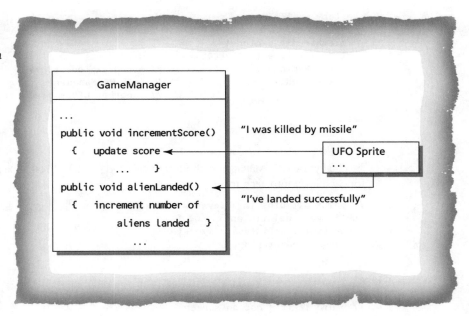

First, let's implement a simple scoring system in which each alien is worth UFO_VALUE points. GameManager needs a public method that the UFO can call when it has been killed. This method is called incrementScore(), and it increases the *score* by the appropriate amount:

```
static final int UFO_VALUE = 130;    // 130 points

private int score;

  // increase score
  public void incrementScore() {
    score += UFO_VALUE;
  }
```

The UFO sprite will call incrementScore() from its hit() method. The variable *game* is assigned in the constructor for UFO, and it refers to the GameManager.

```
// this is called if a missile hits the alien
public void hit() {
  // alien is invulnerable when it's attacking
  //    but it gets "pushed back"
  if (state == ATTACK) {
    locy -= 17;
  }
  // otherwise explode!
  else if (state != EXPLODE) {
    startExplode();                 // start explode state
```

```
      game.incrementScore();     // add to score
      um.killed();               // tell UFOManager
                                 //  another UFO's dead
    }

  }
```

Now *score* gets updated every time you shoot an alien.

Tracking the number of landed aliens involves similar modifications. Define a variable *numLanded* in the GameManager that tracks the current number of aliens landed. The public method alienLanded() provides the interface that the UFO class calls when it lands. If too many aliens land, then gameOver() gets called.

```
static final int MAX_LANDED = 5;    // at most 5 aliens
                                    //   can land

private int numLanded;              // num of aliens landed

// count number of ufo's landed
public void alienLanded() {
  numLanded++;
  if (numLanded == MAX_LANDED) {
    gameOver();
  }
}
```

The call to alienLanded() occurs in the UFO's landingRoutine() method, which is triggered if its y coordinate is high enough. The following is an excerpt from the UFO's update():

```
case LAND:

  if (r1 > LAND_EXIT) {
   startStandby();
  }
  else if (locy >= max_y-height) {
   landingRoutine();
  }
  break;
```

The new version of landingRoutine() is defined as

```
// when the alien lands successfully
protected void landingRoutine() {
  game.alienLanded();        // tell game manager that
                             //   the UFO's landed
  suspend();
}
```

The modifications of this section allow GameManager to keep track of the score and the number of UFOs landed. We'll put the code for displaying *score* and *numLanded* into GameManager's paint() method. In the version in Listing 6-1, the coordinates of the Strings are hardcoded for simplicity. You can also use the FontMetrics class, which you saw in

Chapter 4, Adding Interactivity, to dynamically compute the coordinates based on the length of the string.

If you compile and play the game now, you will rack up pretty good scores, because your missile launcher is immune to alien attacks. Let's change this next!

Modifying GunManager

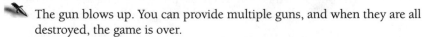

There are at least three ways that the missile gun could respond to alien hits:

🗡 The gun blows up. You can provide multiple guns, and when they are all destroyed, the game is over.

🗡 The gun's ability is impaired. For example, it fires slower, or more missiles are needed to kill a UFO.

🗡 The gun loses energy. When there is no energy left, the game ends.

Let's implement the last option. We'll store the current amount of energy in the GunManager. When the GunSprite gets hit, it tells the GunManager, which updates the energy level. The diagram in Figure 6-5 depicts the communication between the GunSprite and the GunManager.

FIGURE 6-5
◎ ◎ ◎ ◎ ◎ ◎
Communication between GunSprite and GunManager

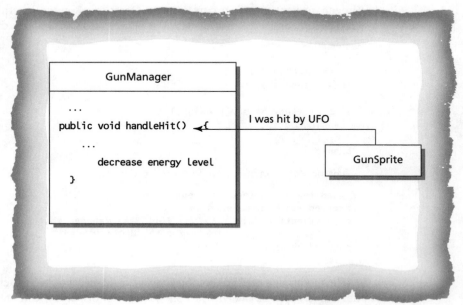

Now for the details. When a UFO collides with the player's gun, it calls the GunSprite's hit() method. This, in turn, calls GunManager's handleHit(). In GunSprite's hit() method, *gm* refers to the GunManager:

```
public void hit() {

  gm.handleHit();          // notify manager of hit

}
```

The GunManager will track the energy level, and decrease it when there is an alien hit. This happens in GunManager's handleHit():

```
// handles a hit from an alien
  public void handleHit() {
    displayHit = true;            // set display hit flag
    energy -= energyDec;          // update energy
    if (energy <= 0) {            // game over if energy <= 0
      game.gameOver();            // notify game manager
      gun.suspend();              // turn off sprites
      missile.suspend();
    }
  }
```

When *energy* reaches 0, GunManager invokes the gameOver() method in GameManager, which you will define in the next section. Otherwise, it sets displayHit, which tells GunManager's paint() to paint a red flash when a hit occurs. The paint() method also provides a status indicator of energy remaining by drawing a rectangle whose width is equal to *energy*. Thus, the rectangle shrinks as the energy level decreases (which is cooler than simply displaying a number!).

Here is GunManager's paint() method:

```
String energyString = "Energy";
public void paint(Graphics g) {
  // if gun is hit, flash a red rectangle
  //    instead of painting gun
  if (displayHit) {
    g.setColor(Color.red);

    g.fillRect(0,gun_y,width,gun_height);
    displayHit = false;
  }
  else {
    gun.paint(g);
  }
  missile.paint(g);

  // display energy left
  g.setColor(Color.red);
  g.drawString(energyString,3,13);
  g.fillRect(0,17,energy,10);
}
```

Compile and try out these changes. (For now, use an empty stub for the gameOver() method in GameManager.) As you will see, the game action is basically finished! But there are two steps remaining before Alien Landing is a complete presentation.

Creating an Opening and Closing

Think of a game as a movie: There are the opening credits, which display the name of the game and the instructions, the actual playing of the game, and the closing credits. The James Bond movies hook you, right from the opening action sequence (sometimes the best part of the movie!). In similar fashion, you can create fantastic opening animations for your games that grab the player.

You won't do that here, but you will see how to modify the GameManager to create openings and closings. Figure 6-6 shows the GameManager structure we will implement.

The idea is to introduce variables that represent the state of the game, and to paint the game, or the opening or closing sequences, based on these variables. The boolean

FIGURE 6-6
◎ ◎ ◎ ◎ ◎ ◎
*GameManager
structure*

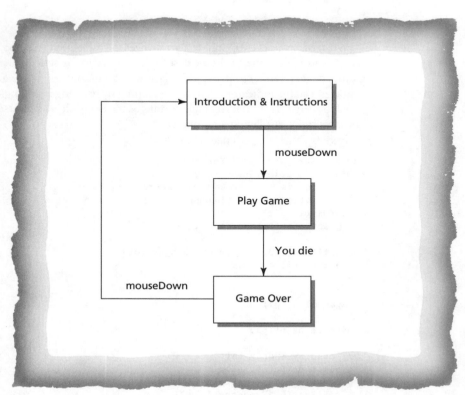

playing records whether the user is actually playing. The *screen* variable can be set to either INTRO or GAME_OVER. GameManager's paint() method will check these variables and draw what's appropriate.

Let's see how these variables are manipulated. The constructor of GameManager first sets the initial values for these variables: The game is not playing, and the introduction screen should be displayed:

```
playing = false;                    // not playing
    screen = INTRO;                 // show intro screen
```

The player will move from the introduction mode to the playing mode, for example, by clicking the mouse. By modifying mouseDown(), you enable this behavior:

```
public boolean mouseDown(Event e,int x,int y) {
  if (playing) {
    gm.fireMissile(x);
  }
  else if (screen == INTRO) {       // start game for mouse
                                    //    down on intro screen
    playing = true;
    newGame();
  }
  else if (screen == GAME_OVER) {   // else go back to intro
    if (e.shiftDown()) {            //    if shift-click
       screen = INTRO;
    }
  }
  return true;
}
```

The other mouse methods will also check if the game is playing before passing input to the GunManager.

Now we need newGame() methods in all the manager classes, which will reset the parameters of the game. For example, GameManager's newGame() will set the *score* back to 0; GunManager's newGame() replenishes the player's energy supply.

```
// GameManager's newGame():
  // initialize params for new game
  public void newGame() {

    score = 0;                          // no score
    numLanded = 0;                      // no aliens landed
    gm.newGame();                       // call newGame in
    um.newGame();                       //    manager classes
    offscreen.setFont(smallFont);       // set font in game
  }

// GunManager's newGame():

public void newGame() {
    gun.setPosition(width/2-gun_width,gun_y);
```

continued on next page

continued from previous page

```
        gun.restore();
        displayHit = false;
        energy = maxEnergy;


}
```

The opposite of newGame() is gameOver(), which is a GameManager method that is called when the player runs out of energy or too many aliens have landed and gameOver() triggers the closing sequence by setting *playing* and *screen*:

```
// handle game over
public void gameOver() {
  if (playing) {
    playing = false;
    screen = GAME_OVER;
  }
}
```

Finally, let's see how to paint the opening and the closing credits. For the opening screen, we will draw instructions for the game. Let's provide an opening animation that underlies the instructions, by including a call to the UFOManager's paint(). This way, the aliens will fly around while the instructions appear. The following excerpt from the GameManager's paint() method draws the introductory screen. The *introString[]* contains the text of the instructions.

```
... if (screen == INTRO) {
      offscreen.setColor(Color.black);
      offscreen.fillRect(0,0,width,height);  // clear buffer
      ...

      um.paint(offscreen);                   // draw UFOs

      ...
      offscreen.setColor(Color.magenta);
      offscreen.setFont(mediumFont);

      // draw instructions
      for (int i=0; i<introString.length-1; i++) {
        offscreen.drawString(introString[i],13,(3+i)*height/12);
      }
      offscreen.setColor(Color.green);
      offscreen.drawString(introString[7],
                (width-stringWidth)/2,
                height*11/12);

      g.drawImage(image,0,0,this);
  }
```

The code for the closing sequence follows the same idea. The closing animation will be provided by the UFOManager, and we will overlay the score and a *gameOverString*. The complete code for GameManager's paint() is in Listing 6-1.

Alien Landing is finished! Now you can show it to your friends.

Source Code for Modified Classes

Listings 6-1 through 6-5 show the source of the classes we've modified in this chapter: GameManager, GunManager, UFOManager, GunSprite, and UFO.

Listing 6-1 *GameManager class*

```java
import java.applet.*;
import java.awt.*;

//////////////////////////////////////////////////////////////////
public class GameManager extends Applet
implements Runnable {

    // animation variables
    static final int REFRESH_RATE = 80; // in ms
    Thread animation;
    Graphics offscreen;
    Image image;

    // game variables used when playing
    static final int UFO_VALUE = 130;    // 130 points
    static final int MAX_LANDED = 5;     // at most 5 aliens
                                         //    can land

    static final int MAX_LEVEL = 9;      //
    static final int MAX_ENERGY = 113;   //

    private int score;
    private int numLanded;               // num of aliens landed

    Image ufoImages[] =  new Image[6];     // 6 ufo Images
    Image attackImages[] =  new Image[6]; // 6 attack Images
    Image explodeImages[] =  new Image[4];// 4 explode Images
    Image gunImage;                        // gun image
    GunManager gm;                         // refers to gun manager
    UFOManager um;                         // refers to ufo manager

    // state of game
    private boolean playing;             // if game playing
    private int screen;                  // which screen to show
    static final int INTRO = 0;          // intro screen
    static final int GAME_OVER = 1;      // game over screen

    AudioClip expsound;                  // explosion sound

    // fonts
    Font smallFont = new Font("Helvetica",Font.BOLD,12);
    Font mediumFont = new Font("Helvetica",Font.BOLD,14);
```

continued on next page

continued from previous page

```
            Font bigFont = new Font("Helvetica",Font.BOLD,18);

            FontMetrics fm;                    // use to center string

            int width, height;                 // applet dimensions

            // strings
            String scoreString = "Score: ";
            String ufoLandedString = "UFOs Landed: ";
            String gameOverString =     "   GAME OVER  ";
            String clickString = "Shift-Click to Continue";
            String alienLandingString = "Alien Landing";
            int stringWidth;
            String introString[] = new String[8];


            public void init() {
              showStatus("Loading Images -- WAIT!");
              setBackground(Color.black);        // applet background
              width = bounds().width;            // set applet dimensions
              height = bounds().height;
              loadImages();

              try {
                 expsound = getAudioClip(getCodeBase(),"Explosion.au");
              }
              catch (Exception e) { }
              um = new UFOManager(2,MAX_LEVEL,width,height,ufoImages,
                             attackImages,explodeImages,
                             this,expsound);
              gm = new GunManager(MAX_ENERGY,5,width,height,gunImage,
                             um.getUFO(),
                             this);
              um.initialize(gm);                // initialize gun parameters

              playing = false;                   // not playing
              screen = INTRO;                    // show intro screen

              image = createImage(width,height); // make offscreen buffer
              offscreen = image.getGraphics();
              offscreen.setFont(bigFont);        // font for intro
              fm = offscreen.getFontMetrics(bigFont); // font metrics
              stringWidth = fm.stringWidth(alienLandingString);

              introString[0] = "You are Humanity's last hope!";
              introString[1] = "Destroy the green Alien Landers";
              introString[2] = "by using the Mouse to Move";
              introString[3] = "your Missile Launcher. Click";
              introString[4] = "to Fire Missile. If 5 Aliens";
              introString[5] = "Land, or Energy Runs Out,";
              introString[6] = "Humans will be Eaten Alive!";
              introString[7] = "Click to start Game";
```

```
}

// load all images used in game
public void loadImages() {

  MediaTracker t = new MediaTracker(this);
  gunImage = getImage(getCodeBase(),"image/gun.gif");
  t.addImage(gunImage,0);
  for (int i=0; i<ufoImages.length; i++) {
    ufoImages[i] = getImage(getCodeBase(),
                     "image/ufo" + i + ".gif");
    t.addImage(ufoImages[i],0);
    attackImages[i] = getImage(getCodeBase(),
                       "image/attack" + i + ".gif");
    t.addImage(attackImages[i],0);
  }
  for (int i=0; i<explodeImages.length; i++) {
    explodeImages[i] = getImage(getCodeBase(),
                       "image/explode" + i + ".gif");
    t.addImage(explodeImages[i],0);
  }


  // wait for all images to finish loading //
  try {
    t.waitForAll();
  } catch (InterruptedException e) {
  }

  // check for errors //
  if (t.isErrorAny()) {
    showStatus("Error Loading Images");
  }
  else if (t.checkAll()) {
    showStatus("Images successfully loaded");
  }

}

// initialize params for new game
public void newGame() {

  score = 0;                       // no score
  numLanded = 0;                   // no aliens landed
  gm.newGame();                    // call newGame in
  um.newGame();                    //   manager classes
  offscreen.setFont(smallFont);    // set font in game
}
```

continued on next page

continued from previous page

```
// handle mouse events //

public boolean mouseMove(Event e,int x,int y) {
  if (playing) {
    gm.moveGun(x);
  }
  return true;
}
public boolean mouseDrag(Event e,int x,int y) {
  if (playing) {
    gm.moveGun(x);
  }
  return true;
}

public boolean mouseDown(Event e,int x,int y) {
  if (playing) {
    gm.fireMissile(x);
  }
  else if (screen == INTRO) {        // start game for mouse
                                     //    down on intro screen

    playing = true;
    newGame();
  }
  else if (screen == GAME_OVER) {    // else go back to intro
    if (e.shiftDown()) {             //    if shift-click
      screen = INTRO;
    }
  }

  return true;
}


// start the Video Game Loop
public void start() {
  showStatus("Starting Game!");
  animation = new Thread(this);
   if (animation != null) {
     animation.start();
   }
}

// update managers. only update gun if playing
public void updateManagers() {
  if (playing) {
    gm.update();
  }
  um.update();
}
```

```
// override update so it doesn't erase screen
public void update(Graphics g) {
  paint(g);
}

// paint the applet depending on mode of game
public void paint(Graphics g) {
  if (playing) {
    offscreen.setColor(Color.black);
    offscreen.fillRect(0,0,width,height);  // clear buffer

    // draw status info
    offscreen.setColor(Color.cyan);
    offscreen.drawString(scoreString+score,width - 113,13);
    offscreen.drawString(ufoLandedString+numLanded,
                  width - 113,27);

    // tell UFOManager and GunManager to paint
    um.paint(offscreen);
    gm.paint(offscreen);


    g.drawImage(image,0,0,this);
  }
  else if (screen == INTRO) {
    offscreen.setColor(Color.black);
    offscreen.fillRect(0,0,width,height);  // clear buffer

    offscreen.setFont(smallFont);
    offscreen.setColor(Color.cyan);
    offscreen.drawString(scoreString+score,width - 113,13);
    offscreen.drawString(ufoLandedString+numLanded,
                  width - 113,27);
    um.paint(offscreen);

    offscreen.setFont(bigFont);

    offscreen.setColor(Color.green);
    offscreen.drawString(alienLandingString,
            (width-stringWidth)/2,
            height/6);

    offscreen.setColor(Color.magenta);
    offscreen.setFont(mediumFont);

    // draw instructions
    for (int i=0; i<introString.length-1; i++) {
     offscreen.drawString(introString[i],13,(3+i)*height/12);
    }
    offscreen.setColor(Color.green);
```

continued on next page

continued from previous page

```
                    offscreen.drawString(introString[7],
                            (width-stringWidth)/2,
                            height*11/12);

            g.drawImage(image,0,0,this);

        }

        else if (screen == GAME_OVER) {
            offscreen.setColor(Color.black);

            offscreen.fillRect(0,0,width,height);  // clear buffer

            // draw status info
            offscreen.setFont(smallFont);
            offscreen.setColor(Color.cyan);
            offscreen.drawString(scoreString+score,width - 113,13);
            offscreen.drawString(ufoLandedString+numLanded,
                            width - 113,27);

            um.paint(offscreen);
            gm.paint(offscreen);

            offscreen.setFont(bigFont);

            offscreen.setColor(Color.red);
            offscreen.drawString(gameOverString,
                            (width-stringWidth)/2,
                            height/2);
            offscreen.setFont(mediumFont);
            offscreen.setColor(Color.green);
            offscreen.drawString(clickString,
                            (width-stringWidth-17)/2,
                            height*11/12);

            g.drawImage(image,0,0,this);


        }
    }

    // the Video Game Loop
    public void run() {
        while (true) {
            repaint();
            updateManagers();
            Thread.currentThread().yield();
            try {
             Thread.sleep (REFRESH_RATE);
            } catch (Exception exc) { };

        }
```

```
      }

      // stop animation
      public void stop() {

        showStatus("Game Stopped");
        if (animation != null) {
          animation.stop();
          animation = null;
        }
      }

      // increase score
      public void incrementScore() {
        score += UFO_VALUE;
      }

      // count number of ufo's landed
      public void alienLanded() {
        numLanded++;
        if (numLanded == MAX_LANDED) {
          gameOver();
        }
      }

      // handle game over
      public void gameOver() {
        if (playing) {
          playing = false;
          screen = GAME_OVER;
        }
      }
    }
```

Listing 6-2 *GunManager class*

```
      ///////////////////////////////////////////////////////////////
      public class GunManager {

        private GunSprite gun;              // your gun
        private int gun_width;              // width of gun
        private int gun_height;
        private MissileSprite missile;      // missile
        private int min_x,max_x;            // min and max x coords
                                            //   for gun movement

        private int gun_min_x,gun_max_x;
        private int mis_min_x,mis_max_x;
        private int gun_y;
```

continued on next page

continued from previous page

```java
        private boolean displayHit;
        private int energy;

        private int maxEnergy;
        private int energyDec;

        private GameManager game;          // ptr to game manager
        static int width, height;          // applet dimensions

        static final int ENERGY_PER_HIT = 5; // energy used per hit

        static final int MISSILE_WIDTH = 3;
        static final int MISSILE_HEIGHT = 27;
        static final int MISSILE_SPEED = -27; // missile flies upward
        static final Color MISSILE_COLOR= Color.red;

        public GunManager(int maxEnergy,int energyDec,int width,int height,
                      Image gunImage,Intersect target[],Applet a) {
          this.maxEnergy = maxEnergy;
          this.energyDec = energyDec;
          this.width = width;
          this.height = height;
          gun = new GunSprite(gunImage,a,this);

          gun_width = gunImage.getWidth(a)/2;
          gun_height = gunImage.getHeight(a);

          gun_y = height - gun_height;
          min_x = gun_width;
          max_x = width - gun_width;
          gun_min_x = 0;
          gun_max_x = width - 2*gun_width;
          mis_min_x = min_x-2;
          mis_max_x = max_x-2;
          gun.setPosition(width/2-gun_width,gun_y);
          missile = new MissileSprite(MISSILE_WIDTH,MISSILE_HEIGHT,
                              MISSILE_COLOR,MISSILE_SPEED,
                              height-gun_height+13,
                              0,target);

          game = (GameManager)a;                // set ptr to GameManager
        }

        // set parameters for the new game
        public void newGame() {
           gun.setPosition(width/2-gun_width,gun_y);
           gun.restore();
           displayHit = false;
           energy = maxEnergy;

        }
```

```
// move gun to the given x coordinate
public void moveGun(int x) {
  if (x <= min_x) {
    gun.setPosition(gun_min_x,gun_y);
    }
  else if (x >= max_x) {
    gun.setPosition(gun_max_x,gun_y);
    }
  else {
    gun.setPosition(x-gun_width,gun_y);
  }
}

// fire missile from given x coordinate
public void fireMissile(int x) {
  if (!missile.isActive()) {      // if missile sprite
                                  //   isn't active

    if (x <= min_x) {
     missile.init(mis_min_x);
     }
    else if (x >= max_x) {
     missile.init(mis_max_x);
     }
    else {
     missile.init(x-1);                  // initialize missile
     }
  }
}

// update all the parameters associated with the
//   gun. In this case, only the missile needs to move
//   automatically.

public void update() {
  missile.update();
}


// paint all sprites associated with gun
// also paint status display for amount of energy left

String energyString = "Energy";
public void paint(Graphics g) {
  // if gun is hit, flash a red rectangle
  //   instead of painting gun
  if (displayHit) {
    g.setColor(Color.red);

    g.fillRect(0,gun_y,width,gun_height);
    displayHit = false;
```

continued on next page

continued from previous page

```
      }
      else {
        gun.paint(g);
      }
      missile.paint(g);

      // display energy left
      g.setColor(Color.red);
      g.drawString(energyString,3,13);
      g.fillRect(0,17,energy,10);
    }

    // accessor function for gun
    public GunSprite getGun() {
      return gun;
    }
    // get the y-coordinate of the gun
    public int getGunY() {
      return gun_y;
    }

    // handles a hit from an alien
    public void handleHit() {
      displayHit = true;              // set display hit flag
      energy -= energyDec;            // update energy
      if (energy <= 0) {              // game over if energy <= 0
        game.gameOver();             // notify game manager
        gun.suspend();               // turn off sprites
        missile.suspend();
      }
    }

    // set the amount of energy lost per hit (energy decrement)
    public void setEnergyDec(int dec) {
      energyDec = dec;
    }
  }
```

Listing 6-3 *UFOManager class*

```
////////////////////////////////////////////////////////////////
public class UFOManager {


    private UFO ufo[];              // array of ufos

    int ufosKilled;                 // count ufos killed
    int level;                      // the level
                                    //    (i.e. #ufos on screen)

    int startLevel;
    int maxLevel;
```

```
      boolean playSound = false;        // initially no sound
      AudioClip expsound;               // sound clip of explosion

      // kill 13 ufos until next level
      static final int KILL_FOR_NEXT_LEVEL = 13;

      static int width, height;         // applet dimensions

      // constructor
      public UFOManager(int startLevel,int maxLevel,int width,int height,
                        Image ufoImages[],
                        Image attackImages[],
                        Image explodeImages[],
                        Applet a, AudioClip exp) {
        this.startLevel = startLevel;
        this.maxLevel = maxLevel;
        this.width = width;
        this.height =  height;

        ufo = new UFO[maxLevel];
        for (int i=0; i<ufo.length; i++) {
          ufo[i] = new UFO(ufoImages,attackImages,explodeImages,
                           width,height,this,a);
        }
        expsound = exp;
        newGame();
      }


      // allow the UFO class to communicate with the gun
      public void initialize(GunManager gm) {
        UFO.initialize(gm);
      }

      // set ufo at a random screen location
      private void initializePosition(Moveable m) {
        m.setPosition(UFO.getRand(width - 100)+50,
                  UFO.getRand(height - 150)+31);

      }

      // initialize parameters of new Game
      public void newGame() {
        ufosKilled = 0;
        level = startLevel;               // start with startLevel ufos
                                          //    on the screen
        for (int i=0; i<ufo.length; i++) {
          initializePosition(ufo[i]);
          if (i >= level) {               // suspend ufos
                                          //    above start level

          ufo[i].suspend();
```

continued on next page

continued from previous page

```
        }
      }
    }


    // return array of ufos
    public UFO[] getUFO() {
      return ufo;
    }

    // paint all ufos in a level
    public void paint(Graphics g) {
      for (int i=0; i<level; i++) {
        ufo[i].paint(g);
      }
    }

    // update all ufos in a level. Otherwise start
    //   ufo if it's not on screen
    public void update() {
      for (int i=0; i<level; i++) {
        if (ufo[i].isActive()) {
          ufo[i].update();
        }
        else {                    // make new ufo
          initializePosition(ufo[i]);
          ufo[i].init();
        }
      }
    }

    // tracks the number of ufos killed. If the
    //   num_killed is divisible by  KILL_FOR_NEXT_LEVEL
    //   increment the level
    public void killed() {
      ufosKilled++;
      if (ufosKilled % KILL_FOR_NEXT_LEVEL == 0) {
        level = (level == maxLevel) ? maxLevel : level+1;
      }
    }

    public void setStartLevel(int start) {
      startLevel = start;
    }

    public void setSound(boolean s) {
      playSound = s;
    }

    public void playExplosion() {
      if (playSound && expsound != null) {
        expsound.play();
```

```
        }
      }
    }
```

Listing 6-4 GunSprite class

```
class GunSprite extends BitmapSprite
implements Moveable,Intersect {

  protected GunManager gm;            // pointer to manager class

  public GunSprite(Image i, Applet a,GunManager gm) {
    super(i,a);
    this.gm = gm;
  }

  // the following methods implement Moveable:

  public void setPosition(int x,int y) {
    locx = x;
    locy = y;
  }

  public void setVelocity(int x,int y) {

  }

  public void updatePosition() {

  }

  // the following methods implement Intersect:

  // compare bounding boxes
  public boolean intersect(int x1,int y1,int x2,int y2) {

    return visible && (x2 >= locx) && (locx+width >= x1)
      && (y2 >= locy) && (locy+height >= y1);

  }


  // tell manager to display the hit
  public void hit() {

    gm.handleHit();              // notify manager of hit

  }
}
```

Listing 6-5 *UFO class*

```
///////////////////////////////////////////////////////////////
public class UFO extends BitmapLoop implements Intersect {

    byte state;

    // UFO states
    static final byte STANDBY = 0;
    static final byte ATTACK = 1;
    static final byte RETREAT = 2;
    static final byte LAND = 3;
    static final byte EXPLODE = 4;

    // probability of state transitions
    static final double STANDBY_EXIT = .95;
    static final double ATTACK_EXIT = .95;
    static final double RETREAT_EXIT = .95;
    static final double LAND_EXIT = .95;
    static final double FLIP_X = 0.9;
    static final int RETREAT_Y = 33;

    // bitmap animations
    protected Image ufo[];              // ufo animation
    protected Image attack[];           // attack animation
    protected Image explode[];          // explosion sequence

    // instance vars
    int max_x, max_y;                   // max coords of this UFO
    int explosion_counter;              // counter for explosion
                                        //   bitmaps

    UFOManager um;

    // class vars
    static Intersect target;            // refers to the gun
    static int gun_y;                   // the y-coord of gun
    static GameManager game;            // ptr to game manager

    // constructor: initialize image references, instance vars
    public UFO(Image ufoImages[],
        Image attackImages[],
            Image explodeImages[],
            int max_x,int max_y,
            UFOManager um,
            Applet a) {
      super(0,0,null,ufoImages,a);
      this.max_x = max_x;
      this.max_y = max_y;
      currentImage = getRand(ufoImages.length);
      ufo = ufoImages;
      attack = attackImages;
      explode = explodeImages;
      game = (GameManager)a;
```

```
      this.um = um;
      startStandby();

   }

   // finish initializing info about the player's gun
   //    this way, the ufo can communicate with the gun
   static public void initialize(GunManager gm) {
      target = gm.getGun();              // refers to gun sprite
      gun_y = gm.getGunY();              // get gun y-coordinate
   }

   // implement Intersect interface:
   public boolean intersect(int x1,int y1,int x2,int y2) {

      return visible && (x2 >= locx) && (locx+width >= x1)
        && (y2 >= locy) && (locy+height >= y1);

   }

   // this is called if a missile hits the alien
   public void hit() {
      // alien is invulnerable when it's attacking
      //    but it gets "pushed back"
      if (state == ATTACK) {
        locy -= 17;
      }
      // otherwise explode!
      else if (state != EXPLODE) {
        startExplode();              // start explode state
        game.incrementScore();       // add to score
        um.killed();                 // tell UFOManager
                                     //    another UFO's dead
      }

   }


   // set state and images loop
   public void init() {
      startStandby();
      images = ufo;
      restore();
   }

   // this implements the state machine
   public void update() {

      // if alien hits target, notify target, and explode if
      //    it's not in attack or explode mode
      //    otherwise retreat
```

continued on next page

continued from previous page

```
  if ((locy + height >= gun_y) && state != EXPLODE &&
    target.intersect(locx,locy,locx+width,locy+height)) {
    target.hit();
    if (state != ATTACK ) {
      startExplode();
      return;
    }
    else {
      startRetreat();
    }
  }

  // otherwise, update alien state

  double r1 = Math.random();
  double r2 = Math.random();
  switch (state) {
  case STANDBY:
    if (r1 > STANDBY_EXIT) {
     if (r2 > 0.5) {
        startAttack();
     }
     else {
        startLand();
     }

    }
    // flip ufo's x-direction if it goes too far right
    //    or left, or if random variable passes threshold
    else if ((locx < width) || (locx > max_x - width) ||
      (r2 > FLIP_X)) {
     vx = -vx;
    }
    break;
  case ATTACK:

    if ((r1 > ATTACK_EXIT) || (locy > gun_y - 17)) {
     startRetreat();
    }

    else if ((locx < width) || (locx > max_x - width) ||
          (r2 > FLIP_X)) {
     vx = -vx;
    }

    break;
  case RETREAT:
    if (r1 > RETREAT_EXIT) {
     if (r2 > 0.5) {
        startAttack();
     }
     else {
```

```
       startStandby();
      }
     }
    else if (locy < RETREAT_Y) {
     startStandby();
    }
    break;
  case LAND:

    if (r1 > LAND_EXIT) {
     startStandby();
    }
    else if (locy >= max_y-height) {
     landingRoutine();
    }
    break;

  case EXPLODE:
    explosion_counter++;      // bump counter

                              // suspend once animation
                              //   is finished
    if (explosion_counter == explode.length) {
     suspend();
    }

  }

  super.update();            // call BitmapLoop's update()
}

// when the alien lands successfully
protected void landingRoutine() {
  game.alienLanded();                // tell game manager that
                                     //   the UFO's landed
  suspend();
}

// start standby state
protected void startStandby() {
  vx = getRand(8)-4 ;
  vy = 0;
  state = STANDBY;
}

// start attack state
protected void startAttack() {
  vx = getRand(10)-5;
  vy = getRand(5)+7;
  images = attack;
  state = ATTACK;
```

continued on next page

continued from previous page

```
        }

        // start retreating state
        protected void startRetreat() {
          vx = 0;
          vy = -getRand(3) - 2;
          images = ufo;
          state = RETREAT;
        }

        // start landing state
        protected void startLand() {
          vx = 0;
          vy = getRand(3) + 2;
          state = LAND;
        }

        // start explosion state
        protected void startExplode() {
          images = explode;          // set bitmap to explosion sequence
          currentImage = 0;          // start at beginning of animation
          explosion_counter = 0;     // count the number of frames
          um.playExplosion();        // play explosion sound
          state = EXPLODE;

        }

        // return a random int from 0 to x
        static public int getRand(int x) {
          return (int)(x * Math.random());
        }
    }
```

Suggestion Box

There are probably a million ways you can extend and improve this game. Here are just a few ideas:

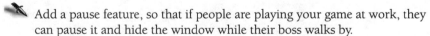 Add a pause feature, so that if people are playing your game at work, they can pause it and hide the window while their boss walks by.

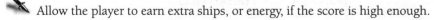 Create aliens with different powers and behaviors. Perhaps the different aliens can appear at later stages of the game.

Allow the player to earn extra ships, or energy, if the score is high enough.

Give the player new powers as the game grows more difficult, such as super missiles or a shield.

Give the player the option of controlling the missile launcher from the keyboard.

 Add more sounds. Right now, the only sound is an explosion that plays when a UFO blows up. You might add sounds for firing missiles, alien landings, and music when the game is over.

 Create a completely new video game. Alien Landing provides code that you can emulate and reuse, so you can develop a new game pretty fast!

Summary

Well, you've finished writing your first Java video game! The key thing to remember about the game development process is that once a good basic design is in place, new features and extensions can be added, piece by piece. (Of course, this development process applies to all types of applications as well.)

In the next chapter, you'll learn how Java's AWT can enable the player to customize your games.

7

Creating Customizable Games with the AWT

Joel Fan

ome bide fare le manobelle le quali si mobano e sal ga
i g ra pesi e iner le mem se a gomesso sa go grano di bo ne
g are nella mob e sa pe rma sesta alla mano bella pe gi qua si
sorga e pib i somo pib bal.

al pere sem... e... me... e...
e li it e resso me... me e... me...
me e... ro mo... se...
l... e... se... me... sesro

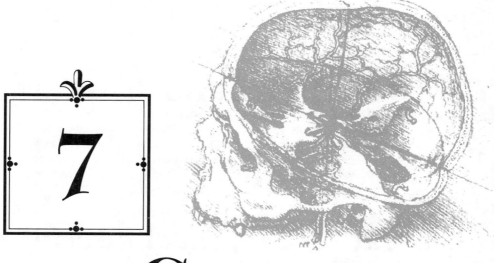

7

Creating Customizable Games with the AWT

Goals:

Use AWT components, containers, and layout managers to create graphical interfaces

Read applet parameters from HTML files

Enable players to customize the Alien Landing video game

The audience for your games is the World Wide Web, and like any large group of people, this audience has diverse tastes and abilities. For any game, some players are more skillful than others and will want greater challenges. Some users might want to enable options, such as sound; others will want to keep the game as quiet as possible, to avoid distracting the boss or waking the baby. In a multiplayer game, you might want the option of playing the computer, if your human opponents don't show up! To accommodate the vast population on the Web, players must be able to *customize* your game.

In this chapter, you'll see how the Java Abstract Windowing Toolkit (AWT) can enable users to modify parameters in your games. The AWT allows you to create graphical user interfaces (GUIs) that are intuitive and easy to use. By the end of this chapter, you'll permit the player to customize our Alien Landing game by interfacing with AWT

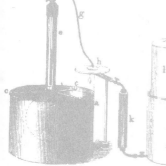

233

components. Of course, you'll be able to apply what you learn about the AWT to create nice interfaces for your own games!

Let's start with a deeper look at the AWT and how its classes work together. After that, you'll learn how to create GUI widgets, such as buttons, checkboxes, and text fields, and how to arrange them in your applets. You'll also see how to interpret the events that these widgets trigger and change the state of your games accordingly. Finally, you'll see how your game applet can read parameters from an HTML file.

Creating Graphical Interfaces with the AWT

The AWT, which we introduced in Chapter 1, Fundamental Java, and Chapter 4, Adding Interactivity, allows you to create graphical user interfaces (GUIs) for your games. In this section, you'll learn how to do this.

Overview of the AWT

The AWT is contained in the package java.awt, and it divides into three kinds of classes:

- Classes that encapsulate GUI windows and widgets (i.e., buttons and checkboxes). Many of these classes derive from the abstract class Component.

- Classes that lay out the onscreen position of GUI components. These classes implement the LayoutManager interface.

- Classes for graphics, images, events, fonts, and other purposes. You've used many of these, such as Graphics, Event, FontMetrics, and MediaTracker, to name a few. We've covered many of these classes in previous chapters.

In this chapter, we'll focus on classes from the first two categories in previous chapters.

First, here's a high-level view of the component and layout manager classes. The AWT classes that derive from Component are shown in Figure 7-1. You'll find a table of Component methods in the Quick AWT Reference section of this chapter.

A notable subclass of Component is the abstract class Container. Classes that derive from Container can contain other Components. For example, a Frame can hold a Button and a Checkbox, as seen in Figure 7-2. This Frame is the parent container of the button and checkbox it holds.

FIGURE 7-1

◎ ◎ ◎ ◎ ◎ ◎

Component hierarchy

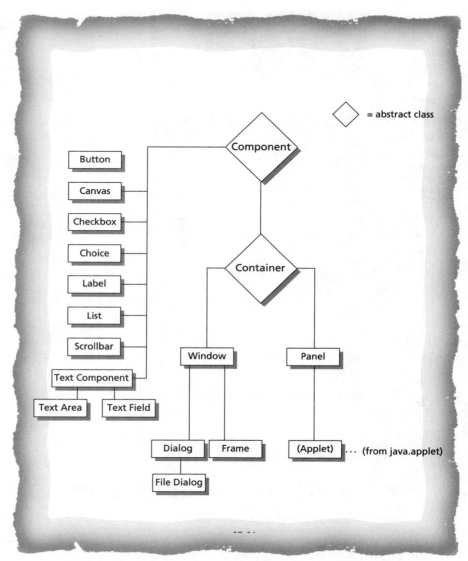

What determines the arrangement of Components in a Container? The arrangement is done by the LayoutManager that is associated with the Container. For example, the Window in Figure 7-2 is using a LayoutManager called FlowLayout. There are several classes of LayoutManagers, each offering different degrees of precision and ease of use. Figure 7-3 shows the available LayoutManagers.

FIGURE 7-2

◎ ◎ ◎ ◎ ◎ ◎

Frame containing Button and Checkbox

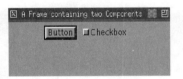

FIGURE 7-3

◎ ◎ ◎ ◎ ◎ ◎

Layout Managers

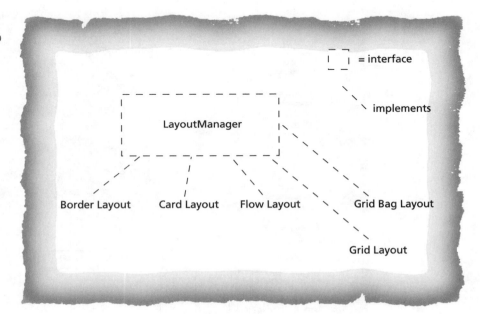

Now let's see how Components, Containers, and LayoutManagers work together to create graphical interfaces.

Creating Graphical Interfaces

Here are the four steps involved in creating and displaying graphical interfaces:

1. Create a Container. (Applet is a subclass of Container, so if you're adding widgets to your applet, this step is already done!)

2. Create the Components that the Container will hold.

3. Associate a particular LayoutManager with the Container, using the Container method setLayout().

4. Add the Components to the Container, by using the add() method of the Container. The order in which you add Components is important.

Let's write an applet that displays a button, using these steps. Although this is a simple example, you'll follow the same basic pattern anytime you use the AWT to create a graphical interface.

First, use the following line:

```
import java.awt.*;
```

to import the classes in the java.awt package. (This means we'll be able to refer to the classes in java.awt directly, without prefixing the package name.)

An Applet is a Container, which means it can contain the button. Let's declare and allocate the button in the applet's init() method:

```
public class ButtonTest extends Applet {
  public void init() {
    Button b = new Button("Hello");
```

The next step is to associate a LayoutManager with the applet container. The simplest LayoutManager is FlowLayout, which places Components, one at a time, in rows from left to right. If a component doesn't fit in a row, FlowLayout puts it in a new row below. Let's tell the applet to use FlowLayout:

```
setLayout(new FlowLayout());
```

The final step is to add the button to the applet:

```
add(b);
```

Pretty easy, right? The complete code is shown in Listing 7-1.

Listing 7-1 ButtonTest applet

```
public class ButtonTest extends Applet {
  public void init() {
    Button b = new Button("Hello");
    setLayout(new FlowLayout());
    add(b);
  }
}
```

If you run this applet, you'll get something like Figure 7-4.

Now let's see how to handle the events generated by components, such as buttons.

Handling Action Events

When you click on a button, it generates an *action* event. Action events are simply events that are triggered by the interaction of the user with a Component. To handle an action event, you'll need to define an event handler called action(). There are two places you can place the action() method:

Within the Component subclass that interacts with the user

 Within a Container subclass containing the component that interacts with the user

Let's start with the second point, since it applies to the ButtonTest applet above.

Defining the Action Handler in the Container

The ButtonTest applet contains the Button object that the user clicks. The following action() method, defined in the ButtonTest class, will catch button clicks.

```
public boolean action(Event e,Object o) {
  if (e.target instanceof Button) {
    System.out.println("Button Click!");
    return true;        // don't pass event
  }
  else return false;    // else pass event to parent container
}
```

The *instanceof* operator checks if the event target is actually a button. If it is, action() returns *true* to prevent the action event from propagating further. If action() returns *false,* the action event passes to the parent container. The same protocol applies to the event handlers we discussed in Chapter 4, Adding Interactivity, such as mouseUp(). Figure 7-5 illustrates this protocol.

You will notice that action() takes two arguments: the event itself and an Object. The particular action event and Object that is passed depends on the component that triggered the action. You'll find a table of action events at the end of this chapter.

Since actions are events, they can also be processed by the handleEvent() method (which is covered in Chapter 4). For example, the following is equivalent to the action() method above:

```
public boolean handleEvent(Event e) {
  // if action event occurs
  if (e.id == Event.ACTION_EVENT) {
    if (e.target instanceof Button) {
    System.out.println("Button Click!");
    return true;        // don't pass event
    }
  }
}
```

FIGURE 7-4

◎ ◎ ◎ ◎ ◎ ◎

ButtonTest

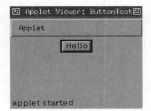

```
      else return false;    // else pass event to parent container
}
```

Defining the Action Handler in the Component

There is another place where the action handler can be defined. You can define the action() (or handleEvent()) method in the Component itself by creating a new subclass. For example, let's derive MyButton from the Button class. MyButton will echo a button click to the screen:

```
public class MyButton extends Button {
  public MyButton(String s) {
    super(s);
  }

  public boolean action(Event e,Object o) {
    if (e.target == this) { // if this object is target
      System.out.println("Button Click!");
```

continued on next page

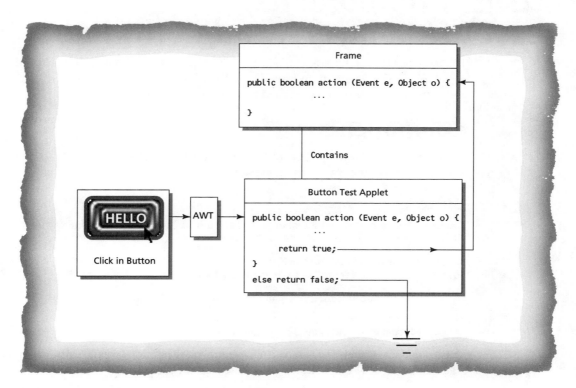

FIGURE 7-5 ◉ *Action event handling*

continued from previous page

```
    return true;          // don't pass event
  }
  else return false;      // else pass event to parent container
 }
}
```

You can instantiate MyButton in an applet. This button will echo clicks automatically, without an event handler in the applet. If the button needs to pass the event to its parent container (the applet), its action() method should return *false*. Defining the event handler in the MyButton allows you to create many buttons that exhibit the same behavior.

Although the AWT contains many possible widgets, layouts, and containers, you will be using the same pattern, seen in these examples, to create your own interfaces and actions!

Now, let's cover the components, containers, and layout managers of the AWT. We'll use these classes to create the customization dialog for Alien Landing.

Using Components, LayoutManagers, and Containers

This is a quick tour of the basic components, layout managers, and containers you'll find useful in creating graphical game interfaces. The Quick AWT Reference section at the end of this chapter lists the classes and methods described here.

Components

Let's discuss the following components: Button, Checkbox, CheckboxGroup, Label, and TextField. Each of these can be seen in Figure 7-6.

Buttons

You can create a Button with a label on it, as you have already seen, or one without a label:

```
Button unlabeled = new Button();
Button OK = new Button("OK");  // labeled with OK
```

There are two Button methods you can use to access the label:

```
String s = OK.getLabel();       //  returns the label
unlabeled.setLabel("No Way");   //  sets the label
```

Clicking on a Button creates an action event, with the button label (a String) as the argument to action().The Button methods are listed in Table 7-1.

FIGURE 7-6

◎ ◎ ◎ ◎ ◎ ◎

Basic
components

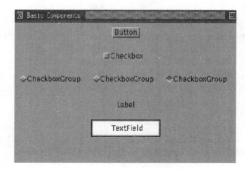

Class	Method

Button	public Button();
	 public Button(String label);
	 public String getLabel();
	 public void setLabel(String label);

TABLE 7-1 ◈ *Button methods*

Checkboxes

A Checkbox records a binary choice. You can create labeled as well as unlabeled checkboxes:

```
Checkbox unlabeled = new Checkbox();
Checkbox chicken = new Checkbox("I like chicken.");
```

As with buttons, you can access the Checkbox label using getLabel() and setLabel(String). To access the state of a Checkbox, use the methods setState(boolean) and getState():

```
Boolean b = chicken.getState()  // true if chicken is selected
chicken.setState(false);        // deselect chicken
```

Clicking on a Checkbox causes an action event, with Checkbox's state as the argument to action(). The Checkbox methods are listed in Table 7-2.

Class	Method
Checkbox	public Checkbox();
	public Checkbox(String label);
	public Checkbox(String label, CheckboxGroup group,boolean state);
	public String getLabel();
	public boolean getState();
	public void setLabel(String label);
	public void setState(boolean state);

TABLE 7-2 ◈ *Checkbox methods*

Checkbox Groups

Sometimes you will want to group checkboxes so that only one can be selected out of the entire group. These are also known as *radio buttons*.

Here's an example. Let's create a CheckboxGroup that allows users to vote for their favorite Internet guru. The first step is to declare a CheckboxGroup:

```
CheckboxGroup vote = new CheckboxGroup();
```

Then create the constituent checkboxes, using *vote* as the second argument and the initial state of the checkbox as the third. Only one Checkbox in a CheckboxGroup can be selected at a time.

```
Checkbox gosling = new Checkbox("James Gosling", vote, false);
Checkbox lee = new Checkbox("Tim Berners-Lee", vote, false);
Checkbox clark = new Checkbox("Jim Clark", vote, false);
Checkbox gates = new Checkbox("Bill Gates", vote, false);
Checkbox bird = new Checkbox("Big Bird", vote, true);
```

To access or change the selected checkbox of a group, use the CheckboxGroup methods getCurrent() and setCurrent(Checkbox box):

```
// gets label of current selection
String s = vote.getCurrent().getLabel();

// changes current selection
vote.setCurrent(bird);
```

The CheckboxGroup methods are listed in Table 7-3.

Class	Methods

CheckboxGroup	public CheckboxGroup();
	public Checkbox getCurrent();
	public synchronized void setCurrent(Checkbox box);

TABLE 7-3 ◈ *CheckboxGroup methods*

Labels

A Label displays text on a single line. Use labels to create headings or to annotate Components, such as CheckboxGroups, that don't have labels. Use a text field if you require user input.

You can specify the alignment of the label using the class constants CENTER, LEFT, and RIGHT. Here are a few examples:

```
// default: left justify
Label l1 = new Label("Junipers and irises");

// a centered label
Label l2 = new Label("Iodine with jujube", Label.CENTER);
```

You can access the text of the label with getText() and setText(String). Furthermore, you can get and set the alignment of the label as well, using getAlignment() and setAlignment(int). For example:

```
// right justify l1
l1.setAlignment(Label.RIGHT);
```

The Label methods are listed in Table 7-4.

Class	Methods

Label	public Label();
	public Label(String label);
	public Label(String label,int alignment);
	public int getAlignment();
	public String getText();
	public void setAlignment(int alignment);
	public void setText(String label);

TABLE 7-4 ◈ *Label methods*

Text Fields

A *text field* allows the user to input text from the keyboard. There are a few TextField constructors available, which allow you the option of specifying the width of the field and the String that it shows once it is initialized. Here are some examples:

```
// empty text field holding 0 characters
TextField t0 = new TextField();

// empty text field holding 13 characters
TextField t1 = new TextField(13);

// initialized to the string, holding 17 characters
Textfield t2 = new TextField("I love jellybeans",17);
```

You can access the contents of the TextField using getText() and setText(String):

```
t1.setText("Chocolate");
String s = t2.getText();
```

The TextField methods are listed in Table 7-5.

Class	Methods

TextField	public Textfield();
	public Textfield(int size);
	public Textfield(String text,int size);
	public String getText(); // inherited from TextComponent
	public setText(String text); // inherited from TextComponent

TABLE 7-5 ◈ *TextField methods*

Now let's see how to place these widgets on the screen by using LayoutManagers.

LayoutManagers

LayoutManagers are responsible for arranging Components within a Container, such as an Applet. To use a LayoutManager, you need methods defined in Container. The basic Container methods you'll need are listed in Table 7-6.

Container Method	Purpose
public Component add(Component c);	Adds the specified component
public Component add(String s,Component c);	Adds component with String argument
public void setLayout(LayoutManager m);	Uses the specified layout manager

TABLE 7-6 ❖ *Basic Container methods*

Here's the sequence of events. First, tell the Container to use a particular LayoutManager:

```
setLayout(LayoutManager);
```

Then, add the Components to the Container:

```
add(Component);
```

For example, the following statement adds a Button:

```
add (new Button("A Button"));
```

The LayoutManager determines the onscreen placement of the Components within the Container.

Let's discuss the three LayoutManagers we'll use: FlowLayout, BorderLayout, and GridLayout.

FlowLayout

This LayoutManager places Components in rows from left to right, in the same way that a word processor lays out words. If the Components do not all fit in a single row, FlowLayout starts a new row below. FlowLayout supports three alignment modes—CENTER, LEFT, and RIGHT—and also allows you to control the horizontal and vertical gaps between each Component. For example:

```
setLayout(new FlowLayout(FlowLayout.RIGHT));
```

will align the components along the right border of the Container. Figure 7-7 shows a group of buttons arranged this way.

The following centers components, with gaps in between of 17 pixels horizontally and 33 pixels vertically:

```
setLayout(new FlowLayout(FlowLayout.CENTER,17,33));
```

Figure 7-8 shows where the buttons appear with this layout. Table 7-7 shows the FlowLayout alignments.

FIGURE 7-7

◎ ◎ ◎ ◎ ◎ ◎

FlowLayout with RIGHT alignment

FIGURE 7-8

◎ ◎ ◎ ◎ ◎ ◎

FlowLayout with CENTER alignment and gaps

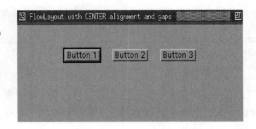

Constant in FlowLayout	Meaning
FlowLayout.CENTER	Center the components
FlowLayout.LEFT	Left-justify the components
FlowLayout.RIGHT	Right-justify the components

TABLE 7-7 ◈ *FlowLayout alignments*

BorderLayout

BorderLayout allows you to insert components along the four borders of the Container—"North," "South," "East," "West"—as well as the "Center," which is the space that's remaining. You can also control the horizontal and vertical gaps that exist between the components. For example, the following uses a BorderLayout with a horizontal space of 17 pixels and a vertical space of 13 pixels between Components.

```
setLayout(new BorderLayout(17,13));
```

To add a Component *comp* to the North border, you need to use another form of the add() method:

```
add("North",comp);
```

Figure 7-9 shows the result of using BorderLayout to arrange five labels, one in each region. Table 7-8 shows the BorderLayout alignments.

FIGURE 7-9
◎ ◎ ◎ ◎ ◎ ◎
*BorderLayout
alignments*

String Argument to Add (String, Component)	Meaning
"Center"	Place component in center
"East"	Place at right border
"North"	Place component at top border
"South"	Place component at bottom border
"West"	Place component at left border

TABLE 7-8 ◈ *BorderLayout alignments*

GridLayout

The GridLayout partitions the Container into a grid of equally sized rectangles. For example, to create a grid of two rows and four columns, use

```
setLayout(new GridLayout(2,4));
```

As with the other LayoutManagers you have seen, you can also specify horizontal and vertical gaps. The following creates a GridLayout with gaps of 13 pixels horizontally and vertically between the grid rectangles:

```
setLayout(new GridLayout(2,4,13,13));
```

As you add Components, GridLayout will arrange them left to right, top to bottom in the grid. Figure 7-10 shows the result of inserting labels from 1 to 8 in consecutive order, using the GridLayout we just defined.

FIGURE 7-10
◎ ◎ ◎ ◎ ◎ ◎
*Labels
arranged by
GridLayout
(2,4,13,13)*

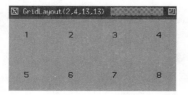

Other Layout Managers

The AWT supports two other LayoutManagers that we won't discuss here: CardLayout and GridBagLayout. GridBagLayout, in particular, is the most powerful and complicated of all the LayoutManagers, and it allows the most precision in the arrangement of Components. Look at Appendix C, Sources of Java Information, for sources of information about these LayoutManagers.

Now let's cover the Container classes in the AWT.

Containers

In this section, you will learn about the Containers in the AWT: Panel, Frame, and Dialog. You'll use these containers for the new interface to Alien Landing. In particular, you will put the Alien Landing applet into a Frame, with a custom menu bar and a crosshair cursor. The player will use a Dialog box to alter the difficulty of the game. And to create proper layouts in the Dialog and Frame, you'll need to use Panels.

First, let's discuss Panel, the simplest Container.

Panels

A Panel is a Container that does not create its own window. For example, Applet is a subclass of Panel, so an applet appears inside the window of the Web browser or the appletviewer, instead of its own window. A Panel may hold Components, including other Panels. Each Panel can use a different LayoutManager, so by nesting Panels, you can create more elaborate layouts.

Here's an example. The following applet, shown in Listing 7-2, uses a GridLayout of two rows and three columns. One of the components added is a Panel, which uses FlowLayout to arrange a series of buttons.

Listing 7-2 *PanelExample applet*

```
public class PanelExample extends Applet{
  public void init() {
    setLayout(new GridLayout(2,3,13,13));
    Panel p = new Panel();    // define a panel

    // set panel layout
    p.setLayout(new FlowLayout(FlowLayout.RIGHT));

    // insert buttons into panel
    p.add(new Button("Buttons"));
    p.add(new Button("in"));
    p.add(new Button("Panel"));

    // add labels
    add(new Label("Label 1", Label.CENTER));
    add(new Label("Label 2", Label.CENTER));
    add(new Label("Label 3", Label.CENTER));
```

```
    add(new Label("Label 4", Label.CENTER));
    add(new Label("Label 5", Label.CENTER));

    // add panel
    add(p);

  }
}
```

Figure 7-11 shows the appearance of this applet.
Now let's move on to Frames.

Frames

Frame is the Container that provides the greatest functionality. Unlike a Panel, which appears inside another window, a Frame provides a separate, resizable, iconifiable window with a title and menu bar. In addition, you can change the cursor within the bounds of the Frame. Figure 7-12 shows what a minimal Frame looks like.

Let's write an applet that creates the Frame of Figure 7-12. This Frame will also use a crosshair cursor. The first step is to construct the Frame, in the applet's init() method:

```
public class FrameExample extends Applet {
  public void init() {
    // create new Frame, with "FrameTest" as the title
    Frame f = new Frame("FrameTest");
```

Now let's set the size of the Frame:

```
f.resize(113,117);
```

Let's also make this Frame unresizable to the user:

```
f.setResizable(false);
```

FIGURE 7-11
◎ ◎ ◎ ◎ ◎ ◎
PanelExample

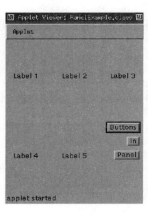

FIGURE 7-12
◎ ◎ ◎ ◎ ◎ ◎
FrameTest

Now let's change the cursor:

```
f.setCursor(Frame.CROSSHAIR_CURSOR);
```

CROSSHAIR_CURSOR is one of several constants in Frame that define cursors. Other commonly used cursors are HAND_CURSOR and DEFAULT_CURSOR (the usual arrow). You'll find the complete list of cursors in the Quick AWT Reference section at the end of this chapter.

Finally, let's pop up the Frame, by calling show():

```
f.show();
```

The opposite of show() is hide(), which will cause the Frame to disappear from view. Listing 7-3 shows the complete applet.

Listing 7-3 *FrameExample applet*

```
public class FrameExample extends Applet {
  public void init() {
    // create new Frame, with "FrameTest"  as the title
    Frame f = new Frame("FrameTest");
    f.resize(113,117);
    f.setResizable(false);
    f.setCursor(Frame.CROSSHAIR_CURSOR);
    f.show();
  }
}
```

Frames are Containers, so you can call setLayout() and add(), as with Panels. However, Frames provide additional functionality, and in the last example in this chapter, you'll see how to create menu bars for them. The basic Frame methods are listed in Table 7-9.

Class	Methods
Frame	public Frame();
	public Frame(String title);
	public synchronized void dispose(); // overrides dispose() from Window
	public MenuBar getMenuBar();
	public boolean isResizable();
	public void setCursor(int cursorType);
	public synchronized void setMenuBar(MenuBar mb);
	public void setResizable(boolean b);

TABLE 7-9 ◈ *Basic Frame methods*

Finally, let's discuss Dialog.

Dialogs

Although a Dialog creates its own window, like a Frame, it doesn't provide certain features, such as menu bars or iconification. Dialogs are somewhat like telephone calls, interrupting the normal flow of activity, and appearing and disappearing when necessary. For example, you might use a Dialog box to confirm a file deletion or to alert the user of an error condition. A Dialog can also be *modal*, which means that it blocks input to all other windows while it is on the screen. In other words, you might say that a modal Dialog is like a telephone call you must answer before doing anything else!

A Dialog always has a parent Frame. For example, the following creates a Dialog with the title A Dialog Box:

```
Frame parent = new Frame("A Frame");
Dialog dialog = new Dialog(parent, "A Dialog Box", false);
```

The last argument to the Dialog constructor, a boolean, indicates whether the Dialog is modal (*true*) or not (*false*).

As with the other Containers, you can use setLayout() and add components to a Dialog window. The Component methods show() and hide(), are of course available too:

```
dialog.show();   // show dialog box
dialog.hide();   // hide dialog box
```

Finally, since Dialogs are used on an interim basis, it's nice to free up system resources when they're done:

```
dialog.dispose();// frees resources used by the dialog
```

The basic Dialog methods are listed in Table 7-10.

Class	Methods
Dialog	public Dialog(Frame parent,boolean modal);
	public Dialog(Frame parent,String title,boolean modal);
	public synchronized void dispose(); // inherited from Window
	public boolean isModal();
	public boolean isResizable();
	public void setResizable(boolean b);

TABLE 7-10 ◈ *Basic Dialog methods*

We'll create a Dialog box in the next section; peek ahead to Figure 7-15 to see what a Dialog object looks like.

Now, let's use what you've learned about the AWT to create a new graphical interface that allows the player to customize the Alien Landing game. You might want to review the design of the game in Chapter 5, Building a Video Game (see the section Dividing Responsibility Among Functional Units).

Customizing Alien Landing

We are going to do three things here.

✦ First, we will put the Alien Landing applet into a Frame, so it can take advantage of the cooler-looking crosshair cursor! The idea is to derive a new class, GameFrame, that we will add (using add()) the applet to.

✦ Second, we will create a menu bar, menus, and menu items for the GameFrame, so that the player can choose a new game, abort a game, or exit the game applet completely. The GameFrame will send messages to the GameManager class depending on the player's selection. In addition, the Options menu will select the customization dialog.

✦ Finally, we will define a subclass of Dialog called OptionsDialog which obtains the player's preferences. The OptionsDialog object will then tell the GameManager to modify the appropriate game parameters.

Figure 7-13 shows the communication that takes place between the new classes we will create and the GameManager class.

Let's get started.

Defining the GameFrame Container

GameFrame will derive from Frame. GameFrame's constructor will take the applet and its width and height as arguments:

```
public GameFrame(Applet app,int width,int height) {
```

The first thing the GameFrame constructor does is call the Frame constructor:

```
super("Alien Landing");
```

Let's set the size of the Frame, and change the cursor as well:

```
resize(width+13,height+65);
setResizable(false);
setCursor(Frame.CROSSHAIR_CURSOR);
```

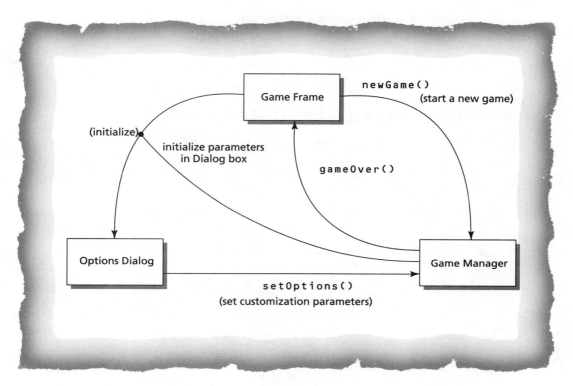

FIGURE 7-13 ◉ *Communication between classes*

Now insert the applet into a Panel, and add this Panel to the GameFrame:

```
p = new Panel();
p.setLayout(new FlowLayout(FlowLayout.CENTER));
p.add(app);
setLayout(new BorderLayout());
add("Center",p);
```

You will also need to construct GameFrame in the init() method of the Alien Landing applet:

```
GameFrame f;

public void init() {
  ...
  width = 240;
  height = 270;
  ...
```

continued on next page

continued from previous page

```
        f = new GameFrame(this,width,height);
        ...
}
```

If you want, you can test these changes right now. But let's go further, by adding a MenuBar to the GameFrame.

Creating a Menu Bar

A MenuBar is the strip at the top of the Frame that lists possible choices. For example, Figure 7-14 shows the menu bar we will create for the Alien Landing GameFrame.

Let's create this MenuBar. All of the following code goes into GameFrame's constructor. First, you must instantiate a MenuBar object:

```
MenuBar menubar = new MenuBar();
```

Then, create each Menu. There are two of them: Game and Options.

```
Menu m1 = new Menu("Game");
Menu m2 = new Menu("Options");
```

At this point, both Menus are empty. If you click on the Game Menu, for example, there aren't any MenuItems to select. You need to insert individual MenuItems into each Menu, using add(). For the Game Menu, you will allow three choices: New Game, Abort Game, and Exit:

```
// newItem,abortItem are MenuItems

newItem = new MenuItem("New Game");
m1.add(newItem);
abortItem = new MenuItem("Abort Game");
abortItem.disable();
m1.add(abortItem);
m1.add(new MenuItem("Exit"));
```

FIGURE 7-14

◎ ◎ ◎ ◎ ◎ ◎

GameFrame
MenuBar

When you call the disable() method of a MenuItem, that item can no longer be selected. For example, the Abort Game item is disabled initially. The enable() method permits an item to be selected.

The Options Menu will have only one choice:

```
m2.add(new MenuItem("Change Options..."));
```

Finally, you must set the MenuBar of the GameFrame:

```
setMenuBar(menubar);
```

The next step is to define actions for the menu items. To do this, we need an action() method in GameFrame.

Handling Menu Actions

The action() method tests whether a given menu item is selected, and makes the appropriate response. For example, when the player chooses New Game, the following occurs:

```
// handle actions
public boolean action(Event e,Object o) {
  if (e.target instanceof MenuItem) {
    String s = (String)o;
    if (e.target == newItem) {
     gm.newGame();
     newItem.disable();
     abortItem.enable();
    }
  ...
```

First, the GameManager starts a new game. Then the New Game menu item is disabled, and Abort Game is enabled.

When the player chooses Exit, the Frame window closes, the applet stops running, and system resources are freed:

```
...
else if (s.equals("Exit")) {
   hide();
   gm.stop();
   gm.destroy();
   dispose();
 }
```

Finally, let's see what happens if the player chooses Change Options...:

```
...
else if (s.equals("Change Options...")) {
 d = new OptionsDialog(this,gm);
 d.show();
}
```

A modal dialog box pops up, awaiting the user's response. Let's lay out this dialog, and enable it to parse user input.

Defining the Customization Dialog

We will let the player alter the difficulty of the game, and enable or disable sound. The two difficulty parameters that we will allow the player to modify are the starting level (the number of aliens on the screen initially) and the energy decrement (the amount of energy the player loses when hit by an alien).

Figure 7-15 shows the Dialog box we will create.

Because we will need to provide actions for this Dialog, let's create a subclass called OptionsDialog. The OptionsDialog window is laid out using a GridLayout. The Labels Starting Level, Energy Decrement, Sound, and the two TextFields are inserted in the following order:

```
public OptionsDialog(Frame parent,GameManager gm) {
  super(parent,"Alien Landing Options",true);
  this.gm = gm;
  setLayout(new GridLayout(4,2,13,13));
  l[0] = new Label("Starting Level",Label.LEFT);
  l[1] = new Label("Energy Decrement",Label.LEFT);
  l[2] = new Label("Sound",Label.LEFT);
  t[0] = new TextField(String.valueOf(gm.startLevel),3);
  t[1] = new TextField(String.valueOf(gm.energyDec),3);
  c[0] = new Checkbox("On",cg,gm.sound);
  c[1] = new Checkbox("Off",cg,!gm.sound);
  add(l[0]);
  add(t[0]);
  add(l[1]);
  add(t[1]);
  add(l[2]);
```

Next is a Panel that contains two Checkboxes, arranged with FlowLayout:

```
p.setLayout(new FlowLayout(FlowLayout.CENTER,3,3));
p.add(c[0]);
p.add(c[1]);
b[0] = new Button("OK");
b[1] = new Button("Cancel");
```

FIGURE 7-15

◎ ◎ ◎ ◎ ◎ ◎

OptionsDialog

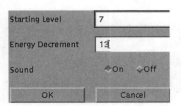

This Panel is then inserted into the grid, along with the two buttons:

```
add(p);
add(b[0]);
add(b[1]);
```

Finally, pack() resizes the window to the preferred size of its components:

```
 pack();
}
```

Now OptionsDialog must process the input from the player. The action() method waits for a click on the OK button or the Cancel button, and then it closes and disposes of the window.

```
// handle actions
 public boolean action(Event e,Object o) {
   if (e.target instanceof Button) {
     String str = (String)o;
      // if user presses OK
     if (str.equals(b[0].getLabel())) {
     parseDialog();
     }
     // else user's pressed cancel, so
     // don't do anything

     hide();
     dispose();
     System.out.println("press d");
     return true;
   }
   else return false;
 }
```

If the player clicked OK, the input is processed by parseDialog(), and is passed along to the GameManager class, which updates the parameters. The static method Integer.parseInt() converts a String to an int.

```
protected void parseDialog() {
   int start = -1,energy = -1;
   boolean sound;
   try {
     start = Integer.parseInt(t[0].getText());
   }
   catch (Exception exc) {
   }

   try {
     energy = Integer.parseInt(t[1].getText());
   }
   catch (Exception exc) {
   }
```

continued on next page

continued from previous page

```
        sound = c[0].getState();
        gm.setOptions(start,energy,sound);
    }
```

That completes the customization dialog for the Alien Landing game!

Customized Source Code for GameManager

The complete code for the GameFrame, OptionsDialog, and the new methods in GameManager is shown in Listings 7-4 through 7-6.

Listing 7-4 *GameFrame class*

```
class GameFrame extends Frame {
    protected Panel p;
    protected MenuItem newItem,abortItem;
    protected GameManager gm;
    protected int width,height;
    protected OptionsDialog d;

    public GameFrame(Applet app,int width,int height) {

        super("Alien Landing");

        this.width = width;
        this.height = height;
        gm = (GameManager)app;

        resize(width+13,height+65);
        setResizable(false);
        MenuBar menubar = new MenuBar();
        Menu m1 = new Menu("Game");
        newItem = new MenuItem("New Game");
        m1.add(newItem);
        abortItem = new MenuItem("Abort Game");
        abortItem.disable();
        m1.add(abortItem);
        m1.add(new MenuItem("Exit"));
        Menu m2 = new Menu("Options");
        m2.add(new MenuItem("Change Options..."));
        menubar.add(m1);
        menubar.add(m2);
        setMenuBar(menubar);
        p = new Panel();
```

```
      p.setLayout(new FlowLayout(FlowLayout.CENTER));
      p.add(app);
      setLayout(new BorderLayout());
      add("Center",p);

      setCursor(Frame.CROSSHAIR_CURSOR);

      show();

  }

  public void gameOver() {
    abortItem.disable();
    newItem.enable();
  }


  // handle actions
  public boolean action(Event e,Object o) {
    if (e.target instanceof MenuItem) {
      String s = (String)o;
      if (e.target == newItem) {
      gm.newGame();
      newItem.disable();
      abortItem.enable();
      }
      else if (e.target == abortItem) {
      gm.gameOver();
      }

      else if (s.equals("Exit")) {
      hide();
      gm.stop();
      gm.destroy();
      dispose();
      }
      else if (s.equals("Change Options...")) {
      d = new OptionsDialog(this,gm);
       d.show();

      }

      return true;
    }
    else return false;
  }

}
```

Listing 7-5 *OptionsDialog class*

```
class OptionsDialog extends Dialog {
  Label l[] = new Label[3];
  TextField t[] = new TextField[2];
  Button b[] = new Button[2];
  CheckboxGroup cg = new CheckboxGroup();
  Checkbox c[] = new Checkbox[2];
  Panel p = new Panel();
  GameManager gm;

  public OptionsDialog(Frame parent,GameManager gm) {
    super(parent,"Alien Landing Options",true);
    this.gm = gm;
    setLayout(new GridLayout(4,2,13,13));
    l[0] = new Label("Starting Level",Label.LEFT);
    l[1] = new Label("Energy Decrement",Label.LEFT);
    l[2] = new Label("Sound",Label.LEFT);
    t[0] = new TextField(String.valueOf(gm.startLevel),3);
    t[1] = new TextField(String.valueOf(gm.energyDec),3);
    c[0] = new Checkbox("On",cg,gm.sound);
    c[1] = new Checkbox("Off",cg,!gm.sound);
    p.setLayout(new FlowLayout(FlowLayout.CENTER,3,3));
    p.add(c[0]);
    p.add(c[1]);
    b[0] = new Button("OK");
    b[1] = new Button("Cancel");
    add(l[0]);
    add(t[0]);
    add(l[1]);
    add(t[1]);
    add(l[2]);
    add(p);
    add(b[0]);
    add(b[1]);

    pack();

  }


  // handle actions
  public boolean action(Event e,Object o) {
    if (e.target instanceof Button) {
      String str = (String)o;
       // if user presses OK
      if (str.equals(b[0].getLabel())) {
      parseDialog();
      }
      // else user pressed cancel, so
      // don't do anything
```

```
        hide();
        dispose();
        return true;
    }
    else return false;
}

protected void parseDialog() {
    int start = -1,energy = -1;
    boolean sound;
    try {
        start = Integer.parseInt(t[0].getText());
    }
    catch (Exception exc) {
    }

    try {
        energy = Integer.parseInt(t[1].getText());
    }
    catch (Exception exc) {
    }

    sound = c[0].getState();
    gm.setOptions(start,energy,sound);
}

}
```

Listing 7-6 *New GameManager variables and methods*

```
// customizable parameters
  int startLevel;
  int energyDec;
  boolean sound;


  int width, height;                    // applet dimensions

// strings
String scoreString = "Score: ";
String ufoLandedString = "UFOs Landed: ";
String gameOverString =     "  GAME OVER  ";
String alienLandingString = "Alien Landing";
int stringWidth;
String introString[] = new String[7];

GameFrame f;

public void init() {
  setBackground(Color.black);           // applet background
```

continued on next page

continued from previous page

```
            width = 240;
            height = 270;
            resize(width,height);
            startLevel = 2;
            energyDec = 5;
            sound = false;

            f = new GameFrame(this,width,height);

            loadImages();

            try {
                expsound = getAudioClip(getCodeBase(),"Explosion.au");
            }
            catch (Exception e) { }
            um = new     UFOManager(startLevel,MAX_LEVEL,width,height,ufoImages,
                            attackImages,explodeImages,
                            this,expsound);
            gm = new GunManager(MAX_ENERGY,energyDec,width,height,gunImage,
                            um.getUFO(),
                            this);
            um.initialize(gm);              // initialize gun parameters

            playing = false;                    // not playing
            screen = INTRO;                     // show intro screen

            image = createImage(width,height); // make offscreen buffer
            offscreen = image.getGraphics();
            offscreen.setFont(bigFont);         // font for intro
            fm = offscreen.getFontMetrics(bigFont); // font metrics
            stringWidth = fm.stringWidth(alienLandingString);

            introString[0] = "You are Humanity's last hope!";
            introString[1] = "Destroy the green Alien Landers";
            introString[2] = "by using the Mouse to Move";
            introString[3] = "your Missile Launcher. Click";
            introString[4] = "to Fire Missile. If 5 Aliens";
            introString[5] = "Land, or Energy Runs Out,";
            introString[6] = "Humans will be Eaten Alive!";

        }

        // handle game over
        public void gameOver() {
          if (playing) {
            playing = false;
            screen = GAME_OVER;
            f.gameOver();      // restore menu items
          }
        }
```

```
// CUSTOMIZE MANAGERS!
public void setOptions(int startLevel,
                int energyDec,boolean sound) {
  if (startLevel >= 1 && startLevel < MAX_LEVEL) {
    this.startLevel = startLevel;
    um.setStartLevel(startLevel);   // set startLevel
  }
  if (energyDec >= 0 && energyDec <= MAX_ENERGY) {
    this.energyDec = energyDec;
    gm.setEnergyDec(energyDec);      // set energy lost
  }
  this.sound = sound;
  um.setSound(sound);                // set sound

  }

}
```

Using Applet Parameters

Finally, let's see how users can customize your game applets by using *applet parameters*.

What Are Applet Parameters?

The APPLET tag allows you (or another user) to refer to your game applet in an HTML file. The PARAM tag allows the user to pass additional parameters that the applet can read. Applet parameters are like command line arguments—the parameters are available when the applet starts running, and interpretation of the parameters is up to the particular applet.

For example, applet parameters might tell the Alien Landing applet where to get image or sound files, how many ships the player should start with, and what the maximum number of aliens is. Here's an APPLET tag that does this:

```
<APPLET code="Alien.class" width=170 height=213>
  <PARAM name="NumShips" value="3">
  <PARAM name="ShipImage" value="ship.gif">
  <PARAM name="MaxAliens" value= 13 >
</APPLET>
```

As you see, the PARAM tag has two attributes:

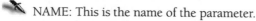 NAME: This is the name of the parameter.

VALUE: This is the value of the parameter.

Reading Applet Parameters

To read applet parameters, use the instance method

```
public String getParameter(String name);
```

defined in the Applet class. For example, the following code fragment reads parameters defined by the APPLET tag above. You could put it in the init() method, for example:

```
// this code occurs in an applet
String numShips = getParameter("NumShips");
String shipImage = getParameter("ShipImage");
```

Then the applet can set game conditions or load image files depending on the parameters it reads.

By using applet parameters, your game can be customized as soon as it starts running!

Quick AWT Reference

The java.awt package offers a rich variety of classes and methods. Here are reference tables for the material we've covered in this chapter.

The Component and Container Classes

Table 7-11 lists some selected Component methods. These methods are sometimes overridden by the subclasses of Component, so their exact behavior varies. You've used most of these methods in this chapter, or in applets from previous chapters (remember, an applet is a Component too!). The key and mouse event handlers discussed in Chapter 4, Adding Interactivity, such as keyUp(), keyDown(), mouseUp(), and mouseDown(), are Component methods that are called by handleEvent().

Component Methods	Purpose
public boolean action(Event e, Object o);	Handles action events
public Rectangle bounds();	Returns bounding rectangle of component
public synchronized void disable();	Disables component from receiving input
public synchronized void enable();	Enables component to receive input
public Color getBackground();	Gets background color

Component Methods	Purpose
public Font getFont();	Gets the font
public Graphics getGraphics();	Gets the Graphics context
public Container getParent();	Gets the parent container
public boolean handleEvent(Event e);	The default event handler
public synchronized void hide();	Hides component
public void paint(Graphics g);	Paints the component
public void repaint();	Repaints the component (calls update())
public void resize(int width,int height);	Resizes the component
public setBackground(Color c);	Sets the background color
public setFont(Font f);	Sets the font
public setForeground(Color c);	Sets the foreground color
public synchronized void show();	Shows the component
public void update(Graphics g);	Updates the component (calls paint())

TABLE 7-11   ◈   *Component methods*

Selected methods in the abstract class Container are listed in Table 7-12.

Container Methods	Purpose
public Component add(Component c);	Adds the specified component
public Component add(String s,Component c);	Adds component with String argument
public Insets insets();	Creates insets
public void setLayout(LayoutManager m);	Uses the specified layout manager
public synchronized void remove(Component c);	Removes the specified component
public synchronized void removeAll();	Removes all components from container

TABLE 7-12   ◈   *Container methods*

Components

Table 7-13 lists the components we've discussed in this chapter and selected methods that are available. Remember that these classes also inherit the Component methods listed above.

Class	Methods

Button	public Button();
	public Button(String label);
	public String getLabel();
	public void setLabel(String label);

Checkbox	public Checkbox();
	public Checkbox(String label);
	public Checkbox(String label,
	CheckboxGroup group,boolean state);
	public String getLabel();
	public boolean getState();
	public void setLabel(String label);
	public void setState(boolean
	state);

CheckboxGroup	public CheckboxGroup();
	public Checkbox getCurrent();
	public synchronized void
	setCurrent(Checkbox box);

Label	public Label();
	public Label(String label);
	public Label(String label,int
	alignment);
	public int getAlignment();
	public String getText();
	public void setAlignment(int
	alignment);
	public void setText(String label);

TextField	public Textfield();
	public Textfield(int size);
	public Textfield(String text,int
	size);
	public String getText(); //
	inherited from TextComponent
	public setText(String text); //
	inherited from TextComponent

TABLE 7-13 ◈ *Components*

Containers

Table 7-14 lists the containers discussed in this chapter and selected methods that are available.

Container	Methods

Dialog	public Dialog(Frame parent,boolean modal);
	 public Dialog(Frame parent,String title,boolean modal);
	 public synchronized void dispose(); // inherited from Window
	 public boolean isModal();
	 public boolean isResizable();
	 public synchronized void pack(); // inherited from Window
	 public void setResizable(boolean b);

Frame	public Frame();
	 public Frame(String title);
	 public synchronized void dispose(); // overrides dispose() from Window
	 public MenuBar getMenuBar();
	 public boolean isResizable();
	 public synchronized void pack(); // inherited from Window
	 public void setCursor(int cursorType);
	 public synchronized void setMenuBar(MenuBar mb);
	 public void setResizable(boolean b);

Panel	public Panel();

TABLE 7-14 ◈ *Container classes*

Cursors

Cursor types are static constants defined within the Frame class. To set the cursor, use the Frame method

```
public void setCursor(int cursorType);
```

Table 7-15 lists the cursors that are available.

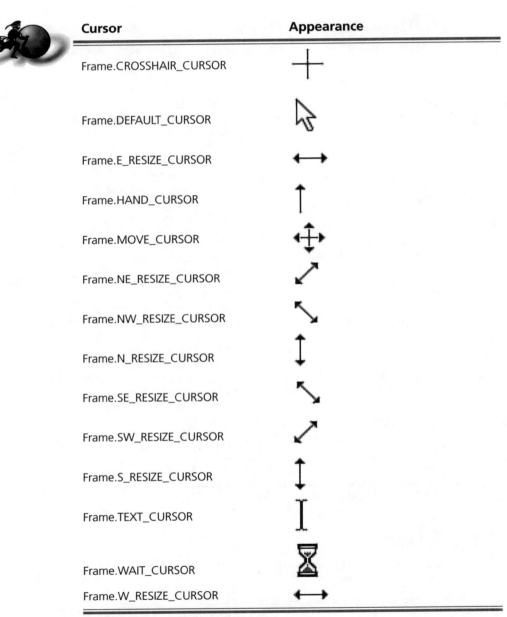

Cursor	Appearance
Frame.CROSSHAIR_CURSOR	
Frame.DEFAULT_CURSOR	
Frame.E_RESIZE_CURSOR	
Frame.HAND_CURSOR	
Frame.MOVE_CURSOR	
Frame.NE_RESIZE_CURSOR	
Frame.NW_RESIZE_CURSOR	
Frame.N_RESIZE_CURSOR	
Frame.SE_RESIZE_CURSOR	
Frame.SW_RESIZE_CURSOR	
Frame.S_RESIZE_CURSOR	
Frame.TEXT_CURSOR	
Frame.WAIT_CURSOR	
Frame.W_RESIZE_CURSOR	

TABLE 7-15 ◈ *Cursor types*

Menu, MenuBar, and MenuItem

Table 7-16 lists selected methods for Menu, MenuBar, and MenuItem.

Class	Methods

Menu	public Menu(String label);
	public synchronized MenuItem add(MenuItem mi);
	public synchronized void remove(MenuComponent item);

MenuBar	public MenuBar();
	public synchronized Menu add(Menu m);
	public synchronized void remove(MenuComponent item);

MenuItem	public MenuItem(String label);
	public void disable();
	public void enable();
	public void enable(boolean cond);

TABLE 7-16 ◈ *Menu, MenuBar, and MenuComponent*

The Event Class

Table 7-17 lists instance variables of the Event class.

Event Instance Variables	Purpose
public Object arg;	Argument that depends on event type
public int clickCount;	The number of consecutive mouse clicks (e.g., clickCount = 2 for a double-click)
public Event evt;	The next event (used to create a linked list of events)
public int id;	The type of event
public int key;	The key (used for key events)
public int modifiers;	Modifier keys used during event
public Object target;	The object that triggered the event
public long when;	Time that event occurred
public int x,y;	x and y coordinates of event

TABLE 7-17 ◈ *Instance variables of the Event class*

The *id* variable tells you the type of the event. Table 7-18 shows the values that *id* can take on. These values are defined as static constants in the Event class.

Event.id Value	Interpretation
ACTION_EVENT	Action event
GOT_FOCUS, LOST_FOCUS	Component got/lost input focus
KEY_ACTION, KEY_ACTION_RELEASE, KEY_PRESS, KEY_RELEASE	Key event
LIST_SELECT, LIST_DESELECT	List event
LOAD_FILE, SAVE_FILE	File event
MOUSE_DOWN, MOUSE_UP, MOUSE_DRAG MOUSE_MOVE, MOUSE_ENTER, MOUSE_EXIT	Mouse event
SCROLL_ABSOLUTE, SCROLL_LINE_UP, SCROLL_LINE_DOWN SCROLL_PAGE_UP, SCROLL_PAGE_DOWN	Scrollbar event
WINDOW_DESTROY, WINDOW_EXPOSE, WINDOW_DEICONIFY, WINDOW_ICONIFY WINDOW_MOVED	Window event

TABLE 7-18 ◈   *Event types*

The interpretation of the Object argument to the action() method depends on the type of component that triggered the event. Table 7-19 associates the component (stored in the *target* variable) with the Object argument.

If evt.target Is an Instance of	Then *obj* Is an Instance of
Button	String (the button label)
Checkbox	boolean (the checkbox state)
Choice	String (the chosen item)
MenuItem	String (the chosen item)
TextField	String (the input text)

TABLE 7-19   ◈   *Interpreting arguments to action(Event evt, Object obj)*

Suggestion Box

Allow the player to customize other features of the game, such as the bitmaps for the missile launcher, the aliens, or the explosions. Other possibilities for customization are the speed of the missiles, the scoring, and the color (or bitmap) for the background.

Explore the other widgets in the AWT. Here are the ones we didn't cover in this chapter: Choice, List, Scrollbar, and TextArea. These aren't hard to learn, and the pattern of creating interfaces remains the same.

Learn how to use GridBagLayout. This LayoutManager is the most powerful that the AWT provides, and you will use it in Java projects to come!

Summary

In this chapter, you've seen how Java's AWT allows players to interact with and customize your games in an easy, intuitive fashion. By allowing customization, your games can appeal to the broadest audience possible. And by using the AWT, your applications and games can have graphical front ends that are portable to any platform that runs Java.

In the next chapter, you'll see how to use networking in your games!

Part II

Advanced Game and Graphics Techniques

8

Implementing a High Score Server on a Network

Eric Ries

ome tredi fare iemanovelle x llequali simoverano illalza
igrapesi inuri leumenne di igoveiso fadograno dibone
gare nellamode nfa pirma testa arfa manovella pegi qua n
forga ex pib isome pib bent.

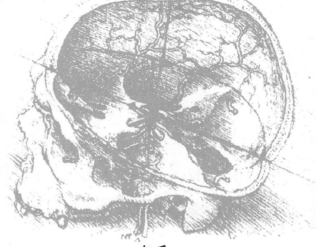

8

Implementing a High Score Server on a Network

Goals:

Understand client-server networking fundamentals

Implement high scores in Java

Use Threads, Sockets, and Files

Build a server

Allowing competition among players enhances the enjoyment of any game. In traditional programming environments, a "high score list" is used to allow players to keep track of their best scores, thus providing an incentive for further play. Java extends this paradigm to a new level. By allowing communications over the Internet, Java allows players to compete against other players worldwide.

Implementing a high score server in Java is relatively simple when compared with older-generation languages. To do this, you need two separate components: the client and the server. The client is the program (your game, in this case) that runs on the user's computer. The server is the program that runs on the machine where your programs were initially located. By obtaining information from, and reporting back to, the server, your Java game can display and continually update a list of the best players of your game. This can be a decisive advantage for your game over other games that compete for users' attention.

In this chapter, there are two things we need to discuss. The first is using Java to handle high scores using concepts this book has already discussed. The second part of the chapter discusses using Java to implement these concepts over a network.

Why Use Java for Network Programming?

Client-server communication over the Internet has obviously been around much longer than Java. Java, however, brings with it an unprecedented level of ease-of-use in network programming. Being game programmers, we have absolutely no need to waste our time with all of the details of Internet communications (and there are *many* details). Java allows us to focus on the more important aspects of the program while it transparently takes care of the messy stuff in the background.

What Is Client-Server Networking?

Most individuals with a reasonable amount of computer experience understand the basics of client-server networking. However, generations of computer science majors have managed to come up with an entire lexicon designed to confuse you. Things like sockets, ports, packets, and streams may sound like they have more to do with fishing than with computers, so let's start with a metaphor to help us along.

Basic Client-Server Terminology

Pretend you are trying to reach customer support at a huge corporation (a painful experience all of us have had). You call the company and reach the receptionist, who asks you for an extension. Luckily, you have the number handy, and you are transferred to the customer representative. The two of you have a delightful conversation, and then you both hang up. The whole process is simple and straightforward; any child could tell you how it's done. Unfortunately, to do something simple like this on a network requires a whole new vocabulary. Let's start with the most common terms we need to know:

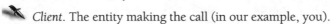 *Client*. The entity making the call (in our example, you).

Server. The entity processing your requests (the company, in our example).

Socket. Computers on the Internet communicate just like you did with your customer service representative. However, instead of telephones, computers use *sockets*. Java provides you with a very handy Socket class, which handles all of the low-level code for network communications. All you have to do is dial.

🗡 *IP address*. For one computer to call another computer, it needs a "phone number." In Internet language this is called an IP (for *Internet protocol*) address. This is a series of numbers and periods that looks something like this: 131.247.1.58. While this may not be too meaningful to a human being, an Internet computer can use it just like a phone number.

🗡 *Domain name server (DNS)*. What if you didn't know the number of a company? For a computer, this is never a problem, because computer memory is flawless. Humans are not so well equipped, so we sometimes rely on a phone book to find the number we're looking for. On the Internet, this is called a *domain name server (DNS)*, and it is what allows you to type in an address like "www.waite.com" instead of all those pesky numbers. Using an IP address or its DNS equivalent, a client program can open a socket connection to a server. Bear in mind that *every* computer connected to the Internet must have a *unique* IP address assigned to it.

🗡 *Port*. What does a client do once it has connected to a server? Just as in our example, it gets the receptionist, who asks it for an extension. In Internet jargon, the extension is called the *port*. On any one machine, any program can access any port, which is usually given a number between 1 and 9999.

🗡 *Service*. No two programs can share a port, so each port represents a different *service* offered by the server. In order for a client and a server to communicate, the server must be listening to the same port that the client is calling on. Otherwise, your client might get sales instead of customer support.

🗡 *Protocol*. Now, when you finally get through to someone on their extension, it doesn't do anybody any good if they speak Korean and you speak Portuguese. In order to do any kind of useful communicating, the client and the server must use the same *protocol*. A protocol is like a language that computers use to speak to each other. A protocol defines the order and type of interactions that can take place in a socket connection. Even though you may not know it, you are probably familiar with many protocols already.

🗡 *HyperText Transfer Protocol (HTTP)*. This is the most popular protocol on the World Wide Web. It is used to send a wide variety of textual and multimedia data. Other common ones include Gopher, Telnet, FTP , WAIS, and SMNP. The protocols that we will be using are far less complex, but the concepts are the same.

A typical phone conversation is shown in Figure 8-1, and its networking equivalent is shown in Figure 8-2.

FIGURE 8-1

◉ ◉ ◉ ◉ ◉ ◉

*Diagram of
telephone
conversation*

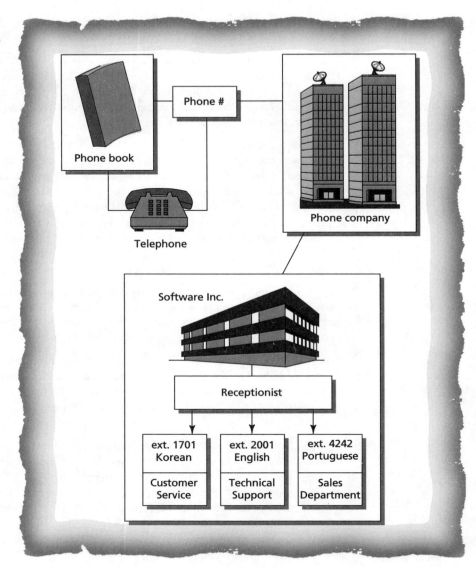

FIGURE 8-2

◉ ◉ ◉ ◉ ◉ ◉

Networking equivalents of telephone metaphor

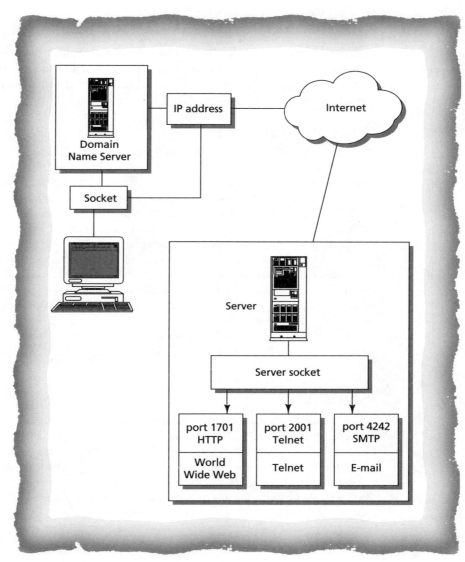

Some Additional Concepts

Before we begin to write the client and server code, there are a few concepts that must be understood. These are not necessarily concepts that are unique to networking, but are used in many higher-level languages. In fact, they might already sound familiar. In Java, they are especially important.

Exception Handling

In Java, whenever an error occurs, an *exception* is *thrown*. This exception must be *caught* and handled by whatever class invoked the method that caused the error. Exception handling is very useful, because usually your program is going to want to know if something went wrong, and, more importantly, exactly what went wrong.

When a problem arises in Java, your program will be sent an Exception object that describes what kind of error took place. What kinds of things can generate exceptions? Well, let's return to our now-overused metaphor for client-server networking, since this is where exceptions are most likely to occur. Let's say you tried to call your "server" company, and instead you got the operator saying "this number has been disconnected." Or what if you got Joe's Bait and Tackle Store instead? Or what if the phone was busy, or the receptionist couldn't find your extension, or the person you reached spoke Latin? All of these things would throw an exception, and you would be expected to do something with it. Now, in most of the code we will write in this chapter, we won't care *what* went wrong. Whether the phone rang through or was busy, we will just abort and try again later.

Streams

In Java, as in many other programming languages, when we want to get data from the outside world, we have to use a *stream*. Streams are classes that allow for data input and output, but they only work in one direction. There are also many kinds of streams, but all of them are subclasses of the InputStream and OutputStream classes. Some examples of these subclasses are DataInputStream, FileOutputStream, and PrintStream. In fact, you are probably already familiar with PrintStream, because it is used whenever you access System. Streams are very important, and you will see them crop up many times in this chapter.

Implementing Our Client Server Game Model

How does all of this client-server information relate to our high score server? You probably have realized by now that, in the client-server model, our game applet running on the user's machine will be the client and that another program running on the host machine will be the server. The client will have to open a socket to the server, request the high score data, and process it. Let's take a look at what the client and the server are going to have to do.

Implementing Client Features

Because Java is an object-oriented language, we can create a high score client "module" that can be plugged into any game you write. Because we do not want to bog down the server machine with many calculations, the client applet will be doing most of the work, and it is necessarily the most complex part of this chapter. The client must perform the following functions:

Request, parse, and sort data. The client must request data from the server, parse it (break it up into usable portions), and then sort it. The data will initially consist of high score names and scores that must be stored together in descending order. Later we will add more types of data.

Report the data. The client must be able to report back to the server a potential high score—however, we do not want the server to be bogged down with superfluous requests, so the client must be able to reject known low scores.

Display the data. The client must display the high scores in a snazzy and flexible manner, so that they can be incorporated into any existing game structure.

Operate independently of the server. The client must be able to perform all of its necessary functions in the absence of a network server. This is important, not only for testing, but also if, for some reason, the high score server is unavailable (or the user does not wish to compare his/her scores with other players).

Check for new data. The client must periodically check the server for new data, and, if necessary, request it.

Creating the HighScoreManager Class

To implement these features, we will first create a new Java class, called HighScoreManager, which will perform the bulk of the work required. The HighScoreManager class will also include a special class called HSob, which will be used for storing the high score data in discrete units. Each HSob will have the following properties:

```
name // a string used to store a player's name
score // a "float" used to store the player's score
```

The HighScoreManager will make use of the following methods and variables:

```
NUM_SCORES     // The number of high score objects in our array
```

continued on next page

continued from previous page

```
scores[]              // The actual array of scores, stored in descending⇐
order

getScoreData()        // Obtains the raw high score data from the server
getScores()    // Parses the raw data into an array of High Score Objects
paintScores()  // Draws the actual high score list with a spiffy⇐
background
addScore()     // Adds a new "HSob" to our array in the proper order
```

How HighScoreManager Reduces Calculations

There are several things that are important to notice at this point. First of all, there is
no sorting method. Because we store the scores in descending order in our *scores[]* array,
it may seem that some kind of sorting mechanism is required. However, such sorting
routines (most commonly, a "bubble sort"), are resource-consuming and altogether inefficient. To avoid using a sorting routine, we make sure to add scores in the proper place
in the list every time. Another important aspect of our design is that it requires almost
no calculation to be done by the server. The server merely needs to send us a string of
raw data that we can parse, and process our occasional updates (more on this later).

Implementing Server Features

Now that we understand the way the client will work, we must be sure that we have
an effective model for our server, so we can certify that the two will work together nicely. Our server model should be one that compliments the strengths of the client.

Effect of Client Design on Server Performance

The advantage of our client design above is that it requires very little processing by the
server. This is ideal for a networking environment for two reasons.

 First, the server could be handling potentially thousands of requests, and if
it had to perform calculations on each one, it would quickly become
bogged down. By distributing the computational load among all of the
client computers, we decrease the burden on the server considerably.

 Second, the server itself need not be implemented in Java. Several methods
of doing simple server requests are available, most commonly the Common
Gateway Interface (CGI), which allows for server programs to be written in
many languages. We will explore different methods of implementing our
server later.

Tasks Performed by the Server

No matter what language our server is written in, it still must perform the following tasks:

 Provide a string of data representing all high scores upon request. This list may be in numerical order, but not necessarily so (remember that our client will parse and order the data later).

 Receive score and name information from clients and, if applicable, add them to the high score list.

Keep track of the last time a change was made to the list of high scores, so that the client can check if it needs to request the data again.

Creating the High Score Objects

The first step in creating both the client and the server is to create a series of object classes that can be used to effectively store, retrieve, and transmit high scores. For this, we will create a special class for a single high score, and a class for a list of many high scores.

The HighScoreList Class

The first class we need to write is one that will be used by both the server and the client. This class keeps track of a bunch of high scores and keeps them in order. Let's start with the most basic skeleton of the HighScoreList class, which we can put in a file called HighScoreList.java:

```
import java.util.*;          // We will need these Java classes
import java.lang.*;


public class HighScoreList extends Object {
int NUM_SCORES = 10;  // Number of scores - default value is ten
public long lastChange = 0;  //Last time a change was made to the list

HighScoreList() {
}
}
```

Scoring Variables

We have started with two important variables in HighScoreList. *NUM_SCORES*, as the name implies, will keep track of the number of scores in our list. The other number is a "long" integer (which means it can get really really really big) called *lastChange*. Even though Java provides a very extensive Date class that can be used to display dates and times, we don't need all of that functionality. Instead, we are only going to keep track of the number of milliseconds since the beginning of the current epoch. This is a huge number, and you probably would not want to have to memorize it, but computers *love* big numbers. Tracking this number gives us a convenient way to see if we need to ask for new data from the server. More on this later.

The HSob Object Class

Before we can have a list of high scores, we are going to need our high score object class, HSob, which is part of the HighScoreList class. Let's add the code for that.

```
class HSob extends Object { // High Score Object class

        public String name;  // Player's name
        public float score;  // Player's score
/* Remember that we can always add more information about the player⇐
later */

        HSob(String n, float sc) {  //Initialization routines
              name=n;
              score=sc;
        }

        HSob() {
              name="noname";
              score=0;
        }
        }
```

You may have noticed that this class has two different initialization routines. The first is used to construct a new object, based on data passed in the new() method. The second is used in case we want to create an object and then add the data later. Next, we should add the HighScoreList itself, which will be an array of HSob. Declare it like this:

```
HSob scores[];
```

Now let's write the initialization routines for the HighScoreList. We are going to provide two different ones, just as we did with HSob. The first will allow us to initialize a HighScoreList that will track a certain number of high scores. It looks like this:

```
HighScoreList(int num) {
     NUM_SCORES = num;
     scores = new HSob[NUM_SCORES];
}
```

The other routine will allow us to create a new HighScoreList that starts out with a certain number of high scores already in it. However, before we can create this routine, we are going to need a new method for parsing data.

Data Parsing

When we get data from the server, it is going to be one long string of values. The art of "parsing" means taking a string of raw data and turning it into something useful (in this case, an array of high scores). Here is what a typical raw data string might look like:

```
"Joe&1000|Bob&250|Gary&52.3|Mary&23|Gabe&5|null|null"
```

This is a string of seven scores. You may have noticed that they are in the form "Name1&score1|Name2&score2|...." We have rather arbitrarily chosen relatively uncommon sets of characters as *delimiters* to separate meaningful data. Each name/score pair is separated by "|", and every name and score is separated by "&". Also, "null" is used to represent empty slots in the list.

The StringTokenizer Class

To break up a string of data into discrete tokens, we use a class already built into Java, called a StringTokenizer. The StringTokenizer class is used to break up a string into smaller substrings (called "tokens"), based on a common separator (now you see why I chose to break up our data with "|"). Here is a summary of the useful methods in the StringTokenizer class:

```
new StringTokenizer(String str, String delim)
/* Creates a new StringTokenizer object based on the String str and the⇐
"delimeter" (or separater) delim */

hasMoreTokens()
/* Returns true if the Tokenizer has more "tokens" left (each substring⇐
is called a "token") */

nextToken()
/* Returns the next substring token */

countTokens()
/* Returns the total number of tokens in the tokenizer */
```

Converting Data to Objects

To successfully parse this string of data, we must take each name/score pair from the list and convert it to an HSob object. We could have just one method do all of this work, but, because we are going to want to be able to convert back and forth between raw data and objects, we are going to teach the HSob class how to handle raw data.

Add a third initialization routine to HSob:

```
HSob(String data) {
    Float fl = null;
    String str;
    StringTokenizer st = new StringTokenizer(data, "&");
```

continued on next page

continued from previous page

```
while (st.hasMoreTokens()) {
        str = st.nextToken();
        if (name == null)
                name = str;
                else
        try {
                fl = Float.valueOf( str );
                score = fl.floatValue();
           } catch (Exception e) {
  other = str;
        }
        }
  }
```

This method has some new things in it that you probably noticed. The first is an extra variable called *other*. This is a String that we are going to use to hold any additional information included besides the name and the score (be sure to declare this variable on the same line where you added the name).

Another new concept is the Float class. In Java, for every primitive data type (like int or float), there is a corresponding object class (like Integer or Float) that has some nifty utility methods useful for that data type. You may not know it, but you have already used one such class extensively: the String class.

A String object is just a special class for representing an array of characters. For now, we are going to use the Float class to transform a string representation of a float (like "1000") into a Float object. You may have realized that this is exactly what we are teaching our HSob class to do! Once we have the Float object, we are then going to extract the actual float number from it, because we really don't care about the object, only its cargo. This is also the first time you have seen an Exception being caught—don't fret, though, it won't be the last.

Before we leave the HSob class for a while, we should add another method that is going to be useful down the line a little bit. This method will take the HSob's current values and convert them into a raw data string.

```
public String toDataString() {        //Convert an HSob into a data string

return name + "&" + score + "&" + other;
}
```

The parseData() Method

It's time to write the data parsing method for the HighScoreList class. Because of all the work we just did with HSob, this is going to be really easy! We are going to have to use our friend the StringTokenizer class, so I hope you haven't forgotten it yet:

```
public void parseData(String str) {  // Parse a string of data
StringTokenizer st1=new StringTokenizer(str,"|");
String theStr;
```

```
                         while (st1.hasMoreTokens()  ) {
                         theStr = st1.nextToken();
                         if (! theStr.startsWith("null"))
                                 addScore( new HSob (theStr));
                                 }
    }
```

This bit of code references a method we haven't yet discussed, so we'd better do that now.

The addScore() Method

This is a very important method, so be sure you understand how it works. Its task is to take an HSob and insert it (if applicable) into the list of scores in its proper place in the sequence. Since the list should already be in descending numerical order, all we have to do is search down the list until we find either (1) a lower score or (2) an empty slot. If we find either of these, we add our new score and drop all of the lower scores down one place. Here is the code:

```
public int addScore(HSob sc) {  // We return the place this score gets
int x,i;
x=0;

if (sc==null) return 0;

while (x<NUM_SCORES) {

if (scores[x] == null || sc.score > scores[x].score) {
      for( i=NUM_SCORES-2 ; i>=x ; i--)
            scores[i+1]=scores[i];
      scores[x]= sc;
lastChange = System.currentTimeMillis();
      return x+1;
      }
x++;
}

return 0;
}
```

So long as we never make any changes to the *scores[]* array except with addScore(), the array will always keep scores in descending order. This means we never have to sort it, which is good news for the speed of our program. Also, here we use the System method currentTimeMillis() to find out how many seconds have transpired since the current epoch began, and we store this in our long variable *lastChange* if and only if we have actually made a change to the list.

The HighScoreList class is almost finished. Only two things remain. Both of these methods allow the outside class a little more access to the list.

The tryScore() Method

The first method is tryScore(), which takes a name/score pair, converts it into an HSob, and passes it to addScore(). If addScore() adds this HSob to the list, tryScore() returns a data string representing HSob. Otherwise, it returns null, indicating that the HSob did not make it onto the list. There are actually two tryScore() methods: The first accepts the name/score/etc. data separately, while the second accepts it as a data string. Only the second method actually does any work; the first method just converts the data it receives into a data string and calls the other tryScore(). Here is the code:

```
public String tryScore( String name, float score, String email, String ⇐
other) {
HSob temp;

temp = new HSob (name, score, email, other);
return tryScore (temp.toDataString());
}

public String tryScore( String data) {

HSob temp = new HSob (data);
if (addScore(temp) > 0)
        return temp.toDataString();
else
        return null;
}
```

The getScore() Method

The last method is getScore(), which will return any individual member of the list if it exists:

```
public HSob getScore(int num) {
if (num < NUM_SCORES)
        return scores[num];
else
        return null;
}
```

That's it! If you really want to, you can compile the HighScoreList, but unfortunately, you cannot run it. In fact, the HighScoreList is utterly useless by itself. You may feel that you have done all of this work for nothing, but you will soon see that putting a lot of work into the foundation classes will make writing the exciting stuff a *lot* easier. This is one of the lessons any OOP programmer has to learn very well.

Creating the HighScoreManager Class

Now it's time to write the object that will plug into the client applet: the HighScoreManager class. The first thing we must do is create a file called HighScoreManager.java. In it, place the basic code for initializing a new class:

```
import java.awt.*;  // These are all java components we will eventually ⇐
need
import java.util.*;
import java.lang.*;


public class HighScoreManager extends Object {


HighScoreManager() { // The object initialization routine — does nothing⇐
for now

}

}
```

In order to test this class without being connected to a server (and without having written the server software yet), let's add a class that pretends it retrieved some data from a server:

```
String getScoreData() {

return "Eric & 1000 | Dave & 200 | Jane & 0 | Mary & 24235";
}
```

If we had really obtained a server connection, this is an example of the type of data we might receive. Recall that our data will be in the form "Name & score | Name & score." Using relatively rare characters like "&" and "|" to separate our data makes it easier to parse. Later on, the getScoreData() method will actually do some work. Another thing we should do is get a new HighScoreList. We can make a new one in the initialization routine for HighScoreManager:

```
HighScoreManager(int max) {
     NUM_SCORES=max;
     L= new HighScoreList(NUM_SCORES);
}
```

The getScores() Method

Now we want to write a method that will take the data from getScoreData() and add it to the list. Here is the code for the getScores() method:

```
void getScores() {
String str;
int x=0;

        str=getScoreData();

if (str==null || str == "none") return ;
/* If there are no scores to parse, we're done */

L = new HighScoreList(NUM_SCORES, str);

}
```

Notice how the HighScoreList really does all the work, and all we have to do is send it the data! Finally, it's time to start providing some methods for interacting with the user. The next method is one that will be called (eventually) from our applet's paint() method.

The paintScores() Method

The paintScores() method will be passed a Graphics context and will be expected to draw the high scores on it. Chief among design considerations for this method is the fact that the high score drawing area may be a rectangle of any size. However, the applet may not want us to draw on the entire rectangle available to us. The Graphics context may be "clipped" to a smaller region—we must account for this. The paintScores() method is passed two arguments: the Graphics context g, and a Rectangle r. The Rectangle defines the total area available for us to draw the scores onto. Here are some Java methods we will use:

```
new Rectangle (int x, int y, int width, int height);
/* create a new Rectangle at (x,y) */
r.intersects (Rectangle);
/* Return true if the two rectangles intersect */

Graphics g.getClipRect();
/* Returns the current "clipping area" of the Graphics context */
fillRect( int x, int y, int width, int height);
/* Fills a rectangle with the current color */
```

Some other methods you will need have to do with Colors and Fonts. These are two more built-in classes in Java.

Methods for Creating Colors

To create a color, you can access it by name (for instance, Color.blue) or create a new color based on red, green, and blue values. The RGB scale uses three integers to represent colors. To create a really neat effect, we are going to divide the screen into a random number (3–53) of even rectangles. We will choose a color for the first rectangle, and then slowly "dissolve" the blue out of each successive rectangle until the last rectangle has no blue in it at all. This will provide us with a very snazzy backdrop for our high scores! Here is the first half of the paintScores() code that handles the background color dissolve:

```
void paintScores(Graphics g, Rectangle r) {

int x;
int b=255;

for(x=r.x  ; x < r.width + r.x  ;x += (int)(r.width/num)) {
      b-=(int)(255/num);
      if (b<0) b=0;
      g.setColor(new Color( red , green , b));
if (g.getClipRect().intersects( new Rectangle(x,r.y,r.width,r.height)))
      g.fillRect ( x , r.y , r.width , r.height);
      }
```

Of course, this code does not create or initialize the variables *red*, *green*, and *num*. For that, we need to declare three more global ints, and create a simple function for choosing random values:

```
private int red,green,num;

...

public void newColors() {
      red=(int)(Math.random()*200)+56 ;
      green= (int)(Math.random()*200)+56;
      num= (int)(Math.random()*50)+2;
}
```

We should also add a call to HighScoreManager() (our init routine, remember?) that calls newColors(). Also, notice that *red*, *green*, and *num* are all *private* variables. This means that they are not accessible by any class outside the HighScoreManager. However, the newColors() routine is public, so our applet can choose to change the background color.

Methods for Creating Fonts

Meanwhile, back at our painting method, we have to do the actual work of writing the scores on the Graphics context. For this, we will need to choose an appropriately sized Font, so that we will have room to display however many scores we have in whatever space we have. We also want to leave a little space between lines of text, say, 5 pixels. Of course, before we can do this, you have to learn a little about the Font class.

A font is created like this:

```
new Font("Times New Roman", Font.PLAIN, 24);
```

This creates a 24-point Times New Roman font that is "plain" (that is, not bold or italic). Another related class is the FontMetrics class, which is used for making calculations based on the current Font and the current Graphics context. The most important method, for our purposes, in FontMetrics is

```
stringWidth(String str);
```

which returns the horizontal width, in pixels, of the specified string, if it were to be drawn using the Font upon which the FontMetrics is based.

Armed with this new information, let's finish off our paintScores() method:

```
fontSize=(int)(r.height/(NUM_SCORES + 4));
g.setFont(new Font("Times New Roman", Font.PLAIN, fontSize));
FontMetrics fm = g.getFontMetrics();

where= 5 + fontSize;
g.setColor(Color.black);
str= "High Scores";
g.drawString( str, (int)((r.width + r.x - fm.stringWidth(str))/2), where);


for (x = 0 ; x< NUM_SCORES ; x ++) {
      where+=fontSize + 5;
if( g.getClipRect().intersects( new Rectangle ( r.x, where-fontSize-5, ⇐
r.width, fontSize))) {
      str="    "+(x+1)+". ";
      if(L.getScore(x) != null) {
            str+=L.getScore(x).name;
            for (i= 5 + fm.stringWidth(str) ; i< r.x + r.width - 6 - ⇐
fm.stringWidth(" " + L.getScore(x).score) ; i+= fm.stringWidth("."))
            str+=".";
            str+=" "+L.getScore(x).score+"  ";
            }
      g.setColor(Color.black);
      g.drawString(str,r.x,where);
}
}


}
```

One extremely important thing to notice in all of this painting code is that we *always* check to see if we are writing within the Clipping rectangle before we waste time doing any drawing. This will help reduce flicker and help the applet refresh itself.

Adding New Scores to HighScoreList

We have yet to provide our applet with the ability to add new scores to the HighScoreList. Let's add that functionality now, within the addScore() method. This method will call the tryScore() method in HighScoreList, which will let us know if the score we tried was successfully integrated into the list. Oftentimes, the score that we try will *not* make it onto the list because it is not high enough. This is also a good time to add another variable that will become useful later on. It is a String called *updateStr*. This String will contain any new scores that have been added to the list. Eventually, we will send these scores to the server so that it can update its list (if applicable), but for now let's just worry about adding new scores. Here's what addScore() looks like:

```
String updateStr = ""; // Don't forget to declare this!
...
public void addScore( String name, float score, String other) {
String temp;

        temp = L.tryScore( name, score, other);
        if (temp != null)  // If the score was added to the list
              updateStr += temp + "|";  // Add it to our update list
}
```

The next set of methods we need to add to the HighScoreManager class allows our applet to get high score data without using the paintScores() method to display it. We will provide four methods for getting high score data:

```
HSob getHighestScore() // Return the highest score
HSob getNextScore()  // Return the "next" score in the list
HSob getScore(int x) // Return the xth score in the list (scores[x-1])
```

These methods are quite simple. They are all public, so an applet can access them easily. They do not do any data manipulation, but are all useful if the applet wants to do something nifty with the score data. Note that these methods are not necessary if our applet uses paintScores() to display the high scores. getHighestScore() and getNextScore() work hand in hand. Both of them obviously require a new global variable to be added to the HighScoreManager (to keep track of what the *last* score requested was). Declare it like this:

```
private int last=0;
```

The actual methods are quite simple, although we must make sure that getNextScore() does not run off the end of the list. If the applet calls for a score that is not there, just return *null*:

```
public HSob getHighestScore() {
return L.getScore(last=0);
}

public HSob getNextScore() {
if(last++ >= NUM_SCORES)
```

continued on next page

continued from previous page

```
            return null;
    return L.getScore(last);
}
```

The last method, getScore(), allows the applet to request a specific score. This method also uses the *last* variable and must check to ensure that the requested element really exists. If not, it returns *null*:

```
public HSob getScore(int x) {

if(x > NUM_SCORES)
        return null;
    return scores[last=(x-1)];
}
```

Well done! We now have a fully functional HighScoreManager class. Ready to do something exciting? Next, we are finally going to write an applet!

Creating a Testing Applet

Now that our HighScoreManager is written, we need an applet that can test it. Because it doesn't actually track any scores over the Internet yet, we can set up a very simple applet to demonstrate how the HighScoreManager works. If you already have a game ready for the HighScoreManager, read this section, and then go ahead and plug the HighScoreManager into your game. Otherwise, we will walk through the creation of a sample applet to see how it's done.

Let's start by making a new file, called testApp.java. In it, we will put the very minimum required for an applet:

```
import java.applet.*; // Our misc. Java classes we will need
import java.awt.*;
import HighScoreManager;  // Don't forget to include this!

public class testApp extends Applet {

void init() { // Does nothing for now
}

}
```

Because our HighScoreManager class does all of the work required, we can test it out by adding a very minimal amount of code. The first thing to do is to create a new HighScoreManager and initialize it:

```
HighScoreManager HS;

void init() {
        HS = new HighScoreManager(10);  // Let's have it track 10 high ⇐
scores
}
```

FIGURE 8-3

◎ ◎ ◎ ◎ ◎ ◎

*testApp.java,
first edition*

Next, we need to tell the applet how to draw itself. This is accomplished via the paint()
method. Because we created a paintScores() method in our HighScoreManager, all we
have to do is pass along some information: a Rectangle indicating where we would like
the HighScoreManager to draw the scores. Because this is just a sample applet, we can
let the HighScoreManager paint all over it, so we pass a Rectangle that "bounds" the entire
applet. In case our applet gets resized, we make sure our method queries the current
size, via the size() method. The HighScoreManager class will do all the work for us! Let's
define our paint method like this:

```
void paint(Graphics g) {
Rectangle r;

r = new Rectangle( 0 , 0 , size().width, size().height);

HS.paintScores(g,r);
}
```

That's it! Go ahead and compile testApp. It should look something like Figure 8-3.
Have fun resizing the applet, and move some other windows in front of it to see how
it handles redrawing the screen. It should do pretty well, but you will notice that the
screen flickers a lot, despite all of the work paintScores() does to try to eliminate this.

Double-Buffering the Testing Applet

In order to eliminate flicker, we will use double-buffered graphics. This technique was
discussed in Chapter 2, Using Objects for Animations, so you should already know how
it works.

```
Image im;      // Declare these globally!
Graphics g;

public void update(Graphics bg) {

// Notice that we changed the name of the local Graphics context from g ⇐
to bg!
```

continued on next page

continued from previous page

```
        Rectangle r= new Rectangle(0,0,size().width,size().height);

        im=createImage(size().width,size().height);  // Create a new Image
        g=im.getGraphics();   // Associate the Graphics context
        HS.paintScores(g,r);  // Do the work

paint(bg);   // Pass it to the paint() method
}

public void paint(Graphics bg) {
        if(im!=null)  // Make sure we have something to draw!
        bg.drawImage(im,0,0,null);   // Do the drawing

}
```

Notice that no drawing happens on the screen until the drawImage() command, even though we call several drawing methods in paintScores().

Because the HighScoreManager currently uses bogus data, it displays the same thing every time. To demonstrate how easy it is to use our HighScoreManager class, we should allow the user of the testApp to enter his/her name and then display a random "score."

The testApp GUI

Because this chapter is more concerned with networking than with Abstract Windowing Toolkit (AWT) fundamentals, we won't spend a lot of time discussing them. For more information, see Chapter 4, Adding Interactivity, and Chapter 7, Creating Customizable Games with the AWT.

Getting back to our testApp applet, let's add some AWT components to it right now. Figure 8-4 shows the results.

FIGURE 8-4

◎ ◎ ◎ ◎ ◎ ◎

*testApp
with AWT
components*

```
Panel p = new Panel();  // This is a global variable

public void init() {

HS = new HighScoreManager(10);

setLayout(new BorderLayout());  // Assign a BorderLayout to the applet

        add("South", p);  // Add Panel p to the "south" region of our ⇐
applet
}
```

If you want, you can compile and run the applet at this point. You should notice two things: First, the applet has a small gray area below the drawing with nothing in it, and second, this area has obscured part of our beautiful high score artwork! Let's deal with the latter effect first. Because the "southern" part of our Applet panel is assigned to a different Panel, the normal drawing did not cover it. Therefore, we need to tell the HighScoreManager *not* to attempt to draw anything in the part of the Applet obscured by Panel *p*. To accomplish this, think back to when we required the applet to pass a Rectangle specifying where the drawing should take place. Because of this, our applet can now tell the HighScoreManager to only draw in a rectangle that does not contain the new Panel. We are therefore going to need to know the height of Panel *p* so we can subtract it from the overall height of the Rectangle. To do this, we use the preferredSize() method in the Panel class. By querying the *height* value of the preferredSize() method, we can obtain the height of the Panel. To put this to work for us, change this line of code:

```
Rectangle r= new Rectangle(0,0,size().width,size().height);
```

to this:

```
int panel_height = p.preferredSize().height;
Rectangle r= new Rectangle(0,0,size().width,size().height-panel_height);
```

Compile and view the applet again just to prove to yourself that we have solved the problem.

The other problem we discussed earlier was the matter of this really ugly gray area in our applet that does nothing. The only way we can fix this problem is by adding some functionality to that gray area. Let's start with a Button.

Creating the Button is easy, and we add it to the Panel the same way we added the Panel *p* to our applet. Add this line to testApp's init() method:

```
p.add( new Button("Change Color"));
```

This adds a Button with the label Change Color to the Panel *p*. Since we didn't specify a Layout for Panel *p*, the Button is, by default, placed in the center. If you want, compile and display testApp and click away! Unfortunately, this doesn't do very much. Although some users may find a bogus button amusing, it won't entertain them for long. In order to add some functionality to the Button, we have to intercept the event message that it sends to the applet. Java provides us with many, many ways of dealing with events, but for this we are going to use the action() method that is built into the Applet class, just for this purpose. The action() method is declared like this:

```
public boolean action(Event evt, Object arg) {
```

Different AWT components cause different types of arguments to be passed to an Applet. Buttons pass String objects with the name of the Button embedded in them. All we have to do, then, is to check and see if the String we were passed matches a String we were expecting, and, if so, take the proper action (in this case, change the color and repaint). Always remember that in event-driven methods we must always return *true* if we handled the specified event, or *false* if we did not. This is important because it allows the event to continue to be processed in another method if it is not the one we are looking for. The code looks like this:

```
public boolean action(Event evt, Object arg) {

        if("Change Color".equals(arg)) {
                HS.newColors();
                repaint();
        return true;
        }
        return false;
    }
```

The AWT classes are so powerful precisely because they allow you to add a great deal of functionality with very little effort. Compile again, and enjoy all the pretty colors! When you're done, we can proceed on to some really useful stuff. This time, we are going to add a TextField object. A TextField is a class of objects designed to allow the user to input/edit a single line of text. We are going to now allow the user to input a name to be added to the high scores list. Since we aren't really playing a game, we will just assign the name a random-number "score" and then let our HighScoreManager handle it. First, we need a global TextField, which we will call *F*. To initialize a TextField, you have to specify the number of columns of text it will hold. We will start with 10 for now, since the user will probably not need more than that (and even if they do, the TextField scrolls!). We will also want a button that will allow the user to add the name currently in the TextField to the high scores list. Here's how it's done:

```
TextField F; // Global
...
F = new TextField(10);  // Add these to init()
p.add(F);
...
// Add this to action() :
      if ("Add".equals(arg)) {
              HS.addScore(F.getText(),(int)(Math.random() * 1000));
              F.setText(null);
              repaint();
          return true;
      }
```

Congratulations! Our testApp is done! Compile and see for yourself. Type in some text, press the Add button, and, voilà! Instant additions.

Threading HighScoreManager

We are almost ready to start writing the network-related code. However, we must first arrange to have HighScoreManager check periodically for new scores. To do this we must use Threads.

Using Threads

Much of the hype surrounding Java and many of today's newest operating systems is that they are *multithreaded*. This is yet another computer jargon term designed to intimidate you into submission. Don't worry, the concept is actually pretty simple. A *thread* is like a program in and of itself. The neat thing about multithreading is that you can have multiple tasks going on at once. Way back in the old days of DOS, you could only have one program—or thread—running at a time. Now you can have as many threads as your computer can handle, all operating concurrently.

In order to periodically check for new scores from the server, we are going to have to have a loop that runs continuously as long as the program is alive. Instead of having our program loop infinitely and freeze up the system forever (which might make our user unhappy), we create a thread to do this in the background. The thread will check for new scores, get them, and then *sleep*. While the thread is asleep, it does not use up precious system resources, and it allows the rest of the computer to run unhindered.

Luckily for us, making our HighScoreManager a thread is not too hard. In Java there are two ways to use threads: you can either *extend Thread*, as we have already done with Object and Applet, or you can *implement Runnable*, which is an *interface*.

Converting HighScoreManager to a Thread

Once the HighScoreManager implements Runnable, you will not be able to compile it. This is because an Object that implements the Runnable interface is aspiring to become a Thread object. Every thread must have a run() method. Unless the HighScoreManager class contains these methods, it can never become a thread, so the compiler will not compile it.

Normally, a Thread object must be started by another object before it can run. This is why we chose to use the Runnable interface rather than just extending the Thread class; Runnable lets HighScoreManager start itself. This is useful because, if you remember, we do not want the applet that makes use of HighScoreManager to have to do very much interacting with it. We want HighScoreManager to do all the work.

So how do we make HighScoreManager into a thread? First, we should implement Runnable in our declaration of HighScoreManager, like this:

```
public class HighScoreManager extends Object implements Runnable {
```

Now, we need to declare a thread object. We are going to call it *kicker* because I like to think of threads being "kicked" into action when they start. This metaphor may work for you, or it may not. Nevertheless, we are going to use *kicker*. Once we declare *kicker*, we are going to need to instantiate it with the new() method, like this:

```
Thread kicker;
kicker = new Thread(this);
```

The variable *this* always points to the current object, in this case to HighScoreManager. The above commands tell the compiler to create a thread, called *kicker*, based on HighScoreManager. When we tell *kicker* to start, it will call HighScoreManager's start() method. Let's put that code we just wrote into HighScoreManager. The thread must be declared as a global variable in HighScoreManager, but it should not be instantiated until HighScoreManager is created with its initialization routine. Also, when HighScoreManager is created, it should start *kicker*, since we don't have any reason to wait. Here's the code:

```
Thread kicker = null;
...
HighScoreManager(int max) {
      NUM_SCORES=max;
      L= new HighScoreList(NUM_SCORES);
      kicker = new Thread(this);
      kicker.start();
      newColors();
}
```

We still haven't created the Thread methods in HighScoreManager, so let's do that now. The first is start(). This is called as soon as Thread is activated, and it returns immediately. The only thing we need to do here is to make sure that *kicker* is active (not set to *null*).

```
public void start() {

if (kicker == null)
      kicker = new Thread(this);

}
```

Now we have to do the actual work of the thread. This is the run() method, which is called right after start(). If run() ever finishes (if it returns), the thread is finished and will be killed. Therefore, we need to make a loop that will run as long as HighScoreManager is alive. We do this by checking to see if *kicker* is equal to *null* (remember that *kicker* is a reference to HighScoreManager, so if HighScoreManager ever dies, so does *kicker*). If it is, we exit; otherwise, we continue. We are also going to make use of the sleep() method, which is how a thread puts itself to sleep for a certain amount of time. To make it easy to change this value later, create a constant (in Java, a *final variable*) with the delay (in milliseconds) you would like between each time the client checks for new scores from the server. To begin with, choose a relatively small value, like 10000 (10 seconds), for easy debugging. Declare it like this:

```
final int DELAY = 10000;
```

Next, write the run() code. All it does is call getScores(), which does the real work anyway, so it, too, is short:

```
public void run() {

while (kicker != null) {
getScores();

try{ kicker.sleep(DELAY); } catch(Exception e);
}
}
```

Here we have another potential exception that we caught, but we don't really care what it has to say, so we just ignore it. However, even though we don't care about it, Java still requires us to catch it.

One last Thread method and then we're finished. Sometimes, someone may want to tell HighScoreManager to stop looking for scores. We know for sure this will happen when HighScoreManager is finished (i.e., when the applet quits), so we'd better be prepared. The stop() method must cause the run() method to finish executing or it must cause the Thread object to be garbage-collected. This stop() method does both, just for good measure:

```
public void stop() {

kicker = null;
}
```

If you compile HighScoreManager again and run testApp, everything should appear normal. However, if you wait a few seconds (however long you set your *DELAY* to) and press the Change Colors button, you will notice that each entry in the list has been repeated. Why? Because each time we call getScores(), it adds the same list of names to the HighScoreList. If you let the program run long enough, it will eventually fill up with the first-place score. The problem lies in the inadequacies of our data-acquisition code, which doesn't do very much, so we just have to be sure we correct this glitch at the same time we add some functionality.

Writing the Networking Code

It is now time to start the second half of our discussion. Up until now, we have been using simulated data, but the time has come to replace this with some actual networking code. The code will create a new socket, try to connect to the server, and, if successful, submit to the server any new scores it has accumulated. Once they have been sent, it will clear our list of new scores so that they do not get sent more than once. In addition, the method will request any new scores that may have been acquired by the server since the last time it checked. If the score list has changed, the client will request that the entire list be re-sent and will replace its current list with the new one.

Creating a New Socket

All of the networking code is contained in the getScoreData() method. Currently, this method returns a string of data, but let's change it. Here's the first part:

```
String getScoreData() {
Socket s;
DataInputStream ds;
PrintStream ps;
String temp = null;


try {
      s = new Socket("localhost",2357);
      ds = new DataInputStream(s.getInputStream());
      ps = new PrintStream(s.getOutputStream());
} catch (Exception e) {
      return null;
}
```

This part creates a new socket, called s, that tries to connect to host *localhost* on port 2357. *localhost* always refers to the computer that the applet is running on, so we use it for testing purposes. Eventually you will want to change this to reflect the real address of your server. Port 2357 is used here, partly to honor the first four prime numbers, but mainly because no other service is using it.

Establishing the Connection

The first *try* block attempts to connect to the server and create new Input and Output streams. If any of this fails, we return *null*. Notice that we don't really need to know what happened; our client aborts and tries again later. If the client was successful in creating a connection and opening streams, we proceed to the next part of the code. This part constitutes the first part of our *protocol*. Our protocol is very simple. The client sends commands to the server in the form "command::parameter," and the server processes these commands as they come. The server will wait until the client sends "bye" before terminating the connection. This type of interaction is called *client-driven*, because it is the client who decides when communication will begin and end.

Updating and Requesting Information: The HighScore Protocol

To handle high scores, we are only going to need two commands: *update* and *request*. These constitute the protocol that we are using. Keep in mind that this protocol is completely arbitrary. Here's how we implement the *update* command:

```
StringTokenizer st;
try {
if ( updateStr != null) {
        st = new StringTokenizer( updateStr , "|");
        while (st.hasMoreTokens())
                ps.println("update::"+st.nextToken());
        updateStr = "";
}
```

This code block sends each high score in the *updateStr* string and then resets *updateStr*. Next, we complete the second part of the communication:

```
ps.println("request::" + lastCheck);
temp = ds.readLine().trim();
ps.println("bye");
}
catch (Exception e) {
        return null;
}
```

Once all the updates are complete, we request any new data that has been received since the last time we checked (which we store in *lastCheck*). The server must respond with something, because the readLine() method (used to read in from our InputStream) is a method that *blocks*.

Understanding Blocking

A method that blocks will not return until it is complete. These methods are dangerous, because if they never complete, the program could hang (freeze and never come back). This is one of the advantages of running the networking in a thread. Even in the unlikely event that the thread did hang, only the thread would be affected and the main program (the game and the HighScoreManager) could continue.

Terminating the Link

Once the server responds to the *request* command, we tell the server "bye". We again catch any exceptions that may have been generated, but we just return *null* and try again later. Now that our conversation with the server is finished, we need to tidy up. First, we display any data we got from the server to the System.out stream, which will print it out in the Appletviewer window. This is useful for debugging, but should be left out of the final version of your program. Next, we close the streams that we were using to communicate with the server, and then we close the Socket connection. This time we really ignore any errors, because we already have the data we want, which we return with

```
System.out.println("Got: "+temp);
try {
ds.close();
ps.close();
```

continued on next page

continued from previous page

```
s.close();
} catch (Exception e);

return temp;
}
```

The HighScoreManager class is finally complete. Unfortunately, we cannot test it until we have a server written. However, you can compile and run the testApp, and notice that, even though there is no server, it still works just fine. This was one of our stated objectives when we started, so it's nice to know we have achieved it!

Creating a Server Application

At long last it is time to write our server code. Earlier, we said that one of the advantages to our client was that it could be used with any kind of server. Because you probably want to learn more about Java, and because it is perhaps the single easiest language for writing servers in, we are going to implement a Java server. However, this should not be regarded as the only way to do it.

The HighScoreServer Class

The HighScoreServer is not going to be a Java applet. Instead it is going to be a full-fledged application. Our server is not going to do anything graphics or multimedia oriented, because no user will ever see the server run. Instead of snazzy sounds and pictures, the server will print out status reports of what it is doing, so that it can be debugged easily. So, let's get started.

Here is the basic code for our Java application. Save it in a file called HighScoreServer.java:

```
import java.net.*;
import java.io.*;
import HighScoreList;

class HighScoreServer{

public static void main(String args[]) {

System.out.println("Hello from the server application.");
System.out.println("This does nothing, so let's quit.");
System.exit(1);
}
}
```

The first thing you should notice is the method main(). Just like in C/C++, this is the method that is invoked as soon as the application starts running. Our simple beginning writes out a little message to the System.out PrintStream, and then exits. Not too impressive. In order to spice this up, we are going to give it some rudimentary networking abilities. However, we are not going to implement our protocol just yet; we'll just write enough code to help you get the picture of how this works. Change main() so it looks like this:

```
public static void main(String args[]) {
try {
        servSock = new ServerSocket(2357);
} catch (Exception e) {
        System.out.println("Tried to set up ServerSocket, but ⇐
failed");
        System.exit(1);
    }

Socket sock = null;
    try {
    sock = servSock.accept();
    System.out.println("Got connection: "+2357);
DataInputStream dis = new DataInputStream(
new bufferedInputStream( sock.getInputStream() ));
PrintStream ps = new PrintStream(
new bufferedOutputStream(sock.getOutputStream(),1024),false);
    } catch (Exception e) {
        System.out.println("Could not get connection");
        System.exit(1);
    }
String inputLine;

while (!inputLine.startsWith("bye")) {
    inputLine = dis.readLine();
    System.out.println("Got: "+inputLine);
    if(inputLine.startsWith("request"))
        ps.println("none");
}

try {
os.close();
is.close();
sock.close();
} catch (Exception e);

System.exit(1);
}
```

Does this code block make sense? It should, but a few things are new and some may be a bit fuzzy. The new class here is ServerSocket, which tries to listen to a specific port and then waits for a connection. The accept() method blocks until it gets a connection, and when it does, it returns a socket that we can read/write to.

This is a good start, but still doesn't do too much. Even worse, as soon as it is done servicing one connection, it quits! This is no good at all. The server should keep waiting for a connection until it is cleared from memory (when someone on the server machine "kills" the server process). Sound familiar? This is very similar to what the HighScoreManager had to do when it checked for scores, and we can solve this problem the same way we did that one: with a thread!

This time, we are going to create a thread that is a subclass of Thread, rather than use the Runnable interface. This is mainly because, later on, we are going to want to create another thread to run concurrently with this one. But don't worry about that yet. It's time to create a new class, the ServerThread class, that will handle all of the server-side networking.

The ServerThread Class

This class is going to do all of the things our previous HighScoreServer did and more. It will implement our simple little protocol, and will actually deal with a HighScoreList. Here is all of the initial code to put in ServerThread.java:

```java
import java.net.*;
import java.lang.*;
import java.io.*;
import java.util.*;
import HighScoreList;

public class ServerThread extends Thread {
ServerSocket servSock = null;  // The server object
long lastChange;  // Track the last time a change was made
HighScoreList L;  // The list of high scores

ServerThread() {
}

public void run() {
}

}
```

Notice that there is no start() or stop() method. Since we don't need these methods to do anything special, we can rely just on the default methods in the Thread class to call run() when needed. Let's start by writing the initialization code for this class. We are going to have the HighScoreServer pass a list of scores. We will then manage it for the server.

Server Initialization Routine

Change the initialization routine to this:

```java
ServerThread(HighScoreList theList) {
      try {
          servSock = new ServerSocket(2357);
      } catch (Exception e) {
          System.out.println("Failed to initialize server");
          System.exit(1);
      }
L = theList;
}
```

Does this make sense? It should. All we did was create a new ServerSocket on port 2357 and then accept the HighScoreList we were given. Because this is the same list used by the HighScoreServer, any changes we make to it will be felt by any threads of HighScoreServer that use the same HighScoreList. This will become very important later on. Before we go on to write the run() method, we should add a small but important method to this class. The finalize() method is called in objects just before they are terminated. Because our run() method might be tied up doing Socket communications, and the stop() method may never get called, we want to be absolutely sure that, if this thread dies, it closes the ServerSocket it opened. Otherwise, we might block off port 2357 forever.

```
public void finalize() {
      try {
            servSock.close();
            } catch(Exception e);
            servSock = null;
}
```

Here we make sure that not only is *servSock* closed, but it is dead, by setting it to *null*.

Coding the run() Method

OK, now for the fun part. Here comes the run() method. The first part gets the time and then enters into the loop that should continue as long as we have a ServerSocket and a HighScoreList to deal with. Remember that the accept() method blocks until it receives a connection request. If any requests come in while we are running this loop, they are queued until we call the accept() method again. Queued requests are answered in the order received (just like when you're on hold for customer service).

```
public void run() {


lastChange = System.currentTimeMillis();
while(servSock != null && L != null ) {

      Socket sock = null;
      try {
      sock = servSock.accept();
      System.out.println("Got connection: "+2357);
       } catch (Exception e) {
            System.out.println("Conneciton request failed");
            System.exit(1);
       }
```

The next bit should look familiar, since we are again trying to open input and output streams to deal with the socket, plus we declare some Strings to use later:

```
try {
            DataInputStream dis = new DataInputStream(  new ⇐
BufferedInputStream(
        sock.getInputStream()));
            PrintStream ps = new PrintStream( new BufferedOutputStream(
        sock.getOutputStream(), 1024), false);

            String inputLine=null, outputLine = "\n";
```

We put the entire section of code, including all of the work we do, in one big *try* block, because the exception we are most likely to get is that the client hung up too early, and we want to immediately recover from that and go back to waiting for a new connection.

The next block of code is the actual protocol implementation, which shouldn't have anything new in it. Notice how it is the exact opposite of the protocol stuff on the client side:

```
String command = "blah";

while( command != null && !command.startsWith("bye") ) {
StringTokenizer st1 = null;

inputLine = dis.readLine().trim();

if(inputLine != null) {
    System.out.println("Got: "+inputLine);
    st1 = new StringTokenizer(inputLine, "::");
    }

if(st1 != null && st1.hasMoreTokens()) {

command = st1.nextToken();

if (command.startsWith("request")) {
    if (st1.hasMoreTokens() && Long.valueOf( ⇐
st1.nextToken()).longValue() < lastChange )
            outputLine = L.toDataString();
    else
            outputLine = "none";
        ps.println(outputLine);
        ps.flush();
}

if(command.startsWith("update")) {

    if (L.tryScore( st1.nextToken() ) != null)
            lastChange = System.currentTimeMillis();
    }
}
}
```

You may recall all that time we spent at the beginning setting up a good foundation for the HSob and HighScoreList classes. This is where it *really* pays off. Believe it or not, we are *done* with this part of the server. All we have to do is tidy up:

```
ps.close();
          dis.close();
          sock.close();


       } catch (Exception e);
}
}
```

It is impossible to emphasize too often the importance of thinking out your program design ahead of time. Because we had a well-written HighScoreList class, the server-side coding was quick and painless.

Trying Out the New Server

Ready to try out this new, improved server? OK, here's what you should change the main() method to:

```
      public static void main(String args[]) {
HighScoreList theList = null;
theList = new
HighScoreList(Integer.valueOf(args[0]).intValue(),"Bob&100|Eric&2000");
      new ServerThread(theList).start();
System.out.println("Server tracking "+args[0]+" scores.");
      }
```

What's that *args[0]* stuff? Well, arguments that are passed to Java applications are stored in that array called *args[]*. You type in each argument, separated by a space. The value at *index 0 (args[0])* is always the first argument passed to the program. In this case, it is an integer specifying how many scores we want the server to track. Now, compile this and run it using the *java* command, *java HighScoreServer 10*. Then, start up the Appletviewer with our client and have it clone itself a few times.

Be sure that you choose to Change Colors in order to see the updated score list, and add all the scores you want to whatever instance of the client you want—they should all update to the same list. Normal games will be doing things other than just displaying high scores, so odds are they will have to refresh periodically anyway. Our poor testApp doesn't do anything, so it has to be manually refreshed when a new score comes in.

Writing Scores Out to a File

A list of high scores isn't too useful if it is lost when the server quits. We therefore need a way to write it out to a file. Luckily, files in Java aren't too tricky. They are just another kind of Stream. The important thing here will be having a delay between file writes, because we don't want to tie down the server with constant writing. Also, we don't want to write anything if there is nothing new to write. It is very, very tricky to do this within the ServerThread thread, because we never know how long the thread is waiting for a connection. (Since accept() blocks, this could potentially be hours or days or years.) The solution is to use another thread, this one designed exclusively for writing the scores to a file, but using the very same HighScoreList as the ServerThread. Because reading and writing a file is just like doing the same to a socket, this should seem pretty straightforward. Here is SaveFileThread.java:

```java
import java.lang.*;
import java.io.*;
import HighScoreList;

public class SaveFileThread extends Thread {
HighScoreList L;
final int FILE_DELAY = 100000;
File f;
long lastWrite;

SaveFileThread(HighScoreList theList, File theFile) {
L = theList;
f = theFile;
}

public void run() {

while( L != null ) {



if(f.exists())
        f.renameTo(new File("test.bak"));

if( L.lastChange > lastWrite) {

try {
PrintStream ps = new PrintStream(new FileOutputStream(f));
ps.println( L.toDataString() );
System.out.println("Writing High Scores to file "+f.getName());
lastWrite = System.currentTimeMillis();
ps.close();
} catch (Exception e);
}
try{ sleep(FILE_DELAY); } catch (Exception e);
}
}


}
```

In order to make use of this, we are going to have to change main() in HighScoreServer. The method now has to read in the values already stored in a user-specified file, pass this data to the HighScoreList, and then pass the File, along with the list, to the

SaveFileThread. It then must start both the SaveFileThread and the ServerThread. Here's what that looks like:

```
import java.net.*;
import java.io.*;
import HighScoreList;
import ServerThread;
import SaveFileThread;

class HighScoreServer{

public static void main(String args[]) {

HighScoreList theList = null;
File theFile = new File(args[1]);
String temp = null;


if (!theFile.exists())
      System.out.println("No such file\nWill create a new one");
else {
try {
      DataInputStream dis = new DataInputStream( new FileInputStream( ⇐
theFile) );
      temp = dis.readLine();
} catch (Exception e) {
System.out.println("Unable to read from file. Terminating...");
System.exit(1);
}
}
if(temp != null)
      theList = new ⇐
HighScoreList(Integer.valueOf(args[0]).intValue(),temp);
else
      theList = new HighScoreList(Integer.valueOf(args[0]).intValue());

if(theList == null) {
      System.out.println("Unable to initzialize. Terminating...");
      System.exit(1);
}
      new ServerThread(theList).start();
      new SaveFileThread(theList, theFile).start();
System.out.println("Server initialized. Tracking "+args[0]+" ⇐
scores.\nUsing "+args[1]);
}

}
```

Running the New Server

Congratulations! You've done it! Compile all your classes, and then start the server with *java HighScoreServer 10 data.txt* or any other values you like. If the server can't find the file you specify, it will create a new one. Otherwise, it will attempt to read in the values contained in the file you specify. If this is successful, it should tell you so, and it will then wait for a connection. Load up a few clients with Appletviewer and have fun! If you or a friend have a WWW page, recompile the client to check *your* IP address and then set it up on the Web page. It will connect seamlessly to your host.

Suggestion Box

This chapter opens up a whole plethora of possibilities to enhance the high score experience. Try these:

- Extend the HSob structure to include even more data. Perhaps comments or messages that can be viewed by other users. Perhaps use an array to have the HSob hold an unlimited amount of data, and allow the applet to decide what each value is used for.

- Enhance the HighScoreManager class to interact with the user. Perhaps allow the user to send e-mail to a high scorer if the user clicks on that person's name. This can be accomplished by having the applet context open a URL that starts with "mailto:". You could also have the HighScoreManager display comments or messages stored as per the previous suggestion.

- Take the code we've written in this chapter and plug it into one of the games you've written so far (I recommend JavaBlaster). This is pretty easy if you make use of HighScoreManager's paintScores() method.

Summary

In this chapter we explored the concept of high scores, and discussed how to implement them in Java, both locally and over a network. Being able to track high scores will make any game more enjoyable, and knowing how to do it will make you a better game programmer.

9

Advanced Networking and Multiplayer Gaming Concepts

Eric Ries

ome tiidi fare le manouelle ... lequali piu obano ... l'alza
i gra pe si ... ... lo men ... a ... gon ... o sa go prano di bo no
... are nella ma d' ... o per ma testa a ... la mano bella po gi qua n
torga ... pio i somo pob vat.

... l p ... ...
... ...
... ...

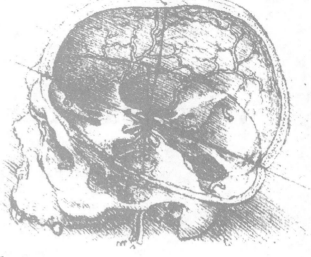

9

Advanced Networking and Multiplayer Gaming Concepts

Goals:

Create a Java Chat Room by using advanced networking concepts

Implement AWT components with the Java API specifications

Learn to use Events to control the flow of an applet

In this chapter, we will build upon the simple networking concepts discussed in Chapter 8, Implementing a High Score Server on a Network, and create a chat room program. If you are familiar with the Internet Relay Chat (IRC) or any of the chat forums on services like America Online or Prodigy, you already know what a chat room is. We are going to build an applet that allows an unlimited number of users to have a conversation in a virtual "room." The user will be able to "say" things to the entire room or "whisper" them to one specific person.

Why Create a Chat Room?

Chat rooms and similar services have been available on the Internet for years. Writing this applet in Java, however, allows anyone with a Java-enabled browser to use our service, so additional software is not needed. Our program will be easy to use and easy to add to a Web page, so you will be able to customize and use this applet to drum up enthusiasm for your own pages. Many users really enjoy getting to meet other people interested in your Web page.

In addition to its practical uses, writing an applet like this is an excellent prelude to writing multiplayer online games. The client-server relationship that you will have to understand in order to write this applet is the same one used by almost every game of this type. In fact, although this chapter deals with the concepts required to create multiplayer games, we will discuss them all in the context of the chat room applet.

First, let's discuss what some of these concepts are.

Fundamentals of Multiplayer Gaming

Almost every game is, in a sense, a multiplayer game. Most computer games pit the user against a variety of computer-generated opponents. This can range from a simulated human opponent, in board games, to a whole alien universe in some space games.

There are many ways that a computer opponent can be made more challenging, and there are many incentives that can be used to lure users into these games (one such device is a high score list, which should sound familiar). Nevertheless, there is nothing that can compare to playing with a real, flesh-and-blood human opponent, because computer opponents have inherent limitations. Sometimes they are too perfect, other times too predictable. But human opponents vary in skill and attitude, and thus are far more exciting. This is true in real-life games as well as computer games. Ever notice that bridge or hearts is much more exciting than solitaire? Or that bowling is more fun in a group? Humans are social by nature, and many successful computer games recognize and appeal to this part of the human psyche.

Types of Multiplayer Games: The User's Perspective

Most likely, you have played a multiplayer game some time in your life. Different games have different ways of allowing multiple players to interact, but from the user's point of view, generally they fall into one of two categories: cooperative and competitive.

Cooperative Gaming

In a cooperative game, players work together toward some common goal. The old arcade game, Gauntlet, is a perfect example of this kind of game play. Up to four players can play on the same screen at the same time. The players must work together to ward off hordes of nasty monsters while collecting treasure and other goodies. If the players refuse to work together, it is nearly impossible to defeat all of the monsters; a good team of players can succeed nicely.

Competitive Gaming

The other style of play is far more common. In a competitive game, players work against each other, and sometimes against the computer, too. Most board and card games are of this type, and victory always comes at your partner's expense. Some games allow players the option of playing cooperatively or competitively. A good example of this kind of game is the now-classic DOOM. DOOM is a pretty typical game in which players roam around different levels and blow the heck out of a whole variety of demons and monsters. One of the things that has propelled DOOM to its current mega-hit status is the fact that multiple players can play simultaneously. Sometimes, players work together to rid a level of all of its monsters, but the game also has an option to let the players hunt each other down. Apparently, getting to "kill" your friends (or even your enemies) without actually damaging them has a huge popular appeal. Despite its apparent popularity, a good game programmer will always keep in mind that there are many people who do *not* enjoy violent competition, and so the very best games often include a variety of modes of play.

Types of Multiplayer Games: The Programmer's Perspective

From a programming perspective, there are two ways of handling a multiplayer game: local and remote.

Local Games

A local game is the more common type. This is the kind of game where all of the players are at the same computer, and they take turns entering their moves. The advantage to writing this type of game is that it is easy to program. The advantage to players is that it requires only one machine. It also has several disadvantages for players. Usually, game play is slow, since each player must wait for all of the other players to complete their moves before he or she moves again. This can be especially aggravating if there are more than a few players. This type of game also presents difficulties for programmers. Especially in games that require each player to keep information secret from other players (like poker, for instance), the fact that all users share a common terminal is disadvantageous.

Remote Games

A remote, or *networked*, game allows multiple players on different computers to compete across some kind of link (often a modem or network). Some programs allow players to play action-type games simultaneously, while others allow them to take turns at strategy games while "chatting" in between moves. This type of game has many advantages, mainly that it allows physically distant players to interact. It also avoids the problem of secret information that local games suffer from. Unfortunately, networked games also present their own set of difficulties from a programming point of view. First of all, they have traditionally been more difficult to write than local games. Another problem is that of speed. Especially for real-time games, each player needs constant updates about the position and status of other players. If this information is too slow in arriving, it makes the game unplayable. Luckily, networks of today have reached the point where sufficient data transfer rates can be attained for even the most rapidly paced games.

Choosing the Proper Networking Architecture

Java makes it easy to write remote multiplayer games because it makes networking so simple. The same skills we used in Chapter 8 to write a high score server can easily be applied to writing a multiplayer game. In Chapter 8, we learned how to implement a client-server networking architecture, but it is important to note that this is not the only architecture suitable for multiplayer games. One method commonly used is called *peer-to-peer* networking.

Peer-to-Peer Networking

Peer-to-peer networking entails having two or more clients connected directly. There is no need for a server (hence each client is said to be a "peer" of the other clients), and clients can choose which other clients will receive information. A good example of peer-to-peer networking that you have probably already used is a modem. When you connect to another computer via a modem, no server is required, and neither client has priority. While this sort of networking scheme works well for two connected clients, it becomes unwieldy when used with more. Think of the complications required for 10 clients connected to each other: the total number of sockets required to make these connections is 10!, or 3,628,800 connections—quite an unacceptable number for only 10 connected clients. Luckily, there are other methods of doing peer-to-peer networking that require fewer connections. One such method is a *ring*.

Networking Rings

In a ring networking structure, each client is connected to two others. By linking each client to the next, network rings allow a message to be sent to many more computers than are connected to any one client. When a client receives a message from one of the two other clients it is connected to, it passes it on to the other client. This type of setup is often used in local area networks, where connections between computers are physical links. However, on the Internet, links between computers take the form of Sockets, which are abstract (and therefore cheaper than physical links). The Internet is largely unsuitable for this type of structure, because if one computer becomes disconnected (which happens often in the dynamic, chaotic world of the Internet), the whole ring suffers. Therefore, this is not an optimal choice for a Java applet running on the Internet.

Peer-to-Peer Networking in Java

Even though peer-to-peer networking may seem attractive for some multiplayer games, most current implementations of Java have special security restrictions that prohibit any applet from communicating with any machine other than the one it was loaded from. There are many practical reasons for this security precaution, but it makes true peer-to-peer networking in Java almost impossible. Therefore, only one choice remains as a viable networking structure for multiplayer games.

Adapting Client-Server Architecture to Multiplayer Games

To get around this security limitation, we must still use client-server networking even for games of only two players. This approach is in many ways superior to the peer-to-peer approach, because client-server networking allows for many players interacting simultaneously. The program we are going to write in this chapter implements this kind of networking relationship. One server will interact with an infinite number of clients *at the same time.*

This is a key difference between this program and the one we wrote in Chapter 8. The high score server only handled one connection at a time. Other connections had to wait in line until the server was finished with the current connection before they could be serviced. This time, the server is going to keep and maintain a list of all of the currently connected clients and interact with all of them. The difference between these two is illustrated in Figures 9-1 and 9-2.

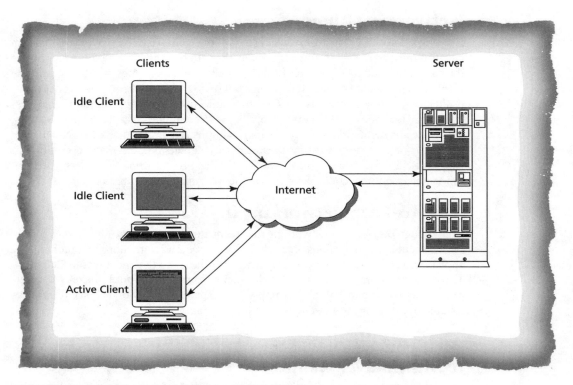

FIGURE 9-1 ◉ *Diagram of clients waiting in line for interaction with server*

Understanding the Chat Room Server

In Chapter 8, we talked first about the client applet. In this chapter, we are going to talk about the *server* side of this applet first. This is because the ChatServer will have many more responsibilities than the client-driven HighScoreServer.

Functions of a Chat Room Server

Let's talk about what the ChatServer has to do:

 Connect to multiple clients simultaneously. In order to have a chat "room," the server must be able to connect to and interact with multiple clients. We will accomplish this by having the server class create special Thread objects to deal with each connection.

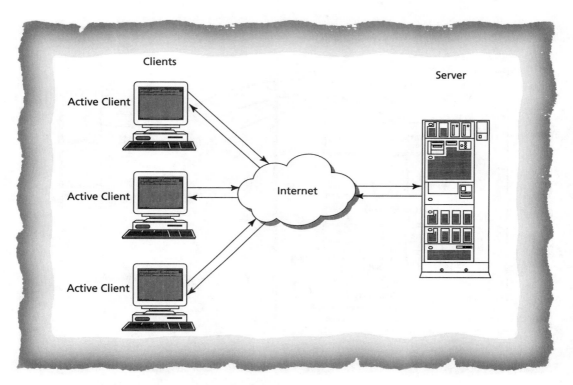

FIGURE 9-2 ◉ *Diagram of server with multiple clients*

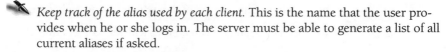 *Receive and process commands from each client.* When the client sends a command to the server, the server must take the specified action by sending a command to one or more additional clients. We will have several types of messages the server and client can send and receive.

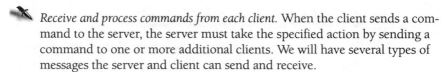 *Keep track of the alias used by each client.* This is the name that the user provides when he or she logs in. The server must be able to generate a list of all current aliases if asked.

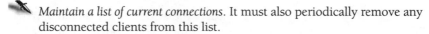 *Maintain a list of current connections.* It must also periodically remove any disconnected clients from this list.

How can we go about writing a program that does all of this? Clearly, we cannot write it all into one application. Luckily, we are using an object-oriented language that will simplify our task greatly. We will create a hierarchy of classes, each with a specific task, and then use them together. Figure 9-3 shows what it will look like. The diagram illustrates how a Socket connection comes in from a client on the Internet and is passed down through the hierarchy until it "plugs in" to a Thread that manages it.

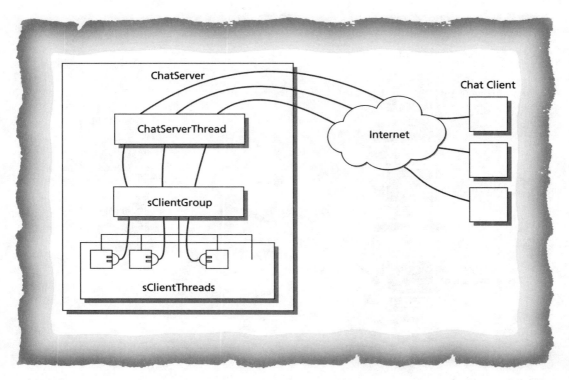

FIGURE 9-3 ◉ *Hierarchy of ChatServer classes*

ChatServer Classes

What are all of these classes? Let's talk about them a little more in-depth:

▸ *ChatServer* is simply the main application class. It will do nothing except create a new ChatServerThread, which will actually do the work.

▸ *ChatServerThread* is a Thread that will wait for a connection. When it receives one, it will pass it along to sClientGroup.

▸ *sClientGroup* does most of the work. It will maintain a *Vector* of all of the current connections. A Vector is a class provided by Java for grouping things similar to an array, but it is dynamic. More on this later. Whenever sClientGroup receives a new connection for ChatServerThread, it will create a new sClientThread to handle the connection, and put this Thread in the Vector list. In addition, sClientGroup is a Thread that periodically checks every connection in the Vector to make sure it is still active. The class also has a function that handles incoming messages from the clients.

sClientThread is a Thread that waits for some input from the Client to which it is assigned. Whenever it gets input, it passes it back to its *parent*, sClientGroup. It also allows sClientGroup to give it a message that it will dutifully pass along to its client. Each sClientThread can handle only one client, and it is up to sClientGroup to assign a client to it when it is created.

This may sound extremely complicated, but it's really not. Pretend you are an important business executive. You have many, many important tasks to complete, far more than you can accomplish on your own. What do you do? You delegate. You take a whole group of your subordinates, and give each one a task. As your boss gives you new tasks, you pass them along to new subordinates. As tasks get completed, you remove them from your to-do list. Most importantly, when subordinates need to talk to each other, they contact you and you send the appropriate memos. This is exactly how the sClientGroup works. The ChatServerThread is your boss, and each sClientThread is a subordinate.

With this metaphor in mind, let's jump straight into the code!

Implementing the Chat Room Server

We are now ready to start writing code. Initially, we must create several classes.

Creating the ChatServer Class

This is the easiest step of all. This class file will simply create a new ChatServerThread and run it. It won't compile, unfortunately, because we haven't written the ChatServerThread program! Create a file called ChatServer.java and put the following into it:

```
import ChatServerThread;

class ChatServer {

public static void main(String args[]) {

     new ChatServerThread().start();

}
}
```

Save this file and then forget about it for a while.

Creating the ChatServerThread Class

This class is not too difficult to write, because it really doesn't do much. Hopefully, you remember how to create and use a ServerSocket from the last chapter, so we won't discuss all the details. This, of course, won't compile either, because we haven't written sClientGroup yet! Nevertheless, we should write it as if there were an sClientGroup and compile it later. Here is what sClientGroup.java should look like:

```java
import java.net.*;
import java.lang.*;
import sClientGroup;

public class ChatServerThread extends Thread {
ServerSocket servSock = null;
sClientGroup group;

ChatServerThread() {
      try {
           servSock = new ServerSocket(1123);
      } catch (Exception e) {
           System.out.println("Could not initialize. Exiting.");
           System.exit(1);
      }
System.out.println("Server successfully initialized. Waiting for
                   connection...");
group = new sClientGroup();
group.start();
}
```

Notice that the server attempts to listen on port 1123, in honor of the first four Fibonacci numbers. If this port is already in use on your system, you can change this value, but be sure you use the same number for the client. Here's the rest of the code:

```java
public void run() {


while(servSock != null ) {
Socket tempSock;
      try {
      tempSock = servSock.accept();
      System.out.println("Received New Connection.");
      group.addClient( tempSock );
      } catch (Exception e) {
           System.out.println("New Connection Failure. Exiting.");
           System.exit(1);
      }


}
}
```

```
public void finalize() {
     try {
            servSock.close();
     } catch(Exception e);
     servSock = null;
}
}
```

Our server here is very temperamental. If it receives any kind of networking error, it immediately exits. A commercial application would, of course, need to be far more robust, and do possible error-correcting steps. Luckily, we don't really have to worry about that at this point because these sorts of errors are relatively rare.

Creating the sClientGroup Class

It's time to do the real work of this application. The object we are about to write is the one that must handle a whole group of clients and carry messages back and forth between them. Before we do this, we will discuss a little bit about the Vector class.

The Vector Class

A Vector is one of the wonderful Java utility classes (just like StringTokenizer). A Vector is an Object that is used to store other Objects. In this case, we are going to use it to hold a group of sClientThreads. Let's take a look at some of the important methods in java.util.Vector:

 new Vector(). This creates a new Vector object and initializes it.

 size(). This returns the number of objects stored in this Vector.

 elementAt(int n). This returns *n*th object (element).

addElement(Object ob). This adds *ob* to the end of the list.

removeElement(Object ob). This removes *ob* from the list.

The sClientGroup.java Startup File

That should be enough to get started with the code. Here's the start of sClientGroup.java, which we won't be able to compile until we write sClientThread:

```
import java.net.*;
import java.io.*;
import java.util.*;
import java.lang.*;

import sClientThread;

public class sClientGroup extends Thread {
Vector theGroup;
```

continued on next page

continued from previous page

```
sClientGroup() {
theGroup = new Vector();
}
}
```

OK, that's the start. It doesn't do anything, so let's add the first function, addClient(), which we called from ChatServerThread. All it needs to do is create a new sClientThread based on a Socket and then add it to *theGroup*, which is our Vector list. Note that when we create the sClientThread, we pass it the special keyword *this*, which always points to the current object. By passing *this* to the sClientThread, we allow for the Thread to call functions that are in sClientGroup. Here's how it goes:

```
public void addClient(Socket s) {
sClientThread tempThread;
    tempThread = new sClientThread( s, this );
    theGroup.addElement( tempThread );
    tempThread.start();
}
```

The sendMessage() Methods

Next, let's write the two methods that will allow us to send messages to different clients. Both have the same name, but one is used for sending messages to all connected clients, while the second only sends the message to one specific client. Messages all have a "type" associated with them that tells the client how to handle them. Messages are sent in the form "type||message". We again use "||" as a separator because it is relatively rare and easy to parse. Here's the code:

```
/* send a message "msg", of type "type", to all Clients */
public void sendMessage(String msg, String type) {
int x;

for(x=0; x<theGroup.size(); x++)
                                    ((sClientThread)theGroup.⇐
elementAt(x)).message(type+"||"+msg);
/* remember that the format for messages is "type||message" */
}


/* send a message "msg", of type "type", to the Client with alias "target" */
public void sendMessage(String msg, String target, String type) {
int x;
sClientThread tempThread;

for(x=0; x<theGroup.size(); x++) {
    tempThread=(sClientThread)theGroup.elementAt(x);
    if( tempThread.getAlias().equals(target) )
        tempThread.message(type+"||"+msg);
}
}
```

Explicit Casting

When we access an element in *theGroup*, you may notice that sClientThread in parentheses immediately precedes it. This is called *explicit typecasting* and is used to convert Objects of different classes. If you've programmed in C, you've probably used this to do such things as convert integers to floats or characters to strings. In Java, you can do this for any object, so long as the two objects share at least one parent class. Vector is used to store any object that subclasses java.lang.Object. This allows the Vector to store objects of any type. However, when we access an object inside a Vector, we need to call methods that are unique to sClientThread. Thus, we must tell the Java compiler that the Object we are accessing is really an sClientThread. This can seem confusing if you've not used a similar language before. If so, don't worry about all the details. Just remember that, to convert an object, you have to *cast* it.

After that is finished, we must write the method that will be called, eventually, by sClientThread whenever it gets some input. There will be many sClientThreads connected at one time, but they will all still use the same protocol method, which is listed here:

```
/* here is where we handle any input received from a Client */
/* This method is called by sClientThread directly */
public void handleInput(String str, sClientThread T) {
StringTokenizer st;

/* this next line is for debugging only. You would not include it in the
final product */
System.out.println("Got: "+str+" from "+T.getAlias());

/* command to disconnect = "bye" */
if( str.startsWith("bye") ) {
      T.stop();
      return;
      }

st = new StringTokenizer( str, "||");

if(st != null ) {
String cmd, val;

cmd = st.nextToken();
val = st.nextToken();

/* "login" = a new person is logging in. Set the alias, send a welcome
message, and then send everyone an updated list of Client names */
if(cmd.equals("login")) {
```

continued on next page

continued from previous page

```
                         T.setAlias( val );
                         sendMessage(T.getAlias()+"||"+T.getAlias()+" has entered the
                                   room.", cmd);
                         sendMessage(calcList(), "list");
                         return ;
                         }

        /* "logout" = one of our clients is finished and wants to disconnect. Let
        everyone know that and then stop the connection. The garbage collection
        method will take care of removing them from the list. */
        if(cmd.equals("logout")) {
                         sendMessage(T.getAlias()+" has left the room.", cmd);
                         T.stop();
                         return ;
                         }

        /* someone wants to "say" something to the whole room */
        if(cmd.equals("say")) {
                         sendMessage(T.getAlias()+" says: "+ val, cmd);
                         return ;
                         }
        /* someone wants to whisper something to a specific person only */
        if(cmd.equals("whisper")) {
                         sendMessage(T.getAlias()+" whispers to you:
                                   "+val,st.nextToken(),cmd);
                         return ;
                         }
        }

        }
```

handleInput() parses the message received and then takes the appropriate action.
Input should always be of the form "command||parameter1||parameter2". Two parameters
are currently plenty for the commands we want to handle (remember that only the *whisper* command even takes that many), although a method that could handle any number
of parameters could easily be developed based on this code.

The calcList() Method

If you looked carefully, you probably noticed a new method, called calcList(), called when
a new user connects and sends the *login* command (which takes the form "login||name").
When someone enters the room, after notifying everyone, a message of type *list* is sent
with an updated list of everyone in the room. This is generated by the calcList()
method below:

```
/* return a list of all currently connected users in the form
"name1&name2&name3" */
public String calcList() {
int x;
StringBuffer buf = new StringBuffer();
String temp;
for(x=0; x<theGroup.size(); x++) {
```

```
        temp = ((sClientThread) (theGroup.elementAt(x))).getAlias();
        if(temp != null)
            buf.append(temp).append('&');
    }
    if (buf.length() >0 )
        buf.setLength(buf.length()-1);
    return buf.toString();
    }
```

The StringBuffer Class

A brief mention of the StringBuffer class is important here. StringBuffers are like Strings, except they are designed to have things added and removed. Whenever you change a String, it is temporarily changed into a StringBuffer, operated on, and then returned to a String. The Java compiler takes care of all this transparently, so it's not something you normally need to worry about. However, if you know you are going to be making a lot of changes to a String (especially adding or removing large chunks), it is much more efficient to operate directly on a StringBuffer, which saves the compiler a lot of time later on. This is just a small optimization to make your code a bit faster.

Automatic Garbage Collection (Reclaiming Unused Memory)

Next we need to talk a little about *garbage collection*. This is a term you may have heard used in reference to Java before. In older-generation languages, you had to allocate memory to objects and variables manually. Once you were done with them, you had to deallocate the affected portions of memory to make them available to the rest of your programs. This was a very tricky business, because if you allocated too much, or didn't deallocate enough, you could easily run out of memory. Even worse, if you deallocated too soon, and then tried to access your variable or object, it was gone and the computer would likely crash! This was no fun at all. Luckily, Java has *automatic garbage collection,* which carefully monitors when objects are no longer being used and then reclaims the memory they once used.

You will probably never be aware of this process, or ever have to interact with it, but you should understand how it works. To demonstrate this concept, we are going to have sClientGroup do some garbage collection of its own.

The cleanHouse() Method

Periodically, sClientGroup has to check to make sure that any inactive threads in the Vector are removed (we will teach each sClientThread to make itself inactive if it loses the connection from its client). This is why we made sure that sClientGroup was a thread, so it can run an infinite loop, and call cleanHouse() every once in a while. Here is the cleanHouse() method that does the actual garbage collecting work:

```
/* go through the Vector, and search for "dead" Threads (which are discon-
nected) and then remove them from the list */
public void cleanHouse() {
int x;
sClientThread tempThread;

for (x=0; x<theGroup.size(); x++) {
    tempThread = (sClientThread)theGroup.elementAt(x);
    if( tempThread==null ||  ! tempThread.isAlive() )
        theGroup.removeElement( tempThread );
    }
}
```

Here is the run() method that will call cleanHouse() and will then "sleep" for a period of time:

```
public void run() {

while( true ) {
try{ sleep(30000); } catch (Exception e);
cleanHouse();
}

}
```

We're almost done! Only one more class to write. Remember, though, that you cannot compile sClientGroup yet, because it imports sClientThread, which hasn't been written
yet! To get around this obstacle, let's write sClientThread.

Creating the sClientThread Class

The sClientThread object, and the previous one, sClientGroup, both need to call each
other. If we wrote them both ahead of time and tried to compile them, the Java compiler would object. Why? Because when sClientThread imports sClientGroup,
sClientGroup is not yet compiled, so the compiler tries to compile it. When sClientGroup
tries to import sClientThread, it finds that it is not yet compiled as well, and tries to compile sClientThread. You probably noticed a most unfavorable pattern developing here.
Therefore, we need to write an intermediate sClientThread file that only implements enough
functionality to allow it and sClientGroup to be compiled.

Here is a watered-down sClientThread with only the methods that are called by
sClientGroup. We will talk more about these methods later, but for now it's important
to get something written and compiled. Here it is:

```
import java.net.*;
import java.lang.*;
import java.io.*;
import java.util.*;
import sClientGroup;

public class sClientThread extends Thread {
Object parent;
```

```
Socket theSock;
DataInputStream dis;
PrintStream ps;
String alias;

sClientThread(Socket s, Object p) {
theSock = s;
parent = p;
}

public boolean message(String str) {
try {
        ps.println(str);
} catch (Exception e) {
        return false;
}
return true;
}

public void finalize() {
        try {
                ps.close();
                dis.close();
                theSock.close();
        } catch(Exception e);
theSock = null;

}

public void setAlias(String str) {
alias = str;
}

public String getAlias() {

return alias;
}

}
```

Input all of this, and compile. It should compile just fine, although it certainly won't run too well. Now that it is compiled, take a moment and go back and compile the other three classes we just wrote. Once you're done with that, we are all set, because now we have compiled versions of all four classes. Now we can work on sClientThread without worrying about crashing the compiler. With that out of our way, let's take sClientThread from the top!

Writing the Real sClientThread Code

Let's start with the basics. Remember that sClientGroup is going to be creating sClientThreads and passing them messages.

The parent Variable

The sClientGroup class expects that these sClientThreads will pass messages back by calling handleInput(). Therefore, not only does sClientGroup need to have a reference to sClientThread, but sClientThread must know who its parent sClientGroup is. That is why we have a variable called *parent*, which is an sClientGroup (although in the code above, it was an Object. This only served to allow compilation—from now on, *parent* will be an sClientGroup). The initialization code is really simple. All we do is declare a group of global variables, and then remember the values passed to us by our parent:

```
import java.net.*;
import java.lang.*;
import java.io.*;
import java.util.*;
import sClientGroup;

public class sClientThread extends Thread {
sClientGroup parent;
Socket theSock;
DataInputStream dis;
PrintStream ps;
String alias;

sClientThread(Socket s, sClientGroup p) { /* called by parent */
theSock = s;
parent = p;
}
```

The run() Method

So far, we haven't done too much. Just make sure you understand what each of the global variables will be used for. (You may want to go back to Chapter 8, Implementing a High Score Server on a Network, to review.) Next, let's write the run() method that continually waits for any kind of input from the Socket we are assigned to. If it ever gets some (remember that readLine() blocks), it passes the input to the parent sClientGroup to be handled. Here's what it looks like:

```
public void run() {

/* try and create new data streams */
      try {
              dis = new DataInputStream( theSock.getInputStream());
                      ps = new PrintStream( theSock.getOutputStream());
      } catch (Exception e);


while (theSock !=null) {
String input = null;
try {
input = dis.readLine().trim();
if(input != null)
```

```
        parent.handleInput(input, this);

} catch (Exception e);
}
}
```

The finalize() Method

sClientThread is very persistent, and will never give up unless someone else disconnects it from its Client. If this happens, finalize() is called and does some housecleaning:

```
public void finalize() {
      try {
            ps.close();
            dis.close();
            theSock.close();
      } catch(Exception e);
theSock = null;

}
```

The message() Method

Proceeding onward, we should write the message() method that gets called by sClientGroup whenever there is a message to be delivered to the client. The sClientThread doesn't really care what the message is; whatever sClientGroup wants to send is fine with us, so we just send it verbatim. We also return *true* for success and *false* for some kind of error (just in case):

```
public boolean message(String str) {
try {
      ps.println(str);
} catch (Exception e) {
      return false;
}
return true;
}
```

The Alias Handling Methods

We are almost finished. We only need to write the last two methods, which are simple. They control the alias of the current client. This is the name the client logged in with, and it is the name the client is referred to in the user list. Here they are:

```
public void setAlias(String str) {
alias = str;
}

public String getAlias() {

return alias;
}
```

The Final Server Compile

We are totally finished with the server now. If you want, you can run it by compiling all the classes and then using the *java* command. On a Windows 95 machine, it looks something like this:

```
c:\java\ChatServer> java ChatServer
```

On UNIX, it would look like this:

```
{/java/ChatServer} java ChatServer &
```

Unfortunately, the server doesn't have a client to connect to. If you are really desperate to see it do something, use Telnet to "telnet localhost 1123" and type something to the server. It should echo that to the screen, but it will only respond to the client if you issue a properly formatted command (as defined in the handleInput() method in the sClientGroup class).

Creating the Chat Room Client

Writing the chat room client is complicated. Because we are interacting with the user on this end, we have to be conscious of our user interface. This means another foray into the realm of the Abstract Windowing Toolkit (AWT). Hopefully, by now you are comfortable with AWT components, like TextFields and Buttons. In addition, we are going to have to review Lists, TextAreas, and, most importantly, Events.

General Design Considerations

Let's talk for a moment about how we are going to go about writing the client applet for the chat room. Its behavior is pretty well defined by the server. We already know the protocol we are going to have to follow, and the types of messages we are going to receive. Most of the processing is done by the server, so there really isn't too much to do beyond receiving and sending specially formatted messages. This is complicated enough on its own. The network stuff can be handled in a thread, so we will definitely have to implement Runnable again.

User Interface Components

Before any code can be written, we have to decide how the applet's user interface will work. There are a variety of ways to do this, but for simplicity's sake, we'll stick with these four components. Although you've worked with them before, here is a little review:

 TextArea. A TextArea is a scrollable box that holds text. It can either be editable (meaning the user can change its contents) or not. We will use this TextArea to display all messages and chat to the user, so we don't want it to be editable (although the user may still select and copy text to the Clipboard from it).

 TextField. A TextField is a one-line text component. We will allow editing of it, because we are going to use it to get input from the user.

 List. A List is a component that allows the user to view a list of Strings. The List also allows the user to select one of these Strings (and can also be configured to allow multiple selections, but we won' be using that feature). We will use the List to display all of the current users who are logged into the chat room. By selecting a name, the user can choose to "whisper" to that person. The top item in the list will always be All Participants which, when selected, causes the user to "say" something to everyone in the room.

 Button. There are two of these. When the applet first loads, one Button will read "login" and, when pressed, will initiate the network connection between the client and the server. The other button, which will read "logout", will be *disabled* at the start. Buttons have two states: enabled and disabled. A Button that is disabled is grayed out and cannot be clicked. Once the connection is established, we will change the name of the first button to "say" and enable the second button. The label of the first button will vary according to the current selection in our List. When the user has selected All Participants, the Button will read "say", but when the user selects one of the names in the List, the Button will read "whisper".

That's it for our Components. The next question is, of course, how are we going to lay them out?

User Interface Design Considerations

Although there are many possible combinations of Components, we will choose a relatively simple one. The scheme involves dividing the applet into two Panels, one for the "north" part and one for the "south" part of the applet window. For this, we are going to need a BorderLayout, which will handle the size and placement of the Panels. In the north Panel, we can put the TextArea and the List, in that order, with a FlowLayout. A FlowLayout is the simplest Layout, and it is also the default choice for Panels (so we don't have to explicitly request it). Remember that all it does is place the Components in nice neat rows in the order they were added. In the south Panel, again using a FlowLayout, we put the TextField, and the two Buttons. Figure 9-4 shows what the end result will look like.

FIGURE 9-4

◉ ◉ ◉ ◉ ◉ ◉

*Picture of chat
room applet
with GUI
layout*

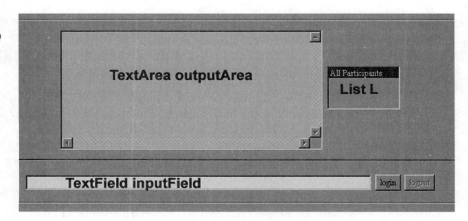

Component Commands and Methods

All Components are subclassed from java.awt.Component. This gives them each a certain amount of common behavior, but each type also has its own commands and methods that you have to learn. First, let's review some of the more important methods that we will use.

Common Component Methods

🗡 enable(), disable(). These enable or disable a Component. Different Components handle being disabled differently.

🗡 getFont(), setFont(). These control the Font being used by a Component. Obviously, this has no effect on Components that do not use text.

🗡 getForeground(), getBackground(), setForeground(), setBackground(). These allow you to control the foreground and background colors of a Component. Use them to spice up your Components whenever you feel the need.

🗡 handleEvent(Event). These are called when an Event must be handled. Each Component should also pass along any unhandled events to its parent using this method.

🗡 layout(). This method causes the Component to restructure and redraw itself. This is a good way to force a Component and all embedded Components to be redrawn.

This list is by no means comprehensive. As you work more with Components, you will have to explore the java.awt.Component class more and more. Some of the Components we will be using in this applet also have their own methods that you should be familiar with. The most important to review at this time are the methods used in the List Component. Here are some of them:

Methods Unique to List

 List.addItem(String). This adds a String item to the List.

 List.clear(). This clears all items off of the List. Unfortunately, as of this writing, this method is broken in the Java language itself—*it does not work properly and should be avoided at all costs until it is fixed.* Hopefully, Sun will have fixed the List class by the time you read this.

 List.select(int), deselect(int). These cause an item to be selected/deselected. Items are kept in the List in an array, so that the first item is always at index 0.

List.getRows(), getItems(). These get the number of rows/items (usually, but not always, the same) in a List.

Planning Your Event-Handling Strategy

A good thing to do before you start writing code is to think about what events you are going to have to handle. Before we can do that, we have to know how exactly an event works. Whenever a Component generates an event, it is sent up the hierarchy until it is either handled or it runs out of Components. For instance, when one of our Buttons is pushed, it generates an Event. This Event is first sent to the Button, then to the Panel in which the Button sits, and then to the Panel in which the first Panel is embedded (which, in this case, would be our Applet). Each Event has certain properties you should be aware of.

Basic Events and Their Properties

Here is a summary of some of the basic ones we will need (assume we are dealing with an Event object named *evt*):

 evt.id is a number that signifies what the Event means. You don't have to memorize *id* numbers, luckily, because the Event class provides a nice long list of constants that you can use. For instance, whenever an item in a List is selected, a LIST_SELECT Event is generated (*evt.id == Event.LIST_SELECT*). The table below lists all of the Event.id constants.

evt.target is the Object that generated the Event. This is most useful along with the *instanceof* operator, which is used to determine if a given Object is a subclass of a particular class. For instance, if *evt* is a LIST_SELECT Event, then (*evt instanceof List*) will evaluate to *true*.

 evt.arg is the argument passed along with the Event. What exactly this is varies from component to component, but Buttons pass a String representing their labels. This is useful for determining which Button has been pressed by the user.

These are the major properties of the Event class that we will use. You will need this information to write this applet's handleEvent() method, but we will get to that later. Just be sure you understand the function and operation of Events before continuing. (Sun's tutorial has especially good examples of how this works.) See Table 9-1 for a list of Event.id constants. (For a more extensive discussion of events and event handling in Java, see Chapter 4, Adding Interactivity.)

Event Constants

The list of Event.id in Table 9-1 is not totally comprehensive, but it covers almost every Event you could possibly receive. For this applet, we are only going to handle those Events caused by the Components we created as part of the graphical user interface (GUI).

Constant	Description
ACTION_EVENT	Generated for different reasons by different Components. For instance, it is called by TextField if the user presses the <ENTER> key after typing. It is also called by List when the user double-clicks on an item.
ALT_MASK	Generated if the <ALT> key is down.
CTRL_MASK	Generated if the <CTRL> key is down.
DOWN	Generated by the down arrow key.
END	Generated if the <END> key is pressed.
ESC	Generated by the <ESC> key.
F1 … F12	Generated by the F1 through F12 function keys.
GOT_FOCUS	Generated when the current Component gains the focus. The "focus" is reserved for one Component at a time, and indicates that the current Component is being used by the user.

Constant	Description
HOME	Generated by the <HOME> key.
KEY_ACTION	Generated when key action has occurred.
KEY_ACTION_RELEASE	Generated when the key action has been released.
KEY_PRESS	Generated when a key has been pressed down.
KEY_RELEASE	Generated when a key has been released (no longer being pressed).
LEFT	Generated by the left arrow key.
LIST_DESELECT	Caused when an item in a List is deselected. This does not happen too often if you only allow one item to be selected at a time.
LIST_SELECT	Caused when an item in a List is selected.
LOAD_FILE	Generated when a File is loaded.
LOST_FOCUS	Generated when a Component loses the "focus."
MOUSE_DOWN	Generated when the mouse button is pressed down.
MOUSE_DRAG	Generated if the mouse moves while being clicked (dragged).
MOUSE_ENTER	Generated when the mouse enters a Component.
MOUSE_EXIT	Generated when the mouse leaves a Component.
MOUSE_MOVE	Generated when the user moves the mouse without pressing the button.
MOUSE_UP	Generated when the mouse button is released.
PGDN	Generated when the <PAGE DOWN> key is pressed.
PGUP	Generated when the <PAGE UP> key is pressed.
RIGHT	Generated when the right arrow key is pressed.

continued on next page

continued from previous page

Constant	Description
SAVE_FILE	Generated when a file is saved by the AWT.
SHIFT_MASK	Indicates that the <SHIFT> key is down.
UP	Generated when the up arrow key is pressed.

TABLE 9-1 ◈ *List of Event.id constants*

Implementing the Client Chat Room Applet Code

First, let's get rid of all of the mundane steps.

The ChatClient.java Startup File

Start with a file called ChatClient.java and put this skeleton in it. It includes *all* of the global variables we will eventually need. You may not recognize them all now, but don't worry, you will.

```java
import java.applet.*;
import java.net.*;
import java.lang.*;
import java.io.*;
import java.awt.*;
import java.util.*;

public class ChatClient extends Applet {

/* network stuff first */
Socket sock;
DataInputStream dis;
PrintStream ps;
String name, theHost;
int thePort;

/* now the Thread */
Thread kicker = null;

/* And finally the AWT stuff */
TextField inputField;
TextArea outputArea;
Button B1,B2;
List L;
Panel p1,p2;
}
```

Text Output

In addition to all of this, let's write up a quick method that will allow us to output text to the server. This really isn't necessary at this point, but it is a good idea to have a method for this in case you ever need to send complicated messages. Don't worry too much about this code. It is only a simple output to a PrintStream. Eventually we'll replace it with something more interesting. We return *true* for success, *false* for failure. Here it is:

```
public boolean output(String str) {
try {
      ps.println(str);
      return true;
} catch(Exception e) {
      return false;
}
}
```

GUI Setup

Now let's set up the GUI. Once this step is complete, you should be able to compile the applet and play with all the neat components! However, because their Events go unhandled, they will be totally useless. Let's write the init() method now:

```
public void init() {

/* first, assign a BorderLayout and add the two Panels */
setLayout( new BorderLayout() );

p1 = new Panel();
p2 = new Panel();

p1.setLayout( new FlowLayout() );

add("South", p1);
add("North",p2);

/* next create the Field used for input. For fun, make it 80 columns wide.
Add it to the south Panel */
inputField = new TextField(80);
p1.add( inputField );

/* create the output Area. Make it 10 rows by 60 columns. Add it to north
Panel */
outputArea = new TextArea(10, 60);
p2.add(outputArea);

/* don't let the user edit the contents, and make the background color
Cyan - because it looks nice */
outputArea.setEditable(false);
outputArea.setBackground(Color.cyan);
```

continued on next page

continued from previous page

```
/* now for the Buttons. Make the first Button to let the user "login" */
B1 = new Button("login");
p1.add(B1);

/* The second Button allows the user to "logout", but is initially
   disabled */
B2 = new Button("logout");
p1.add(B2);
B2.disable();

/* Let's create the List next. Remember that the first item is always "All
Participants" */
L = new List();
p2.add(L);
L.addItem("All Participants");

/* Let's select the first item by default */
L.select(0);

}
```

Event Handling

Once you understand exactly how all of this looks and feels, we can proceed to handle the Events that will be generated by these Components. Normally, Java applets use specialized methods to handle Events, because this is easier than handling the Events directly. This is especially true for mouse-related events, which you are probably very familiar with from all of your Java game experience (see Chapter 4, Adding Interactivity, for more). However, for this applet, we are going to handle Events in the lowest-level Event handler: handleEvent(). Let's step through that code now:

```
public boolean handleEvent(Event evt) {

if( evt != null ) { // just in case

/* first, we handle the List-related Events. The user is not allowed to
talk to nobody, so we default to "All Participants" (index 0) */
if(evt.id == Event.LIST_DESELECT) {
      L.select(0);
      return true;
      }

/* when the user makes a selection in the List, we adjust the label of
Button B1 and then force Panel p1 to redraw and re-layout */
if( evt.id == Event.LIST_SELECT ) {
      if( L.getSelectedIndex() == 0)
            B1.setLabel("say");
      else
            B1.setLabel("whisper");
      p1.layout();
      return true;
      }
```

```
/* if the Event is an ACTION_EVENT generated by a TextField (we only have
one TextField), then it should perform the same action as pressing Button
B1 (either login, say, or whisper) */
if( evt.target.equals( inputField ) && evt.id == Event.ACTION_EVENT)
evt.arg = B1.getLabel();


/* now, we check to see if we have an "arg" */
if( evt.arg != null) {

/* if so, we must check to see if it corresponds to one of the commands we
understand */

/* If it equals "login", we assume the user wants to login and has not
done so already */
if (evt.arg.equals("login")) {
                outputArea.appendText("Logging in...\n");

/* the label of B1 is currently "login", change it to "say" and enable B2
*/
                B1.setLabel("say");
                B2.enable();
/* find out what alias the user wants to use */
                name = inputField.getText();
/* clear the inputField */
                inputField.setText("");

/* create a new Thread and start it */
        kicker = new Thread(this);
        kicker.start();

        return true;
         }

/* if the user wants to "say", then we merely output this command to the
server */
if(evt.arg.equals("say")) {
                output("say||"+inputField.getText());
                inputField.selectAll();
        return true;
        }

/* if the user wants to "whisper", we output this to the server AND we
notify the user of what happened (remember that the server will only echo
a "say" command to all clients. "whisper" is only sent to the target */

if(evt.arg.equals("whisper")) {
                outputArea.appendText("You whisper to "+L.getSelectedItem()+
": "+inputField.getText()+"\n");
        output("whisper||"+inputField.getText()+"||"+L.getSelectedItem() );
                inputField.selectAll();
```

continued on next page

continued from previous page

```
                  return true;
                  }
       }

       /* if the user pressed B2 (yes, we could have checked the "arg" but I
       wanted to show different ways of checking Events, including this one) */
       if(evt.target.equals(B2)) {
                  outputArea.appendText("Logging out...\n");
       /* stop the Thread (which will disconnect) */
                  kicker.stop();
       /* reset our affected GUI components */
                  B2.disable();
                  B1.setLabel("login");
                  p1.layout();

              return true;
              }
       }

       /* if the Event is not one of the ones we can handle, we should pass it
       along the chain-of-command to our super-class */
           return super.handleEvent(evt);;
         }
```

Make sure you understand how this method handles different Events in different ways. Some of the things we can do include the following:

- Check the Event.id.
- Check Event.arg.
- Check the *instanceof* Event.target.
- Check to see whether Event.target equals another Object.

You will need to understand these techniques very well in order to write effective and responsive games.

The above code makes reference to some methods we have not written yet. The most important ones, of course, are those that relate to the Thread part of this applet. Let's get started on that next. You know the drill for writing Thread code by now: First, add *implements Runnable* to the declaration of the ChatClient applet class, so that we can implement some Thread methods, as we did in Chapter 8, Implementing a High Score Server on a Network. Then…

The run() Method

We won't need a special start() method, so let's jump right into the run() method. This method will have two parts, each of which will loop until it is complete. The first loop will try to get a connection from the server. It will try, every five seconds, until it is able to open a Socket to the server, as well as its corresponding input and output Streams. Let's write that part now:

```
public void run() {

while (sock == null && kicker != null) {
    try {
        sock = new Socket(theHost,thePort);
        dis = new DataInputStream( sock.getInputStream() );
        ps = new PrintStream( sock.getOutputStream() );
    } catch (Exception e) {
        System.out.println("Unable to contact host.");
        outputArea.appendText("Unable to contact host.
                            Retrying...\n");
        sock = null;
    }
        try{ sleep( 5000 ); } catch(Exception e);
    }

output("login||"+name);
outputArea.appendText("Logged in to server successfully.\n");
```

That should look fairly familiar. The next part is much harder. Once run() has established a connection, it will attempt to handle any input we get from the server. This is very similar to what the sClientGroup class does on the server. We get a line of input, and then try to parse it into usable commands.

Command Parsing

Here is a list of the commands this client must be able to understand (coincidentally, this is the same as the list of commands the server is able to send):

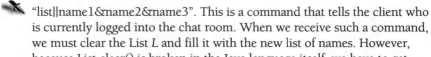 "list||name1&name2&name3". This is a command that tells the client who is currently logged into the chat room. When we receive such a command, we must clear the List *L* and fill it with the new list of names. However, because List.clear() is broken in the Java language itself, we have to get around it by removing *L* from *p2*, reinstantiating it, and then adding it back to *p2*. This is a relatively time-consuming process (compared to clearing the List), but it isn't too bad. Sun should have it fixed by the time you read this.

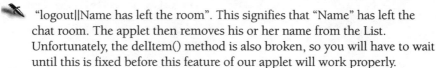 "logout||Name has left the room". This signifies that "Name" has left the chat room. The applet then removes his or her name from the List. Unfortunately, the delItem() method is also broken, so you will have to wait until this is fixed before this feature of our applet will work properly.

"login||Name||Name has entered the room". Signifies that "Name" has entered the chat room. Notice that in this and the command above, it is the server that determines what message to display, and that the client must obey blindly.

If the command was not one of the ones listed above, we assume it is a message command of the form "type||message". Currently, we ignore the type and just display the message. However, a neat extension of this applet would display different types of messages in different styles. See the Suggestion Box for more.

Server Input

Here is the code that handles input from the server in one big loop:

```
while (sock != null && dis != null && kicker != null) {
try {
      String str = dis.readLine();
      System.out.println("Got: "+str);
      if(str != null)
            if(str.indexOf("||") != -1) {
                  StringTokenizer st = new StringTokenizer(str,"||");
                  String cmd = st.nextToken();
                  String val = st.nextToken();
                  if(cmd.equals("List")) {
                        p2.remove(L);
                        L = new List();
                        p2.add(L);
                        p2.repaint();
                        p2.layout();
                        L.addItem("All Participants");
                        StringTokenizer st2 = new StringTokenizer(val,
                                          "&");
                        while(st2.hasMoreTokens())
                              L.addItem(st2.nextToken());
                        L.select(0);
                  }
                  else
                  if(cmd.equals("logout")) {
                  int x;
                        for(x=0;x< L.getRows();x++)
                        if( val.startsWith( L.getItem(x) ) )
                            L.delItem(x);
                        outputArea.appendText(val+"\n");
                  validate();
                  }
                  else
                  if(cmd.equals("login")) {
                        outputArea.appendText(st.nextToken()+"\n");
                   }
                  else
                  outputArea.appendText( val + "\n" );
                  }
            else
                  outputArea.appendText(str + "\n");
```

```
} catch (IOException e) {

/* if we get an IOException, it almost certainly means the connection was
lost */
       System.out.println("Connection lost.");
       kicker.stop();
}
}
}
```

The stop() Method

Because we are such nice, tidy programmers, we must make sure that the Socket and its related streams get closed before we finish. We also want to let the server know that we are logging out. To do this, we override the stop() method and make sure it cleans up before it exits:

```
public void stop() {

output("logout||"+name);
try {
       dis.close();
       ps.close();
       sock.close();
} catch (Exception e);
sock = null;
outputArea.appendText("Logged out from server.\n");
kicker = null;
}
```

That's it! Because we so carefully planned out our server, the client really doesn't have to do too much. Compile, run, and have some fun! Be sure you have the server running before you try to connect.

Suggestion Box

Here are some ideas for extending what you have learned in this chapter. Some are minor additions to the ChatClient, while others explore how you could extend these concepts to other projects.

 Use applet parameters (in the HTML APPLET tag) to embed the host and port the client should use in an HTML page. This first one is in the source code included with this book.

 Allow the server to use a user-defined port, instead of just 1123. (You'll need to use the *args[]* array.)

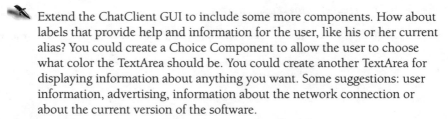

Extend the ChatClient GUI to include some more components. How about labels that provide help and information for the user, like his or her current alias? You could create a Choice Component to allow the user to choose what color the TextArea should be. You could create another TextArea for displaying information about anything you want. Some suggestions: user information, advertising, information about the network connection or about the current version of the software.

Modify the current applet and server to handle multiple selections in the List. This means that the user would be able to "whisper" to multiple people at one time. This will require some modifications to the protocol we use to send *whisper* messages, but, since we already use a flexible protocol for message sending, this is not too hard.

Modify the server to collect and track information about each user logged on, like e-mail addresses, real names, and location. Then, program the client to display this information whenever a user double-clicks on another user in the List. (Remember that java.awt.List generates an ACTION_EVENT whenever an item is double-clicked. You can then check which item is currently selected to find out which one it was.)

Use the protocols and code that we have established here to create a "never-ending story" applet. Each user logged on is invited to add a line to a continuing story, which is prompted by the server. Users may log on and review the current story and then contribute their own sentences to it.

When a user logs into the chat room, he or she should see a summary of what has been said prior to their entry (perhaps the last 10 things said). This list should be kept by the server. Every time something is said, it should be added to a queue that is displayed for new logins.

Have the client display different types of messages differently. There are a number of ways this could be handled. One would be to have *say* messages in normal font and *whisper* messages in bold. Or perhaps different colors.

One last idea that works well with the previous suggestion is to extend the number of types of messages. Perhaps add *shouts* or other emotional messages. One feature of many similar programs is an *emote* command that allows the user to do things rather than say them (i.e., Eric jumps up and down).

Summary

In this chapter, we explored a more advanced networking program than the one we created in Chapter 8, Implementing a High Score Server on a Network. The principles and skills required to implement the Java chat room are the same fundamental concepts you must understand to do any kind of multiplayer gaming on the Internet. Although a chat room is not technically a game (although it certainly is fun), the concepts used in creating it can easily be applied to nearly any online game. From this foundation, you open the door to creating a whole new kind of gaming experience for your user.

In addition to networking concepts, we explored some facets of the Java AWT more fully than we did in previous chapters. Once you understand how to implement the basic AWT Components, you can implement them all by simply reading the Java API specifications to learn what specific methods each Component uses. Perhaps most importantly, we explored the use of Events to control the flow of an applet, which is terribly important for game developers to understand properly.

From here, you can do anything. Once you have firmly mastered the AWT and Sockets, your games can progress from clunky to sophisticated and, most importantly, from local to global!

10

Advanced Techniques

Joel Fan

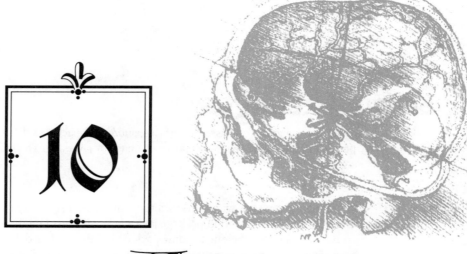

10

Advanced Techniques

Goals:

Learn advanced techniques you can use in games, including the use of
packages, threads, image processing, and data structures in java.util

In this chapter, you'll learn a variety of techniques that will be useful in creating
games and other applications. For example, you'll see:

- How to create packages that organize related collections of classes.

- How to organize games and other applications with threads.

- How to use java.awt.image for simple image processing. In particular,
you'll see how to reduce the download time of a series of bitmaps.

- Data structures in java.util that make writing games easier.

- Tips for creating applets that perform across a wide variety of platforms.

Feel free to skim this chapter and adapt whatever you need for your own projects.
Let's get started!

Using Packages

A *package* is a group of classes, interfaces, and/or subpackages that share a related purpose. Examples of packages are java.awt.image or java.lang. The *fully qualified name* of a class

```
<packagename>.<classname>
```

denotes the given class within the package. For example, the fully qualified name of the Graphics class, contained in package java.awt, is java.awt.Graphics.

All classes in Java belong to some package. Within a class definition, you can refer to another class in the same package by using the class name alone. However, a class must use the fully qualified name when referring to a class outside of its own package.

Importing Packages and Classes

It's inconvenient to type the fully qualified name every time you want to refer to a class in another package. By *importing* a package or a class into your program, you can use class names alone.

Java supports three versions of the *import* statement:

 Import a single class. Use the fully qualified name of the class in the *import* statement. Then, the class name alone will refer to the imported class. For example:

```
// can refer to 'Graphics' in following code
import java.awt.Graphics;
```

 Import all the classes in a package. Use the package name, qualified by *, in the *import* statement. Then, all classes in the packages can be referred to by using only the class names.

```
// can refer to all classes in java.awt using
//   class name alone, i. e. 'Component', 'Graphics', ...
  import java.awt.*;
```

 Import the package. Use the package name in the *import* statement:

```
import java.awt;
```

Then to reference a class, use the last component of the package name, followed by the class name, i.e., "awt.Graphics".

Creating Packages

You can create your own packages of classes and interfaces. This is useful for three reasons:

 To organize related classes and interfaces. A package gives related classes and interfaces conceptual unity. It's a good idea to group libraries of class files into packages that you can import when necessary. An example of a set of related classes is the Sprite class we developed in Chapters 3, 4, and 5. To create a package called "sprite", place the following statement

```
package sprite;
```

at the beginning of each file that contains code to a Sprite class. (The package declaration *must* be the first statement in the file.) If you don't include a package statement at the start of a file, the classes in the file will be members of the default package.

 To avoid name conflicts. By creating packages, you avoid the possibility of naming conflicts while developing applications. Let's say you're writing a program with your friend Ira. By putting all of Ira's classes into a package called "ira", and your classes into your own package, there won't be any problems if you both pick the same names for classes. For example, if each package has a class Shark, the two versions can be distinguished using the fully qualified name:

```
ira.Shark shark1;   // Shark class in package ira
jon.Shark shark2;   // Shark class in package jon
```

 For visibility. The classes in a package have direct access to all variables for which access isn't specified (for example, *public*, *private*, *protected*), and to all classes within the package. You can use this default level of access to make the classes in a package more efficient, by eliminating unnecessary accessor methods while keeping these variables visible only within a package. Only the *public* classes and interfaces of a package are accessible outside of the package. Thus, you can create helper classes that are non-*public*, and invisible outside package boundaries.

Nested Packages and Directory Structure

A package can be nested within another package. The declaration

```
package game.sprite;
```

denotes a package "sprite" in a package called "game". In a similar way, the packages of the Java API, such as java.lang and java.awt, are subpackages of the enclosing "java" package. Thus, packages are organized in hierarchical fashion.

For many installations, the package hierarchy corresponds to the directory structure of the packages. Thus, class files of the package "game" belong in some directory called game/, while class files of package game.sprite are found in the directory game/sprite/. If you don't state the package that a source file belongs to, it is considered part of the *default package*, which corresponds to the directory that the file is in.

When you're developing a game, it's easiest to keep your files as part of the default package. But once you've built up a library of classes you'll use in future games, you can arrange these class files in packages and import them when necessary.

Now, let's move on to threads.

Using Threads

Threads are one of Java's most powerful features. In Chapter 8, Implementing a High Score Server on a Network, you were introduced to threads and how they can be used to create networked games and applications. In this chapter, you will see further advantages and pitfalls of working with a "threaded approach" in your applets. First, let's review the definition of a thread.

A Quick Review of Threads

As we learned in Chapter 8, a thread is a mini-program that runs independently. You can have several threads of execution in a Java application or applet; in fact, the number of threads is limited only by system resources. Threads are useful whenever you need to perform multiple concurrent actions that are inconvenient or impossible to synchronize. The classic example is that of a server process, such as a World Wide Web server, which needs to handle several clients at once.

The Web server talks to each of the connected clients, and at the same time, listens for new requests. With threads, this is easily accomplished. A single thread waits for requests from clients. As each request comes in, a new thread is spawned to communicate with each client. When the conversation is over, the thread disappears. Figure 10-1 shows this sequence of events.

Here's another example. Most games need to track the progress of several independent objects through time, such as a player and his opponents. You can create a separate thread to handle each game object. Interactions in the game world are modeled by communication between the separate threads. You'll see how to structure games in this manner really soon!

Now, let's see how to create threads.

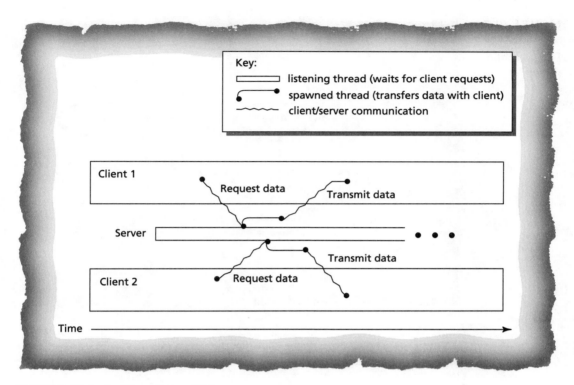

FIGURE 10-1 ◉ *Threads in a Web server*

Creating Threads

The java.lang.Thread class is the base class for all thread objects. To create a separate thread of execution, you create an instance of the Thread class, or one of its subclasses. For example,

```
Thread t = new Thread();
```

instantiates a Thread object *t*. To start and stop the execution of *t*, use the Thread methods start() and stop():

```
t.start();    // start running Thread t
t.stop();     // stop running Thread t
```

You can also suspend the execution of a thread, and resume it afterward:

```
t.suspend();  // suspend execution of t
t.resume();   // resume execution of t
```

A thread can suspend and resume as many times as you'd like, but it can only start and stop once. The life cycle of a thread is illustrated in Figure 10-2.

FIGURE 10-2

⊚ ⊚ ⊚ ⊚ ⊚ ⊚

Life cycle of a thread

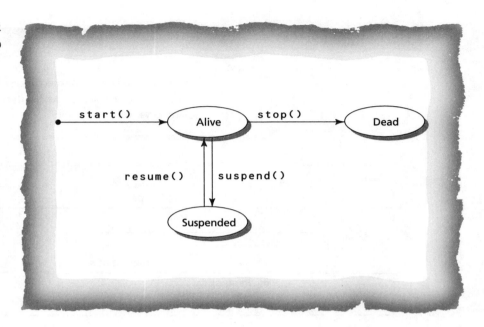

Now let's see how to specify the code that the thread executes, once it's alive. There are two ways of doing this: by creating a subclass of Thread and by doing something else.

Creating a Subclass of Thread

In the first way, you create a subclass of Thread, and define a method called run(). When an instance of your subclass is alive, it will execute the code in the run() method. The thread is destroyed upon completion of the run() method.

As an example, let's derive a subclass of Thread called MyThread:

```
public class MyThread extends Thread {
  ...
  public void run() {
  ...
  }
}
```

Now let's create multiple instances of MyThread, and start them. Each thread will independently execute the code found in run().

```
MyThread t1 = new MyThread();
MyThread t2 = new MyThread();
MyThread t3 = new MyThread();

// start all three threads.
t1.start();
```

```
t2.start();
t3.start();

...
// suspend t1
t1.suspend();
...
// stop t3
t3.stop();
```

Creating a Class That Implements Runnable

The second way of telling a thread to execute your code is to create a class that implements the Runnable interface. You have already used this method to create animations in Chapter 2, Using Objects for Animation.

A class that implements the Runnable interface provides the definition of a method called run():

```
class MyClass implements Runnable {
  ...
  public void run() {
    ...
  }
}
```

Let's create an instance of MyClass:

```
MyClass c = new MyClass();  // create MyClass object
```

Now create an instance of Thread while passing in the Runnable object.

```
Thread t = new Thread(c);
```

Once *t* starts, it executes the run() method of MyClass as a separate thread. The animation applets you've written work in this way. This method of creating threads comes in handy, for classes like Applet that don't derive from Thread.

Now let's see how a single CPU handles the concurrent execution of several threads.

Understanding Thread Scheduling

Unlike most humans, computers can do more than one thing at a time (or so it seems). Since there's usually a single CPU per computer, you might wonder how it executes multiple threads concurrently. The answer is simple: The CPU executes only one thread at a given moment, but it alternates between the various threads, running each in turn. For example, Figure 10-3 shows how processing time might be divided if you have three living threads in a Java program. As you see, each thread has the CPU for a moment. Then it waits for the CPU to execute it again.

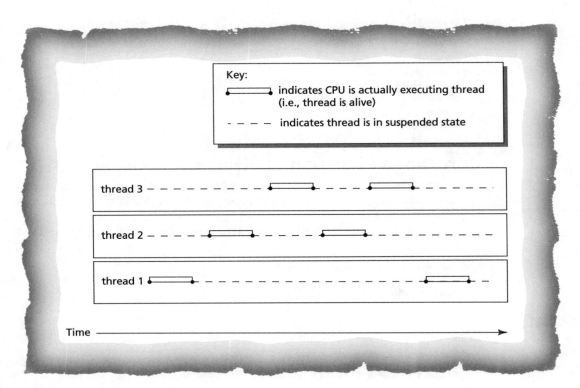

Key:

———→ indicates CPU is actually executing thread
(i.e., thread is alive)

– – – – indicates thread is in suspended state

thread 3

thread 2

thread 1

Time

FIGURE 10-3 ◉ *Execution of three threads*

The process of deciding which thread to run is called *thread scheduling*, and it's done by the runtime environment. All threads have a *priority*, and those with higher priority are executed before those of lower priority. Priorities are integers between Thread.MIN_PRIORITY and Thread.MAX_PRIORITY, and you can access the priority of a thread using the methods getPriority() and setPriority(int):

```
Thread t = new Thread();
t.setPriority(Thread.NORM_PRIORITY);
System.out.println("Priority:" + t.getPriority());
```

When two threads have equal priority, the manner in which these threads are executed depends on the particular platform. For time-slicing systems (such as those running UNIX), the two threads will alternate execution. On other platforms, the scheduler will execute one thread until it's finished, before moving on to other threads of equal priority. (Needless to say, this sounds a little unfair!)

However, a thread can *yield* to other threads of equal priority, using the instance method yield():

```
t.yield();
```

This allows other threads that are waiting for processing time to be executed. Figure 10-4 shows how two threads that use yield() might be executed.

When you're writing a program that uses multiple threads, it's good practice to use yield(), as you'll see later on. Of course, a thread also gives up the CPU to other threads when it executes sleep(), suspend(), or stop().

Now, let's look at a simple example of threads in action!

Creating a Simple Multithreaded Animation

Let's create a multithreaded animation applet. Although this example is simple, it'll highlight the differences of programming with threads.

First of all, let's define an abstract class, Actor, that specifies the essential methods and variables of objects that move independently on the screen. This class is shown in Listing 10-1.

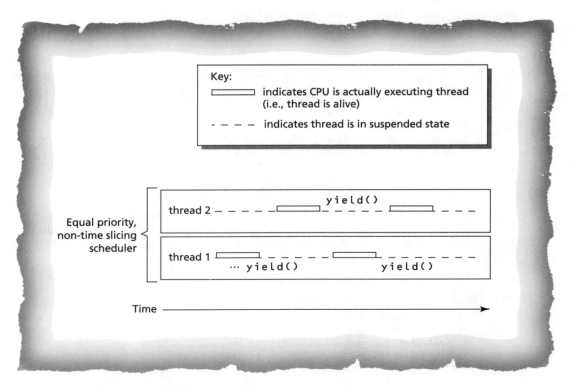

FIGURE 10-4 ◉ *Using yield()*

Listing 10-1 *Actor class*

```
abstract class Actor extends Thread {
  Applet applet;
  protected boolean drawNow;
  abstract void paint(Graphics g);
}
```

Each Actor object is a separate thread that runs independently. When it needs to paint itself (for example, after a change in color or position), it will set *drawNow* to *true*, and notify the mother applet. For example, here is the run() method of an Actor subclass, called CycleColorActor, which paints a rectangle that changes colors every few milliseconds:

```
public void run() {
  while (true) {
    drawNow = true;
    applet.repaint();
    updateColor();
    try {
     sleep(delay);
    }
    catch (InterruptedException e) {
    }
  }
}
```

The repaint() method of the applet eventually triggers a call to each Actor's individual paint() method. Here's the paint() of the CycleColorActor:

```
public void paint(Graphics g) {
  if (drawNow) {
    g.setColor(new Color(red,green,blue));
    g.fillRect(locx,locy,73,73);
    drawNow = false;
  }
}
```

As you see, only those Actors that need to paint will draw themselves.

The full definition of the CycleColorActor is shown in Listing 10-2. The constructor allows you to specify the location of the rectangle, the delay, and the starting (*r,g,b*) triple.

Listing 10-2 *CycleColorActor class*

```
class CycleColorActor extends Actor {
  protected int locx,locy;        // location
  protected int red,green,blue;   // color
  protected int delay;            // delay in ms

  public CycleColorActor(Applet a,int x,int y,
              int r,int g,int b,int d) {
    // initialize inherited variables
```

```
      applet = a;
      drawNow = false;

      // initialize other variables
      locx = x;
      locy = y;
      red = r;
      green = g;
      blue = b;
      delay = d;
      start();              // start thread running!
    }

    // override run() -- each thread executes this
    //    when it's alive

    public void run() {
      while (true) {
        drawNow = true;
        applet.repaint();
        updateColor();
        try {
         sleep(delay);
        }
        catch (InterruptedException e) {
        }
      }
    }


    public void updateColor() {
      red = (red + 4) % 256;
      green = (green + 4) % 256;
      blue = (blue + 4) % 256;
    }

    // provide implementation of abstract methods:

    public void paint(Graphics g) {
      if (drawNow) {
        g.setColor(new Color(red,green,blue));
        g.fillRect(locx,locy,73,73);
        drawNow = false;
      }
    }
  }
}
```

Finally, Listing 10-3 shows the applet (ActorTest) that will define three Actors and set them running. Figure 10-5 shows how this applet works in conjunction with the Actors.

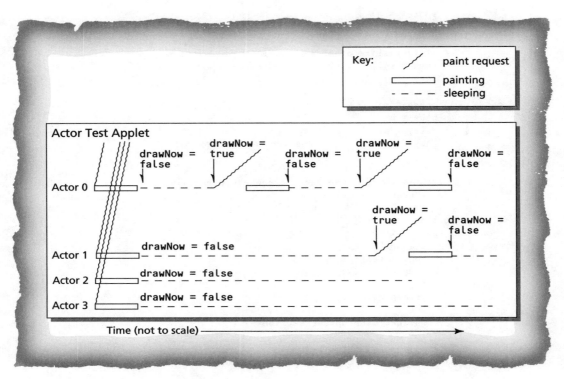

FIGURE 10-5 ◉ *ActorTest applet execution*

ActorTest doesn't implement Runnable, as our previous animation applets did. Study the following code so you understand how things work!

Listing 10-3 *ActorTest applet*

```
import java.applet.*;
import java.awt.*;

public class ActorTest extends Applet {

  Actor actors[] = new Actor[4];

  public void init() {
    int width = size().width;
    int height = size().height;
    setBackground(Color.black);
    // define 4 Actors:
    // this changes color every 50 ms
    actors[0] = new CycleColorActor(this,0,0,
                         90,150,0,50);
```

```
    // this changes color every 100 ms
    actors[1] = new CycleColorActor(this,width-73,0,
                      90,150,0,100);
    // this changes color every 200 ms
    actors[2] = new CycleColorActor(this,0,height-73,
                      90,150,0,200);
    // this changes color every 400 ms
    actors[3] = new CycleColorActor(this,width-73,height-73,
                      90,150,0,400);

  }


  // override update so it doesn't erase screen
  public void update(Graphics g) {
    paint(g);
  }

  public void paint(Graphics g) {

    for (int i=0; i<actors.length; i++) {
      actors[i].paint(g);      // paint each rectangle
    }

  }

}
```

Next, let's see how you can structure games with threads. The ActorTest applet contains the basic idea.

Structuring Games with Multiple Threads

First, let's review how we've written games without using multiple threads. The key to our previous approach is the Video Game Loop, diagrammed in Figure 10-6.

In this scheme, the run() loop contained in the applet acts as the master clock, telling each of the classes used in the game when to update and paint.

With multiple threads, a different approach is possible. Each Actor in the game will update at an individual rate, based on its own internal clock. When it's ready to paint, it notifies the mother applet. The mother applet passes the graphics context to the individual Actors, which paint if necessary. This scheme is diagrammed in Figure 10-7.

FIGURE 10-6

◉ ◉ ◉ ◉ ◉ ◉

*The Video
Game Loop
revisited*

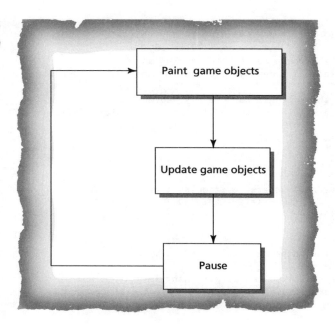

FIGURE 10-6

◉ ◉ ◉ ◉ ◉ ◉

*The Video
Game Loop
revisited*

Incorporating Multiple Threads into the Alien Landing Game

Let's see how this scheme might work for the Alien Landing video game we've already written. You might want to review this game in Chapters 5, 6, and 7. Each Sprite object of the original game—the UFOs, the missile launcher, and the missile—will be a distinct Actor object in the threaded version of the game. As before, the Manager classes will track information about the game state. For example, if a UFOActor is hit, it calls the method in UFOManager that increments the number of UFOs killed:

```
// method in UFOManager that tracks
//    number of UFOs killed
public void killed() {
  ufosKilled++;
  ...
}
```

At this point, we have to be careful! When multiple threads modify shared information, unexpected effects, or *race conditions*, may occur. Let's see why. Each Java instruction, even "simple" ones such as

```
ufosKilled++;
```

FIGURE 10-7
◎ ◎ ◎ ◎ ◎ ◎
*Multithreaded
Video Game
structure*

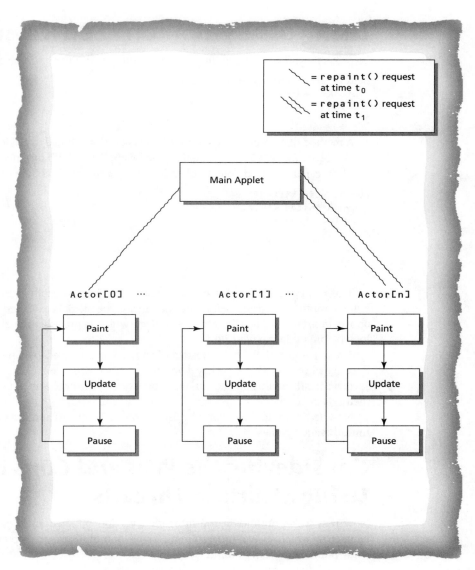

actually gets compiled to several machine instructions. A thread may be in the process of executing some of these instructions when it gets suspended. Another thread can update *ufosKilled*, but when the original thread resumes, it won't take the updated value into account. The net result is that one of the updates is lost!

Using the synchronized Keyword

To protect against the possibility of race conditions, use the *synchronized* keyword:

```
public synchronized void killed() {
  ufosKilled++;
  ...
}
```

A method that's declared *synchronized* allows only one thread to call it at a time, which neatly solves our problem. *synchronized* can be applied to both instance and class methods. You can also declare blocks of code to be *synchronized*, as in the following:

```
public void killed() {
  synchronized (this) {
    ufosKilled++;
    ...
  }
  ...
}
```

This form of the *synchronized* statement allows you to specify the object that must enforce mutual exclusion before the code inside the block is executed. In the example above, *this* refers to the UFOManager object, which is precisely the object we need to lock before updating *ufosKilled*.

The remainder of the multithreaded Alien Landing can be adapted pretty directly from the original version. Here's the key point to remember: when you're writing code in which several threads modify shared variables, be aware of the necessity of using *synchronized* methods or blocks.

Now, let's sum up this section by listing some advantages and drawbacks of writing multithreaded games.

Considering the Pros and Cons of Using Multiple Threads

Now that we've outlined a multithreaded version of Alien Landing, you might be wondering which style of programming (single or multithreaded) is preferable. Here are a few pointers to keep in mind.

Some advantages of multithreaded games are:

 Conceptual clarity. Most game worlds have several independent processes that operate concurrently. By modeling these processes as separate threads, you simplify the transition from concepts to actual Java code.

 Asynchronous capability. Sometimes, using multiple threads will be the best available option. This is the case when there are several processes in the gaming environment that can't be coordinated with a master clock.

Some disadvantages of multithreaded games are:

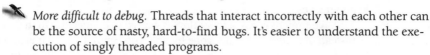 *More difficult to debug.* Threads that interact incorrectly with each other can be the source of nasty, hard-to-find bugs. It's easier to understand the execution of singly threaded programs.

Greater runtime expense. Tracking several threads increases the burden on the runtime system. Executing *synchronized* methods is particularly slow, since the appropriate locks must be acquired.

Finally, here's a rule of thumb you can use when writing Java games (and other applications): *Use as few threads as necessary to accomplish your programming goals. In the case of our Alien Landing game, the multithreaded approach outlined above is not necessary. However, in more complex games, you may find it easier to use multiple threads.*

Now let's explore a package we haven't used before.

Improving Performance with Image Processing

This section introduces java.awt.image, a package of classes that enable you to perform image processing. You will learn how the facilities provided in java.awt.image can help speed up the downloading of images in your games. In particular, you'll learn how to use the ImageProducer interface and the ImageFilter classes to create new bitmaps dynamically. But let's see why you'd want to use these classes in the first place!

Why Be Concerned with Image Processing?

Once your game is published on the Web, users around the world can download it to their own computers. Unfortunately, modem speeds are relatively slow for the average user, and it can take quite a while to load a game applet and the associated images. As a result, it behooves you, the game designer, to explore ways of reducing download times.

Creating Image Strips

If your code is lean and mean, as it should be, there won't be much opportunity for reducing the download time of the game applet itself. However, multiple bitmaps that are used in the game can take significant amounts of time to load, and you *can* reduce this. The idea is pretty simple. The HTTP protocol used by the Web is *stateless*, which means that every time your browser wants to download an image, it needs to connect to the server and request the image. For multiple images, this means multiple connections and requests.

Figure 10-8 illustrates the steps involved in loading a single image, versus loading several images.

As you might guess, a lot of time is wasted in connecting to the server for each image. Instead of requesting images one by one, you can put all the images you need into a single image file, and get this file in one fell swoop. We'll call this file an *image strip*. For example, Figure 10-9 shows how an image strip might look for the Alien Landing game of Chapter 5, Building a Video Game.

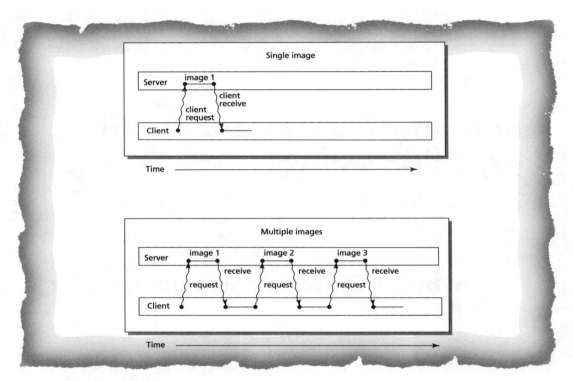

FIGURE 10-8 ⊙ *Loading images*

FIGURE 10-9

⊙ ⊙ ⊙ ⊙ ⊙ ⊙

Partial image strip for Alien Landing

Loading an image strip is more efficient than loading several images separately, simply because you don't waste time on multiple connects and requests to the server.

Filtering the Images

Once the strip is loaded, you can extract the original bitmaps by filtering the image strip. Let's see how to filter images using the interfaces and classes defined in java.awt.image. It's not hard at all!

First, you need to have an object that implements the ImageProducer interface. An ImageProducer, as the name implies, is an object that can generate an image. With an ImageProducer you can create an image dynamically:

```
// this code appears in a Component
ImageProducer p;
... // assign an ImageProducer object to p
Image i = createImage(p);
```

The Component method createImage() takes an ImageProducer argument and returns a reference to an image.

Now let's see what kinds of ImageProducers are out there. The simplest are associated with the Images themselves, and they generate the data that's in the image. Use the Image method getSource() to get its ImageProducer:

```
Image i = getImage(getCodeBase(),"strip.gif");
...
ImageProducer p = i.getSource();
```

This suggests a way to copy an Image: Get its ImageProducer, and then use the Component method createImage(). To continue the example above, let's create another copy of strip.gif:

```
Image j = createImage(p); // copies Image i
```

Now let's see how to filter image data. The idea is to create a new ImageProducer, which takes data from the original image (using getSource()) and processes it with an ImageFilter object. Figure 10-10 illustrates this sequence.

An example of an ImageFilter is CropImageFilter. This class implements a filter that crops an image to the rectangle defined in the arguments

```
ImageFilter filter = new CropImageFilter(x,y,width,height);
```

Next, create an ImageProducer that will generate the filtered image. To do this, construct an instance of FilteredImageSource, specifying the original ImageProducer, and the filter to be used:

```
ImageProducer filterProducer =
    FilteredImageSource(image.getSource(),filter);
```

The last step is to create the filtered image:

```
Image filteredImage = createImage(filteredProducer);
```

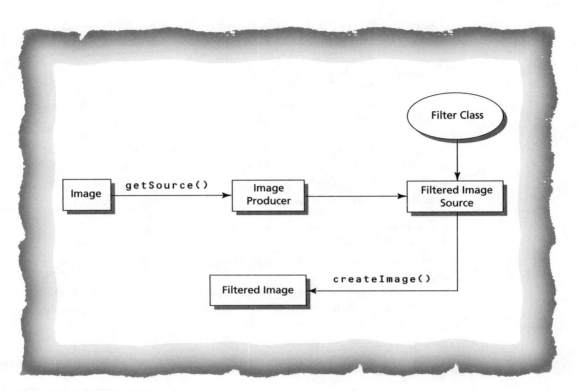

FIGURE 10-10 ◉ *Filtering an Image*

Once you've created the filtered image, you can display it, or even pass it through another image filter!

Extracting Images from an Image Strip

Now you're ready for the applet shown in Listing 10-4, which takes an image strip and creates and displays the constituent images. The dirty work's done by the extractImages() method, which iterates through the strip and extracts each bitmap in turn.

Listing 10-4 *ExtractImageTest applet*

```
// Demo of how to extract images from an image strip

import java.applet.*;
import java.awt.*;
import java.awt.image.*;

public class ExtractImageTest extends Applet {
  Image strip;         // the image strip
```

```
Image images[];      // the constituent images
int num_images = 0;  // number of images in strip
int width = 10;      // width of each image in strip
int height;

public void init() {
  Image strip = getImage(getCodeBase(),"strip.gif");

  // wait for image to load
  //   (here's how to do it without using MediaTracker)
  while (strip.getWidth(this) <0);

  // define number of images in strip
  num_images = strip.getWidth(this)/width;

  // define height of each image
  height = strip.getHeight(this);

  // define array of constituent images
  images = new Image[num_images];

  // extract constituent images
  extractImages(strip,images,num_images,width,height);
}

/////////////////////////////////////////////////////////////////
// Extract the constituent images from a strip.
// There are num_images to extract, each with the
// specified width and height.

public void extractImages(Image strip,
                          Image images[],
                          int num_images,
                          int width,
                          int height) {
  ImageProducer source = strip.getSource();

  for (int i = 0; i<num_images; i++) {
    // define filter to pull image at (i*width,0) with
    //   dimensions (width,height)
    ImageFilter extractFilter = new CropImageFilter(i*width,
                                                    0,
                                                    width,
                                                    height);

    // define producer from source and filter
    ImageProducer producer =
     new FilteredImageSource(source,extractFilter);

    // extract the subimage!
    images[i] = createImage(producer);
```

continued on next page

continued from previous page

```
      }
    }

    // display constituent images in a diagonal
    public void paint(Graphics g) {
      for (int i=0; i<num_images; i++) {
        g.drawImage(images[i],i*width,i*13,this);

      }
    }
}
```

You can use a method such as extractImages() to reduce the loading time of images in your applets. java.awt.image contains other filters and image producers that you can use, so be sure to check them out!

Table 10-1 shows the methods we've covered in this section.

Class/Interface	Methods
java.awt.Component	public Image createImage(ImageProducer producer);
java.awt.Image	public abstract ImageProducer getSource();
java.awt.image.CropImageFilter	public CropImageFilter(int x,int y,int w,int h); // constructor
java.awt.image.FilteredImageSource	public ImageFilterSource(ImageProducer orig, ImageFilter imgf); // constructor

TABLE 10-1 ◈ *Methods for image processing*

Now, let's talk about java.util.

Using the java.util Classes

The package java.util defines several classes that will come in handy when you're creating games (and other applications). In fact, other classes of the API use this package as well. A quick look at the class hierarchy, shown in Figure 10-11, will tell you why.

In this section, you'll see how the following classes might be used in gaming situations:

 Date

 Vector

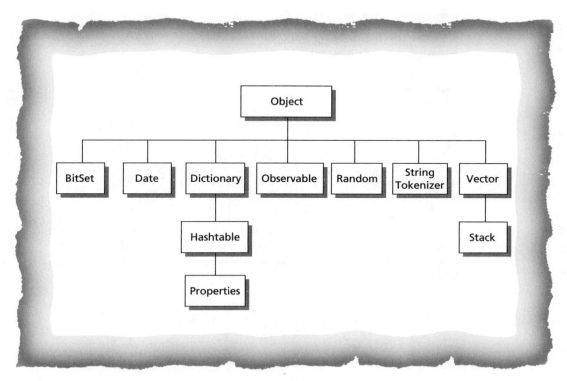

FIGURE 10-11 ◉ *Class hierarchy of java.util*

 Stack

Hashtable

Random

The Date Class

The Date class encapsulates methods that manipulate time in a platform-independent manner. If you're writing a game or application with real-time requirements, such as a video game, you can use this class to access the system clock. For example, the following fragment creates a Date object with the current time and date:

```
// contains the current time and date
Date d = new Date();
```

You can also initialize a Date to a given value:

```
// initialized to the date April 9, 1969
```

```
Date e = new Date(69,4,9);
```

To compare dates, use the instance methods after(Date), before(Date), and equals(Date), all of which return a *boolean*:

```
boolean b1 = d.after(e);  // true
boolean b2 = d.before(e); // false
boolean b3 = d.equals(e); // false
```

Here's how you can access the various components of the Date object:

```
int year = d.getYear();        // get years since 1900
int month = d.getMonth();      // get month (1..12)
int date = d.getDate();        // get date in month (1..31)
int hours = d.getHours();      // get hour (0..23)
int minutes = d.getMinutes();// get minute (0..59)
int seconds = d.getSeconds();// get second (0..59)
```

You can set these components using the corresponding methods: setYear(int), set Month(int), setDate(int), setHours(int), setMinutes(int), and setSeconds(int).

Finally, to get the time in milliseconds since GMT 12:00:00 A.M. of January 1, 1970, use getTime():

```
long time = d.getTime();
```

You can use this method to dynamically measure the performance of your games. For example:

```
long before = new Date().getTime();  // time before
...                                  // some code here
long after = new Date().getTime();   // time after
long elapsed = after - before;       // elapsed time
```

Then, your program might alter some parameters, based on the value of *elapsed*. For example, if *elapsed* is too high, your game might reduce the number of objects it's tracking.

An equivalent to the getTime() method is currentTimeMillis() in the java.lang.System class. Table 10-2 shows the methods in the Date class.

Class	Methods
Date	public Date();
	public Date(int year, int month, int date);
	public boolean after(Date when);
	public boolean before(Date when);
	public boolean equals(Object obj);
	public long getTime();

TABLE 10-2 ◈ *Methods in java.util.Date*

The Vector Class

A Vector stores an ordered collection of objects that can grow or shrink dynamically. As a result, it offers more flexibility than an array, which requires that the number of elements be known prior to allocation. You can use a Vector for game situations in which the number of objects to be stored changes as the game progresses. Keep in mind, though, that a Vector is more complex than an array, and it's correspondingly slower.

It's easy to create a Vector:

```
Vector v = new Vector();
```

Here's how you add objects to and remove objects from the Vector:

```
// obj1, obj2, obj3 are arbitrary objects
v.addElement(obj1);
v.addElement(obj2);
v.addElement(obj3);
v.removeElement(obj2);
```

You can address the elements of a Vector directly, using an index starting from 0:

```
Object obj4 = v.elementAt(0);  // get the element at 0
v.removeElementAt(1);          // delete the element at 1
```

To figure out the number of objects stored in the Vector, use the instance method size():

```
int size = v.size();  // num elements in v
```

Finally, here's how you read the elements of the Vector, using the Enumeration interface. The methods declared by the Enumeration interface allow you to iterate through the elements of a collection class, such as a Vector. An object that implements Enumeration refers to a set of elements that you can step through, one at a time, without using an explicit index. There are two Enumeration methods: nextElement(), which returns the next object in the Enumeration, and hasMoreElements(), which returns *true* if there are elements left.

Here's an example. The first step is to define an Enumeration that refers to the elements of the Vector. The Vector method elements() does just that:

```
Enumeration e = v.elements();
```

Now, the following loop

```
while (e.hasMoreElements()) {
  Object obj = e.nextElement();
  ...
}
```

will set the variable *obj* to each element of the Vector, for each iteration of the loop.

Table 10-3 shows the methods in the Enumeration interface and the Vector class.

Class/Interface	Methods
Enumeration	public abstract boolean hasMoreElements(); public abstract Object nextElement() throws NoSuchElementException;
Vector	public new Vector(); public final synchronized void addElement(Object obj); public final synchronized Enumeration elements(); public final synchronized Object elementAt(int index) throws ArrayOutOfBoundsException public final synchronized boolean removeElement(Object obj); public final synchronized void removeElementAt(int index) throws ArrayOutOfBoundsException public final int size();

TABLE 10-3 ◈ *Methods in java.util.Enumeration and java.util.Vector*

The Stack Class

A Stack implements last-in, first-out storage (as in a stack of dirty dinner plates to be cleaned!). Stacks are fundamental data structures that come in handy in numerous programming situations. You can push() an element onto the top of the Stack, or remove the top element, using pop(). To look at the top element, without removing it, use peek(). empty() returns *true* if there are no elements on the Stack. Table 10-4 shows the methods in the Stack class.

Here's an example using a Stack:

```
Stack s = new Stack();
// obj1, obj2 are arbitrary objects
s.push(obj1);
s.push(obj2);
Object obj3 = s.pop();
Object obj4 = s.peek();
boolean isEmpty = s.empty();
```

Class	Methods

Stack	public Stack();
	public boolean empty();
	public Object peek() throws EmptyStackException;
	public Object pop() throws EmptyStackException;
	public Object push(Object item);

TABLE 10-4 ◈ *Methods in java.util.Stack*

The Hashtable Class

A Hashtable stores pairs of keys and objects. You can retrieve the object using the key. A key can be any arbitrary object, so you might consider a Hashtable as an array that allows arbitrary objects to serve as indices.

Hashtables are a convenient and natural way to store dictionary data, such as a word and its definition. For example, you could use a Hashtable to record a player's name, and his high scores.

Here's an example. First, instantiate the Hashtable:

```
Hashtable h = new Hashtable();
```

Keys can be arbitrary objects. To associate an object with a particular key in the Hashtable, use

```
// keys key1, key2 are arbitrary objects
// objects obj1, obj2 are arbitrary objects also

h.put(key1, obj1);    // associate obj1 with key1
h.put(key2, obj2);    // associate obj2 with key2
```

Now you can look up the entries in the table by using get() for a given key:

```
Object obj3 = h.get(key1);
```

You can also remove the element corresponding to a given key:

```
h.remove(key2);
```

The methods in the Hashtable class are shown in Table 10-5.

Class	Methods

Hashtable	public Hashtable();
	public synchronized Object get(Object key);
	public synchronized Object put(Object key,Object value) throws NullPointerException;
	public synchronized Object remove(Object key);

TABLE 10-5 ◈ *Methods in java.util.Hashtable*

The Random Class

Random number generators are used to give games variety and unpredictability. The Random class provides several methods for producing *pseudo-random* values. The numbers generated aren't truly random, but computed with a formula that takes a seed value.

Here's how. To create a Random object, seeded with the current time, use:

```
// seeded with current time
Random r1 = new Random();
```

You can specify the seed (a long) in the constructor, or using the instance method setSeed(long):

```
// seed in constructor
Random r3 = new Random(1317L);
r1.setSeed(1713L);
```

By specifying a seed, you can fix the sequence of random numbers, which is invaluable in debugging.

Here's how to get random numbers of different types:

```
// get int between Integer.MIN_VAL and Integer.MAX_VALUE
int i = r1.nextInt();

// get long between Long.MIN_VAL and Long.MAX_VALUE
long l = r3.nextLong();

// get float between 0.0f and 1.0f
float f = r1.nextFloat();

// get double between 0.0 and 1.0
double d = r3.nextDouble();
```

Another way to get a random double between 0.0 and 1.0 is to use the static method Math.random():

```
double d2 = Math.random();
```

The methods in the Random class are shown in Table 10-6.

Class	Methods
Random	public Random();
	public Random(long seed);
	public double nextDouble();
	public float nextFloat();
	public int nextInt();
	public long nextLong();

TABLE 10-6 ◈ *Methods in java.util.Random*

In the next section, you'll get some tips for writing game applets that perform across different platforms.

Writing for Multiple Platforms

The Java environment is designed to exhibit similar behavior across a wide range of platforms. However, there are times when your code might run properly on one platform, only to crash and burn on another. Here are some things to keep in mind.

Yield Threads

You've already seen how time-slicing systems execute two threads of equal priority differently from non-time-slicing systems. If your code depends on one form of scheduling, you shouldn't be surprised when a friend of yours downloads your applet and tells you it doesn't work on his machine! When you have a program with multiple threads, it's wise to explicitly yield() at natural intervals. For example, if the run() method of some thread has a loop, you might want to yield() every iteration:

```
// the run() method of some thread
public void run() {
  for (int i = 0; i < 1713; i++) {
    ...                  // some code here
    yield();             // yield the thread
  }
}
```

Aligning Text

Each windowing toolkit has a different look and feel, and GUI components take up different amounts of space, depending on the particular toolkit. One way to lay out text in a window (such as an Applet or a Frame) is to define the text String, and write it to the window at the given coordinates:

```
// g is Graphics context
// draw textString at (130,170)
g.drawString(textString, 130, 170);
```

Although this is the simplest way to lay out text, the text might not align properly across all platforms. If alignment is important, it's better to define Labels and use the appropriate LayoutManager. For example, you can center or right-justify text in this way. If the user resizes the window, the LayoutManager will automatically center the label for the new screen size.

LayoutManagers and Labels don't provide the fine-grained control that you sometimes need. In this case, use the java.awt.FontMetrics class to determine the height and width of the particular string under a particular font, and position it accordingly.

Determining System Properties

Let's face it—not all systems are created equal. You might be slaving away in front of a 13-inch monitor, while your more fortunate brethren are basking in the glow of huge Sony Trinitrons and tremendous screen resolution. Thus, a game that looks just right on the latter system might take up too much space on the former; likewise, an applet that looks fine on the 13-inch screen seems invisible on bigger ones. What to do?

Determining Screen Parameters

One solution is to pick a size for your game that seems to work well across different installations. This is a bit approximate, but it's the simplest alternative.

The second solution takes a bit more work. The API allows you to determine the screen size, screen resolution, and other system properties as well. Then, you can adjust parameters in your games at runtime, depending on characteristics of the particular system.

Here's how you can determine the screen size and resolution that your applet's running on by using the class java.awt.Toolkit. First, use the Component method getToolkit() (you can put this in an applet, for example):

```
Toolkit t= getToolkit();
```

Then, the Toolkit method getScreenResolution() returns the screen resolution in dots per inch:

```
int dpi = t.getScreenResolution();
```

and the method getScreenSize() returns the screen dimensions:

```
Dimension d = t.getScreenSize();
int screen_width = d.width;
int screen_height = d.height;
```

Obtaining System Properties

It's also possible to determine other system properties as well. For example, your game applet can determine the architecture of the system that it's running on, and adjust parameters accordingly. (For slower systems, your game might perform fewer computations.)

The first step is to get the table of system Properties:

```
Properties p = System.getProperties();
```

Properties is a class defined in java.util that extends Hashtable. To look up values in a Properties object, use the instance method getProperty(String). Table 10-7 shows some keys available in the Properties object returned by the System class.

Key	Property
"java.version"	Java interpreter version
"java.class.version"	Java API version
"os.arch"	Host architecture
"os.name"	Host operating system
"os.version"	Operating system version

TABLE 10-7 ◈ *System property keys*

For example, here's how your game can determine the API version of the host installation:

```
Properties p = System.getProperties();
String version = p.getProperties("java.class.version");
```

Then, your applet can proceed accordingly, perhaps taking advantage of features found in newer versions of the API.

Ask the Player

Finally, you should not overlook the simplest way to determine system properties, which is to ask the player. You can have an introductory screen that allows the player to select the platform the applet is running on. Another option is to place the list of platforms on the HTML page. The platform that the player chooses runs the applet with a certain set of applet parameters, or even runs a different applet altogether.

Allowing Customization

Each user has a particular range of preferences, such as preferred colors, preferred sounds, and level of difficulty. By allowing your game to be customizable, not only can the user adjust the applet to the platform it's running on, he or she can tailor it to his or her particular preferences. This is one of the best ways of smoothing out bumps as your applet travels from computer to computer, and we cover it in Chapter 7, Creating Customizable Games with the AWT.

Testing Your Games on Multiple Platforms

This is an important step to take before unleashing your applet on the world. Have your friends across the Web test your game, if possible. They can tell you how long it takes to download, how it looks, and how it runs. Be prepared for some surprises—and another round of modifications—before you're done!

Suggestion Box

🗡 Create a graphics simulation of bouncing objects by using a separate thread for each. You can start by extending the Actor class, which we defined above. You can also model other real-time systems using threads, such as a nuclear power plant, a city, or an airplane.

🗡 MemoryImageSource is an ImageProducer that allows you to specify the image data, pixel by pixel. Use this class to create a color wheel that displays the possible combinations of red, green, and blue.

🗡 RGBImageFilter is an ImageFilter that allows you to change the colors in an image. See how easy it is to swap the red and green component of each pixel in an Image. Then experiment with various filtering formulas to create cool-looking images.

🗡 Allow your next graphics applet to adjust automatically to the screen size and resolution of the computer that it's executing on.

Summary

In this chapter, you've learned some finer points of creating multithreaded games in Java. Multiple threads allow you to model independent, concurrent processes in your games. You've learned how to filter images and speed up the process of loading image data into a game application. You've also covered important classes in java.util and have seen ways of making your applets as portable as possible.

11

Into the Third Dimension

Calin Tenitchi

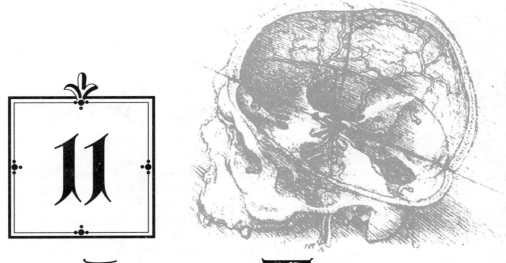

Into the Third Dimension

Goals:

Build the classes needed for a small 3D engine

Understand Java/object-oriented concepts of inheritance, abstract classes, and methods

This chapter will take you step by step through the process of defining, transforming, projecting, and painting 3D models. By the end of the chapter we will have a couple of classes that can be used to make a simple 3D engine.

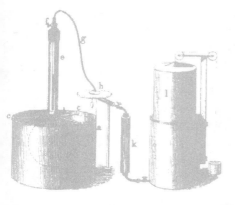

Performance Issues with 3D in Java

The only way a game can truly give the player a firsthand perspective of a virtual world is by using 3D graphics. Walking, driving, or flying around in a virtual world is a great experience that cannot be created by any two-dimensional techniques. Unfortunately, the performance hit of using 3D graphics is very large compared to the much simpler two-dimensional approach even if the application is compiled to native code. So why in the world would anybody want to develop 3D applications in Java? The answer is simple: Because it can be done.

Even in the "stone age" of 10 years ago, enthusiasts developed 3D games on computers with less horsepower than a modern calculator has. Considering that Java is at this point an interpreted language, it is definitely not the platform for developing games that squeeze every hertz of the processor. It will be a true challenge to write a fairly fast 3D application. What can you do to improve the performance, then?

Improving Performance Through Simple Rendering

One way to improve performance is to restrict ourselves to simple rendering techniques. We have the choice of using filled or wire-frame polygons, but wire frame is as out as it can be and should not even be considered as an option. Fortunately, the performance gained from using wire-frame instead of filled polygons is barely noticeable. This is because most video cards nowadays support hardware-implemented polygon filling. Since Java's polygon filling routines call the host platform's API, these operations are very fast, so this is not the place to try to improve performance.

Improving Performance Through Optimizing the Overall Model

The optimizations have to be done on a different level. Instead of optimizing some inner loop, we should try optimizing the overall application model. Low-level optimizations that improve the performance on a certain machine can have the opposite effect on some other machine with different hardware architecture. We always have to keep in mind that Java is supposed to run on a variety of computers that can differ very much from each other. Still, one sure common denominator among them is object orientation. As long as the application model is truly object-oriented and optimized within these frames, it should be considered a good solution. On the way, we will take some shortcuts, but only tiny ones to smooth out performance in tight corners.

Future Optimization of Java Itself

Not long from now, all Java applications will hopefully be "just-in-time compiled," which means that the bytecode is compiled to native machine code before being executed. This will erase the sharp performance gap between native and Java code. But for now, we simply have to accept that Java is sluggish, especially in graphics-intensive applications. The performance hit is very high. A good guess is a double-digit number possibly starting with two thousand percent, or 20 times slower in graphic intensive applications. On the other hand, Java wasn't designed to be lightning fast and from a speed standpoint isn't the platform of choice for writing games. The power of Java is that a game that runs on a 486-Intel machine also runs on Sun's Pulsar or on Apple's Macintosh.

Polygon-Based Modeling

The art of 3D graphics is the art of fooling the brain into thinking that it sees a 3D object painted on a flat screen. This impression is stronger or weaker depending on the way the 3D objects are represented. A good balance between fast rendering and accurate representation is achieved with models that use flat polygons as building blocks. There are hybrids that use both flat polygons and scaled sprites to give the 3D impression.

Doom, the die-hard classic, uses this technique. Just look at the bodies on the ground and notice how they somehow always point their feet at you. Other games like Descent, another die-hard classic, or classic flight simulators make use of polygon-based models to represent the 3D objects. Whether it is sprite based or polygon based doesn't matter as long as the ultimate goal is achieved: to give the impression of space.

The Polyhedron

A 3D model that is built from flat polygons connected to each other is called a polyhedron. Most 3D objects can be more or less accurately represented using polygons. The accuracy depends mainly on the number of polygons used and the general shape of the object. Figure 11-1 shows a six-sided polyhedron with eight vertices. As fancy as it may sound, it is nothing more than a simple cube.

As you can see, the shape of a cube with its flat surfaces is especially suited to be represented by a polyhedron. Most objects in the civilized world are made from flat surfaces that can be represented fairly well with a polyhedral structure. Curved objects like spheres are not as polyhedron-friendly, since either a large number of polygons would be needed to represent them accurately, or other polygon rendering techniques, like Gouraud or Phong shading, would need to be used. Both of these alternatives are out of the question, especially the latter ones, because of the limitations of Java. We must try to stick to relatively simple polyhedrons and solid color-filled polygons to come close to real-time rendering speeds.

FIGURE 11-1

◎ ◎ ◎ ◎ ◎ ◎

A simple poly-
hedron

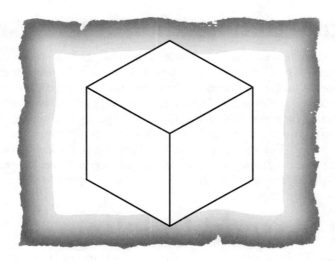

The good thing about a polyhedral structure is that it can be dissected into two components: vertices and polygons. As you can see in Figure 11-2, the vertices mark the corners
and the polygons bind the vertices together into flat surfaces.

This kind of whispers to us that we should have two classes that represent these features: an array of 3D coordinates that represents the vertices, and a polygon class that

FIGURE 11-2

◎ ◎ ◎ ◎ ◎ ◎

A dissected
polyhedron

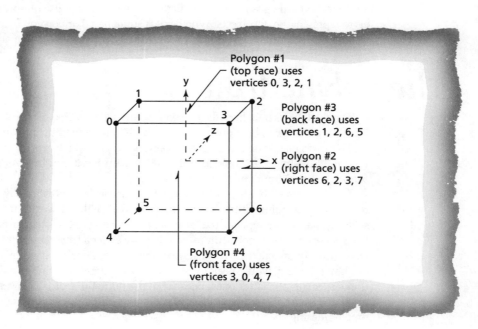

represents the faces of the polyhedron. These classes should then be used in a polyhedron class. Let's look at how these classes could be implemented.

Vertices

Taking a closer look at Figure 11-2, you should notice that polygons share vertices with each other. This means that a vertex is used in more than a single polygon, because all the polygons are connected to each other. Since a vertex is used in at least three polygons, it would be a waste of memory and calculations to let every polygon have its own 3D coordinates. Instead of eight different coordinates, we would end up with 24, out of which two-thirds are identical. Rotating the polyhedron would mean rotating three times as many vertices. That is a deadly sin. Rule #1 in the list of things that you shouldn't do is this: Don't ever make the same calculation twice.

Understanding the Structure of a Polyhedron

The structure of a polyhedron is described as a list of vertices and a list of polygons. How the polygons are defined will be described later. The vertices in Figure 11-2 can, however, be comfortably expressed using vectors. The vectors contain the coordinates of each vertex.

```
//- vertex # 0  1  2  3  4  5  6  7
double x[]={-1,-1, 1, 1,-1,-1, 1, 1}
double y[]={ 1, 1, 1, 1,-1,-1,-1,-1}
double z[]={ 1,-1,-1, 1, 1,-1,-1, 1}
```

To make life easier, we will implement a support class that encapsulates an array of 3D coordinates using three vectors of doubles. The data encapsulation is not very strict, and it can be accessed by any class in the module. The reason for this somewhat repulsive implementation is that the vertices of a polyhedron are treated and looked upon as an entity and not a bunch of independent 3D coordinates. All transforms will be applied on all vertices every time.

We will use a class with three vectors of doubles instead of an array of 3D points because such a class is effectively handled by Java. It is an implementation decision and will not affect the overall design.

Implementing an Array of 3D Points

Parts of the code shown in Listing 11-1 include reading and writing to streams, which will not be covered in this chapter. Except for the use of streams, the implementation is pretty much straightforward without any unpleasant surprises.

Listing 11-1 *An array of 3D points*

```
/**
 * A class that encapsulates an array of 3D points.
 */
class fArrayOf3dPoints extends Object {
   double x[],y[],z[];
   int npoints;
   /**
    * Constructs an array of 3d points with the supplied vectors.
    */
   fArrayOf3dPoints(double x0[],double y0[],double z0[],int n){
      x=x0; y=y0; z=z0; npoints=n;
   }
   /**
    * Constructs an empty array of 3d points with size "n"
    */
   fArrayOf3dPoints(int n){
      npoints=n;
      x=new double[n]; y=new double[n]; z=new double[n];
   }
   /**
    * construct an array of 3d points from a stream
    */
   fArrayOf3dPoints(InputStream is) throws IOException{
      fromString(is);
   }
   /**
    * ovrrides the Object method
    */
   public String toString(){
      String str=new String();
      //-- the number of vertices
      str=" "+npoints+"\n";
      //-- concat the coordinates to the string
      for(int n=0;n<npoints;n++){
         str=str+x[n]+" "+y[n]+" "+z[n]+"\n";
      }
      return str;
   }
   /**
    * Returns a clone.
    */
   fArrayOf3dPoints makeClone(){
      double xnew[],ynew[],znew[];
      System.arraycopy(x,0,xnew=new double[npoints],0,npoints);
      System.arraycopy(y,0,ynew=new double[npoints],0,npoints);
      System.arraycopy(z,0,znew=new double[npoints],0,npoints);
      return new
fArrayOf3dPoints(xnew,ynew,znew,npoints);
   }
```

```
/**
 * Reads an array from a stream
 */
void fromString(InputStream is) throws IOException {
    //-- make a stream tokenizer
    StreamTokenizer stream = new StreamTokenizer (is);
            stream.commentChar('#');

    //-- get the # points
    stream.nextToken(); npoints=(int)stream.nval;

    //-- create the vectors
    x=new double[npoints];
    y=new double[npoints];
    z=new double[npoints];

    //-- read the coordinates
    for(int n=0;n<npoints;n++){
        stream.nextToken(); x[n]=(double)stream.nval;
        stream.nextToken(); y[n]=(double)stream.nval;
        stream.nextToken(); z[n]=(double)stream.nval;
    }
 }
}
```

Polygons

Each face in a polyhedron is defined by specifying the vertices it contains in a certain order. The order is either clockwise (CW) or counterclockwise (CCW). We will use the CCW standard. The easiest way to understand what CW and CCW means is to look at Figure 11-2. Polygon #4 is the front face of the cube and it is turned toward the camera. The vertices it uses are 3, 0, 4, and 7. The numbers don't seem to have any apparent order, but there is a logic behind this arrangement. If the polyhedron is rotated in such a way that the polygon we are looking at is facing us, then its vertices will always go in a CCW fashion. Figure 11-3 illustrates this for polygon #4.

It takes a little bit of training to be able to rotate polyhedrons in your head and visualize vertices moving around, so don't worry if it feels awkward. Also notice that we indirectly use the two-dimensional representation of the polyhedron to decide if a polygon is CW or CCW.

Understanding Polygon Orientation and Visible Surface Determination

The polygons in a polyhedron are a little bit special because they can be thought to have two sides. Think of a hollow box made out of plywood sheets. The plywood sheets, like the polygons, have two sides. One is facing inward, into the box, and the other one is

FIGURE 11-3

Ⓞ Ⓞ Ⓞ Ⓞ Ⓞ Ⓞ

Polygon with its vertices defined CCW

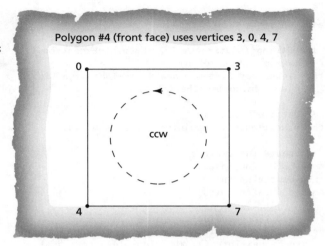

Polygon #4 (front face) uses vertices 3, 0, 4, 7

0 ——— 3

CCW

4 ——— 7

facing outward. Since the box is totally enclosed and there are no holes, we can never look inside. This means that we can never see the back side of a plywood sheet. This leads us to the conclusion that only the front sides of the plywood sheets will be visible.

We can also make an interesting observation at this point. A polygon that is facing the camera (as shown in Figure 11-4), meaning that we look at its front side, has a CCW orientation. But if the polygon is "turned" away from the camera, the orientation switches from CCW to CW. Figure 11-5 illustrates this by emphasizing polygon #4.

These facts lead us to the conclusion that a polygon can only be visible if its orientation is CCW. The next problem is to find a way of determining the orientation of a polygon with a few simple operations.

Luckily, with some linear algebra we can decide the orientation of a convex polygon with some cheap calculations. What convex means will be explained below. For now it is not important. If you know your linear algebra, then these calculations will seem simple. If you don't, just use the results in good health.

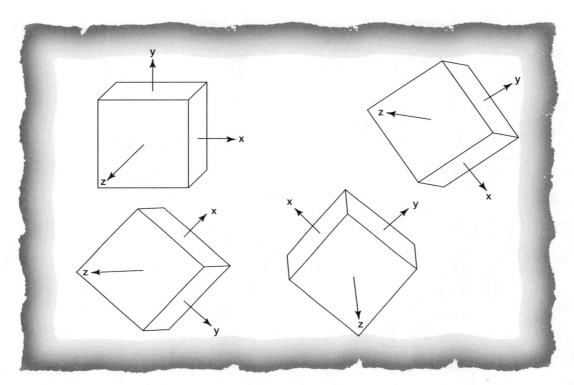

FIGURE 11-4 ⊚ *Only polygons facing the camera can be seen*

Calculating the determinant of the vectors V1 and V2 indirectly gives us the orientation in a swift and precise way. The result is the area of the parallelogram that V1 and V2 make. What is interesting, though, is the sign of the result. The sign is determined by the way that V1 and V2 are in relation to each other. The result is positive when the smallest rotation that takes V1 and places it on top of V2 is CCW, just as in cross-product. Looking at Figure 11-6, we realize that a positive result would mean that the polygon is CCW.

There are other methods of determining if a polygon is visible or not involving the polygon's normal and vector operations in 3D, but these methods are less effective for several reasons. First, the calculations are not done in two dimensions, where it really counts, and can therefore give wrong results for the border cases. Second, we would need to keep track of each polygon's normal.

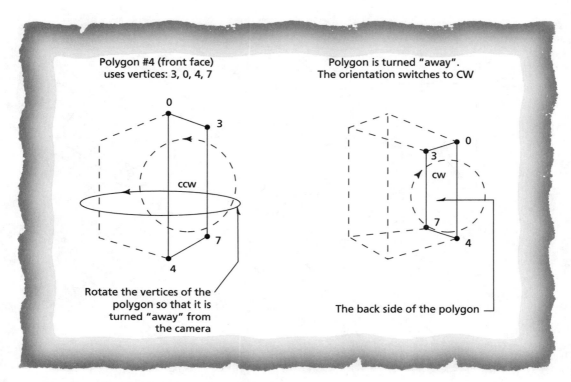

FIGURE 11-5 ◉ *A polygon switching orientations*

Implementing an Indexing Polygon (fIndexingPolygon)

We now have all we need to implement an abstract indexing polygon class. There are a few tricky details in the implementation that should be commented on. You should browse through Listing 11-2 and then read the comments below if you feel that something is unclear. This listing also contains reading and writing to streams. All the classes will have that. It is important that classes support this feature, because it automatically gives the application the ability to communicate through streams.

FIGURE 11-6

◎ ◎ ◎ ◎ ◎ ◎

Same triangle has different orientation when viewed from opposite sides

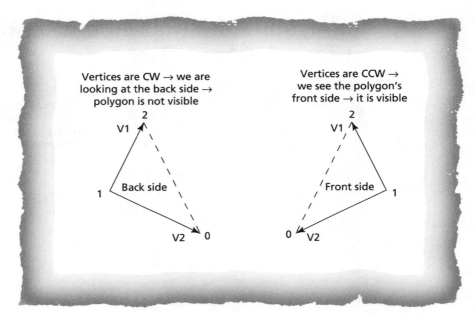

Why Is the Indexing Polygon an Abstract Class?

The fIndexingPolygon represents the abstract class of an indexing polygon and nothing more. It is not intended to be used directly "as is" but is supposed to be extended by a polygon class that implements a specialized polygon. This class will be extended by a filled polygon.

The Static "Scratch-Pad" Polygon

At some point in time we would like to render an indexing polygon, but there is no direct way of doing that. Here are some alternatives:

 Constructing an instance of Java's Polygon, rendering it and then letting the garbage collector do the rest each time we want to paint a polygon. The problem is that we will probably want to paint about 500 polygons per second, and that would mean a lot of unnecessary memory allocation and deallocation.

 Letting fIndexingPolygon extend Java's Polygon. This means that every indexing polygon will contain a copy of its two-dimensional coordinates whether they are needed or not. Keep in mind that a scene might contain hundreds of polygons, but only a fraction of them are visible. The rest will not even get past first base, and therefore their two-dimensional coordinates are totally uninteresting and would only take up RAM.

A polygon's orientation and visible surface determination

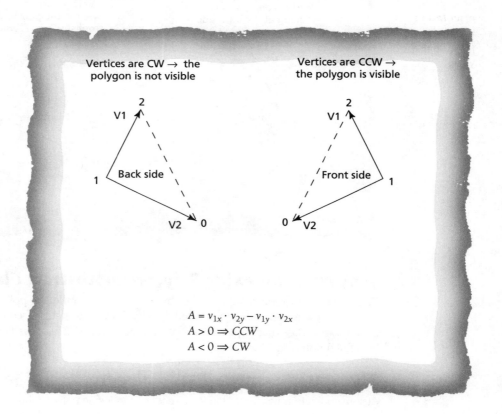

This somewhat odd problem can be effectively solved using a so-called "scratch-pad" polygon (see Figure 11-7). The scratch pad is used as a direct hook to Java's API. Anytime an indexing polygon needs to be rendered, it will "borrow" the scratch pad, fill in the screen coordinates, and then use Java's API to paint it. The reason it is declared as static is because we only need one scratch pad for all the indexing polygons. We assume that only one polygon is rendered at a time. If we have multiple threads that paint simultaneously, we must use some protection, but at this point it is not necessary.

The scratch pad can be thought of as being a common property of all instances of fIndexingPolygon. Another reason for using this method is to break any intimate contact with Java's AWT. As it is now, the scratch pad is one of the few direct links to Java's AWT.

The Abstract paint() and copyIndexedPoints() Methods

An indexing polygon doesn't contain any absolute coordinates. It has an array of integers that are indices in some list. These indices are worthless by themselves and are only useful in combination with an array of coordinates. What the paint() method needs is an array of two-dimensional coordinates so that the indexing polygon can poke out its coordinates using copyIndexedPoints() as in Figure 11-8. These coordinates are stored in the static "scratch-pad" polygon explained earlier. At this point, the scratch-pad is all set and ready to be painted using fillPolygon() or drawPolygon().

One thing that should be pointed out is that the 2D coordinates are actually the vertices of the polyhedron projected on the screen. How this is done will be explained later.

The Static orientation() Method

Once the scratch pad contains the two-dimensional coordinates, the method orientation() can be called to find out if it is CW or CCW using the calculations described earlier. This method will be used to determine if a polygon should be painted or not.

Listing 11-2 *An indexing polygon*

```
import java.awt.*;
import java.io.*;
/**
 * Describes an abstract indexing polygon.
 */
abstract class fIndexingPolygon extends Object{
   /**
    * construct a polygon with the supplied indices
    */
   protected fIndexingPolygon(int indices[],int n){
      myIndices=indices;
      nbrIndices=n;
   }
   /**
    * construct a polygon from a stream
    */
   public fIndexingPolygon(InputStream is) throws IOException {
      fromString(is);
   }
   /**
    * paints a polygon. the 2d list of coordinates must be supplied
    */
   public abstract void paint(Graphics g,int x[],int y[]);
   /**
    * read a polygon from a stream
```

continued on next page

continued from previous page

```
*/
public void fromString(InputStream is) throws IOException {
   //-- make a stream tokenizer
   StreamTokenizer stream = new StreamTokenizer (is);
   stream.commentChar('#');

   //-- get the # of indicies in this polygon
   stream.nextToken(); nbrIndices=(int)stream.nval;
   //-- allocate the vector
   myIndices=new int[nbrIndices];
   //-- read all indices
   for(int i=0;i<nbrIndices;i++){
       stream.nextToken(); myIndices[i]=(int)stream.nval;
   }
}
/**
 * make a string representation of a polygon
 */
public String toString(){
```

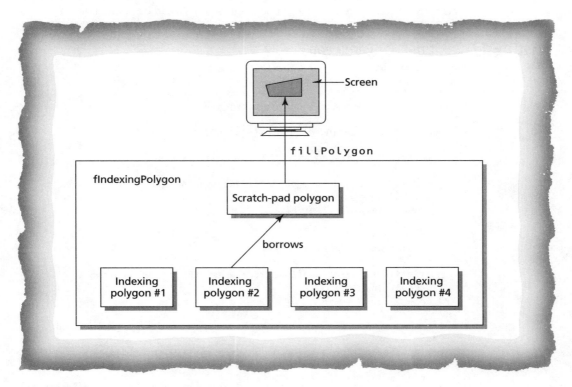

FIGURE 11-7 ◉ *Using a scratch pad as a hook to Java API*

FIGURE 11-8

◎ ◎ ◎ ◎ ◎ ◎

Poking the screen coordinates

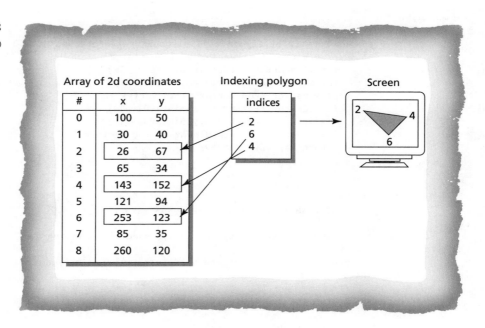

```
    String str=new String();
    str=str+nbrIndices;
    for(int n=0;n<nbrIndices;n++){
        str=str+" "+myIndices[n];
    }
    return str;
}
/**
 * pokes out the 2d coordinates and stores them into the
 * scratch polygon.
 */
protected void copyIndexedPoints(int x[],int y[]){
    for(int n=0;n<nbrIndices;n++){
        int i=myIndices[n];
        ourScratchPoly.xpoints[n]=x[i];
        ourScratchPoly.ypoints[n]=y[i];
    }
    ourScratchPoly.npoints=nbrIndices;
}
/**
 * determine the orientation of the scratch polygon.
 * if the result is positive then it is CW.
 */
protected static int orientation() {
```

continued on next page

continued from previous page

```
        int
p1x=ourScratchPoly.xpoints[1],p1y=ourScratchPoly.ypoints[1];
        //-- vector from vertex #1 to vertex #2
        int v1x=ourScratchPoly.xpoints[2]-p1x;
        int v1y=ourScratchPoly.ypoints[2]-p1y;
        //-- vector from vertex #1 to vertex #0
        int v2x=ourScratchPoly.xpoints[0]-p1x;
        int v2y=ourScratchPoly.ypoints[0]-p1y;
        //-- return the determinant of the vectors
        return v1x*v2y-v2x*v1y;
    }
    /**
     * make a clone of this polygon
     */
    public abstract fIndexingPolygon makeClone();
    /**
     * the "scratch" polygon that is used for painting
     */
    protected static Polygon ourScratchPoly=new Polygon(new int[50],new
int[50],50);
    /**
     * the indices that define this polygon
     */
    protected int myIndices[];
    /**
     * number of indices in this polygon.
     */
    protected int nbrIndices;
}
```

We now have an abstract polygon class that describes the key elements of a polygon, but the polygon doesn't know how to paint itself. It is time to extend the indexing polygon with a class that knows how to do that.

Implementing a Filled Polygon

The filled polygon is an extension of the indexing polygon. It implements the paint() method and contains one additional piece of data: its color. A couple of things should be said about the implementation.

The paint() Method

This method is called with an array of 2D screen coordinates supplied by the caller. The first thing that is done is to prepare the scratch-pad polygon by poking out the absolute coordinates. The second step is to check the orientation using the method with the same name. We know that if the orientation is CW, then the polygon is not visible and therefore no further action is taken. If the orientation is CCW, then the scratch-pad will be rendered using the Java API.

It might seem strange that this check is done in the polygon's paint() method, but remember that the fIndexingPolygon is tailor-made to be used in polyhedrons and it is very well aware of that.

Listing 11-3 *The filled polygon, an extension of indexing polygon*

```java
import java.awt.*;
/**
 * A solid color polygon.
 */
class fFilledPolygon extends fIndexingPolygon {
  /**
   * The color of this polygon.
   */
  protected fColor myColor;
  /**
   * Create a polygon with the supplied data.
   */
  public fFilledPolygon(int indices[],int n,fColor color){
    super(indices,n);
    myColor=color;
  }
/**
 * Create a polygon from a stream.
 */
public fFilledPolygon(InputStream is) throws IOException {
  super(is);
}
/**
 * paints the polygon if it is cw
 */
public void paint(Graphics g,int x[],int y[]){
  //-- copy the indexed coordinates from the 2d list to
  //-- the scratch-pad
  copyIndexedPoints(x,y);
  render(g);
}
/**
  * The actual rendering.
  */
protected void render(Graphics g){
  //-- check orientation
  if(orientation()>0){
    g.setColor(myColor.getColor());
    g.fillPolygon(ourScratchPoly);
  }
}

/**
```

continued on next page

continued from previous page

```
          * overrides fIndexingPolygon.toString()
          * the color must also be written to the string.
          */
         public String toString(){
            //-- make the string for fIndexingPolygon
            String str=super.toString();
            //-- add the color and line break
            str=str+" "+myColor.toString()+"\n";
            return str;
         }
         /**
          * overrides fIndexingPolygon.toString()
          * the color must also be read from the stream.
          */
         public void fromString(InputStream is) throws IOException {
            super.fromString(is);
            //-- read the color
            myColor=new fColor(is);
         }
         /**
           * Makes a clone of this polygon.
          */
            public fIndexingPolygon makeClone(){
               int i[];
               System.arraycopy(myIndices,O,i=new int[nbrIndices],O,nbrIndices);
               return new fFilledPolygon(i,nbrIndices,myColor.makeClone());
            }
         }
```

The fColor Class

The fColor class wraps Java's Color. The implementation, shown in Listing 11-4, is pretty much straightforward and needs no further comments. The reason that this class exists is to break intimate contact with Java's AWT.

Listing 11-4 *A wrap-around for Java's Color*

```
         import java.awt.*;
         import java.io.*;
         /**
          * Wraps Java's color
          */
         public class fColor extends Object {
            public int r,g,b;
            protected Color myBaseColor;

            /**
             * construct a color with the RGB supplied.
             */
```

```
    public fColor(int r0,int g0,int b0){
        r=r0; g=g0; b=b0;
        myBaseColor=new Color(r,g,b);
    }
    /**
     * constructs a color from a stream
     */
    public fColor(InputStream is) throws IOException{
        fromString(is);
    }

    /**
     * returns the base color
     */
    public Color getColor(){
        return myBaseColor;
}
    /**
     * read the color from a stream
     */
    public void fromString(InputStream is) throws IOException{
        //-- make a stream tokenizer
        StreamTokenizer stream = new StreamTokenizer (is);
        stream.commentChar('#');

        //-- read the RGB triple
        stream.nextToken(); r=(int)stream.nval;
        stream.nextToken(); g=(int)stream.nval;
        stream.nextToken(); b=(int)stream.nval;
    }
    /**
     * make a string representation
     */
    public String toString(){
        return new String(" "+r+" "+g+" "+b+" ");
    }
    /**
     * Makes a clone of this color.
     */
    public fColor makeClone(){
        return new fColor(r,g,b);
    }
}
```

We now have all the classes we need to describe a polyhedron. The next step is to look at how it should be implemented.

Implementing the Polyhedron Class

Now that all support classes have been implemented, we can put them together and make the abstract polyhedron class (see Listing 11-5). There are some comments that should be made, though.

The Abstract paint() Method

The paint() method is now called with an array of two-dimensional coordinates as an argument. The array contains the polyhedron's vertices projected to the screen. Projection will be explained later.

The paint() method used here is abstract and must be implemented in an extension. The reason for this is that some types of polyhedrons are especially easy to paint, and we wouldn't want to miss the chance of using this.

Reading and Writing Polyhedrons from/to Streams

Since every support class implements the toString() and fromString() methods, a polyhedron can be transparently constructed from a stream. We now have a way of storing and retrieving 3D models.

Listing 11-5 *The abstract polyhedron class*

```
import java.awt.*;
import java.io.*;
/**
 * A polyhedron class that is made out of a list of vertices
 * and a list of indexing polygons.
 */
abstract class fPolyhedron extends Object {
   //-- the 3d coordinates for the model
   protected fArrayOf3dPoints myVertices;
   //-- the polygons
   protected fIndexingPolygon myPolygons[];
   protected int nbrPolygons;
   /**
    * construct a polyhedron with the supplied vertices and polygons.
    */
   protected fPolyhedron(fArrayOf3dPoints points,fIndexingPolygon
polys[],int npolys){
      myVertices=points;
      myPolygons=polys;
      nbrPolygons=npolys;
   }
   /**
    * construct a polyhedron from a stream.
    */
   protected fPolyhedron(InputStream is) throws IOException {
      fromString(is);
```

```
   }
   /**
    * paint the polyhedron using the supplied 2d coordinates.
    */
   public abstract void paint(Graphics g,fArrayOf2dPoints point2d);
   /**
    * make a string representation of this polyhedron
    */
   public String toString(){
      String str=new String();
      //-- make the array of 3d points into a stream
      str=myVertices.toString();
      //-- write to stream how many polygons there are
      str=str+nbrPolygons+"\n";
      //-- write all polygons to the stream
      for(int n=0;n<nbrPolygons;n++){
         str=str+myPolygons[n].toString();
      }
      return str;
   }
   /**
    * read the polyhedron from a stream
    */
   public void fromString(InputStream is) throws IOException {
      //-- make a stream tokenizer
      StreamTokenizer stream = new StreamTokenizer (is);
      stream.commentChar('#');

      //-- get the points
      myVertices=new fArrayOf3dPoints(is);
      //-- get the # polygons
      stream.nextToken(); nbrPolygons=(int)stream.nval;
      //-- create the vector
      myPolygons=new fIndexingPolygon[nbrPolygons];
      //-- read each polygon
      for(int n=0;n<nbrPolygons;n++){
         myPolygons[n]=new fFilledPolygon(is);
      }
   }

   public fArrayOf3dPoints getVertices(){
      return myVertices;
   }
}
```

A Two-Dimensional Point Array

The class fArrayOf2dPoints, shown in Listing 11-6, is used because it is a convenient way of shuffling vectors around. It is quite simple and no further comments are needed.

Listing 11-6 *The array of two-dimensional points*

```
class fArrayOf2dPoints extends Object {
   int x[],y[];
   int npoints;

   fArrayOf2dPoints(int x0[],int y0[],int n){
      x=x0; y=y0; npoints=n;
   }
}
```

The Convex Polyhedron and Polygon Sorting

Although a polyhedron can look just about any way you can imagine, we will restrict ourselves to convex polyhedrons for now. The general shape of a convex polyhedron brings some benefits that we simply cannot ignore.

What Does Convex Mean?

Explaining what convex means is easier done in two dimensions by first looking at a polygon, as shown in Figure 11-9. Imagine that each vertex in a polygon is a spike on a plank, and the outline of the polygon is drawn on the plank. Now imagine that an elastic band is placed around the spikes. If the outline of the polygon matches the elastic band, then the polygon is convex. Otherwise it is concave or complex.

This way of thinking can be generalized to 3D, but instead of using an elastic band, you could think of using an elastic surface, as shown in Figure 11-10. If all faces in the polyhedron touch the elastic surface, then it is convex.

For example, a cube, sphere, cone, or cylinder is convex, while a torus is nonconvex. The doughnutlike shape of the torus would leave a hole in the middle if it was covered with an elastic surface.

The Advantages of Using Convex Polyhedrons

Before they are rendered, the polygons in a polyhedron have to be sorted so that the polygon nearest the camera is rendered last. This must be done to ensure that the polyhedron is rendered properly; otherwise, surfaces that are visible may be rendered in the wrong order, and that can ruin your whole day. This is called the painter's algorithm and is the simplest of the bunch.

FIGURE 11-9
◎ ◎ ◎ ◎ ◎ ◎
A convex and a nonconvex polygon

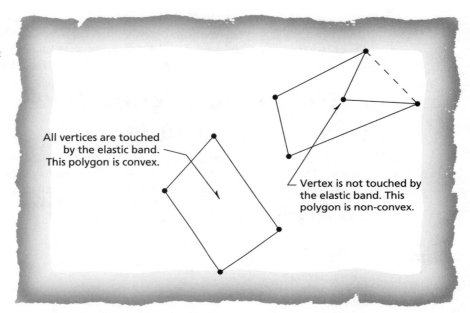

All vertices are touched by the elastic band. This polygon is convex.

Vertex is not touched by the elastic band. This polygon is non-convex.

FIGURE 11-10
◎ ◎ ◎ ◎ ◎ ◎
A convex and a nonconvex polyhedron

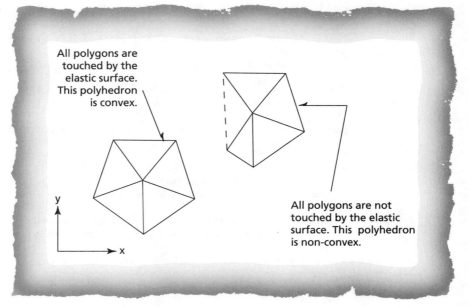

All polygons are touched by the elastic surface. This polyhedron is convex.

All polygons are not touched by the elastic surface. This polyhedron is non-convex.

Polygons in a convex polyhedron don't have to be sorted before they are rendered because two visible surfaces never overlap each other. Throwing away the polygons that do not face the camera and rendering the rest is enough to produce a proper rendering. This makes the process very effective and pretty much straightforward.

Implementing a Convex Polyhedron (fConvexPolyhedron)

The only thing that a convex polyhedron (shown in Listing 11-7) is doing is implementing the paint() method, which is abstract in its superclass, the fPolyhedron.

The paint() method calls all its polygons and instructs them to paint themselves. A convex polyhedron doesn't need to sort the polygons, so it is pretty much a matter of going through the list and calling the paint() method.

Listing 11-7 The convex polyhedron

```
import java.io.*;
import java.awt.*;

public class fConvexPolyhedron extends fPolyhedron {
   /**
    * construct a polyhedron with the supplied data.
    */
   public fConvexPolyhedron(fArrayOf3dPoints points,fIndexingPolygon
polys[],int npolys){
      super(points,polys,npolys);
   }
   /**
    * construct a polyhedron from a stream.
    */
   public fConvexPolyhedron(InputStream is) throws IOException   {
      super(is);
   }
   /**
    * overrides fPolyhedron.paint(..)
    * the polygons don't need to be sorted.
    */
   public void paint(Graphics g,fArrayOf2dPoints point2d){
      //-- the polygons don't have to be sorted, simply paint them
      for(int n=0;n<nbrPolygons;n++){
         myPolygons[n].paint(g,point2d.x,point2d.y);
      }
   }
}
```

The Classes Used So Far

We now have all the classes we need to completely describe a convex polyhedron. We could also theoretically paint the polyhedron if the vertices were transformed to screen coordinates and then the paint() method was called. The first stage is now completed. It is now time to move on to the second stage: the 3D pipeline. But before we do that, let's reflect on what we have achieved so far, as shown in Figure 11-11.

We have an abstract class fPolyhedron that contains an array of 3D coordinates and an array of fIndexingPolygons. This abstract inner core describes pretty much the structure of a polyhedron but cannot be used as it is because several methods are declared as abstract. The reason for this is that the painting procedure differs depending on the type of polyhedrons and polygons used. The class fConvexPolyhedron extends fPolyhedron and implements the paint() method, which in the case of an convex polyhedron is exceptionally simple.

FIGURE 11-11

◎ ◎ ◎ ◎ ◎ ◎

The classes used so far

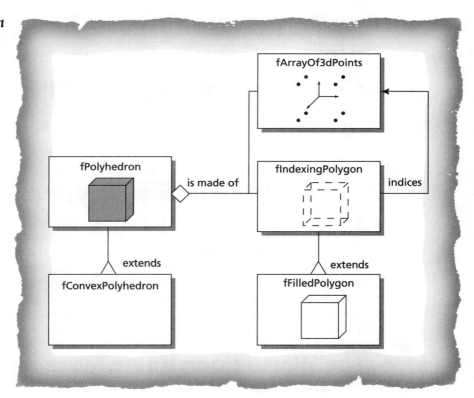

The abstract indexing polygon is extended to fFilledPolygon, which implements the paint() method. The fFilledPolygon, knowing that it is part of a polyhedron, first checks its orientation before rendering. Since all the polygons are defined CCW, the polygon can decide if it is visible or not by simply checking its orientation using the method with the same name.

Constructing a Simple 3D Pipeline

The process of rendering a 3D scene can be divided into several discrete steps, also referred to as the 3D pipeline. In this pipeline a polyhedron's vertices will be transformed several times and then ultimately projected to the screen. At this point, the paint() method can be called with the resulting two-dimensional coordinates, and a polyhedron can render itself.

Let's examine a simple 3D pipeline that assumes that all polyhedrons in a scene are visible, just to get acquainted with the different transforms. In a more complex pipeline, we would try to exclude as many objects as possible before they even get inside the pipeline, so that no unnecessary calculations are done. There are some really good methods of doing that.

The Four Coordinate Systems

The 3D pipeline involves transforming an object from one coordinate system to another. These coordinate systems only exist in the mathematical world and can be explained with equations. I will try to give a more down-to-earth explanation by using a parallel.

The Model Coordinate System (MCS)

Think of an architect sitting at his desk drawing a house. See Figure 11-12. Imagine that he is using a sheet of paper with a coordinate system that is conveniently centered somewhere in the middle of the building. The building that he is drawing is also suitably scaled down so that it fits on the paper. This scaled-down representation is created in the model coordinate system (MCS), so-called because that is where the model is defined.

There are no real strict guidelines on how MCS should be defined. One thing that we should keep in mind is that all rotations will be done about the principal axes in MCS, so it is a good idea to try to put the origin of the MCS in the middle of the object.

The World Coordinate System (WCS)

The house that the architect is designing will eventually be built in a small town. This small town has decided that it needs to have its own coordinate system, and that the origin is in the middle of the town hall, with the x-axis going east and y-axis going north, as in Figure 11-13. Let's call this the world coordinate system (WCS). The house will be built at an exact coordinate in the WCS. The building will also be scaled, because nobody wants to live in a 10-inch by 20-inch house.

FIGURE 11-12

◎ ◎ ◎ ◎ ◎ ◎

A building in MCS

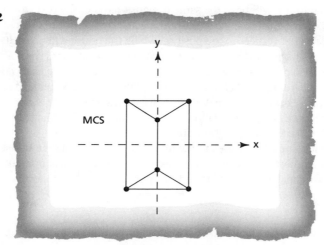

FIGURE 11-13

◎ ◎ ◎ ◎ ◎ ◎

The building placed in the WCS

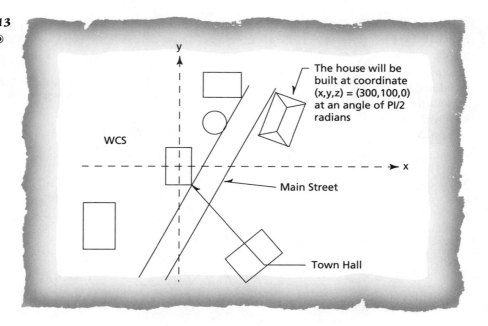

One day the architect gets the idea to calculate the exact coordinates that the vertices of his model will have in the real world. He knows the exact position where his house will be built and also the angle with respect to the town hall. So he enters the magic world of math. He takes his blueprint to the town hall and places it so that the axis in the MCS coincides with the axis in the WCS. He then recalculates the vertices by first scaling them so that the house will have the same dimensions as in the real world. Next he rotates the vertices by the same angle as the house will be rotated with respect to the WCS. Then he translates the vertices to the position where the house will be built. The coordinates resulting from these calculations are saved, and he waits until the construction work is done. He then checks the calculated vertices and measures the exact coordinates of each corner in the real house. Behold, they are exactly identical. What he does is in fact a series of transforms as discussed in Appendix E, 3D Transforms. At this point you should be acquainted with matrix operation. If you aren't, just take the results for given. Figure 11-14 shows the results of the architect's calculations.

Let's pick one single vertex in the MCS and call it v, and then transform it from MCS to WCS. Mathematically this can be expressed using matrix operations in the following way (the matrixes can be found in Appendix E, 3D Transforms):

$$v_{WCS} = T \cdot R \cdot S \cdot v_{MCS}$$

Using the generic matrix class implemented in Appendix E, this series of transforms can be coded like this:

FIGURE 11-14

◉ ◉ ◉ ◉ ◉ ◉

The town populated by 3D models, each with its own MCS

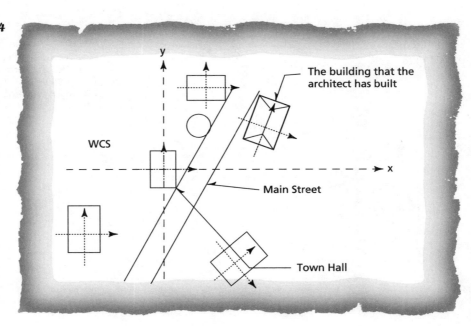

```
//-- transform the vertices from MCS to WCS
matrix.makeIdentity();           //-- make the identity matrix
matrix.concatS(Sx,Sy,Sz);        //-- scaling
matrix.concatRx(Ax);             //-- rotate about X-axis
matrix.concatRy(Ay);             //-- rotate about Y-axis
matrix.concatRz(Az);             //-- rotate about Z-axis
matrix.concatT(Xpos,Ypos,Zpos); //-- translate
matrix.transform(Vm,Vw);         //-- transform points
```

This series of transforms can be called the MCS to WCS transform. Since this is a tedious procedure, we will expand the generic matrix and hide these transforms in a convenient method called makeMCStoWCStransform(...). This way all the math will be hidden and make the code into a math-free zone.

After our architect discovers that he can mathematically transform vertices from MCS to WCS, he gets all carried away and wonders how his house would look if somebody took a picture of it from an arbitrary angle and position. He knows the position of the camera in WCS and also its orientation (angle). Figure 11-15 illustrates this.

The View Coordinate System (VCS)

Since the camera is now the center of attention, we could think of its position as the center of the universe. The direction of the principal axes depends on the angle of the camera.

FIGURE 11-15

◎ ◎ ◎ ◎ ◎ ◎

The camera has a position and angle in the world

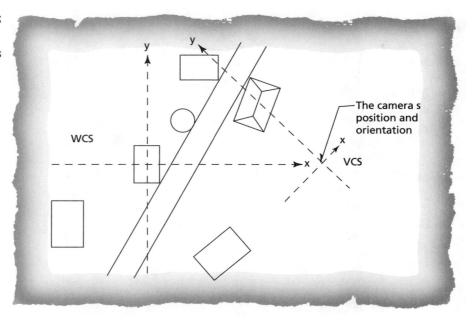

Suppose that the architect has all the coordinates defined in WCS. The same vertices will not have the same coordinates in the VCS. This is realized by comparing a vertex with the principal axes of WCS and VCS. What he needs to do is to somehow calculate the coordinates of the vertices with respect to the VCS as in Figure 11-16.

This transformation is not as intuitive as the MCS to WCS transform but is actually closely related to it. Mathematically the matrix can be calculated by first making the MCS to WCS matrix and then calculating its inverse. This would, however, take a massive amount of calculations, so we must find a simpler method.

The inverse can be constructed using the generic 3D matrix with the following code:

```
//-- make a matrix that transforms a vertex from WCS to VCS
matrix.makeIdentity();
matrix.concatT(-Xpos,-Ypos,-Zpos);
matrix.concatRz(-Az);
matrix.concatRy(-Ay);
matrix.concatRx(-Ax);
//-- transform the vertices from WCS to VCS
matrix.transform(Vw,Vm);
```

These operations will be "hidden" inside a method called makeWCStoVCStransform(..) in the extended generic matrix. The implementation will be shown later. Just keep in mind that you don't necessarily need to know the math behind these transforms to use them.

FIGURE 11-16

◎ ◎ ◎ ◎ ◎ ◎

Vertices have different coordinates in VCS than in WCS

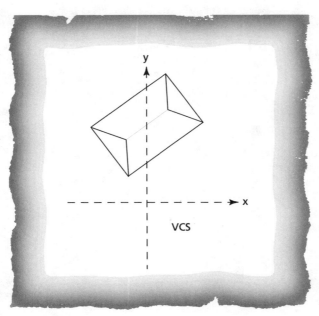

Projecting 3D Points on a Plane

Projection means transforming 3D coordinates to a 2D plane. It is not as tedious as it sounds. All the 3D figures that you have seen thus far are actually 3D figures projected on a piece of paper. The software in our head can see the depth of a flat picture if it contains enough information. To help our brain "see" the depth without straining it too much, it is helpful to include objects that we know from real life, shade the polygons depending on the light source, and include shadows. A wire-frame model, for example, contains very little depth information, because we have no way of knowing which lines are in front of which. If you look at Figure 11-17 long enough, you will see what I mean.

The art of 3D graphics is to pack so much information in a picture that the brain immediately perceives the depth. What you might not be aware of is that every time you look at a picture, your brain makes a massive number of calculations in order to approximate distances and perceive the depth, especially if the picture is taken in some environment unfamiliar to us. Fortunately, all the calculations are done "behind the scenes" without our noticing. For example, try driving your car on small streets with one eye closed. You will need to concentrate much harder, since the brain will start a "thread" that does all the calculation necessary to compensate for the loss of 3D sight. At this point you still have a perfectly rendered picture updated at 25 frames per second. Think of the problems you would have if you started blinking 10 times a second and were driving at noon, when there are no shadows, on a winding mountain road. You would probably end up over the side.

FIGURE 11-17

◎ ◎ ◎ ◎ ◎ ◎

Wire-frame models contain very little depth information

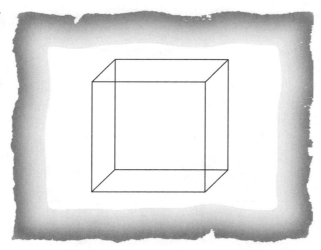

One necessary piece of information that we definitely need to approximate distances is that objects are perceived as being smaller as they get farther away. This is the way we are used to seeing the world, and this kind of projection is called perspective projection. Although there are lots of ways to make projections, this type is the most useful to us, since it is the one that most closely resembles reality.

The Screen Coordinate System (SCS)

What makes this transform different from the others we have examined is that it cannot be expressed with a matrix operation.—at least not completely. The reason for this is that it is not a linear transform.

The projection of 3D points to a two-dimensional plane can be theoretically done from an arbitrary angle and position, but it is most effectively done when the vertices are in the VCS. This is one of the few reasons that we do the WCS to VCS transformation.

The 3D coordinates are projected on a two-dimensional plane called the view plane, which in our case is the screen shown in Figure 11-18. The coordinate system that defines the screen is called the screen coordinate system (SCS), shown in Figure 11-19.

The amount of perspective depends on the distance of the view plane from the origin of the VCS. The smaller the distance, the more exaggerated the perspective, because the distance indirectly determines the view angle. Beyond a certain value, the projection will be so exaggerated that the objects will be distorted.

FIGURE 11-18

⊚ ⊚ ⊚ ⊚ ⊚ ⊚

Projection of a 3D coordinate on a view plane

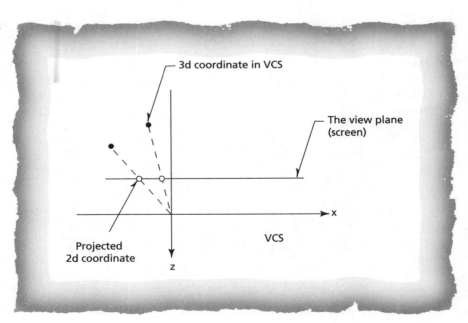

FIGURE 11-19

⊙ ⊙ ⊙ ⊙ ⊙ ⊙

The screen coordinate system (SCS)

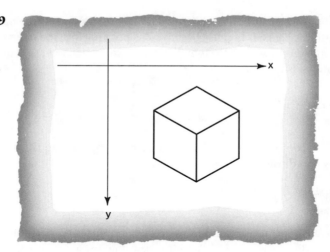

The math behind perspective projection is based on Figure 11-20 which gives us the following equation:

$$\frac{X_{VCS}}{X_{SCS}} = \frac{-Z_{VCS}}{ScrDist}$$

FIGURE 11-20

⊙ ⊙ ⊙ ⊙ ⊙ ⊙

The projection can be calculated using triangles

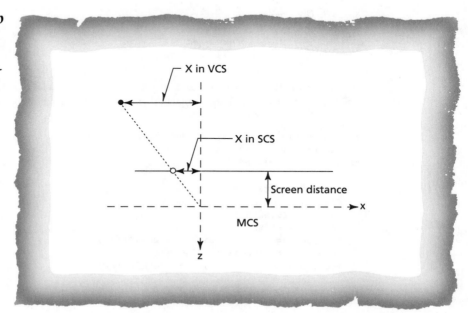

Notice that Z is negative. If it weren't, then the projection would be mirrored along the z-axis. All this hassle is because negative Z is pointing into the screen.

The only unknown and the term that we are interested in in the equation is *Xscreen*. The equation is rewritten:

$$X_{SCS} = ScrDist \cdot \frac{X_{VCS}}{-Z_{VCS}}$$

The *Yscs* coordinate is calculated using almost the same equations but now involving the y coordinate instead of the x:

$$Y_{SCS} = ScrDist \cdot \frac{Y_{VCS}}{Z_{VCS}}$$

Notice that Z is *not* negative in this equation. This is because the y-axis in the SCS is pointing downward while in VCS it is pointing upward. If Z were negated, then we would have a projection that is mirrored along the x-axis.

One more problem is that the *Xscs* and *Yscs* will have (x,y)= (0,0) as origin and can even be negative. But the SCS has its origin in the top-left corner. What we have to do is move the origin to the middle of the screen. This implies that we should translate the resulting x and y values by half the screen width and half the screen height, respectively. The resulting equations would be:

$$X_{SCS} = ScrDist \cdot \frac{X_{VCS}}{-Z_{VCS}} + \frac{ScreenWidth}{2}$$

$$Y_{SCS} = ScrDist \cdot \frac{Y_{VCS}}{Z_{VCS}} + \frac{ScreenHeight}{2}$$

This transform, the final one in the chain, can be coded using a *for* loop that goes through all the coordinates in VCS and projects them to SCS in the following way:

```
..
//-- calculate the center of the screen
int x0=ScreenWidth>>1;
int y0=ScreenWidth>>1;
..
for(int n=0; n<pts; n++){
    //-- copy the z value
    double z=Zview[n];
    //-- project the X-coordiante
    Xscreen[n]=-(int)(ScrDist*Xview[n]/z)+x0;
    //-- project the Y-coordiante
    Yscreen[n]= (int)(ScrDist*Yview[n]/z)+y0;
}
..
```

As you see when the dust clears, we end up with a few lines of simple code. This is only because the 3D coordinates were in the VCS, which simplified the projection stage. As I mentioned earlier, the projection can be done using vertices in the WCS, but it would be more complicated. In fact we would just "hide" the WCS to VCS transform in the equations. The gains would not be very dramatic.

◾ Projecting a 3D Point on the Screen

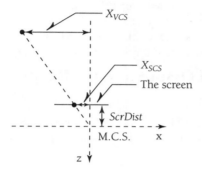

$$X_{SCS} = ScrDist \cdot \frac{X_{VCS}}{-Z_{VCS}} + \frac{ScreenWidth}{2}$$

$$Y_{SCS} = ScrDist \cdot \frac{Y_{VCS}}{Z_{VCS}} + \frac{ScreenHeight}{2}$$

It is now time to implement a class that can do the projection and the WCS to VCS transform transparently, so that from now on you can forget the math.

The Camera

The camera has a very important role. It will transform a set of WCS vertices through the VCS and then project them to SCS. A caller can feed the camera with an array of 3D points, and in return it gets to "borrow" an array of two-dimensional coordinates. This array will be used to call the paint() method of an fPolyhedron. And with this array, we have completed the chain of transformations.

The camera can have any position and orientation. Just place it in the WCS and tell it which direction to look.

Implementing a Generic Camera (fGenericCamera)

A few details in the implementation need to be discussed before we study the code for the fGenericCamera (Listing 11-8).

The Static Buffers

The static buffer of 3D coordinates is used for storing the VCS vertices before the projection. It is static because only one camera at a time will use it.

The static buffer of two-dimensional coordinates is used for projection. It will be "borrowed" to the caller so that it can use it for rendering the polyhedrons.

Calculating Screen Distance with Respect to the View Angle

When constructing a camera, the view angle has to be specified. Using this argument and the width of the screen, we can calculate the screen distance with a trigonometric operation, as in Figure 11-21.

FIGURE 11-21

◉ ◉ ◉ ◉ ◉ ◉

Calculating the screen distance

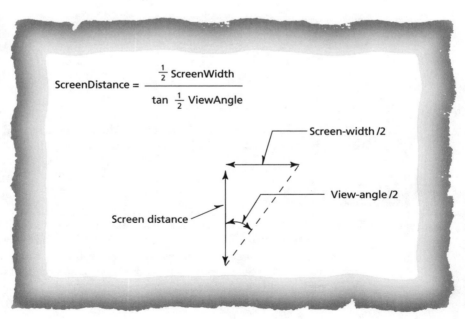

$$\text{ScreenDistance} = \frac{\frac{1}{2} \text{ ScreenWidth}}{\tan \frac{1}{2} \text{ ViewAngle}}$$

Screen-width /2

View-angle /2

Screen distance

The Private updateMatrix() Method

Every time the position or orientation changes, the transformation matrix is marked as "dirty." The updateMatrix() method checks to see if the matrix is dirty, and if it is, it is recalculated.

The project() Method

The project() method is fed with an array of 3D coordinates from the WCS. The coordinates will be transformed to the VCS and then projected into the 2D buffer. The 2D buffer will be returned from the method so that the caller can use it.

Listing 11-8 *A very generic camera*

```
/**
 * A generic camera.
 */
public class fGenericCamera extends Object {
   //-- a temporary buffer used for projection
      protected static fArrayOf2dPoints our2dBuffer=
               new fArrayOf2dPoints(new int[100],new int[100],100);
   //-- a temporary buffer used for WCS to VCS transform
   protected static fArrayOf3dPoints our3dBuffer=
               new fArrayOf3dPoints(new double[100],new double[100],new
double[100],100);
      //-- the screen distance
      protected double screendist;
      //-- screen origo
      protected int x0,y0;
      //-- the viewangle
      protected double myViewAngle;
      //-- the matrix used for the WCS to VCS tranform
      fMatrix3d myWCStoVCSmatrix;
      //-- mark if the matrix is dirty
      boolean matrixIsDirty;
      //-- the position and angle of the camera in WCS
      fPoint3d myPosition;
      fAngle3d myAngle;

   /**
    * constructs a camera by specifying the width, height and viewangle
    */
      public fGenericCamera(int width,int height,double viewAngle){
            myViewAngle=viewAngle;
            //-- calculate the screen origo
            x0=width>>1; y0=height>>1;
            //-- calculate the screen distance
            screendist=(double)x0/(Math.tan(viewAngle/2));
            //-- construct the matrix
```

continued on next page

continued from previous page

```
                                myWCStoVCSmatrix=new fMatrix3d();
                                //--
                                myPosition=new fPoint3d();
                                myAngle=new fAngle3d();
                                matrixIsDirty=true;
                        }
                        /**
                        * sets the position and angle of the camera.
                         */
                        public void setOrientation(fPoint3d pos,fAngle3d agl){
                                if(myPosition.equals(pos)==false){
                                myPosition.set(pos);
                                matrixIsDirty=true;
                                }
                                if(myAngle.equals(agl)==false){
                                        myAngle.set(agl);
                                        matrixIsDirty=true;
                                }
                        }
                        /**
                        * projects an array of 3d points to the temporary 2d buffer
                        */
                        public fArrayOf2dPoints project(fArrayOf3dPoints p3d){
                            //-- updates the matrix if it needed
                            updateMatrix();
                            //-- transform the WCS vertices to VCS storing the results
                            //-- in a buffer
                                    myWCStoVCSmatrix.transform(p3d,our3dBuffer);
                                    //-- project the VCS coordiantes to SCS storing the results
                                    //-- in a buffer
                                    for(int n=0;n<p3d.npoints;n++){
                                    double z=our3dBuffer.z[n];
                            our2dBuffer.x[n]=-(int)(screendist*our3dBuffer.x[n]/z)+x0;
                            our2dBuffer.y[n]= (int)(screendist*our3dBuffer.y[n]/z)+y0;
                            }
                            //-- lend the buffer to the caller.
                            return our2dBuffer;
                        }
                        /**
                         * updates the matrix
                         */
                        private void updateMatrix(){
                            if(matrixIsDirty==true){
                                //-- only remake the matrix if it is "dirty"
                                myWCStoVCSmatrix.makeWCStoVCStransform(myPosition,myAngle);
                                matrixIsDirty=false;
                            }
                        }
                }
```

Implementing the 3D Point Class (fPoint3d)

To make the handling of 3D coordinates smoother, a 3D point class is introduced in Listing 11-9. There are no surprises in this class, and it needs no further comments.

Listing 11-9 *The fPoint3d class*

```
public class fPoint3d{
    public double x;
    public double y;
    public double z;
    public fPoint3d (double x0, double y0, double z0) {
         x=x0; y=y0; z=z0;
    }

    public fPoint3d () {
         x=y=z=0;
    }

    boolean equals (fPoint3d p) {
         return (p.x==x)&&(p.y==y)&&(p.z==z);
    }

    void set (fPoint3d p) {
         x=p.x; y=p.y; z=p.z;
    }
}
```

Implementing the 3D Angle Class (fAngle3d)

The fAngle3d class, shown in Listing 11-10, simplifies the handling of 3D angles. The x, y, z values contain the angle of rotation about the principal axes.

Listing 11-10 *The fAngle3d class*

```
public class fAngle3d{
    double x;
    double y;
    double z;
    fAngle3d (double x0, double y0, double z0) {
        x=x0; y=y0; z=z0;
    }
```

continued on next page

continued from previous page

```
        fAngle3d () {
            x=y=z=0;
        }

        fAngle3d (fAngle3d a) {
            x=a.x; y=a.y; z=a.z;
        }

        boolean equals (fAngle3d a) {
            return (a.x==x)&&(a.y==y)&&(a.z==z);
        }

        void set (fAngle3d a) {
            x=a.x; y=a.y; z=a.z;
        }
    }
```

Implementing the 3D Matrix Class (fMatrix3d)

The generic 3D matrix, fGeneric3dMatrix, from Appendix E, 3D Transforms, only contains the basic transforms such as scaling, rotation, and translation. The extension of the generic matrix, fMatrix3d, shown in Listing 11-11, simply "hides" the actual series of transforms by introducing new methods.

Listing 11-11 *The fMatrix3d class*

```
/**
 * A 3d matrix that hides the making of the different
 * transforms
 */
class fMatrix3d extends fGeneric3dMatrix {
    /**
     * construct the matrix
     */
    public fMatrix3d(){
        super();
    }
    /**
     * let matrix contain the MCS to WCS transform
     */
    public void makeMCStoWCStransform(fPoint3d pos,fAngle3d agl,fPoint3d
scale){
        makeIdentity();
        concatS(scale.x,scale.y,scale.z);
        concatRx(agl.x);
        concatRy(agl.y);
        concatRz(agl.z);
        concatT(pos.x,pos.y,pos.z);
```

```
   }
   /**
    * let matrix contain the MCS to WCS transform, without scaling
    */
   public void makeMCStoWCStransform(fPoint3d pos,fAngle3d agl){
      makeIdentity();
      concatRx(agl.x);
      concatRy(agl.y);
      concatRz(agl.z);
      concatT(pos.x,pos.y,pos.z);
   }
   /**
    * let matrix contain the WCS to MCS transform
    */
   public void makeWCStoVCStransform(fPoint3d pos,fAngle3d agl){
      makeIdentity();
      concatT(-pos.x,-pos.y,-pos.z);
      concatRz(-agl.z);
      concatRy(-agl.y);
      concatRx(-agl.x);
   }
}
```

The Complete Chain of Transforms

In the previous section we looked at the 3D pipeline that transforms a set of vertices all the way from MCS to SCS. Let's summarize the results with Figure 11-22.

We now have quite a few classes (and we are not done yet), so let's look at how the chain in Figure 11-22 works.

1. The vertices of a polyhedron are transformed from MCS to WCS.

2. The transformed vertices are fed to a camera (fCamera).

3. The camera transforms the vertices from WCS to VCS, simplifying the projection stage.

4. The vertices are projected from VCS to SCS.

5. The screen coordinates are returned and used as arguments to the polyhedron's paint() method.

6. The fIndexingPolygons are instructed to paint themselves using the two-dimensional coordinates supplied by the camera.

7. The scratch-pad polygon is used as a hook to Java's API, and the polygons are rendered.

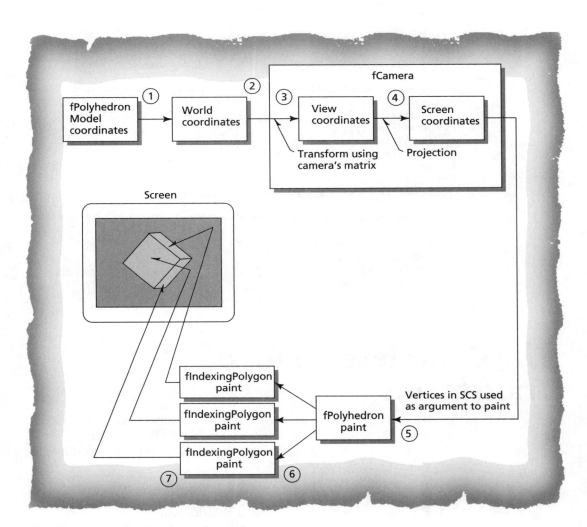

FIGURE 11-22 ◉ *The chain of transforms*

The Polyhedron Instance Class

As you might have noticed, there is a missing link in the chain. Nowhere have we mentioned how the vertices of a polyhedron are transformed from MCS to WCS. This issue was saved until last because it can be solved in a number of ways that may all seem equally good at first glance. What we need is to somehow specify the position and orientation of a polyhedron in the WCS. One solution would be to extend the fPolyhedron and add these features to it. But think about the following scenario.

We want to model a city made of hundreds of buildings. Half of them are identical in that they use the exact same 3D model. This would mean that we would waste memory storing the same model vertices over and over again as in Figure 11-23.

Another solution would be to not store the world coordinates at all. This can be solved with a matrix multiplication, as in Appendix E. On the other hand, buildings are pretty much static. They don't move around unless there is an earthquake. Recalculating the vertices of a static object from MCS to WCS every time the object needs to be rendered seems like a waste of calculations. Even dynamic objects that change their world coordinates a lot, such as cars, stand still most of the time, whether they are in garages or traffic.

A good solution would be to have a class that is an *instance* of a polyhedron. The easiest way of understanding this is to look at Figure 11-24.

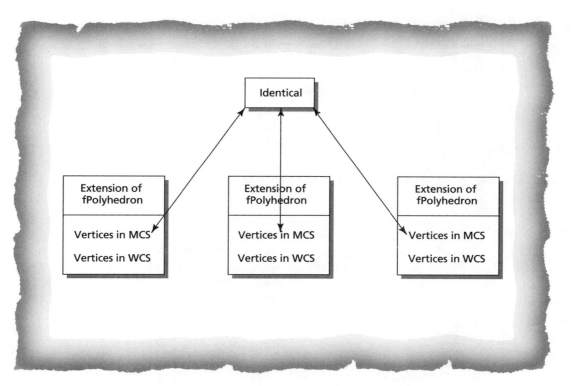

FIGURE 11-23 ◉ *Same vertices stored in several instances of a extension of fPolyhedron*

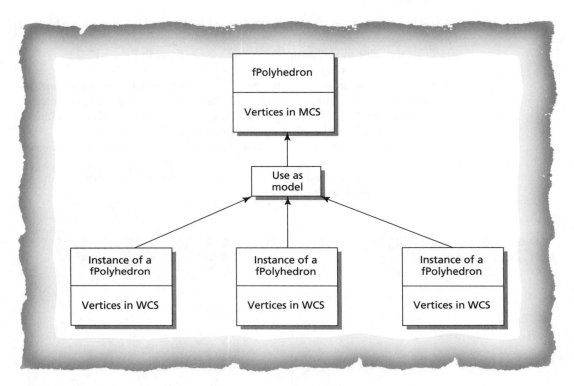

FIGURE 11-24 ◉ *A polyhedron instance using a polyhedron as a model*

In this arrangement, a polyhedron instance contains the vertices transformed to WCS but doesn't contain a copy of the model vertices. This kind of structure would cut the memory use almost by half. It is also a good optimization, since it avoids redundant MCS to WCS transforms. There are also other factors that we should consider. Many objects are very short-lived. For example, a missile only lives a couple of seconds, but the overhead of constructing it is the same as for a never-dying mountain. This means that we must try minimizing the overhead of constructing new instances of a polyhedron. Using this class structure, the model coordinates don't have to be copied to every instance. But there are also disadvantages to this approach. An instance of a polyhedron cannot change its model coordinates, since doing so would have an impact on all instances using the same model. This problem can be solved by assigning a personal polyhedron by simply cloning it before any changes are made to the model vertices.

Implementing the Polyhedron Instance

The implementation (see Listing 11-12) will turn out to be simpler than you might think, but since it might contain unpleasant surprises, there are a few comments to be made.

The Array transformedVertices

This array is used for storing the world coordinates of the polyhedron's vertices. Since many objects are static, it is a good idea to save this information to eliminate redundant recalculations.

Understanding the paint() Method

The paint() method first checks to see if the world coordinates are up-to-date. If an object's orientation has changed in any way, then the world coordinates will be "dirty," meaning that they have to be recalculated. This transform only needs to be done on objects that will be rendered and are actually visible to the camera. Notice that a static object never needs to be updated, since the position and angle never change.

The paint() method is supplied with a camera. Once the world coordinates are up-to-date, the method project() in camera is called with them as an argument. This method will return an array of 2D coordinates that are fed to the polyhedron's paint() method. The rest is taken care of by the fPolyhedron.

Listing 11-12 The fPolyhedronInstance

```java
import java.awt.*;
/**
 * Class that represents an instance of a polyhedron.
 */
public class fPolyhedronInstance extends Object {
   //-- the transformed vertices
   protected fArrayOf3dPoints transformedVertices;
   //-- the matrix used for transformations
    protected fMatrix3d myTransformMatrix;
   //-- the polyhedron
   protected fPolyhedron thePolyhedron;
   //-- position in WCS
   protected fPoint3d myPosition;
   //-- the angle in WCS
   protected fAngle3d myAngle;
   //--
    protected boolean positionIsDirty,angleIsDirty;

   /**
    * construct an instance of the supplied polyhedron.
    */
```

continued on next page

continued from previous page

```
            public fPolyhedronInstance(fPolyhedron poly){
            //-- the polyhedron that this instance is using
            thePolyhedron=poly;
            //-- create the vertices to be used for storing transformations
            try{

transformedVertices=(fArrayOf3dPoints)thePolyhedron.getVertices().makeClo
ne();
                } catch(Exception e){e.printStackTrace();}

                myPosition=new fPoint3d();
                myAngle=new fAngle3d();
                myTransformMatrix=new fMatrix3d();
                }

        /**
         * set the position and angle for this polyhedron instance.
         */
        public void setOrientation(fPoint3d pos,fAngle3d agl){
        if(myPosition.equals(pos)==false){
            //-- if position has changed then mark the matrix
            //-- as "dirty" meaning that the transformed points
            //-- need to be updated.
            myPosition.set(pos);
            positionIsDirty=true;
            }
            if(myAngle.equals(agl)==false){
                myAngle.set(agl);
                angleIsDirty=true;
        }
        }

        /**
         * paint the polyhedron instance.
         */
        public void paint(Graphics g,fGenericCamera camera){
          if(positionIsDirty || angleIsDirty){
          //-- position or angle has changed and the transformed
          //-- vertices need to be updated.
          myTransformMatrix.makeMCStoWCStransform(myPosition,myAngle);
          //-- transform the polyhedron model coordinates to world coords.

myTransformMatrix.transform(thePolyhedron.getVertices(),transformedVertic
es);
          //--
          positionIsDirty=angleIsDirty=false;
          }
          //-- project the WCS to the screen with the supplied camera
          //-- and then call the paint method of the polyhedron with
          //-- the returned 2d array
          thePolyhedron.paint(g,camera.project(transformedVertices));
        }
        }
```

Putting It All Together

We have now designed a couple of classes that can be used to construct dynamic 3D scenes viewed through arbitrary cameras. This is actually part of a 3D engine, a very small part. It is now time to put these classes to work.

The applet shown in Figure 11-25 will only scratch the surface of what can be done with these classes. As you will see, it will be a quick and dirty implementation just to show you how we can put them to work. In a complete 3D engine we would use another layer of classes representing scenes and actors.

The applet will construct nine instances of a polyhedron and a camera. The polyhedrons will be rotated around while the camera moves backward.

To avoid flickering, we will use an offscreen image to do the rendering and then blit it to the screen. The implementation of the no-flicker applet is not a 3D issue, so it will be presented as a black-box class. Use it in good health. It can be found on the CD.

Implementing the Rotating Cubes Applet

Most of the code in Listing 11-13 is standard applet code, but some sections might prove a bit more difficult to understand.

FIGURE 11-25

◎ ◎ ◎ ◎ ◎ ◎

The rotating cubes applet

Initiating the Applet

Initiating this applet consists of four steps:

1. Construct a camera with a view angle of 90 degrees. This is about three times as large as a handy-cam's view angle.

2. Load the model of the cube from the file cube.f3d and construct nine instances.

3. Create an array of coordinates containing the positions of the models with respect to WCS.

4. Start a thread.

The run() Method

The position and orientation of the camera and models are updated. Then a repaint is requested.

Listing 11-13 The rotating cubes applet

```
import java.awt.*;
import java.net.*;
import java.io.*;
/**
 * A rotating cubes applet
 * .. putting the classes to work with a quick and dirty
 * applet.
 */
public class Cube extends fNoFlickerApplet implements Runnable{
    fGenericCamera camera;
    fPoint3d CamPos;
    fAngle3d CamAngle;

    fPolyhedron cube;
    fPolyhedronInstance cubeInstance[];
    fPoint3d pos[];
    fAngle3d agl;

    Thread myThread;
    /**
     * initiate the applet.
     */
    public void init(){
      //--
      //-- create a camera
      //--
      camera=new fGenericCamera(400,400,Math.PI/2);
      CamPos=new fPoint3d(0,0,5);
      CamAngle=new fAngle3d();
```

```
     //--
     //-- load a model from the file cube.f3d
      //--
        try{
           InputStream is=new URL(getCodeBase(),"cube.f3d").openStream();
           cube=new fConvexPolyhedron(is);
         } catch(Exception e){e.printStackTrace();}

     //-- create 9 instances of the cube
  cubeInstance=new fPolyhedronInstance[9];
       for(int n=0; n<9; n++){
       cubeInstance[n]=new fPolyhedronInstance(cube);
        }

     //--
     //-- create the positions and angle
       //--
       pos=new fPoint3d[9];
       int n=0;
       for(int y=-5; y<=5; y+=5){
          for(int x=-5; x<=5; x+=5){
             pos[n]=new fPoint3d(x,y,0);
             n++;
          }
       }
       agl=new fAngle3d();
      //--
      //-- start the thread
     //--
       myThread=new Thread(this);
       myThread.start();
  }

  public void run(){
     while(true){
         //--
         //-- sleep 1/10 of a second
         //--
          try {
             myThread.sleep(100);
          } catch ( InterruptedException e) {}

         //--
         //-- update the angle of the models
         //--
         agl.x+=Math.PI/20; agl.y+=Math.PI/30;

         //--
         //-- update camera angle and position
         //--
         CamPos.z+=0.2; CamAngle.z+=Math.PI/50;
```

continued on next page

continued from previous page

```
        camera.setOrientation(CamPos,CamAngle);

        //--
        //-- request a repaint
        //--
            repaint();
    }
}
public void start(){
    if(myThread==null){
        myThread=new Thread(this);
        myThread.start();
    }
}
public void stop(){
    if(myThread!=null){
        myThread.stop();
        myThread=null;
    }
}

 public void paint(Graphics g){
   //-- clear screen
   g.clearRect(0,0,size().width,size().height);

   //--
   //-- paint the models
   //--
   for(int n=0; n<9; n++){
       cubeInstance[n].setOrientation(pos[n],agl);
       cubeInstance[n].paint(g,camera);
   }
 }
}
```

Suggestion Box

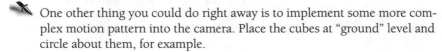 At this point you could start experimenting with different models. Find an .f3d file on the CD and change the line in the code that loads the "cube.f3d" to the model of your choice.

One other thing you could do right away is to implement some more complex motion pattern into the camera. Place the cubes at "ground" level and circle about them, for example.

Another thing could be to extend the indexing polygon class with a wire frame polygon. It will be almost the same as the filled polygon class except for the paint method, which must be changed to actually draw a polygon instead of filling it.

Summary

As you have seen, the process of designing even a small fraction of a 3D engine can be pretty tricky. And the sad part is that there are still some complex issues that need to be taken care of, like 2D, 3D clipping, polygon shading, visible objects determination, and so on. The list goes on and on. And these topics pertain only to the visual parts of a 3D engine. The nonvisual part is just as important and covers issues such as collision detection, construction of virtual worlds, creating objects with behaviors, and so on.

In this chapter you have learned some basic 3D programming. Abstraction, one of the most important parts of object-oriented programming, was also illustrated. With the knowledge acquired in this chapter, you could build your own 3D Java engine. You must, however, consult other literature for the issues not covered here. Try *Black Art of 3D Programming* if you are especially interested in 3D graphics.

12

Building 3D Applets with App3Dcore

Calin Tenitchi

ome bede fore le manoue lle ... le quali fimoђano e llalga
gra pe fi i euer lecommete di ... genito fa de grano di бone
gare nella man ... e fa per man tella alla mano bella pegi qui n
orga ... pio i fomo pib bat.

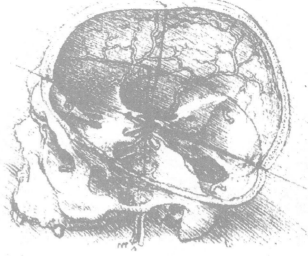

12

Building 3D Applets with App3Dcore

Goals:

Use an advanced 3D core to create a 3D game

Improve your understanding of Java/OO concepts: inheritance, abstract classes, and methods

In this chapter the Application 3D Core, or App3Dcore, is introduced. The vital classes are described as we go along. This chapter is meant to show you how the core works and how you can use it to develop some simple 3D applets and an advanced 3D game.

What Is the App3Dcore?

The App3Dcore is a set of classes that can be used to construct 3D applications very quickly. What makes this package interesting is that it hides the actual 3D graphics deep inside the core. Although it was designed to be a general 3D system, App3Dcore has turned out to be an excellent game-making platform. The package consists of around 30 classes, but luckily only a handful of them are used directly outside the package,

443

while the rest are part of the internal workings of App3Dcore. The vital classes are a virtual world class, static and moving objects, and a couple of different cameras.

The core itself is partitioned into two subsystems, the 3D engine, which does the rendering, and the virtual world, which handles the objects. This ensures the core's expandability and flexibility. Because of the sheer amount of code and the complexity of the core, it is impossible to explain in a single chapter. It would take a whole book just to describe the inner workings. What we will do instead is learn how to *use* the vital parts and also explain some must-know things. Although we will only scratch the surface of the App3Dcore, you will be surprised how easy it is to construct objects with complex behaviors by writing a few lines of code.

The Core's Internal Structure

This section will give an overview of how the core works. The classes mentioned here will be described in more detail later.

The virtual world consists of three cornerstone classes: the static object, the moving object, and the virtual world. These classes make a generic abstract representation of a virtual world. Figure 12-1 shows the vital classes and the relationship between them.

The 3D engine, on the other hand, takes care of the rendering. The cornerstone classes in this subsystem are the various cameras and the polyhedron classes.

The only similarity between these two systems is that each virtual object has a polyhedron instance that can be rendered by the 3D engine. A gimped version (in which large parts have been removed for the sake of clarity) of the polyhedron instance class was described in Chapter 11, Into the Third Dimension. Figure 12-2 shows the vital classes in the 3D engine and the relationship between them.

FIGURE 12-1

◉ ◉ ◉ ◉ ◉ ◉

The vital virtual world classes

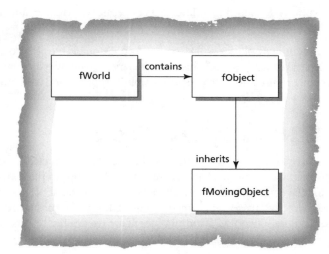

FIGURE 12-2
◎ ◎ ◎ ◎ ◎ ◎
*The vital
classes in the
3D engine*

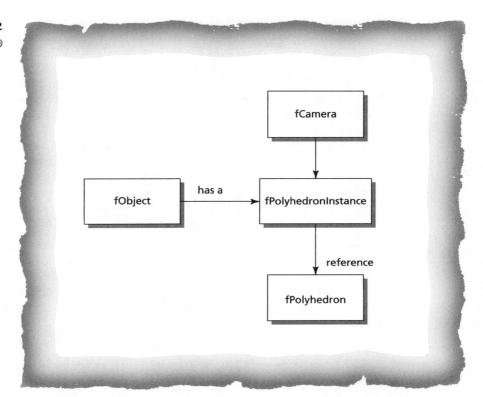

Understanding the Virtual World in the Core

The class that simulates the virtual world is fWorld. It works pretty much as a container for all the objects. The objects that reside in the world are the actual building blocks, and without them there wouldn't be much to simulate except an empty space. The mother of all objects is fObject, which is a static object that once inserted into the world will remain there until removed. A direct extension of this class is fMovingObject, which has the ability to change position and angle. These two classes divide all new objects into two branches: moving and static objects.

The world runs in discrete time intervals. In one time interval a set of actions is taken in certain precise order, as in a board game. Because time is of the essence, a great deal of attention was paid to make sure that it is simulated properly. Here is a light description of what takes place in the core during each time interval.

Each fWorld keeps track of its own time starting with zero at creation. In order to simulate time, a world must be updated. Updating is done by calling the method update() with one argument: the amount of time that the core should update. This method will be called by an "outsider"—probably a thread in the application.

This feature gives us the ability to run the world in slow motion or fast forward, but most important of all, we can make two identical worlds run equally fast on different machines. For example, if you run the same game on a very fast machine and a very slow machine that stand one foot from each other, the worlds will still be synchronized. One of them will run much more smoothly, since it will be updated more often and with shorter time intervals, while the other one will chop forward with jerky motions but will still keep up as much as possible. Some parallels can be drawn with the bouncing rectangles in Chapter 2, Using Objects for Animation, except that the applet shown there will run at different speeds depending on the host machine.

Each time the world is updated the following things take place:

🗡 All objects are updated. At this stage all the objects in the world make changes to their internal state. A static object will not do much except age, while a moving object will update its position and angle. Extensions of the generic core objects will take additional actions that will give them their own personal behavior. This will be shown in the basic examples.

🗡 Collisions are detected. Before the core checks for a collision between two objects, it will first ask them both: Is either of you interested in a collision with other? If that is the case, then a detection will be done and the interested parties will be notified. This notification will be turned into an event that is taken care of at the next stage. How to use collision notification will be shown in one of the basic examples.

🗡 All objects are instructed to handle their events. Since the world runs at discrete time intervals, it must be ensured that things happen in a certain order. For example, you wouldn't want to start changing the position of an object in the middle of a collision detection. To ensure the integrity of the core, most actions on an object will be done through events that are taken care of at this stage. The event making, posting, and handling is hidden within the objects. An example is the collision notification. When objects collide, their collisionWith(..) method is called. In this method the object will make an event and put it in its event list. At the event handling stage (this stage), the event will be cracked, and another method, handleCollisionWith(..), is called. It might seem like a lot of beating around the bush, but this way guarantees that things happen when they should.

I jumped over two stages that do not play a major role in understanding the core. One of them is the divineIntervention(..) method, and the other is the insertion of new objects stage, both of which are reserved for networking capabilities in later versions.

Understanding the 3D Engine in the Core

The 3D engine is a subsystem to the core. It is responsible for rendering the world as seen through a camera. As weird as it may sound, the world can be represented in any way you like. You can use a 2D engine and make a 2D representation, if you like. You can also skip this stage altogether and settle for watching lots of numbers in a console window, but that would be kind of boring.

The 3D representation is done using three different cameras: a basic static camera, a ground-faking camera, and a tracking camera that can be hooked to an object.

The static camera, fCamera, is a regular camera that has a position and an orientation that can be changed at will. The ground-faking camera, fMagicCamera, can fake ground by drawing a horizon and a grid at ground level, giving a vague impression that there is a ground. The tracking camera, fTrackerCamera, can be hooked to an object. This camera will try to follow the hooked object. By follow, I don't mean look at it, but try to keep up with its position and orientation. This is similar to the spotting camera seen in all flight simulators.

All cameras have a method paint(). When this method is called, they will render the world by first determining which objects are visible and then calling the paint() method on each visible fObject. This method is propagated to the fPolyhedronInstance, where the actual painting takes place.

The cameras are not part of the virtual world but are only used as a tool to view it. You can place them in the world or hook them to objects, and then at regular time intervals tell them to paint the world as they see it. You can insert an arbitrary number of cameras in your applet that view the world from different positions and angles. This will have a major impact on the performance, though.

Building an Application on Top of the Core

Now that you know a little about the core, we can start looking at how to use it. The best way to learn something is by looking at examples. Below are two examples that show some of the things that you can do.

A Small Example: The Bouncing Boxes

In the following example you will see how you can use the core by extending the cornerstone classes. You should read the description and look at the code at the same time to get the most out of it. The "headers" for the core classes mentioned can be found on the CD-ROM.

We will first extend the generic fMovingObject with a BouncingBox object. After that the fWorld class will be extended by the BouncingBoxWorld. Finally, these classes will be put together in an applet.

We will start by looking at how the generic core class fMovingObject can be extended to make a bouncing box, as shown in Listing 12-1 and Figure 12-3.

Listing 12-1 *The bouncing box*

```
class BouncingBox extends fMovingObject{
  BouncingBox(fWorld w, fPoint3d p ) {
    //-- construct the base class
    super(w,p,new fAngle3d(0,0,0),
          new fPoint3d(0,0,0),new fAngle3d(0,Math.PI,0));
    //--
    //-- every non-abstract object MUST have a polyhedron instance.
    //-- this line of code MUST be somewhere in the constructor
    //--
    usePolyhedronInstance(new
      fPolyhedronInstance(ourDefaultPolyhedron,ourScale));
  }

  //-- override the update method
  public void update (double dt) {
    //-- always let the base class do the default action for
    //-- an overridden method. Never forget this!
    super.update(dt);

    //-- retrieve the position and velocity of the box
    fPoint3d dp=getdPosition();
    fPoint3d p=getPosition();

    //-- check if the box has hit the ground
    if(p.y<ourScale.y){
      //-- the bottom of the box has hit the ground
      //-- switch the sign of the velocity and
      //-- decrease it a bit
      dp.y=-dp.y*ourBounciness;
      //-- make sure the box is not below ground level
      p.y=ourScale.y;
      //-- set the new position
      setPosition(p);
    }
    //-- make sure gravity does it's share
    dp.y-=BouncingBoxWorld.gravity*dt;

    //-- set the new velocity
    setdPosition(dp);
  }
```

```
    //-- inititates the class
    public static void initiateClass (Applet app) {
       //--
       //-- get the static "constants" that all bouncing boxes have
       //--
       try{
          //-- load the default polyhedron for all bouncing boxes
          //-- this MUST be done in all non-abstract classes
          String polyfile=
           app.getParameter("BouncingBox_ourDefaultPolyhedron");
          InputStream is=url.openStream();
          ourDefaultPolyhedron=new fConvexPolyhedron(is);
       } catch(Exception e) {
          e.printStackTrace();
       }
       //-- the scaling of the polyhedron
       double xscale=new
Double(app.getParameter("BouncingBox_scalex")).doubleValue();
       double yscale=new
Double(app.getParameter("BouncingBox_scaley")).doubleValue();
       double zscale=new
Double(app.getParameter("BouncingBox_scalez")).doubleValue();
       ourScale=new fPoint3d(xscale,yscale,zscale);
       //-- the bounciness of this box
       ourBounciness=new
Double(app.getParameter("BouncingBox_bounciness")).doubleValue();
       }
    //-- class constants
    protected static fPolyhedron ourDefaultPolyhedron;
    protected static double ourBounciness;
    protected static fPoint3d ourScale;
}
```

The BouncingBox Constructor

 The constructor of a bouncing box takes two parameters: the world in which it should be inserted and the starting position. The base class, fMovingObject, is constructed by setting the velocity and angle to zero. The angular velocity is set to PI, making the moving object rotate about the y-axis with an angular velocity of PI rad/s.

 The next line in the constructor tells the base class fObject which polyhedron instance to use. Without a polyhedron instance, the object cannot be painted by a camera.

FIGURE 12-3

◎ ◎ ◎ ◎ ◎

*The
BouncingBox
class*

The Overridden Update

🔪 The first thing we do here is let the base class update itself. This is a must, or fMovingObject will not get the chance to update the position and angle.

🔪 The position and velocity are retrieved, since they will both be used.

🔪 Check whether the box has hit the ground by looking at the scale of the model. The scale of the model decides how large the object is. This is because the vertices of the models are defined between -1 and 1 on all axes.

🔪 If the box has hit the ground, invert the speed and multiply it by a factor that controls the bounciness of the box.

🔪 The position of the model is set so that we ensure that the bottom of the box is at ground level.

🔪 The method setPosition() is used to set the new position of the object. This is a must, since getPosition() and getdPosition() return clones. This is to ensure the integrity of the core.

🔪 Outside the *if* statement, the velocity is affected by the gravity, and the new velocity is set using setdPosition().

The initiateClass() Method

This method is only called once: at the beginning of the application. This method can be seen as a *class* constructor, meaning that it prepares a class before creating instances. Let's look at the advantages gained from using this method. All bouncing boxes have something in common. They are all represented by a polyhedron that has a certain scaling. They all have a certain "bounciness," too. Instead of hardcoding these constants, we would like to retrieve them when the application starts. All these constants are stored in the HTML (HyperText Markup Language) file as parameters to the applet. This way you can change all "constants" without recompiling the code but by simply restarting the application with another HTML file.

This method will save you LOTS of time once the application is done and only the final tuning is left. When I wrote Asteroids96, a game that is not featured in this book, I spent over a third of my time compiling, looking at the applet for three seconds, then changing a number and recompiling.

All class constants are of the types static and start, with the prefix "our" to emphasize that this is not a class variable but a constant for all instances of this class. Let's look at what actually takes place in this method:

 Retrieve a 3D model from an F3D file. The name of the file is stored as a parameter in the HTML file, as shown below:

```
<param name=BouncingBox_ourDefaultPolyhedron value=cube.f3d>
```

The parameter name starts with the class name, followed by an underscore and then the name of the constant. The value depends on the parameter type. In this case it is a string that refers to a filename.

 The next thing that is in common for all bouncing boxes is that their 3D model is scaled. This is because all the vertices in an F3D file are between -1 and 1 on all axes. The actual file format and how models can be imported from external applications will be described at the end of the chapter.

 Finally, the "bounciness" of the boxes is retrieved. This bounciness determines how much of the initial energy is saved after a bounce (see Listing 12-2).

Listing 12-2 *The BouncingBoxWorld class*

```
class BouncingBoxWorld extends fWorld {
  BouncingBoxWorld(Applet app){
    //-- make a world which is 200x200 meters with the left top corner
    //-- at -100,-100. The world is divided into 5x5 grids
    super(app,-100,-100,200,5);

    //-- insert a couple of boxes at random height
    for(double x=-10;x<=10;x+=10){
      for(double z=-10;z<=10;z+=10){
```

continued on next page

continued from previous page

```
                    new BouncingBox(this,new fPoint3d(x,Math.random()*30,z));
            }
        }
    }

    protected void initiateClasses (Applet app) {
        BouncingBox.initiateClass(app);

        gravity=new
Double(app.getParameter("BouncingBoxWorld_gravity")).doubleValue();
    }

    public static double gravity;
}
```

The BouncingBoxWorld Constructor

➤ The constructor of this class takes a single parameter, the applet that has constructed it.

➤ The superclass fWorld is constructed by specifying the dimensions of the world.

➤ A couple of boxes are inserted into the world at random height above the ground.

The initiateClasses() Method

➤ This method sees to it that all classes used in this world are initiated. It also retrieves a parameter, the gravity, from the bouncing boxes applet file (see Listing 12-3).

Listing 12-3 *The bouncing boxes applet*

```
public class BouncingBoxes extends NoFlickerApplet implements Runnable {
    //-- the world and the camera
    BouncingBoxWorld world;
    fCamera camera;

    //-- standard-fare applet stuff
    Thread myThread;
    boolean alive;

    public void init () {
        //-- construct the world
        world=new BouncingBoxWorld(this);
        //-- construct the camera
        double viewangle=Math.PI/3;
        double viewdist=100;
```

```
        fPoint3d campos=new fPoint3d(0,15,30);
        fAngle3d camagl=new fAngle3d(0,0,0);
        double gridsize=15;
        double fading=0;
        camera=new fMagicCamera(world,viewangle,viewdist,campos,
                                camagl,gridsize,fading);

        //-- applet stuff
        myThread=new Thread(this);
        myThread.start();
        alive=true;
    }

    protected long lastUpdate;

    public void run () {
        lastUpdate=System.currentTimeMillis();
        while(alive){
            long currentTime=System.currentTimeMillis();
            long dtmillis=currentTime-lastUpdate;
            double dt=(double)dtmillis/1000;
             lastUpdate=currentTime;
             //-- make sure the update doesn't take to large "steps"
            if(dt>0.2) dt=0.2;

            world.update(dt);
            camera.update(dt);

            //-- to speed up the repaint we tell the Applet to update
            //-- directly instead of calling repaint
            if(getPeer()==null) return;
            Graphics g=getGraphics();
            if(g==null) return;
            Dimension dim=size();
            if(dim.width==0 || dim.height==0) return;
            update(g);
        }
    }

    public void start () {
        if(myThread==null){
            myThread=new Thread(this);
            myThread.start();
            alive=true;
        }
    }

    public void paint(Graphics g){
        //-- update the screen size for the camera
        camera.setScreenSize(size().width,size().height);
        //-- erase the screen
        g.clearRect(0,0,size().width,size().height);
```

continued on next page

continued from previous page

```
        //-- paint the world
        camera.paint(g);
    }

    public void stop () {
        if(myThread!=null){
            myThread.stop();
            myThread=null;
            alive=false;
        }
    }
}
```

The init() Method

The first line of code constructs a bouncing boxes world. After that, a magic camera is constructed, through which we will view the world.

The run() Method

 In the run() method we keep track of how long a frame takes to render. If a frame takes more than 0.2 seconds to render, then the hardware is too slow or the OS is too busy, so we set the update time to 0.2 seconds.

 The world and the camera are updated.

 The next thing we would like to do is paint the world as seen through the camera. To accelerate the rendering, we will ignore the repaint() request and simply tell Java's AWT to paint. This method will drastically increase the rendering speed but can also cause problems due to the inner workings of Java. To insure that no major malfunction occurs, a couple of checks are done: Is there an actual window to paint on? If so, is the window real or a bogus window with no dimension?

The paint() Method

 In the paint() method we ensure that the camera has the right screen dimensions and then tell it to paint.

Listing 12-4 *The HTML file*

```
<HTML>
<HEAD>
<TITLE>Bouncing Boxes 96 - Calin Tenitchi</TITLE>
</HEAD>
```

```
<BODY>
<center><HR>
<applet code="BouncingBoxes.class" width=400 height=400>
<param name=BouncingBox_ourDefaultPolyhedron value=cube.f3d>
<param name=BouncingBox_ourBounciness          value=0.6>
<param name=BouncingBox_scalex                 value=2>
<param name=BouncingBox_scaley                 value=4>
<param name=BouncingBox_scalez                 value=1>
<param name=BouncingBoxWorld_gravity           value=9.82>
</applet>
<hr></center>
Bouncing boxes by Calin Tenitchi
```

As you can see in Listing 12-4, the HTML file contains quite a few parameters that can be changed to customize the applet. You can experiment by changing the *ourDefaultPolyhedron* parameter, telling the bouncing box to use some other 3D model, or you can change the gravity of the world if you like.

As you may have guessed, the HTML file for the game will be VERY large, with hundreds of parameters that can be changed at will, changing the behavior of the game without any additional coding.

Building on the Example: Collisions and Object Interactions

The last example illustrated how the core class fMovingObject and fWorld can be extended. This example (see Figure 12-4) will show collision handling, extending fObject, and removing an object from the world.

We will start by extending the core class fObject with StaticBox, shown in Listing 12-5.

Listing 12-5 *The static box*

```
class StaticBox extends fObject{
   StaticBox(fWorld w, fPoint3d p ) {
      //-- construct the base class by specifying position and angle
      super(w,p,new fAngle3d(0,0,0));
      //--
      //-- every non-abstract object MUST have a polyhedron instance.
      //-- this line of code MUST be somewhere in the constructor
      //--
      usePolyhedronInstance(new
fPolyhedronInstance(ourDefaultPolyhedron,ourScale));
   }

   public void update (double dt) {
      super.update(dt);
      if(getAge()>ourLifeTime){
         die();
```

continued on next page

continued from previous page

```
            }
        }

    public static void initiateClass (Applet app) {
        //--
        //-- get the static "constants" that all bouncing boxes have
        //--
        try{
            //-- load the default polyhedron for all bouncing boxes
            //-- this MUST be done in all non-abstract classes
            String polyfile=
                app.getParameter("StaticBox_ourDefaultPolyhedron");
            URL url=new URL(app.getCodeBase(),polyfile);
            InputStream is=url.openStream();
            ourDefaultPolyhedron=new fConvexPolyhedron(is);
        } catch(Exception e) {
            e.printStackTrace();
        }
        //-- the scaling of the polyhedron
        double xscale=new
Double(app.getParameter("StaticBox_scalex")).doubleValue();
        double yscale=new
Double(app.getParameter("StaticBox_scaley")).doubleValue();
        double zscale=new
Double(app.getParameter("StaticBox_scalez")).doubleValue();
        ourScale=new fPoint3d(xscale,yscale,zscale);
        ourLifeTime=new
Double(app.getParameter("StaticBox_ourLifeTime")).doubleValue();
    }

    //-- class constants
    protected static fPolyhedron ourDefaultPolyhedron;
    protected static fPoint3d ourScale;
    protected static double ourLifeTime;
}
```

The Constructor

The StaticBox constructor is similar to the BouncingBox's constructor except that this class has fObject as a base class. The base class is constructed by specifying its position and angle.

The update() Method

This object doesn't do anything except age. When its lifetime has been exceeded, it will remove itself from the world with the die() method.

FIGURE 12-4

◉ ◉ ◉ ◉ ◉ ◉

Collisions in the bouncing boxes example

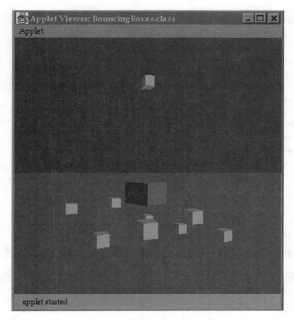

Collision Handling

Listing 12-6 shows the bouncing box with collision handling. To conserve space, only the changes to Listing 12-1 are shown. The complete source code can be found on the CD-ROM.

Listing 12-6 *The bouncing box, with collision handling*

```
class BouncingBox extends fMovingObject{
   ..
   ..
   public boolean interestedOfCollisionWith (fObject obj){
      //-- i'm interested in collisions with static boxes
      if(obj instanceof StaticBox) return true;

      //-- none of the objects I know, let the base class decide
      return super.interestedOfCollisionWith (obj);
   }

   protected boolean handleCollisionWith (fObject obj,double dt){
      //-- if it is one of my "interest" objects
      if(obj instanceof StaticBox){
         //-- retrieve the position and velocity of the box
         fPoint3d dp=getdPosition();

         dp.y=-dp.y;
         //-- make sure gravity does it's share
```

continued on next page

continued from previous page

```
                    dp.y-=BouncingBoxWorld.gravity*dt;

                    //-- set the new velocity
                    setdPosition(dp);

                    //-- event has been handled, get more events
                    return true;
                }
                //-- if I don't know what this object is then it
                //-- means that a super class is interested.
                //-- let it take care of it
                return super.handleCollisionWith(obj,dt);
            }
            ..
            ..
            ..
    }
```

The interestedOfCollisionWith() Method

Collision detection is an expensive operation. In order to optimize the core, one has to be very selective about which collisions objects should be interested in. Say that an object of type LargeTruck has collided with an object of type Maggot. From the large truck's point of view, this is not an important event, but for the maggot this might be a turning point in its life. To express interest in a collision, an object has to override this method. In this case a BouncingBox is interested in collisions with all objects of the type StaticBox. If it doesn't recognize the object type or it is not interested, it will let its base class make the decision. The base class in this case is fObject, and since this is a core object, it is very ignorant and will return *false*.

The handleCollisionWith() Method

When a collision with an object of interest has occurred, this method will be called. In this case a collision with a StaticBox will result in a bounce.

Using a Template to Simplify Designing New Objects

To make the designing of new objects easier, I have put together a template, shown in Listing 12-7, with the basic methods that can be overridden.

Listing 12-7 *The template*

```
class MyCoolObject extends fObject{
    /**
     * Constructor.
     */
    MyCoolObject(fWorld world){
```

```
        super(world,new fPoint3d(0,0,0),new fAngle3d(0,0,0));
        usePolyhedronInstance(new
fPolyhedronInstance(ourDefaultPolyhedron,ourScale));

        //--
        //-- insert code here
        //--
    }
    /**
     * Updates this object by dt seconds.
     */
    public void update (double dt) {
        super.update(dt);

        //--
        //-- insert code here
        //--
    }


    /**
     * The core will ask this object if it is interested of
     * collision with some other object. Return true if the object
     * is interested otherwise let the base class decide.
     */
    public boolean interestedOfCollisionWith (fObject obj) {
        //--
        //-- insert code here, example
        //--     if(obj instanceof MyCoolClass) return true;
        //--

        return super.interestedOfCollisionWith(obj);
    }
    /**
 * Handles a collision with a object. Returns false if there
     * is no point in checking more collisions. I.e. the object is dead.
     */
    protected boolean handleCollisionWith (fObject obj,double dt) {
        //--
        //-- insert code here, example
        //--     if(obj instanceof AtomicBomb) {die();return false;}
        //--

        return super.handleCollisionWith(obj,dt);
    }
    /**
     * Kills this object.
     */
    protected void die () {
        super.die();

        //--
        //-- insert code here, example
        //--    largeExplosion();
```

continued on next page

continued from previous page

```
    }
    /**
     * Inititates this class by loading the static parameters from
     * the applet.
     */
    public static void initiateClass (Applet app) {
      try{
        //-- load the default polyhedron for all bouncing boxes
        //-- this MUST be done in all non-abstract classes
        String polyfile=
          app.getParameter("MyCoolObject_ourDefaultPolyhedron");
        URL url=new URL(app.getCodeBase(),polyfile);
        InputStream is=url.openStream();
        ourDefaultPolyhedron=new fConvexPolyhedron(is);
      } catch(Exception e) {
        e.printStackTrace();
      }
      //-- the scaling of the polyhedron
      double xscale=new
Double(app.getParameter("MyCoolObject_scalex")).doubleValue();
      double yscale=new
Double(app.getParameter("MyCoolObject_scaley")).doubleValue();
      double zscale=new
Double(app.getParameter("MyCoolObject_scalez")).doubleValue();
      ourScale=new fPoint3d(xscale,yscale,zscale);

      //--
      //-- load your other constants here
      //--
    }

    //-- class "constants"
    protected static fPolyhedron ourDefaultPolyhedron;
    protected static fPoint3d ourScale;
    //--
    //-- insert your static stuff here
    //--
}
```

▨ Things to Watch out For

1. When overriding a method, copy it from the template or you might misspell it.

2. Always be sure to initiate all classes in yourWorld.initiateClasses().

3. Always make sure to add the new parameters to the HTML file when you create a new class.

4. Make sure the parameters are loaded properly and that they are not misspelled, or they'll be null or zero and possibly crash the core.

5. When using getPosition(), getAngle(), getdPosition(), or getdAngle(), you will receive a clone of that object. You have to call setPosition(), etc., in order to really change the state of the object; otherwise you will only change the clone.

6. Do not forget to call the method usePolyhedronInstance(..) in all non-abstract classes or the object will not have a 3D model.

7. Be sure you have checked points 1, 2, 3, 4, 5, 6, and 7.

Creating the Game Layer

In this section, a layer of classes called the game layer will be developed. This layer of classes will turn the general App3Dcore into a game engine. This layer also breaks the intimate contact with the core. Figure 12-5 shows an abstract representation of how the classes are extended layer by layer.

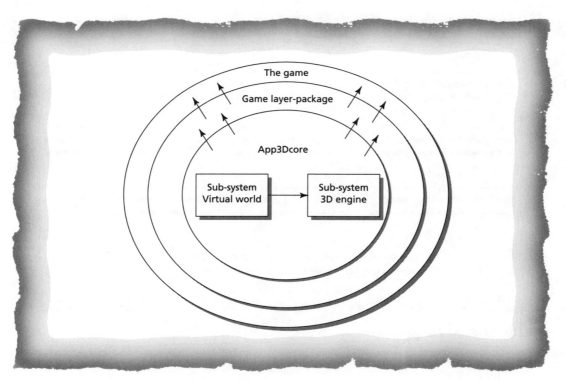

FIGURE 12-5 ◉ *Extending the App3Dcore*

How the Game Layer Works

In all 3D games we find buildings, vehicles, weapons, and scenery, among other things. All objects within such sets have something in common. All buildings, for example, are static objects. All vehicles have a maximum velocity, turning rate, and so on. To make the development of games easier, we will implement a set of abstract classes that cover most types of objects. This abstract layer will also implement their default behavior. Once this layer is implemented, the designing of new objects is trivial. The game layer will be a tree of classes, as shown in Figure 12-6.

Since Java lacks multiple inheritance, the game layer is divided into two major branches: moving objects and static objects. Each of these branches is further divided into specialized types of moving/static objects. For example, the cmAbstractStaticStructure implements the default behavior and what is in common to all buildings.

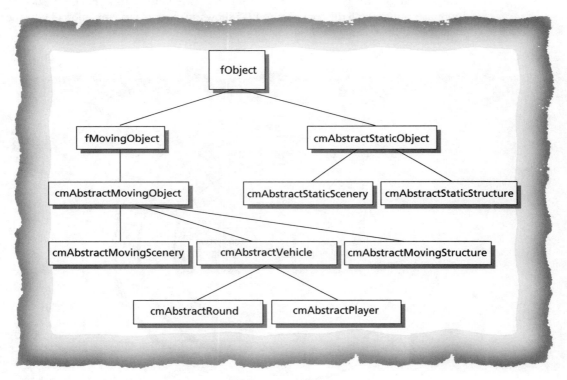

FIGURE 12-6 ◉ *The game layer*

The good thing about this tree structure is that an object can express interest in collisions with a whole branch of classes. For example, if a vehicle is interested in collisions with buildings, it will get all collisions with all buildings, whether the building is the Empire State Building or a small cottage in the Canadian wilderness. This is because both of these buildings are subclasses of cmAbstractStaticStructure. If a new object is introduced into the game, the already-implemented objects will react to it in a somewhat realistic manner. Say that all objects know what to do if they collide with a structure. Suppose we wish to insert a new type of structure called PentagonBuilding. Even though the rest of the objects in the world don't know exactly what PentagonBuilding is, they know that it is a cmAbstractStaticStructure and treat it accordingly. This means that no additional coding is needed if the objects don't have a reason to treat it differently.

The classes in the game layer implement the default behavior for the different types of objects. For example, all vehicles are interested in collisions with structures. If a vehicle collides with a building, its default behavior is to stop. On the other hand, structures are never interested in collisions with vehicles. This can, of course, be discussed, since a small cottage should definitely be interested in collisions with bulldozers, for example.

The behavior of a game layer class can be extended but should not be ignored. An extension of cmAbstractVehicle might be interested in collisions with other objects on top of the default for cmAbstractVehicle. It can also change the behavior when a collision occurs. Another thing that all vehicles have in common is that they can be steered and are limited by their capabilities. Some vehicles might be able to take tighter turns than others, or accelerate faster, for example. The steering of a vehicle is done through the methods that cmAbstractVehicle supplies. This means that all extensions of this class can be controlled through these methods.

The Game Layer Classes

Most of these classes contain very little or trivial code, except for the cmAbstractVehicle, which contains large amounts of code.

The cmAbstractStaticObject Class

This is the abstract representation of a static object. The code for it is shown in Listing 12-8. The only reason this class exists is to draw a clear line between App3Dcore and the game layer. It also contains a variable that specifies the amount of "health" this object has. If no health is specified, then it is assumed that this object is indestructible.

Listing 12-8 *The abstract static object*

```
abstract class cmAbstractStaticObject extends fObject{
   protected cmAbstractStaticObject (fWorld w, fPoint3d pos,
                                     fAngle3d ang)
   {
      super(w,pos,ang);
      myHealth=Double.MAX_VALUE;
   }
   protected cmAbstractStaticObject (fWorld w, fPoint3d pos,
                                     fAngle3d ang,double health)
   {
      super(w,pos,ang);
      myHealth=health;
   }
   public double getHealth(){
      return myHealth;
   }
   public void setHealth(double e){
      myHealth=e;
   }
   protected double myHealth;
}
```

The cmAbstractMovingObject Class

This is an abstract representation of a moving object. The code is shown in
Listing 12-9.

Listing 12-9 *The abstract moving object*

```
abstract class cmAbstractMovingObject extends fMovingObject{
   protected cmAbstractMovingObject (fWorld w, fPoint3d pos,
                                     fAngle3d agl, fPoint3d dpos,
                                     fAngle3d dagl)
   {
      super(w,pos,agl,dpos,dagl);
      myHealth=Double.MAX_VALUE;
   }
   protected cmAbstractMovingObject (fWorld w, fPoint3d pos,
                                     fAngle3d agl, fPoint3d dpos,
                                     fAngle3d dagl,double health)
   {
      super(w,pos,agl,dpos,dagl);
      myHealth=health;
   }
   public double getHealth(){
      return myHealth;
   }
   public void setHealth(double h){
```

```
        myHealth=h;
    }
    protected double myHealth;
}
```

The cmAbstractStaticStructure Class

The static structure is the root of all static buildings. Since all static structures are placed at ground level, the constructor only needs to know the coordinates of the structure in 2D. It then decides how high above the ground the object should be placed so that the bottom touches the ground. This, once again, is because of the way the vertices in an F3D file are centered and scaled.

All structures are interested in collisions with weapon rounds like bullets and missiles. The default action taken in such a collision is to decrease the "health," depending on the impact damage of the round. Extensions of this class might take additional actions.

Extensions of this class might be buildings, rocks, or anything that can be considered as an impassable structure. Listing 12-10 shows the abstract static structure class.

Listing 12-10 *The abstract static structure*

```
abstract class cmAbstractStaticStructure extends cmAbstractStaticObject{
    protected cmAbstractStaticStructure (fWorld world, double x, double z,
        fAngle3d agl, double w, double b, double h)
    {
        super(world,new fPoint3d(x,h,z),agl);
        myHealth=Double.MAX_VALUE;
    }

    protected cmAbstractStaticStructure (fWorld world, double x, double z,
        fAngle3d agl, double w, double b, double h, double health)
    {
        super(world,new fPoint3d(x,h,z),new fAngle3d(0,0,0),health);
    }

    public boolean interestedOfCollisionWith (fObject obj) {
        if(obj instanceof cmAbstractRound) return true;
        return super.interestedOfCollisionWith(obj);
    }

    protected boolean handleCollisionWith (fObject obj,double dt) {
        if(obj instanceof cmAbstractRound){
            myHealth-=((cmAbstractRound)obj).getImpactDamage();
            if(myHealth<0) {
                die();
            }
        }
        return super.handleCollisionWith(obj,dt);
    }
}
```

The cmAbstractMovingStructure Class

This class, shown in Listing 12-11, represents a moving structure, which is nearly the same as a static structure except that it can move around.

Extensions of this class might be, for example, a huge moving gate or a large asteroid.

Listing 12-11 *The abstract moving structure*

```
abstract class cmAbstractMovingStructure extends cmAbstractMovingObject{
    protected cmAbstractMovingStructure (fWorld w, fPoint3d p, fAngle3d a,
                                         fPoint3d dp, fAngle3d da)
    {
        super(w,p,a,dp,da);
        myHealth=Double.MAX_VALUE;
    }
    protected cmAbstractMovingStructure (fWorld w, fPoint3d p, fAngle3d a,
                                         fPoint3d dp, fAngle3d da,
                                         double health)
    {
        super(w,p,a,dp,da,health);
    }

    public boolean interestedOfCollisionWith (fObject obj) {
        if(obj instanceof cmAbstractRound) return true;
        return super.interestedOfCollisionWith(obj);
    }

    protected boolean handleCollisionWith (fObject obj,double dt) {
        if(obj instanceof cmAbstractRound){
            myHealth-=((cmAbstractRound)obj).getImpactDamage();
            if(myHealth<0) {
                die();
            }
        }
        return super.handleCollisionWith(obj,dt);
    }
}
```

The cmAbstractStaticScenery Class

This class, shown in Listing 12-12, is the mother of all static scenery. Scenery is the type of object that does not interact with the rest of world. Its only purpose in life is to make things look prettier. No object should be interested in collisions with scenery, and no scenery should be interested in collisions with other objects.

Extensions of this class might be small rocks, bushes, and so on.

Listing 12-12 *The abstract static scenery*

```
abstract class cmAbstractStaticScenery extends cmAbstractStaticObject{
   protected cmAbstractStaticScenery (fWorld w, fPoint3d p, fAngle3d a) {
      super(w,p,a);
   }
}
```

The cmAbstractMovingScenery Class

This class is just like the static one, but this scenery is moving. The code is shown in
Listing 12-13.

Extensions of this class might be small fragments, clouds, and so on.

Listing 12-13 *The abstract moving scenery*

```
abstract class cmAbstractStaticScenery extends cmAbstractStaticObject{
   protected cmAbstractStaticScenery (fWorld w, fPoint3d p, fAngle3d a) {
      super(w,p,a);
   }
}
```

The cmAbstractVehicle Class

This is the most comprehensive class in the game layer. What distinguishes a vehicle
from all other moving objects is that it can be controlled. It also travels in the direction
that it faces. Controlling the vehicle is done through the methods supplied in the class.
The abstract vehicle is interested in collisions with structures, and the default behavior is to stop.

The steering of the vehicle is done through methods like turnLeft(), turnRight(), and
so on. The *factor* argument in these methods must be between 0 and 1 and tells the vehicle how much of its steering capability it should use. If we used an analogous joystick
to control an object, then the factor would depend on the position of the stick.

Listing 12-14 shows the abstract vehicle class. Due to the very large source, only the
"header" is shown. The full source can be found on the CD-ROM.

Listing 12-14 *The abstract vehicle*

```
abstract class cmAbstractVehicle extends cmAbstractMovingObject{
   //-- the constructor for flying vehicles
   protected cmAbstractVehicle (fWorld w, fPoint3d pos,
            fVelocityVector v, double turningrate,
            double pitchrate, double acceleration,
            double brakingrate, double maxVelocity,
            double climbrate, double decentrate,
            double pitchClimbrateRelation)
```

continued on next page

continued from previous page

```
            //-- the constructor for ground vehicles
            protected cmAbstractVehicle (fWorld w, fPoint3d pos,
                    fVelocityVector v, double turningrate0,
                    double acceleration0, double brakingrate0,
                    double maxVelocity0)

    public void addWeapon(cmAbstractWeapon wep)

    public void removeWeapon(cmAbstractWeapon wep)

    public boolean selectWeapon(int wepnbr)

    public void update (double dt)

    //--
    //-- event creating methods
    //--
    public void fireSelectedWeapon()

    public void turnLeft (double factor, double dt)

    public void turnRight (double factor, double dt)

    public void increaseVelocity (double factor, double dt)

    public void decreaseVelocity (double factor, double dt)

    public void brake (double factor, double dt)

    public void climb (double factor, double dt)

    public void decent (double factor, double dt)

    public void pitchUp (double factor, double dt)

    public void pitchDown (double factor, double dt)
}
```

The cmAbstractPlayer Class

An abstract player is an extension of a vehicle. The code for this class is shown in Listing 12-15. A player can either be controlled directly by a human or by a computer-controlled player. The computer players are controlled by the cmAbstractBrain. Describing how to implement an artificial intelligence is, however, beyond the scope of this chapter; therefore it will not be discussed.

Listing 12-15 *The abstract player*

```
abstract class cmAbstractPlayer extends cmAbstractVehicle{
    protected cmAbstractPlayer (fWorld w, fPoint3d pos, fVelocityVector v,
```

```
                              double turningrate, double pitchrate,
                              double acceleration, double brakingrate,
                              double maxVelocity, double climbrate,
                              double decentrate,
                              double pitchClimbrateFactor)
    {
    super(w,pos,v,turningrate,pitchrate,acceleration,
        brakingrate,maxVelocity,climbrate,
        decentrate,pitchClimbrateFactor);
    }

    protected cmAbstractPlayer(fWorld w, fPoint3d pos,fVelocityVector v,
                              double turningrate,double acceleration,
                              double brakingrate,double maxVelocity)
    {
        super(w,pos,v,turningrate,acceleration,brakingrate,maxVelocity);
    }

    public void update (double dt) {
        super.update(dt);
        if(myBrain!=null){
            myBrain.update(dt);
        }
    }

    public void setBrain(cmAbstractBrain brain){
        myBrain=brain;
    }

    protected cmAbstractBrain myBrain;
}
```

The cmAbstractWeapon Class

This class, shown in Listing 12-16, implements the abstract behavior of a weapon. All weapons are mounted on a host vehicle at a relative position. Every weapon has a loading time and ammo.

This class must be extended and the fire() method must be overridden by creating the actual projectile or round of this particular weapon.

Listing 12-16 *The abstract weapon*

```
abstract class cmAbstractWeapon extends Object {
    protected cmAbstractWeapon(cmAbstractVehicle host,fPoint3d relPos,
                              double loadingTime0,int ammo0)
    {
        loadingTime=loadingTime0;
        ammo=ammo0;
        theHost=host;
        relOrigin=relPos;
```

continued on next page

continued from previous page

```
      }

      public void addAmmo(int nbr){
         ammo+=nbr;
      }

      public void update(double dt){
         lastFire-=dt;
         if(lastFire<0){
            lastFire=0;
         }
      }

      public boolean fire(){
         if(lastFire>0) return false;
         if(ammo<=0) return false;
         ammo--;
         lastFire=loadingTime;
         return true;
      }

      public int getAmmo(){
         return ammo;
      }

      public String getName(){
         return null;
      }

      protected fPoint3d relOrigin;
      protected double loadingTime;
      protected double lastFire;
      protected int ammo;
      protected cmAbstractVehicle theHost;
   }
```

The cmAbstractRound Class

An abstract round, shown in Listing 12-17, is what is fired from an abstract weapon. Its base class is cmAbstractVehicle, since that class already implements most of the methods needed. Most "rounds" have a simple behavior. For example, a bullet travels with its maximum velocity straight forward. Other "rounds," like missiles, accelerate.

Each weapon has an "impact damage." This damage is by default inflicted on any object interested in collision with rounds. Some objects might take special actions when colliding with certain weapons. Think of a tank getting hit by an antitank missile. This weapon will inflict extra damage on that particular object.

Homing missiles and other smart weapons have a more complex behavior, which involves steering toward the target. This is where the methods in the base class cmAbstractVehicle come into really good use.

Listing 12-17 *The abstract round*

```
abstract class cmAbstractRound extends cmAbstractVehicle{
    protected cmAbstractRound (fWorld w, fObject shooter, fPoint3d pos,
                               fVelocityVector v, double turningrate0,
                               double pitchrate0, double acceleration0,
                               double brakingrate0, double maxVelocity0,
                               double climbrate0, double decentrate0,
                               double pitchClimbrateRelation0,
                               double impactDamage)
    {
    super(w,pos,v,turningrate0,pitchrate0,acceleration0,
        brakingrate0,maxVelocity0,climbrate0,decentrate0,
        pitchClimbrateRelation0);
       theShooter = shooter;
       this.impactDamage=impactDamage;
    }

    public fObject getShooter () {
       return theShooter;
    }

    protected boolean handleCollisionWith (fObject obj,double dt) {
       die();
       return false;
    }

    public double getImpactDamage(){
       return impactDamage;
    }

    protected fObject theShooter;
    protected double impactDamage;
}
```

Implementing a Simple 3D Game

In this section, we will look at a simplified version of the fully developed Combat Machines 96 (see Figure 12-7). This version will include a small city and two different vehicles: a tank and an airborne vehicle. Each of these objects can carry three different weapons: a mini-cannon, missiles, or bombs.

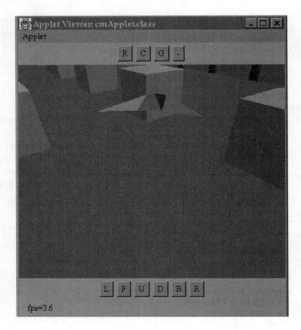

FIGURE 12-7

◎ ◎ ◎ ◎ ◎ ◎

*Combat
Machines 96*

The classes used in the game are direct extensions of the classes in the game layer. The source code for the classes is shown below.

Parts of the source code like the initiateClass methods will not be shown here, since they take large amounts of space, even though they involve simple and uninteresting operations. However, the full source code can be found on the CD-ROM.

The Tank, Extending cmAbstractPlayer

The tank (see Figure 12-8 and Listing 12-18) is a rapid, maneuverable light vehicle armed with a mini-cannon and light missiles. It doesn't have any special behavior on top of what is already implemented in the abstract vehicle class.

Listing 12-18 *The Fesse tank*

```
class cmFesseTank extends cmAbstractPlayer{
    cmFesseTank (fWorld w, double x, double z, double a) {

        super(w,new fPoint3d(x,ourScale.y,z),
            new fVelocityVector(a,0,0),turningRate,acceleration,
            brakeRate,maxVelocity,ourHealth);

        usePolyhedronInstance(
            new fPolyhedronInstance(ourDefaultPolyhedron,ourScale));
```

```
      addWeapon(new cmMinicannon(this,new fPoint3d(0,ourScale.y,0)));

      addWeapon(new cmMissileLauncher(this,
         new fPoint3d(0,ourScale.y,0)));
      selectWeapon(0);
   }

   protected void die () {
      super.die();
      for(int n=0;n<fragmentsWhenDead;n++){
      new cmGenericFragment(getWorld(),fragmentSize,getPosition(),
         fragmentSpread,fragmentGenerations,fragmentSpeed,3);
      }
      new cmFesseTankRemains(getWorld(),this);
   }

   public static void initiateClass (Applet app) {
      //--
      //-- lots of code with that can be found on the CD
      //--
   }
   //--
   //-- lots of class constants that can be found on the CD
   //--
}
```

The Constructor

🗡 The base class is constructed with the default values for the tank.

🗡 The object is instructed to use the default polyhedron for this class.

🗡 A mini-cannon and a missile launcher are mounted on top of the tank.

🗡 The mini-cannon, being the first weapon, is selected.

FIGURE 12-8
◉ ◉ ◉ ◉ ◉ ◉
The tank

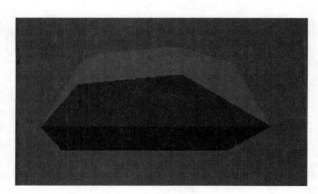

The die() Method

Since the tank doesn't have any special behavior, it is treated as a regular vehicle. When it is hit by rounds, its health will decrease and eventually the tank will be destroyed. This is, however, taken care of in the base class. When the tank is removed from the world, the die() method is called. This method is overridden to insert some new features instead of just letting the tank disappear:

- At death the tank creates fragments.
- The remains of a tank are created.

The Tank Remains, Extending cmAbstractMovingScenery

I have always hated games in which things just explode into nothing. For this reason I have decided that each dead object of significant size should leave something after its death—as does the tank in Figure 12-9. The remains class, shown in Listing 12-19, is constructed when a tank is killed. The behavior is to be thrown up in the air at a random rotation. When this object hits the ground it will remain there for the rest of the game.

Listing 12-19 *The Fesse tank remains*

```
class cmFesseTankRemains extends cmAbstractMovingScenery {

    cmFesseTankRemains(fWorld w, cmFesseTank deadTank){
        super(w,deadTank.getPosition(), deadTank.getAngle(),
            deadTank.getdPosition(), deadTank.getdAngle());

        usePolyhedronInstance(new fPolyhedronInstance(
            ourDefaultPolyhedron,ourScale));

        //-- throw the remaining tank up in the air
        fPoint3d dp=getdPosition();
        dp.y=fWorld.rand(0,ourSpeedUp);
        setdPosition(dp);
        //-- set a random rotation on the remaining tank
        setdAngle(new fAngle3d(fWorld.rand(-ourRandRot,ourRandRot),
            fWorld.rand(-ourRandRot,ourRandRot),
            fWorld.rand(-ourRandRot,ourRandRot)));
    }

    public void update(double dt){
        super.update(dt);
        fPoint3d p=getPosition();
        //-- check if hit the ground
        if(p.y<ourScale.y){
            fPoint3d dp=getdPosition();
```

```
            p.y=ourScale.y;
            dp.x=dp.y=dp.z=0;
            setPosition(p);
            fAngle3d a=getAngle();
            a.x=a.z=0;
            setAngle(a);
            setdAngle(new fAngle3d(0,0,0));
            setdPosition(dp);
        } else if(p.y>ourScale.y) {
            fPoint3d dp=getdPosition();
            dp.y+=((cmWorld)getWorld()).gravity*dt;
            setdPosition(dp);
        }
    }
    public static void initiateClass (Applet app) {
        //--
        //-- lots of simple monotone code that retrieves the class
        //-- constants. The full source can be found on the CD
        //--
    }
    //--
    //-- lots of class constants
    //--
}
```

FIGURE 12-9

◎ ◎ ◎ ◎ ◎ ◎

The tank remains

The Constructor

 The superclass is initiated with the dead tank's position, angle, velocity, and angular velocity.

 The velocity with respect to the y-axis is set to a random value so that the remains of the tank lift off the ground.

 The angular velocity is set to a random value so that the tank remains spin in the air.

The update() Method

 Let the base class do the default updating.

 Check if the object has hit the ground.

 If that is the case, then set velocity to zero and the angle about the x- and z-axes to zero.

 If it is still airborne, just let the gravity do its share.

The Glider, Extending cmAbstractPlayer

The glider in Combat Machines 96 (see Figure 12-10 and Listing 12-20) is some sort of an airplane that can hover and turn in any direction it wants. It is not your regular Kmart glider, but a vehicle with special abilities. The glider carries three weapons: a mini-cannon, dumb missiles, and bombs. The only additional behavior for this vehicle is that it can hit the ground, in which case it will lose health depending on the velocity.

FIGURE 12-10

◎ ◎ ◎ ◎ ◎ ◎

The glider

Listing 12-20 The glider

```
class cmGlider extends cmAbstractPlayer{
  cmGlider (fWorld w, double x, double z, double y,
    double turn, double pitch)
  {
    super(w,new fPoint3d(x,ourScale.y+y,z),
      new fVelocityVector(turn,pitch,0),turningRate, pitchRate,
      acceleration, brakeRate, maxVelocity, climbRate, decentRate, 1,
      ourHealth);

    //-- use the default polyhedron instance
    usePolyhedronInstance(new
fPolyhedronInstance(ourDefaultPolyhedron,ourScale));

    //-- add the weapons
    addWeapon(new cmMinicannon(this,new fPoint3d(0,ourScale.y,0)));
    addWeapon(new cmMissileLauncher(this,
      new fPoint3d(0,ourScale.y,0)));
    addWeapon(new cmBombBay(this,new fPoint3d(0,ourScale.y,0)));
    selectWeapon(0);
  }

  public void update (double dt) {
    super.update(dt);

    //-- check collision with ground
    fPoint3d p=getPosition();
    if(p.y<ourScale.y){
    p.y=ourScale.y;
      setPosition(p);
      fVelocityVector dp=(fVelocityVector)getdPosition();
      dp.setAngleAboutXaxis(0);
    dp.setVelocity(0);
    setdPosition(dp);
    //-- some damage depending on the speed
    double vel=((fVelocityVector)getdPosition()).getVelocity();
    setHealth(getHealth()-vel);
    }
  }

  protected void die(){
    super.die();
    for(int n=0;n<fragmentsWhenDead;n++){
      new cmGenericFragment(getWorld(),fragmentSize,getPosition(),
      fragmentSpread, fragmentGenerations, fragmentSpeed,3);
    }
    new cmGliderRemains(getWorld(),this);
  }

  public static void initiateClass (Applet app) {
```

continued on next page

continued from previous page

```
            //--
            //-- lots of simple monotone code that retrieves the class
            //-- constants. The full source can be found on the CD
            //--
        }
        //--
        //-- lots of class constants
        //--
}
```

The Constructor

The constructor is pretty much a copy of the constructor for cmFesseTank, except that it contains more parameters. The new parameters are specific for airborne vehicles and are pretty much self-explanatory.

The glider also has a new weapon: the bomb.

The update() Method

The position of the glider is checked to be sure that it is above the ground. If that is not the case, then the glider has crashed and the health is decreased depending on the velocity.

The die() Method

The glider leaves some fragments and some remains after its unfortunate death.

The Glider Remains, Extending cmAbstractMovingScenery

This class, shown in Listing 12-21, is almost identical to the remains of the tank. The only difference is that the junk left after a glider is destroyed will simply fall to the ground instead of being thrown up in the air. Figure 12-11 displays the glider remains.

FIGURE 12-11
◎ ◎ ◎ ◎ ◎ ◎
The glider remains

Listing 12-21 *The glider remains*

```
class cmGliderRemains extends cmAbstractMovingScenery {
   cmGliderRemains(fWorld theWorld,cmGlider g){
      super(theWorld,g.getPosition(),g.getAngle(),
         ((fPoint3d)g.getdPosition()),g.getdAngle());

      //-- use the default polyhedron instance
      usePolyhedronInstance(new
fPolyhedronInstance(ourDefaultPolyhedron,ourScale));

      //-- set a random rotation on the remaining glider
      setdAngle(new fAngle3d(fWorld.rand(-ourRandRot,ourRandRot),
         fWorld.rand(-ourRandRot,ourRandRot),
         fWorld.rand(-ourRandRot,ourRandRot)));
   }

   public void update(double dt){
      super.update(dt);
      fPoint3d p=getPosition();

      //-- check if collision with ground
      if(p.y<ourScale.y){
         fPoint3d dp=getdPosition();
         p.y=ourScale.y;
         dp.x=dp.y=dp.z=0;
         setPosition(p);
         fAngle3d a=getAngle();
         a.x=a.z=0;
         setAngle(a);
         setdAngle(new fAngle3d(0,0,0));
         setdPosition(dp);
      } else if(p.y>ourScale.y) {
         //-- gravity
         fPoint3d dp=getdPosition();
         dp.y+=((cmWorld)getWorld()).gravity*dt;
         setdPosition(dp);
      }
   }

   public static void initiateClass (Applet app) {
      //--
      //-- lots of simple monotone code that retrieves the class
      //-- constants. The full source can be found on the CD
      //--
   }
   //--
   //-- lots of class constants
   //--
}
```

The Buildings, Extensions of cmAbstractStaticStructure

There are a couple of different buildings in the game, but the only difference between them is their 3D model and scaling—both types are shown in Figure 12-12 and Listing 12-22. The buildings have no additional behavior on top of the default for their base class. They simply stand there until they are destroyed. The code for these two classes is similar, so only one of the listings is shown.

Listing 12-22 *The generic buildings*

```
class cmGenericBuilding extends cmAbstractStaticStructure{
  /**
   * Generic building with an angle.
   */
  cmGenericBuilding (fWorld world, double x, double z, fAngle3d agl,
    double w, double b, double h)
  {
    super(world,x,z,agl,w,b,h,ourHealth);
    //-- make a building
    myWidth=w; myBredth=b; myHeight=h;
    usePolyhedronInstance(new
        fPolyhedronInstance(ourDefaultPolyhedron,new fPoint3d(w,h,b)));
  }
  /**
   * Generic building with the default 0,0,0 angle.
   */
  cmGenericBuilding (fWorld world, double x, double z, double w,
     double b, double h)
  {
    super(world,x,z,new fAngle3d(),w,b,h,ourHealth);
     //-- make a building
      myWidth=w; myBredth=b; myHeight=h;
      usePolyhedronInstance(new
fPolyhedronInstance(ourDefaultPolyhedron,new fPoint3d(w,h,b)));
    }

  protected void die () {
    super.die();
    fPoint3d pos=getPosition();
    new cmGenericBuildingRuin(getWorld(),pos.x,pos.z,getAngle(),
       myWidth,myBredth,myHeight*.2);
    int nbr=(int)(relFragsWhenDead*myHeight);
    for(int n=0;n<nbr;n++){
      new cmGenericFragment(getWorld(),relFragSize*myHeight,
          getPosition(),relFragSpread*myHeight,
```

>

```
                    (int)(myHeight*relFragGens),myHeight*relFragSpeed,
                    myHeight*relFragRot);
        }
    }

    public static void initiateClass (Applet app) {
        //--
        //-- lots of simple monotone code that retrieves the class
        //-- constants. The full source can be found on the CD
        //--
    }
    //--
    //-- lots of class constants
    //--
}
```

The Missile Launcher, Extension of cmAbstractWeapon

The missile launcher, shown in Listing 12-23, is a weapon that shoots missiles. The terms "weapon" and "round" are very abstract in these circumstances. This means that the round for this weapon is a missile.

FIGURE 12-12

◎ ◎ ◎ ◎ ◎ ◎

The generic buildings

Listing 12-23 *The missile launcher*

```java
class cmMissileLauncher extends cmAbstractWeapon {
    cmMissileLauncher(cmAbstractVehicle host,fPoint3d relPos){
        super(host,relPos,loadingtime,defaultammo);
    }

    public boolean fire(){
        if(super.fire()){
            //-- create a new missile
            fPoint3d p=theHost.getPosition();
            p.plus(relOrigin);
            new cmGenericMissile(theHost.getWorld(), theHost,
                p, theHost.getAngle());
            return true;
        }
        return false;
    }

    public String getName(){
        return name;
    }

    public static void initiateClass (Applet app) {
        //--
        //-- lots of simple monotone code that retrieves the class
        //-- constants. The full source can be found on the CD
        //--
    }
    //--
    //-- lots of class constants
    //--
}
```

The Constructor

The only parameters are the host vehicle and the relative position where the weapon is mounted. The relative position decides where the actual round for this weapon is created.

The fire() Method

If the fire() method of the abstract weapon returns *true*, then the weapon has succeeded in firing a round. The round for this weapon is a generic missile that is created. The rest is taken care of in the missile class.

The Missile, Extension of cmAbstractRound

The generic missile (see Figure 12-13 and Listing 12-24) is a primitive missile that simply travels in the direction that it is fired until it hits something. Upon impact with an object or the ground, it will explode into a fireworks of fragments.

Listing 12-24 *The generic missile*

```
class cmGenericMissile extends cmAbstractRound{
   cmGenericMissile (fWorld w, fObject shooter,
      fPoint3d pos, fAngle3d agl)
   {
      super(w, shooter, pos, new fVelocityVector(agl.y,agl.x,0),
         turningRate, pitchRate, acceleration, brakeRate,
         maxVelocity, 0, 0, 1,impactDamage);

      usePolyhedronInstance(new
fPolyhedronInstance(ourDefaultPolyhedron,ourScale));
   }

   public void update (double dt) {
      super.update(dt);
      increaseVelocity(1,dt);

      fPoint3d p=getPosition();
      if((getAge()>4) || (p.y<0)){
         p.y=0;
         setPosition(p);
         die();
      }
   }

   protected void die () {
      super.die();
      for(int n=0;n<fragmentsWhenDead;n++){
         new cmGenericFragment(getWorld(),fragmentSize,getPosition(),
            fragmentSpread,fragmentGenerations,fragmentSpeed,3);
      }
   }

   public static void initiateClass (Applet app) {
      //--
      //-- lots of simple monotone code that retrieves the class
      //-- constants. The full source can be found on the CD
      //--
   }
   //--
   //-- lots of class constants
   //--
}
```

FIGURE 12-13

◎ ◎ ◎ ◎ ◎ ◎

The missile

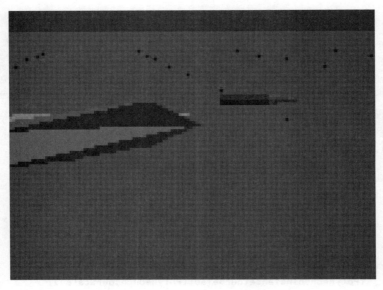

The Constructor

No surprises here.

The update() Method

The missile has a lifetime. If it exceeds a certain "age" or hits the ground, it will die. Otherwise, it just keeps accelerating.

The die() Method

When the missile dies, it will produce fragments.

The Mini-Cannon, Extension of cmAbstractWeapon

This weapon, shown in Listing 12-25, is very much like the missile launcher except that the round for this weapon is a mini-cannon round. Other than that, this class is identical to the missile launcher.

Listing 12-25 The mini-cannon

```
class cmMinicannon extends cmAbstractWeapon {
   cmMinicannon(cmAbstractVehicle host,fPoint3d relPos){
      super(host,relPos,loadingtime,defaultammo);
   }

   public boolean fire(){
      if(super.fire()){
         fPoint3d p=theHost.getPosition();
         p.plus(relOrigin);
         new cmMinicannonRound( theHost.getWorld(), theHost, p,
            theHost.getAngle());
         return true;
      }
      return false;
   }

   public String getName(){
      return name;
   }
   public static void initiateClass (Applet app) {
      //--
      //-- lots of simple monotone code that retrieves the class
      //-- constants. The full source can be found on the CD
      //--
   }
   //--
   //-- lots of class constants
   //--
}
```

The Mini-Cannon Round, Extension of cmAbstractRound

The mini-cannon round (see Figure 12-14 and Listing 12-26) is an object with a simple behavior. It is very much like the missile, except that this round doesn't accelerate but starts with its maximum velocity and travels until it hits something or dies because of old age.

FIGURE 12-14

ⓐ ⓐ ⓐ ⓐ ⓐ ⓐ

*A mini-cannon
projectile*

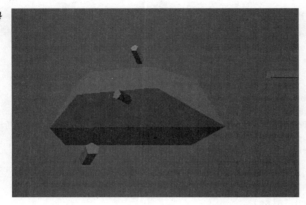

Listing 12-26 *The mini-cannon round*

```
class cmMinicannonRound extends cmAbstractRound{
    cmMinicannonRound (fWorld w, fObject shooter,
        fPoint3d pos, fAngle3d agl)
    {
        super(w,shooter,pos,new fVelocityVector(agl.y,agl.x,maxVelocity),
            0,0,0,0,maxVelocity,0,0,1,impactDamage);

        //-- the polyhedron instance
        usePolyhedronInstance(new
fPolyhedronInstance(ourDefaultPolyhedron,ourScale));
        //-- create an empty shell
        new cmMinicannonShell(getWorld(),pos,agl,
            ((cmAbstractMovingObject)shooter).getdPosition());
    }

    public void update (double dt) {
        super.update(dt);
        //-- check if it is time to die
        if(dieNextUpdate==true){
            die();
            return;
        }

        fPoint3d p=getPosition();
        //-- if bullet hits the ground then die
        //-- next round so that a collision detection
        //-- can be done
        if(p.y<0){
            p.y=0;
            setPosition(p);
            dieNextUpdate=true;
        }
        //-- if life is out
```

```
        if(getAge()>lifeTime){
           deadOfAge=true;
           die();
        }
     }

     protected void die () {
        super.die();
        //-- if this round has died by hitting something
        if(deadOfAge==false){
           for(int n=0;n<fragmentsWhenDead;n++){
              new cmGenericFragment(getWorld(), fragmentSize,
                 getPosition(), fragmentSpread, fragmentGenerations,
                 fragmentSpeed, fragmentRotation);
           }
        }
     }
     protected boolean dieNextUpdate;
     protected boolean deadOfAge;

     public static void initiateClass (Applet app) {
        //--
        //-- lots of simple monotone code that retrieves the class
        //-- constants. The full source can be found on the CD
        //--
     }
     //--
     //-- lots of class constants
     //--
  }
```

The Constructor

 The superclass is a vehicle with very few capabilities. As you can see in the constructor, this round can only travel forward at maximum velocity.

 The standard assignment of a 3D model.

 An empty shell is created to enhance the effect.

The update() Method

Since a bullet travels at very high speeds, a collision can be "missed." The bullet might travel right through the object without ever actually touching the object. This is especially annoying when the round is fired from an airborne vehicle at a ground vehicle. For this reason, when a round hits the ground, it will remain there one frame so that a possible collision will be detected.

A round can also die of different reasons. If it dies of age, then that is marked, because the round should just disappear without producing any fragments. On the other hand, if the round dies because of the result of an impact, it should produce fragments.

🗡 If this round is already dead, complete it by calling die() and return.

🗡 If the round is below ground level, then set it to ground level and mark it as dead.

The die() Method

If the bullet has died of old age and not because of an impact, then just die without any further actions; otherwise, make a nice exit.

The Abstract Shell, Extension of cmAbstractMovingScenery

Every time a projectile is fired, an empty shell will be tossed out of the weapon. There are different kinds of shells, but they all have something in common. The common behavior is that they are all tossed up and have a random spread and rotation.

Note that this is an abstract class and therefore does not have the initializeClass() method. Like all abstract classes, the constructor is full of arguments. Listing 12-27 shows the abstract shell.

Listing 12-27 The abstract shell

```
abstract class cmAbstractShell extends cmAbstractMovingScenery{

    protected cmAbstractShell (fWorld w, fPoint3d origin,
        fAngle3d agl, fPoint3d dpos, fAngle3d dagl, double randomSpread,
        double randomRotation, double lifeTime0)
    {
    super(w,origin,agl,
        new fPoint3d(dpos.x+fWorld.rand(-randomSpread,randomSpread),
                    dpos.y+fWorld.rand(-randomSpread,randomSpread),
                    dpos.z+fWorld.rand(-randomSpread,randomSpread)),
        new fAngle3d(dagl.x+fWorld.rand(-randomRotation,randomRotation),
                    dagl.y+fWorld.rand(-randomRotation,randomRotation),
                    dagl.z+fWorld.rand( randomRotation,randomRotation))
        );
    lifeTime = lifeTime0;
    }

    public void update (double dt) {
        super.update(dt);
```

```
        fPoint3d v=getdPosition();
        v.y+=((cmWorld)getWorld()).gravity*dt;
        setdPosition(v);

        if( (getPosition().y<0) || (getAge()>lifeTime) ){
            die();
        }
    }

    protected double lifeTime;
}
```

The Constructor

The velocity and angular velocity of the object is affected by the random values supplied in the construct.

The update() Method

If the shell hits the ground or exceeds its lifetime, it will die.

The Mini-Cannon Empty Shell, Extension of cmAbstractShell

The mini-cannon shell, unlike other shells, has a certain size and certain 3D model, except that it is just a regular shell. (Refer to Figure 12-14 for examples of shells.) A mini-cannon shell will fly perpendicular to the right of the projectile. Listing 12-28 shows the empty mini-cannon shell.

Listing 12-28 *The empty shell*

```
class cmMinicannonShell extends cmAbstractShell{
    cmMinicannonShell (fWorld w, fPoint3d origin, fAngle3d agl,
        fPoint3d vel)
    {
        super(w,origin,agl,
            new fPoint3d(vel.x+speed*Math.sin(agl.y+Math.PI/2),
            vel.y+speed, vel.z+speed*Math.cos(agl.y+Math.PI/2)),
            new fAngle3d(angleX,angleY,angleZ),
            randomSpread, randomRotation,lifeTime);

        usePolyhedronInstance(new
fPolyhedronInstance(ourDefaultPolyhedron,ourScale));
    }

    public static void initiateClass (Applet app) {
```

continued on next page

continued from previous page

```
        //--
        //-- lots of simple monotone code that retrieves the class
        //-- constants. The full source can be found on the CD
        //--
      }
//--
//-- lots of class constants
//--
}
```

The Constructor

The superclass is initialized by tossing the shell perpendicularly to the right of the projectile.

The Bomb Bay, Extension of cmAbstractWeapon

This class is, as strange as it might sound, a weapon that has bombs as rounds. Other than that, it is just like any other weapon. It creates a bomb when fired. The bomb bay is shown in Listing 12-29.

Listing 12-29 *The bomb bay*

```
class cmBombBay extends cmAbstractWeapon {
   cmBombBay(cmAbstractVehicle host,fPoint3d relPos){
      super(host,relPos,loadingtime,defaultammo);
   }

   public boolean fire(){
      if(super.fire()){
         fPoint3d p=theHost.getPosition();
         p.plus(relOrigin);
         new cmGenericBomb(theHost.getWorld(), theHost.getPosition(),
            theHost.getAngle(), theHost.getdPosition(), 15);
         return true;
      }
      return false;
   }

   public String getName(){
      return name;
   }
```

```
public static void initiateClass (Applet app) {
   //--
   //-- lots of simple monotone code that retrieves the class
   //-- constants. The full source can be found on the CD
   //--
}
//--
//-- lots of class constants
//--
}
```

The Bomb, Extension of cmAbstractMovingScenery

The bomb (see Figure 12-15) is a bit special, since it is not the actual casing of the bomb that does the damage but the explosion. This is the reason why it is just scenery. The action takes place when it hits the ground.

This class, shown in Listing 12-30, is technically more advanced than the other objects, since it uses more features and has to do some tricks to get the wanted results.

FIGURE 12-15

◎ ◎ ◎ ◎ ◎ ◎

The bomb

Listing 12-30 *The generic bomb*

```
class cmGenericBomb extends cmAbstractMovingScenery{
    cmGenericBomb (fWorld w, fPoint3d p, fAngle3d a,
        fPoint3d dp, double strength0 )
{
    super(w,p, a, new fPoint3d(0,0,0),
        new fAngle3d(
            fWorld.rand(-randRotation,randRotation),
            fWorld.rand(-randRotation,randRotation),
            fWorld.rand(-randRotation,randRotation))
    );      //--
    usePolyhedronInstance(new
fPolyhedronInstance(ourDefaultPolyhedron,ourScale));
    //--
    strength=strength0;
}

public void update (double dt) {
    super.update(dt);

    fPoint3d v=getdPosition();
    v.y+=cmWorld.gravity;
    setdPosition(v);

    fPoint3d p=getPosition();
    if(p.y<0){
        die();
    }
}

protected void die () {
    super.die();
    //-- create an explosion that is proportional to the strength
    //-- of the bomb
    new cmGenericExplosion(getWorld(),getPosition(),
        strength*0.25,0.5,strength,0.6,strength*0.1);

    //-- create an explosion round since
    cmAbstractRound wep=new cmExplosion(getWorld(),10*strength);

    //-- get all objects within a radius and check feed them with
    //-- the impact of the bomb
    vect.removeAllElements();
    getWorld().getAllObjectsInRadius(getPosition(),strength*3,vect);
    int nbr=vect.size();
    for(int n=0;n<nbr;n++){
        fObject obj=(fObject)vect.elementAt(n);
        if(obj.interestedOfCollisionWith(wep)){
            obj.collisionWith(wep,1);
        }
    }
    wep.die();
```

```
    }
    protected double strength;

    public static void initiateClass (Applet app) {
        //--
        //-- lots of simple monotone code that retrieves the class
        //-- constants. The full source can be found on the CD
        //--
    }
    //--
    //-- lots of class constants
    //--
}
```

The Constructor

The bomb will have the same initial velocity and angle as the host vehicle, but the angular velocity will be affected by a random value so that the bombs fall differently from each other.

The update() Method

 The bomb keeps falling until it hits the ground.

 If the bomb has hit the ground, it is time to die.

The die() Method

When the bomb hits the ground, an explosion is created. The explosion itself is just scenery and has no function except for giving the impression of an explosion. The actual damage is done through the "dummy" object cmExplosion, which is a cmAbstractRound. All the objects within the radius of the explosion will be notified of a collision with this round.

Let's look at what takes place in this method:

 An explosion is created with a set of parameters that affects the way it looks.

 The "dummy" round cmExplosion is created with the same strength as the bomb itself.

 All objects within the radius of the bomb are asked: Are you interested in a collision with an explosion? If that is the case, then they are notified about the collision.

 The dummy explosion is killed to remove it from the world.

The Explosion, Extension of cmAbstractRound

This is a very abstract round that is produced by the bomb when it hits the ground. This class, shown in Listing 12-31, is only used as a sort of notification to objects that they have collided with something that "hurts." Since an explosion is just a lot of heat, it cannot be represented satisfactorily by a 3D model. That is the reason why this somewhat odd object exists.

Listing 12-31 *The explosion*

```
class cmExplosion extends cmAbstractRound {
   cmExplosion(fWorld world, double strength){
      super(world,null,new fPoint3d(),new fVelocityVector(0,0,0),
         0,0,0,0,0,0,0,1,strength);
   }
}
```

The Constructor

The superclass is initiated with some dummy values.

The Explosion, Extension of cmAbstractMovingScenery

The somewhat abstract object shown in Figure 12-16 and Listing 12-32 represents the explosion of a bomb. The 3D model for this object expands and then contracts to give the impression of brute force.

Listing 12-32 *The explosion*

```
class cmGenericExplosion extends cmAbstractMovingScenery{
   public cmGenericExplosion (fWorld w, fPoint3d p, double s0,double t0,
      double s1,double t1,double s2)
   {
      super(w,new fPoint3d(p.x,s0,p.z),new fAngle3d(),
         new fPoint3d(),new fAngle3d(0,3,0));

      //-- set the polyhedron instance
      usePolyhedronInstance(new fPolyhedronInstance(
         ourDefaultPolyhedron,new fPoint3d(s0*2,s0*0.33,s0*2)));

      //-- create some fragments
      for(int n=0;n<(int)(nbrOfFragments*s1);n++){
```

```
            new cmGenericFragment(getWorld(),s1*fragmentsSize,p,
                s0*fragmentsSpeed,1,s1*fragmentsSpeed,s0*fragmentsRotation);
        }

        //-- calculate the delta scaling
        strength=s1;

        time1=t0;
        dScale1=(s1-s0)/t0;

        time2=t1;
        dScale2=(s2-s1)/t1;
    }

    public void update (double dt) {
        super.update(dt);
        double age=getAge();

        //-- adjust the scaling of the polyehdron
        fPoint3d scale=getPolyhedronInstance().getScalingFactor();
        if(age>(time1+time2)){
            die();
        }else if(age>time1){
            scale.plus(dScale2*dt);
        } else {
            scale.plus(dScale1*dt);
        }
        getPolyhedronInstance().setScalingFactor(scale);

        //-- adjust the position so that the bottom always touches
        //-- the ground
        fPoint3d p=getPosition();
        p.y=scale.y;
        setPosition(p);
    }

    public double getStrength(){
        return strength;
    }
    protected double dScale1,time1,dScale2,time2;
    protected double strength;

    public static void initiateClass (Applet app) {
        //--
        //-- lots of simple monotone code that retrieves the class
        //-- constants. The full source can be found on the CD
        //--
    }
    //--
    //-- lots of class constants
    //--
}
```

FIGURE 12-16
◎ ◎ ◎ ◎ ◎ ◎
The explosion

The Constructor

The arguments of the constructor control with what speed the explosion expands and contracts, as shown in Figure 12-17.

FIGURE 12-17
◎ ◎ ◎ ◎ ◎ ◎
*The explosion
expansion and
contraction*

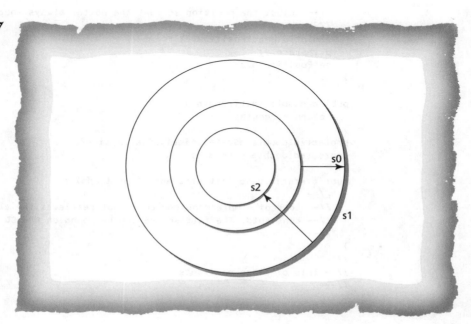

s0 is the initial scale of the polyhedron. In *t0* seconds the explosion will expand to the maximum size of *s1*. Immediately after that, the explosion will start contracting, and in *t1* seconds it will reach the minimum scale of *s2* and then disappear.

Uses a polyhedron scaled depending on arguments to the constructor.

Creates some fragments to give the impression of things flying up in the air from the power of the explosion.

Calculates the growth and contraction rate for the explosion.

The update() Method

The scale of the polyhedron instance is changed.

The position of the object is adjusted so that the bottom of the model always touches the ground.

Putting Together a Virtual World

We now have all the objects we need to make a virtual world. The construction of the world is simple but hard work, since we don't have access to a world editor.

The cmWorld, Extension of fWorld

The extension of fWorld (see Listing 12-33) is our own customized virtual world. In the constructor all objects are created (several hundreds), which are then left to the mercy of the core. The full source code can be found on the CD-ROM.

The class variable *theActivePlayer* is the player that is controlled from the keyboard while all other players are controlled by the computer. By default the player is a tank, but you can change it to an arbitrary abstract player. You can even make your own machine of destruction, armed to the teeth and possessing extreme capabilities.

Listing 12-33 *The cmWorld*

```
class cmWorld extends fWorld{
   cmWorld (Applet app) {
      //-- create a world with the size 1km x 1km divided into
      //-- 20x20 squares
      super(app,-500,-500,1000,20);
      app.showStatus(" Creating CombatMachines96 world.");
      //-- reset the virtual world
      reset();
   }
   /*
```

continued on next page

continued from previous page

```
* Returns the active player that is controlled by the keyboard.
*/
   public cmAbstractPlayer getActivePlayer(){
      return theActivePlayer;
   }

   protected cmAbstractPlayer theActivePlayer;
   public static final double gravity=-10;

   /*
    * Override the base class method.
    */
   public void reset(){
      super.reset();
      //--
      //-- creating the initial world by
      //-- making new objects
      //-- the full source is on the CD
      //--
      //--
   }
```

The Display Panel

The display panel that will be used in the final applet is a simple class with standard Java coding. There shouldn't be any problems for you at this point.

There are a few buttons that change the function of the panel from camera to radar to vehicle gauges and so on. There is really nothing tricky about it. The source code is self-explanatory and can be found on the CD-ROM.

The Applet

It is now time to wrap it all up and make the actual applet (see Listing 12-34) in which the world will be displayed. The applet contains a display panel with the camera that tracks the active player in the world.

The player can be controlled from the keyboard with a set of commands that apply to all vehicles. The commands are easily deduced by looking at the source of the applet.

Listing 12-34 *The applet*

```
public class cmApplet extends Applet implements Runnable{
   Thread myThread;
   boolean alive;
   boolean key [ ];
   cmWorld world;
   cmAbstractPlayer player;
   cmDisplayPanel display1;
   Panel panel;
```

```
public void init () {
    double viewAngle=new
Double(getParameter("cmApplet_viewAngle")).doubleValue();
    viewDistance=new
Double(getParameter("cmApplet_viewDistance")).doubleValue();
    gridSize=new
Double(getParameter("cmApplet_gridSize")).doubleValue();

    key=new boolean[100];

    showStatus(" Initiating Combat Machines 96 ");

    world=new cmWorld(this);

    setLayout(new GridLayout(1,1));
    //-- add a display panel with a camera
    add(display1=new cmDisplayPanel(world.getActivePlayer(),"C"));

    myThread=new Thread(this);
    myThread.start();
    myThread.setPriority(Thread.MAX_PRIORITY);
    alive=true;
}

public final void run () {
    lastUpdate=System.currentTimeMillis()    ;
    while(alive){
        long currentTime=System.currentTimeMillis();
        long dtmillis=currentTime-lastUpdate;
        double dt=(double)dtmillis/1000;
        lastUpdate=currentTime;

        if(dt>0.2) dt=0.2;
        //-- get the active player
        player=world.getActivePlayer();
        //-- handle keyboard events
        handleKeyboard();
        //-- update the world
        world.update(dt);
        //-- update the display
        display1.update(dt);
    }
}

public final void start () {
    showStatus(" Starting Combat Machines 96 (gimped)");
    if(myThread==null){
        myThread=new Thread(this);
        myThread.setPriority(Thread.MAX_PRIORITY);
        myThread.start();
        alive=true;
```

continued on next page

continued from previous page

```
            }
        }

        public final synchronized void stop () {
            showStatus(" Stoping applet.");
            if(myThread!=null){
                myThread.stop();
                myThread=null;
                alive=false;
            }
        }

        public boolean keyDown (Event ev, int k) {
            keyboardEvent(ev.key,true);
            return true;
        }

        public boolean keyUp (Event ev, int k) {
            keyboardEvent(ev.key,false);
            return true;
        }

        protected void keyboardEvent (int k, boolean pressed) {
            switch(k){
                case 'h': key[cmEventSteeringCommand.TURN_LEFT]=pressed;break;
                case 'k': key[cmEventSteeringCommand.TURN_RIGHT]=pressed;break;
                case 't':
key[cmEventSteeringCommand.INCREASE_VELOCITY]=pressed;break;
                case 'g': key[cmEventSteeringCommand.BRAKE]=pressed;break;
                case 'y': key[cmEventSteeringCommand.CLIMB]=pressed;break;
                case 'i': key[cmEventSteeringCommand.DECENT]=pressed;break;
                case 'u': key[cmEventSteeringCommand.PITCH_DOWN]=pressed;break;
                case 'j': key[cmEventSteeringCommand.PITCH_UP]=pressed;break;
                case 'a': key[cmEventWeaponCommand.FIRE]=pressed;break;
                case '1': key[cmEventWeaponCommand.MINICANNON]=pressed;break;
                case '2': key[cmEventWeaponCommand.MISSILE]=pressed;break;
                case '3': key[cmEventWeaponCommand.BOMB]=pressed;break;
            }
        }

        protected void handleKeyboard () {
            //-- handle keyboard;
            if(key[cmEventSteeringCommand.TURN_LEFT]) player.turnLeft(1,0.1);
            if(key[cmEventSteeringCommand.TURN_RIGHT]) player.turnRight(1,0.1);
            if(key[cmEventSteeringCommand.INCREASE_VELOCITY]) {
                player.increaseVelocity(1,0.1);
            }
            if(key[cmEventSteeringCommand.BRAKE]) player.brake(1,0.1);
            if(key[cmEventSteeringCommand.CLIMB]) player.climb(1,0.1);
            if(key[cmEventSteeringCommand.DECENT]) player.decent(1,0.1);
            if(key[cmEventSteeringCommand.PITCH_UP]) player.pitchUp(1,0.1);
            if(key[cmEventSteeringCommand.PITCH_DOWN]) player.pitchDown(1,0.1);
```

```
      if(key[cmEventWeaponCommand.FIRE]) player.fireSelectedWeapon();
      if(key[cmEventWeaponCommand.MINICANNON]){
         int com=cmEventWeaponCommand.SELECT;
         int arg=cmEventWeaponCommand.MINICANNON;
         player.addEvent(new
cmEventWeaponCommand(world.getTime(),com,arg));
      }
      if(key[cmEventWeaponCommand.MISSILE]){
         int com=cmEventWeaponCommand.SELECT;
         int arg=cmEventWeaponCommand.MISSILE;
         player.addEvent(new
cmEventWeaponCommand(world.getTime(),com,arg));
      }
      if(key[cmEventWeaponCommand.BOMB]){
         int com=cmEventWeaponCommand.SELECT;
         int arg=cmEventWeaponCommand.BOMB;
         player.addEvent(new
cmEventWeaponCommand(world.getTime(),com,arg));
      }
   }

   protected long lastUpdate;
   static double viewAngle;
   static double viewDistance;
   static double gridSize;
}
```

Suggestion Box

As you have seen by now, developing 3D games using the App3Dcore in conjunction with the game layer is very easy, since most of the work is done for you behind the scenes. You can, at this point, build your own objects and insert them in the virtual world using the template supplied to you.

You can, for example, change the HTML file, giving the tank extreme capabilities.

Other extensions might be to design your own weapons. By changing the source for the generic missile, you could turn it into a homing missile. You can design mines easily by using the source for the bomb. Just let it rest on the ground, and when a collision occurs, let it explode.

Summary

In this chapter you have learned how to use the core by extending the most vital classes. You have seen how to implement some simple behavior, like the bouncing boxes. The behavior was implemented by overriding methods in the core classes. You have also seen how the core can be extended with a whole layer of classes that turned it from a bare-bones engine into a more specialized game engine. The classes developed in the game layer implemented all the basic behavior of the most commonly used objects in games. With this platform to stand on, we have developed a small but relatively complex 3D game.

Part III

Game Gallery

13

Building the JAVAroids Game

Joel Fan

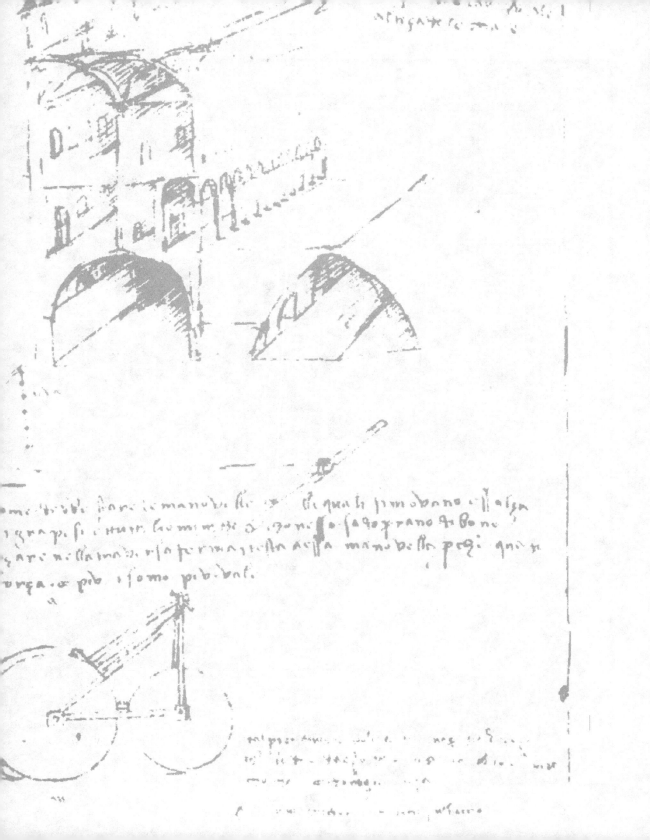

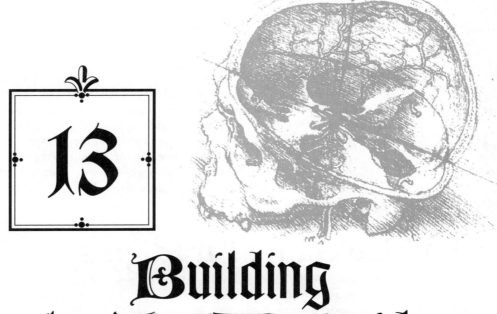

13

Building the JAVAroids Game

In this chapter, you're going to build a full-fledged video game called JAVAroids. You'll make use of the fundamental techniques we've explored in the earlier parts of this book, such as object-oriented design and inheritance, to construct and manage a complex applet. In addition, you'll apply your knowledge of Java's multimedia capabilities to create fast-paced entertainment for players around the World Wide Web! So without further ado, let's start by seeing what this game is about.

The Game Plot

Imagine: You are lost in space, searching desperately for a friendly space station, when your ship strays into an asteroid belt. To make matters worse, this area of space is infested with enemy aliens who would like nothing better than to blow your ship to bits! This is the plot behind Asteroids, one of the classics of the video game canon.

By building a Java version of Asteroids, you'll apply a variety of techniques that can be used to write millions of other video games. In fact, you'll see how easy it is to add features above and beyond the classic Asteroids, due to the object-oriented nature of Java. Our version of Asteroids will be called JAVAroids, in honor of the programming language it's written in.

For those of you who don't remember Asteroids, here's some detail of the game action. Your ship is initially situated at the center of the screen, and can rotate, thrust, and fire in arbitrary directions. As the asteroids approach, you can fire at them to protect yourself. If you hit an asteroid, it splits into two smaller ones, unless it's too small to be split any further. And once in a while, the enemy ships come out firing at you. We're going to add a bunch of features to the original Asteroids: color, rotating asteroids, a shield, and a "powerup," which gives your ship extra shield strength. And soon, you'll be adding your own cool extensions.

Video Game Paradigms

In Asteroids, the ship you control is in the center of the screen, and you can rotate and thrust it in space. Of course, when your ship drifts off the edge of the screen, it doesn't disappear—it appears on the opposite side. The same is true for the asteroids. This effect is called *wrap-around graphics*, and it's a common device used in 2D games with a landscape that doesn't scroll, or a *fixed landscape*. Figure 13-1 shows the effect of wrapping a sprite from the right side of the screen to the left.

In contrast, some 2D games give the illusion of existing in a larger universe than what is currently seen on the display. Such games are said to have a *scrolling landscape*. Figure 13-2 gives an example of a scrolling landscape. Games with scrolling displays are a bit more complex than their fixed-landscape counterparts, as we'll see in a few chapters. One nice feature of scrolling-landscape games is that they port naturally to 3D.

FIGURE 13-1

◉ ◉ ◉ ◉ ◉ ◉

Wrapping a sprite from right to left

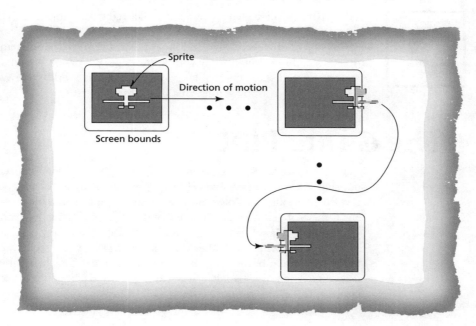

FIGURE 13-2

◎ ◎ ◎ ◎ ◎ ◎

A scrolling landscape

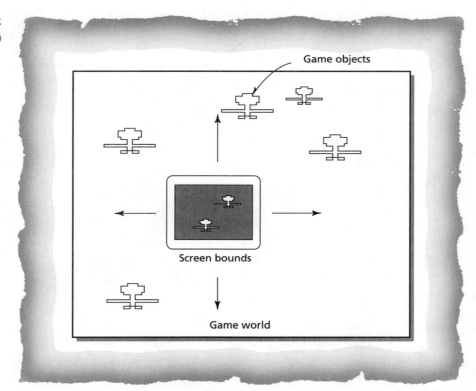

JAVAroids is a fixed-landscape game, and we need to implement the wrap-around effect for all the sprites in the game: the player's ship, the asteroids, the enemy ships, and firing. These sprites are represented with polygons that move across the screen, and rotate if necessary. Let's implement these sprites by inheriting from the Sprite framework we developed in Chapter 3, Animating Sprites. (You won't have to go back there; all the information you need is below.)

Deriving Sprites

Games and graphics applications often have multiple objects on the screen that move independently of one another. The Sprite framework gives us a uniform way of encapsulating and controlling these screen objects, regardless of their internal structure, whether they're bitmaps or rectangles. For example, Figure 13-3 diagrams the Sprite hierarchy we built earlier.

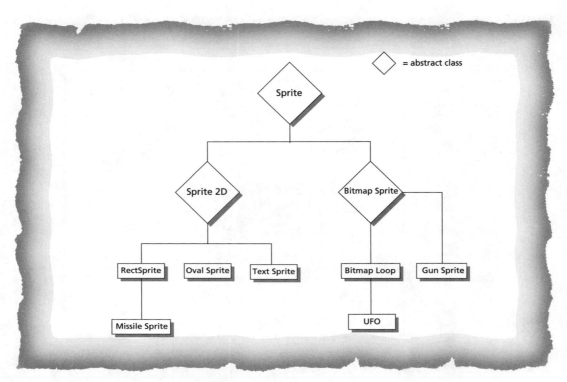

FIGURE 13-3 ◉ *Sprite hierarchy from Part I*

For JAVAroids, we need classes that encapsulate moving and rotating polygons. We will call these classes PolygonSprite, MoveablePolygon, and RotateablePolygon, and we'll derive them from existing Sprite classes. The first step is to choose an appropriate parent class.

Choosing a Parent for the PolygonSprite Class

What is the best parent class for a PolygonSprite? This would be the most specific class in our Sprite hierarchy that provides functionality that we can build upon. We're not going to use bitmaps to represent the polygons, so the BitmapSprite or BitmapLoop provides unnecessary functionality. On the other hand, a RectSprite displays rectangles, so it's a bit too specific. The best choice of parent class for a PolygonSprite is Sprite2D, which encapsulates sprites that rely on methods defined in the Graphics class. Listing 13-1 shows the definition of Sprite2D and its parent, Sprite.

Listing 13-1 *Sprite and Sprite2D classes*

```java
abstract class Sprite {
  protected boolean visible;            // is sprite visible
  protected boolean active;             // is sprite updatable

  // abstract methods:
  abstract void paint (Graphics g);
  abstract void update();

  // accessor methods:
  public boolean isVisible() {
    return visible;
  }

  public void setVisible(boolean b) {
    visible = b;
  }

  public boolean isActive() {
    return active;
  }

  public void setActive(boolean b) {
    active = b;
  }

  // suspend the sprite
  public void suspend() {
    setVisible(false);
    setActive(false);
  }

  // restore the sprite
  public void restore() {
    setVisible(true);
    setActive(true);
  }

}


abstract class Sprite2D extends Sprite {

  protected int locx;                   // x location
  protected int locy;                   // y location

  protected Color color;                // the color of sprite
  protected boolean fill;               // filled or not

  public boolean getFill() {
    return fill;
  }
```

continued on next page

continued from previous page

```
        public void setFill(boolean b) {
          fill = b;
        }

        public void setColor(Color c) {
          color = c;
        }

        public Color getColor() {
          return color;
        }

    }
```

After deriving PolygonSprite, we'll subclass MoveablePolygon to represent the firing and the enemy ships, and RotateablePolygon to display the player's ship and the asteroids.

Defining PolygonSprite

To implement PolygonSprite, we need some way of representing a polygon. Fortunately, java.awt provides a Polygon class that's convenient to use.

java.awt.Polygon

Variables

    npoints: The number of points in the polygon

    xpoints: The array of x coordinates

    ypoints: The array of y coordinates

Selected Methods

    Polygon(): Creates an empty polygon

    Polygon(int xpoints[], int ypoints[], int npoints):

        Creates and initializes a polygon with the specified parameters

    addPoint(int x, int y): Appends point (x,y) to polygon

To paint a Polygon *p* in Graphics context *g*, use

```
g.drawPolygon(p);
```

    or

```
g.fillPolygon(p);
```

Of course, it's possible to draw a polygon by using a sequence of g.drawLine() commands, but it's definitely faster to use the polygon-draw from the Graphics class. Let's use java.awt.Polygon to help us with the PolygonSprite class, shown in Listing 13-2.

Listing 13-2 *PolygonSprite class*

```
////////////////////////////////////////////////////////////////////
//
// PolygonSprite class: encapsulates polygon, position
//                           it appears, visibility
//
////////////////////////////////////////////////////////////////////

class PolygonSprite extends Sprite2D {

  protected Polygon p;

  // methods:

////////////////////////////////////////////////////////////////////
// constructor: take absolute coords
////////////////////////////////////////////////////////////////////

  public PolygonSprite(int x[], int y[], int n, Color c) {
    p = new Polygon(x,y,n);
    color = c;
    visible = true;
    fill = false;                              // don't fill polygon
    locx = locy = 0;
  }


////////////////////////////////////////////////////////////////////
// add point to the polygon
////////////////////////////////////////////////////////////////////

  public void addPoint(int x, int y) {
    p.addPoint(x,y);
  }


////////////////////////////////////////////////////////////////////
// paint polygon based on variables from Sprite and Sprite2D
////////////////////////////////////////////////////////////////////

  public void paint(Graphics g) {
    if (visible) {
      g.setColor(color);
      if (fill)
        g.fillPolygon(p);

      else
        g.drawPolygon(p);
```

continued on next page

continued from previous page

```
      }
    }

//////////////////////////////////////////////////////////////
// no update operation
//////////////////////////////////////////////////////////////

  public void update() {
  }


}
```

As you see, it's pretty straightforward! Now the MoveablePolygon can be derived from PolygonSprite. In Listing 13-3, we'll use the Moveable interface (defined in Chapter 3, Animating Sprites), which specifies methods to move a Sprite class.

Listing 13-3 *Moveable interface*

```
public interface Moveable {
  public abstract void setPosition(int x, int y);
  public abstract void setVelocity(int x, int y);
  public abstract void updatePosition();
}
```

Remember that a class implements an interface by providing the code for methods specified in the interface. One way of moving the polygon (as required by updatePosition()) is to store the polygon in *local* coordinates, and compute the *screen* coordinates before painting. Using a local coordinate system is also going to make rotating a polygon really easy, since we can store the points in *polar* coordinates. Did you catch all that? If not, here's a little review...

Doing a Little Vector Math

In this section, we're going to cover the math necessary to implement moving and rotating polygons. In particular, you'll learn about local and screen coordinate systems, as well as Cartesian and polar coordinates.

Local vs. Screen Coordinates

To implement polygon sprites that will move and rotate, the polygon will be represented as a sequence of vectors that start at the origin. Figure 13-4 shows an example of five vectors that comprise a house (a.k.a. a pentagon).

FIGURE 13-4

◎ ◎ ◎ ◎ ◎ ◎

Simple house

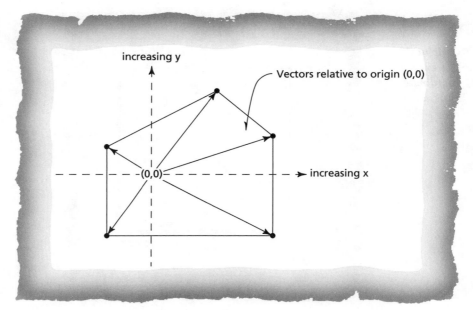

This house is represented in a local coordinate system, since all vectors are relative to the local origin (0,0) and don't tell us where the polygon will appear on the screen. In contrast, screen, or *absolute,* coordinates tell us exactly where the house will be displayed. Figure 13-5 shows the coordinate system used by the graphics context. Remember that points beyond the extents of the graphics context, such as points with negative coordinates, are not displayed. And since (0,0) is at the upper-left corner, y coordinates increase as you go down the screen, in contrast to local coordinates, where increasing y means going up.

To display the house at some location on the screen, the local coordinates must be *transformed* into screen coordinates. It's really easy to do this. First decide where the origin of the house should be in screen coordinates. Let's call the screen position of the origin (*locx,locy*). Then the screen coordinates for each point of the house can be found by adding the vector for that point to the new origin (*locx,locy*). Figure 13-6 shows the house with origin at (200,200).

Wait! The house is upside down. This is because of the opposite orientation of the y-axes in the local and screen coordinate systems. To orient the local y-axis properly, multiply each vector's y coordinate by -1 before transforming to screen coordinates. Figure 13-7 shows the result of performing this transformation.

FIGURE 13-5

◉ ◉ ◉ ◉ ◉ ◉

Graphics context coordinate system

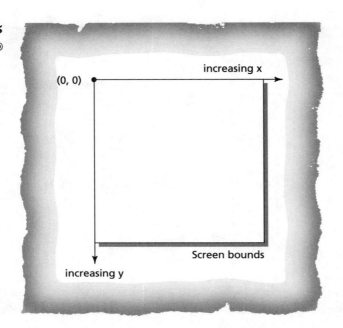

FIGURE 13-6

◉ ◉ ◉ ◉ ◉ ◉

House coordinates transformed to screen coordinates

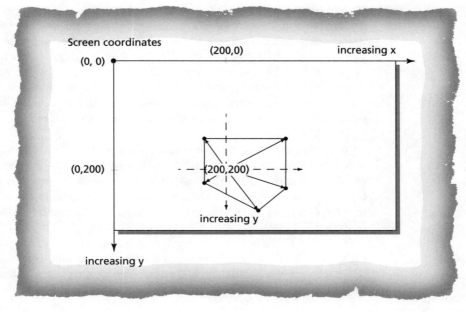

FIGURE 13-7

◎ ◎ ◎ ◎ ◎ ◎

The correct house to screen transformation

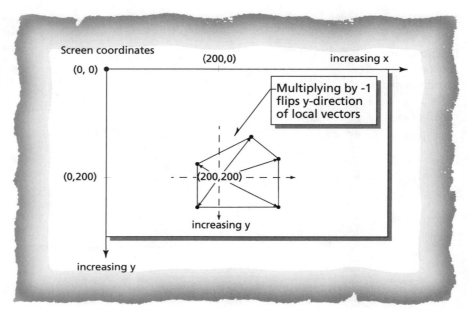

In summary, a local vector (x,y) transforms to screen coordinates (s,t) by

```
s = locx + -1 * x;
t = locy + -1 * y;
```

where (*locx,locy*) is the screen position of the local origin. By applying this formula to each vector of a polygon, we can move the polygon anywhere on the screen! When the orientation of the polygon is unimportant, as in our case, we'll omit the multiplication by -1.

Cartesian vs. Polar Coordinates

Now we will learn how to rotate a polygon about its origin. This is really easy in *polar* coordinates, so we're going to transform the *Cartesian* coordinates we're familiar with (that is, the standard x and y) into polar form.

Polar coordinates (*r,theta*) are just another way of specifying points in the 2D plane. As Figure 13-8 shows, *r* is the distance from (*x,y*) to the origin, or the *magnitude* of vector (*x,y*); *theta* is the angle from some distinguished axis, such as the x-axis. Equations 13-1 and 13-2 relate (*x,y*) to (*r,theta*).

FIGURE 13-8
⊚ ⊚ ⊚ ⊚ ⊚ ⊚
*Relationship
between
Cartesian and
polar
coordinates*

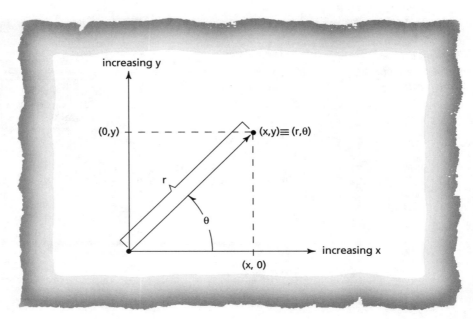

Equation 13-1 *Converting polar to Cartesian coordinates*

```
// (r,theta) => (x,y)

x = r * Math.cos(theta);
y = r * Math.sin(theta);
```

Equation 13-2 *Converting Cartesian to polar coordinates*

```
// (x,y) => (r,theta)

r = Math.sqrt(x*x + y*y);    // Pythagorean theorem
theta = Math.atan2(y/x);     // the arctangent of y/x
```

Figure 13-9 shows that the result of rotating (*r*,*theta*) about the origin by *alpha* degrees is (*r*, *theta+alpha mod 360*). As you see, it's trivial to rotate a vector about the origin in polar coordinates!

To sum up, this is one way to rotate a vector (*x*,*y*) about the origin:

1. Convert (*x*,*y*) into its polar coordinate representation (*r*, *theta*) using Equation 13-2.

2. Compute *theta1 = theta+alpha mod 360*.

3. Convert (*r*,*theta1*) into its Cartesian representation (*x1*,*y1*) using Equation 13-1.

FIGURE 13-9
◎ ◎ ◎ ◎ ◎ ◎
*Rotating a
vector about
the origin*

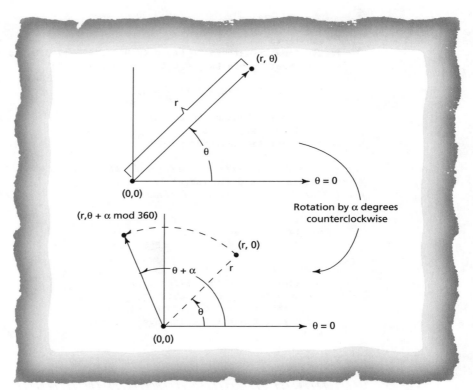

These mathematical operations occur so often in this game that it makes sense to define a helper class, GameMath, that encapsulates useful routines. GameMath is declared a *final* class, which means it can't be subclassed. GameMath includes conversion factors between degrees and radians, as well as a lookup table for sine and cosine. The lookup tables are used to reduce computation during game play, and they're computed with a static initializer. (A static initializer initializes static variables when the class is loaded.) Listing 13-4 shows the definition of the GameMath class.

Listing 13-4 *GameMath class*

```
///////////////////////////////////////////////////////////////
//
// the GameMath class contains mathematical routines for our
// graphics and games programs
//
///////////////////////////////////////////////////////////////


   public final class GameMath {
```

continued on next page

continued from previous page

```
// constants
static final float DEG_TO_RAD = (2.0f*3.14159f)/360.0f;
static final double RAD_TO_DEG = 1.0/DEG_TO_RAD;

static final int TABLE_SIZE = 360;

// storage for lookup tables
static float cos_table[];
static float sin_table[];
```

```
//////////////////////////////////////////////////////////////
// initialize cos and sin tables
//////////////////////////////////////////////////////////////

static {
   cos_table  = new float[TABLE_SIZE];
   sin_table  = new float[TABLE_SIZE];

   double temp;
   for (int i=0; i<TABLE_SIZE; i++) {
     temp = DEG_TO_RAD*(double)i;
     cos_table[i] = (float)Math.cos(temp);
     sin_table[i] = (float)Math.sin(temp);
   }

}
```

```
//////////////////////////////////////////////////////////////
// return value of cos from lookup table
//////////////////////////////////////////////////////////////

public static float cos(int degree) {
   if (degree >= 360) {
    degree = degree % 360;
   }
   else if (degree < 0) {
    degree = (-degree)%360;
   }

    return cos_table[degree];
}
```

```
//////////////////////////////////////////////////////////////
// return value of sin from lookup table
//////////////////////////////////////////////////////////////

public static float sin(int degree) {
   if (degree >= 360) {
    degree = degree % 360;
   }
   else if (degree < 0) {
```

```
        degree = (-degree)%360;
      }
      return sin_table[degree];
  }
//////////////////////////////////////////////////////////////
// computes angle, in degrees, from the x-axis
// returns angle in degrees between 0.0 and 360.0
// where 90.0 degrees is the y-axis.
//////////////////////////////////////////////////////////////

  public static double computeAngle(int v1x,int v1y) {
    double t= Math.atan2((double) v1y, (double)v1x);
    t *= RAD_TO_DEG;
    if (t < 0.0) t += 360.0;
    return (double)t;
  }


//////////////////////////////////////////////////////////////
// compute magnitude of a vector
//////////////////////////////////////////////////////////////

    public static float computeMagnitude(int v1x,int v1y) {
      return (float)Math.sqrt((double)(v1x*v1x+v1y*v1y));
    }

//////////////////////////////////////////////////////////////
// return random numbers of specified type between 0 and Max
//////////////////////////////////////////////////////////////

    public static int getRand(int Max) {
      return (int)(Math.random() * Max);
    }

    public static float getRand(float Max) {
      return (float)(Math.random() * Max);

    }

    public static double getRand(double Max) {
      return (Math.random() * Max);

    }

  }
```

Now let's implement moving and rotating polygons!

Moving and Rotating Polygons

We're going to subclass two Sprite classes now: MoveablePolygon and RotateablePolygon.

The MoveablePolygon Class

MoveablePolygon will subclass from PolygonSprite, which we defined above. The polygon will be stored in the int arrays *tx []* and *ty []*, which are the x and y coordinates of polygon's vectors in its local coordinate system:

```
protected int tx[],ty[];                        // offset vectors
```

The MoveablePolygon constructor will receive the local vectors and store them in *tx []* and *ty []*. By storing these vectors, it'll be easy to compute the new screen coordinates of the polygon every time it moves. Since it's so convenient to specify a polygon in a local system, we will also provide, in Listing 13-5, a new constructor for PolygonSprite that takes local coordinates and converts them to the screen coordinates required by Polygon *p*.

Listing 13-5 *PolygonSprite constructor for local coordinates*

```
///////////////////////////////////////////////////////////////
// constructor: take center and offset vectors
///////////////////////////////////////////////////////////////

    public PolygonSprite(int tx[], int ty[], int n,
                    int centerx, int centery, Color c) {
      int x[], y[];
      x = new int[n];
      y = new int[n];
      for (int i=0; i<n; i++) {                 // compute abs coords
        x[i] = centerx + tx[i];
        y[i] = centery + ty[i];
      }
      p = new Polygon(x,y,n);
      locx = centerx;
      locy = centery;
      color = c;
      visible = true;
      fill = false;                             // don't fill polygon
    }
```

The MoveablePolygon constructor will call this PolygonSprite constructor before storing the local vectors. In addition, MoveablePolygon declares the instance variables *height* and *width*, which store the screen bounds, and *max_radius*, which is the approximate maximum radius of the polygon. The method updatePosition() uses *max_radius* to decide if the polygon should wrap around to the other side. Here's a small excerpt of updatePosition() (from MoveablePolygon), which wraps the polygon from the right side of the screen to the left.

```
// if polygon is off the rhs of display
// move it to the left

if (locx - max_radius > width) {
locx -= (width + 2*max_radius);
}
```

Another important method is updatePoints(), which accomplishes the local to screen coordinate transformation:

```
//////////////////////////////////////////////////////////////
// convert from local coords to screen coords of the
//    polygon points
//////////////////////////////////////////////////////////////


  public void updatePoints() {

    for (int i=0; i<p.npoints; i++) {
      p.xpoints[i] = locx + tx[i];
      p.ypoints[i] = locy + ty[i];

    }
  }
```

The source for the MoveablePolygon is shown in Listing 13-6. Note how this class builds upon the PolygonSprite.

Listing 13-6 *MoveablePolygon class*

```
//////////////////////////////////////////////////////////////
//
// MoveablePolygon: encapsulates a moveable PolygonSprite
//
//////////////////////////////////////////////////////////////

class MoveablePolygon extends PolygonSprite
implements Moveable

{

  protected int tx[],ty[];                     // offset vectors
  protected int vx;                            // velocity x;
  protected int vy;                            // velocity y;
  protected int height = 1000,
            width = 1000;               // default screen limits
  protected int max_radius = 0;         // max radius of polygon
```

continued on next page

continued from previous page

```
              // methods:

              ///////////////////////////////////////////////////////////////
              // Constructor: construct with offset vectors
              ///////////////////////////////////////////////////////////////

                public MoveablePolygon(int tx[], int ty[], int n,
                                 int centerx, int centery, Color c) {
                  super(tx,ty,n,centerx,centery,c);              // constructor
                  vx = vy = 0;
                  this.tx = new int[n];
                  this.ty = new int[n];
                  for (int i=0; i<n; i++) {
                    this.tx[i] = tx[i];                          // save offset vectors
                    this.ty[i] = ty[i];
                  }

                }


              ///////////////////////////////////////////////////////////////
              // Constructor: construct with offset vectors,
              //             initialize screen bounds and max_radius
              ///////////////////////////////////////////////////////////////


                public MoveablePolygon(int tx[], int ty[], int n,
                                 int centerx, int centery, Color c,
                                 int w, int h, int r) {
                  super(tx,ty,n,centerx,centery,c);              // constructor
                  vx = vy = 0;
                  this.tx = new int[n];
                  this.ty = new int[n];
                  for (int i=0; i<n; i++) {
                    this.tx[i] = tx[i];                          // save offset vectors
                    this.ty[i] = ty[i];
                  }
                  height = h;
                  width = w;
                  max_radius = r;

                }

              ///////////////////////////////////////////////////////////////
              // implement Moveable methods
              ///////////////////////////////////////////////////////////////

                // move polygon to specifiedlocation
                public void setPosition(int x, int y) {
                  locx = x;
                  locy = y;
```

```
    // compute screen coords of polygon from local coords
    for (int i=0; i<p.npoints; i++) {
      p.xpoints[i] = locx + tx[i];
      p.ypoints[i] = locy + ty[i];
    }
  }


  // set velocity of polygon
  public void setVelocity(int x, int y) {
    vx = x;
    vy = y;
  }


  public void scale(double factor) {
    for (int i=0; i<p.npoints; i++) {    // scale offset vectors
      tx[i] = (int)Math.round(factor*tx[i]);
      ty[i] = (int)Math.round(factor*ty[i]);
    }
    updatePoints();
  }


  // update position of center of polygon. Wrap center
  //    to other side of screen if polygon exits screen bounds
  public void updatePosition() {
    locx += vx;
    locy += vy;

    // if center of polygon is off the rhs of display
    // move it to the left
    if (locx - max_radius > width) {
      locx -= (width + 2*max_radius);
    }

    // if center of polygon is off the lhs of display
    // move it to the right
    else if (locx < -max_radius ) {
      locx += (width + 2*max_radius);
    }

    // if center of polygon is off the bottom of display
    // move it to the top
    if (locy - max_radius > height) {
      locy -= (height + 2*max_radius);
    }

    // if center of polygon is off the top of display
    // move it to the bottom
    else if (locy < -max_radius ) {
      locy += (height + 2*max_radius);
```

continued on next page

continued from previous page

```
      }
    }

//////////////////////////////////////////////////////////////////
// convert from local coords to screen coords of the
//    polygon points
//////////////////////////////////////////////////////////////////

  public void updatePoints() {

    for (int i=0; i<p.npoints; i++) {
      p.xpoints[i] = locx + tx[i];
      p.ypoints[i] = locy + ty[i];

    }
  }

//////////////////////////////////////////////////////////////////
// default update method
//////////////////////////////////////////////////////////////////

  public void update() {
    if (isActive()) {
      updatePosition();        // move center
      updatePoints();          // compute polygon points
    }
  }

}
```

The RotateablePolygon Class

Making our polygons rotate is going to take just a little more effort than making them move. Implementing rotation according to the equations above requires computing the polar form of the offset vectors.

Here are the instance variables in class RotateablePolygon that will store the polar coordinates:

```
protected float magnitude[];        // magnitudes of vectors
protected int angle[];              // angles of vectors
```

The magnitudes of the offset vectors are stored in float *magnitude[]*, and the angles in int *angle[]*. The *magnitude[]* and *angle[]* arrays are computed in the constructor for RotateablePolygon, which is shown in Listing 13-7.

Listing 13-7 *RotateablePolygon class*

```
//////////////////////////////////////////////////////////////////
//
// RotateablePolygon: encapsulates a MoveablePolygon that also
//                    rotates
//////////////////////////////////////////////////////////////////

class RotateablePolygon extends MoveablePolygon {

  // variables:

  protected float magnitude[];        // magnitudes of vectors
  protected int theta = 0;            // current angle of
                                      //     orientation
  protected int angle[];              // angles of vectors
                                      // (offset from theta)
  protected int rate = 0;             // rate of rotation


  // methods:

  //////////////////////////////////////////////////////////////////
  // Constructor: take local vectors, center,color,screen bounds,
  //              and approximate max radius of polygon
  //////////////////////////////////////////////////////////////////

  public RotateablePolygon(int tx[], int ty[], int n,
                           int centerx, int centery, Color c,
                           int w, int h, int r) {


    super(tx,ty,n,centerx,centery,c,w,h,r);
    magnitude = new float[n];
    angle = new int[n];

    // compute magnitude and angle for each local vector
    // this is the Cartesian ==> Polar coordinate transformation
    for (int i=0; i<n; i++) {
      magnitude[i] =
      (float)GameMath.computeMagnitude(tx[i],ty[i]);

      angle[i] =
      (int)Math.round(GameMath.computeAngle(tx[i],ty[i]));
    }

  }
```

FIGURE 13-10

◉ ◉ ◉ ◉ ◉ ◉

*Polygon at
different values
of* theta

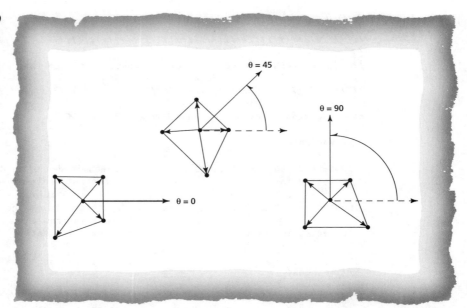

Now, we want these polygons to rotate on their own, with each call to update(). The variable *theta* represents the current angle of orientation. Figure 13-10 illustrates a polygon at various orientations of *theta*.

The variable *rate* supplies the rotation rate of the polygon, in degrees per update() call. Here are a few methods that enable other classes to access *theta* and *rate*:

```
////////////////////////////////////////////////////////////
// set the angle of orientation
////////////////////////////////////////////////////////////

  public void setAngle(int a) {
    theta = a;
  }


////////////////////////////////////////////////////////////
// set rate (in degrees) for continuous rotation
////////////////////////////////////////////////////////////

  public void setRotationRate(int r) {
    rate = r;
  }


////////////////////////////////////////////////////////////
// update the angle of orientation by the rotation rate
////////////////////////////////////////////////////////////

  public void updateAngle() {
    theta = checkAngleBounds(theta + rate);
```

```
    }

    ///////////////////////////////////////////////////////////////////
    // update the angle of orientation with a parameter
    ///////////////////////////////////////////////////////////////////

    public void updateAngle(int a) {
      theta = checkAngleBounds(theta + a);
    }


    ///////////////////////////////////////////////////////////////////
    // check that th is between 0 to 359
    ///////////////////////////////////////////////////////////////////

    public int checkAngleBounds(int th) {
      if (th >= 360)
        th -= 360;
      else if (th < 0)
        th += 360;
      return th;
    }
```

Rotation of the sprite is performed by the rotate() method. Each vector's angle, stored in array *angle[],* is added to the current amount of rotation stored in *theta.* Then, the rotated vector, oriented at this new angle, is transformed to screen coordinates and stored in the Polygon *p.* One subtlety: using Math.round() to round doubles before casting to ints really improves the appearance of the rotating polygon.

```
///////////////////////////////////////////////////////////////////
// rotate polygon by 'a' degrees.
// this is accomplished by using the polar representation
// of the polygon, then converting back to Cartesian coordinates
///////////////////////////////////////////////////////////////////

    public void rotate(int a) {
      // compute new angle of orientation
      theta = checkAngleBounds(theta + a);

      // for each offset vector,
      //    compute the new angle that its facing
      //    compute the coords associated with this angle
      //    update the polygon representation

      for (int i=0; i<p.npoints; i++) {
        double tempx, tempy;

        tempx = (magnitude[i]*GameMath.cos(theta)) ;
        tempy = (magnitude[i]*GameMath.sin(theta)) ;
        tx[i] = (int)Math.round(tempx);
        p.xpoints[i] = (int)Math.round(tempx + (double)locx);
        ty[i] = (int)Math.round(tempy);
        p.ypoints[i] = (int)Math.round(tempy + (double) locy);
```

continued on next page

continued from previous page

```
      }

  }
```

By precomputing and storing the polar coordinates, we've reduced the complexity of rotation to two multiplies per vector, and two more additions to translate the vector to screen coordinates.

Finally, update() is just

```
//////////////////////////////////////////////////////////////
// default update -- assumes continuous rotation //
//////////////////////////////////////////////////////////////
  public void update() {
    updatePosition();            // update location of sprite
    rotate(rate);                // rotate the sprite
    updateAngle();               // update the orientation
  }
}
```

As you can see, RotateablePolygon inherits several methods and instance variables from its superclasses. Inheritance lets you write code in an incremental, modular fashion, and allows you to easily extend the functionality of the graphics engine.

Now it's time to start building JAVAroids! We're going to proceed incrementally, by building each sprite class that's used in the game, and then defining the manager classes. First, it's important to organize a strong overall structure before moving on to the details.

Allocating Responsibility

Now that we've spent much of this chapter building sprite classes, it's time to think of how JAVAroids is going to be organized at the top level. Let's see how we can organize the sprites involved.

The Top-Level Organization

First, the asteroids. Since there will be lots of asteroids floating around, and each one is going to have similar characteristics, such as shape, color, or the number of points it's worth, it makes sense to have an asteroid manager that takes care of initializing the right number of asteroids with the proper attributes. The asteroid manager will also be in charge of game situations that involve more than one asteroid, such as asteroid division, and counting the number of asteroids. The asteroid manager will communicate to the asteroids and tell them when to appear and disappear.

Each asteroid will be represented by an Asteroid sprite. The Asteroid sprite will be in charge of painting itself and keeping track of individual Asteroid characteristics, such as its radius, color, value, and position. The Asteroid sprite will derive from the RotateablePolygon sprite.

The Ship sprite will also be subclassed from the RotateablePolygon sprite, and it controls the appearance of the ship on the screen. It makes sense to have a ship manager class that keeps track of ship characteristics, such as the number of shots or shield strength, and translates instructions from the player (such as "rotate left") into messages to the Ship sprite. The ship manager also tracks the sprites that the player fires (which we'll call Fire sprites).

Similarly, we'll have an Enemy sprite that draws enemy ships, and an enemy manager that controls when the enemy ships appear and when they fire. The effect manager will handle explosions (by creating an Explosion sprite) and sound effects from collisions. Finally, the game manager will be responsible for tasks that involve the entire game: initialization, displaying instructions and "Game Over" messages, and tracking score, to name a few.

Table 13-1 sums up the manager classes and the sprite objects that they control.

Manager Classes	Sprites
Game manager	None
Asteroid manager	Asteroid sprite
Ship manager	Ship sprite, Fire sprite
Enemy manager	Enemy sprite, Fire sprite
Effect manager	Explosion sprite

TABLE 13-1   ◈   *Manager classes and sprite objects*

Figure 13-11 illustrates the division of responsibility that we've outlined above. It's quite general, but it illustrates how you can split the basic tasks of any game into smaller, logically coherent units. The arrows in the diagram show how the manager classes and the sprites get initialized. The managers are like puppeteers that manipulate the puppet sprites.

Handling Collisions

Objects in JAVAroids interact with one another when they collide. There are many types of collisions that can happen in this game. It's up to the manager classes to handle the results of collisions between the sprites. Let's say, arbitrarily, that the asteroid manager will be responsible for handling all collisions involving asteroid sprites. There are three types of collisions here:

➤ Asteroid with player's ship

➤ Asteroid with enemy ships

➤ Asteroid with player fire or enemy fire

FIGURE 13-11

◉ ◉ ◉ ◉ ◉ ◉

*Division of
responsibility in
JAVAroids*

Now, we'll say that the enemy manager will track collisions between the objects that
it's responsible for and the player's ship. In particular, there are three more types of collisions here:

 Enemy ship with player's ship

 Enemy ship with player fire

 Enemy fire with player's ship

FIGURE 13-12

◎ ◎ ◎ ◎ ◎ ◎

Collision handling graph

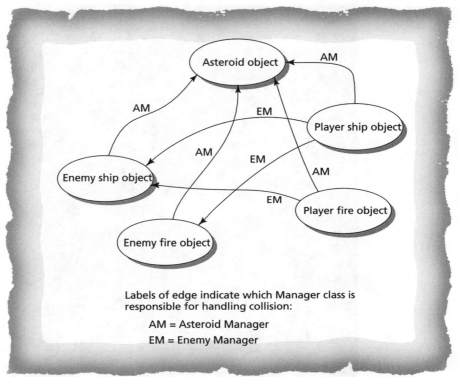

Figure 13-12 graphs the six types of collisions that are possible in the current implementation. The edges along the graph define which manager class is responsible for handling the collision.

Now let's start building the game. Although it may seem like a daunting task, the key is to construct the program piece by piece. First, let's define the five new Sprite classes we need. Don't worry—the definition of most of these classes is really easy, since we've built most of the functionality in the MoveablePolygon and RotateablePolygon classes!

Building the Game Sprites

There are five types of sprites in JAVAroids:

 Enemy: the enemy ship

 Fire: the fire from the enemy ship or the player's ship

 Asteroid: the colored, rotating slab of rock

 Ship: what the player controls

 Explosion: the result of a collision

FIGURE 13-13

◎ ◎ ◎ ◎ ◎ ◎

*JAVAroids
sprites*

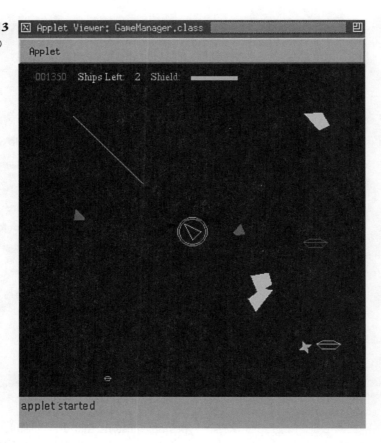

Figure 13-13 shows what these sprites look like, and Figure 13-14 shows where the Sprite classes will inherit from.

Let's define these sprites, one by one.

The Enemy Sprite

The Enemy sprite, shown in Listing 13-8, will be a MoveablePolygon. In addition to all the functionality from its parent, the Enemy will also track its *value* (how much it's worth when it's hit). The Enemy contains methods to determine if an intersection with a Ship or Fire sprite has occurred.

FIGURE 13-14

◎ ◎ ◎ ◎ ◎ ◎

*Inheritance
hierarchy for
JAVAroids
Sprite classes*

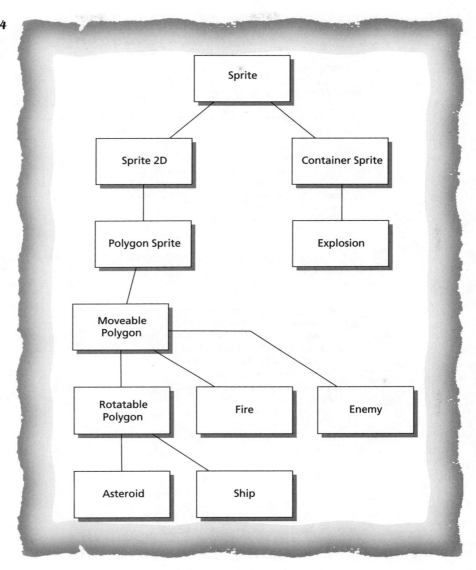

Listing 13-8 *Enemy class*

```
///////////////////////////////////////////////////////////////
//
// Enemy sprite class
//
///////////////////////////////////////////////////////////////

public class Enemy extends MoveablePolygon {
  public int value;   // value of this enemy

  public Enemy(int tx[], int ty[], int n,
               int centerx, int centery, Color c,
               int w, int h, int r,int v) {
    super(tx,ty,n,centerx,centery,c,w,h,r);
    value = v;
    setFill(false);  // don't fill polygon
  }

  ///////////////////////////////////////////////////////////////
  // intersection routines
  ///////////////////////////////////////////////////////////////

  // check for intersection with fire:
  //    compute midpt of the fire
  //    and see if it's within the max_radius of this enemy
  public boolean intersect(Fire f) {
    if (isActive() && f.isActive()) {
      int midptx = (f.p.xpoints[1] + f.p.xpoints[0]) / 2;
      int midpty = (f.p.ypoints[1] + f.p.ypoints[0]) / 2;
      return (Math.abs(midptx - locx) < max_radius) &&
        (Math.abs(midpty - locy) < max_radius);
    }
    else
      return false;
  }

  // check for intersection with Ship
  //     see if ship's center is within max_radius of this
  //     asteroid, with 2 pixels of leeway on each side
  public boolean intersect(Ship s) {
    return isActive() && s.isActive() &&
      (Math.abs(s.locx - locx+2) < max_radius) &&
      (Math.abs(s.locy - locy+2) < max_radius) ;
  }

}
```

The intersection algorithm is simple, but sufficient. If the center of the Fire sprite or the Ship sprite is within *max_radius* pixels of the Enemy's center, we'll say there's an intersection. Thus, collisions occur only when there are direct hits to the middle of the Enemy sprite. Figure 13-15 illustrates when a collision with the Enemy sprite is detected.

FIGURE 13-15

◎ ◎ ◎ ◎ ◎ ◎

*Enemy sprite
collision
detection*

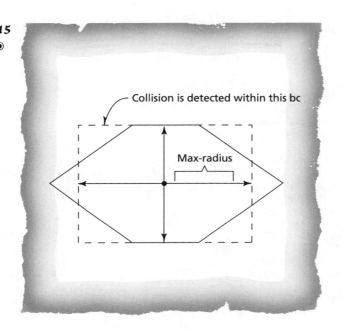

Collision is detected within this bc

Max-radius

The Fire Sprite

The Fire class, shown in Listing 13-9, also derives from MoveablePolygon, and in the current implementation, it's a straight line (i.e., polygon with two points). To start a Fire sprite in motion at a given location (x,y), and an angle a, use the instance method initialize(x,y,a). The Fire sprite has a finite lifetime when it's active, and each time it's updated, *count* is incremented. When *count* hits a threshold, the Fire sprite automatically suspends. In this way, the fire from an enemy or player's ship stops after traveling a certain distance.

Listing 13-9 *Fire class*

```
/////////////////////////////////////////////////////////////////
//
// Fire sprite class: this sprite automatically after a
//                    certain number of updates
//
/////////////////////////////////////////////////////////////////

public class Fire extends MoveablePolygon {


    // fire is a polygon with two points, i. e. a straight line
    static final int firex[] = { 0, 0};
    static final int firey[] = { 0, 0};
```

continued on next page

continued from previous page

```
            // length of the fire sprite
            static final int DEFAULT_LENGTH = 23;
            int fire_length = DEFAULT_LENGTH;

            // fire sprite lasts for this many updates
            int max_updates = 14;

            // count the number of updates
            int count = 0;


    ///////////////////////////////////////////////////////////////
    // Fire sprite constructors
    ///////////////////////////////////////////////////////////////

      public Fire(Color c,int w, int h ) {
        super(firex,firey,2,
            0,0,c,
            w,h,DEFAULT_LENGTH);
        setFill(false);
      }


      public Fire(Color c,int w, int h,int length,int updates ) {
        super(firex,firey,2,0,0,c,w,h,length);
        fire_length = length;
        max_updates = updates;
        setFill(false);
      }

    ///////////////////////////////////////////////////////////////
    //initialize a fire sprite from x,y at specified angle
    ///////////////////////////////////////////////////////////////

      public void initialize(int x, int y, int angle) {
        tx[1] = (int)Math.round((fire_length*GameMath.cos(angle)));
        ty[1] = (int)Math.round((fire_length*GameMath.sin(angle)));
        setPosition(x,y);
        setVelocity(tx[1],ty[1]);
        count = 0;
        restore();
      }


    ///////////////////////////////////////////////////////////////
    // update fire sprite: bump counter, suspend sprite if
    //                     counter's high enough
    ///////////////////////////////////////////////////////////////

      public void update() {
        if (isActive()) {
          count++;
          if (count == max_updates) {
```

```
        suspend();
      }
      else
       super.update();
    }
  }

  // check if fire intersects the ship
  public boolean intersect(Ship s) {
    return isActive() && s.isActive() &&
      (Math.abs(s.locx - locx+2) < max_radius) &&
      (Math.abs(s.locy - locy+2) < max_radius) ;
  }

}
```

There's also a method that checks if the Fire sprite hits the player's ship; this is analogous to the intersection routine used by Enemy.

The Asteroid Sprite

The Asteroid sprite, shown in Listing 13-10, derives from RotateablePolygon. The variable *value* stores the number of points the player gets for shooting it There are three intersection calculations in the Asteroid definition—one for each type of asteroid-object collision. Again, we use the simple algorithm of determining whether the object's center is within *max_radius* of the Asteroid.

Listing 13-10 Asteroid class

```
///////////////////////////////////////////////////////////////
//
// Asteroid sprite class
//
///////////////////////////////////////////////////////////////


public class Asteroid extends RotateablePolygon {

  // maximum rate of rotation
  static final int MAX_ROTATE_RATE = 8;

  // value of this asteroid
  public int value;

  public Asteroid(int tx[], int ty[], int n,
            int centerx, int centery, Color c,
            int w, int h, int r, int v) {
    super(tx,ty,n,centerx,centery,c,w,h,r);
    value = v;                  // set value
                                // set rotation rate
```

continued on next page

continued from previous page

```
    rate = GameMath.getRand(2*MAX_ROTATE_RATE)-MAX_ROTATE_RATE;
    setFill(true);          // fill the polygon
  }


  ////////////////////////////////////////////////////////////////
  // intersection routines
  ////////////////////////////////////////////////////////////////

    // check for intersection with fire:
    //    compute midpt of the fire
    //    and see if it's within the max_radius of this asteroid
    public boolean intersect(Fire f) {
      if (isActive() && f.isActive()) {
        int midptx = (f.p.xpoints[1] + f.p.xpoints[0]) / 2;
        int midpty = (f.p.ypoints[1] + f.p.ypoints[0]) / 2;
        return (Math.abs(midptx - locx) < max_radius) &&
         (Math.abs(midpty - locy) < max_radius);
      }
      else
        return false;
    }


    // check for intersection with Ship
    //    see if ship's center is within max_radius of this
    //    asteroid, with 2 pixels of leeway on each side
    public boolean intersect(Ship s) {
      return isActive() && s.isActive() &&
        (Math.abs(s.locx - locx+2) < max_radius) &&
        (Math.abs(s.locy - locy+2) < max_radius) ;
    }

    // check for intersection with Enemy
    //    see if Enemy's center is within max_radius of this
    //    asteroid, with 2 pixels of leeway on each side
    public boolean intersect(Enemy e) {
      return isActive() && e.isActive() &&
        (Math.abs(e.locx - locx+2) < max_radius) &&
        (Math.abs(e.locy - locy+2) < max_radius) ;
    }
  }
```

The Ship Sprite

Ship is the sprite that the player controls. It inherits from RotateablePolygon, and provides methods for rotating left, rotating right, and thrusting. Ship overrides RotateablePolygon's update() method (which provides the continuous rotation used by Asteroid). The new update() method rotates the ship only in response to a rotateLeft()

or rotateRight() message. The thrust() method updates the ship's velocity, based on the angle *theta* (inherited from RotateablePolygon). The Ship class is shown in Listing 13-11.

Listing 13-11 *Ship class*

```
////////////////////////////////////////////////////////////////////
//
// Ship sprite: adds a few methods to RotateablePolygon
//
////////////////////////////////////////////////////////////////////


public class Ship extends RotateablePolygon {

  // default rate of rotation is 15 degrees
  static final int ROT_RATE = 15 ;

  // has ship rotated?
  boolean rotated = false;

  // actual amount of rotation
  int rotation_amount;




  ////////////////////////////////////////////////////////////////////
  // Ship constructor
  ////////////////////////////////////////////////////////////////////

  public Ship(int tx[], int ty[], int n,   // coordinates
              int centerx, int centery,    // location
              Color c,                     // color
              int w, int h,                // screen bounds
              int r) {                     // ship length

    super(tx,ty,n,centerx,centery,c,w,h,r);

    // align the nose of the ship with theta = 0
    // this is necessary because the direction of ship's
    // thrust is based on theta, so the angles must be
    // rotated so that the angle of the ship's nose
    // and theta match.
    for (int i=0 ; i < angle.length; i++) {
      angle[i] = checkAngleBounds(angle[i]-90);
    }
    rotate(-90);                               // initially ship
                                               //   faces up

  }
```

continued on next page

continued from previous page

```
///////////////////////////////////////////////////////////////
//
// Rotation methods: called by ShipManager
//
///////////////////////////////////////////////////////////////


///////////////////////////////////////////////////////////////
// rotate left => decreasing theta in screen coordinate system
///////////////////////////////////////////////////////////////
  public void rotateLeft() {
    rotated = true;
    rotation_amount = -ROT_RATE;
  }


///////////////////////////////////////////////////////////////
// rotate right => increasing theta in screen coordinate system
///////////////////////////////////////////////////////////////
  public void rotateRight() {
    rotated = true;
    rotation_amount = ROT_RATE;
  }


///////////////////////////////////////////////////////////////
// override update to prevent continuous rotation
///////////////////////////////////////////////////////////////

  public void update() {
    if (isActive()) {
      updatePosition();

      if (rotated) {
       rotate(rotation_amount);
       rotated = false;
      }
      else {
       updatePoints();
      }

    }
  }


///////////////////////////////////////////////////////////////
//
// handle ship thrusting:
//    update ship's velocity based on direction it's pointed
//
///////////////////////////////////////////////////////////////
```

```
static final double ACCEL_FACTOR = 1.0;

public void thrust() {

  vx = (int)Math.round((double)vx +
                 GameMath.cos(theta)*ACCEL_FACTOR);
  vy = (int)Math.round((double)vy +
                 GameMath.sin(theta)*ACCEL_FACTOR);

}

}
```

The Explosion Sprite

The Explosion sprite is actually a series of lines that blows apart. Each of these lines will be a distinct Sprite that the Explosion will contain. Since the concept of a container sprite is so useful, let's define it, in Listing 13-12.

Listing 13-12 ContainerSprite class

```
///////////////////////////////////////////////////////////
//
// ContainerSprite: Container class for sprites
//
///////////////////////////////////////////////////////////

public class ContainerSprite extends Sprite {
  // vector of the constituent sprites
  protected Vector sprites;

///////////////////////////////////////////////////////////
// constructor
///////////////////////////////////////////////////////////

  public ContainerSprite() {
    sprites = new Vector();
  }

///////////////////////////////////////////////////////////
// add a new sprite
///////////////////////////////////////////////////////////

  public void addSprite(Sprite s) {
    sprites.addElement(s);
  }

///////////////////////////////////////////////////////////
// paint each constituent sprite in sprites vector
///////////////////////////////////////////////////////////
```

continued on next page

continued from previous page

```java
public void paint(Graphics g) {
  if (isVisible()) {
    Enumeration e;
    e = sprites.elements();
    while (e.hasMoreElements()) {
     Sprite s = (Sprite) e.nextElement();
     s.paint(g);
    }
  }
}

/////////////////////////////////////////////////////////////////
// update each constituent sprite in sprites vector
/////////////////////////////////////////////////////////////////

public void update() {
  if (isActive()) {
    Enumeration e;
    e = sprites.elements();
    while (e.hasMoreElements()) {
     Sprite s = (Sprite) e.nextElement();
     s.update();
    }
  }
}
}
```

As you see, the sprites in the container are stored in a Vector. The paint() and update() methods iterate through the constituent sprites, painting and updating each one individually.

An Explosion is a ContainerSprite that animates a collection of MoveablePolygons. In this implementation of Explosion, the constituent polygons are straight lines (though you can easily define your own shape). Each time an Explosion is updated, it moves the subsprites farther outward, like shock waves from the center of an explosion. When the Explosion updates a certain number of times, it sets the *done* flag, which will be used by the effect manager.

Figure 13-16 illustrates the action of the Explosion sprite, and Listing 13-13 shows the implementation of this class.

FIGURE 13-16

◎ ◎ ◎ ◎ ◎ ◎

Explosion sprite

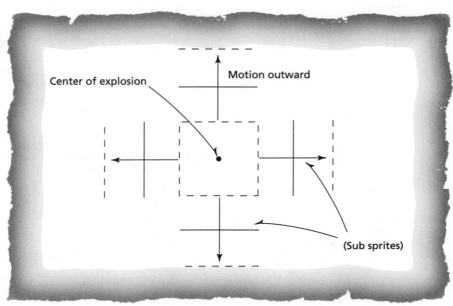

Listing 13-13 *Explosion class*

```
/////////////////////////////////////////////////////////////////
//
// Explosion sprite class: contains lines that blow apart
//
/////////////////////////////////////////////////////////////////

public class Explosion extends ContainerSprite {
  // center of explosion
  protected int locx,locy;

  // size of lines of explosion
  static final int EXP_SIZE = 13;

  // how long explosion lasts
  protected int max_updates = 0;

  // updates so far
  protected int updates;

  // the constituent lines in the container
  static final int ex[][] = { {0,0} , {-EXP_SIZE,EXP_SIZE},
                              {0,0}, {-EXP_SIZE,EXP_SIZE}};
  static final int ey[][] = { {-EXP_SIZE,EXP_SIZE}, {0,0},
                              {-EXP_SIZE,EXP_SIZE}, {0,0} };
```

continued on next page

continued from previous page

```java
                    // the constituent edge sprites in container
                    MoveablePolygon edges[] = new MoveablePolygon[ex.length];

                    // size of explosion
                    protected float size;

                    // is explosion over?
                    protected boolean done = false;

            //////////////////////////////////////////////////////////////
            // Explosion constructor: color, position, #updates
            //////////////////////////////////////////////////////////////

                    public Explosion(Color color, int x, int y, int u) {

                      // define edge sprites of explosion

                      for (int i=0; i<edges.length; i++) {
                        edges[i] = new MoveablePolygon(ex[i],ey[i],ex[i].length,
                                                x,y,color);
                        edges[i].restore();              // show all edges

                        // add each edge to container
                        addSprite(edges[i]);
                      }

                      // initialize how long the explosion lasts
                      max_updates = u;

                      // initialize counter
                      updates = 0;

                      // set explosion at the given coordinates
                      locx = x;
                      locy = y;

                      // restore explosion sprite
                      restore();

                      // set size
                      size = 1.0f;

                      // reset boolean
                      done = false;
                    }


            //////////////////////////////////////////////////////////////
            // update explosion or suspend if it reaches maximum size
            //    (assumes 4 edges in the container, which move apart
            //      along x,y coordinates.)
            //////////////////////////////////////////////////////////////
```

```
public void update() {
  if (updates++ < max_updates) {
    // blow the lines apart!
    size *= 1.7f;                    // increase size

    int isize = (int)size;      // cast size to int
    edges[0].setPosition(locx + isize,locy );
    edges[1].setPosition(locx ,locy + isize);
    edges[2].setPosition(locx - isize,locy);
    edges[3].setPosition(locx,locy - isize);

  }
  else
    done = true;

}


/////////////////////////////////////////////////////////////////
// return explosion status
/////////////////////////////////////////////////////////////////

public boolean isDone() {
  return done;
}
}
```

Now it's time to define the manager classes!

Defining the Managers

There are five manager classes in JAVAroids:

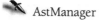 AstManager

 ShipManager

 EnemyManager

 EffManager

 GameManager

Each manager class will have two methods: update(), which updates the individual sprites and handles collisions between them, and paint(), which draws the sprites. Before defining the managers, let's see how they'll work with each other. Figure 13-17 diagrams the interaction of the managers during the main loop of the game.

FIGURE 13-17

ⓞ ⓞ ⓞ ⓞ ⓞ ⓞ

Interaction of Managers during Main Loop

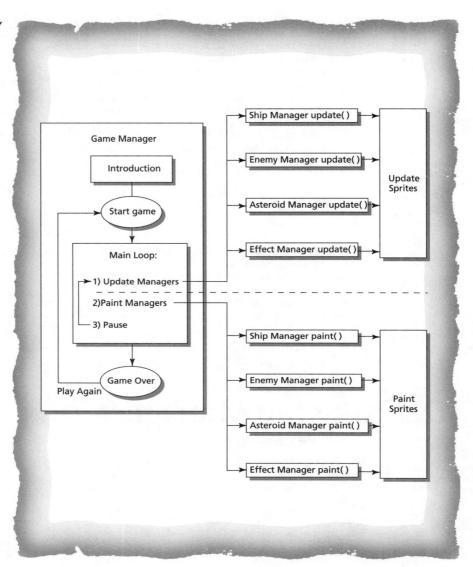

As Figure 13-17 shows, the game manager class acts as a master clock that synchronizes the update() and paint() operations of the other four managers. Each manager in turn instructs the sprites it controls to update() and paint(). The main functionality of the game is implemented in the update() methods of the managers. For example, the asteroid manager's update() moves the asteroids, checks for collisions with other game objects, and divides the asteroids when necessary. Another example is the update() method of the ship manager, which instructs the Ship sprite how to move, based on the keys that the player is holding down.

Now let's define the manager classes. By the time this is done, you'll have the full game!

The Asteroid Manager

The first thing the AstManager class does is create the individual asteroids used in the game. Instantiating an object is a complex and relatively slow operation, so it makes sense to allocate all the asteroids needed in the constructor. Afterward, you can control the visibility of the asteroid by suspending or restoring it.

The asteroids are stored in an array *a[]*. There are three sizes of asteroids: large, medium, and small. Large asteroids divide into two medium ones, and a medium asteroid splits into two small ones. As a result, we'll use the indexing scheme shown in Figure 13-18 to implement asteroid division.

More precisely, if a large asteroid *a[i]* is hit, you'll suspend the *a[i]* sprite, and restore the two medium asteroid sprites at *a[2*i + NUM_LARGE]* and *a[2*i + 1 + NUM_LARGE]*, where *NUM_LARGE is the maximum number of large asteroids.*

How do we obtain the shapes for these asteroids? One way is to hardcode the polygonal coordinates. In the current implementation, asteroid shapes are created dynamically in the method MakeVectors(), by randomly perturbing the points about a polygonal template, as shown in Figure 13-19.

Once the asteroids are constructed, the AstManager controls their interactions in its update(). Let's take a closer look at this method.

update() iterates through all sprites in the asteroid array *a[]*. If no sprites are active, update() calls newBoard() to start a new rack of asteroids. If an asteroid sprite is active, it goes through a series of intersection checks. For example, here's the code that handles a collision between an asteroid and the enemy ship objects:

```
/////////////////////////////////////
// CHECK FOR ENEMY INTERSECTION
//
for (int j=0; j<enemy.length; j++) {
  if (a[i].intersect(enemy[j])) {
    Divide(i);
    em.destroyEnemy(j);
  }
}
```

The Divide() method creates the effect of splitting asteroids by suspending the larger one, and activating the two smaller sprites using the indexing scheme we've described.

The remainder of the update() method handles the other types of collisions similarly. A collision between the ship and a "powerup" asteroid increases the shield power of the ship.

FIGURE 13-18

◎ ◎ ◎ ◎ ◎ ◎

Asteroid array
indexing

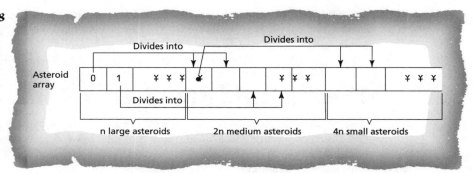

FIGURE 13-19

◎ ◎ ◎ ◎ ◎ ◎

Creating a new
asteroid shape

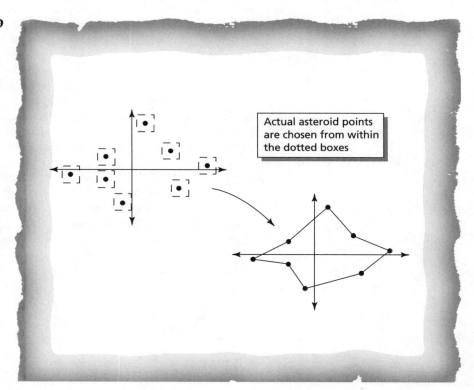

Finally, the AstManager paint() method is really simple: it iterates through the array of asteroid sprites, telling each Asteroid to paint itself.

The source to the AstManager class is shown in Listing 13-14. The long series of constants at the beginning of the class definition is for constructing random asteroid shapes, so you can skip over it and look at the methods.

Listing 13-14 AstManager class

```
///////////////////////////////////////////////////////////////
//
// the Asteroid Manager class -- handles all things relating
//                                  to asteroids, as well as
//                                  collisions with other
//                                  game objects
//
///////////////////////////////////////////////////////////////


public class AstManager extends Object {


///////////////////////////////////////////////////////////////
// constants -- these control the size, basic shape, and speed
//              of the asteroids
///////////////////////////////////////////////////////////////

  // max speed
  static final int MAX_VX = 4;
  static final int MAX_VY = 4;

  // max size
  static final int MAX_RADIUS = 30;

  // size ratio between large:medium, and medium:small asteroids
  static final int SIZE_RATIO = 2;

  // constants that refer to asteroid size
  static final int SMALL = 2;
  static final int MEDIUM = 1;
  static final int LARGE = 0;

  // how much each asteroid's worth
  static final int VAL_SMALL = 90;
  static final int VAL_MEDIUM = 60;
  static final int VAL_LARGE = 30;

  // large:small asteroid size ratio
  static final int SRAT = SMALL*SIZE_RATIO;

  // large:medium asteroid size ratio
  static final int MRAT = MEDIUM*SIZE_RATIO;

///////////////////////////////////////////////////////////////
// templates for the asteroids
///////////////////////////////////////////////////////////////

  static final int PX0 =
    (int)(Math.cos(0.0*GameMath.DEG_TO_RAD)*MAX_RADIUS);
```

continued on next page

continued from previous page

```java
            static final int PX1 =
              (int)(Math.cos(72.0*GameMath.DEG_TO_RAD)*MAX_RADIUS);
            static final int PX2 =
              (int)(Math.cos(144.0*GameMath.DEG_TO_RAD)*MAX_RADIUS);
            static final int PX3 =
              (int)(Math.cos(216.0*GameMath.DEG_TO_RAD)*MAX_RADIUS);
            static final int PX4 =
              (int)(Math.cos(288.0*GameMath.DEG_TO_RAD)*MAX_RADIUS);
            static final int PY0 =
              (int)(Math.sin(0.0*GameMath.DEG_TO_RAD)*MAX_RADIUS);
            static final int PY1 =
              (int)(Math.sin(72.0*GameMath.DEG_TO_RAD)*MAX_RADIUS);
            static final int PY2 =
              (int)(Math.sin(144.0*GameMath.DEG_TO_RAD)*MAX_RADIUS);
            static final int PY3 =
              (int)(Math.sin(216.0*GameMath.DEG_TO_RAD)*MAX_RADIUS);
            static final int PY4 =
              (int)(Math.sin(288.0*GameMath.DEG_TO_RAD)*MAX_RADIUS);

            // the x-coordinates of large, medium, and small template

            static final int px[][] =  {
              {0,MAX_RADIUS/2,MAX_RADIUS,MAX_RADIUS/2,0,-MAX_RADIUS/2,
               -MAX_RADIUS,-MAX_RADIUS/2,0},
              {PX0/MRAT,PX1/MRAT,PX2/MRAT,PX3/MRAT,PX4/MRAT},
              {PX0/SRAT,PX1/SRAT,PX2/SRAT,PX3/SRAT,PX4/SRAT}
            };

            // the y-coordinates of large, medium, and small template

            static final int py[][] = {
              {MAX_RADIUS,MAX_RADIUS/2,0,-MAX_RADIUS/2,-MAX_RADIUS,
               -MAX_RADIUS/2,0,MAX_RADIUS/2,MAX_RADIUS},
              {PY0/MRAT,PY1/MRAT,PY2/MRAT,PY3/MRAT,PY4/MRAT},
              {PY0/SRAT,PY1/SRAT,PY2/SRAT,PY3/SRAT,PY4/SRAT}

            } ;

    /////////////////////////////////////////////////////////////
    // coordinates of the powerup
    /////////////////////////////////////////////////////////////

      static final int powerx[] = {
        10,2,0,-2,-10,-2,0,2,10
        };
      static final int powery[] = {
        0,2,10,2,0,-2,-10,-2,0
        };


      // variance in asteroid shape
      static final double AVAR = 1.7;
```

```
// used for intersection calcs
static final int MAX_RAD_LARGE =
   MAX_RADIUS+(int)(MAX_RADIUS/AVAR);
static final int MAX_RAD_MEDIUM =
   MAX_RADIUS/MRAT+(int)(MAX_RADIUS/AVAR/MRAT);
static final int MAX_RAD_SMALL =
   MAX_RADIUS/SRAT+(int)(MAX_RADIUS/AVAR/SRAT);

// num of large asteroids
static final int NUM_LARGE = 6;

// num of medium asteroids
static final int NUM_MEDIUM = 2*NUM_LARGE;

// num of small asteroids
static final int NUM_SMALL = 2*NUM_MEDIUM;

// total number of asteroids
static final int NUM_ASTS = NUM_LARGE+NUM_MEDIUM+NUM_SMALL;

// color of asteroids
static final Color LARGE_COLOR = new Color(150,150,233);
static final Color MEDIUM_COLOR = Color.cyan;
static final Color SMALL_COLOR = Color.magenta;


//////////////////////////////////////////////////////////////
// variables
//////////////////////////////////////////////////////////////

// level of play
static int level;

// array of asteroids
private Asteroid a[] = new Asteroid[NUM_ASTS];

// the powerup
private Asteroid powerup;

// screen bounds
static int width,height;


// references to other game objects
// the ship
ShipManager sm;
Ship ship;
Fire[] fire;

// the enemies
EnemyManager em;
```

continued on next page

continued from previous page

```
                Enemy[] enemy;
                Fire[] enemyfire;

                // the effect manager
                EffManager efm;
                // game manager
                GameManager game;


        /////////////////////////////////////////////////////////////
        // AstManager constructor:
        //     create all Asteroids used in game. This is done
        //     at beginning to improve performance
        /////////////////////////////////////////////////////////////

            public AstManager(int w, int h,
                          ShipManager sm,EnemyManager em,
                          EffManager efm, GameManager g) {
            ship = sm.getShip();            // get ship-- needed for
                                            // collision detection
            fire = sm.getFire();            // -- same
            this.sm = sm;
            enemy = em.getEnemy();          // get enemies-- needed for
                                            // collision detection
            enemyfire = em.getFire();       // -- same
            this.em = em;
            this.efm = efm;
            game = g;
            width = w;
            height = h;

            // create storage for actual asteroids:

            // storage for large ast
            int tx0[] = new int[px[LARGE].length];
            int ty0[] = new int[px[LARGE].length];

            // storage for medium ast
            int tx1[] = new int[px[MEDIUM].length];
            int ty1[] = new int[px[MEDIUM].length];

            // storage for small ast
            int tx2[] = new int[px[SMALL].length];
            int ty2[] = new int[px[SMALL].length];


            // initialize powerup sprite
            powerup = new Asteroid(powerx,powery,powerx.length,
                            0,0,
                            Color.green,w,h,
                            8,0);
```

```
        powerup.setRotationRate(3);

        // make large asts
        for (int i=0; i<NUM_LARGE; i++) {
          MakeVectors(tx0,ty0,LARGE);
          a[i] = new Asteroid(tx0,ty0,px[LARGE].length,
                          MAX_RAD_LARGE-
                          (int)(MAX_RADIUS/AVAR/2.0),
                          VAL_LARGE);
        }

        // make medium asts
        for (int i=NUM_LARGE; i<NUM_LARGE+NUM_MEDIUM; i++) {
          MakeVectors(tx1,ty1,MEDIUM);
          a[i] = new Asteroid(tx1,ty1,px[MEDIUM].length,
                          0,0,MEDIUM_COLOR,w,h,
                          MAX_RAD_MEDIUM-
                          (int)(MAX_RADIUS/AVAR/MRAT/2.0),
                          VAL_MEDIUM);


        // make small asts
        for (int i=NUM_MEDIUM;
            i<NUM_LARGE+NUM_MEDIUM+NUM_SMALL;
            i++) {
          MakeVectors(tx2,ty2,SMALL);
          a[i] = new Asteroid(tx2,ty2,px[SMALL].length,
                          0,0,SMALL_COLOR,w,h,
                          MAX_RAD_SMALL-
                          (int)(MAX_RADIUS/AVAR/SRAT/2.0),
                          VAL_SMALL);
        }

      newGame();
    }


//////////////////////////////////////////////////////////////////
// initialize a new Game: set the level, and create
//    a new board of asts at that level
//////////////////////////////////////////////////////////////////

    public void newGame() {
      level = 1;
      newBoard(level);
    }


//////////////////////////////////////////////////////////////////
//
// The Update method:
//    handle collisions between:
```

continued on next page

continued from previous page

```
//         asts and (ship, ship fire, enemies, enemy fire)
//         powerup and ship
//////////////////////////////////////////////////////////////////

  public void update() {

    // update powerup
    if (powerup.isActive()) {
      powerup.update();

      // if ship touches powerup, increase shield
      if (powerup.intersect(ship)) {
       powerup.suspend();
       sm.increaseShield();
      }
    }

    ///////////////////////////////////
    // iterate through all asteroids
    ///////////////////////////////////

    boolean asts_left = false;

    for (int i=0; i<NUM_ASTS; i++) {
      if (a[i].isActive()) {
       asts_left = true;
       a[i].update();

       ///////////////////////////////////
       // CHECK FOR SHIP INTERSECTION
       // if the ship's grace period isn't over,
       //   update the grace period
       if (gracePeriod > 0) {
      gracePeriod--;
       }

       // else check if the ast hits the ship
       else {
         if (a[i].intersect(ship)) {
           // divide Asteroid i
           Divide(i);

           game.updateScore(a[i].value);
           // tell ShipManager to destroy ship
           sm.destroyShip();
         }
       }

       ///////////////////////////////////
       // CHECK FOR ENEMY INTERSECTION
       //
       for (int j=0; j<enemy.length; j++) {
```

```
                  if (a[i].intersect(enemy[j])) {
                    Divide(i);
                    em.destroyEnemy(j);
                   }
              }

              ///////////////////////////////////////
              // CHECK FOR INTERSECTION WITH SHIP FIRE
              //

              for (int j=0; j<fire.length; j++) {
                if (a[i].intersect(fire[j])) {
                  // stop fire sprite
                  sm.stopFire(j);
                  Divide(i);

                  game.updateScore(a[i].value);
                }
              }

              ///////////////////////////////////////
              // CHECK FOR INTERSECTION WITH ENEMY FIRE
              //
              for (int j=0; j<enemyfire.length; j++) {
                if (a[i].intersect(enemyfire[j])) {
                  // stop fire sprite
                  em.stopFire(j);
                   Divide(i);

                }
              }
            }
          }

        // IF NO ASTEROIDS LEFT, CREATE A NEW BOARD
        if (!asts_left) {
          newBoard(++level);
        }
      }

  ///////////////////////////////////////////////////////////////
  // set the level of play
  ///////////////////////////////////////////////////////////////

    public void setLevel(int i) {
      level = i;
    }


  ///////////////////////////////////////////////////////////////
  // split an asteroid into two smaller ones
  ///////////////////////////////////////////////////////////////
```

continued on next page

continued from previous page

```java
private void Divide(int i) {
  int child1, child2;
  int vertex;
  // suspend asteroid i, and create an explosion there
  a[i].suspend();
  efm.addAstExplosion(a[i].locx,a[i].locy);

  // don't do anything if it's a small asteroid
  if (i >= NUM_LARGE + NUM_MEDIUM)
    return;

  // if it's a large ast, split it into two mediums
  if (i < NUM_LARGE) {
    child1 = NUM_LARGE + 2*i;          //  indices of med asts
    child2 = NUM_LARGE + 2*i + 1;
  }
  // else medium ast => two smalls
  else {                              //  indices of small asts
    child1 = (NUM_LARGE+NUM_MEDIUM) + 2*(i-NUM_LARGE);
    child2 = (NUM_LARGE+NUM_MEDIUM) + 2*(i-NUM_LARGE) + 1;
  }


  vertex = a[i].p.npoints - 1;      // last vertex

  // set location of children to midpt betw center and vertex
  a[child1].setPosition(a[i].tx[vertex]/2 + a[i].locx,
                        a[i].ty[vertex]/2 + a[i].locy);

  a[child2].setPosition(a[i].tx[0]/2 + a[i].locx,
                        a[i].ty[0]/2 + a[i].locy);

  // set velocity of children
  a[child1].setVelocity(a[i].vx +
                        GameMath.getRand(2*MAX_VX)-MAX_VX,
                        a[i].vy +
                        GameMath.getRand(2*MAX_VY)-MAX_VY);

  a[child2].setVelocity(a[i].vx +
                        GameMath.getRand(2*MAX_VX)-MAX_VX,
                        a[i].vy +
                        GameMath.getRand(2*MAX_VY)-MAX_VY);

  // restore these sprites
  a[child1].restore();
  a[child2].restore();

}
```

```
///////////////////////////////////////////////////////////////
// paint the powerup and asteroids
///////////////////////////////////////////////////////////////

  public void paint(Graphics g) {
    powerup.paint(g);
    for (int i=0; i<NUM_ASTS; i++) {
      a[i].paint(g);
    }
  }


///////////////////////////////////////////////////////////////
// Accessor methods
///////////////////////////////////////////////////////////////

  public Asteroid[] getAsts() {
    return a;
  }
  public Asteroid getPowerup() {
    return powerup;
  }


///////////////////////////////////////////////////////////////
// Create a new board of asteroids
//    based on the given level 'n'
///////////////////////////////////////////////////////////////

  // period of invulnerability for ship
  //    every time there's a new board
  static int gracePeriod;


  public void newBoard(int n) {
    int x,y;
    int vx,vy;

    // define the number of large asts in this board
    int num_asts = n/2 + 1;
    if (num_asts >= NUM_LARGE) {
      num_asts = NUM_LARGE;
    }

    // set the position and speed of these large asteroids
    //    and restore these sprites
    for (int i=0; i<num_asts; i++) {
      x = GameMath.getRand(width-2*MAX_RADIUS)+MAX_RADIUS ;
      y = GameMath.getRand(height-2*MAX_RADIUS)+MAX_RADIUS ;
      vx = GameMath.getRand(2*MAX_VX)-MAX_VX;
      vy = GameMath.getRand(2*MAX_VY)-MAX_VY;
      a[i].setPosition(x,y);
      a[i].setVelocity(vx,vy);
```

continued on next page

continued from previous page

```
                    a[i].restore();
                 }

                 // set the powerup
                 if (!powerup.isActive()) {
                   x = GameMath.getRand(width-2*MAX_RADIUS)+MAX_RADIUS ;
                   y = GameMath.getRand(height-2*MAX_RADIUS)+MAX_RADIUS ;
                   powerup.setPosition(x,y);
                   powerup.restore();
                 }

                 // set the grace period for the ship
                 gracePeriod = 50;

                 // suspend the remaining sprites
                 for (int i= num_asts; i<NUM_ASTS; i++) {
                   a[i].suspend();
                 }
              }


       /////////////////////////////////////////////////////////////
       // Make the vectors of the individual Asteroids,
       //    by randomly perturbing the given template
       /////////////////////////////////////////////////////////////

         private void MakeVectors(int tpx[], int tpy[],int size) {
           int n = tpx.length;         // number of points in asteroid
           int deviation;              // max deviation from template

           // compute max deviation from template

           if (size == LARGE) {
             deviation = (int)(MAX_RADIUS/AVAR);
           }
           else {
             // else a small or medium size asteroid
             //    so reduce max deviation by the corresponding amount
             int factor = size*SIZE_RATIO;
             deviation = (int)(MAX_RADIUS/factor/AVAR);
           }

           // compute the first and final point of asteroid
           int fx =
             (int)(GameMath.getRand(2*deviation)-deviation) +
             px[size][0];
           int fy =
             (int)(GameMath.getRand(2*deviation)-deviation) +
             py[size][0];

           // close polygon
```

```
      tpx[0] = tpx[n-1] = fx;
      tpy[0] = tpy[n-1] = fy;


      // compute the rest of the points in asteroid
      for (int i = 1; i < n-1 ; i++) {
        tpx[i] =
         (int)(GameMath.getRand(2*deviation)-deviation) +
          px[size][i];
        tpy[i] =
         (int)(GameMath.getRand(2*deviation)-deviation) +
          py[size][i];

      }

    }

  }
```

The Ship Manager

The ShipManager class is in charge of initializing the player's ship and the Fire sprites (which draw the missiles that the player fires). As usual, this initialization occurs in the ShipManager's constructor.

The next function of the ShipManager is translating player input into messages to the Ship sprite. To process user input, we'll keep a buffer that tracks whether a key is pressed or not. This allows the game to react to multiple keystrokes, so you can fire and thrust simultaneously, for example. If we didn't keep a key state buffer, the game would only respond to a single keystroke at a time!

Here's the code that defines and sets the appropriate booleans in the key buffer. The keyboard event handlers in the main applet will call these keyUp() and keyDown() methods of the ShipManager:

```
// declare the key buffer
  static boolean keyState[] = new boolean[5];

  public void keyDown(Event e,int k) {
    switch(k) {
    case LEFT:
      keyState[LEFTINDEX] = true;
      break;
    case RIGHT:
      keyState[RIGHTINDEX] = true;
      break;
    ...
  }
  public void keyUp(Event e,int k) {
    switch(k) {
    case LEFT:
      keyState[LEFTINDEX] = false;
```

continued on next page

continued from previous page

```
      break;
   case RIGHT:
     keyState[RIGHTINDEX] = false;
     break;
   ...
 }
```

The ShipManager's update() method does two things. First, it updates the Fire sprites associated with the player, stored in the array *f[]*:

```
public void update() {

  // update fire sprites
  for ( int i=0 ; i<MAX_SHOTS; i++) {
    f[i].update();
  }
```

Then, it reads the key buffer, and tells the Ship sprite what to do based on buffer contents. Here's an excerpt of this:

```
// if ship's alive
if (shipAlive) {

  // check the key buffer and perform the
  //   associated action

  if (keyState[LEFTINDEX])
    s.rotateLeft();
  if (keyState[RIGHTINDEX])
    s.rotateRight();
  ...
```

Thus, multiple keystrokes are handled successfully!

Finally, the paint() method of this manager class tells the Fire sprites and Ship sprite to paint. In addition, it creates a status display of the number of ships left, and the shield power remaining. If the shield button is down, paint() also draws the shield around the Ship sprite.

Listing 13-15 shows the ShipManager code.

Listing 13-15 *ShipManager class*

```
//////////////////////////////////////////////////////////////////
//
// ShipManager class -- responsible for tracking ship data
//                        (e.g. shipsLeft, shield)
//
//                      -- responsible for translating player input
//                         to Ship sprite methods
//////////////////////////////////////////////////////////////////


public class ShipManager extends Object {
```

```
            // coordinates of the Ship sprite polygon
            static final int tpx[] = { 0, -7, 7, 0};
            static final int tpy[] = { 13, -7, -7, 13};

            // 5 shots at a time
            static final int MAX_SHOTS = 5;

            // length of ship's nose
            static final int SHIP_LENGTH = 13;


            static int width,height;              // screen dimensions
            private int shipsLeft;
            private boolean shipAlive;
            private boolean shieldOn;
            private int shieldStrength;
            private boolean gameOver;

            private Ship s;                       // Ship sprite
            private Fire f[] = new Fire[MAX_SHOTS]; // Fire sprites
            EffManager efm;
            GameManager game;

        //////////////////////////////////////////////////////////////
        // ShipManager constructor
        //////////////////////////////////////////////////////////////
            public ShipManager(int width,int height,
                        EffManager efm,GameManager game) {


              // initialize Ship sprite
              s = new Ship(tpx,tpy,tpx.length,       // coords of Ship
                        width/2,height/2,            // initial position
                        Color.yellow,                // color
                        width,height,                // screen bounds
                        SHIP_LENGTH);                // length of ship

              // initialize Fire sprites
              for ( int i=0 ; i<MAX_SHOTS; i++) {
                f[i] = new Fire(Color.white,width,height);
                f[i].suspend();
              }

              // initialize variables
              this.efm = efm;
              this.game = game;
              this.width = width;
              this.height = height;
              shipsLeft = 2;
              shipAlive = true;
              shieldOn = false;
```

continued on next page

continued from previous page

```
        shieldStrength = 100;
        gameOver = false;

        // activate Ship sprite
        s.restore();
    }


//////////////////////////////////////////////////////////////////
// Accessor methods : provide access to privates:
//                       Ship and Fire sprites
//////////////////////////////////////////////////////////////////

    // return Ship sprite
    public Ship getShip() {
      return s;
    }

    // return array of Fire sprites
    public Fire[] getFire() {
      return f;
    }

    // suspend the given Fire sprite
    public void stopFire(int i) {
      f[i].suspend();
    }

    // give an extra ship
    public void extraShip() {
      shipsLeft++;
    }


//////////////////////////////////////////////////////////////////
// Destroy the Ship
//////////////////////////////////////////////////////////////////

    // waiting period for the next ship
    static int waitPeriod;

    public void destroyShip() {
      if (gameOver) return;

      // if there's no shield on, destroy the ship
      if (!(keyState[SHIELDINDEX] && shieldStrength > 0)) {

        shipAlive = false;              // set boolean
        s.suspend();                    // suspend sprite
        shipsLeft--;                    // update count
        if (shipsLeft < 0) {            // if no ships left
          game.setGameOver();           //    then game's over
```

```
        gameOver = true;
      }
      waitPeriod = 50;                    // set wait period
      clearKeyState();                    // clear key buffer
                                          // create explosion
      efm.addShipExplosion(s.locx,s.locy);
    }
  }


//////////////////////////////////////////////////////////////////
// clear key buffers
//////////////////////////////////////////////////////////////////
  private void clearKeyState() {
    for (int i=0; i<keyState.length; i++) {
      keyState[i] = false;
    }
  }


//////////////////////////////////////////////////////////////////
// Pad a number n with zeroes, up to the given length 1
//////////////////////////////////////////////////////////////////

  public String PadNumber(int n,int 1) {
    StringBuffer s;
    s = new StringBuffer(Integer.toString(n));
    while (s.length () < 1) {
      s.insert(0,"0");
    }
    return s.toString();
  }




//////////////////////////////////////////////////////////////////
// Paint all information related to the Ship:
//    Ship sprite
//    Fire sprites
//    Shield
//    Shield status
//    Ships left
//////////////////////////////////////////////////////////////////


  // text Strings needed
  String shieldString = new String("Shield:");
  String noShieldString = new String("No Shield");
  String shipsLeftString = new String("Ships Left:");

  public void paint(Graphics g) {
    g.setColor(Color.yellow);
```

continued on next page

continued from previous page

```
                  // draw ships left indicator
                  g.drawString(shipsLeftString,69,20);
                  g.drawString(PadNumber(shipsLeft,1),135,20);

                  // if ship's alive:
                  if (shipAlive) {

                    // if shield's on, draw it!
                    if (keyState[SHIELDINDEX] && shieldStrength > 0) {
                     g.setColor(Color.green);
                     g.drawOval(s.locx-15,s.locy-15,30,30);
                     g.drawOval(s.locx-17,s.locy-17,34,34);
                    }

                    // draw shield status
                    if (shieldStrength > 0) {
                     g.setColor(Color.green);
                     g.drawString(shieldString,153,20);
                     g.fillRect(199,15,shieldStrength, 5);
                    }


                    else {
                     g.setColor(Color.red);
                     g.drawString(noShieldString,153,20);
                    }


                    // paint the Ship sprite
                    s.paint(g);

                    // paint the Fire sprites
                    for ( int i=0 ; i<MAX_SHOTS; i++) {
                     f[i].paint(g);
                    }
                  }
                }


  //////////////////////////////////////////////////////////////
  // Translate keyboard input into Ship sprite actions
  //////////////////////////////////////////////////////////////

   // declare the key buffer
   static boolean keyState[] = new boolean[5];

   // key bindings
   static final int LEFTINDEX = 0;
   static final int LEFT = 'q';            // rotate left

   static final int RIGHTINDEX = 1;
```

```
static final int RIGHT = 'w';          // rotate right

static final int THRUSTINDEX = 2;
static final int THRUST = 'o';          // thrust

static final int FIREINDEX = 3;
static final int FIRE = 'p';            // fire


static final int SHIELDINDEX = 4;
static final int SHIELD = ' ';          // shield




/////////////////////////////////////////////////////////////////
// update Ship and Fire sprites based on key buffer
/////////////////////////////////////////////////////////////////
public void update() {

  // update fire sprites
  for ( int i=0 ; i<MAX_SHOTS; i++) {
    f[i].update();
  }

  // if ship's alive
  if (shipAlive) {

    // check the key buffer and perform the
    //   associated action

    if (keyState[LEFTINDEX])
     s.rotateLeft();
    if (keyState[RIGHTINDEX])
     s.rotateRight();
    if (keyState[THRUSTINDEX])
     s.thrust();
    if (keyState[FIREINDEX])
     handleFire();
    if (keyState[SHIELDINDEX])
     updateShield();

    // update the Ship sprite
    s.update();
  }

  // otherwise, the ship's not alive!
  else {

    // if the waiting period's over,
```

continued on next page

continued from previous page

```
         //    initialize a new Ship sprite
         if (!gameOver && (waitPeriod-- <= 0)) {
          s.setAngle(270);
          s.setPosition(width/2,height/2);
          s.setVelocity(0,0);
          s.rotate(0);
          shieldStrength = 100;
          shipAlive = true;
          s.restore();
         }
       }
      }


///////////////////////////////////////////////////////////////
// initialize parameters for a new game
///////////////////////////////////////////////////////////////

   public void newGame() {
        s.setAngle(270);
        s.setPosition(width/2,height/2);
        s.setVelocity(0,0);
        s.rotate(0);
        shieldStrength = 100;
        shipAlive = true;
        shipsLeft = 2;
        gameOver = false;
        s.restore();
       }


///////////////////////////////////////////////////////////////
// increase Shield strength (when the Ship touches a powerup
///////////////////////////////////////////////////////////////

   public void increaseShield() {
     shieldStrength += 30;
     if (shieldStrength > 250)
       shieldStrength = 250;
   }


///////////////////////////////////////////////////////////////
// handle keyDown events by setting the appropriate
//    field in the key buffer
///////////////////////////////////////////////////////////////

   public void keyDown(Event e,int k) {
     switch(k) {
     case LEFT:
       keyState[LEFTINDEX] = true;
       break;
     case RIGHT:
       keyState[RIGHTINDEX] = true;
```

```
        break;
      case FIRE:
        keyState[FIREINDEX] = true;
        break;
      case THRUST:
        keyState[THRUSTINDEX] = true;
        break;
      case SHIELD:
        keyState[SHIELDINDEX] = true;
        break;

      default:
        break;
      }
    }


    ///////////////////////////////////////////////////////////////
    // handle keyDown events by setting the appropriate
    //    field in the key buffer
    ///////////////////////////////////////////////////////////////
      public void keyUp(Event e,int k) {
        switch(k) {
        case LEFT:
          keyState[LEFTINDEX] = false;
          break;
        case RIGHT:
          keyState[RIGHTINDEX] = false;
          break;
        case FIRE:
          keyState[FIREINDEX] = false;
          break;
        case THRUST:
          keyState[THRUSTINDEX] = false;
          break;
        case SHIELD:
          keyState[SHIELDINDEX] = false;
          break;

        default:
          break;
        }
      }


    ///////////////////////////////////////////////////////////////
    // update Shield strength (when the player's activating Shield)
    ///////////////////////////////////////////////////////////////
      private void updateShield() {
        if (--shieldStrength <= 0) {
          shieldStrength = 0;
```

continued on next page

continued from previous page

```
          }
        }

//////////////////////////////////////////////////////////////////
// start a new Fire sprite
//////////////////////////////////////////////////////////////////

   private void handleFire() {
     for (int i=0; i<MAX_SHOTS; i++) {
       if (!f[i].isActive()) {

         // start fire from ship's nose at angle theta
         f[i].initialize(s.p.xpoints[0],s.p.ypoints[0],s.theta);
         break;
        }
      }
    }
  }
```

The Enemy Manager

By now, you should be getting a better idea of how these managers are organized! The EnemyManager class is responsible for the Enemy sprites and their Fire sprites, which it initializes in its constructor. The update() method checks for collisions between the enemy objects and the ship (and this code is really similar to the AstManager's update()). In addition, update() starts new enemy ships, using the method NewEnemy(), and initiates enemy firing at random intervals. Finally, the paint() method cycles through all enemy ship sprites and enemy fire sprites, and tells each one to paint itself.

Listing 13-16 shows the EnemyManager class.

Listing 13-16 *EnemyManager class*

```
//////////////////////////////////////////////////////////////////
//
// EnemyManager -- responsible for controlling the
//                 Enemy alien sprites, and Enemy Fire
//
//////////////////////////////////////////////////////////////////


public class EnemyManager extends Object {

    // constants to define two sizes of enemy ships
    static final int LARGE = 0;
    static final int SMALL = 1;
    static final int SRATX = 3;      // x-ratio of large to small
    static final int SRATY = 2;      // y-ratio of large to small

    // the enemy ship templates
    //   x-coordinate template
```

```
static final int tpx[][] =  {
  {14,11,8,-8,-11,-14,-6,6,14,-14},
  {14/SRATX,11/SRATX,8/SRATX,-8/SRATX,-11/SRATX,-14/SRATX,
   -6/SRATX,6/SRATX,14/SRATX,-14/SRATX} } ;

//    y-coordinate template
static final int tpy[][] =  {
  {0,3,6,6,3,0,-4,-4,0,0},
  {0/SRATY,3/SRATY,6/SRATY,6/SRATY,3/SRATY,0/SRATY,-4/SRATY,
   -4/SRATY,0/SRATY,0/SRATY} } ;

// screen boundaries
static int width,height;

// constants parameters for enemy ships
static final int MAX_ENEMIES = 3;
static final int MAX_SHOTS_PER_ENEMY = 2;
static final int MAX_SHOTS = MAX_ENEMIES*MAX_SHOTS_PER_ENEMY;

// arrays for color, length, and value of various enemy ships
static final Color ENEMY_COLOR[] =
  {Color.green,Color.red,Color.orange};
static final int ENEMY_LENGTH[] = {14,14,5};
static final int VALUE[] = {500,750,1000};

// maximum speed
static final int MAX_VX = 9, MAX_VY = 9;

// how often enemies appear, and how often they fire
static double enemy_freq = 0.995 ;
static double fire_freq = 0.995;

// array of Enemy sprites
private Enemy e[] = new Enemy[MAX_ENEMIES];

// array of Fire sprites
private Fire f[] = new Fire[MAX_SHOTS_PER_ENEMY*MAX_ENEMIES];

// references to other game objects
ShipManager sm;
EffManager efm;
Ship ship;
Fire[] shipfire;
GameManager game;

/////////////////////////////////////////////////////////////////
// EnemyManager constructor
/////////////////////////////////////////////////////////////////

  public EnemyManager(int width,int height,
                      ShipManager sm,
                      EffManager efm,
```

continued on next page

continued from previous page

```
                          GameManager g) {
        ship = sm.getShip();              // get ship-- needed for
                                          //   collision detection
        shipfire = sm.getFire();          // get ship's fire for
        this.sm = sm;                     //   collision detection
        this.efm = efm;
        game = g;

        // initialize the three enemy sprites
        e[0] = new Enemy(tpx[0],tpy[0],tpx[0].length, // template
                    0,0,                              // initial loc
                    ENEMY_COLOR[0],            // color
                    width,height,              // screen bounds
                    ENEMY_LENGTH[0],VALUE[0]); // length,value
        e[1] = new Enemy(tpx[0],tpy[0],tpx[0].length,
                    0,0,ENEMY_COLOR[1],
                    width,height,
                    ENEMY_LENGTH[1],VALUE[1]);
        e[2] = new Enemy(tpx[1],tpy[1],tpx[1].length,
                    0,0,
                    ENEMY_COLOR[2],
                    width,height,
                    ENEMY_LENGTH[2],VALUE[2]);

        // suspend the three enemy sprites
        for (int i=0; i<MAX_ENEMIES; i++) {
          e[i].suspend();
        }

        // create and suspend the Fire sprites
        for ( int i=0 ; i<MAX_SHOTS; i++) {
          f[i] = new Fire(ENEMY_COLOR[i/MAX_SHOTS_PER_ENEMY],
                      width,height);
          f[i].suspend();
        }

        // save screen bounds
        this.width = width;
        this.height = height;

      }


    ///////////////////////////////////////////////////////////
    // initialize for new game
    ///////////////////////////////////////////////////////////

      public void newGame() {
        for (int i=0; i<MAX_ENEMIES; i++) {
          e[i].suspend();
        }
```

```
      for (int i=0 ; i<MAX_SHOTS; i++) {
        f[i] = new Fire(ENEMY_COLOR[i/MAX_SHOTS_PER_ENEMY],
                     width,height);
        f[i].suspend();
      }
    }


    //////////////////////////////////////////////////////////////
    // update enemy ships and enemy fire
    //      CHECK FOR COLLISIONS WITH SHIP OR SHIP FIRE
    //////////////////////////////////////////////////////////////

    public void update() {


      // check if any of the fire sprites hit the Player's ship.
      // If so, tell the ShipManager to destroy the ship

      for ( int i=0 ; i<MAX_SHOTS; i++) {
        f[i].update();
        if (f[i].intersect(ship)) {
          sm.destroyShip();

        }
      }

    //////////////////////////////////////////////////////////////
      // cycle through all enemies
      for ( int i=0 ; i<MAX_ENEMIES; i++) {

        // place a new enemy on the screen at random intervals
        if (!e[i].isActive()) {
         if (Math.random() > enemy_freq) {
         NewEnemy(i);
         }
        }

        // else update and check for collisions
        else {
         e[i].update();

         // if it intersects the ship
         if (e[i].intersect(ship)) {

           // increase score
           game.updateScore(e[i].value);

           // tell sm to destroy ship
           sm.destroyShip();

           // suspend enemy and create explosion
```

continued on next page

continued from previous page

```
                        e[i].suspend();
                    efm.addEnemyExplosion(e[i].locx,e[i].locy);
                }

                // check if enemy intersect's ship's fire
                for (int j=0; j<shipfire.length; j++) {
                  if (e[i].intersect(shipfire[j])) {
                    sm.stopFire(j);                // stop fire sprite
                    e[i].suspend();                // stop enemy sprite
                      efm.addEnemyExplosion(e[i].locx,e[i].locy);
                      game.updateScore(e[i].value);
                  }
                }

                // create new enemy fire at random intervals
                if (Math.random() > fire_freq) {
                  Fire(i);
                }
              }
            }
          }


    /////////////////////////////////////////////////////////////
    // Accessor methods
    /////////////////////////////////////////////////////////////

      public Enemy[] getEnemy() {
        return e;
      }

      public Fire[] getFire() {
        return f;
      }

      public void destroyEnemy(int i) {
        e[i].suspend();
      }

      public void stopFire(int i) {
        f[i].suspend();
      }


    /////////////////////////////////////////////////////////////
    // make new enemy at slot i of the Enemy array e
    /////////////////////////////////////////////////////////////

      private void NewEnemy(int i) {
        // set the enemy speed
        e[i].setVelocity(GameMath.getRand(2*MAX_VX)-MAX_VX,
                    GameMath.getRand(2*MAX_VY)-MAX_VY);
        // set the enemy position
        int px = (Math.random() > 0.5) ? 0 : width;
        int py = GameMath.getRand(height);
```

```
        e[i].setPosition(px,py);
        // restore the sprite
        e[i].restore();
    }


//////////////////////////////////////////////////////////////
// initialize enemy fire for enemy ship i
//////////////////////////////////////////////////////////////

    private void Fire(int i) {
      for (int j = i*MAX_SHOTS_PER_ENEMY;
          j < (i+1)*MAX_SHOTS_PER_ENEMY;
          j++) {

        // if there's a slot in enemy fire array,
        //    initialize and restore the fire sprite
        if (!f[j].isActive()) {
         f[j].initialize(e[i].locx,e[i].locy,
                    GameMath.getRand(360));  // random angle
          f[j].restore();

        }
      }
    }


//////////////////////////////////////////////////////////////
// paint the enemy ships and their fire
//////////////////////////////////////////////////////////////


    public void paint(Graphics g) {
      for ( int i=0 ; i<MAX_ENEMIES; i++) {
        e[i].paint(g);
      }

      for ( int i=0 ; i<MAX_SHOTS; i++) {
        f[i].paint(g);
      }
    }
}
```

The Effect Manager

For the effect manager, we're going to depart from our policy of avoiding object instantiations during game play. This is because the number of explosions is tricky to judge beforehand, so it's easier to keep a Vector of explosions, and insert new explosions when the other manager classes detect collisions. Thus, EffManager provides the public methods addShipExplosion(), addEnemyExplosion(), and addAstExplosion(), which the other managers can invoke. These methods create new Explosion objects that are added to the explosions Vector.

Listing 13-17 contains the complete effect manager class.

Listing 13-17 *EffManager class*

```
/////////////////////////////////////////////////////////////////
//
// EffManager: handles effects, such as explosions and sound
//
/////////////////////////////////////////////////////////////////

public class EffManager extends Object {

  Vector explosions;
  AudioClip expsound;

/////////////////////////////////////////////////////////////////
// EffManager constructor
/////////////////////////////////////////////////////////////////

  public EffManager(AudioClip expsound) {
    explosions = new Vector();
    this.expsound = expsound;
  }

/////////////////////////////////////////////////////////////////
// make a ship explosion at x,y
/////////////////////////////////////////////////////////////////

  public void addShipExplosion(int x,int y) {
    Explosion exp = new Explosion(Color.red,x,y,20);
    Explosion exp1 = new Explosion(Color.yellow,x+2,y+2,25);
    explosions.addElement(exp);
    explosions.addElement(exp1);
    if (expsound != null) {
      expsound.play();
    }
  }

/////////////////////////////////////////////////////////////////
// make an asteroid explosion at x,y
/////////////////////////////////////////////////////////////////
  public void addAstExplosion(int x,int y) {
    Explosion exp = new Explosion(Color.white,x,y,15);
    explosions.addElement(exp);
    if (expsound != null) {
      expsound.play();
    }
  }

/////////////////////////////////////////////////////////////////
// make an asteroid explosion at x,y
/////////////////////////////////////////////////////////////////
```

```java
  public void addEnemyExplosion(int x,int y) {
    Explosion exp = new Explosion(Color.orange,x,y,15);
    explosions.addElement(exp);
    if (expsound != null) {
      expsound.play();
    }
  }

//////////////////////////////////////////////////////////////////
// make an explosion of the given color at x,y
//////////////////////////////////////////////////////////////////
  public void addExplosion(Color c,int x, int y, int u) {
    Explosion exp = new Explosion(c,x,y,u);
    explosions.addElement(exp);
    if (expsound != null) {
      expsound.play();
    }
  }

//////////////////////////////////////////////////////////////////
// paint the explosions by stepping through the
//    explosions Vector
//////////////////////////////////////////////////////////////////
  public void paint (Graphics g) {
    Enumeration e;
    e = explosions.elements();
    while (e.hasMoreElements()) {
      Sprite exp = (Sprite) e.nextElement();
      exp.paint(g);
    }
  }

//////////////////////////////////////////////////////////////////
// update the explosions by stepping through the
//    explosions Vector
//////////////////////////////////////////////////////////////////
  public void update() {
    Enumeration e;
    e = explosions.elements();
    while (e.hasMoreElements()) {
      Explosion exp = (Explosion) e.nextElement();
      exp.update();
      // if the explosion's finished, remove it from vector
      if (exp.isDone()) {
        explosions.removeElement(exp);
      }
    }
  }
}
```

The Game Manager

The GameManager class contains the top-level structure of JAVAroids. The game opens with an introductory screen, which lists the point values of the objects in the game. After this, the player can test drive his ship, and learn the controls. Then, the player can start the game. The transition between these screens is triggered by a mouseUp event.

GameManager implements the Runnable interface by defining a method called run(). The heart of the run() method is the Video Game Loop, which we covered back in Chapter 5, Building a Video Game. This loop coordinates the sequence of actions that take place in Figure 13-17. GameManager also defines handlers for key events, which it passes along to the ShipManager.

Finally, the GameManager source is presented in Listing 13-18. JAVAroids is finished!

Listing 13-18 GameManager class

```
/////////////////////////////////////////////////////////////
//
// GameManager:
// responsible for tracking status of game and keeping score
//
/////////////////////////////////////////////////////////////

public class GameManager extends Applet implements Runnable {


    // variables for double buffering and animation
    Thread animation;
    Graphics gbuf;
    Image im;
    static final int REFRESH_RATE = 72;        // in ms

    // size of the game applet: change as needed
    static final int MAX_HEIGHT = 400;
    static final int MAX_WIDTH = 400;

    // game parameters
    private int score;                          // score
    private boolean playing;                    // playing or not
    private boolean gameOver;                   // is game over
    private int intro_screen;                   // which screen
    static final int EXTRA_SHIP = 10000;    // #pts for extra ship
    private int current_extra = 0;              // counts extras

    // constants for the introduction part of the game
    static final int INSTRUCTIONS  = 1;
    static final int TEST_DRIVE  = 2;
    static final int INTRO_OVER  = 3;

    // references to manager classes
```

```
        AstManager am;                          // asteroids
        ShipManager sm;                         // ship
        EnemyManager em;                        // enemy ships
        EffManager efm;                         // effects

        // sound
        URL codebase;
        AudioClip expsound = null;

        // variables to monitor performance during game
        Date time;
        long t1,t2,dt;

        // fonts
        static Font bigfont = new Font("TimesRoman", Font.BOLD,24);
        static Font medfont = new Font("TimesRoman", Font.PLAIN,18);
        static Font smallfont = new Font("TimesRoman", Font.PLAIN,12);

//////////////////////////////////////////////////////////////////
// initialize applet
//////////////////////////////////////////////////////////////////
  public void init() {

    // initialize screen
    setBackground(Color.black);
    setFont(smallfont);

    // initialize double buffer
    im = createImage(MAX_WIDTH,MAX_HEIGHT);
    gbuf = im.getGraphics();

    // initialize sound
    codebase = getCodeBase();
 // System.out.println(codebase.toString());

    resize(MAX_WIDTH,MAX_HEIGHT);

    // initialize game state
    gameOver = true;
    intro_screen = 1;
    playing = false;

  }


//////////////////////////////////////////////////////////////////
// start applet
//////////////////////////////////////////////////////////////////
  public void start() {
    // load sound

    try {
```

continued on next page

continued from previous page

```
              expsound = getAudioClip(getCodeBase(),"Explosion.au");

    }
  catch (Exception exc) {
    System.out.println("Sound not loaded");
  };

    // initialize manager classes

    efm = new EffManager(expsound);

    sm = new ShipManager(MAX_WIDTH,MAX_HEIGHT,efm,this);

    em = new EnemyManager(MAX_WIDTH,MAX_HEIGHT,sm,efm,this);

    am = new AstManager(MAX_WIDTH,MAX_HEIGHT,sm,em,efm,this);


    // start animation
    if (animation == null) {
      animation = new Thread(this);
      if (animation != null) {
        animation.start();
      }
      else
        System.out.println("Insufficient memory to fork thread!");
    }
  }


//////////////////////////////////////////////////////////////////
// stop applet
//////////////////////////////////////////////////////////////////
  public void stop() {
    if (animation != null) {
      animation.stop();
      animation = null;
    }
  }


//////////////////////////////////////////////////////////////////
// set gameOver flag
//////////////////////////////////////////////////////////////////
  public void setGameOver() {
    gameOver = true;
  }


//////////////////////////////////////////////////////////////////
// start a new game
//////////////////////////////////////////////////////////////////
```

```
private void newGame() {
  // tell managers to start a new game
  em.newGame();
  am.newGame();
  sm.newGame();

  // set font for game
  gbuf.setFont(smallfont);

  // initialize parameters
  current_extra = 0;
  score = 0;
  gameOver = false;
  playing = true;

}


//////////////////////////////////////////////////////////////////
//
// Event Handlers
//
//////////////////////////////////////////////////////////////////

// if mouseUp occurs, proceed to next screen of introduction.
// if game's being played, restart the game.

public boolean mouseUp(Event e,int x,int y) {

  if (intro_screen == INSTRUCTIONS) {
    intro_screen = TEST_DRIVE;
    sm.getShip().setPosition(385,75);
    sm.getShip().restore();
  }
  // else restart the game
  else if (intro_screen == TEST_DRIVE) {
    intro_screen = INTRO_OVER;
    newGame();
  }
  else
    newGame();

  return true;
}

// pass key events to the ShipManager
public boolean keyDown(Event e, int k) {
  sm.keyDown(e,k);
  return true;
}
// pass key events to the ShipManager
```

continued on next page

continued from previous page

```
        public boolean keyUp(Event e, int k) {
          sm.keyUp(e,k);
          return true;
        }




        /////////////////////////////////////////////////////////////
        // the game driver
        /////////////////////////////////////////////////////////////
          public void run() {
            startInstructions();

            // the Video Game Loop
            while (true) {

              if (playing) {
              time = new Date();              // track time
              t1 = time.getTime();
              if (!gameOver) {
              sm.update();                 // update ship
              }
              em.update();                 // update enemies
              am.update();                 // update asteroids
              efm.update();                // update effects
              repaint();

              Thread.currentThread().yield();
              time = new Date();            // track time
              t2 = time.getTime();
              dt = t2-t1;                   // how long did it take?

                                           // sleep
              try {
              Thread.sleep (REFRESH_RATE-(int)dt < 0
                ? 8
                : REFRESH_RATE-(int)dt);
              } catch (Exception exc) { };

              }

              // else not playing
              else {
               updateOpening();              // update opening
               repaint();
               Thread.currentThread().yield();
               try {
               Thread.sleep (REFRESH_RATE);// sleep
               } catch (Exception exc) { };
              }
            }
          }
```

```
/////////////////////////////////////////////////////////////////
// initialize the AstManager and EnemyManager for the
// INSTRUCTIONS screen.
/////////////////////////////////////////////////////////////////
  private void startInstructions() {
    Asteroid a[] = am.getAsts();
    Asteroid p = am.getPowerup();
    // set asteroids in instruction screen
    a[0].setPosition(270,98);
    a[0].setRotationRate(4);
    a[0].setVelocity(1,2);
    a[0].restore();
    a[am.NUM_LARGE].setPosition(330,138);
    a[am.NUM_LARGE].setRotationRate(-4);
    a[am.NUM_LARGE].setVelocity(-1,-1);
    a[am.NUM_LARGE].restore();
    a[am.NUM_LARGE+am.NUM_MEDIUM].setPosition(370,178);
    a[am.NUM_LARGE+am.NUM_MEDIUM].setRotationRate(5);
    a[am.NUM_LARGE+am.NUM_MEDIUM].setVelocity(2,-1);
    a[am.NUM_LARGE+am.NUM_MEDIUM].restore();

    // set powerup in intro screen
    p.setPosition(330,340);
    p.restore();

    // set enemies for intro screen
    Enemy e[] = em.getEnemy();
    e[0].setPosition(10,214);
    e[0].setVelocity(2,0);
    e[0].restore();
    e[1].setPosition(390,254);
    e[1].setVelocity(-3,0);
    e[1].restore();
    e[2].setPosition(7,294);
    e[2].setVelocity(4,0);
    e[2].restore();
  }


/////////////////////////////////////////////////////////////////
// update the opening screens
/////////////////////////////////////////////////////////////////
  private void updateOpening() {
    if (intro_screen == INSTRUCTIONS) {
      am.update();
      Enemy e[] = em.getEnemy();
      e[0].update();
      e[1].update();
      e[2].update();
      efm.update();
    }
    else if (intro_screen == TEST_DRIVE) {
```

continued on next page

continued from previous page

```
        sm.update();
      }
    }


    //////////////////////////////////////////////////////////////
    // update the score. If the score passes threshold
    // (every EXTRA_SHIP points) give an extra ship!
    //////////////////////////////////////////////////////////////
      public void updateScore(int val) {
        score += val;
        if ((score / EXTRA_SHIP) > current_extra) {
          sm.extraShip();                    // give extra ship
          current_extra = score/EXTRA_SHIP;
        }
      }


    //////////////////////////////////////////////////////////////
    // override update() to eliminate flicker
    //////////////////////////////////////////////////////////////
      public void update(Graphics g) {
        paint(g);                            // don't clear screen
      }


    //////////////////////////////////////////////////////////////
    // return a string of n that is 0-padded with the given length
    //////////////////////////////////////////////////////////////
      public String PadNumber(int n,int len) {
        StringBuffer s;
        s = new StringBuffer(Integer.toString(n));
        while (s.length () < len) {
          s.insert(0,"0");
        }
        return s.toString();
      }



    //////////////////////////////////////////////////////////////
    // define Strings used in the Opening screens
    //////////////////////////////////////////////////////////////

      // Strings used in INSTRUCTIONS screen
      String javaroidsString = new String("JAVAroids!");
      String galleryString = new String("The Lineup...");
      String largeAstString =
        new String("30 points for Big Asteroid");
      String mediumAstString =
        new String("60 points for Medium Asteroid");
      String smallAstString =
        new String("90 points for Small Asteroid");
```

```
        String greenAlienString =
          new String("500 points for Green Alien");
        String redAlienString =
          new String("750 points for Red Alien");
        String orangeAlienString =
          new String("1000 points for Orange Alien");
        String clickMouseString1 =
          new String("Click mouse to continue...");
        String powerupString1 =
          new String("Touch PowerUp for");
        String powerupString2 =
          new String("extra shield strength:");

        // Strings used in the TEST_DRIVE screen
        String shipControlString =
          new String("Test Drive your ship NOW ---> ");
        String rotLeftString = new String("Press 'q' to Rotate Left");
        String rotRightString =
          new String("Press 'w' to Rotate Right");
        String thrustString = new String("Press 'o' to Thrust");
        String fireString = new String("Press 'p' to Fire");
        String shieldString =
          new String("Press <space bar> for Shield");

        String extraShipString =
          new String("Extra Ship every 10,000 points");
        String goodLuckString =
          new String("GOOD LUCK!");
        String clickMouseString =
          new String("Click mouse to begin!");
        String byMeString = new String("by Joel Fan");

        String gameOverString = new String("GAME OVER");
        String clickMouseString2 =
          new String("Click mouse to play again!");

  ///////////////////////////////////////////////////////////
  // paint to the screen, depending on mode of game
  ///////////////////////////////////////////////////////////
    public void paint(Graphics g) {

      // clear offscreen buffer
      gbuf.setColor(Color.black);
      gbuf.fillRect(0,0,MAX_WIDTH,MAX_HEIGHT);

      if (playing) {

        // if game's not over, show the ship.
        if (!gameOver) {
         sm.paint(gbuf);
        }
```

continued on next page

continued from previous page

```
                // otherwise, display the Game Over message
                else {
                 gbuf.setFont(bigfont);
                 gbuf.setColor(Color.cyan);
                 gbuf.drawString(byMeString,
                           MAX_WIDTH/2 - 55, MAX_HEIGHT/2-60);

                 gbuf.setColor(Color.magenta);
                 gbuf.drawString(gameOverString,
                           MAX_WIDTH/2 - 65, MAX_HEIGHT/2);


                 gbuf.drawString(clickMouseString2,
                           MAX_WIDTH/2 - 120, MAX_HEIGHT/2+35);
                 gbuf.setFont(smallfont);
                }

                // tell other manager classes to paint themselves
                em.paint(gbuf);                     // paint enemies
                am.paint(gbuf);                     // paint asteroids
                efm.paint(gbuf);                    // paint effects

                // draw the score
                gbuf.drawString(PadNumber(score,6),20,20);

                // draw offscreen image to screen
                g.drawImage(im,0,0,this);
            }

            else if (intro_screen == INSTRUCTIONS) {
              paintInstructions(g);
            }

            else if (intro_screen == TEST_DRIVE) {
              paintTestDrive(g);
            }
        }


      /////////////////////////////////////////////////////////////
      // paint Instructions screen
      //    coordinates are hardcoded for simplicity
      /////////////////////////////////////////////////////////////
        public void paintInstructions(Graphics g) {

          gbuf.setFont(bigfont);

          // set a random color
          gbuf.setColor(new Color(GameMath.getRand(155)+100,
                          GameMath.getRand(155)+100,
                          GameMath.getRand(155)+100));
          gbuf.drawString(javaroidsString,MAX_WIDTH/2 - 60, 30);
```

```
            gbuf.setColor(Color.yellow);
            gbuf.setFont(medfont);
            gbuf.setColor(Color.magenta);
            gbuf.setFont(bigfont);
            gbuf.drawString(largeAstString,25,80);
            gbuf.drawString(mediumAstString,25,120);
            gbuf.drawString(smallAstString,25,160);
            gbuf.setColor(Color.green);
            gbuf.drawString(greenAlienString,25,200);
            gbuf.setColor(Color.red);
            gbuf.drawString(redAlienString,25,240);
            gbuf.setColor(Color.orange);
            gbuf.drawString(orangeAlienString,25,280);
            gbuf.setColor(Color.green);
            gbuf.drawString(powerupString1,25,320);
            gbuf.drawString(powerupString2,50,350);
            gbuf.setColor(Color.yellow);
            gbuf.drawString(clickMouseString1,MAX_WIDTH/2-120,385);
            am.paint(gbuf);
            Enemy e[] = em.getEnemy();
            e[0].paint(gbuf);
            e[1].paint(gbuf);
            e[2].paint(gbuf);
            efm.paint(gbuf);
            // dump offscreen buffer to screen
            g.drawImage(im,0,0,this);

        }


    /////////////////////////////////////////////////////////////
    // paint the test drive screen
    //    coordinates are hardcoded for simplicity
    /////////////////////////////////////////////////////////////
      public void paintTestDrive(Graphics g) {

        gbuf.setFont(smallfont);
        sm.paint(gbuf);              // paint the ship
        gbuf.setFont(bigfont);

        gbuf.setColor(new Color(GameMath.getRand(155)+100,
                        GameMath.getRand(155)+100,
                        GameMath.getRand(155)+100));
        gbuf.drawString(javaroidsString,MAX_WIDTH/2 - 60, 50);
        gbuf.setColor(Color.magenta);
        gbuf.drawString(shipControlString,25,80);
        gbuf.setColor(Color.orange);
        gbuf.drawString(rotLeftString,25,130);
        gbuf.drawString(rotRightString,25,170);
        gbuf.drawString(thrustString,25,210);
        gbuf.drawString(fireString,25,250);
        gbuf.drawString(shieldString,25,290);
        gbuf.setColor(Color.cyan);
```

continued on next page

continued from previous page

```
        gbuf.drawString(extraShipString,25,340);
        gbuf.setColor(Color.green);
        gbuf.drawString(clickMouseString,MAX_WIDTH/2-120,385);
        g.drawImage(im,0,0,this);

    }

}
```

Recommended Applet Tag to Run JAVAroids

<applet code="GameManager.class" width=400 height=400>

Suggestion Box

This game's only a starting point. Here are a few ideas for further extensions and improvements to the game:

 Make the enemy ships more intelligent. For example, they could follow the player's ship, or exhibit different behaviors. You can use a state machine to implement multiple behaviors, as you've seen in Chapter 5, Building a Video Game.

 Change the way the game objects move. One change you can implement almost immediately is to bounce the sprites off the edges of the screen, instead of wrapping them around to the other side. Just modify the updatePosition() method of MoveablePolygon, and you can alter the dynamic of the game dramatically!

 Another way of handling explosions and sound effects is by incorporating this functionality in the Sprite subclasses themselves. Thus, the sprites would be responsible for the sounds that occur when they collide, and the way that they explode. In this scenario, the effect manager might tell the individual sprites when to make sounds or explode, but the actual sound or explosion is the responsibility of the sprite itself. Think about the benefits of encapsulating explosion and sound effects in the Sprite subclasses, and implement it.

Optimize the game. Here are some ways of doing this. First, precompute the coordinates of the rotated polygons, and store them in a lookup table. This way, you can avoid the floating-point multiplications while the game is playing. Secondly, use final methods whenever possible (such as accessor methods) to eliminate the overhead from dynamic method binding. A third optimization is to flatten the inheritance hierarchy, and reduce unnecessary method calls by inlining functions as much as possible.

Allow multiple players to compete, either in alternation or at the same time. (You'll need a big keyboard!)

Summary

You've constructed a fairly intricate video game in this chapter. However, you've built the game, and managed its complexity, by making use of inheritance- and responsibility-driven design. These are concepts you can take with you in designing any object-oriented application, whether it's a game or not!

14

Daleks!

Ethan Koehler

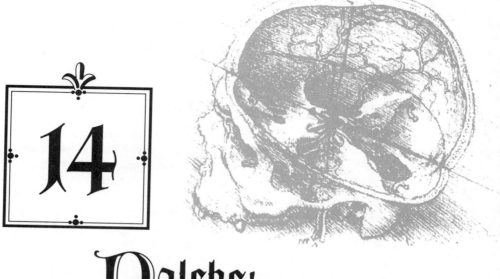

14

Daleks!

This chapter presents an enhanced version of a classic computer game. You must help Dr. Who evade his ruthless but dim-witted enemies, the Daleks. The Daleks will move closer to you every turn. If they reach your square, the game is over. At your disposal are a limited number of sonic screwdrivers (handy devices that destroy adjacent Daleks), an ability to teleport to random destinations, and your superior intellect. The Daleks can also be killed when they attempt to move into the same square on the board, which reduces them to a pile of rubble. Any Daleks trying to move into a square containing rubble will also be destroyed.

In developing this applet, I paid a lot of attention to the issues of bandwidth and processor speed. The sounds, graphics, and animations used are simple but effective. The result is a program that loads and runs quickly—features that are easy to overlook with Java. In addition, many game parameters are customizable from HTML, meaning the game board, images, and intro screen can be modified to incorporate different themes and challenges.

Playing the Game

When the applet first runs, the player is greeted with an animated intro screen and a bar showing the progress of loading images. When the images are done loading, the player can press any key to begin the game. Figure 14-1 shows a typical board setup on level 1. The player's character always begins in the center of the screen. The Daleks are scattered randomly around the board and move one square in the direction of the player every turn. The numeric keypad is used to control movement (diagonal movement is allowed). The player may press "S" to activate a sonic screwdriver to destroy adjacent Daleks. The number of remaining screwdrivers is displayed in the info bar at the bottom of the screen. The player may teleport at any time by pressing "T". This will move the player to a random space on the board, which may be adjacent to one of the Daleks, resulting in the player's capture and the end of the game. Finally, the player can press "L" to make a "last stand," allowing the Daleks to move continuously until the player or all the Daleks are destroyed.

Setting Up the Game

The applet is contained in two classes, daleks14 and animatedIntroClass. A daleks14 object contains all the game routines and directs the traffic throughout the game. An animatedIntroClass object contains the methods necessary to create the title screen shown between games. Listing 14-1 shows the init() method of the daleks14 class, which is automatically called when the applet is loaded.

FIGURE 14-1

◎ ◎ ◎ ◎ ◎ ◎

The Daleks!
board

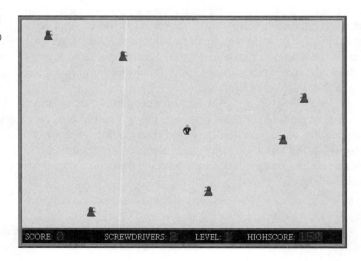

Listing 14-1 The daleks14.init() method

```java
public void init()  {
// get parameters from the calling HTML file
getHTMLParameters();

    // initialize dalek arrays
    dalX = new int[maxEnemies];
    dalY = new int[maxEnemies];
    dalF = new int[maxEnemies];

    drStartX = maxX / 2;
    drStartY = maxY / 2;

    // create enough room to fit gameboard and status bar
    resize(maxX*imgW,maxY*imgH+25);

    // load game graphics
    doctorPic[0] = getImage(getCodeBase(),"dw1l.gif");
    doctorPic[1] = getImage(getCodeBase(),"dw1r.gif");
    doctorPic[2] = getImage(getCodeBase(),"dw2l.gif");
    doctorPic[3] = doctorPic[2];
    doctorPic[4] = getImage(getCodeBase(),"dw3l.gif");
    doctorPic[5] = doctorPic[4];
    doctorPic[6] = getImage(getCodeBase(),"dw4l.gif");
    doctorPic[7] = getImage(getCodeBase(),"dw4r.gif");
    doctorPic[8] = getImage(getCodeBase(),"dw5l.gif");
    doctorPic[9] = getImage(getCodeBase(),"dw5r.gif");
    dalekPic[0] = getImage(getCodeBase(),"dalekl.gif");
    dalekPic[1] = getImage(getCodeBase(),"dalekr.gif");
    rubblePic[0] = getImage(getCodeBase(),"daldl.gif);
    rubblePic[1] = getImage(getCodeBase(),"daldr.gif");
    deadPic = getImage(getCodeBase(),"drdead.gif");

    // load graphic digits
      for (int j=0; j<10; j++)
          digit[j] = getImage(getCodeBase(),"green"+j+".gif");

      for (int j=0; j<10; j++)  {
          tracker.addImage(doctorPic[j], j);
          tracker.addImage(digit[j], j+10);
          }
      for (int j=0; j<2; j++)  {
          tracker.addImage(dalekPic[j], 20+j);
          tracker.addImage(rubblePic[j], 22+j);
          }
    tracker.addImage(deadPic, 24);

    // start loading images
    tracker.checkAll(true);

    // create the off-screen bitmap
    nextScreen = createImage(maxX*imgW,maxY*imgH+25);
```

continued on next page

continued from previous page

```
offScreenGC = nextScreen.getGraphics();

prepareScreen();

animateIntro.setInfo(nextScreen, maxX, maxY, imgH, imgW, title,
                     flyingWidget, numWidgets);
animateIntro.start();
animIntro = true;
repaint();
}
```

This procedure sets up the game. First, a call is made to getHTMLParameters(void), which allows the user to customize many aspects of the game. The arrays of Dalek information are initialized at this point. By waiting to allocate the arrays, the method allows any number of Daleks in the game. A call to resize(int, int) ensures that the game graphics will fit in the applet window. The method then assigns each graphic image to the appropriate Image object. The various Images contained in the *doctorPic* array are needed because the player's appearance changes at certain levels (mimicking Dr. Who's ability to regenerate on the TV show). Each player and Dalek has a right- and left-facing Image. All the Image objects are given to a newly created MediaTracker object *tracker*, which handles loading the graphics and reports on their progress. The *nextScreen* variable is basically a worksheet Image where we build each successive game screen, which can be accessed by using *offScreenGC*, its graphics context. The call to prepareScreen() draws the current game status on the offscreen Image. Finally, the animatedIntroClass object is initialized and run.

▓ Programming Tip

Java addresses some of the complexity of C++ by eliminating the ability to dynamically allocate memory. After an array is initialized, it cannot be extended, which can greatly reduce the flexibility of Java applets. Daleks! avoids this problem by waiting to initialize the Dalek arrays until the maximum number of Daleks allowed is determined (this can be set through an HTML <param> tag).

Animating the Title Screen

The animated intro screen displays a cloud of question marks flying from the middle to the edges of the screen, as shown in Figure 14-2. It displays the applet title, version number, author, and an info bar on the bottom of the screen. If the animatedIntroClass object is running for the first time, it will display a progress bar that grows as the Image variables are loaded. When loading is complete, the progress bar is replaced with the standard info bar showing the player status (i.e., last score, screwdrivers, level number, and so on).

FIGURE 14-2

◎ ◎ ◎ ◎ ◎ ◎

*The animated
intro screen*

Before the title screen is run, however, a new Thread must be created. This allows the daleks14 object to monitor the keyboard while another Thread loops continuously to create the animation effect of the title screen.

Preparing to Animate

The title screen features a number of customizable items, and so we cannot assume anything about the applet title, screen size, and flying widgets (question marks by default). We need to have a procedure to ensure that when displayed, the graphics and text on the intro screen will be properly aligned and displayed. To do this, the setInfo(…) method examines the dimensions of the String objects to be displayed and determines their horizontal and vertical positions. Listing 14-2 shows a portion of the setInfo(…) method, which determines how to center the game title on the screen.

Listing 14-2 *The animatedIntroClass.setInfo(…) method*

```
// handle Font creation and sizing
int halfWayX = maxX * imgW / 2;
int totalHeight = maxY * imgH;

titleFont = new Font("Helvetica", Font.PLAIN, 36);
offScreenGC.setFont(titleFont);
titleX = halfWayX - offScreenGC.getFontMetrics().stringWidth(gameTitle) ⇐
/ 2;
titleY = (int)(totalHeight * 0.3);
```

The value of *halfWayX* is the horizontal center of the applet window in pixels (number of horizontal board squares * horizontal width of game pieces / 2). The *totalHeight* variable is the height of the game board in pixels. The code creates a new Font object *titleFont*, which defines the display characteristics of the String object *gameTitle*. To calculate dimensions, the procedure must make *titleFont* the current font, which is done by setting it on the offscreen graphics context *offScreenGC*. The variable *titleX* is then given the value for center of the screen minus half the width (in pixels) of the *gameTitle* String. The procedure also calculates a new vertical position for the text, 30 percent of the way down from the top of the applet window (remember both the height and width of the intro screen are customizable!).

Another preparation involves initializing the arrays for the flying String objects on the title screen. The trajectory and speed of each question mark is predetermined. Listing 14-3 shows a portion of code that may seem a rather roundabout way of animating a number of randomly moving objects. This code was chosen because it minimizes the number of calculations done in the animation loop itself, and therefore increases the speed at which the animation runs.

Listing 14-3 *The animatedIntroClass.start() method*

```java
public void start() {
        //   determine question mark trajectory, velocity, and color
//    *before* they are ever drawn
        for (int j=0; j<numQmarks; j++) {
                int angle = (int)(Math.random()*360);
                int numSteps = (int)(Math.random()*30) + 20;
                qMarkSteps[j] = numSteps;
                int bright = 255 - numSteps * 3;
                qMarkColor[j] = new Color(85, bright, 85);
                qMarkXinc[j] = (int)(Math.cos(angle) * radius / numSteps);
                qMarkYinc[j] = (int)(Math.sin(angle) * radius / numSteps);
                qMarkCnt[j] = 0 - (int)(j/2);
                qMarkX[j] = maxX * 8 + 2 + qMarkXinc[j];
                qMarkY[j] = maxY * 8 + 2 + qMarkXinc[j];
                }
        }
```

As will be seen later, the number of question marks on the title screen is variable, and can be changed within the source code or from HTML. The *for* loop determines a trajectory, velocity, and Color object for each question mark (later referred to as "flying widgets," because they can be any valid String object). The total number of steps needed for each question mark to go from the center of the screen to the screen's edge is placed in *qMarkSteps[x]* (this is technically a measure of velocity). The fewer the steps needed to reach the edge, the faster the question mark will move. Based on this velocity, faster question marks are displayed using brighter Color objects. The arrays *qMarkXinc[x]* and *qMarkYinc[x]* are determined based on velocity and a randomly determined trajectory (angle) calculated for each question mark. These values represent the amount the question mark will be moved horizontally and vertically from its last position.

What is the end result? The question marks can be drawn and moved with a minimum of logical steps. The *qMarkCnt[x]* array tracks how many steps each question mark has taken. When this becomes larger than the value of *qMarkSteps[x]*, the question mark is simply returned to the middle of the screen and sent right back along the same path. Because of the large number of question marks being displayed, the animation still retains a random feel, even though it really just continually shows the same thing.

Creating a New Thread

Because the daleks14 class is implemented as Runnable, a method called start() is called when the applet is run, as shown in Listing 14-4. This method handles the creation of the new Thread for animation.

Listing 14-4 *The daleks14.start() method*

```
public void start() {
if (kicker == null) {
kicker = new Thread(this);
kicker.start();
}
repaint();
}
```

The *kicker* Thread can be controlled using its start() and stop() methods. The Thread object also contains methods for adjusting its priority, or its share of CPU resources. This allows applet programmers to adjust performance and distribute processing power to the methods or objects that need it most.

The Animation Loop

Now that two Thread objects are active, one can be concentrated on the animation loop while the other waits for keyboard input (a keypress indicates it is time for the game to begin). Nothing fancy is required here. The update() procedure will call the animatedIntro object whenever *animIntro* (a boolean variable) is set to *true*. Therefore, the animation loop will start whenever repaint() is called and *animIntro* is *true*, as demonstrated in Listing 14-5.

Listing 14-5 *The daleks14.update(...) method*

```
public synchronized void update(Graphics g) {
    //   draw between-move animations and repaint the game board, or
    //   call the intro screen's drawing routine
    repaintDone = false;
    if (animIntro) {
```

continued on next page

continued from previous page

```
                        animateIntro.drawIntroScreen(g, doneLoading, currentPic);
                        if (!doneLoading) {
                            if (tracker.checkID(currentPic, true))
                                currentPic ++;
                            if (currentPic > 24) {
                                doneLoading = true;
                                prepareScreen();
                                }
                            }
                        repaint();
                        }
                else {
                    ...
                    }
```

This is the portion of the update() procedure that comprises the animation loop. Notice that the loop will only continue so long as *animIntro* remains *true*. When a key is pressed and image loading is complete, the keyDown() method sets *animIntro* to *false* and stops the second Thread object, effectively ending the animation loop.

Notice that the actual drawing routine is handled by the animateIntro object. Its drawIntroScreen() method is called with arguments for the current graphics context (telling it where to draw!), Image loading status, and the number of the picture currently being loaded.

The last important point of the animation loop is the use of the MediaTracker object *tracker*. As a picture is loaded, the value for *currentPic* is incremented. The value of *currentPic* is passed to the animateIntro() method and is used to determine the length of the progress bar on the bottom of the screen, as shown in Figure 14-3. When the last Image file is loaded, *doneLoading* becomes *true*, and the progress bar is replaced by the normal status bar.

FIGURE 14-3

◎ ◎ ◎ ◎ ◎ ◎

The progress bar while an image is loading

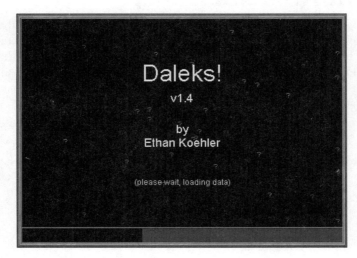

The Game Begins

Once the game begins, nothing happens in the Daleks! applet until the player presses a key. In a real-time game this would be unacceptable, but it is perfect for turn-based games. A large number of boolean variables are used in the daleks14 object to help direct traffic, but we will only examine the important ones to get a feel for the structure of the game itself.

Starting a Turn

A new turn begins when the player presses a key, which automatically calls the keyDown() method, shown in Listing 14-6.

Listing 14-6 *The daleks14.keyDown(...) method*

```
public synchronized boolean keyDown(Event evt, int x)  {
     if (doneLoading)
           handleKeyPress(x);
     return false;
     }
```

Notice that nothing will happen unless *doneLoading* is *true*. This variable will not become *true* until the *tracker* object is done loading all the Image files necessary to play the game. Ideally, the audio files would also be tracked, but Java's beta API does not currently implement this function. As a result, the game will pause to load audio files the first time they are played.

Directing Traffic

Now that a new turn has started, what should be done? The game can be in many states–we could be waiting to start a new level (if all the Daleks have been destroyed), in the middle of a level, or waiting to reanimate the title screen (if the player has been captured). Each of these possibilities requires an additional boolean variable to help the handleKeyPress(int) method decide what to do. Listing 14-7 gives the skeleton of this procedure.

Listing 14-7 *Basic logic/skeleton of handleKeyPres(int whichKey)*

```
public void handleKeyPress(int whichKey)
     { if (animIntro) {
           // stop the intro screen and begin the game
           ...
           }
     else if (levelComplete) {
           // set up for the next level
```

continued on next page

continued from previous page

```
                ...
                }
else if (playerDead) {
                // animate the intro screen
                ...
                }
else {
                // analyze keypress and execute the next turn
                ...
                }
}
```

The *if* statement checks the current status of the game and calls the appropriate methods. Let's examine what happens if we are in the middle of a level and the player has pressed a key. In this case, the boolean variables *animIntro*, *levelComplete*, and *playerDead* are *false*, and the code in the final *else* clause will be executed.

Making the Right Moves

We can only hope for the player's sake that he or she has made a wise move. Fortunately, the applet's only job is to analyze the player's input and update the game board according to the rules of the game. The final *else* clause (with the comment "analyze keypress and execute the next turn") is where the entire turn unfolds, shown in Listing 14-8.

Listing 14-8 *Executing player's move in handleKeyPress(int whichKey); executing next turn in handleKeyPress(int whichKey)*

```
public void handleKeyPress(int whichKey) {
    if (animIntro) {
        // stop the intro screen and begin the game
        ...
        }
    else if (levelComplete) {
        // set up for the next level
        ...
        }
    else if (playerDead) {
        // animate the intro screen
        ...
        }
    else {
        // analyze keypress and execute the next turn
        char ASCIImove = (char)whichKey;
        boolean validMove = movePlayer(ASCIImove);

        if (validMove) {
                if (lastStand)
                repaint();
            else {
                    if (screwdriverUsed) {
```

```
                                    calcSonic();
                                    play(getCodeBase(), "sonic.au");
                                    }
                            moveDaleks()
                    if (newRubble)
                                    play(getCodeBase(), "crash.au");
                    }
            }
        repaint();
    checkDaleks();
        if ((drA) && (allDead))
            levelComplete = true;
        else if (!drA) {
            prepareScreen();
            repaint();
            playerDead = true;
            }
        }
    }
```

First, the player's move is converted from an integer to an ASCII character for simplification. Then the movePlayer(char) method is called. This method returns a boolean value—*true* if the player's move was valid and *false* otherwise. If the player's move checks out, several things can happen. If the player has chosen to make a last stand (by pressing "L"), the repaint() procedure is called. This will be examined in a later section.

Analyzing Input

The movePlayer(char) method shown in Listing 14-9 takes care of the gritty details of keyboard processing. The end result of this method is a boolean value indicating whether or not the player's move is a valid one.

Listing 14-9 *The daleks14.movePlayer(...) method*

```
public boolean movePlayer(char input) {
        int newX = drX;
        int newY = drY;
        int newF = drF;
        boolean pass = false;
        // player may elect to not move (hit '5')
        boolean teleport = false;
        // player may teleport (hit 'T' or 't')
        boolean validMove = true;
        switch (input) {
            // numeric keypad movement options
            case '1': newX--;    newY++;    newF = faceLeft;    break;
            case '2':            newY++;                        break;
            case '3': newX++;    newY++;    newF = faceRight;   break;
            case '4': newX--;               newF = faceLeft;    break;
            case '5': pass = true;                              break;
```

continued on next page

continued from previous page

```
                              case '6': newX++;                        newF = faceRight;   break;
                              case '7': newX--;        newY--;         newF = faceLeft;    break;
                              case '8':                newY--;                             break;
                              case '9': newX++;        newY--;         newF = faceRight;   break;

                              // alternative keys for movement
                              case 'N': newX--;        newY++;         newF = faceLeft;    break;
                              case 'n': newX--;        newY++;         newF = faceLeft;    break;
                              case 'M':                newY++;                             break;
                              case 'm':                newY++;                             break;
                              case ',': newX++;        newY++;         newF = faceRight;   break;
                              case 'H': newX--;                        newF = faceLeft;    break;
                              case 'h': newX--;                        newF = faceLeft;    break;
                              case 'J': pass = true;                                       break;
                              case 'j': pass = true;                                       break;
                              case 'K': newX++;                        newF = faceRight;   break;
                              case 'k': newX++;                        newF = faceRight;   break;
                              case 'Y': newX--;        newY--;         newF = faceLeft;    break;
                              case 'y': newX--;        newY--;         newF = faceLeft;    break;
                              case 'U':                newY--;                             break;
                              case 'u':                newY--;                             break;
                              case 'I': newX++;        newY--;         newF = faceRight;   break;
                              case 'i': newX++;        newY--;         newF = faceRight;   break;

                      // other valid commands
    case 'T': teleport = true;                                break;
    case 't': teleport = true;                                break;
    case 'S': screwdriverUsed = true;                         break;
    case 's': screwdriverUsed = true;                         break;
    case 'L': lastStand = true;                               break;
    case 'l': lastStand = true;                               break;
    default: validMove = false;
    }

// check if the move is out-of-bounds
        if ((newX<0) || (newX>maxX-1) || (newY<0) || (newY>maxY-1))
                validMove = false;

// find an empty location if teleporting
        if (teleport) {
boolean okLoc = false;
// loop until valid coordinates are found
while (!okLoc) {
okLoc = true;
                        newX = (int)(Math.random()*maxX);
                        newY = (int)(Math.random()*maxY);
                        for (int j=0; j<numDaleks; j++)
                        if ( ((newX==dalX[j])&&(newY==dalY[j])) &&
        ((dalA[j])||(dalR[j])) )
                        okLoc = false;
                        }
                animTele = true;
```

```
            }

        // check if the player is allowed to use the screwdriver
        if ((screwdriverUsed) && (screwdrivers==0)) {
            validMove = false;
            screwdriverUsed = false;
            }

        // check if attempting to move to a location containing rubble
        for (int j=0; j<numDaleks; j++)
            if ((newX==dalX[j]) && (newY==dalY[j]) && (dalR[j]))
                validMove = false;

        // if everything is ok, record new position & orientation
        if (validMove) {
            drX = newX;
            drY = newY;
            drF = newF;
            }

        return validMove;
        }
```

The heart of this method is the *switch* command, which tests all the valid possibilities and sets the game variables accordingly. The various logical tests that follow the *switch* statement check the validity of the player's proposed move (e.g., whether the player actually has any screwdrivers to use). If the player's move is valid, the temporary values are copied into the actual variables and the method returns the value *true*. If the method returns *false*, the turn is aborted and the applet resumes waiting for keyboard input.

The Daleks Pursue

Assuming the player has entered a valid command, the applet must move the Daleks toward the player, and check whether the player has been captured or all the Daleks have been destroyed. The handleKeyPress() method calls moveDaleks() and checkDaleks() to handle these functions, demonstrated in Listing 14-10.

Listing 14-10 *The daleks14.moveDaleks() method*

```
public void moveDaleks() {
    // move each dalek toward player
    for (int j=0; j<numDaleks; j++)
    // only move if dalek is alive
        if (dalA[j]) {
        if (dalX[j] < drX) dalX[j]++;
        if (dalY[j] < drY) dalY[j]++;
        if (dalX[j] > drX) dalX[j]--;
```

continued on next page

continued from previous page

```
                           if (dalY[j] > drY) dalY[j]--;
                           if ((dalX[j]==drX) && (dalY[j]==drY))
                // player has died
                               drA = false;
                       }

                   // check for collisions between daleks
                   newRubble = false;
                   for (int j=0; j<numDaleks; j++) {
                   for (int k=j+1; k<numDaleks; k++)
                         if ( (dalX[j]==dalX[k]) && (dalY[j]==dalY[k]) &&
                ((dalA[j]) || (dalR[j])) && ((dalA[k] || dalR[k])) )
                   {
                       if (dalA[j]) {
score += level * 2; newRubble = true; }
                       if (dalA[k]) {
score += level * 2; newRubble = true; }
                       dalA[j] = dalA[k] = false;    // both daleks are dead
                       dalR[j] = dalR[k] = true;     // both daleks are rubble
                   }
                       }
```

The first loop evaluates every Dalek on the board. If the Dalek is alive (the value of the boolean variable *dalA[x]* is *true*), its position will be evaluated relative to the player's current position. Each surviving Dalek is allowed to move to one adjacent square. Daleks destroyed with the sonic screwdriver or turned into rubble will not be moved, because the corresponding *dalA[x]* variable will be *false*. If a Dalek has moved onto the same square as the current player, the boolean variable *drA* is set to *false*, indicating the player has been captured.

The block of code evaluates the updated Dalek positions. Any Daleks that have attempted to move onto the same square must be turned into rubble. The outside *for* loop cycles through the entire array of active Daleks (numbered 0 to *numDaleks*). The inside loop checks the position of the Dalek pointed to by the outside loop against all higher-numbered Daleks. There is no need for both loops to cycle through the entire array, and doing so would have a number of negative effects. First, performance would be decreased. When many Daleks are on the current board, these nested loops take up a large proportion of processor time each turn. Second, if the inner loop cycled through the entire array, each pair of Daleks would be compared more than once. And Daleks would also be compared to themselves! Try tracing through the code by hand to get a feel for the logic behind the way the code is written.

Programming Tip

The performance of a game can often be dramatically improved by paying close attention to the algorithms it uses. An algorithm is a set of logic that evaluates the status of the game and makes decisions. It is common for programmers to realize large performance increases simply by rewriting small portions of code.

Between-Move Animations

Once a valid move is entered and the Daleks have moved, the handleKeyPress() method plays any appropriate sounds. The method plays audio files when Daleks crash into each other or the player uses the sonic screwdriver. Then the update() method is called with repaint(). Animations are drawn directly to the old game board for teleportation, the sonic screwdriver, or a level change. For example, the animateTele() method (shown in Listing 14-11) is called when the player presses "T" to teleport to a new location, as seen in Figure 14-4.

Listing 14-11 *The daleks14.animateTele(...) method*

```
public void animateTele(Graphics g) {
    //  animate pairs of gray lines when teleporting
    g.clipRect(0,0,maxX*imgW,maxY*imgH);
    g.setColor(Color.lightGray);
    for (int j=maxX*imgW+8; j>8; j-=8) {
        g.drawLine(drX*imgW-j,drY*imgH-j,drX*imgW+j,drY*imgH-j);
        g.drawLine(drX*imgW-j,drY*imgH+j,drX*imgW+j,drY*imgH+j);
        pause(800);
        }
    animTele = false;
    }
```

The code clips the screen to the actual game board so that the information bar on the bottom is not drawn on. Then the *for* loop draws a series of horizontal lines starting from the edges of the board and moving toward the player. The routine was specifically written to be independent of the size of the current board. Instead of using absolute coordinates, the functions use *maxX*, *maxY*, *imgH*, and *imgW*, which can be easily changed. This is common throughout the graphics routines in the Daleks! classes, allowing the game board to be made larger or smaller by adjusting only a couple values instead of every graphics function in the applet.

FIGURE 14-4

◉ ◉ ◉ ◉ ◉ ◉

*Teleporting to a
new location*

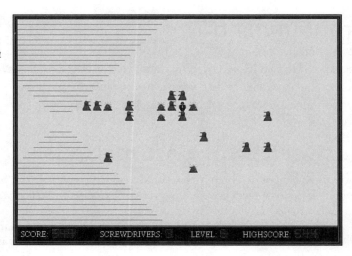

Redrawing the Board

Once the player and Daleks have moved, and the sounds and animations are done, it is time to draw the updated board to the offscreen bitmap. The update() method calls prepareScreen() to take care of this, given in Listing 14-12.

Listing 14-12 *The daleks14.prepareScreen() method*

```
public synchronized void prepareScreen() {
        //    draw the current game status on the off-screen bitmap
        offScreenGC.setColor(Color.white);
        offScreenGC.clipRect(0,0,maxX*imgW,maxY*imgH+25);
        offScreenGC.fillRect(0,0,maxX*imgW,maxY*imgH+4);

        // draw info bar on bottom
        offScreenGC.setColor(Color.darkGray);
        offScreenGC.drawLine(0, maxY*imgH+1, maxX*imgW, maxY*imgH+1);
        offScreenGC.drawLine(0, maxY*imgH+3, maxX*imgW, maxY*imgH+3);
        offScreenGC.setColor(Color.lightGray);
        offScreenGC.drawLine(0, maxY*imgH+2, maxX*imgW, maxY*imgH+2);
        offScreenGC.setColor(Color.black);
        offScreenGC.fillRect(0, maxY*imgH+4, maxX*imgW, 21);
        if (doneLoading) {
                offScreenGC.setFont(new Font("TimesRoman", Font.PLAIN, 12));
                if (score > highScore)
                        highScore = score;
                int yPos = maxY*imgH + 19;
                offScreenGC.setColor(Color.white);
                offScreenGC.drawString("SCORE: ", 5, yPos);
                paintNumber(score, 51, yPos);
```

```
                    offScreenGC.drawString("SCREWDRIVERS: ", 124, yPos);
                    paintNumber(screwdrivers, 221, yPos);

                    offScreenGC.drawString("LEVEL: ", 260, yPos);
                    paintNumber(level, 303, yPos);

                    offScreenGC.drawString("HIGHSCORE: ", 338, yPos);
                    paintNumber(highScore, 415, yPos);

                // draw the daleks
                for (int j=0; j<numDaleks; j++) {
                        if (dalA[j]) {  // if the dalek is alive..
checkFace(j);
            offScreenGC.drawImage(dalekPic[dalF[j]],
dalX[j]*imgW,dalY[j]*imgH,this);
                        }
                    else if (dalR[j])
// if dalek is rubble..
                                    offScreenGC.drawImage(rubblePic[dalF[j]],
dalX[j]*imgW,dalY[j]*imgH,this);
                    }

                // draw the doctor
                if (!playerDead)
                    offScreenGC.drawImage(doctorPic[drF+whichDoc],
drX*imgW,drY*imgH,this);
                else {
                        offScreenGC.setColor(Color.white);
                        offScreenGC.fillRect(drX*imgW, drY*imgH, imgW, imgH);
                        offScreenGC.drawImage(deadPic, drX*imgW, drY*imgH, ⇐
this);

                        offScreenGC.setColor(Color.black);
                        offScreenGC.setFont(new ⇐
Font("Helvetica",Font.PLAIN,36));
                        offScreenGC.drawString("GAME OVER",maxX*imgW/2-⇐
100,75);
                    }
                }
            }
```

A lot happens in this method. First the offscreen Image is covered with a fresh coat of white pixels to erase the previous graphics. Then the words and graphic are placed in the information bar to update the player's status (see Painting by Number, below). The appropriate Dalek graphics are drawn to the game board. If a Dalek is alive, the right- or left-facing image is drawn, depending on its position relative to the player. If the Dalek has been reduced to rubble, a right- or left-facing rubble pile is drawn at its location.

Finally, an Image for the player is drawn. The Image object drawn is dependent on the current level and the direction the player last moved. For instance, above level 5, the graphics for the second actor to play the role of Dr. Who are drawn. All possible player Images are contained in the *doctorPic[]* array, which is set up as shown in Table 14-1.

Array Index	Array Contents
0	Left-facing graphic, first Doctor
1	Right-facing, first Doctor
2	Left-facing graphic, second Doctor
3	Right-facing graphic, second Doctor
…	…
9	Right-facing graphic, fifth Doctor

TABLE 14-1   ◈   *The doctorPic[] array*

The variable *drF* is either 0 (the player is facing left) or 1 (facing right), and the value of *whichDoc* points to the left-facing position of the currently active Doctor. The correct Image index can be calculated by adding both values together. If the player is facing right, and on level 5 (where *doctorPic[]* will equal 2), the calculated index value would be 3, indicating the Image object for the right-facing, second Doctor should be displayed.

If the player is captured, the words "Game Over" are displayed in large, imposing letters, and the graphic of a skull is shown in place of the normal player picture, as shown in Figure 14-5. In psychology, this is known as positive reinforcement, though players tend to view it as a fairly unpleasant experience.

When the offscreen Image is complete, it is drawn to the screen in update() to replace the previous board. The update() method is now finished, and control is returned to handleKeyPress().

FIGURE 14-5
◉ ◉ ◉ ◉ ◉ ◉
Captured—the end of the road

Painting by Number

Sometimes very simple additions can greatly enhance the visual appeal of an applet. For Daleks!, the paintNumber(int) routine (shown in Listing 14-13) is used to draw the player's current status using counter-style digits instead of the traditional awt.Font objects (which are limited in variety and rather plain-looking).

Listing 14-13 The daleks14.paintNumber(int) method

```
public void paintNumber(int num, int xPos, int yPos)  {
    //   draw the number as a graphic at the specified position
    Integer numObj = new Integer(num);
    String stringNum = numObj.toString();
    for (int j=0; j < stringNum.length(); j++)  {
        char charDigit = stringNum.charAt(j);
        int intDigit = Character.digit(charDigit, 10);
        offScreenGC.drawImage(digit[intDigit],xPos+j*12, yPos-⇐
13,this);
    }
}
```

The first step is to convert the number from an integer to a String. The *for* loop then examines each successive character in the String, converts it to its integer equivalent, and paints the corresponding counter-style Image object to the offscreen bitmap. Unlike the rest of the Daleks! methods, this routine assumes that the counter digits will be twelve pixels in width. It would be a nice touch to make this routine independent of the size of the graphic digits used.

Better Housekeeping

A bit of tidying up remains to be done before the turn can end. In particular, we need to evaluate whether the level has been completed. The handleKeyPress() method calls checkDaleks() to perform this function, shown in Listing 14-14.

Listing 14-14 The daleks14.checkDaleks() method

```
public void checkDaleks()  {
    //   evaluate whether all the daleks are dead
    //   and set the 'allDead' variable accordingly.
    allDead = true;
    for (int j=0; j<numDaleks; j++)
    if (dalA[j])
            allDead = false;
}
```

This method begins by assuming that all the Daleks have been destroyed. It then checks each Dalek's *dalA[x]* boolean variable. If the value of that variable is *true*, indicating the Dalek is still alive, we can no longer say all the Daleks have been destroyed, and the *allDead* variable is set to *false*.

Meanwhile, back at the handleKeyPress() method, the last few chores are completed, as given in Listing 14-15.

Listing 14-15 *Status update portion of handleKeyPress(int whichKey)*

```
public void handleKeyPress(int whichKey) {
        if (animIntro) {
                // stop the intro screen and begin the game
                ...
                }
        else if (levelComplete) {
                // set up for the next level
                ...
                }
else if (playerDead) {
                // animate the intro screen
                ...
                }
else {
                // analyze keypress and execute the next turn
                ...
                checkDaleks();
                if ((drA) && (allDead))
                        levelComplete = true;
                else if (!drA)
playerDead = true;
                }
}
```

After the call to checkDaleks(), handleKeyPress() checks to see if the player is still alive and all of the Daleks have been destroyed. If so, the level is complete, and *levelComplete* is set to *true*. The next call to handleKeyPress() will now give control to the routines under the comment "set up for the next level".

Another possibility is that the player has been captured. If this is the case, the boolean variable *playerDead* is set to *true*, and the next call to handleKeyPress() will resume animation of the title screen.

Customizing the Game

The graphics routines in Daleks! were written to be flexible. In addition, users can adjust aspects of the game without having to return the source code, change variables, and recompile the classes. Allowing users to customize the applet means that different challenges and game themes can be created with ease.

FIGURE 14-6

◉ ◉ ◉ ◉ ◉ ◉

Giving the intro screen a custom look

Changing the Title Screen

Several aspects of the animated title screen can be customized from HTML. The following HTML code includes tags that change various variables in the applet, as shown in Listing 14-16 and Figure 14-6.

Listing 14-16 *Modifying the intro screen*

```
<applet code="daleks14.class" width=576 height=313>
...
<param name="title" value="Skeletons!">
<param name="flyingWidget" value="*">
<param name="numWidgets" value=300>
...
</applet>
```

The "Skeletons!" String replaces the usual "Daleks!" title. In addition, instead of animating 100 question marks, the animatedIntroClass object will display 300 asterisks. Currently the color and size of these Fonts cannot be changed from HTML.

Changing the Board Size

In a similar way, the size of the board and the graphics displayed on the board can be changed. The code shown in Listing 14-17 sets new dimensions for the game board and the graphics in the game. By replacing the GIF files loaded by the applet, users can create new themes for the game, like the one shown in Figure 14-7.

FIGURE 14-7

◎ ◎ ◎ ◎ ◎ ◎

Creating new themes with new GIFs

Listing 14-17 *Adjusting board size through HTML*

```
<applet code="daleks14.class" width=576 height=313>
...
<param name="maxX" value=18>
<param name="maxY" value=9>
<param name="imgH" value=32>
<param name="imgW" value=32>
...
</applet>
```

The values of the *maxX* and *maxY* parameters will become the new dimensions for the size of the game board in squares. The *imgH* and *imgW* parameters specify the size of the graphics to be displayed in those squares, in this case standard 32x32 Images. Note that the *height=* modifier in the <applet> tag is 25 pixels taller than the value of *imgH * maxY*. The extra height is necessary to create enough room for the information bar at the bottom of the screen.

Balancing Play

The most important customizing options are those that change the nature of the game itself. While limited, Daleks! does allow several options to fine-tune the actual play of the game. Listing 14-18 shows one such possibility.

Listing 14-18 *Play-balancing through HTML*

```
<applet code="daleks14.class" width=576 height=313>
...
<param name="maxX" value=18>
<param name="maxY" value=9>
<param name="levelMultiple" value=3>
```

```
<param name="baseNum" value=2>
<param name="maxEnemies" value=100>
...
</applet>
```

As seen before, *maxX* and *maxY* can be changed to adjust the overall size of the board. The value of *levelMultiple* becomes the number of Daleks added each level, while *baseNum* is an unchanging number of Daleks. The formula used in the game is

numDaleks = level * levelMultiple + baseNum

Finally, *maxEnemies* puts an upper limit on the number of Daleks the player must contend with. This parameter can be used to keep the game from quickly getting out of hand (or to consciously let it get out of hand!).

Allowing Customization

There are currently 10 parameters that can be specified from HTML to adjust some aspect of the game. The getHTMLParameters() method (shown in Listing 14-19) checks for each of these parameters and adjusts game variables as necessary.

Listing 14-19 *The daleks14.getHTMLParameters() method*

```
public void getHTMLParameters() {
      // read the parameters within the HTML applet tags
      if (getParameter("maxX") != null)
            maxX = Integer.parseInt(getParameter("maxX"));
      if (getParameter("maxY") != null)
            maxY = Integer.parseInt(getParameter("maxY"));
      if (getParameter("imgH") != null)
            imgH = Integer.parseInt(getParameter("imgH"));
      if (getParameter("imgW") != null)
            imgW = Integer.parseInt(getParameter("imgW"));
      if (getParameter("levelMultiple") != null)
            levelMultiple = ⇐
Integer.parseInt(getParameter("levelMultiple"));
      if (getParameter("baseNum") != null)
            baseNumDaleks =  Integer.parseInt(getParameter("baseNum"));
      if (getParameter("maxEnemies") != null)
            maxEnemies = Integer.parseInt(getParameter("maxEnemies"));
      if (getParameter("numWidgets") != null)
            numWidgets = Integer.parseInt(getParameter("numWidgets"));
      if (getParameter("flyingWidget") != null)
            flyingWidget = getParameter("flyingWidget");
      else
            flyingWidget = "?";
      if (getParameter("title") != null)
            title = getParameter("title");
      else
            title = "Daleks!";
      }
```

Because we cannot assume that any <param> tags are actually contained in the HTML document, we have to first test for their existence. This is done using *if* statements. The value of the Strings will be *null* if the parameter is not included. There are two kinds of values that are contained in the <param> tags, although they all are read in as String objects. The Integer.parseInt(String) method is used to convert Strings to integers where necessary.

Suggestion Box

- Base animation speed on actual timing rather than a *for* loop (which allows animations to vary according to processor speed)

- Rewrite the applet in a more object-oriented way to represent the game objects more logically, enhance reusability of the code, and allow for future customization

- Add graphics for the actors who played the role of Dr. Who but are left out of the game in ego-crushing obscurity

- Include additional enemies from the Dr. Who TV show and imbue them with styles of attack even more clever than that of the Daleks

- Give the player additional options—like the ability to pick up objects that enhance the player's abilities for a limited period of time

- Add *<param>* tags which would rename the Sonic Screwdrivers and change how many are added each level

- Make any fundamental changes optional so players can choose between playing the "classic" and "enhanced" versions of the game

Comments

In this chapter we covered the essence of a Java board game with a number of additional features. The applet makes use of such fundamental Java concepts as multiple threads, double-buffered animation, and event-oriented processing. The end result is a fairly simple, but effective game which puts a minimal strain on bandwidth and processor speed. The ability to customize the appearance and game play of the applet can greatly extend its interest to players. New themes and challenges for Daleks! can be created with a minimum of development effort.

15

NetOthello

Eric Ries

come uedi fare le manouelle le quali si muouano e alza
e grapesi cuore lo monte di ponso fa fa grano di bo no
fare nella manouella per ma questa alla mano della pegi qui si
orga e più isomo pibibuti

15

NetOthello

In this chapter we are going to build upon our networking skills to create a networked implementation of the classic game Othello. In case you've never played Othello before (you may have played it under a different name; sometimes it is called reversi), let's run down how the game is played. Figure 15-1 shows what the board looks like at the start of the game.

FIGURE 15-1

◉ ◉ ◉ ◉ ◉ ◉

Generic Othello board with initial four pieces

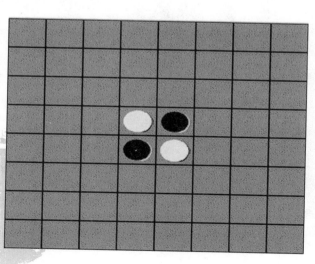

Each of the circles is a piece, much like a checker piece, except that Othello pieces are double-sided: One side is white and the other black. Two players take turns adding pieces of their own color to the board. A legal move is one in which the piece you place, in conjunction with a piece of yours already on the board, surrounds one or more of your opponent's pieces, in the same row, column, or diagonal. Once a move is made, any pieces of your opponent's color that are between the piece you placed and another piece of your own color are flipped so that they become your color. Game play continues until all of the empty spaces on the board are used up. The player with the most pieces of his or her own color is the winner. Figures 15-2 through 15-4 illustrate a three-move sequence of Othello game play.

FIGURE 15-2

◎ ◎ ◎ ◎ ◎ ◎

An initial Othello move

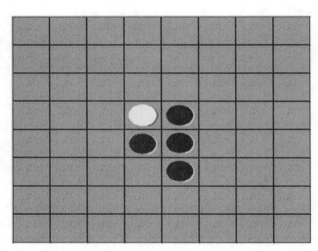

FIGURE 15-3

◎ ◎ ◎ ◎ ◎ ◎

A second Othello move

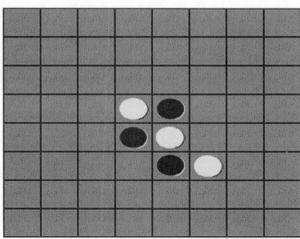

FIGURE 15-4
◉ ◉ ◉ ◉ ◉ ◉
A third Othello move

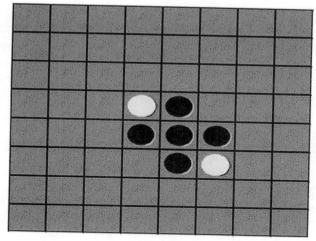

Got the hang of it? Good. Othello's motto is "a minute to learn, a lifetime to master"; although it may seem like a simple game, it in fact can be very challenging, once you get the hang of it. This is not a book on Othello strategy, although volumes have certainly been written on that subject. If it interests you, I suggest you consult the Othello World Wide Web page.

Why Othello?

Why did we choose Othello as a game to write in Java? Surely there are enough versions of Othello floating around on different platforms. There are even versions that let you play against a computer over the Internet. Well, our motivation for writing Othello is twofold. First, as mentioned before, it is a relatively simple game that is still interesting. This is important, because you will want to learn how to do this kind of multiplayer gaming with a game that has relatively simple rules. (Imagine trying to write a chess or bridge game at the same time as learning networking fundamentals.) But we also want our final product to be something interesting and not too boring. (Imagine doing all this work for tic-tac-toe—the *last* thing the world needs is another tic-tac-toe game!) Furthermore, Othello is one of those games that gets boring with a computerized opponent, because even the best Othello algorithms are boring and predictable. For it to be really exciting, Othello must have a human opponent. That is exactly what we are going to do in this chapter.

Implementing a Board Game

We are going to create a series of Java classes that can be used for any game similar to Othello—one that uses a checkered board with black and white pieces. Of course, this could also be extended to be used with all kinds of similar games, perhaps Chinese checkers or even chess. We'll talk a little bit later about how we could expand our capabilities. For now, let's think about Othello.

Implementing the Class Hierarchy

The first thing we need is a hierarchy of classes and then we need to determine who will do what. The most basic component of this game is a "piece," which is a circle that can be either black or white. These pieces are placed on an 8×8 board that keeps track of them all in a two-dimensional array. This board is governed by certain rules that allow certain pieces to be moved by certain users at certain times. Each of these tasks (including rule handling) will be coded into a Java class.

The GamePiece Class

The GamePiece class will be responsible for keeping track of its state (black or white) and its location on the screen. It will also be called upon to draw itself in a designated rectangle. It should also know some other basics, like how to "flip" itself from one state to another.

The gameBoard Class

The gameBoard object will keep track of a specified number of GamePieces in a 2D array. It will also be responsible for drawing itself and all of its pieces in a specified area. It should be able to count the number of pieces of each color in the board, and know how many empty spaces are left. It should be able to add pieces as well as return individual pieces, based on screen or board coordinates. These two classes could be used by any similar board game. The actual game-specific functions are carried out by the Othello applet itself. It is responsible for user input, for finding valid moves, making moves, and deciding when the game is over. In addition, it will also be responsible for network connections, but we'll talk about this later. For now, let's concentrate on the game portion of the applet.

Another very common feature of programs such as this is the ability for the user to play against a computer *or* a human player. We are not going to implement the former option in this program (writing the AI code for a decent Othello player is outside the scope of this project); however, it is important to realize how easy it would be to add this functionality later.

The NetOthello Class

This is the Java class that handles all game rules and functions. Often, you would want to write this as a separate class, but for Othello, we will just integrate its functions into the applet itself. The functions that the NetOthello class (or any similar managing class) must implement are discussed in the next section.

Controlling Game Play

Here are the tasks that must be carried out by whatever class is in charge of handling the game itself (in this case, NetOthello.class).

Taking Turns

In this program, we need to use variables to represent black and white. This is necessary to set the state of pieces, track whose turn it is, and so on. Because there are only two possibilities, we are going to use boolean variables to represent color. WHITE is *true* and BLACK is *false*. We will use constants (final variables) to represent these values, in case we ever want to change them. (For instance, if we had a five-color game, we might use integer instead of boolean.) Boolean is nice because it allows us to use a statement like *color=!color;* to switch the *color* of a variable.

Teaching a Computer the Rules

To create this applet, we are going to have to teach the computer how to play Othello. Specifically, we must teach the computer about three things: what constitutes a valid move, how to make a move, and how the game ends. Here is how the computer does each of these things:

- To determine a valid move, the computer must check in all eight directions (up, down, left, right, plus four diagonals) to see if there is a contiguous line of opposite-colored pieces followed by one similarly colored piece. If so, this is a valid move. Otherwise, it is not.

- To make a move uses an algorithm very similar to the one above. The computer checks in the eight directions and, if it finds a valid line, it must flip all the pieces in between.

- An Othello game is over if there are no more valid moves for either player. This happens when there are no spaces left on the board or if all of the remaining spaces are not valid moves. This requires that the computer check all available spaces to see if they are valid after every move. When the game is over, the player with the most pieces is the winner.

Now that we have the fundamentals of writing the Othello game code down, let's go on to discuss the networking part.

The Server Side

The server we need is going to be very similar to the ChatServer we wrote in Chapter 9, Advanced Networking and Multiplayer Gaming Concepts. However, since each game of Othello can have only two players, we are going to need to change the server design slightly. Instead of putting everyone in the same Group object, we are going to create a special kind of group designed to hold a limited number of users (in this case, two, but you may want to write three- or four-player games in the future). As users connect to the server, they are placed in a Group, if one is waiting. If no Group exists, a new Group is created, and the user must wait for another player to log on.

This system is going to be completely client-driven; all the server will do is echo any messages it receives. The server's sole responsibility will be to decide who plays white and who plays black at the start of each game. Other than that, the server just sits and waits for client input. Just like before, we can use threads to control each connection and each group, as well as do garbage collection on clients that have disconnected.

The Client Side

The client is responsible for doing all the work. The client interacts with the user, gets his or her move, and sends it to the server. The server echoes this input back to each client, which must process the move it receives and display it. In addition, the client will allow the two players to chat with each other (accomplished using a simplified version of the chat program we wrote in Chapter 9).

Writing the Client Code

In writing the client, we will write the code in the same general order in which we discussed it. First, we must write the game-specific code (including the game classes). Next, we will discuss and build the Othello GUI. Last, but certainly not least, we will write the networking code.

Writing the Game Code

The most complicated code, which we should finish first, is the code that controls the game itself. We discussed the different goals of this code already; now we must deal with the practical issue of implementing it.

The GamePiece Class

We already spent some time discussing the game-related classes we will need. Let's go about implementing them now. The first class we discussed was the GamePiece class, so start with a file called GamePiece.java and put in the basics:

```java
import java.awt.*;

public class GamePiece {

final boolean BLACK = false;
final boolean WHITE = true;

public boolean color;
public Rectangle rect;

GamePiece( boolean c) {
        color=c;
}

}
```

Notice the two final variables. We will declare these in each file so that we don't have to remember which value represents white and which represents black. This may seem unnecessary when there are only two colors, but if there were 10 or 100 colors, you would not want to try to remember all of the numeric constants, so we use final variables to make life easier. All GamePieces must have a color associated with them.

The first real method we need is one that flips the piece from white to black or vice-versa. Luckily, all we have to do is use the "!" operator in order to invert the value of color like this:

```java
public void flip() {
        color=!color;
}
```

To complete the GamePiece class, only one thing remains—drawing. The GamePiece class must be able to paint itself in a specified rectangle. It should also remember what this rectangle is, in case it ever gets asked to draw itself without a rectangle specified. We use the now familiar two-methods-with-the-same-name trick to accomplish this.

```java
public void paintPiece(Graphics g) {
        paintPiece( g, rect );
}

public void paintPiece(Graphics g, Rectangle r ) {

rect = r;

if( ! r.intersects(g.getClipRect()) ) return;

if ( color == WHITE )
        g.setColor(Color.white);
else
        g.setColor(Color.black);

g.fillOval( rect.x, rect.y, rect.width, rect.height );

}
```

Note that we *never* do any drawing unless our current rectangle intersects with the clipping rectangle of the Graphics context. That's all the GamePiece has to do; now on to the GameBoard.

The GameBoard Class

The GameBoard is mainly responsible for keeping track of a 2D array of GamePieces. Let's dive right in with GameBoard.java:

```
import java.awt.*;
import GamePiece;

public class GameBoard {

final boolean BLACK = false;
final boolean WHITE = true;

public int pieceWidth, pieceHeight;
public int rows, cols;  // number of rows/columns
GamePiece board[][]; // the actual board itself
public int empty;

GameBoard( int w, int h) {
      board = new GamePiece[w][h];
      cols = w;
      rows = h;
      empty = w*h;
}
}
```

A GameBoard must be initialized with row and column data. Although Othello is designed specifically for an 8×8 board, GameBoard could easily accommodate any number of rows and columns. The *pieceWidth* and *pieceHeight* variables refer to the screen dimensions of each square on the board.

To paint the board onto the screen, we simply pass the Graphics context to each of the pieces on the board. We also draw a green backdrop and lines to separate each square. The GameBoard expects that it will be passed a rectangle defining the total area that it is allowed to draw in. This rectangle is then divided into even squares, which are passed on to the GamePieces. Here's how it works:

```
public void paintBoard(Graphics g, Rectangle r) {

int x;
int y;

pieceWidth = (int) (r.width/cols);
pieceHeight = (int) (r.height/rows);

g.setColor(Color.green);
g.fillRect( r.x, r.y, r.width, r.height );
```

```
for( x=0; x<cols; x++) {
        g.setColor( Color.black );
        g.drawLine( x* pieceWidth, 0, x*pieceWidth, r.height );
        for(y=0; y< rows; y++) {
                g.setColor( Color.black );
                g.drawLine(0, y* pieceHeight, r.width, y*pieceHeight );
                if( board[x][y] != null )

board[x][y].paintPiece( g, new Rectangle( r.x + pieceWidth*x, r.y +⇐
pieceHeight*y, pieceWidth, pieceHeight), (board[x][y].color));
                }
        }
}
```

We want to provide a few methods that provide access to the individual pieces themselves. This will aid us in interacting with the GameBoard later on. The methods we create should allow access to the pieces on the board in a few different ways, to allow for a variety of interactions later. We will provide two such methods, one that will return the piece at a certain row and column, and one that will return the piece located at a certain screen coordinate:

```
public GamePiece pieceAt(int x, int y) {

if( x>=cols || x<0 || y>= rows || y<0 ) return null;

return board[x][y];
}


public GamePiece pieceAtXY( int x, int y) {
int i,j;

for(i=0; i<cols; i++)
        for(j=0; j<rows; j++)
                if( board[i][j].rect.inside(x,y) )
                        return board[i][j];
return null;
}
```

Notice that these two methods will both return *null* if there is no piece that matches the *x* and *y* parameters passed *or* if the *x* and *y* parameters fall outside of the current board. This is extremely useful when writing move-checking code, as you will soon see.

The last method in GameBoard is one that will count the number of pieces of a specified color (used to determine the winner at the end of Othello, but also useful for a variety of other applications):

```
public int count( boolean color) {
int i,j,num=0;

for(i=0; i<rows; i++)
for(j=0; j<cols; j++)
        if(board[i][j] != null && board[i][j].color == color )
                num++;
return num;
}
```

That's it for GameBoard.class. The classes we've created so far provide the infrastructure for a generic Othello-style board game. It's now time to write the code that teaches the computer how to play the game.

The NetOthello Class

This is the applet itself. NetOthello is the class that actually implements all of Othello's game-specific features. When writing a program like this, it is good to start the applet part simple, to ensure that you can work out any bugs that may have developed in the foundation classes. Then, as you add features, you can slowly build the applet to its final form. This is the strategy we are going to take.

Let's start by declaring a whole long list of variables that we know we are going to need. Although we won't use them all for a while, we should already have a pretty good sense of what we are going to need. Here's how NetOthello.java starts:

```java
import java.applet.*;
import java.awt.*;
import java.util.*;
import java.net.*;
import java.io.*;
import GameBoard;

public class Othello extends Applet implements Runnable {

final boolean WHITE = true;
final boolean BLACK = false;

/* the Game stuff */
GameBoard theBoard;
boolean turn;  // whose turn is it?
boolean local; // What color is the local computer?

/* the GUI stuff */
TextArea dispA;
Panel inputPanel, turnPanel;
promptFrame pf;

/* the Thread */
Thread kicker;

/* the network stuff */
PrintStream ps;
Socket s=null;
DataInputStream dis = null;
String name, theHost="localhost";
int thePort=8314;

public void run() {
}
}
```

In addition to variables, we added a run() method so that NetOthello will compile, despite the fact that it implements Runnable. We will come back later and make the run() method do something, but in the meantime we want to write the initialization routine. To start out with, it'll just call a single method to set up the GameBoard:

```
public void init() {


newGame();
}

public void newGame() {

initBoard();
}

public void initBoard() {
turn = WHITE;
     theBoard = new GameBoard( 8, 8, im);
     theBoard.addPiece( 3,3, WHITE);
     theBoard.addPiece( 3,4, BLACK);
     theBoard.addPiece( 4,3, BLACK);
     theBoard.addPiece( 4,4, WHITE);
}
```

Now let's do the method that will actually paint the board on the applet:

```
public void paint(Graphics g) {
     Dimension d = size();
     theBoard.paintBoard(g, new Rectangle( 0,0, d.width, d.height ) );
}
```

If you compile the applet at this point, you should see the initial state of the Othello board: two white and two black pieces. This probably indicates that our game classes are working well, but let's add a little more functionality just to be sure.

```
public boolean mouseDown(Event evt, int x, int y) {
int xx,yy;
     xx= (int)(x/theBoard.pieceWidth);
     yy=(int)(y/theBoard.pieceHeight);
theBoard.addPiece( xx,yy, turn = !turn );
repaint( xx*theBoard.pieceWidth, yy*theBoard.pieceHeight,
theBoard.pieceWidth, theBoard.pieceHeight);
return true;
}
```

This will allow you to click on any square and place an alternatively black or white piece on that square. One of the really cool programming things you should notice is that this method calls repaint() for a specific section of the screen only. This allows the paint methods to be called with a very small clipping rectangle, so that only the affected square will redraw itself. This will substantially decrease the amount of time required for a repaint. In fact, this makes painting so efficient that using double-buffered graphics is unnecessary. Of course, you could still use an offscreen drawing area, but in this case it's a waste of memory, as long as you always remember to call a limited repaint() whenever you want a square redrawn.

Creating Game-Specific Functionality

Once you're done playing with this version of NetOthello, it's time to get down to some serious work. As we discussed earlier, we have some game-specific tasks to complete. First, there is the method that determines if a certain move is valid. To make this a bit easier, we are going to add two utility functions: one that converts screen coordinates to board coordinates, and another that returns the total number of valid moves for a specific player:

```
/* check if the screen coordinates x,y are in a valid square */
/* validMove() does the work, all we do is convert the numbers  */
boolean validMoveXY( int x, int y, boolean color) {
      return validMove( (int) (x/theBoard.pieceWidth), (int)⇐
(y/theBoard.pieceHeight), color );
}

/* ok, check if x,y is a valid square for color */
boolean validMove(int x, int y, boolean color) {

/* if there already is a piece at x,y */
if( theBoard.pieceAt(x,y) != null ) return false;

int a,b,i,j, num;
GamePiece temp=null;

/* check in all four directions */
for(i=-1;i<=1;i++)
for(j=-1;j<=1;j++)
if( !(j == 0 && i == 0) ) {  /* can't check in the 0 direction */
a=x;
b=y;
num=0;
        do {
                        a+=i;
                        b+=j;
                        temp = theBoard.pieceAt(a,b);
                        if( temp != null && temp.color == !color )
                            num++;
                        if( temp != null && temp.color == color )
                        if( num > 0) return true; /* this is the only thing⇐
that returns true */
                        else temp = null;
                } while (temp != null);
}
return false;

}
```

```
/* count the number of valid moves for color */
int validMoves( boolean color ) {
int i,j,num=0;

for(i=0; i<8; i++)
      for( j=0; j<8; j++)
            if( validMove( i,j, color ) )
                              num++;
return num;
}
```

Does all of that make sense? Even if you are still confused, don't worry. The goal of this chapter is not to teach you specifics of Othello programming, but the fundamentals of networked game programming. Keep this in mind as you read through the next two game-specific functions, which actually do most of the Othello work in the applet:

```
/* this actually makes a move. Very similar to validMove() */
public void doMove(int x, int y, boolean color) {

int a=x,b=y,i,j, num;
GamePiece temp=null;


theBoard.addPiece( x,y,color );
repaint( a * theBoard.pieceWidth, b * theBoard.pieceHeight,⇐
theBoard.pieceWidth, theBoard.pieceHeight);

for(i=-1;i<=1;i++)
for(j=-1;j<=1;j++)
if( !(j == 0 && i == 0) ) {
a=x;
b=y;
num=0;
      do {
            a+=i;
            b+=j;
            temp = theBoard.pieceAt(a,b);
            if( temp != null) {
            if( temp.color == !color )
                  num++;
            else if( temp.color == color ) {
                  if( num > 0) {
                      a=x+i;
                              b=y+j;
                              temp = theBoard.pieceAt(a,b);
                                    while( temp.color == !color) {
                                    theBoard.pieceAt(a,b).flip();
                                        repaint( a * theBoard.pieceWidth,⇐
b * theBoard.pieceHeight, theBoard.pieceWidth, theBoard.pieceHeight);
                                      a+=i;
                                      b+=j;
                                    temp = theBoard.pieceAt(a,b);
```

continued on next page

continued from previous page

```
                                        }
                                    }
                                    temp = null;
                                }
                            }
                        }
                    } while (temp != null);
}

int bl,wh;

if( validMoves( !turn ) > 0 )
/* if the other player has valid moves, switch turns */
        turn = !turn;

/* if the game is over */
        if( endGame() )
                if( (wh=theBoard.count(WHITE)) > (bl=theBoard.count(BLACK)) )
                        display("White wins!");
                else if(wh<bl)
                        display("Black wins!");
                else if(bl==wh)
                        display("It's a TIE!");


/* check if the game is over */
public boolean endGame() {

        if( theBoard.empty == 0)
                return true;
        else
        if( theBoard.count( BLACK ) == 0 || theBoard.count(WHITE) ==0 )
                return true;
        else
        if( validMoves( BLACK ) ==0 && validMoves( WHITE ) ==0)
                return true;
return false;
}
```

Phew! All the Othello code is now done! However, before you try to compile it, you had better provide it with a method called display(), which is referenced in doMove(). Eventually, this will display a message with the GUI, but for now we'll just send it to System.out:

```
/* display a string in the TextArea (for now just System.out) */
public void display(String str) {
        System.out.println(str);
}
```

Congratulations! You are now totally capable of playing a game of Othello with yourself, if you change the mouse-handling code to this:

```
public boolean mouseDown(Event evt, int x, int y) {

if( validMoveXY(x,y,turn) ) { /* if we got a valid move */
        int xx,yy;
                xx= (int)(x/theBoard.pieceWidth);
                yy=(int)(y/theBoard.pieceHeight);
        doMove( xx,yy, turn);
        turn=!turn;
        return true;
        }
}


return false;
}
```

Well done! Go play around a bit. You deserve it!

Writing the GUI Code

Let's switch gears for a while and work on the user interface for this applet. We've already seen how the user will interact with the GameBoard, but what about getting other kinds of input and displaying other kinds of output? For this, we are going to need to do some GUI layout. There are many ways you could write a user interface for this applet, but here is a simple GUI version:

First, the user will be presented with a dialog box asking for his or her name.

Once we have the user's name, we can proceed with all of the game and network parts of the game.

While the user is playing, messages from the game and the user's opponent are displayed in a TextArea below the GameBoard.

The user can also reply to messages from the opponent by entering them into a TextField and then pressing <ENTER>.

Implementing this is not very difficult, because of Java's AWT. However, to get all of the components laid out exactly the way you want is a bit tricky (unless you have an expensive Visual Java tool), and involves some hefty use of Panels. Also, we are going to have to review some things in order to implement the dialog box. First, though, let's get the easy stuff out of the way.

NetOthello's GUI Layout

All of the components are created and added to the applet in the init() method, like this:

```
/* set up all GUI components */
setLayout( new BorderLayout() );
```

continued on next page

continued from previous page

```
inputPanel = new Panel();
inputPanel.setLayout( new BorderLayout() );
inputPanel.add( "West", dispA=new TextArea( 5,35));
inputPanel.add( "South",new TextField(20) );
inputPanel.add("Center", turnPanel=new Panel() );
turnPanel.add( new Button("Logout") );
turnPanel.add( new Button("New Game") );
add( "South", inputPanel );
```

Try compiling NetOthello now. You should recognize that something is very wrong:
The board gets cut off by the inputPanel. Why? Because in paint(), we told the
GameBoard that it could draw all over the full dimension of the applet. This is no longer
the case. The available space for the board to be drawn has shrunk, because there is a
panel obscuring part of the applet! Let's inform the GameBoard of the change like this:

```
public void paint(Graphics g) {
      Dimension d = size();
      d.height -= inputPanel.preferredSize().height;
      theBoard.paintBoard(g, new Rectangle( 0,0, d.width, d.height ) );
}
```

Now when you compile, the board should fit nicely above the panel. You may want
to play around with the size of the applet so that the squares don't look like rectangles.

Handling Events

All of these components are going to generate events that must be handled by
NetOthello. You should already be pretty familiar with the procedure used to do this,
so just dive on in:

```
public boolean handleEvent(Event evt) {

/* if the user entered text in the TextField and hit enter */
if( evt.target instanceof TextField && evt.id == Event.ACTION_EVENT ) {
      ps.println("say|"+name+" says: "+((TextField)evt.target).getText()⇐
);
      ((TextField)evt.target).setText("");
      return true;
      }

/* if the user clicked on the restart button */
if( evt.target instanceof Button && evt.arg.equals("Restart") ) {
      kicker.stop();
      newGame();
      repaint();
      return true;
      }
return super.handleEvent(evt);
}
```

Now that the events are handled, we are almost done with the GUI code. The only
thing left is the dialog box.

Implementing a Dialog Box

Java provides programmers with a Dialog class designed to be used for dialog boxes that pop up and get information from the user. Unfortunately, Dialogs can only be created by Window objects, and, at present, applets are not considered Windows. Eventually, Sun will probably add some way of getting around this, but for now, we must create our own dialog box class. This involves the use of a Frame.

 # Frames: Windows with an Attitude

You may be used to using Frames to hang pictures, but in Java, the Frame class is a special subclass of Window that allows you to do some pretty nifty things. What makes a Frame so special? A Frame has a title bar, can be resized, has close/maximize/shrink buttons, can be iconified, and can hold a menu bar and menus. Frames can even control the state of the mouse cursor within them (something not even Applet can do).

We're not going to use Frame to its full potential, but we'll at least get our feet wet. Frame is a class that is just dying to be subclassed, and we are going to do precisely that. We are going to create a special kind of Frame, called promptFrame, which will have the singular purpose of getting a particular kind of input from the user. Here's the code:

```
/* this is a simple window that gets a name from the user */
class promptFrame extends Frame {
TextField TF;
public String gotName;
promptFrame() {
        super("Ready to play Othello?");
        setLayout( new FlowLayout() );
        add( "West",new Label("Input your name: ") );
        add("West",TF = new TextField(20) );
        add("Center",new Button("Login") );
        gotName = null;
}


public boolean handleEvent(Event evt) {

if( (evt.target instanceof TextField && evt.id==Event.ACTION_EVENT) ||
(evt.target instanceof Button && evt.arg.equals("Login")) ) {
        if( TF.getText() == "" )
                gotName = "Noname";
        else
                gotName = TF.getText();
        return true;
        }
return super.handleEvent(evt);
}

}
```

You are probably wondering what good it does to get some name from the user and then store it in a variable (which is all promptFrame does). What will eventually happen is that the Thread executing in NetOthello will take this String and dispose of the promptFrame that was created. To assist, let's add some more code to NetOthello itself. This next method will create a new promptFrame, resize it, and show it to the user:

```
/* pops up a new promptFrame */
public void promptUser() {

pf = new promptFrame();
pf.resize(300,100);
pf.show();
}
```

Let's also now rewrite the newGame() method to incorporate the promptFrame:

```
public void newGame() {
/* initialize the board, then pop up a window */
        initBoard();
        promptUser();
}
```

You can recompile at this point if you like, although you will find that it is pretty darn hard (i.e., impossible) to get rid of that prompt window. We'll remedy this later.

Writing the Networking Code

Time to get NetOthello to live up to the "Net" part of its name. Ideally, a game like this could simply open up a socket to a user-specified host and port and play with another person running the program on that machine. However, the current implementation of Java prohibits any applet from making arbitrary Socket connections. An applet is only permitted to make Socket connections to the host on which it originally resided. So, that is what NetOthello must do. It will connect to the server, which will be responsible for pairing it up with another client so that they can play together.

Threading NetOthello

To handle all of the network tasks, we are going to use a Thread. Here is how we'll get the Thread started in newGame():

```
/* start the thread */
        kicker = new Thread(this);
        kicker.setPriority(Thread.MIN_PRIORITY);
        kicker.start();
```

The run() method for this Thread is very complicated, and so we have to approach it in stages. Each stage consists of a loop that runs until that stage is complete. Always keep in mind that, in any loop, we must always be sure to "sleep" for a little so that we do not hog all available system resources.

Getting the User Info

The first stage is used to get the user's name from the promptFrame and then dispose of the Frame. It is pretty simple, so let's take a look:

```
/* the main Thread loop */
public void run() {

/* first, wait for pf to get a name from the user */
name = null;
while( name == null) {
        name = pf.gotName;
        try { kicker.sleep(500); } catch(Exception e);
        }
/* get rid of pf */
pf.dispose();
```

Connecting to the Server

Once we have the user's name (and the user has pressed the "login" button on the promptFrame), we can proceed to connect to the server. Since we cannot connect to anyone except the server, we can always use getCodeBase() to find out the server's DNS name. However, we can still allow the port to be defined in the HTML tag. To do this, add the following to init():

```
/* check applet parameters */
try{
        thePort = Integer.valueOf( getParameter("port") ).intValue();
} catch(Exception e) {
        thePort = 8314;
}
```

Notice that we default to 8314 (after the chemistry constant, R, which is 8.314) if the port is not defined by the <APPLET> tag. Now, here is the next stage of run():

```
s = null;

/* ok, now make the socket connection */
while( s == null )
try{
      theHost = getCodeBase().getHost();
      display("Attempting to make connection");
      s = new Socket(theHost,thePort);
      dis = new DataInputStream( s.getInputStream() );
      ps = new PrintStream( s.getOutputStream() );
} catch( Exception e) {
      try { kicker.sleep(7500); } catch(Exception ex);
}

display("Connection established");
display("Waiting for another player...");
```

This repeatedly tries to connect to the server, and once it does, we can proceed to the main part of the run() loop.

Handling Server Input

This stage handles input from the server and processes it, taking any appropriate action. First, we loop and wait for input:

```
/* here is the main event loop */
while( kicker != null) {
String input=null;
StringTokenizer st = null;

while( input == null)
try {
      kicker.sleep(100);
      input = dis.readLine();
} catch (Exception e) {
      input = null;
}
System.out.println("Got: "+input); //used for debugging purposes
```

Now that we have some input from the server, we can try to process it. There are several commands that the client understands, so let's walk through each one separately. The first is the *bye* command, which will be generated in the NetOthello stop() method. It is used to signal that the client has disconnected, and if we receive this message, it is safe to assume that our opponent has logged off and abandoned our game. In this case, we display a message and restart:

```
/* if the other person disconnected for any reason... start over */
if( input.equals("bye" ) ) {
      display("Your partner has left the game... Restarting");
      newGame();
      repaint();
      return;
      }
```

The remainder of the command is assumed to be in the format "command|value1|value2|value3|..." (look familiar?). We will use a StringTokenizer to parse the input into commands and values. The first command we check for is the *start* command. This signals the beginning of the game, and it also tells the client whether it will be playing white or black. The *local* variable is then set accordingly:

```
st = new StringTokenizer(input,"|");
String cmd = st.nextToken();
String val = st.nextToken();

/* if we are ready to start a game */
if( cmd.equals("start") ) {
      display("Got another player.");
      if( val.equals("black") ) local = BLACK;
```

```
else local = WHITE;
display("You will play "+val);
repaint();
}
```

Next, check for the *move* command, which lets us know that the person whose turn it is currently (as defined by the *turn* variable) has made a move. We must then pass the two integer parameters to the doMove() method, which will do the actual move-making. Here's how it works:

```
else /* if we got a move, make it */
if( cmd.equals("move"))
        doMove( Integer.valueOf(val).intValue(), ⇐
Integer.valueOf(st.nextToken()).intValue(), turn);
```

The last command we might get is the *say* command, which, just as it did in ChatRoom, signals that our opponent has something to say to us. In this case, we just display the message:

```
else /* if this is a message from a player */
if(cmd.equals("say"))
        display( val );
}
}
```

That's all there is to it! All we have left to do is stop() to ensure that NetOthello tidies up before it quits. Here's what that looks like:

```
/* if the Thread stops, be sure to clean up! */
public void stop() {

try {
        ps.println("bye");
        dis.close();
        ps.close();
        s.close();

} catch (Exception e);
}
```

Sending Moves

The last thing we have to do in NetOthello is change the mouseDown() method to reflect all of the changes we have been making. It must check to see if it is the user's turn or not. Most importantly, we are not going to have mouseDown() call doMove() directly. Rather, it will send a message to the server that will get echoed back so that both clients will update at the same time. (We wouldn't want to give either client an advantage.) This is the very last piece of networking code we have to write. Here's how mouseDown() should work:

```
public boolean mouseDown(Event evt, int x, int y) {

if( turn == local) { /* if it's our turn */
     if( validMoveXY(x,y,turn) ) { /* if we got a valid move */
          int xx,yy;
              xx= (int)(x/theBoard.pieceWidth);
              yy=(int)(y/theBoard.pieceHeight);
          boolean flag=false;
/* be SURE the move gets sent */
     while( !flag )
          try{
              ps.println("move|"+xx+"|"+yy);
              ps.flush();
          System.out.println("Sent move: "+xx+","+yy);
          flag = true;
          } catch (Exception e) {
              flag = false;
              }
          return true;
          }
}

return false;
}
```

Congratulations! The networking code is finished. NetOthello can now successfully interact with a server and play Othello against another client applet running on another machine. Unfortunately, there is no server yet! Obviously, we are going to have to write that code next.

Writing the GameServer

Our goal with GameServer is to create a generic multiplayer game server that can be used with only slight modifications by any similar game client. The concepts behind it are very similar to those used to create the ChatServer in Chapter 9, Advanced Networking and Multiplayer Gaming Concepts, as is the class hierarchy, so be sure you understand that program before you proceed here.

Step 1: Creating GameServer.class

This class doesn't actually do very much except create a GameServerThread and start it. Its one responsibility is to get a port number from the user, or else default to 8314.

```
import GameServerThread;

class GameServer {
public static void main(String args[]) {
int thePort;
```

```
try{
        thePort = Integer.valueOf(args[0]).intValue();
} catch (Exception e) {
        thePort = 8314;
}

new GameServerThread(thePort).start();
}
}
```

Step 2: Writing GameServerThread.class

This class has the responsibility of setting up a ServerSocket and accepting Socket connections from clients. It must also manage a list of GameGroups (again stored in a Vector) and pass the new connection along to the next open GameGroup to be handled. If there are no open GameGroups, it must create a new one. Once a GameGroup is full, it must be started by GameServerThread. GameServerThread also performs garbage collection on the list it maintains and weeds out any dead or disconnected GameGroups.

The GameServerThread begins by establishing a server presence on the designated port:

```
import java.net.*;
import java.lang.*;
import java.util.*;
import GameGroup;

public class GameServerThread extends Thread {
ServerSocket servSock = null;
Vector v;

GameServerThread(int port) {
        try {
            servSock = new ServerSocket(port);
        } catch (Exception e) {
            System.out.println("Could not initialize. Exiting.");
            System.exit(1);
        }
System.out.println("Server successfully initialized. Waiting for connec-
tion on port "+port);
v = new Vector();
}
```

Once the GameServerThread is started, it waits, accepting connections and handing them off to GameGroups as necessary:

```
public void run() {
GameGroup tempGroup=null;

while(servSock != null ) {
Socket tempSock;
      try {
      tempSock = servSock.accept();
      System.out.println("Received New Connection.");
      if( !v.isEmpty() ) {
            tempGroup = (GameGroup)v.lastElement();
            if( tempGroup.full() )
          v.addElement(  new GameGroup( tempSock ) );
            else {
                  tempGroup.addClient(tempSock);
                  if( tempGroup.full() )
                        tempGroup.start();
            }
        } else
                  v.addElement(new GameGroup( tempSock ) );
for( int x=0; x<v.size()-1;x++)
      if( !((GameGroup)v.elementAt(x)).isAlive() )
            v.removeElementAt(x);

      } catch (Exception e) {
          System.out.println("New Connection Failure. Exiting.\n"+e);
        System.exit(1);
      }

try{ sleep(100); } catch (Exception e);
}
}
```

It weeds out any dead threads from the Vector here. The last thing the GameServerThread
has to do is clean up after itself when it is destroyed. This can only happen when the
whole program is about to exit, so we can get rid of the ServerSocket:

```
public void finalize() {
      try {
            servSock.close();
      } catch(Exception e);
      servSock = null;
}
}
```

Was that easy enough? Well, for a little more challenge, check out this next class.

Step 3: Coding GameGroup.class

GameGroup is designed to be an all-purpose multigame server handler. It receives a Socket
from GameServerThread and spins it off into a GameClientThread, which it adds to an
array. GameGroup does not need a Vector, because it is used for games where there is
a known, predetermined number of players. In the case of Othello, this is two players,

but we want to be as general as possible. The basic setup is quite simple. Remember that GameGroups are created with a specific number of players in mind:

```
import java.lang.*;
import java.net.*;
import java.io.*;
import java.util.*;
import GameClientThread;

public class GameGroup extends Thread {

GameClientThread arr[];
final int SIZE=2;

GameGroup ( Socket s ) {
    arr = new GameClientThread[SIZE];
    addClient( s );
}
}
```

Notice that all that is required to change the number of players in a GameGroup is to change the constant SIZE. Next, let's write the method that adds a Socket to the array:

```
public void addClient( Socket s ) {
int x;

for( x=0; x<SIZE; x++)
    if( arr[x] == null || !arr[x].isAlive() ) {
        arr[x] = new GameClientThread(s,this);
        arr[x].start();
        return ;
        }

}
```

As soon as we create a GameClientThread, we have to start() it so that it will immediately start processing input. GameGroup's Thread is not started until the GameGroup is full. This signals the start of the game, so GameGroup must assign colors to each of the players and let them know to start playing. This is the only really proactive thing that GameGroup does. This is done in the run() method along with some garbage collection that makes sure all of the clients are still alive. If anyone leaves, everyone is sent the *bye* command, and the GameGroup stops itself (so it can be garbage collected):

```
public void run() {
int x;

arr[0].message("start|white");
arr[1].message("start|black");


while( true ) {
    for(x=0;x<SIZE;x++)
```

continued on next page

continued from previous page

```
                              if( arr[x] == null || !arr[x].isAlive() ) {
                                  output("bye");
                                  stop();
                                  }
              try{ sleep( 10000 ); } catch(Exception e);
              }
        }
```

Like any good object, GameGroup cleans up after itself, in the finalize() method:

```
public void finalize() {
int x;

output("bye");
try {
for(x=0; x<SIZE; x++)
        if( arr[x] != null ) {
              arr[x].stop();
              }
} catch(Exception e);

}
```

The GameGroup also has a method that is eventually called by GameClientThread to output a message to all currently connected clients. It is quite simple:

```
public void output(String str) {
int x;

for(x=0;x<SIZE;x++)
        if(arr[x] != null)
              arr[x].message(str);

}
```

GameGroup does one last thing. GameServerThread needs a way of determining if GameGroup is "full," which means that all of its slots are full and no more clients may be added. This is done with the full() method:

```
public boolean full() {
int x;

for(x=0;x<SIZE;x++)
        if( arr[x] == null )
                return false;
return true;
}
```

Even though we've now written all of GameGroup's methods, you still can't compile it, because GameGroup requires a compiled version of GameClientThread. However, GameClientThread needs a compiled version of GameGroup in order to compile. Hopefully, you remember the trick we learned in Chapter 9 for dealing with this dilemma: Compile a dumbed-down version of one class, compile its partner, and then change and recompile the first one. Or you could just use the precompiled binaries that come with the CD-ROM. Either way, you're almost done!

Step 4: Building GameClientThread.class

This is a puny little class that just watches a Socket and passes any input it receives to its parent GameGroup. It also has a little method for sending a message to its client, if needed. Here's what it looks like:

```
import java.net.*;
import java.lang.*;
import java.io.*;
import java.util.*;
import GameGroup;

public class GameClientThread extends Thread {
GameGroup parent;
Socket theSock;
DataInputStream dis;
PrintStream ps;
String alias;

GameClientThread(Socket s, GameGroup p) {
theSock = s;
parent = p;
}
}
```

Setting that up was pretty easy. Here is what the run() method looks like:

```
public void run() {

    try {
            dis = new DataInputStream( new BufferedInputStream(
            theSock.getInputStream()));
          ps = new PrintStream( theSock.getOutputStream());
    } catch (Exception e) {
          stop();
/* notice that, if there is any problem, we stop immediately */
      }


while (theSock !=null) {
String input = null;
try {
input = dis.readLine().trim();
if(input != null) {
    parent.output(input);
```

continued on next page

continued from previous page

```
            if(input.equals("bye"))
                    stop();
            }
} catch (Exception e) {
        stop();
        theSock = null;
}
try{ sleep(100); } catch(Exception e);
}
}
```

And top it off with a little method for receiving messages:

```
public boolean message(String str) {
boolean flag = false;

while (!flag)
try {
        ps.println(str);
        flag = true;
} catch (Exception e) {
        flag = false;
}
return true;
}
```

Now, don't forget to clean up!

```
public void finalize() {
        try {
                ps.close();
                dis.close();
                theSock.close();
        } catch(Exception e);
theSock = null;

}
```

Ta dah! NetOthello is now fully functional, and you and a friend can play if you have a Web server. If you don't, that's OK; run the server (from a command line) and two clients (in appletviewer) and you can play against yourself! Enjoy, have some fun, and, when you're ready, we'll start making some improvements.

Adding Some Features

NetOthello is a pretty cool applet already, but let's see if we can make it even cooler.

Multimedia Enhancements

One fairly simple thing to do would be to use some nifty rendered graphics instead of simple circles for pieces, and maybe a textured background instead of that plain old green. Even more spiffy would be to devise an animation sequence for the pieces as they flip, and maybe even play a sound to accompany it. These tiny things are the keys to enhancing the end-user's experience. The users aren't ever going to see the elegant code you used to write the game, or the brilliant insights required to write the code, but they will forever remember a cleverly done animation or a cool graphic.

Adding Graphics

Let's start simple. To begin with, let's say we have three images: empty.gif, white.gif, and black.gif, which represent the three states that any piece can have. Each piece includes the textured background and is framed by a black rectangle, so there is no longer a need to draw that ugly green thing anymore. This feature requires a few changes to each of the classes used in NetOthello, but not anything major.

The first change to make is, of course, to GamePiece.class. GamePiece now expects to be passed an array of Images, which indicate the possible states it might have. For all the methods we use, the first Image will be the empty square, the second a white piece, and the third a black piece. All of this will only really affect paintPiece(), which will now look like this:

```
public void paintPiece(Graphics g, Image im[]) {
        paintPiece( g, rect, im );
}

public void paintPiece(Graphics g, Rectangle r, Image im[] ) {
Image temp;
rect = r;

if( ! r.intersects(g.getClipRect()) ) return;

if ( color == WHITE )
        temp = im[1];
else
        temp = im[2];

g.drawImage(im, rect.x,rect.y,rect.width, rect.height, null );

}
```

The next affected class is obviously GameBoard.class, which must act as an intermediary between NetOthello (which retrieves the Images) and GamePiece (which displays them). Here's what the initialization method looks like with the added Image handling:

```
Image im[];

GameBoard( int w, int h, Image images[]) {
      board = new GamePiece[w][h];
      cols = w;
      rows = h;
      empty = w*h;
      im = images;
}
```

And here is the resulting paintBoard() method:

```
public void paintBoard(Graphics g, Rectangle r) {

int x;
int y;

pieceWidth = (int) (r.width/cols);
pieceHeight = (int) (r.height/rows);

for( x=0; x<cols; x++) {
      for(y=0; y< rows; y++) {
            if( board[x][y] != null )
                        board[x][y].paintPiece( g, new Rectangle( r.x +
                        pieceWidth*x, r.y + pieceHeight*y, pieceWidth,
                        pieceHeight), im);
            else
                        g.drawImage(im[0],  r.x + pieceWidth*x, r.y +
pieceHeight*y, pieceWidth, pieceHeight, null);
                  }
            }
}
```

Nothing too complicated. Next, we must instruct the NetOthello applet to load the images from the server. We will use a relative URL that assumes that the images are located in a directory named "images" off of the same directory in which the applet is located. We can just change the init() method like this:

```
Image im[];

public void init() {

im= new Image[3];
im[0] = getImage( getCodeBase(), "images/empty.gif" );
im[1] = getImage( getCodeBase(), "images/white.gif" );
im[2] = getImage( getCodeBase(), "images/black.gif" );
...
```

We must also change the way the GameBoard is instantiated in initBoard():

```
public void initBoard() {
turn = WHITE;
      theBoard = new GameBoard( 8, 8, im);
...
```

And now we're all set! Create a directory named "images" and put in it your three GIFs (or JPEGs). What? You say you don't have any GIFs (or JPEGs)? Well, that is the same problem I ran into, so I convinced a very graphically talented friend of mine, Jessica Ruble-English, to create them for me. If you want to use hers, they are included on the CD-ROM, but you are welcome to create your own. As long as they are square, Java will scale them to exactly the right dimensions.

Suggestion Box

Because we made our game system so open and general, there are many, many extensions possible. Let's examine a few here.

First, I would like to make a confession. The system we used for objects in this chapter is *not* the best way to do it. It works just fine, but there is a more elegant solution, which I deliberately left to you to implement. All of the game-specific code for Othello should not be located in the NetOthello applet itself. Rather, there should be a subclass of GameBoard called OthelloBoard that knows the rules of Othello and acts as an intermediary between NetOthello and GameBoard. In fact, GameBoard should really be an *abstract* object designed to be extended by a more specialized type of board.

Another good extension of GameBoard would be to make it extend Panel. This way, it could be laid out just like any other GUI component. This would also mean that the applet could be solely concerned with the GUI part of the program while OthelloBoard deals with all of the drawing, etc.

Of course, the logical progression from here is to write another board game, perhaps checkers, perhaps chess (depending on what level you feel like working on) and use the model we have created here to implement it. Do your best to reuse as much code as possible, since there is never a good reason to reinvent the wheel.

Another extension would be to create a similar game environment, except instead of pieces, use something different. A good example would be a card game of some sort; perhaps start with something like blackjack. Think of the obvious parallels to what we have created here: you could have a PlayingCard object, and a CardDeck object that would be responsible for tracking, shuffling, and drawing the entire deck of cards. You could then have a BlackJack applet that knew the rules of the game. You could even have the server be used for keeping track of money and bets—perhaps even start your own online virtual casino! With Java, the possibilities are endless!

Summary

In this chapter, we combined our knowledge of networking, GUI, and all-around cool programming skills to create an online Java board game, NetOthello. While this is a totally cool purpose in its own right, it also serves as an excellent conceptual base for similar games you may write in the future. Although we discussed a few in the Suggestion Box section, there are many others. Java is the ideal language for combining these elements into interesting and, most importantly, *fun* applications!

16

WordQuest

Eric Ries

me tribli fiore iemanouille : si quali primovano : l'alzra
i gra pesi i turri huomini che d igoni o fagografano di bene
gari nellamano rsa per raugrella arssa mano bella pegi qui si
orga o pib i somo pibibus.

16

WordQuest

No doubt you've noticed that the most popular computer games on the market are violent shoot-'em-up, testosterone-charged games. There is, however, a large niche market for nonviolent games. Board and strategy games fall in this category, as does a third kind of game we have not yet discussed: educational games. The computer has proved itself a powerful tool for learning as well as entertainment, and the best results are often achieved through a combination of the two. In this chapter, we will create a Java game specifically designed to teach vocabulary, but which could easily be extended to teach a plethora of other concepts.

What Is WordQuest?

WordQuest combines certain elements of an action-adventure game with an educational purpose. For educational games, a believable plot is often unnecessary, but can add to the fun. In WordQuest, the player is on a secret nighttime mission to penetrate the enemy's defenses. To successfully save his or her country/planet/galaxy from certain destruction, the player must pass through an advanced defense system designed to thwart would-be infiltrators by testing their vocabulary skills. As the player flies in a high-speed hovercraft, the enemy defense system will ask multiple-choice questions. The defense system uses massive force fields to thwart the player's aim, but luckily, friendly agents have infiltrated the enemy base. These agents have managed to weaken each section of the force field at a specific point to allow the player to succeed in penetration. As the player approaches the force field, he or she will find that it has been divided into sections, each with an answer written on it. The user must "shoot" the correct answer to find the weak point in the force field and penetrate it. Figure 16-1 shows what the final game looks like.

Plan of Attack

WordQuest will be written in several stages. First, we are going to create a generic scrolling-action game environment that could be used for any kind of action game. This will help get the fundamentals of this type of game out of the way. This will also provide a useful set of classes that can be used and reused—a nice bonus for any program. Once we've got this generic game engine running to our satisfaction, we will proceed to alter it to meet the needs of an educational game. This will entail adding, removing, and changing some parts of our original code, but if we do a good job with the first part, we won't have to do too much work.

Building an Action Environment

The game we are creating takes place in a mythical realm in which the programmer gets to specify the laws of physics. Our goal, as always, is to create a set of classes that we can reuse later for any similar type of game. To this end, we are going to create a special Sprite class that can handle any kind of onscreen entity. By modifying and extending

FIGURE 16-1

◉ ◉ ◉ ◉ ◉ ◉

WordQuest final product

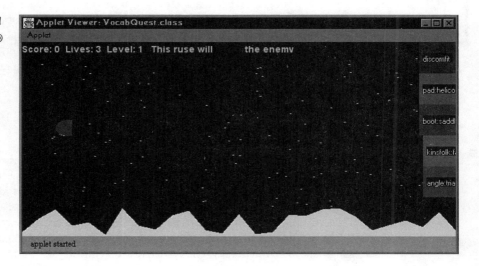

this class, we can easily create spaceships, birds, or flying oysters—all without having to do much more that make some cute graphics.

Simulating 3D

We're not going to write a 3D game in this chapter. However, we do want to give players the illusion that they are traveling forward at a tremendous speed. The two ways to simulate motion in a game of this type are to either move the user's Sprite very fast, or to leave the player stationary and scroll the background very fast behind him or her. For this environment, we are going to choose the latter option.

Whenever you drive, you'll notice that when you look to the side, things that are closer to you appear to move quickly, while things far away appear to move slowly. We will take advantage of this property to fool the user. In the "foreground" we will scroll a fast-moving terrain, while in the background we will scroll a slow-moving star field that will give the illusion of night. These two things combined will give users the feeling that they are hurtling forward toward certain death, even though their "ship" is not moving at all.

This technique is very common. Video games systems, like Nintendo, make extensive use of it to achieve the very same illusion we seek. However, most games like that scroll a bitmapped background/foreground over and over again. This is obviously repetitive, and while it works pretty well, is not the best method. Because of some nifty Java features, we can have a *dynamic* background/foreground that is not repetitive, and has greater realism. We'll discuss this implementation a little later.

Understanding Sprite Theory

Each Sprite will be its own thread. Each Sprite will be responsible for keeping track of its current location, moving appropriately, and drawing itself when requested by the applet. Furthermore, each Sprite should know what to do when it collides with another Sprite, and it should take action depending on the type of Sprite with which it collides. In order to accomplish this, we are going to need to assign each Sprite an ID number that designates what sort of sprite it is. That way, when two Sprites collide, each one simply checks what it has collided with and acts appropriately. For instance, if a "rock" Sprite collides with a "window" Sprite, you would expect the rock to emerge unscathed but the window to be completely destroyed. Game Sprites must exhibit these same behaviors.

Writing the Code

Let's jump right in and create a Sprite class with the basic features we've discussed so far. Once we've done that, we can figure out how to alter it to meet the needs of our specific game. Note that we will not make use of double-buffered graphics yet, as adding that later often leads to more efficient code.

Implementing Sprite.java Variables

The first thing we must do with this class is define a whole slew of variables. Here's what each of them is for:

- ⚔ int WIDTH, HEIGHT. These variables are the default Sprite width and height values. Most sprites will override these initial values.

- ⚔ double *speedX, speedY.* These variables are used to determine Sprite's velocity in the X and Y directions.

- ⚔ int *x, y.* These variables determine the Sprite's current position.

- ⚔ int *lastX, lastY.* These variables are the previous x and y coordinates of the Sprite; they are used to erase the Sprite when not using double-buffered graphics.

- ⚔ Rectangle *bounds.* A Rectangle (usually based on *x,y* and WIDTH,HEIGHT) that contains the entire Sprite.

- ⚔ int DELAY. This variable is the time, in milliseconds, that the Sprite's Thread should pause before advancing the Sprite. This is used to ensure that no one Sprite takes up all available resources.

- ⚔ static Graphics *theG.* This variable is used to allow all Sprites to use the same Graphics context to draw in. Thus, once the parent applet sets this property, every Sprite has someplace to draw.

- ⚔ static int *warp.* This variable is a "warp factor." Every Sprite multiplies its speed by this number, which is usually one. However, if we want to quickly increase the speed of every Sprite (including the background), we can increase this number.

- ⚔ public Image *anim[].* This variable is an array of Images that can be set if we want a Sprite to use a series of Images to animate itself. Otherwise, we must provide a default drawing behavior for the Sprite.

- ⚔ int *animIndex, animMax.* These variables contain the "current" *anim[]* frame and the size of the *anim[]* array, respectively.

- ⚔ public Image *im.* This variable is an Image used for offscreen drawing, when necessary (especially when we start doing double-buffered graphics). Each Sprite must have this variable set by the applet (only Abstract Windowing Toolkit (AWT) components can create offscreen Image space).

- ⚔ Color *theColor.* This is used for the default drawing color of this Sprite (only used by some Sprites).

- ⚔ public int *id.* This variable contains the Sprite's ID, which is one of the constants declared in the Sprite class (we'll declare the actual values later).

Here's what the initial class declaration looks like:

```
import java.awt.*;


public class Sprite extends Thread {

int WIDTH=40,HEIGHT=25;

double speedX=0,speedY=0;
int x,y, animIndex,animMax;
int lastX,lastY;
int DELAY=300;
public Image anim[], im;

static Graphics theG;
static int warp=1;

Rectangle bounds;
Color theColor;
int id=0;
}
```

Defining Sprite IDs

Next, we should decide on a system of Sprite IDs. For starters, we should define five different types of Sprites (although adding more later is simple): ENEMY, BULLET, USER, EXPLOSION, and MESSAGE. It would be simple and feasible to assign each of these Sprites a number between 1 and 5, and then use a series of *if* statements to check what sort of collision has taken place. However, if we use a little mathematics, we can come up with a far more versatile system. Suppose we used the simple 1–5 numbering scheme mentioned before. To check a collision, we could do something like this:

```
public void collision(int num) { // num == ID of the colliding object

if( num==BULLET && this.id==ENEMY)
      stop();
}
```

A whole slew of *if* statements, or a large *case* statement, could probably handle all possible permutations for a two-Sprite collision. However, consider what would happen if we wanted to have three Sprites collide? four Sprites? 100 Sprites? Clearly the colossal nature of such a *case* statement makes this method impractical. How, then, should we proceed? One method that is very effective is to assign a prime number to each ID. Whenever a collision takes place, we pass the product of all of the IDs in the collision to each Sprite, which then can act accordingly. Because every collision number is the product of a unique set of prime numbers, we can use the modulus operator to determine what type of collision has taken place. Don't let all this math stuff scare you. If you aren't quite sure how all this works, try an example. Let's use the following set of ID definitions in Sprite:

```
static final int ENEMY = 2;
static final int BULLET = 3;
static final int USER = 5;
static final int EXPLOSION = 7;
static final int MESSAGE = 11;
```

Now any collision involving a bullet will yield 0 if it is "%" (modulus division) by Sprite.BULLET. Keep in mind that the default ID of the Sprite class is 0, so that Sprites that do not get collided with (like the background) produce a "zero" collision that we can safely ignore. Here is some simple code that handles the most basic of collisions:

```
public void collision( int num ) {

if( num == 0 ) return;
if( id == MESSAGE ) return;


if( id == BULLET || num%BULLET == 0)
      stop();
else
if( num == USER*ENEMY )
      stop();
}
```

For more complicated games, of course, this method could become quite complex. One interesting idea would be to have a Sprite that is "killed" replace itself with an EXPLOSION Sprite. For more on this, see the Suggestion Box at the end of this chapter.

Initializing the Variables

To make this class easier to use, let's define a couple of methods that allow easy initialization of key variables. These are pretty straightforward and aren't especially exciting, so let's get them out of the way quickly:

```
public void setXY(int x, int y) {
      this.x=x;
      this.y=y;

if( bounds == null)
      bounds = new Rectangle( x,y,WIDTH,HEIGHT );
else {
      bounds.x=x;
      bounds.y=y;
      }

}

public void setBounds( Rectangle r) {
      bounds = r;
```

```
                x = bounds.x;
                y = bounds.y;
        }

        public void setID(int id) {
                this.id = id;
        }

        public int queryID() {
                return id;
        }

        public void setSpeed( double X, double Y ) {
                speedX=X;
                speedY=Y;
        }

        public void setSpeed( double factor ) {
                speedX=factor;
                speedY=factor;
        }

        public int getSpeed() {
                if( speedY!=0 )
                        return warp*(int)(speedX/speedY);
                else
                        return warp*(int)(speedX+.5);
        }
```

Defining the Sprite Images

Next comes the tedious job of defining each type of Sprite's default "look". This is used in the absence of an animation array of Images. To speed things up, rather than actually drawing the Sprite every time it is required, we will have the program generate an offscreen Image and put it in the animation array. Subsequent calls can simply make use of the default Image. Besides raw speed, the advantage of this is that the same code can be used whether the Sprite is preanimated or not. Here's the method that will take care of creating the default Image:

```
public synchronized void generateImage() {

if( im==null) return;

                Graphics blah = im.getGraphics();
                anim = new Image[1];
switch( id ) {
        case ENEMY: {
                theColor = new Color( (int)(Math.random()*255),(int)(Math.ran-
dom()*255),(int)(Math.random()*255));
                blah.setColor( theColor );
```

continued on next page

continued from previous page

```
                            blah.fillRect( 0,0,bounds.width,bounds.height);
                            break;
                            }
                    case BULLET: {
                            theColor = Color.green;
                            blah.setColor( theColor );
                            blah.fillRoundRect( 0,0,bounds.width,bounds.height,5,5);
                            break;
                            }
                    case USER: {
                            theColor = Color.blue;
                            blah.setColor( Color.black );
                            blah.fillRect( 0,0,bounds.width,bounds.height );
                            blah.setColor( Color.white );
                            blah.drawOval( 0,0, bounds.width, bounds.height);
                            blah.setColor( theColor );
                            blah.fillOval( 0,0, bounds.width, bounds.height);
                            break;
                            }
                }


                    anim[0]=im;
                    animIndex=0;
                    animMax=1;
        }
```

This takes care of all of our default IDs except MESSAGE, which we will handle later. We declare this method to be *synchronized* because we don't want the Sprite to try to draw the Image before it is finished being created. Next, let's actually create the drawing methods:

```
public void paintSprite( Graphics g ) {

g.setColor( Color.black );


if( lastX!=x || lastY!=y)
        g.fillRect( lastX,lastY,bounds.width,bounds.height);


        if( anim == null )
                generateImage();
g.drawImage(anim[animIndex],x,y,null);
}
```

Animating the Sprites

Notice how this method works just fine whether or not we have given this Sprite a nifty animation array. However, if there is an animation array, we need a method that will advance it as necessary. This method should also move the Sprite to its new location based on the speed attributes:

```
public void advance() {

if( anim != null ) {
        animIndex++;
        if( animIndex >= animMax )
                animIndex = 0;
        }

lastX=x;
lastY=y;
x += warp*(int)(speedX+.5);
y += warp*(int)(speedY+.5);

bounds.move(x,y);
}
```

Be sure to understand that a negative *speedX* or *speedY* value is totally legitimate, and is used to move the Sprite in the left or up directions, respectively. The last method required for a fully functional Sprite class is the one that makes it actually do something. If you remember that Sprite extends Thread, you should realize it needs a run() method:

```
public void run() {
        while(true) {
                try{ sleep(DELAY); } catch(Exception e);
                paintSprite( theG );
                advance();
                }
        }
}
```

Scrolling the Background

The scrolling background is best accomplished in two parts: the terrain (foreground) and the star field (background). Because the Terrain uses some pretty wacky methods to achieve great speed, we will write it as its own class, and not as a subclass of Sprite. However, just to demonstrate how useful the Sprite class is, we will write the StarField class as an extension of it.

Understanding the Terrain Class

How does one write a scrolling foreground? Many games use a graphic that is longer than the active playing field and that looks exactly the same at both ends. This can then be scrolled at high speeds past the user, and when it "runs out," another copy of it (or another compatible graphic) is added. This works pretty well, but the repetitive nature of it can be quite annoying to the user if the graphic is not large enough. Of course, the drawback to a large graphic is that it requires large amounts of memory to store, and time to develop.

To avoid the drawbacks associated with predrawn terrains, we are going to create a "dynamic" terrain that is continuously generated by a Thread specifically written for this task. A "terrain" looks something like Figure 16-2.

This may seem complicated to draw. However, if you look at the terrain as a series of polygons, each with four sides, a way of creating it should become clear. Figure 16-3 gives an example.

To create this effect we will call upon the Polygon class. The terrain will be composed of a series of Polygons, each the same width, that have at least two points in common. This is highlighted in Figure 16-4. Every time the terrain is "scrolled," the leftmost Polygon is removed and a new one is generated at the far right. At high speeds, this gives the illusion that the user is whizzing by a landscape tremendously fast.

FIGURE 16-2

◎ ◎ ◎ ◎ ◎ ◎

Terrain to be scrolled

FIGURE 16-3

◎ ◎ ◎ ◎ ◎ ◎

Same terrain divided into quadrilaterals

FIGURE 16-4
◉ ◉ ◉ ◉ ◉ ◉
*Terrain
coordinate
system*

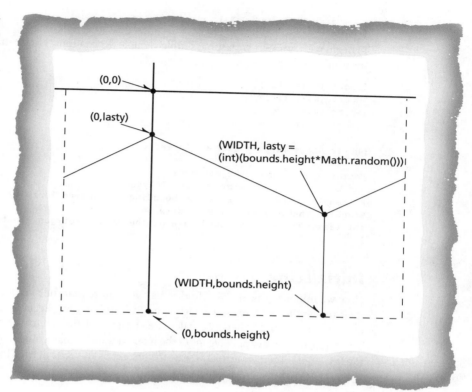

(0,0)

(0,lasty)

(WIDTH, lasty =
(int)(bounds.height*Math.random()))

(WIDTH,bounds.height)

(0,bounds.height)

Coding the Terrain Class

The Terrain class will use a Vector to store the number of Polygons of a specified width. In order to avoid using double-buffered graphics (which are just too slow for this) and to also avoid much flicker (which would ruin the high-speed effect), we will be using some tricky Graphics methods.

Declaring Variables

To begin with, we start with some simple variable declarations. Notice that many of them are similar to ones we used in the Sprite class.

```
import java.awt.*;
import java.util.*;
import java.lang.*;
import Sprite;

public class Terrain extends Thread {

Vector v; // stores the Polygons
int WIDTH; // pixel width of one Polygon
Rectangle bounds; // Rectangle bounding the entire Terrain
Graphics theG; // Graphics to draw on
int lasty=0; // the y-coordinate of the "last" Polygon created
}
```

Initializing

Now we initialize the Terrain. To do this, we require that the creating class pass along three things: the width of each Polygon, the Terrain's bounding Rectangle, and the Graphics context to be used. Then, we calculate the size of the Vector needed to store the Polygons (the number of Polygons of the requested width that would fit within the bounding Rectangle). Then we actually create the first set of Polygons needed to draw the Terrain:

```
Terrain( int w, Rectangle r, Graphics g ) {
WIDTH = w;
bounds = r;
theG = g.create();

int num = (int) (r.width/WIDTH);
v = new Vector(num);
while( num-- >= 0 )
        v.addElement(nextPoly());
}
```

Creating the nextPoly() Method

Of course, we haven't written the nextPoly() method, so let's do that next. It creates a Polygon of random height starting with the Y coordinate of the last Polygon created:

```
Polygon nextPoly() {
Polygon p = new Polygon();
        p.addPoint( (int)(WIDTH/2), (int)(bounds.height * Math.random())
);
        p.addPoint( 0, lasty );
        p.addPoint( 0, bounds.height );
```

```
        p.addPoint( WIDTH, bounds.height );
        p.addPoint( WIDTH, lasty = (int)(bounds.height * Math.random() )
);
return p;
}
```

Notice that we create the Polygon using x and y coordinates that are relative to an X coordinate of zero. When we draw the actual Polygon onto the screen, we are going to need to shift it over before it is drawn, and for that we need a new method:

```
void paintPolyXY(Graphics g, Polygon p, int x, int y) {
    for(int i=0;i<p.npoints;i++) {
            p.xpoints[i]+=x;
            p.ypoints[i]+=y;
            }
    g.fillPolygon(p);
}
```

Drawing Terrain onto the Screen

Next, let's write the method that actually draws the entire Terrain onto the screen. For this, we must take each Polygon out of the Vector and make a copy of it, because the method we just wrote for painting the Polygon actually changes its X and Y coordinates. We then send the copy to be painted, and leave the original alone:

```
public void paintAll( Graphics g, Rectangle r) {

g.setColor(Color.black);
g.fillRect(bounds.x,bounds.y,bounds.width,bounds.height);

g.setColor( Color.yellow );
for(int x=0;x<v.size();x++) {
        Polygon p2 = (Polygon) v.elementAt(x);
        Polygon p = new Polygon(p2.xpoints,p2.ypoints,p2.npoints);
        paintPolyXY(g,p,r.x+x*WIDTH,r.y);
        }
}
```

Using copyArea() to Enhance Performance

Although we could go ahead now and write the Thread code that makes the Terrain go, the result would be horrendously slow. Even if we used double-buffered graphics to draw each successive frame of the Terrain, the method is simply not fast enough, especially when there are many Threads running simultaneously (as there will be in the final product). The key to solving this problem is to recognize that 90 percent of the Terrain (all but one Polygon) doesn't change each time. Therefore, it is wasteful and inefficient (not to mention slow) to have to redraw the entire Terrain for each frame. Rather, we can take advantage of a Graphics method called copyArea(), which actually copies a rectangular set of bits from one location on a Graphics context to another. Using this method, we can easily copy the majority of the Terrain to the left, and then only draw the one remaining Polygon right next to it. Here's the code:

```
public void paintChange( Graphics g, Rectangle r) {
      g.copyArea( r.x,r.y,r.width,r.height,-WIDTH,0);
      g.setColor(Color.black);
      g.fillRect( r.x+r.width-WIDTH,r.y,WIDTH,r.height);
      g.setColor(Color.yellow);
      paintPolyXY(g, (Polygon)v.lastElement(), r.x+r.width-WIDTH,r.y);
}
```

Finishing the Thread Methods

Now it's time to finish up the Thread-related methods of Terrain.class. First, there is a method that will be called each frame to dispose of the oldest Polygon and to add a new one:

```
public void advance() {

v.removeElementAt(0);
v.addElement( nextPoly() );


}
```

Next, we add a new variable and method that will allow the applet to request that the entire Terrain (and not just the new Polygon) be redrawn at the next available instant. This method also makes reference to the Sprite class "warp" factor that is used to increase the drawing frequency of the Terrain when necessary. This, of course, assumes that the applet using Terrain is also using Sprite. If this is not the case, you can always give Terrain a separate "warp" variable (or just leave this feature out altogether).

```
boolean repaint=true;

public void repaint() {
      repaint=true;
}
```

Adding Functionality

And last but not least, we create the run() method in order to actually give this class some functionality!

```
public void run() {
      while(true) {
            if( repaint ) {
                  paintAll(theG,bounds);
                  repaint = false;
                  }
            else
                  paintChange(theG,bounds);
```

```
                        advance();
                        try{ sleep(200/Sprite.warp); } catch(Exception e);
            }
    }
```

Terrain is finished! I would recommend writing up a simple applet to prove this to yourself, or if you wish, you can proceed straight to the rest of our background drawing.

Coding the StarField Class

The StarField is quite simple, really. All we have to do is keep track of a big array of X and Y coordinates. At each coordinate, we draw a tiny little white line, on a black background, to represent a star. Because we will make StarField an extension of Sprite, we can use its "speed" to determine not only the amount each star will move, but also the length of each star. Thus, when the Sprite "warp" factor is set to a large number, the stars will appear to streak by at amazing warp speeds! Like the Sprite class, this first version of StarField will use simple onscreen graphics, but eventually we will convert it to double-buffered form.

We begin with two integer arrays for the X and Y coordinates. We initialize the arrays so that they are full of -1. The method we will write for creating new stars will search the array for a star that is off the screen (that is, one with an X or Y coordinate that is less than zero).

Let's get started:

```
import java.awt.*;
import java.lang.*;

public class StarField extends Sprite {

int x[],y[];
int NUM_STARS;

Graphics g;

StarField( int num, Rectangle r, Image im) {

        this.im=im; // we'll use this later for double-buffered graphics
        DELAY = 300;
        NUM_STARS = num;
        bounds = r;

x = new int[num];
y = new int[num];
for(int i=0;i<NUM_STARS;i++) {
        x[i]=-1;
        y[i]=-1;
        addStar(i);
        }
}
```

The initialization method makes a call to a method that adds a star to the array at position i, so let's code that:

```
public void addStar(int min) {
int i,j;

for(i=0;i<NUM_STARS;i++)
        if(x[i]==-1 && y[i]==-1) {
                x[i] = bounds.x+min+(int)((bounds.width-min)*Math.⇐
random());
                y[i] = bounds.y+(int)(bounds.height*Math.random());
                }
}
```

This picks a random Y position and a random X position (near the right edge) and adds the "star" to the coordinate arrays. Next let's write a little method to "kill" a star that is no longer needed (i.e., one that has scrolled off the screen):

```
public void killStar(int i) {
        x[i]=-1;
        y[i]=-1;
}
```

The default advance method for Sprite will obviously not work for StarField, so let's code that next:

```
public void advance() {
int i, spd = (int)(speedX+.5);


for(i=0;i<NUM_STARS-1;i++) {
        x[i]-=spd;


if( !bounds.inside(x[i],y[i]) ) {
        killStar(i);
        addStar(bounds.width-50);
        }
}
}
```

Of primary importance is the painting method. We can safely assume that the applet will start with a nice black background, so all we have to do is erase the previous stars' locations and then draw the new ones. As previously mentioned, we use Sprite's default getSpeed() method to determine the length of each star (remember that getSpeed() takes the "warp" factor into account):

```
public void paintSprite(Graphics g) {
int i;
Rectangle r=bounds;

g.setColor( Color.black );
g.fillRect( r.x,r.y,r.width,r.height );
```

```
for(i=0;i<NUM_STARS;i++)
    if( r.inside(x[i],y[i] ) ) {
    g.setColor(Color.black);
    g.drawLine(x[i]+getSpeed(),y[i], x[i]+2*(int)(speedX+.5), y[i]);
    g.setColor(Color.white);
            g.drawLine( x[i], y[i], x[i]+(int)(speedX+.5), y[i] );
    }
}
```

We're done! This perhaps comes as a surprise, since we haven't yet coded any of the Thread methods (run(), start(), stop). This is one of the great advantages of modular code design—the Sprite class (which is our superclass) takes care of all of that for us! Because our methods (like advance() and paintSprite()) use the same conventions as Sprite, the preexisting run() method is quite sufficient.

Checking Out the Environment

If you want to see what all that we have accomplished looks like put together, you should take the time now to code up a very simple applet that uses the classes as we've developed them so far. A simple applet that creates a StarField, Terrain, and Sprite is just fine. Although we won't walk through the code for such a game right now (WordQuest should demonstrate how it all works), you can find the source code to a game called SpaceDeath on the CD-ROM that accompanies this book. That game shares many attributes with WordQuest (including some things we haven't yet talked about), but isn't nearly as refined. I would recommend it only as an example of how these classes can be used to create other games. If you want to really see them in action, move right along to the next section...

On with the Quest

It's time to start talking about our primary goal for this chapter: WordQuest. There are many refinements that need to be made to the classes we just developed in order to get them ready for WordQuest. In addition, we need to create some new classes and the very lengthy WordQuest class itself. WordQuest is so long mainly because it has the responsibility of coordinating all of the various elements involved in the game: It must play referee, scorekeeper, and line judge. To accomplish all of this, we should start by creating some new classes to help with the task.

Creating the Question Class

WordQuest works by presenting a question to the user and then presenting several possible answers. In order to manage this data, we should create a data structure for storing a question and its possible answers. We will assume that all questions are meant to have five possible answers, but it is quite easy to change this number for games you may create in the future. Another feature of the Question class is a static Vector that we will use to store all of the answers to all of the questions. This will enable the Question class to generate random incorrect answers in case there is a question with less than five options specified.

Since Question is a small class used only by WordQuest, there is no reason for it to be a public class. Therefore, we add it to the same file that the WordQuest class itself will be added to, WordQuest.java. We begin with a static Vector used to store the big list of all answers. This is used by every instance of Question that is created. We also have regular instance variables to store the text of the question, the correct answer, and another Vector to store the list of possible answers for this question:

```
class Question {

static Vector biglist = new Vector();

public String question,correct;
Vector answers;
}
```

Every Question must be instantiated with the text of the question and the correct answer. This answer is also added to the big list via the addAnswer() method:

```
Question(String q, String a) {
      question = q;
      correct  = a;
      answers = new Vector(5);
      addAnswer(a);
}

public void addAnswer(String a) {
      answers.addElement( a );

if( !biglist.contains(a))
      biglist.addElement(a);

}
```

Notice that we carefully avoid duplicating any answers in the big list.

Next, we add a few more methods for accessing the Question. The first simply provides the text of the Question to be asked. The second extracts (and removes) an answer from the Question's list of possible answers. If this list is empty, it returns *null*:

```
public String getQuestion() {
      return question;
}

public String takeAnswer() {

if( answers.isEmpty() )
      return null;

int rand = (int)(Math.random()*answers.size());
```

```
      String temp = (String)answers.elementAt(rand);
      answers.removeElementAt(rand);
return temp;
}
```

The last method required is one that returns a random answer from the big list. This will usually be used when takeAnswer() returns *null*:

```
public static String randAnswer() {
int rand = (int)(Math.random()*biglist.size());

return (String)biglist.elementAt(rand);
}
```

That's all there is to the Question class. It doesn't seem like much, but it makes handling the question and answer data superlatively easier.

Getting the Question Data

The Question data must be stored in a data file on the same server as the applet. Rather than make the applet do the work of reading and parsing that data, we can create another small helper class for WordQuest, a Thread that reads data into a Vector of Questions. This class is instantiated with a URL that points to a data file, as well as a Vector in which the data should be stored:

```
class dataThread extends Thread {
URL theURL;
Vector questions;

dataThread( Vector v, URL u ) {
questions = v;
theURL = u;
}
```

Nothing happens until the Thread is started; then it goes to work. The actual reading is done using a now familiar DataInputStream, and the parsing is done by our friend, the StringTokenizer. The data must be in the following format:

```
Q: This is a question
A: This is the correct answer
A: This is an incorrect answer
A: This is also an incorrect answer
Q: This is the next question
A: This is the next question's correct answer
  etc.
```

Note that the correct answer is assumed to be the one immediately following the Question, and that the file may specify as many as four incorrect answers (five answers total). If there are fewer than five total answers, wrong answers will be drawn from another question set. Here is how the Thread does its thing:

```
public void run() {

DataInputStream dis;

try {

        dis = new DataInputStream( theURL.openStream() );

Question temp=null;
String q = null;
for( String str= dis.readLine(); str != null; str = dis.readLine() ) {
StringTokenizer st = new StringTokenizer(str,"||");

//System.out.println(str);
if( st.countTokens() >= 2 )
        switch( st.nextToken().charAt(0) ) {

                case 'Q': {
                        q = st.nextToken();
                        if( temp != null ) {
                                questions.addElement( temp );
                                temp = null;
                                }
                        break;
                }
                case 'A': {
                        if(temp == null)
                            temp = new Question(q, st.nextToken());
                        else
                                temp.addAnswer(st.nextToken());
                        break;
                }
        }
/* use this for debugging
if( temp != null ) {
        System.out.println(temp.getQuestion());
        }
*/
}
if( temp != null )
        questions.addElement( temp );

} catch (Exception e) {
        System.out.println("Data file not found.\n"+e);
}

}

}
```

Notice that several lines are commented out; these are useful for debugging but are not needed in the final product.

Writing the Prompt Frame

Just like NetOthello in Chapter 15, WordQuest will use a Frame to get input from the user at the start of the game. However, this promptFrame will also track and display high scores using the HighScoreManager created in Chapter 8, Implementing a High Score Server on a Network. We aren't doing anything new in this code, so it should look familiar. If not, you should refer back to Chapters 8 and 15. This code is only used to help out the main WordQuest class, so add it to the same file:

```
class promptFrame extends Frame {
TextField TF;HighScoreManager HS = new HighScoreManager(10);Panel p;⇐
public String gotName;boolean ready
promptFrame() {            super("Ready for a new game?");      setLayout( new⇐
 BorderLayout() );p = new Panel();        p.setLayout( new FlowLayout() );⇐
p.add( "West",new Label("Input your name: ") );     p.add("West",TF = new⇐
TextField(20) );     p.add("Center",new Button("OK") );     add⇐
("South",p);     gotName = null;     ready=false;}

public void paint(Graphics g) {
Graphics offG;Dimension d = size();d.height-⇐
=p.preferredSize().height;Image im=createImage(d.width,d.height);
Rectangle r = new
Rectangle(0,0,d.width,d.height);offG=im.getGraphics();HS.paintScores⇐
(offG,r);g.drawImage(im,0,0,null);}
public boolean handleEvent(Event evt) {
if( (evt.target instanceof TextField && evt.id==Event.ACTION_EVENT) ||⇐
(evt.target instanceof Button && evt.arg.equals("OK")) ) {
      if( TF.getText() != "" )                     gotName = TF.getText();⇐
ready = true;     return true;     }return super.handleEvent(evt);}
}
```

Using ThreadGroups to Synchronize Enemy Sprites

We want the enemy Sprites to come at the user in unison; that is, we want them to be *synchronized*. One excellent way of doing this is to make sure that they are all in the same ThreadGroup. This also makes them more manageable, and allows us to call certain methods (like suspend() and stop()) on the entire group at once. Furthermore, if we make the group containing the enemy Sprites part of a larger group that encompasses all Sprites, we can call these methods in all of the Sprites in the game at once. The hierarchy looks something like Figure 16-5.

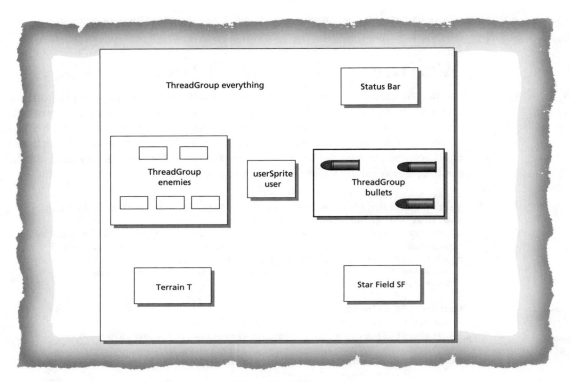

FIGURE 16-5 ◉ *ThreadGroup hierarchy in WordQuest*

In order to implement these ThreadGroups, we must declare each Sprite to be part of a ThreadGroup at the time it is instantiated. Once a Thread is in a group, it is there for good. This requires a few changes to the initialization method of Sprite:

```
Sprite( ThreadGroup p, String d) {
     super(p,d);
}
```

When you create a Thread within a ThreadGroup, you must assign it a name. The name is not terribly important, unless you want to do some Thread operations on only specific Threads to which you do not have a pointer. Even though we have no need to do this, we still must provide a name, because that is one of Java's quirky rules.

Extending the Sprite Class

There are a couple of changes to the Sprite class we should make next. The first thing we need to do is to add the capacity for each Sprite to have a certain data string associated with it. This will be used mainly for the enemy Sprites, each of which must display a potential answer to the question WordQuest poses. This mainly affects two methods, setXY() and generateImage() in Sprite.class. They need to be altered as follows:

```
public String data;
...
public void setXY(int x, int y) {
        this.x=x;
        this.y=y;
if( data != null && !data.equals("user")) {
        FontMetrics fm = theG.getFontMetrics();
        WIDTH = fm.stringWidth( data ) + 10;
    }

    if( bounds == null)
            bounds = new Rectangle( x,y,WIDTH,HEIGHT );
    else {
            bounds.x=x;
            bounds.y=y;
            }
    }
...
public synchronized void generateImage() {
...
        case ENEMY: {
                theColor = new Color(
(int)(Math.random()*255),(int)(Math.random()*255),(int)(Math.⇐
random()*255));
                blah.setColor( theColor );
                blah.fillRect( 0,0,bounds.width,bounds.height);
                blah.setColor(Color.black);
                blah.fillRect( 5, (int)(bounds.height/2-⇐
theG.getFont().getSize()/2-1),WIDTH-10,theG.getFont().getSize()+2);
                blah.setColor(Color.white);
                blah.drawString( data, 5,⇐
(int)(bounds.height/2+theG.getFont().getSize()/2)
);
                break;
                }
...
```

This will enable enemy Sprites to be resized to adequately display their data, and will draw it on top of their Image. Note that these Sprites will not draw any text if they are using a custom animation Image array. Any such array must either have the words imprinted on it (not very practical) or Sprite needs another method for adding the text to the Image (this is far easier and is left as an exercise for the user).

Because most Sprites will be instantiated with their data as their name, we can change the initialization slightly:

```
Sprite( ThreadGroup p, String d) {
        super(p,d);
        data=d;
}
```

The statusBar Class

Even though we used ID constants to represent different kinds of Sprites, there are still some instances when extending the Sprite class is appropriate. One such instance is for the status bar that appears above the playing area. This is merely a Sprite that stays still, and whose data is comprised of several numeric variables. Instead of moving every time it is advanced, it recalculates the value of its data string. The status bar uses the MESSAGE ID in the Sprite class, so first we should add a case for MESSAGE to the generateImage() method:

```
public synchronized void generateImage() {
...
     case MESSAGE: {
             blah.fillRect(0,0,bounds.width,bounds.height);
             blah.setFont( new Font("Times New Roman",Font.BOLD,14));
             blah.setColor(theColor);
             blah.drawString(data,0,bounds.height);
             break;
             }
...
```

Now we can create the statusBar class itself. There are four properties we need to track:

🗡 int *score*. This represents the user's score.

🗡 int *level*. This is the current "level" the user has attained.

🗡 int *lives*. This is the number of "lives" the user has left (number of times the user can die).

🗡 String *quest*. This is the text of the current question to be displayed.

In order to create the data string to be displayed, we must concatenate all of these values like this:

```
data="Score: "+score+"  Lives: "+lives+"  Level: "+level+"    "+quest;
```

This is what happens every time the status bar is advanced. However, it is inefficient to do these calculations if nothing has changed since the last time they were performed, so we use a boolean variable to keep track of whether any change has occurred to any of the values that the status bar tracks. Here's the first bit of code:

```
import java.awt.*;
import Sprite;

public class statusBar extends Sprite {
String quest;
int score=0, lives=3, level=1;
boolean update=true;

statusBar(ThreadGroup tg, String d) {
     super(tg,d);
     data = null;
```

```
        setID( MESSAGE );
        theColor = Color.cyan;
        advance();
    }
}
```

There's nothing fancy here yet, but you'll notice that we make a call to advance(), which is defined in Sprite, but which will only cause trouble if used as is. We had better override it:

```
public void advance() {

if( !update )
      return;

data="Score: "+score+"  Lives: "+lives+"  Level: "+level+"    "+quest;

generateImage();
update=false;
}
```

You see here how the update variable helps save time. However, this means that whenever a data variable is accessed, the update variable must get switched to *true*. Thus, no data variable can be accessed directly. Here are the wrapper functions that we will need:

```
public void addScore(int amt) {
      score+=amt;
      update=true;
}

public void addLives(int amt) {
      lives+=amt;
      update=true;
}

public void addLevel(int amt) {
      level+=amt;
      update=true;
}

public void setQuestion( String str ) {
      quest=str;
      update=true;
}
```

That's all there is to this class. All other methods are taken care of by Sprite.

The userSprite Class

There are several properties that we could decide to give the user's object, but for now we just want to be sure that the user doesn't try to leave the clipping Rectangle of the current Graphics context (which means we'd better be sure to clip it to the playing field):

```
import Sprite;
import java.awt.*;

public class userSprite extends Sprite {
int WIDTH = 25;
int HEIGHT = 25;

userSprite(ThreadGroup tg, String name) {
super(tg,name);
setID(Sprite.USER);
data = null;
}

public void move( int x, int y) {
        if( theG.getClipRect().inside(x,y) )
                super.move(x,y);
        else
                return;
}
}
```

Writing WordQuest

At long last, it is time to write the actual code for WordQuest. This is a long and arduous task, but if we don't proceed, all of our efforts to date will have been for naught. Courage, my friends…

Getting Started

Let's get all of our variables declared. WordQuest uses a very long list of variables, so let's deal with them in small groups, based on what they're used for. First, let's get the importing done:

```
import java.applet.*;
import java.awt.*;
import java.util.*;
import java.net.*;
import java.io.*;
import Terrain;
import StarField;
import Sprite;
import userSprite;
import HighScoreManager;

public class WordQuest extends Applet implements Runnable {
}
```

Variable Declarations

Next, the Sprite variables:

```
Thread kicker;
StarField SF=null;
Terrain T=null;
statusBar bar;
userSprite user;
```

And then the ThreadGroups:

```
ThreadGroup group,bullets,everything;
```

The three groups are for the enemies, bullets, and the master group, respectively. Now the AWT variables:

```
Rectangle SFrect, Trect,statRect;
Dimension d;
promptFrame PF;
Image im;
Graphics offScreenG;
```

The three Rectangles are used to divide the screen into regions. The Graphics and Image are for doing offscreen double-buffered graphics stuff. The next few variables deal with Questions:

```
Vector questions;
Question currentQ;
String name;
```

And lastly, we use a boolean variable to keep track of whether the user is playing the game or looking at the high scores:

```
boolean playing = false; // start with high scores
```

The init() Method

Getting everything initialized is a pretty tough task, but let's get it done. Start by dividing the screen into three distinct regions for the status bar, the StarField (playing area), and the Terrain, respectively:

```
public void init() {
      d = size();
      statRect = new Rectangle(0, 0, d.width, 16);
      SFrect = new Rectangle( 0,statRect.height,⇐
d.width,(int)(d.height*.8));
Trect = new Rectangle( 0, statRect.height+SFrect.height, d.width,⇐
(int)(d.height-statRect.height-SFrect.height) );
```

Next, give the Sprite class a copy of the applet's Graphics context:

```
Sprite.theG = getGraphics().create();
```

Define our ThreadGroups:

```
everything = new ThreadGroup( "all" );
group = new ThreadGroup( everything,"enemies" );
bullets = new ThreadGroup(everything,"bullets");
```

Create the status bar and prompt window:

```
bar = new statusBar(everything, "statusbar");
bar.setBounds( statRect );
bar.im = createImage( statRect.width, statRect.height );
bar.setPriority(Thread.MIN_PRIORITY);
bar.start();

PF = new promptFrame();
PF.resize(d.width,d.height);
PF.show();
```

And last, but not least, get the "kicker" started:

```
        kicker = new Thread(this);
        kicker.setPriority(Thread.MAX_PRIORITY);
        kicker.start();
}
```

Using Double-Buffered Graphics

Because we want to do the run() method next, we need to convert all of our Sprite classes to use double-buffered graphics. This isn't too hard, especially since we decided to have each Sprite create its own Image before it actually does any drawing. Here's the game plan: We have each Sprite work on creating its Image and then tracking its own location. Each time WordQuest wants to redraw, it simply queries each Sprite in the game, and draws that Sprite's Image at the proper location. Keep in mind that this means the StarField *must* be drawn first, or some Sprites may appear to vanish.

Double-Buffering the Sprite Class

The only real change to the Sprite class that is required is that it no longer has to draw itself on the Graphics context. This means we can change run() to look like this:

```
public void run() {
      while(true) {
            try{ sleep(DELAY); } catch(Exception e);
            advance();
            }
}
```

In addition, we want to add another method to make it easier to query the current Image:

```
public Image currentImage() {
if( anim== null)
      generateImage();
return anim[animIndex];
}
```

Other than that, Sprite remains the same. You could even remove the painting method, since it is no longer called. However, future games might still require such a method, so it's best to leave it in.

Double-Buffering StarField

The main changes that need to be made to StarField are in the run() method. Some minor changes also have to be made to handle the Image referenced herein, but you should be able to figure those out on your own:

```
public void run() {
Graphics bg = im.getGraphics();
      while(true) {
              flag = true;
              paintSprite( bg );
              flag = false;
              anim[0]=im;
              im.flush();
              advance();
              try{ sleep(300); } catch(Exception e);
      }
}
```

StarField uses a boolean flag that is only *false* after it is done creating its Image. This is necessary because Java allows other classes to access the Image while it is still being generated, and this allows incomplete versions of it to be drawn onto the screen—a very tacky effect.

See WordQuest Run

The WordQuest run() method does the following: First, it checks to see if we are playing. If so, it runs the check method to handle any collisions, and so on. Then, it creates a new offscreen Image, and prepares it for drawing. It draws the StarField, and then all other Sprites on the Image, and then it draws the Image onto the current Graphics context.

If the user is not playing, it checks to see if the promptFrame is "ready" (i.e., if the user has pressed the OK button). If so, it starts the game up again by calling all the game-starting methods. If the user is not ready to start playing, it just goes to sleep for a bit and checks again later.

That's how the run() method works, and we are going to code it before we code any of the methods to which it refers. This is so you can get a better handle on how the various methods interact as we write them.

Here's the run() code:

```
public void run() {


while(true)
if( playing ) {
        try{kicker.sleep(50); }catch(Exception e);
        doCheck();

        im = createImage(d.width, d.height-Trect.height);
        offScreenG = im.getGraphics();
/* don't draw the StarField until it is ready (flag == false) */
try{    while(SF.flag) kicker.sleep(100); } catch(Exception e);
        offScreenG.drawImage(SF.currentImage(),SF.x,SF.y,null); //}⇐
catch(Exception e);
try {
        Sprite s[]=new Sprite[everything.activeCount()];
        everything.enumerate( s );
        for(int i=0;i<everything.activeCount();i++)
                    if( s[i] != SF )
                        try {

offScreenG.drawImage(s[i].currentImage(),s[i].x,s[i].y,null);
                        } catch(NullPointerException e);
} catch(ArrayIndexOutOfBoundsException e);

        getGraphics().drawImage(im,0,0,null);

} else {
        if( PF.ready ) {
                PF.ready=false;
                name=PF.gotName;
                playing=true;
                PF.hide();
                initUser();
                nextQuestion();
                everything.resume();
                T.resume();
        }
                try{kicker.sleep(500);}catch(Exception e);
        }

}
```

To accompany the run() code we'll need those other crucial Thread methods, start() and stop():

```
public void start() {
questions = new Vector();
        try{
                URL theURL = new URL(getCodeBase(), "data.txt");
                new dataThread( questions, theURL ).start();
```

```
        } catch (Exception e);
}

public void stop() {
        everything.stop();
}
```

Handling the Rules

Arguably the most crucial method in WordQuest is the method that does all of the game-related checking. This implements the "rules" of WordQuest. This method decides the fate of every Sprite and imposes the rules of the game on everyone. First, it turns all active enemies and bullets into arrays of Sprite:

```
public void doCheck() {
int i,j;
Sprite sprites[]=new Sprite[group.activeCount()],bul[]=new Sprite
[bullets.activeCount()];

group.enumerate( sprites );
bullets.enumerate( bul );
int x;
```

Next, it checks to see whether the user's Sprite is alive. If it is not, the user has suffered an ignominious defeat, and his or her score must be adjusted, and the high scores must be displayed:

```
if( !user.isAlive() ) {
        System.out.println("You lose!\n");
        bar.addScore(-10);
        bar.addLives(-1);
        bullets.stop();
        T.suspend();
        if( bar.lives==0 ) {
                playing=false;
                PF.HS.addScore(name,bar.score,null,null);
                PF.show();
                return;
                }
        initUser();
        nextQuestion();
        return;
        }
```

Undoubtedly you would want to replace "You lose" with a friendlier message (maybe even a graphic or pop-up window); this is left as an exercise. Next, we do all of the Sprite checking. Whenever a collision occurs, we call the collision() method in the affected Sprites. In order to save processing time, we only check those Sprites that have an effect on each other (i.e., user vs. Enemy). However, if we wanted to, we could just check every Thread in the "everything" group against every other Thread, and call the appropriate collision methods. Also, notice that we suspend a Sprite while we are checking it, in order to ensure that it does not move while it is being checked (that is cheating!). Another nifty feature is that when a bullet hits an incorrect answer, it is deflected back at the user. This adds a bit more action to the game, although some players might find it a bit too difficult to handle. If you find this to be the case, the feature can easily be disabled.

```
for( x=0;x<group.activeCount();x++) {
sprites[x].suspend();
      if( !sprites[x].intersects( SFrect ) )
            sprites[x].stop();
      else
      if( user.intersects( sprites[x].bounds )) {
            user.collision( user.id * sprites[x].id );
            sprites[x].collision( user.id * sprites[x].id );
            }
      for(int y=0; y < bullets.activeCount(); y++ ) {
      Sprite bullet = bul[y];
      bullet.suspend();
            if( ! bullet.intersects( SFrect ) || bullet.getSpeed() == ⇐
0 )
                  bullet.stop();
            else
            if( bullet.intersects(user.bounds) ) {
                  user.stop();
                  bullet.stop();
            } else
            if( sprites[x].intersects( bullet.bounds ) )
                  if( currentQ.correct.equals( sprites[x].data ) ) {
                        sprites[x].stop();
                        bullet.stop();
                        bar.addScore(50);
                  } else
                        bullet.setSpeed( - bullet.getSpeed(),0 );
            bullet.resume();
            }
            sprites[x].resume();
      }

if( group.activeCount() <= 2 )
      nextQuestion();


}
```

Selecting a Question

The next method we need to write selects a question from the list that the dataThread we wrote earlier gets from the data file. The method must also take the information contained in the Question object and create the appropriate enemy groups.

 We start by stopping any currently active enemy Sprites. Then, we check to see if there are any questions available from which to choose. If not, we spawn a new dataThread to read some in from the data file:

```
public void nextQuestion() {

group.stop();

if( questions.isEmpty() )
      try{
            URL theURL = new URL(getCodeBase(), "data.txt");
            new dataThread( questions, theURL ).start();
      } catch (Exception e);
```

 Next, we wait until there is at least one Question in the Vector that the dataThread is supposed to fill:

```
currentQ=null;
do {
      try {
      currentQ = (Question)questions.elementAt((int)(Math.random()⇐
*questions.size()));
      questions.removeElement(currentQ);
      } catch(Exception e);
} while( currentQ == null );
```

 Once that is complete, we assign the new question to the status bar, and then attempt to find a list of five possible answers to the question. We want to be especially sure that the correct answer appears once and only once in every set of five:

```
bar.setQuestion( currentQ.question );

String dataArray[],temp;

dataArray = new String[ 5 ];

boolean flag = false;
for(int x=0; x<5; x++) {
            temp = currentQ.takeAnswer();
            if( temp == null )
            do {
            flag = false;
                  temp = Question.randAnswer();

            for(int i =0;i<x;i++)
                  if( temp == null || temp.equals(dataArray[i]) )
                        flag = true;
            } while( flag );

            dataArray[x]=temp;
            }
```

Once we have the text of the answers, we can create the enemy Sprites themselves. Once we have them started, we suspend them immediately. Once they are all created and in the appropriate ThreadGroup, we resume them all at one time. This helps ensure that they are closely synchronized.

```
double spdX;

int h = (int)(SFrect.height/5);
spdX = 20*Math.random()+5*bar.level;

Sprite s;
for(int x=0; x<5; x++) {
s = new Sprite( group, dataArray[x] );
s.HEIGHT=h;
s.setXY( SFrect.width+SFrect.x-25, SFrect.y+(h*x));
        s.setSpeed( -spdX, 0);
        s.setID( Sprite.ENEMY );
s.im=createImage(s.WIDTH,s.HEIGHT);
s.start();
s.suspend();
        }
group.resume();
T.resume();

}
```

Initializing Once More

One method that was called from doCheck() was designed to create the user's object and initialize it properly. This also creates a new StarField and/or Terrain if one has not been instantiated already (although this could have been accomplished elsewhere).

This method is pretty straightforward, and here's what it looks like:

```
void initUser() {

    if( SF == null ) {
        SF = new StarField(100, SFrect, createImage(SFrect.width,⇐
SFrect.height), everything, "sf");
        SF.setBounds( SFrect );
        SF.setSpeed(2,0);
        SF.start();
        }
    if( T == null || !T.isAlive()) {
        T = new Terrain(50,Trect,getGraphics());
        T.start();
        T.suspend();
        }
    if( user != null && user.isAlive() ) user.stop();
    user = new userSprite(everything, "user");
    user.setID( Sprite.USER );
```

```
user.setXY( 50, (int)(SFrect.height/2) );
user.im = createImage( user.WIDTH, user.HEIGHT );
user.setSpeed(0);
user.start();
}
```

Creating a Firing Mechanism

Whenever the user wants to "shoot" an answer, we need to create a bullet and send it hurtling toward its destination. To add a little intrigue to the scoring mechanism, we also dock the user one point for each bullet he or she fires. Here's the code for a method that creates a new bullet at a given X and Y coordinate:

```
public Sprite newBullet(int x, int y) {
Sprite b;
Rectangle temp = new Rectangle( x+user.bounds.width+5,
y+(int)(user.bounds.width/2), 15,3 );

        b = new Sprite(bullets,"bang");
        b.setBounds( temp );
        b.im = createImage(temp.width, temp.height);
        b.setSpeed(25,0);
        b.setID( Sprite.BULLET );
bar.addScore(-1);
return b;
}
```

A related method that is useful only for debugging purposes is one that allows you to fire bullets at any location with the mouse. This makes it easy to test different questions without actually having to play the game. Just remember to remove it in the final product!

```
public boolean mouseDown(Event evt, int x, int y) {
Sprite b= newBullet(user.x,user.y);
b.start();
return true;
}
```

Giving the User Control

We added one control for debugging purposes above, but let's also add the code that allows the player to move his or her ship around. First, we need to handle movement. This is accomplished with the numeric keypad. We use the numbers 1–9 to represent eight different directions that the user could travel in (N, W, S, E, NE, NW, SE, SW):

```
public boolean keyDown(Event evt, int key) {

switch( key ) {
```

continued on next page

continued from previous page

```
case '8': {
        user.move( user.x,user.y-5);
        return true;
        }

case '2': {
        user.move( user.x,user.y+5);
        return true;
        }

case '4': {
        user.move( user.x-5,user.y);
        return true;
        }
case '6': {
        user.move( user.x+5,user.y);
        return true;
        }
case '1': {
        user.move( user.x-5,user.y+5);
        return true;
        }
case '3': {
        user.move( user.x+5,user.y+5);
        return true;
        }
case '7': {
        user.move( user.x-5,user.y-5);
        return true;
        }
case '9': {
        user.move( user.x+5,user.y-5);
        return true;
        }


}
return false;
}
```

Next, we add handling to allow the user to fire a bullet:

```
case ' ': {
        Sprite b=newBullet(user.x,user.y);
        b.start();
        return true;
        }
```

We also add two keys that are useful for debugging but should be disabled in the final version. <P> and <R> are used to pause and resume the game. This can be easily accomplished by appropriate calls to the "everything" ThreadGroup:

```
case 'p' : {
     everything.suspend();
     return true;
     }
case 'r' : {
     everything.resume();
     return true;
     }
```

Last, we add one of WordQuest's neatest special effects: the warp factor. When the user holds down the <W> key, his or her ship kicks into warp mode, and everything flies past much faster. The StarField also makes a cool streaking effect. To do this, we must first have a keyDown event that turns on the warp effect:

```
case 'w': {
     Sprite.warp= 5;
     return true;
     }
```

This, however, requires a corresponding keyUp event that turns off the effect:

```
public boolean keyUp(Event evt, int key) {

switch(key) {

case 'w': {
     SPEED=1;
     Sprite.warp=1;
     return true;
     }
}
return false;
}
```

A Few Enhancements

Although WordQuest is practically finished, there is still one small matter that we have not resolved. We discussed earlier the idea of Thread *synchronization*. This is very important in Java, and is something worth discussing further. If you have played WordQuest at all, you will notice that although the enemy Sprites, being in the same group, run pretty much at the same rate, they are not totally synchronized. Some Sprites run faster, some slower, depending on how resources get allocated in each cycle. This effect is not visually appealing, so we need to come up with a way of having absolute synchronization among Sprites.

The key to synchronization is having each Sprite keep in touch with all of the other Sprites it needs to synchronize with. While there are many ways to accomplish this, we will explore one simple way. Once you understand the basic concept, it is trivial to extend it to more complicated examples.

The syncSprite Class

To achieve Thread synchronization among enemy Sprites, we are going to create a new subclass of Sprite, called syncSprite. Each syncSprite will not advance itself until all of the other syncSprites in its ThreadGroup have advanced. To do this, we use a counter variable. When each syncSprite finishes advancing, it increments this counter in every syncSprite in the Group. When the value of this counter reaches the number of syncSprites in the Group, it is reset and the process repeats. The syncSprite will not advance until this condition is met. The net result of all this inter-Thread communication is that no syncSprite can get more than one frame ahead or behind its siblings. The main drawback is that all syncSprites move as slowly as the one with the least amount of resources allocated to it. However, if all the syncSprites have the same priority level, this should not be much of a problem.

The code for this class is not very complicated once you understand the concepts involved. We use a simple integer as a counter, and we use a boolean flag to ensure that each Sprite gets run for the first frame (without this, if one Sprite advanced ahead of the others, their counters would be set to 1, and they would never advance). We also take advantage of the yield() method to give up the Sprite's time slice to another waiting Thread (most likely another syncSprite in the same Group).

```
import Sprite;
import java.lang.*;

public class syncSprite extends Sprite {
int count=0;
boolean flag=true;

syncSprite(ThreadGroup tg, String d) {
       super(tg,d);
       count=0;
       flag=true;
       DELAY=50;
}

public void run() {
       while(true) {
               try{ sleep(DELAY); } catch(Exception e);
//             paintSprite( theG );
               if( flag || count==0 || count >= getThreadGroup().activeCount() ) {
                       =0;
                       advance();
               flag = false;
               int i;
               syncSprite s[]= new syncSprite[i=getThreadGroup().activeCount()];
               enumerate(s);

               while(i-- > 0)
                       s[i].count++;
               } else
```

```
        yield();
        }
    }

}
```

To take advantage of this new class, we need to make only one change to WordQuest. In the nextQuestion() method, change the following line:

```
s = new Sprite( group, dataArray[x] );
```

to

```
s = new syncSprite( group, dataArray[x] );
```

That's All Folks!

Congratulations! WordQuest is totally functional now. Go ahead and compile it. Of course, you will need some questions to be in a data file called data.txt, in the same directory as your compiled class files. If you want, you can borrow some that I created that are on the CD-ROM that accompanies this book. They are mainly taken from preparatory material for the Scholastic Aptitude Test (SAT-1). Note that although WordQuest was designed for vocabulary training, it could easily be used for math or other subjects.

Beautiful Friend, the End

WordQuest is now ready to go! Compile it, play it, show it off to your friends. Who knows, you might even learn some new words!

Suggestion Box

There are many, many things you could do to make WordQuest even more fun. This list includes a few:

 Like any other game, WordQuest would benefit from some dazzling graphics or sound effects. Inserting these into the game is very easy, since we have already established methods and structures for handling arrays of Images designed to animate Sprites. Sounds would require a few lines of new code, but nothing tricky.

 Now that our enemy Sprites are synchronized, you could have them fly in formation. This would require having a method that was aware of different patterns that the Sprites could be staggered in, and that set them up in cool patterns. Because the Sprites are synchronized, they will maintain this pattern almost exactly.

Implement different levels. Although we have a variable in the status bar for "level," we never actually use it in WordQuest. You could have each level use a different set of questions, so that the game gets progressively more difficult. Or, perhaps the Sprites could move faster as levels increase. You make the call.

 Write the EXPLOSION Sprite! This is simply an array of Images that animate an explosion. Write a special explosionSprite class that displays itself and then stops; then write up a method in either Sprite or WordQuest itself that calls for an explosion to replace dead Sprites.

Summary

In this chapter, we created a nifty educational game while getting some practical experience with some Java concepts, like Thread synchronization. In addition, we combined many of the techniques learned throughout the book into an integrated gaming adventure. WordQuest is a formidable game in its own right, and it lays the foundation for many enjoyable action games to come. Education and action are both game genres with a considerable audience, and it is important for any game programmer to understand the underlying concepts that make both possible.

17

The Magic Squares Puzzle

Kyle Palmer

ome truove fare le manouelle e le quali prinderano i llalça
i grapeſi i nuovi lecomento e i gonoſſo ſa do grano de bono
e are nella moue ſa per moue tella della manouelle peʒi quo n
forʒa e peʒo i ſomo pro boue

17

The Magic Squares Puzzle

The applet developed in this chapter takes the form of a deceptively simple, yet challenging puzzle game. The game consists of nothing more than a grid of variously colored squares, which change color in a seemingly random way when you click on them. The goal is to discover the pattern that the colors follow, and deduce the correct squares to click on to make the entire grid the same color. The difficulty of the puzzle can be changed in order for it to always remain challenging. This is a game for the kind of puzzle lovers who could spend hours twisting Rubik's Cubes. Although this game is simple, it uses Java features such as multiple classes, threaded classes, and GUI components, and is therefore a good example of effectively using the power of Java to create an elegant program.

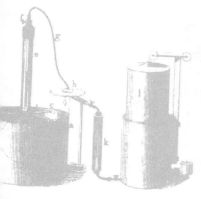

Playing Magic Squares

Playing this game is similar to most puzzle games, in that it is simple and easy to learn. Figure 17-1 shows the layout of the applet on the HTML page. The grid of squares at the top is what the user clicks on to play the game. Clicking on this grid causes the squares to begin a color-cycling routine.

Rules of the Game

When a square is clicked on, that square and its neighbors above, below, to the right, and to the left are cycled forward one color. Thus, if a square being cycled is at color one, it becomes color two. Colors are cycled in this manner, and return to color one if an attempt is made to cycle past their maximum color value. If a neighbor does not exist because of the grid boundary, that neighbor is ignored.

The color cycling makes it difficult for a player to follow the color rotation, which in turn creates the challenge of this game.

Below the game board are various buttons that control the difficulty of the game. With these buttons, you can increase or decrease the number of colors that are possible. You can also change the number of squares in the grid. Below these are the Solve and Restore buttons. The Solve button will cause the applet to save the current state of the puzzle and to begin solving the puzzle in the background. The Restore button restores the state

FIGURE 17-1

⊚ ⊚ ⊚ ⊚ ⊚ ⊚

The Magic Squares applet running

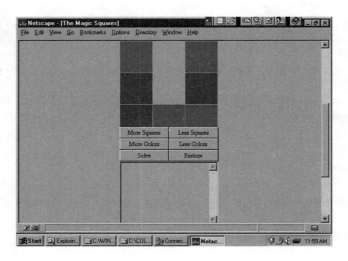

of the puzzle to the time that it was saved. This allows the puzzle to be worked on while the solve algorithm is running, and provides the option of returning to the puzzle once the solve has finished.

This solve algorithm is mostly academic and cannot handle boards much more complex than nine squares with two or three colors; however, Java's implementation of classes would make it easy to change the solve algorithm if a better method of doing so were found. The information on the status of the solve is displayed in a text window below the buttons to let the player know whether a solution has been found, what the solution is, and how many boards have been checked in finding the solution.

The Classes

When I was first introduced to object-oriented programming, (C++ at the time), my professor told us that to figure out what classes we needed, we should express the intended product in a sentence and make an object for every noun. I used this idea to write the Magic Squares applet, with the modification of adding verbs to the list of objects to make use of the multithreading capabilities of Java.

The game is basically an applet in which the player makes moves on a board, and can request that the computer perform a solve. The sentence we are working on here logically breaks down into three classes:

- A class to provide a game board
- An *Applet* class to handle the input and display the board
- A class that extends Thread to provide a background solve

The *solver* class is the only threaded class in the game, and its threaded nature allows it to be run in the background while the user continues clicking away. The *solver* class and the *Applet* class both depend heavily on the data and methods provided by the board class. We will discuss this board class first.

The game_board Class

In order to completely encapsulate the game board, I had to store all data that would be necessary in the class (see Listing 17-1 and Figure 17-2), and ensure that any method that would ever have to be done on a board is provided by the class itself. This encapsulation reduces the code necessary by calling methods, and makes everything easy to understand. This allows the rest of the applet to tell the board what to do to itself, and then have the board do its own operations.

Listing 17-1 *The data defined in the game_board class*

```
class game_board {  //the board class to hold and manipulate a board
  int board[][];   //the 2D array to hold the board itself
  int side_squares; //to store the number of squares to a side
  int max_color; //store the maximum color of a square
  int side_length;  //the length of one side
```

The class begins by defining all of the data it uses both internally and externally, that is, by the outside world. The two-dimensional array *board* contains the actual state of the board. The board is stored in the rows and columns of this array in integers, representing the color of the square. The integer *side_squares* indicates how many squares compose one side of the board. The board is always a square, so only one number is needed to represent its dimensions. The *max_color* integer stores the maximum color that a square can assume. This number is used when color cycling takes place, in that if a cycling pushes a square past this color, the square is reset to color zero. The final data item *side_length* is important in drawing the board onto the screen. This value indicates how many pixels should be drawn per side. The size of each square is calculated using this value and the value of *side_squares* to fit the board into the required space.

FIGURE 17-2

The game_board class does most operations on itself

The game_board Class Constructors

Two constructors are implemented for the game_board class (see Listing 17-2) to act in different situations.

 The first constructor creates a board from given parameters and is used primarily when the applet is initialized, as illustrated later. This constructor allocates the memory for the board and sets the number of colors and the dimensions of the board, allowing for a board to be created to exact specifications.

 The second constructor is used, in most cases, to create a game_board exactly like an existing board. This one behaves exactly as the other constructor does; however, it gets the parameters from the existing *game_board source*. The colors to be stored in the *board* array are then copied from the source by the local copy_board() method.

Listing 17-2 *The constructors for the game_board class*

```
game_board(int squares,int side_pixels,int colors){ //constructor
   board = new int[squares][squares]; //get the data for the board
   side_squares = squares;  //save the size of the board
   side_length = side_pixels;  //save the size in pixels of the board
   max_color = colors - 1;  //-1 because colors start at zero
}

game_board(game_board source){ //a copying constructor
   board = new int[source.side_squares][source.side_squares];
   side_squares = source.side_squares; //save the number of squares to
side
   max_color = source.max_color;      //save the maximum color
   side_length = source.side_length; //save the length in pixels
   copy_board(source);      //copy over the board data
}
```

The randomize() Method

The public method randomize() fulfills the role of randomizing an existing board. It simply goes through each square and uses a Random object to determine its color from zero to the maximum color allowed. The case of the color being returned negative has to be taken care of, because the Java modulo (%) operator returns a positive or negative value based on the dividend. Individuals with a mathematics background will realize that this does not make a great deal of sense, but it is that way nonetheless. The randomize() method is given in Listing 17-3.

Listing 17-3 *The randomize() method*

```
public void randomize(){ //randomize the board
  Random num_gen = new Random(); //random number generator
  int i,j;

  for (i=0;i<side_squares;i++)
    for (j=0;j<side_squares;j++){
      board[i][j]=(num_gen.nextInt()%(max_color+1));
      if (board[i][j] < 0)
    board[i][j]*=-1;
    }
}
```

Three Methods Used to Apply a Move to the Board

The following three methods listed and described are responsible for acting on a mouse click, and are what the calling program will use whenever it has to change the state of the board for any reason.

The increment_square() Method

The increment_square() method (Listing 17-4) is responsible for the lowest level of board manipulation. Given an x and y coordinate of a square in the array, it increases the color value of this square by one and checks whether it is greater than the maximum color allowed, in which case the square's color is set to zero. This method does nothing if the square passed to it is out of bounds given the size of the board, and this simplifies the procedures that call this method.

Listing 17-4 *The increment_square() method*

```
public  void increment_square (int x1,int y1){  //increments this square
  if (x1<0 || x1 > side_squares -1 || y1 <0 || y1 > side_squares-1)
    return;                       //return if not a valid square
  else{                           //otherwise increment the square
    board[x1][y1]++;
    if (board[x1][y1]>max_color)
    board[x1][y1] = 0;
  }
 }
```

The apply_move_s() and apply_move_p() Methods

The apply_move_s() and apply_move_p() are the brains of the board and actually apply the move. Both these methods perform the same task: to take in the coordinates of a square and apply the appropriate move to them. However, this action comes in two flavors:

The method apply_move_s() (Listing 17-5) takes in the absolute coordinates of a square in the grid. Thus, these parameters can be used to directly call increment_square() on the given squares and the four squares around it. The increment_square() method performs all out of bounds checking, so this method can blindly call increment_square() on all of the necessary squares whether they exist or not.

Listing 17-5 The apply_move_s() method

```
public  void apply_move_s (int x,int y){  //what to do on a click,takes
squares
  //first convert from pixels to squares

  //now increment the appropriate squares
  increment_square(x,y);       //invalid squares handled in increment_square
  increment_square(x-1,y);
  increment_square(x+1,y);
  increment_square(x,y-1);
  increment_square(x,y+1);
}
```

 The apply_move_p() method (Listing 17-6) takes in the coordinate as pixel values relative to the top-right-hand corner of the board. These coordinates are translated into a square, and apply_move_s() is called to make the move.

Listing 17-6 The apply_move_p() method

```
public void apply_move_p(int xpix,int ypix){ //apply click, takes pixels
  int x,y;

  if (xpix>side_length || ypix >side_length) //only take valid moves
    return;

  x = xpix/((int)(side_length/side_squares)); //convert pixels to loca-
tion
  y = ypix/((int)(side_length/side_squares));

  apply_move_s(x,y);  //call the square version of apply_move
}
```

In the true spirit of object-oriented programming, the two methods apply_move_s() and apply_move_p() should have been overloaded into one method name. They have not been, because they both take the same types of parameters: two integers. For this reason, overloading cannot be used here.

Now that moves can be made, all that is really essential is to be able to draw the board onto the screen, as shown in Listing 17-7.

Listing 17-7 *The game_board methods to draw the board onto the screen*

```
public void draw_board(int x,int y,Graphics g){ //draws the board
  int i,j;

  //now fill the squares
  for (i=0;i<side_squares;i++)
    for (j=0;j<side_squares;j++)
      fill_square(x+i,y+j,g);   //fill in all the appropriate squares
}


public void fill_square(int x1,int y1,Graphics g){//fills the square based
  int x,y,side;  //the x and coordinates, and the length of the square

  //set appropriate colors

  if (board[x1][y1]==0)
    g.setColor(Color.lightGray);
  else if (board[x1][y1]==1)
    g.setColor(Color.red);
  else if (board[x1][y1]==2)
    g.setColor(Color.blue);
  else if (board[x1][y1]==3)
    g.setColor(Color.green);
  else if (board[x1][y1]==4)
    g.setColor(Color.pink);
  else if (board[x1][y1]==5)
    g.setColor(Color.yellow);


  x = x1 * (int)(side_length/side_squares)+1;  //calculate the x and y
  y = y1 * (int)(side_length/side_squares)+1;

  side = (int)(side_length/side_squares)-1;  //offset 1, leave outline
  g.fillRect(x,y,side,side); //fill the rectangle
}
```

These two methods, draw_board() and fill_square(), are all that is necessary to draw the board onto the screen. The basic method is simply to loop through all the squares and draw them to the screen in their appropriate location.

The draw_board() Method

The first method, draw_board(), is all that the outside world really needs to see to draw the whole board. One call to this high-level method will cause one call to fill_square() for each square on the board. The draw_board() method is passed an (x,y) coordinate pair though two integers and a Graphics on which to draw the square. The x and y coordinates specify where the upper-right-hand corner of the board should be placed on the Graphics, and the Graphics is passed so that the routine can place the board on any surface necessary. draw_board() then calls fill_square() for each square and passes the indices of the square, plus the coordinates of the board. In this way, the coordinates of the board act as an offset for each square's position, which places each square in its appropriate position on the Graphics.

The fill_square() Method

The fill_square() method performs the translation of a given square to its actual location on the given Graphics, and draws it accordingly. The color value is retrieved by comparing the square's color number to six possible colors, and the corresponding one is chosen. The Graphics position of the upper-right-hand corner is then determined by using the length of a side and the number of squares to a side, and the square is drawn. Since the square's size and location on the Graphics is calculated each time instead of being hard-coded, the size and number of squares in the board can be any number, and the draw_square() and draw_board() routines will work just as well.

Only two more methods are needed to make the functional board class. It becomes necessary in the game to be able to copy boards simply, and the solve requires a method for determining whether a board is in a solved state or not.

The copy_board() Method

The copy_board() method (shown in Listing 17-8) simply copies the value of each square over to the destination board.

Listing 17-8 *The copy_board() method*

```
public boolean copy_board(game_board source){ //copy in a board
  if (source.side_squares != side_squares)  //if boards are not the same
                                            //size
    return false;              //return that couldn't complete

  int i,j;

  for (i=0;i<side_squares;i++)
    for (j=0;j<side_squares;j++)
      board[i][j] = source.board[i][j];  //copy over every square

  return true;   //everything succeeded
}
```

The is_completed() Method

This final board method, is_completed(), is a necessary method in order for the solve to operate. As might be expected, it returns a boolean value, indicating whether the board is completed or not. Since a completed board occurs when all of the squares are the same color, such a board can be tested for easily. The method merely gets the color in location (0,0) and compares this with all of the other squares. As soon as a square with a different color is found, the method knows that all the squares cannot be the same color, and the method returns *false*. If no such square is found, the routine returns *true* by default, and the calling method can be sure that the board is all one color. This method is shown in Listing 17-9.

Listing 17-9 *The is_completed() method*

```
public boolean is_completed(){ //return if this is a solved board
  int color;
  int i,j;

  color = board[0][0];  //compare this color with all others

  for (i=0;i<side_squares;i++) //go through, checking for if color not
same
    for(j=0;j<side_squares;j++)
      if (board[i][j] != color)
    return false;

  return true;
}

}
```

The squares Class

With a solid, fully functioning board class, the main Applet class, *squares*, doesn't have much work to do. All that the *squares* class (given in Listing 17-10) really does is check for mouse clicks, button pushes, and call board methods accordingly. Since this game does very little work and only responds to mouse clicks from the player, the whole functionality of the game has been built into the event handling methods. This is a nice feature in that the game uses very little CPU time, and allows more time to be given to the background solve.

The class extends Java.applet.Applet because my intention in writing this program was to have it available on the Web. It can be run as an application through the appletviewer, or a main() method could be added to make it an application if you don't want to fire up your Web browser every time you want to play.

Listing 17-10 *The data defined in the squares class*

```
public class squares extends Java.applet.Applet {
  int squares;  //the number of squares to a side
  int length;   //the length of one side
  int colors;   //the current number of colors working with
  game_board main_board;  //the main board to play with
  game_board save_board;  //a board to save when solving
  Panel buttons;  //the panel for the buttons
  TextArea solve_area;  //a text area to put the solve status on
  Panel main_panel;  //a main panel to put buttons and textarea on
  solver solve_thread;
```

The above code is documented quite well to show the function of each variable in the applet. The dimensions and maximum number of colors of the current board are stored, and two game_boards are used in the game. The Panels are used to display the buttons, and the TextArea is used by the solve to display information about the status of the solve. The final item, *solve_thread*, is a member of the *solver* class, which is used to perform the solving of a board.

The init() Method

The first method to look at is the init() method, which is given in Listing 17-11. This method sets up all of the starting characteristics of the game, places all of the *buttons* and the TextArea on the screen, and allocates the memory for the game_boards to be used.

Listing 17-11 *The init() method*

```
public void init(){  //initialize this applet

    squares = 3;      //start with 3 squares to a side
    length = 350;     //start with 100 pixels to a side
    colors = 2;       //start with two colors
    main_board = new game_board(squares,length,colors); //create the board
    main_board.randomize();  //randomize the board

    //set up the panels, is simple, so not given own class

    setLayout(new BorderLayout()); //set the layout

    main_panel = new Panel();  //get the main panel

    main_panel.setLayout(new BorderLayout()); //want a border layout on main

    buttons = new Panel();  //create the panel
    buttons.setLayout(new GridLayout(3,2));  //arrange buttons in a grid
    buttons.add(new Button("More Squares")); //add the buttons
    buttons.add(new Button("Less Squares"));
    buttons.add(new Button("More Colors"));
    buttons.add(new Button("Less Colors"));
    buttons.add(new Button("Solve"));
    buttons.add(new Button("Restore"));

    solve_area = new TextArea(8,25);  //create the window for solve text
    solve_area.setEditable(false); //don't want to edit this

    main_panel.add("North",buttons); //add the button panel to top
    main_panel.add("South",solve_area); //add the panel to the main panel

    add("South",main_panel);  //add buttons and window to screen
}
```

The game starts out with a board with nine squares on it, and has only two colors. A new game_board is created to those specifications, and is randomized by calling the randomize() method in order for each game to start differently. The rest of the init() method sets up the buttons and the TextArea on the screen using Panels. It is laid out with two Panels. The Panel that is placed on the screen, *main_panel*, uses the BorderLayout layout manager so that the buttons and the TextArea are equally spaced. The six Buttons relating to the size and number of colors and the actions of solving and restoring boards are first placed on their own Panel with the GridLayout, so that they are stuck together in a grid. The Panel containing these buttons is then placed on the top of the *main_panel*. The *main_panel* is finally added to the bottom of the screen to give the look that appears in Figure 17-1.

The paint() Method

The paint() method (Listing 17-12) is very simple and could be improved upon. It merely redraws the entire board, which, although slow and flickery, is a lot simpler than keeping track of which squares need to be redrawn.

Listing 17-12 *The paint() method*

```
public void paint (Graphics g){ //just draw the board to repaint
  main_board.draw_board(0,0,g); //draw the board at 0,0
}
```

The mouseDown() Method

The simplicity of the mouseDown() method (Listing 17-13), which is called most frequently over the course of a game, comes from the modularity of the game_board class. All that has to be done on a mouse click is to tell the board to apply the move, and then repaint the screen, which will redraw the board.

Listing 17-13 *The mouseDown() event handler*

```
public boolean mouseDown (Event ent,int x,int y){ //handle mouse click
  main_board.apply_move_p(x,y); //apply the move
  repaint();  //redraw the board
  return true;
}
```

The action() Method

The action() Method is given in Listing 17-14 and diagrammed visually in Figure 17-3. I use this method to trap all of the input events that occur when the player clicks on buttons to modify the game or to start or restore from a solve. It begins by converting the *Object* parameter into a string so that its name can be compared with the names of the buttons that have been defined. This allows the method to determine which button has been pressed by using a simple comparison by way of the *Equals* method of the

String class. If the solve button has been pressed, the thread for the solve is stopped if it is active and a new instance of the *solver* class is allocated and started. The current board is also saved in *save_board* to be restored later, and the method *returns* from there. The saved board is restored when the Restore button is called, in which case the old *main_board* is replaced by the saved version. If there has been no board saved, nothing is done, and the method ends. For the buttons pertaining to the number of colors and number of squares, the variable that stores the number of squares or colors is incremented and decremented as necessary, checked for limits, and a new board is created with the new specification.

Listing 17-14 *The action() event handler*

```
public boolean action (Event evt, Object arg){ //process buttons
  String label = (String)arg;  //converts the button to a string
  if (label.equals("Solve")) { //if request to start solving the board
    if (solve_thread != null){ //potentially running solve
      solve_thread.stop();  //stop the thread
      solve_thread = null;  //allow garbage collecting
    }
    save_board = new game_board(main_board);  //save the board

    solve_thread = new solver(main_board,solve_area); //create the solver
    solve_thread.setPriority(Thread.MIN_PRIORITY); //lower priority
    solve_thread.start();                    //start solving in background
    return true;
  }
  if (label.equals("Restore")){ //restore the board to when started solve
    if (save_board == null) //don't do anything if no board saved
      return true;

    main_board = new game_board(save_board); //otherwise create a new
                                             //board
    repaint();
    return true;     //return here so we don't randomize

  }

  if (label.equals("More Colors")){ //if request for more colors
    colors ++;
  }
  else if (label.equals("Less Colors")){
    colors --;
  }
  else if (label.equals("More Squares")){
    squares += 2;
  }
  else if (label.equals("Less Squares")){
    squares -= 2;
  }
```

continued on next page

continued from previous page

```
        if (squares > 35)   //max 35x35 squares
          squares = 35;
        if (squares < 3)
          squares = 3;
        if (colors > 5)   //maximum 5 colors
          colors = 5;
        if (colors < 2)   //at least two colors
          colors = 2;

        main_board = new game_board(squares,length,colors); //create new board
        main_board.randomize();  //randomize the new game board

        repaint();  //copy new board to screen
        return true;
      }
```

FIGURE 17-3

◉ ◉ ◉ ◉ ◉ ◉

*The inner
workings of the
action() method*

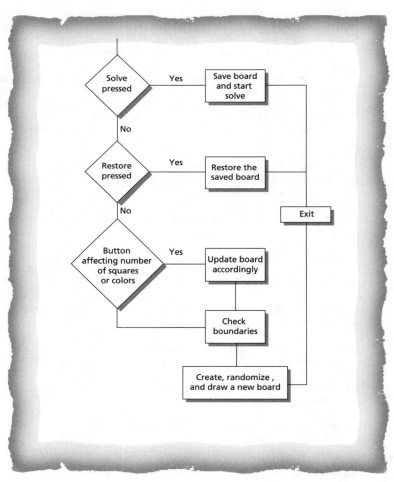

Buttons

On a press of the solve Button, any thread that is working on a solve is stopped to allow for a new thread to be started on the current board. The board that is being solved is saved in *save_board* so that it can be restored later if the user wants to try out the solve. The board can then be restored by clicking on the restore Button, which merely loads in the new board, draws this board, and returns.

The Buttons pertaining to the number of squares and colors on a board are straightforward in that they modify the global variables that hold the attributes for the current board, so that they can be applied at the end of the method. At the end of the method, the attribute bounds are checked and applied, and the board is randomized and redrawn.

The solver Class

The *solver* class (see Listing 17-15) is the most interesting class in this otherwise elementary puzzle game. The techniques involved in solving this puzzle can be applied to almost any puzzle or board game from tic-tac-toe to chess (to a limited extent), and although inefficient, it is an important concept that should be understood. The solve algorithm is very simple to understand if you leave the implementation details aside and just look at it logically.

The Basic Idea Behind the Solve Algorithm

To discover how to get from any board to a finished state, you simply have to try every combination of moves from the starting board until you find one that makes all of the squares the same color.

This technique used by the solve algorithm is known as an exhaustive search in computing science terms and is aptly named. It is as inefficient, as you might think, but it should also be clear that it would work in any case given enough time, if the board can be solved. Anyone who was very meticulous could even employ this method manually and be guaranteed to always succeed, although maybe not in the person's lifetime.

Unfortunately, even with today's fast computers, this method is not really very practical. In fact, I've never been able to solve a board with more than nine squares using the solver class, but I am currently trying to look at the problem from different angles to see if a better method exists. One nice feature of the solve algorithm is that it always finds the shortest, or one of the shortest, possible sequences of moves to solve the puzzle. This stems from the fact that the solve routine first looks for a solve of one move, then two moves, then three, and so on until one is found, or until a preset maximum depth has been hit. This will be discussed as it is seen in the run() method.

Listing 17-15 *The data items defined in the solver class*

```
class solver extends Thread{ //a class to solve a board,run in background
  game_board start_board; //the board to start from
  TextArea solve_window; //The textarea to put the solve info into
  int max_depth = 12;  //the maximum depth to probe to
  int current_depth = 1; //current depth in the solve
  int visited = 0;  //the number of boards that have been visited
  int solved[][] = new int[max_depth+1][2]; //hold the moves
```

The commented code in Listing 17-15 speaks for itself and contains all of the global variables necessary for the solver to operate. The *start_board* initially has the same state as the board to solve and is modified to test the results of different combinations of moves. The *solve_window* is a TextArea supplied by the calling method to tell the class where to place its text output. The remaining variables serve to store information about the current state of the solve at any given time.

The solver Class Constructor

This class employs only one constructor (given in Listing 17-16), which takes and stores its parameters. These parameters direct the class where to put the text information and what board configuration to solve for. The modularity of the game_board class and the presence of a copying constructor makes this method very simple.

Listing 17-16 *The constuctor for the solver class*

```
solver (game_board board,TextArea t){ //thread constructor
  start_board = new game_board(board);  //create and copy new board
  solve_window = t;   //get the textarea to write to
}
```

The solver Class run() Method

The run() method for this class (shown in Listing 17-17) acts mostly as a driver for the try_all_squares() method. From the run() method's perspective, the try_all_squares() method returns *true* if a board solution can be found within *i* moves. The run method thus tests try_all_squares() with integers increasing from one to a set maximum value to make sure that the shortest solve is found. If a path is found, the loop is broken and the thread stops.

Listing 17-17 *The run() method for the solver class*

```
public void run(){  //The thread's run method, what to do on start
  int i;

  visited = 0;
  solve_window.appendText("Beginning solve.\n");  //little greeting
```

```
for (i=1;i<=max_depth;i++){ //go through each depth of search
  solve_window.appendText("Attempting depth search of "+i+"\n");
  if (try_all_squares(i) == true){   /*try every position from here*/
    break;
  }
  solve_window.appendText("No solution found in "+visited+" boards.\n");
}
solve_window.appendText("Done solving\n");

}
```

The try_all_squares() Method

The run() method behaves without any concern for the implementation of try_all_squares(), which is important so that another implementation could be quickly integrated if a better one were found. Before looking at the current try_all_squares() method, some discussion of how it works is in order. The try_all_squares() method is recursive and brings all of the headaches that come with trying to understand any recursive method. For people who have managed to avoid using recursion, a recursive method is a method that calls itself. This would lead to infinite cycles and the like except that a check called "the basis" is put in the method to make it terminate on some condition. Recursion is seen in things like maze searching, tree traversals, and the solve routine for simple puzzles like the Towers of Hanoi and this one. The algorithm for the solve without the recursion looks like Listing 17-18.

Listing 17-18 *The algorithm for the try_all_squares() method without the recursion*

```
starting with the board you want to solve

  Make the first move. (ie. click on square one)
  Check if this move completed the board
      if so, quit
  If not, take back the move and try the next move in the sequence
```

If the algorithm in Listing 17-18 were implemented, it would successfully check to determine whether there were any one move that would solve the puzzle. Unfortunately, that would not solve any general puzzle, and most one-move puzzles could be solved by hand anyway. This is where the power of recursion comes in. To complete the algorithm, one extra step is needed. Instead of just checking whether the move solved the board, the try_all_squares() method is applied to the board after the move has been made, to try all of the possible moves one board away from that. In this way, a tree structure of calls is made that systematically tries all possible moves.

What keeps this calling from infinitely occurring is the parameter *depth*. In each recursive call, the current depth is compared with *depth*, and the method terminates if the calls become too deep. Thus, if try_all_squares() is called with *depth* being three, the moves demonstrated in Figure 17-4 and Listing 17-19 would be made.

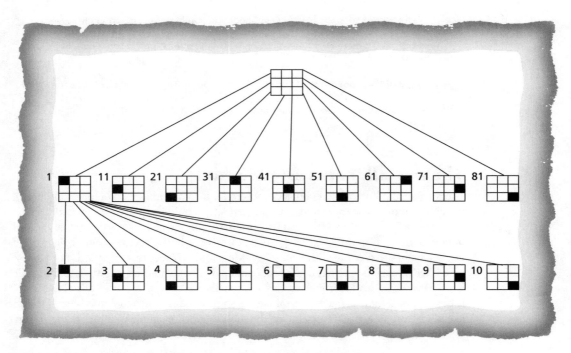

FIGURE 17-4 ◉ *The first few moves of a solve with depth of 3*

Listing 17-19 *The try_all_squares() method*

```
public boolean try_all_squares(int depth){ //do a board search of depth
                                           //depth
  int i,j,k,l,m;  //counter variables

  i=j=0;

  if (start_board.is_completed()){ //start off the bat checking if
completed
    print_solution();
    return true;
  }

  if (current_depth > depth)  //basis, don't recurse too far
    return false;             //return didn't find anything


   try {
    this.sleep(7);  //Brief sleep to appease netscape
   } catch (InterruptedException e){}
```

```
for (i=0;i<start_board.side_squares;i++) //go through each possible move
  for (j=0;j<start_board.side_squares;j++){
    start_board.apply_move_s(i,j);  //apply the current move
    solved[current_depth][0]=i; //save the current move on solved stack
    solved[current_depth][1]=j;

    if (is_repeat()){  //if this move would be a repeated move
      start_board.undo_move(i,j);  //undo the last move so can resume
      continue;        //skip this move, should have some savings
    }
    visited++;  //count the number of boards seen


    if (start_board.is_completed()){ //if this move completed the board
      print_solution();  //print out the solution
      return true;
    }

    else { //didn't solve the board with this move

      current_depth++;            //go to next depth
      if (try_all_squares(depth)==true) //if next depth found a solution
        return true;                //then done, return
      else
        current_depth--;    //come back to this depth and try another

    }
    start_board.undo_move(i,j);  //undo the last move so can continue
  }
  start_board.undo_move(i,j); //restore the board
  return false;
}
```

After the declaration and initialization of the local variables, this method starts by checking whether or not the board has been completed. This line is really only important if the *solver* class is called to solve a board that is already in a solved state. If the board has been completed, print_solution() is called to print out the solution, which in this case would only indicate that the board is already solved. The next *if* statement checks to see whether the depth boundary has been crossed, and returns if the recursion has gone too deep. The thread is then told to sleep for a short time to free up some CPU cycles, as the solve tends to require a lot of CPU resources. The huge nested loops that follow do the work of the method by looping the row and column through all of the squares on the board. The inner code is thus executed once for each square. The loop follows the series of steps given in Listing 17-20.

Listing 17-20 *The algorithm for the main loop of the try_all_squares() method*

```
for each possible move
   apply the move
   store the move in the array of moves made to get to this position
   If the move is redundant, undo the move and continue
   count the move
   if this move completed the board
      print the solution and return true
   else
      increase the depth by one
      if try_all_squares finds a solution with this modified board
         return true
      else
         decrease the depth back to this level
   undo the move
   continue
```

This sequence will systematically check every possible sequence up to the specified depth of recursion. If the loop exists normally, then a solution has not been found and the method returns *false*. If a solution has been found, the moves to solve the board will be saved in the *solved* array. This array acts like a stack, saving each move at depth *I* in locations *solved[i][0]* and *solved[i][2]* for the x and y coordinates, respectively. Figure 17-5 shows the contents of a typical *solved* array.

FIGURE 17-5

◉ ◉ ◉ ◉ ◉ ◉

The contents of a typical solved *array*

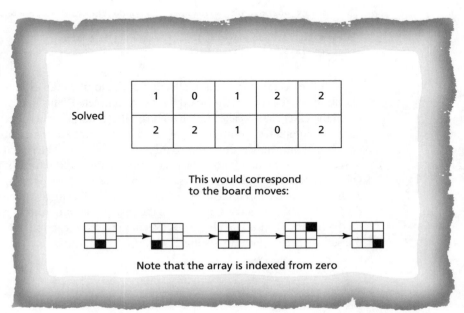

The print_solution() Method

When the try_all_squares() method has found a set of moves that solve the board, the moves are stored in the *solved* array from one to the depth of the solve, which will be stored in *current_depth*. The print_solution() method (Listing 17-21) prints out these values as coordinates so that the user can try out the solve. Figure 17-6 shows the results of a typical solve.

Listing 17-21 *The print_solution() method*

```java
public void print_solution(){ //print out the found solution
   int m;

   solve_window.appendText("Board solution found after "+visited+"
boards.");
   solve_window.appendText("\nMoves are:\n");


   if (current_depth >= 1 && visited > 0) //if actually had to make a move
      for (m=1;m<=current_depth;m++)  //print out each stored move
         solve_window.appendText((solved[m][0]+1) +"," +⇐
(solved[m][1]+1)+"\n");
      else  //didn't have to make a move
         solve_window.appendText("Board already solved.\n");
}
```

FIGURE 17-6

◉ ◉ ◉ ◉ ◉ ◉

The results of a typical solve

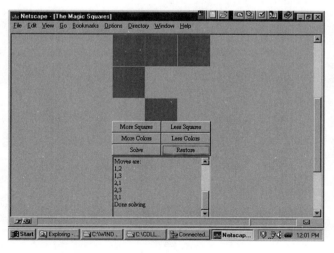

The is_repeat() Method

The is_repeat() method (Listing 17-22) is by no means a necessary method for the solve to operate, but it does make it slightly more efficient. When playing with the puzzle, it becomes noticeable that if you click on the same square enough times, the puzzle will eventually cycle back to its original state. The phenomenon can be seen in Figure 17-7.

Listing 17-22 *The is_repeat() method*

```
public boolean is_repeat(){ //finds redundant repeats
  int tx,ty,j;
  int count=0;                   //holds the number of repeated

  if (current_depth < start_board.max_color+1) //if not deep enough
    return false;  //there could not possibly be a repeat

  tx = solved[current_depth][0];  //get the last move made
  ty = solved[current_depth][1];

  j = current_depth;   //count down from the current depth

  while ((tx == solved[j][0]) && (ty == solved[j][1]) && j >= 1){
    count++;       //count the repeat
    j--;           //go back one depth
  }
  return (count >= start_board.max_color+1);//return if redundant
}

}
```

FIGURE 17-7

⊙ ⊙ ⊙ ⊙ ⊙ ⊙

A cycle formed by repetitively clicking on the same square

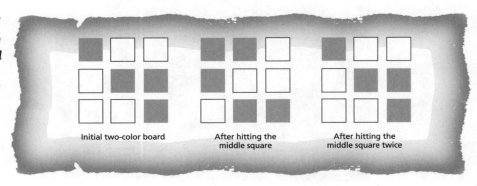

Initial two-color board

After hitting the middle square

After hitting the middle square twice

The *solver* class takes advantage of this by looking at the moves that have been made and doesn't consider sequences that have these repeats. This has the advantage of saving not only the board check for that move, but also for all of the recursive calls that would have resulted from that board. This is known as "pruning the tree" that results from the recursion. is_repeat() finds these cycles by checking whether a move has been repeated the same number of times as there are colors, which is the condition that causes a cycle. This will never result in a missed solution because if there is a solution involving that cycle, there is a shorter solution starting from the repeated move in the cycle.

The undo_move() Method

The undo_move() method (Listing 17-23) uses the same principle of repeating moves as the is_repeat() method, except in this case the idea is employed to undo a move. Assuming that the move passed to undo_move() has already been made, it can be undone by repeating the same move once for each possible color. This method is more efficient than saving and restoring whole boards to back up in the solve, but it gets less efficient as the numbers of colors in the board increases. It benefits mostly from the fact that no extra memory is needed to save the state of past boards; only the moves to get that board from the original need be saved.

Listing 17-23 *The undo_move() method*

```
public void undo_move(int x,int y){ //undoes a given move
  int i;

  for (i=0;i<max_color;i++)  //apply the same move once for each color-1
    apply_move_s(x,y);
}
```

Suggestion Box

The academic nature of this game, combined with its encapsulation into the *game_board* class, creates some possiblities for enhancements and variations. Here are some suggestions.

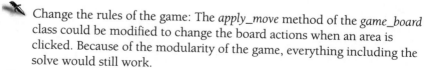

Change the rules of the game: The *apply_move* method of the *game_board* class could be modified to change the board actions when an area is clicked. Because of the modularity of the game, everything including the solve would still work.

Modify the *solver* class: The exhaustive search used is by no means efficient, and there is bound to be a better way. Figuring out new algorithms can be quite challenging and fullfilling (however, implementing them is another story).

Use the board elsewhere: Want an interesting front page for your Web site that only allows access to those who deserve it? Integrate the game into a password scheme and watch your hit count decrease.

Expand on the techniques presented: There is a whole world of computing science problems out there just waiting to be solved. Try using the exhaustive search method elsewhere, such as in writing a tic-tac-toe game or something similar.

Summary

That's the Magic Squares game. It is an example of a simple puzzle game implemented mostly through event handling, but makes good use of multiple classes and has a background thread thrown in for fun. The *game_board* class encapsulates all the data and actions pertaining to a board complete with high level methods for applying moves and for drawing the board. The *solver* class demonstrates an exhaustive search approach to solving problems and shows the power that a multithreaded language like Java can provide. It is not a very complex game, but I think there's always room for academic games like these to challenge puzzle lovers.

18

The Internet Mah Jong Server

Zuwei Thomas Feng

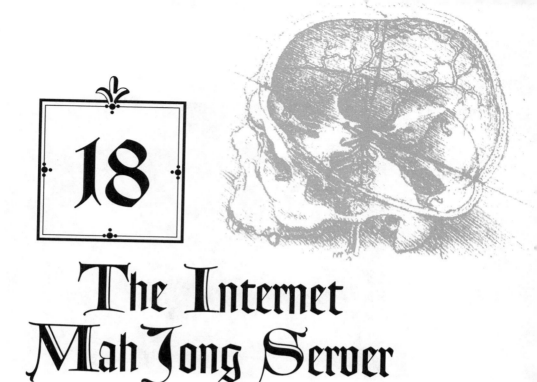

18

The Internet MahJong Server

MahJong is an ancient Chinese game of strategy and luck. It is very popular in East Asian countries, and is attracting many American players as well. It is similar to some card games, except that it is played with tiles instead of cards. In a typical game, players take turns playing and try to win by arranging their tiles into certain "MahJong" patterns.

My Internet MahJong Server is a software package that allows people to play MahJong with each other online. The concept is not new; there are such servers for games like chess, bridge, Go, and so on, and even a text-based package for MahJong exists. What makes my program unique is that it's written entirely in Java. It comes with a graphical user interface (GUI), and is portable. The biggest advantage, as far as players are concerned, is that they can use any Java-capable Web browser and don't need to compile or install a special client program. Figure 18-1 shows a screenshot of a typical session on the server.

FIGURE 18-1

◎ ◎ ◎ ◎ ◎ ◎

*A typical
session on the
MahJong server*

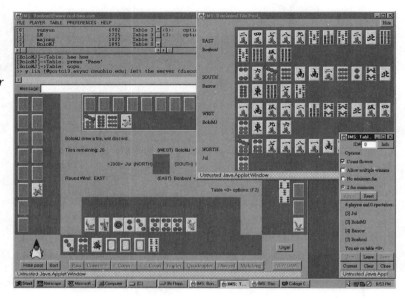

In this chapter, I will lead you through the design and implementation of my programs step by step. There is really nothing special about MahJong here; the same principles
apply to other multiplayer games as well.

A Brief Introduction to MahJong

MahJong has very complicated rules. What I will attempt to give here is a minimal version that suffices for playing online. For more complete rules, the reader is referred to
standard textbooks on MahJong.

Game Pieces and Components

The game is played with a total of 144 tiles, which can be arranged into three categories.
First, there are three *suits*: the *characters*, the *balls*, and the *bamboos*, each suit containing the values 1 to 9 and four tiles for each value. Then there are seven kinds of *honor*
tiles (four *winds* and three *dragons*,) again with four tiles for each kind. Finally, there are
eight distinct *flower* tiles.

A number of tiles can form a *set*. There are three types of sets in MahJong. A *chow*
(or connection, sequence) is a set of three tiles in the same suit with consecutive values. A *pong* (or triplet) is a set of three identical tiles. And finally, a *gong* (quadruplet)
is a set of four identical tiles. There is also the notion of a *pair*, which obviously consists of two identical tiles. A *MahJong pattern* consists of four sets and one pair, plus any
number of flower tiles. Thus, there are 14 or more tiles, depending on the number of
gongs and flower tiles. See Figure 18-2 for details.

FIGURE 18-2

◎ ◎ ◎ ◎ ◎ ◎

MahJong tiles and patterns

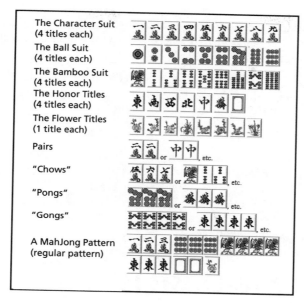

Rules of Play

Typically, four players are involved in a MahJong game. All the tiles are made into a stock-pile, and each player initially draws 13 tiles from it to form a concealed hand. If someone gets a flower tile, he immediately reveals it and draws another tile. The whole game evolves around drawing and discarding tiles, and constructing sets to get a MahJong pattern. One player is the dealer, and he gets a 14th tile and the *turn* to play. The player, in turn, has to eventually discard a tile. After he does so, the other three players can make *bids* for the next turn:

- The player sitting to the right of the discarding person can bid to *draw* a new tile, or to *grab* the discarded tile if it would make a set with two (or three in the case of a gong) other tiles in his concealed hand.

- The other two players can also bid to grab, but only if they can form a pong or a gong (no chows allowed for them).

- A player can also claim to win the game if by taking the discarded tile, he would have a MahJong pattern.

Among the various bids, winning has the highest precedence, followed by pong or gong, with chow or draw the lowest. The player with the highest bid gets the next turn. If his bid involves grabbing the discard, he has to reveal his new set, and draw another tile if the set is a gong. Revealed tiles are fixed for the remainder of the game. Now he has the chance to make the following plays:

If he has four identical concealed tiles, he may form a concealed gong. These tiles are not actually revealed but have the same fixed status. He then draws another tile.

 If he has a revealed pong and the fourth tile in his concealed hand, he may form a gong with it. Doing this might let other players win by grabbing this fourth tile. If the play is safe, he draws another tile.

If he has a MahJong pattern, he wins the game.

Eventually, if the player cannot win yet, he has to make a discard, and we are back to the bidding stage. This process is repeated until either a winner is produced or the stockpile is exhausted, in which case the game is a draw.

That's it. The most complicated thing is perhaps drawing an extra tile after a gong. This is to ensure that right before a player makes a discard, the number of his concealed tiles is always two modulo three.

Overall Game Design

The software package is designed to allow many people to play online with each other, and to act as a referee. This design is based on a client-server architecture, where a central server manages everything from players to game play, and each player runs a client program that interacts with him through a GUI. Players would connect with the client program, and log in under a certain user name. They should be able to communicate with other players using messages, join or serve a table, and play games. Usually, in such a client-server model, it is the server's responsibility to keep track of everything. The client, despite its fancy graphics, is only a messenger between the player and the server.

Classes, Protocols, and Packets

It's a good idea to decide now what sort of "things" we will be dealing with on the server. Under the object-oriented paradigm, we are talking about *classes*. A couple of classes should immediately come to mind: We need a Player class to encapsulate information about each player, and a Table class for a virtual MahJong table. We also need classes such as Tile and Hand in order to keep a MahJong game going.

The client and the server talk to each other in a language that's usually called a *protocol*. Individual sentences of this language are called *packets*. When a player wants to log in, his client sends the server a login packet, which contains his user name. The server decides if he can log in, and sends back a reply packet. Thus, we need many types of packets, each type carrying a certain piece of information. Java provides several classes for networking. I use ServerSocket and Socket, because they provide reliable point-to-point communication and don't impose a particular data format. I choose to send packets in binary, because it is the most bandwidth-efficient.

Threads

The server keeps two threads for each player. One is a "listener" that receives packets from the player's client and processes them. The other is a "replier" that sends packets back to the client. I will explain later why I chose to use two threads instead of one. MahJong is not an action game, so the threads will be blocked most of the time and not cause load problems. The client only needs one listener thread. Its job is to receive and process packets from the server. Client to server packets are only sent in response to user actions.

Source Code Tree Structure

For such a big project there are inevitably a huge number of classes. I chose to group them into four packages: a server package for all server-specific classes (e.g., Player and Table), a client package for the Client and GUI-related classes, a common package for classes that are used by both the server and the client (e.g., Tile and Hand), and finally, a types package for auxiliary classes that are useful for other programming projects. This arrangement makes the source tree much easier to maintain.

This is pretty much all the designing we can do at this stage. The client-server structure is summarized in Figure 18-3. From now on, we will keep this "grand picture" in mind, and work our way up from the bottom.

Protocols and Packets

Since we are writing a network game, it's a good idea to first get the networking part right. I've taken a quick-and-dirty approach to this.

The Packet Class

To think abstractly, we have a socket connected to a remote site, and several types of packets that we would like to send and receive through this socket. As far as the socket is concerned, each packet is simply a byte stream. We can make the first byte a special tag that tells us which type of packet it is. For the rest of the packet, we use the DataInputStream and DataOutputStream classes for binary I/O. The Packet class is simply a ByteArrayOutputStream buffer wrapped with a DataOutputStream:

```java
import java.io.*;
public class Packet extends DataOutputStream {
  ByteArrayOutputStream b_out;              // holds binary data

  private Packet (ByteArrayOutputStream buf) {
    super(buf);
    b_out = buf;
  }
  private byte[] buf () {
    return b_out.toByteArray();
```

continued on next page

continued from previous page

```
    }
    private static Packet New (int size) {  // make a new packet
      ByteArrayOutputStream buf = new ByteArrayOutputStream(size);
      return new Packet(buf);
    }
    // constants and methods here
  }
```

FIGURE 18-3

◉ ◉ ◉ ◉ ◉ ◉

The client-server structure

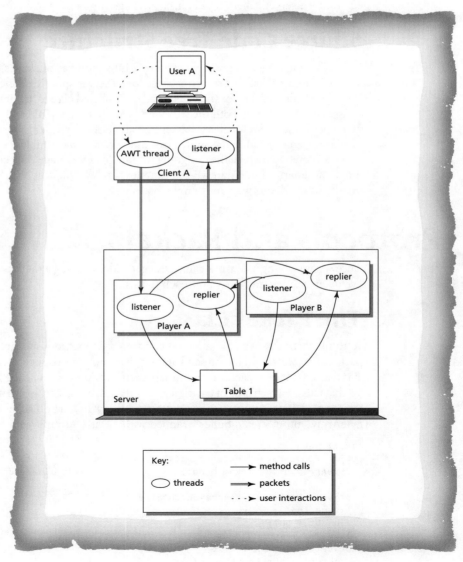

Say we have a type of packet sent from the server to the client (let's call it SP_SOME_PACKET), carrying the information of a byte *b*, an int *i*, and a String *s*. We would define in the Packet class a unique tag (among all server-to-client packets; client-to-server packets are tagged separately) and a static method to construct it:

```
public static final byte SP_SOME_PACKET = 0;  // unique tag
public static byte[] SPSomePacket (byte b, int i, String s) {
  try {
    Packet p = New(10);                     // estimated size
    p.writeByte(SP_SOME_PACKET);            // write tag first
    p.writeByte(b);                         // write fields
    p.writeInt(i);
    p.writeUTF(s);
    return p.buf();                         // return the buffer
  } catch (IOException e) { return null; }  // shouldn't happen
}
```

Sending Packets

Suppose we are given a DataOutputStream out; then sending SP_SOME_PACKET to it involves only two steps:

```
// construct it first
byte[] buf = Packet.SPSomePacket(0, 1, "Hi");
// send it out
out.write(buf, 0, buf.length);       // send it out
```

Receiving Packets

Receiving and processing packets is slightly trickier. I use a *packet dispatcher* plus multiple handlers for this purpose. Suppose we are given a DataInputStream in. The packet dispatcher is just a loop that reads in a byte that is the tag of the packet that follows, and calls the appropriate handlers. The handlers are methods that actually read in packet data and act upon them.

```
public void run () {
  // ...
  // A typical packet handler for server->client packets.
  // Here we assume given a DataInputStream in.
  // This code resides in a run() method of the Client class.
loop:
  while (true) {
  try {
    byte tag = in.readByte();  // read in the packet tag
    switch (tag) {
    case SP_SOME_PACKET:
      hdSomePacket();
      break;
      // handle other packets here
```

continued on next page

continued from previous page

```
      default:                    // invalid tag
        break loop;
      }
    } catch (IOException e) {    // bad connection?
      break loop;
    }
    // handle bad connection here
    // ...
}
```

In the handler method hdSomePacket(), we read in data in the order our SPSomePacket() method encodes it, minus the first tag byte, which has been read in the *while* loop already:

```
private void hdSomeThing () throws IOException {
  // read in the data fields
  byte b = in.readByte();
  int i = in.readInt();
  String s = in.readUTF();
  // do something with the data...
}
```

Other Possible Approaches

You may have noticed that my approach isn't very object-oriented. This is true; a "better" way to do networking is to define a separate class for each packet type, and embed methods in those classes to convert the packet to and from binary data. In fact, I did exactly this in the first version of my game. However, as I added more features, I had to add more packet types and hence define more classes. At some point, Netscape started to crash, because I had too many classes! That is why I use the current method. It's not very elegant, but cuts down the number of classes to one.

I'd also like to point out that when Java gets more mature, for example, when Sun finalizes its RMI (Remote Method Invocation) library, the networking task will become much easier. But at this moment, we are on our own.

The Basic Server

We are now ready to start writing the server, which is a Java application that runs forever. It's always a good idea to write a simple version first. In this case, it only handles login, logout, communications, and joining and leaving tables. The packets needed for this task are summarized in Table 18-1. Client-to-server packets start with "CP" and vice versa with "SP".

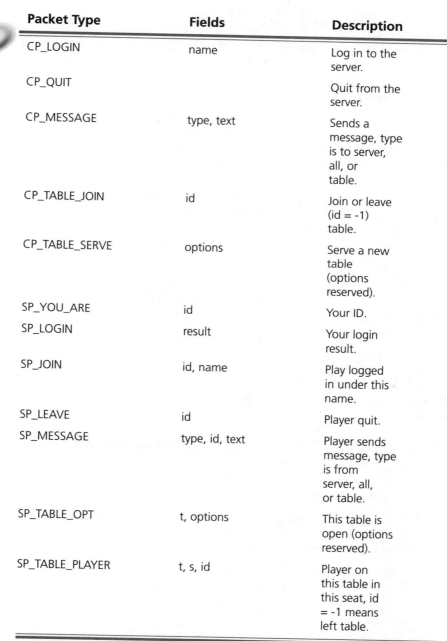

Packet Type	Fields	Description
CP_LOGIN	name	Log in to the server.
CP_QUIT		Quit from the server.
CP_MESSAGE	type, text	Sends a message, type is to server, all, or table.
CP_TABLE_JOIN	id	Join or leave (id = -1) table.
CP_TABLE_SERVE	options	Serve a new table (options reserved).
SP_YOU_ARE	id	Your ID.
SP_LOGIN	result	Your login result.
SP_JOIN	id, name	Play logged in under this name.
SP_LEAVE	id	Player quit.
SP_MESSAGE	type, id, text	Player sends message, type is from server, all, or table.
SP_TABLE_OPT	t, options	This table is open (options reserved).
SP_TABLE_PLAYER	t, s, id	Player on this table in this seat, id = -1 means left table.

TABLE 18-1 ◈ *A basic list of packets*

The Server Class

The server class contains the main() method. Its job is to do some initialization, create a ServerSocket, and accept connections.

```
package server;
import java.net.*;
import java.io.*;

class FullServerException extends Exception;
class Server {
  public static void main (String args[]) {
    ServerSocket main_sock = null;
    try {
      main_sock = new ServerSocket(5656);  // default port
    } catch (IOException e) {
      System.out.println;
      System.exit(1);
    }
    while (true) {
      try {
        Socket s = main_sock.accept();        // accept connection
        DataInputStream i = new DataInputStream(s.getInputStream());
        DataOutputStream o = new DataOutputStream(s.getOutputStream());
        (new Player(s, i, o)).start();        // start thread
      } catch (Exception e) {
        System.out.println;
      }
    }
  }
}
```

The Player and PlayerOutput Classes

We first group some information about a player into the Player class:

```
package server;
import java.net.*;
import java.io.*;
class Player extends Thread {
  public static Player[] global = new Player[100];
  public int id = -1;
  public String name = null;
  private Socket sock;
  private DataInputStream in;
  private DataOutputStream out;
  public boolean connected = true;
  private PlayerOutput out_thread = null;
  public Table table = null;
  public int seat = -1;
}
```

The above definition includes the player's name, his socket connection, table and seat, and so on. There is a static array *global* that holds all the players on the server. Each player has a unique ID, which is an index into this array. To construct a new Player instance, we need to find an empty slot. Here it is important to use the *synchronized* statement on the array *global*, because our server will be a multithreaded program, and other threads may want to modify *global*, too. In case the server is full, we throw a FullServerException to inform our caller, Server.main().

```
public Player (Socket s, DataInputStream in, DataOutputStream out)
throws FullServerException {
  synchronized (global) {              // find a unique player id
    for (int i = 0; i < global.length; i++) {
      if (global[i] == null) {
        id = i;
        global[i] = this;
        break;
      }
    }
  }
  if (id == -1)                        // all slots full
    throw new FullServerException();
  sock = s;
  this.in = in;
  this.out = out;
  (out_thread = new PlayerOutput(this, out)).start();
  output(Packet.SPYouAre(id));         // notify the player
}
```

We need methods to send out packets. Player.output() sends a packet to a player. I will explain it in more detail soon. The static method outputAll() sends a packet to everyone on the server. It works by first acquiring the monitor associated with *global* and then calling every player's output() method. We also need a disconnect() method, called when a player decides to quit (his client sends the server a CP_QUIT packet for this purpose) or when his network connection is somehow dead.

```
public void output (byte[] p) {
  if (connected)
    out_thread.output(p);
}
public static void outputAll (byte[] p) {
  synchronized (global) {              // critical section
    for (int i = 0; i < global.length;  i++) {
      Player him = global[i];
      // only send to players who have logged in
      if (him != null && him.name != null)
        him.output(p);
    }
  }
}
public synchronized void disconnect () {
  if (id == -1) return;                // we do it only once
```

continued on next page

continued from previous page

```
      connected = false;
      if (table != null)              // leave the table
        table.leave(this);
      synchronized (global) {         // critical section
        global[id] = null;            // will GC eventually
      }
      try {                           // close the socket
        in.close();
        out.close();
        sock.close();
      } catch (IOException e) {
      }
      if (name != null)               // announce leave
        outputAll(Packet.SPLeave(id));
      id = -1;                         // we're done here
    }
  // ...
  }
```

The Listener Thread

As explained earlier, we need a listener thread for each player. This is why Player extends
Thread. It is clear that its run() method should basically be a packet dispatcher:

```
private Integer working = new Integer(0);
public void run () {
loop:
  while (connected) {
    try {
      byte tag = in.readByte();
      // don't stop until we finish with this packet
      synchronized (working) {
        switch (tag) {
        case CP_QUIT:
          break loop;
        case CP_MESSAGE:
          hdMessage();
          break;
        // call other packet handlers
        }
      }
    } catch (IOException e) {
      break loop;
    }
  }
  connected = false;
  out_thread.stop();
  disconnect();
}
public void stopOnWait () {
  connected = false;              // so that run() won't loop again
```

```
synchronized (working) {    // stop only if blocked on input
  stop();
}
}
```

The stopOnWait() method is called when an abnormal event happens to a player, for example, when the server decides his network connection is dead and wants to clear his slot. The run() method may be in the middle of handling a packet, so we don't want to stop it immediately and potentially leave the server in an inconsistent state. However, we do make sure that the thread dies before it reads in the next packet.

I only present here a handler method for CP_MESSAGE. It first determines whether a message is directed to all players on the server or only to those on the player's table (I chose not to allow personal messages as a countermeasure against cheating), then constructs a corresponding SP_MESSAGE packet and sends it to targeted players. Other packet handlers are similar in nature, so I will skip them.

```
void hdMessage throws IOException {
  // CP_MESSAGE contains a target type (MSG_SERVER,
  // MSG_TABLE, or MSG_ALL), and a text message.
  byte type = in.readByte();
  String text = in.readUTF();
  if (type == Packet.MSG_SERVER)
    System.out.println("Msg from " + id + ": " + text);
  else if (type == Packet.MSG_TABLE && table != null)
    table.outputTable(Packet.SPMessage(Packet.MSG_TABLE, id, text));
  else
    outputAll(Packet.SPMessage(Packet.MSG_ALL, id, text));
}
```

The Replier Thread

It remains to explain the use of PlayerOutput *out_thread*. This is the replier thread for our player. Let me first convince you that there is a need for two threads per player. Sending packets is done via the output() method. Its naive implementation is to just do an out.write() call. However, this may cause problems. Player A's listener thread may need to send another player B's client a packet (this happens, for example, when A sends everyone a message); thus, somewhere inside A.run() we have a call to B.output(). But as we know, network connections are far from perfect, so such a call, implemented the naive way, might take an arbitrarily long time to finish. This would prevent A.run() from handling more packets in a timely manner. Indeed, a general rule of thumb is that all packet handlers must do their job quickly.

To solve this problem, I let the output() method simply add the packet to a queue. The replier thread of the player pops them off the queue and sends them out. First, let me give a version of the Queue class:

```
package types;
class QueueLink {              // a linked list node for our Queue
  public QueueLink next;
  public Object obj;
  public QueueLink (Object o) {
    obj = o;
    next = null;
  }
}
public class Queue {           // first-in, first-out
  private QueueLink head = null, tail = null;
  public synchronized Object pop () {
    while (head == null) {
      try {
        wait();                // block until we get an item
      } catch (InterruptedException e) {
      }
    }
    Object o = head.obj;       // pop the first item
    head = head.next;
    if (head == null) {
      tail = null;
    }
    return o;
  }
  public synchronized void push (Object o) {
    if (head == null) {
      head = tail = new QueueLink(o);
    } else {
      tail.next = new QueueLink(o);
      tail = tail.next;
    }
    notify();                  // wake up blocked threads
  }
}
```

The actual class for the replier thread is PlayerOutput:

```
package server;
import java.io.*;
class PlayerOutput extends Thread {
  private static Player the_player;
  private DataOutputStream out;
  private Queue pkt_queue = new Queue();

  public PlayerOutput (Player p, DataOutputStream o) {
    the_player = p;
    out = o;
  }
  public void output (byte p[]) {
    pkt_queue.push(p);
  }
  public void run () {
  loop:
```

```
    while (true) {                          // keep sending packets out
      byte p[] = (byte[])pkt_queue.pop();
      if (p != null && p.length > 0) {
        try {
          out.write(p, 0, p.length);
        } catch (IOException e) {   // bad connection
          break loop;
        }
      }
    }
    the_player.stopOnWait();        // stop the listener thread
    the_player.disconnect();        // make the player leave
  }
}
```

Note that since we keep two threads for each player, abnormal conditions like a dead network connection could occur in either thread. Some care needs to be taken to stop both threads (when they can be safely stopped) on such occasions.

The Table Class: A Simple Version

For the basic server, we only need to record which players are on a table, and provide methods for players to join and leave tables. As with players, we keep a list of all the tables on the server in an array. The following is a sketch of the Table class.

```
package server;
class Table {
  public static Table[] global = new Table[25];
  int id = -1;
  Player[] players = new Player[8];  // including 4 spectators

  public Table () throws FullServerException {
    // assign a unique table id
    synchronized (global) {                 // critical section
      for (int i = 0; i < global.length; i++) {
        if (global[i] == null) {
          id = i;
          global[i] = this;
          break;
        }
      }
    }
    if (id == -1) throw new FullServerException();
  }
  public synchronized void outputTable (byte[] p) {
    for (int i = 0; i < players.length; i++) {
      if (players[i] != null)
        players[i].output(p);
    }
  }
  public synchronized void join (Player him, boolean play) {
```

continued on next page

continued from previous page

```
              join:
                {
                  // seats 0 - 3 are for players, the rest spectators
                  int s0 = play ? 0 : 4;
                  int s1 = play ? 4 : players.length;
                  for (int i = s0; i < s1; i++) {
                    if (players[i] == null) {
                      players[i] = him;
                      him.table = this;
                      him.seat = i;
                      Player.outputAll(Packet.SPTablePlayer(id, i, him.id));
                      break join;
                    }
                  }
                  him.output(Packet.SPMessage(Packet.MSG_GOD, 0,
                                          "Table is full."));
                  return;
                }
                // MahJong-related stuff here
              }
              public void leave (Player him) {
                synchronized (global) {           // critical section
                  synchronized (this) {
                    if (him.table != this) return;
                    // announce to all;  player id of -1 means leaving table
                    Player.outputAll(Packet.SPTablePlayer(id, him.seat, -1));
                    players[him.seat] = null;
                    him.table = null;
                    him.seat = -1;
                    for (int i = 0; i < 4; i++)
                      if (players[i] != null)
                        return;
                    // now the table has only spectators, so we close it
                    for (int i = 4; i < players.length; i++) {
                      if (players[i] != null) {
                        Player.outputAll(Packets.SPTablePlayer(id, i, -1));
                        players[i].table = null;
                        players[i].seat = -1;
                        players[i] = null;
                      }
                    }
                    global[id] = null;
                  }
                }
              }
              public synchronized void update (Player him) {
                for (int i = 0; i < players.length; i++) {
                  if (players[i] != null)
                    him.output(Packet.SPTablePlayer(id, i, t.players[i].id));
                }
              }
              // other methods...
            }
```

I will say more about the leave() method later.

Handling Login Requests

There is one last loose end to tie up: login. For the basic server, we let a player log in whenever he isn't on the server already. Passwords can be added later.

After a player logs in, we need to send him updates on all the players and tables currently on the server. This is done in the hdLogin() method that handles login requests:

```
void hdLogin () throws IOException {
  String n = in.readUTF();                    // read in packet data
  synchronized (global) {                      // critical section
    for (int i = 0; i < global.length; i++) {
      if (global[i] != null && n.equals(global[i].name)) {
        output(Packet.SPLogin(Packet.LOGIN_TWICE));
        return;                                // reject his login
      }
    }
    name = n;                                  // accept his login
  }
  output(Packet.SPLogin(Packet.LOGIN_OK));
  // send updates on all the players
  synchronized (global) {                      // critical section
    for (int i = 0; i < global.length; i++) {
      if (global[i] != null && global[i].name != null)
        output(Packet.SPJoin(i, global[i].name));
    }
  }
  // send updates on all the tables
  synchronized (Table.global) {                // critical section
    for (int i = 0; i < Table.global.length; i++) {
      if (Table.global[i] != null) {
        output(Packet.SPTableOpt(i, null));    // update this table
        Table.global[i].update(this);          // update players
      }
    }
  }
}
```

Synchronization and Deadlock Prevention

As you've seen in the code I've given so far, in the Player and Table classes we often need to acquire monitors on certain objects—four kinds of them, to be exact:

🗡 The Player.global array

🗡 The Table.global array

🗡 A particular Player instance

🗡 A particular Table instance

Often, two or more monitors have to be acquired. For instance, in the process of updating all the tables to a certain player, we need to acquire the monitor of Table.global first and then of each individual Table instance. As the server code gets complicated, we face potential deadlock situations.

A deadlock occurs when several threads are competing for monitors, yet each holds a monitor that another thread needs to acquire in order to proceed. As an example, suppose I defined Table.leave() like this (which is actually more "natural" than the first version):

```
// an alternative problematic Table.leave()
public synchronized leave (Player him) {
  // get him off the table here, and check for empty table
  // suppose table is empty:
  synchronized (global) {              // remove table
    global[id] = null;
  }
}
```

Now imagine two players, A and B. A just logged in, so we are informing him about all the tables. We are about to reach table T, on which B just happens to be the only player, and he happens to decide to leave at this very moment. Say T.leave() is called first, then T.update() must wait for it to finish. In T.leave() we find out that the table should be removed because it is now empty. However, to do this we need to acquire the monitor on Table.global, which is currently held by player A. Thus, these two threads are now in a deadlock. Granted, the chance of this happening is rare, but it's likely to happen after an extended period of time, and we have to deal with it to get a robust server.

One way to prevent such deadlocks is to make all threads acquire these monitors only in a certain order. In my case, the order is Player instances first, then Table.global, then Table instances, and finally Player.global. The particular ordering isn't a big deal; what matters is consistency. If all monitors are acquired in order, then deadlock cannot happen. This is why the first version of Table.leave() is used.

The Basic Client

The client is a Java applet that's accessible from a user's Web browser. However, unlike most Java applets, the MahJong client needs to live in its own window (a Frame in Abstract Windowing Toolkit (AWT) terminology). This allows the user to continue using his browser while on the server, and also makes it easier to integrate menu bars. In fact, as I added more features, I found it necessary to open multiple windows.

I therefore define two classes, first a Greeting class that extends Applet and lives inside a Web page, and then a Client class that extends Frame. The Greeting applet simply presents a clickable button. When the button is clicked on, it connects to the server, and creates a new Client instance, whose job is to carry on.

The Greeting Class and the HTML Document

The Greeting class is straightforward to write:

```
package client;
import java.net.*;
import java.io.*;
import java.awt.*;
import java.applet.*;

public class Greeting extends Applet {
  Button main_button = new Button("Connect NOW!");
  Client main = null;

  public void init () {
    add(main_button);
    show();
  }
  public void restart () {
    main = null;
    main_button.setLabel("Connect again");
    main_button.enable();
  }
  public synchronized boolean action (Event evt, Object what) {
    if (evt.target == main_button) {
      main_button.disable();
      try {
        Socket s = new Socket(getParameter("ServerHost"), 5656);
        DataInputStream i = new DataInputStream(s.getInputStream());
        DataOutputStream o = new DataOutputStream(s.getOutputStream());
        main_button.setLabel("Connected!");
        main = new Client(this, s, i, o);
      } catch (IOException e) {
        restart();
      }
    }
    return true;
  }
}
```

We also need to write an HTML document, say mj.html, and embed our applet in it. This is done via the <applet> tag:

```
<html>
<applet CODE="client.Greeting.class" WIDTH=200 HEIGHT=40>
<param NAME="ServerHost" VALUE="localhost">
</applet>
</html>
```

If you run a public server, the ServerHost parameter should contain the actual host-name of the machine on which you are running your server; otherwise, people won't be able to connect to it. Of course, you also want to explain the game in the HTML document.

The Client Class

On the client side, we also have the notion of players and tables. I define classes CPlayer and CTable. They are miniature versions of their server-side counterparts. We need to define their toString() methods. For a player, it formats his ID, name, and table ID. For a table, it formats the IDs of the table and the players on that table. For reasons I'll get to later, the toString() methods need to save a copy of their output to be retrieved later by a getString() method. I won't go into more details here.

The client needs a listener thread to receive and dispatch packets from the server. Therefore, we need to make Client implement Runnable. Its run() method is roughly sketched out in an earlier section on packet handling. The code shown below is quite similar to the Player class, except that here we do not need a replier thread.

```
package client;
import java.awt.*;
import java.io.*;
import java.net.*;

class Client extends Frame implements Runnable {
  Greeting greeter;
  Socket sock;
  DataInputStream in;
  DataOutputStream out;
  Thread listener;
  CPlayer[] g_players = new CPlayer[100];
  CTable[] g_tables = new CTable[25];
  int myID = -1;

  Client (Greeting g, Socket s,
          DataInputStream i, DataOutputStream o) {
    sock = s;
    in = i;
    out = o;
    greeter = g;
    // spawn listener thread
    (listener = new Thread(this)).start();
    // other initializations here...
  }
  void output (byte[] p) {
    if (p != null && p.length > 0) {
      try {
        out.write(p, 0, p.length);
      } catch (IOException e) {
        disconnect();
        listener.stop();
        dispose();
```

```
        greeter.restart();
      }
    }
  }
  void disconnect () {
    try {
      in.close();
      out.close();
      sock.close();
    } catch (IOException e) { }
  }
  public void run () {
  loop:
    while (true) {
    // packet dispatcher code here, shown earlier
    }
    // handle bad connection
    disconnect();
    dispose();
    greeter.restart();
  }
  void hdYouAre () throws IOException { // packet handler for SP_YOU_ARE
    myID = (int)in.readByte();
  }
  // ...
}
```

The Client GUI

The first GUI element of the client is a login window. It should be presented as soon as we get the connection to the server. To simplify matters, I use here only a text input field to accept a login name. Patch up the constructor of Client and define an action() method:

```
// in class Client
TextField login_name;

public Client ( ... ) {
  // ...
  login_name = new TextField(20);
  setLayout(new FlowLayout());
  add(login_name);
  pack();
  show();
}
public synchronized boolean action (Event evt, Object what) {
  if (evt.target == login_name) {
    login_name.setEditable(false);
    // exercise: write Packet.CPLogin()...
    output(Packet.CPLogin(login_name.getText()));
  }
  // other events
  return true;
}
```

The server is supposed to process our request and send back an SP_LOGIN packet. We handle it in the following way:

```
void hdLogin () throws IOException {
  byte result = in.readByte();          // read in packet data
  if (result != Packet.LOGIN_OK) {      // login rejected
    login_name.setEditable(true);
    login_name.setText("");
    return;
  } else {                              // login accepted
    after_login();
  }
}
```

The after_login() method is called when we successfully log in. Its job is to remove the login GUI and present a big window that will be the player's workspace, or the *console*. I will take a moment here to explain what kind of GUI components the MahJong client uses for the console window. First of all, there is the menu bar. The most important menu items are probably File, which has a Quit item, and Table, which has Join, Leave, and Serve items. There are also two text panels that list all the players and tables on the server. These two lists are updated in real time from the server. We also need a text panel to hold all messages, and of course, a text input field plus a couple of buttons to allow sending messages. Finally, I reserve a big panel to hold subcomponents for the MahJong table. These AWT components are added as field variables, as shown below:

```
// field variables for AWT components
MenuBar menu_bar;
Menu file_menu;
Menu table_menu;
MenuItem m_file_quit;
MenuItem m_table_join;
MenuItem m_table_leave;
MenuItem m_table_serve;
TextArea player_list;      // list of players
TextArea table_list;       // list of tables
TextArea msg_list;         // list of messages
TextField msg_out;         // out-going message
Choice msg_choice;         // to GOD, TABLE, ALL
Button msg_send;           // send out a message
Panel table_panel;         // mahjong table
```

I use a GridBagLayout to lay out these AWT components. Figure 18-4 shows a reasonable way to lay them out, and Table 18-2 gives the appropriate values for GridBagConstraints fields. The components are all expanded to full grid size, by the way.

FIGURE 18-4

The client GUI illustrated

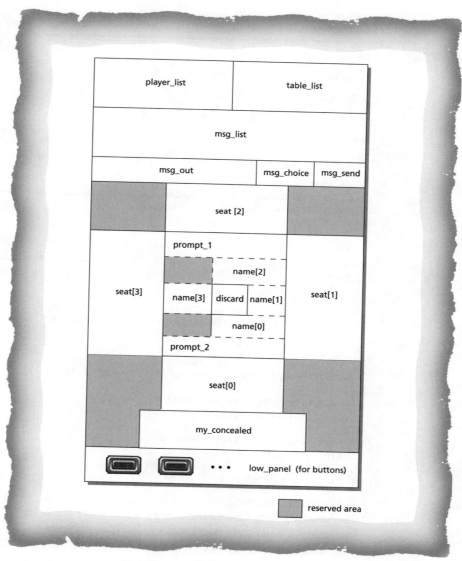

Component	gridx, gridy	gridwidth, gridheight	weightx, weighty
player_list	0, 0	1, 1	1.0, 0.0
table_list	1, 0	3, 1	1.0, 0.0
msg_list	0, 1	4, 1	0.0, 1.0
msg_out	0, 2	2, 1	0.0, 0.0
msg_choice	2, 2	1, 1	0.0, 0.0
msg_send	3, 2	1, 1	0.0, 0.0
table_panel	0, 3	4, 1	0.0, 0.0

TABLE 18-2 ◈ *Laying out the console*

Given the listing of components and Table 18-2, it is easy to write after_login() to create and arrange them. Note that the *m_table_leave* menu item should be disabled initially. Next, expand action() to let the player send messages and join/leave tables:

```
// in action()...
if (evt.target == msg_out || evt.target == msg_send) {
  output(Packet.CPMessage(msg_choice.getSelectedItem(),
                   msg_out.getText()));
}
if (evt.target == m_table_serve) {
  output(Packet.CPTableServe(null));   // no options yet
}
if (evt.target == m_table_leave) {
  output(Packet.CPTableJoin((byte)-1, (byte)0));
}
if (evt.target == m_table_join) {
  JoinTable jt = new JoinTable(this);
  jt.show();
}
```

To join a table, the user is presented a dialog window to input the table ID and choose whether he wants to join as a player or a spectator. This can be implemented with a class JoinTable that extends Dialog. I won't go into details here.

Finally, we need to update the player, table, and message lists whenever the server sends us the appropriate packets. I will show you how to implement the player list using the AWT component TextArea. Others are similar. The AWT component List can also be used for this purpose, if you can do without a horizontal scrollbar.

```
void hdJoin () {
  int id;
  String name;
  // exercise: write Packet.SPJoin() and read it in here...
  CPlayer him = g_players[id] = new CPlayer(id, name);
  player_list.appendText(him.toString());
}
```

```
void hdLeave () {
  int id;
  // exercise: write Packet.SPLeave() and read it in here...
  CPlayer him = g_players[id];
  int i = player_list.getText().indexOf(him.getString());
  int j = i + him.getString().length();
  player_list.replaceText("", i, j);
}
void hdPlayerTable () {
  int t_id, p_id, seat;
  // exercise: write Packet.SPPlayerTable() and read it here...
  CTable table = g_players[t_id];
  CPlayer him;
  if (p_id == -1) {                    // this player left the table
    him = g_players[table.players[seat]];
    him.table = null;
    him.seat = -1;
    table.players[seat] = null;
  } else {
    him = g_players[p_id];
    him.table = table;
    him.seat = seat;
    table.players[seat] = him;
  }
  int i = player_list.getText().indexOf(him.getString());
  int j = i + him.getString().length();
  player_list.replaceText(him.toString(), i, j);
  // update table list too...
}
```

Here you see the use of storing the old string value of a player during the toString() call so it can be retrieved later with getString(), even though the player information may have changed already.

At this point, we should have a functional server and client pair. This is what I suggest you do first if you are writing your own game. Although they don't do much, it's very important to debug them thoroughly, now!

Incorporating MahJong

The following describes how to actually implement the MahJong game. We will start out on the client side, which mainly handles user-interface considerations, and eventually move to the server side, which actually handles the game play. This approach lets you see the game in action as soon as possible.

Setting Up the MahJong Table on the Client

In a graphical representation of the table, "myself" (he who runs the client) is always put in the "south" position. Other players' positions are uniquely determined by this setup. See the lower half of Figure 18-4 for the layout of the MahJong table. (Note: In MahJong, the four words for compass directions have another meaning, so it's important not to confuse players with overloaded notions. The server always refers to players by name rather than seat position.)

There is a table area for displaying each player's tiles. For "myself," I use another area near the bottom to display the tiles that are concealed from others; other players' concealed tiles show up facedown in their respective tile areas. In the center is a small area to show the current discarded tile, and around it I display player names and other information. At the bottom of the table panel, I display a row of buttons, each corresponding to a certain MahJong play (pass, chow, etc.). The server determines which buttons are clickable at any particular stage of the game; clicking on a button makes the corresponding play.

The table panel uses a GridBagLayout, with the bottom row of buttons in a subpanel managed by a FlowLayout. I summarize the values for GridBagConstraints fields in Table 18-3.

Component	gridx, gridy	gridwidth, gridheight	weightx, weighty
seat[0]	1, 6	3, 1	0.0, 0.0
seat[1]	4, 1	1, 5	0.0, 0.0
seat[2]	1, 0	3, 1	0.0, 0.0
seat[3]	0, 1	1, 5	0.0, 0.0
discard	2, 3	1, 1	0.0, 0.0
my_concealed	0, 7	5, 1	1.0, 0.0
name[0]	2, 4	1, 1	0.0, 0.0
name[1]	3, 3	1, 1	0.0, 0.0
name[2]	2, 2	1, 1	0.0, 0.0
name[3]	1, 3	1, 1	0.0, 0.0
prompt_1	1, 1	3, 1	0.0, 1.0
prompt_2	1, 5	3, 1	0.0, 1.0
low_panel	0, 8	5, 1	0.0, 0.0

TABLE 18-3 ◈ *Laying out the MahJong table*

The Tile and Hand Classes

Since there are a total of 42 distinct tiles in MahJong, a tile can be represented by a byte. I use the numbers 1 to 42 and reserve 0 for a concealed tile.

The Tile class only needs static methods that figure out the category and value of a tile given its byte representation.

The Hand class stores a sequence of tiles, together with the following information:

🗡 Subsets of tiles can be grouped together. Typically, a group may be a *set* or a *pair* in MahJong terminology.

🗡 A number of tiles/groups may be marked. Marks would cause highlighting when the hand is displayed.

🗡 Operations like grouping and deletion take effect on marked tiles.

Thus, the prototype of the Hand class would pretty much be

```
packet common;
public class Hand {
  // the following 3 arrays have 1 element for each tile
  private byte[] tiles;
  private byte[] groups;
  private boolean[] select;
  private int length;                   // number of tiles

  // constants for groups:
  public static final byte SINGLE = 0;  // singleton tile
  public static final byte HEAD = 1;    // head of a group
  public static final byte MIDDLE = 2;  // middle of a group
  public static final byte TAIL = 3;    // tail of a group

  // construct a hand with buffer size
  public Hand (int size) {}
  // return the length variable
  public int length () {}
  // truncate the hand to given length
  public synchronized int setLength (int len) {}
  // return the tile at given location
  public synchronized byte tileAt (int pos) {}
  // set the tile at given location
  public synchronized byte setTileAt (int pos, byte tile, byte gp) {}
  // return the group info at given location
  public synchronized bytre groupAt (int pos) {}
  // return the marker info at given location
  public synchronized boolean isSelected (int pos) {}
  // add a tile to the end of the hand, returns the hand itself
  public synchronized Hand addTile (byte t, byte g, boolean s) {}
  // remove a tile at given location
  public synchronized Hand killTile (int pos) {}
  // insert a tile at given location
  public synchronized Hand insertTile (int pos, byte t,
```

continued on next page

continued from previous page

```
                                              group g, boolean s) {}
  // append another hand to this one
  public synchronized Hand append (Hand h) {}
  // mark a tile/group, return the pos of the 1st tile in the group
  public synchronized int select (int pos) {}
  // undo the above process
  public synchronized int unselect (int pos) {}
  // unmark all the tiles
  public synchronized void unselectAll () {}
  // make all tiles SINGLE and unmarked
  public synchronized void clearAll () {}
  // group together all marked tiles, return false if none marked
  public synchronized boolean group () {}
  // make all marked tiles SINGLE, return false if none marked
  public synchronized boolean ungroup () {}
  // see whether the marked tiles form a single group
  public synchronized boolean isGroup () {}
  // remove all marked tiles, return false if none marked
  public synchronized boolean delete () {}
  // mark the first n of the given tile, return actual number found
  public synchronized int search (byte t, int n) {}
  // return a new hand with marked tiles
  public synchronized Hand selection (boolean keep_orig) {}
  // return a new hand with unmarked tiles
  public synchronized Hand unselected (boolean keep_orig) {}
  // randomly shuffle the tiles in this hand
  public synchronized void shuffle () {}
  // sort the tiles in this hand
  public synchronized void sort() {}
}
```

There will inevitably be packets that contain tiles and hands. For a tile we can simply use its byte representation. For hands, however, we need to write two methods to read and write them. They are best put in the Packet class:

```
// in class Packet
public static void writeHand (DataOutputStream S, Hand h)
throws IOException {
  S.writeInt(h.length());
  for (int i = 0; i < h.length(); i++) {
    S.writeByte(h.tileAt(i));
    S.writeByte(h.groupAt(i) | (byte)(h.isSelected(i) ? 16 : 0));
  }
}
public static Hand readHand (DataInputStream S, Hand h)
throws IOException {
  int len = S.readInt();
  if (h == null)
    h = new Hand(len);
  h.setLength(0);
  for (int i = 0; i < len; i++) {
    byte t = S.readByte();
    byte g = S.readByte();
```

```
    boolean s = ((g & (byte)16) != 0);
    h.addTile(t, (byte)(g & 15), s);
  }
  return h;
}
```

A Generic Shuffling Algorithm

I present here an algorithm for shuffling an array *list[]* of N objects. Assuming a good random number generator, it gives each possible permutation equal probability, and has complexity O(N). It works, thanks to some elementary facts from combinatorics.

```
import java.util.Random;
Random rand = new Random();
for (int i = 1; i < list.length; i++) {
  int j = Math.abs(rand.nextInt()) % (i + 1);  // 0 <= j <= i
  if (i != j) {                                 // swap list[i]
    Object temp = list[i];                      // with list[j]
    list[i] = list[j];
    list[j] = temp;
  }
}
```

MahJong Tile Images

Clay Breshears (http://www.cs.utk.edu/~clay/) has made an excellent collection of color GIF images for MahJong tiles. The tile images I use for my MahJong client are based on his, with some minor modifications and the addition of eight flower tiles (see Figure 18-2).

To use these images, first put them in a subdirectory "tiles" on the server machine, and name the files T0.gif through T42.gif. On the client side, arrange them into an array:

```
// in class Greeting
public static Image tiles[] = new Image[43];
```

I spawn a thread in Greeting.init() to load all the images. It uses the MediaTracker class:

```
// run() method of Greeting which now extends Runnable
public void run () {
  MediaTracker tracker = new MediaTracker(this);
  Object errors[] = null;
  for (int i = 0; i < 43; i++) {
    tiles[i] = getImage(getDocumentBase(), "tiles/T" + i + ".gif");
    tracker.addImage(tiles[i], 0);
  }
  while (true) {
    try {
      tracker.waitForAll();
    } catch (InterruptedException e) {}
    if ((errors = tracker.getErrorsAny()) == null)
      break;                                    // all images loaded
```

continued on next page

continued from previous page

```
        for (int i = 0; i < 43; i++) {
          if (tiles[i] == errors[j]) {
            tiles[i] = getImage(getDocumentBase(), "tiles/T" + i + ".gif");
            tracker.addImage(tiles[i], 0);
          }
        }
      }
    }
```

Displaying and Manipulating a Hand

Now we are ready to define a new AWT component, TileWindow, that can display a hand with these tile images. In the actual MahJong client, this component can display several rows and columns, and handles several drawing directions. To illustrate the point, I present here a simplified version that only draws horizontally from left to right, in one row. To mimic real MahJong games, all tiles in a group are displayed right next to each other; there is a padding space between different groups or single tiles.

```
package client;
import java.awt.*;
import common.*;

class TileWindow extends Canvas {
  private static final int XSIZE = 30, YSIZE = 40, PAD = 8;
  private Hand hand = null;
  private int size;

  public TileWindow (int n_tiles) {
    size = n_tiles;
    setBackground(Color.gray);
  }
  public synchronized void setHand (Hand h) {
    hand = h;
    repaint();
  }
  public Dimension minimumSize () {
    return preferredSize();
  }
  public Dimension preferredSize () {
    return new Dimension(size * (XSIZE + PAD) + PAD, 2 * PAD + YSIZE);
  }
  public synchronized void paint (Graphics g) {
    if (hand == null) return;
    int i_tile = 0, n_grp = 0, p_col = PAD;
    while (i_tile < hand.length()) {
      if (hand.groupAt(i_tile) == Hand.SINGLE) {
        n_grp = 1;
      } else {
        int i = i_tile + 1;
        n_grp = 2;
```

```
        while (hand.groupAt(i) != Hand.TAIL) {
          i++;
          n_grp++;
        }
      }
      if (hand.isSelected(i_tile))  // highlight bounding rectangle?
        g.setColor(Color.yellow);
      else
        g.setColor(getBackground());
      g.drawRect(p_col - 2, PAD - 2, XSIZE * n_grp + 3, YSIZE + 3);
      for (int n = 0; n < n_grp; n++) {
        g.drawImage(Greeting.tiles[(int)hand.tileAt(i_tile++)],
                    p_col, PAD);
        p_col += XSIZE;
      }
      p_col += PAD;
    }
  }
}
```

A player can arrange his concealed tiles by clicking and dragging tiles around. Note that it does not make much sense to let the player group his tiles, because all the groups should correspond to MahJong sets and pairs, and I would rather let the server decide whether they can be formed. So I add an option for a TileWindow to be "editable," and handle certain mouse events:

```
private boolean editable = true;
private boolean draggable = false, dragged = false;
private int drag_dx = 0, down_x = 0, down_pos = 0, drag_x0 = 0;

public synchronized void setEditable (boolean e) {
  editable = e;
}
public synchronized boolean mouseDown (Event evt, int x, int y) {
  if (!editable) return true;
  int pos = x / (XSIZE + PAD);
  if ((x % (XSIZE + PAD)) < PAD || pos < 0 ||
      pos >= hand.length()) {                // cancel selection
    dragable = false;
    hand.unselectAll();
    paint(getGraphics());
    return true;
  }
  hand.unselectAll();
  hand.select(pos);                          // select this tile
  dragable = true;                           // prepare for dragging
  drag_dx = (XSIZE + PAD) * pos + PAD - 2 - x;
  down_x = x;
  down_pos = pos;
  paint(getGraphics());
  return true;
}
```

continued on next page

continued from previous page

```
public synchronized boolean mouseDrag (Event evt, int x, int y) {
  if (!editable || !dragable) return true;
  Graphics g = getGraphics();
  if (!dragged) {                        // first drag event
    dragged = true;
    drag_x0 = x;
    g.setColor(Color.black);
    g.setXORMode(Color.white);
    g.drawRect(x + drag_dx, PAD - 2, XSIZE + 3, YSIZE + 3);
    g.setPaintMode();
  } else {                               // more dragging
    g.setColor(Color.black);
    g.setXORMode(Color.white);
    g.drawRect(x + drag_dx, PAD - 2, XSIZE + 3, YSIZE + 3);
    g.setPaintMode();
  }
  return true;
}
public synchronized boolean mouseUp (Event evt, int x, int y) {
  if (!editable || !dragged) return true;
  dragged = false;
  dragable = false;
  Graphics g = getGraphics();
  g.setColor(Color.black);
  g.setXORMode(Color.white);
  g.drawRect(drag_x0 + drag_dx, PAD - 2, XSIZE + 3, YSIZE + 3);
  g.setPaintMode();
  int pos;
  if (x < down_x - 3)                    // move left
    pos = (x + drag_dx + XSIZE) / (XSIZE + PAD);
  else if (x > down_x + 3)               // move right
    pos = (x + drag_dx - PAD) / (XSIZE + PAD);
  else return true;
  byte tile = hand.tileAt(down_pos);
  boolean sel = hand.isSelected(down_pos);
  hand.killTile(down_pos).insertTile(pos, tile, Hand.SINGLE, sel);
  repaint();
  return true;
}
```

A Client-Server Model for MahJong

There are several models for client-server applications. I propose to use a simple one: The server handles everything about game play. The client keeps information locally, but doesn't do any decision-making. When the user takes an action, the client simply forwards it to the server for further scrutiny; when the server responds, the client updates the GUI components to restrict the user's future actions. Another possible model is to let the client deal with the user's actions locally, and only inform the server when a legal play is made. I prefer the former, because it is consistent, less prone to synchronization problems, copes well with future changes in the game structure, and keeps "hackers" from running a modified client program and getting unfair advantage.

This approach also makes the client extremely simple. For each user action, it just sends a packet to the server, and the setup to wait for the response, which it displays graphically. For playing MahJong, it suffices to use the TileWindow class to update tiles and enable/disable MahJong related buttons. They are easy to write, so I won't give any code examples here.

I define only one type of client-to-server packet for MahJong games: CP_PLAY. It contains an action and a reference tile. Table 18-4 shows the kind of information this packet type carries.

Action	Uses tile?	Description
PASS = 0	no	Acknowledgement only.
DRAW = 1	no	Bid to draw a new tile.
CONN_UP = 2	no	Bid to make a chow, with two higher tiles.
CONN_MD = 3	no	Bid to make a chow, with two sandwiching tiles.
CONN_DN = 4	no	Bid to make a chow, with two lower tiles.
TRIP = 5	no	Bid to make a pong.
QUAD = 6	no	Bid to make a gong.
DISCARD = 7	yes	Make a discard.
FOUR = 8	yes	Make a gong with a concealed tile.
WIN = 9	no	Claim to win the game.

TABLE 18-4 ◈ *CP_PLAY fields and values*

From the server's point of view, a MahJong table is a finite-state machine. It has a status plus a set of variables. Figure 18-5 shows how a table reacts to game plays.

FIGURE 18-5

◎ ◎ ◎ ◎ ◎ ◎

*MahJong as a
finite-state
machine*

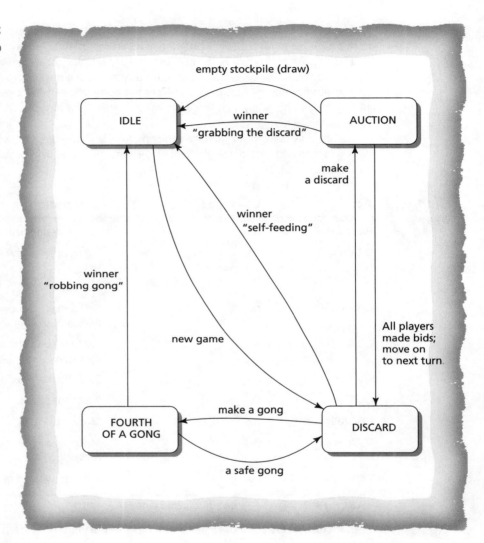

Accordingly, the following field variables should be added to the Table class:

```
// constants for Table.status:
public static final int IDLE = 0;      // no game in progress
public static final int DISCARD = 1;   // someone's turn to discard
public static final int AUCTION = 2;   // tile discarded, bid for it
public static final int FOURTH = 3;    // gong with a 4th tile
public int status = IDLE;               // table status
public int turn = -1;                   // seat of player having turn
public int dealer = -1;                 // seat of dealer
public byte active = 0;                 // discarded tile
public byte[] actions =                 // plays made by the players
```

```
    { -1, -1, -1, -1 };
public byte[] action_masks =              // acceptable plays
    { 1, 1, 1, 1 };
Hand stockpile = new Hand(144);           // stockpile to draw tiles from
Hand[] pri_hands = new Hand[4];           // concealed hands
Hand[] pub_hands = new Hand[4];           // revealed hands
Hand[] semi_pubs = new Hand[4];           // concealed gongs
Hand[] out_tiles = new Hand[4];           // previously discarded tiles
Hand[] winning = new Hand[4];             // mahjong pattern
```

A player's hand could be stored in the Player class, but I chose to think of it as belonging to that player's seat rather than the player himself. This way, if a player leaves the table, someone else can take his seat and continue the game with his hand.

The server needs to send the clients various types of packets. They typically contain the game state or each player's hand. These packets are summarized in Table 18-5.

Packet Type	Fields	Description
SP_GAME	dealer	New game and the dealer.
SP_TURN	seat	His turn to discard.
SP_DISCARD	tile	A tile is discarded, or fourth of a gong.
SP_TILES	seat, hand	Tiles of a player.
SP_YOUR_PRIV	hand	Your concealed tiles.
SP_YOUR_DRAW	tile	The tile you just drew in.
SP_YOUR_PLAY	result	Was your last play accepted?
SP_YOUR_CHOICES	flags	You can make these plays.
SP_OUT_TILES	seat, hand	Previous discards.
SP_WIN	seat	He wins the game.

TABLE 18-5 ◈ MahJong-related server packets

Starting a New Game

A new game starts when the table gets four players. First, in Table.join(), we check if the table has four players. If so, we call the NewGame() method, which does the following things:

1. Tells everyone that a new game has started, by sending an SP_GAME.

2. Creates and shuffles a stockpile of 144 tiles.

3. Deals 13 tiles to each player, and a 14th tile to a selected dealer.

4. Sends updates on all tiles with the appropriate SP_TILES and SP_YOUR_PRIV packets. See the Table.play() method below to see how this is done.

5. Tells everyone the dealer has the turn to discard, by sending an SP_TURN.

The NewGame() method is also called when a game ends and all four players agree to start a new one (say, by sending a CP_PLAY packet with action PASS).

Adding the Server Code for Game Play

Now we can finally add server code to handle a MahJong game. This involves writing a play() method in the Table class, and a handler hdPlay() in Player that reads in a CP_PLAY packet and calls the play() method of that player's table.

```
// in class Table
public synchronized void play (Player him, byte action, byte tile) {}
```

This method is declared with a *synchronized* keyword, because it is potentially called by multiple players' threads. Now, you might recall from previous discussion that all packet handlers, hence play(), must return quickly. Fortunately, for most board and card games this is not a problem—the rules are simple and easy to check.

So what is involved in the play() method? Let's just take one case, where a Player *him* makes a discard. First check whether he has that tile:

```
if (action == DISCARD) {                  // he wants to discard
  int s = him.seat;
  pri_hands[s].unselectAll();             // unmark everything
  if (pri_hands[s].search(tile, 1) == 0) {
    him.output(Packet.SPYourPlay(false)); // reject this play
    return;
  }
  him.output(Packet.SPYourPlay(true));    // confirm play
  pri_hands[s].delete();                  // delete from hand
  active = tile;                          // make the discard
  outputTable(Packet.SPDiscard(tile));    // tell everyone
```

Then, tell everyone about the discarded tile, and what this player's hand looks like now:

```
// conceal the concealed tiles to the other players
Hand to_other = new Hand();
to_other.append(pub_hands[s]);
for (int i = 0; i < semi_pubs[s]; i++) {
  to_other.addTile((byte)0, semi_pubs[s].groupAt(i), false);
}
for (int i = 0; i < pri_hands[s]; i++) {
  to_other.addTile((byte)0, Hand.SINGLE, false);
}
for (int i = 0; i < 4; i++) {              // send to others
  if (players[i] != null && i != s)
    players[i].output(Packet.SPTiles(s, to_other));
}
```

We also have to determine what the other players can do with the discarded tile, and tell them that:

```
for (int i = 0; i < 4; i++) {
  if (i == s) {                            // he can only wait
    actions[s] = PASS;
    action_masks[s] = 0;
    him.output(Packet.SPYourChoices(0));
    continue;
  }
  actions[i] = -1;
  Hand h = pri_hands[i];
  if (i == (s + 1) % 4) {                  // immediate right
    action_masks[i] = 1 << DRAW;           // he can draw
    boolean up1 = h.search(Tile.stepUp(tile), 1) != 0;
    boolean up2 = h.search(Tile.stepUp(Tile.stepUp(tile)), 1) != 0;
    boolean dn1 = h.search(Tile.stepDn(tile), 1) != 0;
    boolean dn2 = h.search(Tile.stepDn(Tile.stepDn(tile)), 1) != 0;
    if (up1 && up2)
      action_masks[i] |= 1 << CONN_UP;  // he can chow
    if (up1 && dn1)
      action_masks[i] |= 1 << CONN_MD;  // he can chow
    if (dn1 && dn2)
      action_masks[i] |= 1 << CONN_DN;  // he can chow
  } else action_masks[i] = 1 << PASS;   // he can pass (not draw)
  int n_id = h.search(tile, 3);
  if (n_id >= 2) {
    action_masks[i] |= 1 << TRIP;         // he can pong
    if (n_id == 3)
      action_masks[i] |= 1 << QUAD;       // he can gong
  }
  h.unselectAll();                         // unmark everything again
  if ((winning[i] = CheckMahJong(s, tile)) != null)
    action_masks[i] |= 1 << WIN;          // he can win
  if (players[i] != null)                  // tell him his choices
    players[i].output(Packet.SPYourChoices(action_masks[i]));
}
```

The other cases are quite similar to this, just tedious to write down fully. If you are writing your own game, be sure to produce something like Figure 18-5 first. Then it's just a matter of translating it into code.

Checking for a MahJong Pattern

The CheckMahJong() method we call above looks at a player's hand (revealed tiles together with concealed ones) and determines if he has a MahJong pattern. If so, the method returns a Hand with all the tiles grouped up into four sets and a pair. Otherwise, it returns *null*. This can be achieved with a simple recursive algorithm.

The recursive function takes as arguments a fixed hand of tiles that are already grouped up, a boolean value indicating whether the fixed hand contains a pair or not, and another hand of tiles to test on. We simply look at the first tile of the test hand, and see if we can make chows, a pong, or a pair (if the fixed hand doesn't have one already) with it and other tiles in the test hand. If no groups can be formed, we return *null*. Otherwise, in each possible case, we construct a new set of arguments using the new group we form, call the function itself again, and return the first non-*null* return value from the recursive calls. In the final situation, we have an empty test hand, which means the fixed hand is a MahJong pattern, which is returned all the way up the calling stack. The implementation is tedious yet straightforward.

Given this recursive function, our CheckMahJong() method simply calls it with the fixed hand being the revealed tiles plus concealed gongs, which also have fixed status, the boolean value being *false*, and the test hand being the concealed tiles.

Adding Finishing Touches

After the first release of my software, I kept adding features to it. They are not fancy, but either make the server a more robust environment or increase players' convenience. I will discuss them briefly here.

A Flexible Scoring System

No game will attract players unless it calculates score. For MahJong, there are well-defined scoring systems, but alas, too many of them. I have chosen a large common subset of the most popular conventions, and allow some minor variations that are adjustable as table options. Implementing them is relatively straightforward after what we've been through. It's just a matter of adding variables to the Table class, patching up the protocol to transmit the options, and finally, making a new GUI window for the players to view and change them. To prevent chaos, I only allow the creator of a table to change the options, and only when no game is in progress.

A Player Database

The database records a player's name, password, score, and optional data such as e-mail address, home page URL, a "plan," and his preferred client setup. Since I did not own a database server, I had to write my own. What I came up with is the RecordFile class, based on the library RandomAccessFile. Abstractly, a RecordFile holds an arbitrary number of *records*, which are simply byte streams whose length can vary. The physical file is chopped into *blocks* of fixed length, and a record can occupy any number of blocks. As records shrink or grow, some blocks may be freed and reused later. Thus, a RecordFile can be thought of as an extremely simple file system! I associate to each player such a record, and use DataOutput and DataInput calls to store and retrieve player records.

The RecordFile class is in the types package. You may find it useful for your own games.

To make the database easy to access, I also expanded the protocol and the client GUI a little, to let you "finger" other players. This brings up a window to show the other player's personal information as he put it on the server.

Dealing with Bad Connections

The Internet is not perfect. Many a time the network connection between a player's client and the server breaks down. In this situation, it's advisable to free up that player's slot. Unfortunately, the current Java implementations make this task harder than it ought to be. Instead of immediately throwing an IOException on dead sockets, Java may simply block forever on read/write calls.

My solution is using *ping packets*. On the client side, we spawn a thread that sends a ping packet once every 30 seconds. The ping packet carries no information other than that it has reached the server. On the server side, every time a player's listener thread reads in a ping packet, it increases a ping counter. We use one extra server thread, too, called the WatchDog, which is usually sleeping, but wakes up once every minute or so to check the counters of all players. A counter's being 0 means that player's network connection is hosed, and we disconnect him. Otherwise, we reset his counter to 0 for the next round.

Adding Timeout Functionality

The ping method has the added bonus of being able to gauge a user's idle time. If a player is playing on a table, and the ping counter reaches 2 before we receive any CP_PLAY packet from him, we can make a safe guess that he is probably answering the phone or busted by his boss; in either case we can kick him off the table to let someone else play.

An Urge! feature comes with the timeouts. There is an Urge! button that, when clicked on, will ask the server to alert everyone on the table to pay more attention to the gare. The alert comes in the form of a "Duke" figure waving at you, accompanied by a sound (which can be turned off). A timer on the server side makes sure this feature isn't abused.

Debugging the Game

After implementing everything up to this point, we are looking at tens of thousands of lines of source code. Debugging is tough even if you have the best development tools at your disposal. It is therefore important to divide the code into functional chunks, write one at a time, then fully debug and gradually add onto it. For example, I finished the basic client-server pair before adding MahJong features, and then used subsets of MahJong rules before handling the complete game.

Another way to speed up debugging is to write some extra code to get you started in a midgame situation. I created a back-door on the server, such that I could send to the server a specially formatted message string that encodes a particular hand I want to have, and the server will give me that hand. This way I can test game play without betting my luck on drawing the tiles I want to test on.

Comments

There are several sites running public servers with my software. You can access them from my Internet MahJong Meta-Server Web page at URL http://www.math.princeton.edu/~ztfeng/mj_servers.html. You can also find there more information about MahJong, documentation of server features, and the most recent source code release.

The companion CD-ROM of this book also contains the source code. However, it has not been polished as I've done to the code segments given in this chapter; indeed, some code that achieves more or less the same functionality looks much uglier there! Look for future releases, which will contain more features, bug fixes, and which may or may not be more readable.

To summarize, Java's platform independence, built-in networking, multithreading, and the still-immature but promising AWT library make developing multiplayer Internet games like the MahJong Server quite easy. Indeed, it took me less than three weeks to get the first version running. If I had started this project in C and Motif or Win32, I would have eventually given up as I had done with several previous endeavors. Let's wish Java well-being, and enjoy programming in it!

Suggestion Box

🗡 When writing a multiplayer game, first get a simple client and sever pair working, and gradually add to the client-server protocol to do fancy things.

🗡 Use multiple threads to keep track of different players, but handle synchronization with care.

🗡 For a game with complicated rules, it's often a good idea to express it as a finite-state machine, as I have done with MahJong. The game is in one of several states, and valid game play moves the game from one state to another.

🗡 If your game needs an extensible player database, you may want to look at the RecordFile class in the IMS source.code. You can read/write variable-length records with it. For simple score-keeping, the RandomAccessFile class in java.io probably suffices.

🗡 The easiest way to write a multiplayer game is probably to study somebody else's code and replace appropriate chunks with your own. If you start your own game from the latest version of IMS, then you will already have a lot of raw functionality!

Summary

This chapter covered the design and implementation of a multiplayer Internet game. We studied the client-server architecture, the protocol, socket programming, the use of threads, and how to implement a complicated game like MahJong. You also saw plenty of examples of AWT in action. Now you are ready to bring games to the Internet, where Java is intended to rule!

19

Slider Puzzle

Steve Green

me troule fiare le manouelle e lle quali sono vano e llalsa
gran pesi e uure li omini a sopene o sago grano di boue
hare nellamo uso per malstesti della manouella pegi qui n
orga o pio i somo pribi bnts.

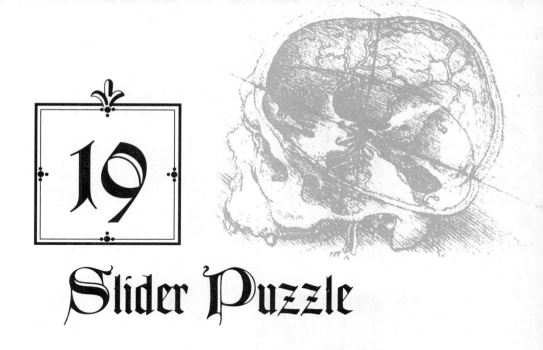

19

Slider Puzzle

This chapter describes how to write a Java applet for a simple slider puzzle. The aim of the game is simple. After mixing up the numbers, or blocks, you return the blocks to their original positions by sliding them about. Most people are familiar with this game, whether it uses numbers or a picture.

On starting the puzzle, the player hears some ambient thinking music while the applet draws the blocks. A mouse click over a wood block indicates that this block should move, if it is free to do so. More than one block may be manipulated in a single move by clicking the lead block. For example, if the number 13 block shown in Figure 19-1 is selected, then it and the two blocks to the right are moved to the right. The resulting configuration is shown in Figure 19-2.

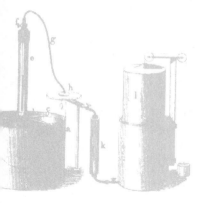

FIGURE 19-1

◎ ◎ ◎ ◎ ◎ ◎

*The puzzle
solved*

FIGURE 19-2

◎ ◎ ◎ ◎ ◎ ◎

After a move

During each move, a *clink* sound can be heard to provide audible feedback. Selecting a block that is not free to move will generate a sound of smashing glass. On completion of the puzzle, the sound of hysterical laughter will ring out from the player's speakers.

Of course it would be pointless starting with the puzzle already solved, so the Randomize button was added to allow the player to mess things up. Figure 19-3 shows what it could look like after this button is clicked.

FIGURE 19-3

◎ ◎ ◎ ◎ ◎ ◎

*Randomized
puzzle*

Creating the Basic Program

The aim when developing this program is to learn the basics of how to display and animate graphics, and how to synchronize sounds with the animation.

Understanding the Game's Logic

Before getting into the nitty gritty of the applet, let's look at the overall logic.

First, the init() method (shown in Figure 19-4) is called by the Web browser or applet viewer. This method sets up everything the game needs to work with, including the wood block images and the sounds.

Once the applet is running, it waits for the execution environment to send events to it. The only event that this applet is interested in is mouse clicks. Mouse clicks over the game's only button, Randomize, are treated differently from mouse clicks over other parts of the applet area. Both mouseDown and mouseUp events may be intercepted and processed by your applet. The mouseDown event has been chosen to be acted on simply because it makes the game feel better to use. The mouseDown() method is shown in Figure 19-5.

FIGURE 19-4

◎ ◎ ◎ ◎ ◎ ◎

The init()
method

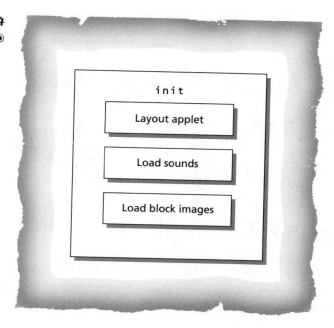

FIGURE 19-5
◎ ◎ ◎ ◎ ◎ ◎
*The
mouseDown()
method*

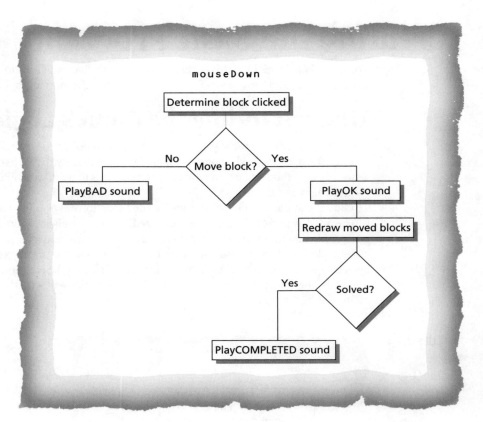

The only other event this applet needs to be concerned about is one generated in response to the Randomize button being clicked. The execution environment calls a method called action() with the name of the button clicked. By simply including this method in your applet, you can determine which button was pressed and take appropriate action. Figure 19-6 shows the logic flow of this method, as used in this applet.

Creating the Graphics

First, let's get the graphics. A large image that contains all the beautiful wood blocks will be "cut up" into smaller GIF images that can be individually displayed and animated in the program. These images should be saved in separate files named 1.GIF to 64.GIF, the file number corresponding to the block number. The block images are shown in Figure 19-7.

FIGURE 19-6
◎ ◎ ◎ ◎ ◎ ◎
*The action()
method*

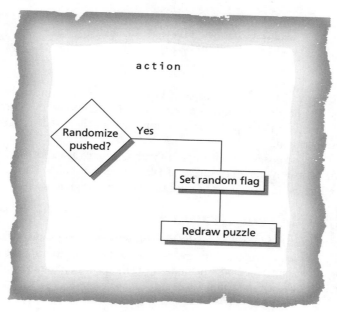

FIGURE 19-7
◎ ◎ ◎ ◎ ◎ ◎
*The block
images*

Loading the Graphics

In order to display a graphic, it must first be loaded into the program. The code in Listing 19-1 details how this is accomplished.

Listing 19-1 *Loading the graphics*

```
// Load the blocks..

maxBlocks = GridSize.height * GridSize.width;

for (y=0;y<GridSize.height;y++)
    for (x=0;x<GridSize.width;x++) {
        if ( block < maxBlocks ) {
            name = "graphics/" + block + ".gif";
            grid[y][x] = newTile(getImage(getCodeBase(),name),block,name);
            block++;
        }
```

continued on next page

continued from previous page

```
    else {
        grid[x][y] = new Tile(null,0,null);
        blank = new Point(x,y);
    }
}
```

The correct number of GIF files will be loaded, corresponding to the numbered wood blocks. The height and width are determined by examining the amount of space that was allocated for the applet. The maximum size for the puzzle is 8x8, only limited by the number of images.

The last grid position is left empty, providing a single space for blocks to slide around.

This code also creates the array of Tile objects that holds, for each image, the corresponding wood block number and the name of the graphics file.

Displaying the Graphics

The paint() method is called by the Web browser or applet viewer whenever the whole image needs to be redrawn. The update() method is called in response to the applet itself calling the repaint() method. The update() method is set up to call another method called drawGrid(), shown in Listing 19-2.

Listing 19-2 *Displaying the graphics*

```
private void drawGrid(Graphics g) {

    int x,y;

    // Only draw blocks that have changed to improve display speed.

    for (y=0;y<GridSize.height;y++)
        for (x=0;x<GridSize.width;x++) {
            if ( grid[y][x].changed ) {
                if ( grid[y][x].number != 0 )
                    g.drawImage(grid[y][x].img,x*48,y*48,this);
                else
                    g.clearRect(x*48,y*48,48,48);
                grid[y][x].changed = false;
            }
        }
}
```

You'll notice from the code that only blocks that have the *changed* variable set to *true* are redrawn. This greatly improves the efficiency of the code, especially on slower machines. The *changed* flags are set by the move() method, in response to a mouse click on a movable wood block, or by drawAll(), which is called by paint() in response to something dramatic like the browser window being resized.

Moving the Blocks

In order to get the blocks moving, you need to detect any mouse clicks and work out which block has been selected, as shown in Listing 19-3.

Listing 19-3 *Responding to mouse clicks*

```
public boolean mouseDown(Event evt, int x, int y) {

    // Mouse clicked somewhere

    Point from;

    // Translate to block coordinates

    from = new Point(x/48,y/48);

    // Kill the intro sound if still playing...

    if ( intro )
        introSound.stop();
    intro = false;

    if ( from.x >= GridSize.width || from.y >= GridSize.height )
        return true;

    // If on the same row or column as the blank we can move

    if ( move(from) ) {
        clinkSound.play();

        // Wait for about 250ms so that the sound and the
        // animation appear to be in sync.

        try {
            Thread.sleep(250);
        } catch (InterruptedException e) {}
        repaint();
        if ( solved() )
            winSound.play();
    }
    else
        badSound.play();
    return true;
}
```

This mouseDown() method is really what makes everything happen. It is called by the Web browser or applet viewer in response to a mouseDown event within the region of the screen under your applet's control. The absolute applet coordinates are then converted to block coordinates.

The move() method then attempts to move the block, or blocks. If it succeeds, then the clink sound is played and the blocks that have been affected are redrawn. A smashing glass sound is played if the block cannot be moved.

The 250ms delay was added to synchronize the sound and image motion.

You'll notice from the code above that the move() method does most of the work, as demonstrated in Listing 19-4.

Listing 19-4 *The move() method*

```
private boolean move(Point from) {

    Point to,by;

    by = new Point(delta(from.x,blank.x),delta(from.y,blank.y));

    if ( (by.x == 0 && by.y == 0) || (by.x != 0 && by.y != 0) )
        return false;

    to = new Point(from.x + by.x, from.y + by.y);

    // Try and move, if blocked by another block, move it first...

    if ( grid[to.y][to.x].number != 0 )
        move(to);

    // Move the block and repaint

    grid[to.y][to.x].number = grid[from.y][from.x].number;    // here...
    grid[to.y][to.x].img = grid[from.y][from.x].img;
    grid[to.y][to.x].changed = true;

    grid[from.y][from.x].number = 0;                          // from here...
    grid[from.y][from.x].img = null;
    grid[from.y][from.x].changed = true;

    blank = from;                                             // blank is now here...
    return true;
}
```

The move() method accepts the coordinates, in block units, of the block that is clicked on. It then calculates a unit movement vector, that is, which way to move, in order to put it onto the blank position. If this vector has an x and a y component, then the block is not in the same row or column as the blank square and, therefore, cannot move. The value is also checked to see if the user has clicked on the blank square itself.

Once it is determined that this block can move, the target coordinates for the move are calculated. If a block is present at this position, then this block must be moved first before the selected block can move. A recursive call to the move() method is performed to see if the next block can be moved, and so on down the line, until finally, the target position is the blank square.

Each block affected by the move has its *changed* flag set to ensure it is redrawn by the next update. This method returns *true*, if the block moved, to let the mouseDown() method know to play the right sound and repaint() the screen.

Adding the Sound

Just like the graphics, the sounds must be loaded into the program before they can be played. The sounds used must be supported by the browser or applet viewer. All the sounds are in AU format. Listing 19-5 gives the code for loading the sounds.

Listing 19-5 *Loading the sounds*

```
//      Load sounds...

    try {
        introSound = getAudioClip(
                        newURL(getDocumentBase(),"sounds/spacemusic.au"));
        introSound.loop();
        clinkSound = getAudioClip(
                        new URL(getDocumentBase(),"sounds/clink.au"));
        winSound = getAudioClip(
                        new URL(getDocumentBase(),"sounds/laugh.au"));
        badSound = getAudioClip(
                        new URL(getDocumentBase(),"sounds/crash.au"));
    } catch ( java.net.MalformedURLException e) {}
```

The getAudioClip() method loads the audio file into an object of class AudioClip. This class has several methods to control the playing of audio clips. The loop() method plays the click continuously until the program executes the stop() method on the same AudioClip object. The play() method plays the sound once.

If you look closely at Listing 19-5, you will see that the loop() method is executed for *introSound* immediately after it has been loaded. This sound continues to play while the other sounds and images are loaded. It is not until the user presses the mouse button for the first time that this sound is stopped (refer to Listing 19-3).

Adding Some Complexity

So far the basics of what makes the program work have been described. This section will outline other aspects of the program that were added to improve the playability of the puzzle.

The Image Observer

The imageUpdate() method is without doubt the most mysterious method in the applet. This method is an ImageObserver that receives messages regarding the status of images being drawn by the drawImage() method.

But why do you need a method to observe the status of graphics being drawn? Because drawImage() draws the graphics asynchronously. That is, after the drawImage() method returns to the calling method, the graphic is not necessarily displayed. If the image takes a little while to be displayed, like a GIF image, then an ImageObserver will be notified when some or all of this image is ready to be displayed.

Have a look at the drawImage() method called in Listing 19-2. You can see that the last parameter is *this*. *this* informs the Abstract Windowing Toolkit (AWT) that this applet wants to be notified when some or all of any graphics being displayed are ready.

The final thing to do is to declare a method called imageUpdate() to receive these messages and take appropriate action, as shown in Listing 19-6.

Listing 19-6 *The image observer*

```
public boolean imageUpdate(Image img, int flags, int x, int y, int w,⇐
inth) {

// When image is drawn, redraw THIS BLOCK.
// This is done by first finding where the block in the grid.
// THIS IS A BIT CRUDE!

    int iy,ix;

    if ((flags & (SOMEBITS|FRAMEBITS|ALLBITS)) != 0) {
        for (iy=0;iy<GridSize.height;iy++)
            for (ix=0;ix<GridSize.width;ix++)
                if ( grid[iy][ix].img == img ) {
                    grid[iy][ix].changed = true;
                    repaint(100);
                    return (flags & (ALLBITS|ERROR)) == 0;
                }
    }
    return (flags & (ALLBITS|ERROR)) == 0;
}
```

The first thing this method does is check the flags that have been set to determine if the graphic is to be drawn again. If some of the graphic (SOMEBITS), a complete frame (FRAMEBITS), or the whole thing (ALLBITS) is ready, then call drawImage() again to display whichever of the parts is complete.

The next trick to work out is which graphic is to be redrawn. The array of blocks is searched, looking for an image that matches the one passed to imageUpdate(), the image's *changed* flag is set, and repaint(100) is called to signal the AWT to call update() within 100 milliseconds.

The Randomize Button

So far, you have seen how the program interacts with the user by the use of the mouse. You also need to understand how the Randomize button works.

Before a button can be used, it must be drawn, as done in Listing 19-7.

Listing 19-7 *Drawing the button*

```
setLayout(new BorderLayout());
...
Panel p = new Panel();
add("South",p);
p.add(new Button("Randomize"));
```

Here, an object of class Panel was created and placed at the bottom of the applet ("South"), then a single button was added to it. "South" is a container of the BorderLayout class. The BorderLayout class probably offers the simplest way to arrange things in an applet window.

Whenever a button is clicked, the Web browser or applet viewer calls the action() method. You can intercept these events by defining a method of the same name in your applet, as in Listing 19-8.

Listing 19-8 *Detecting whether a button has been selected*

```
public boolean action(Event evt, Object arg) {
    if ( arg.equals("Randomize") ) {
        random = true;
        repaint();
    }
    return true;
}
```

The applet can then simply check to see if the value of the argument passed equals the name of the button drawn earlier, and then take the appropriate action.

Here a *random* flag is set and a call made to repaint(). The repaint() method causes update() to be called "as soon as possible." The update() method detects the *random* flag and then executes another method to mix up the position of the blocks, rather than draw the grid as normal.

The randomize() method animates the movement of the blocks by performing a sequence of moves, ensuring that the grid is redrawn between each movement so that the user can observe the blocks being jumbled about. This is demonstrated in Listing 19-9.

Listing 19-9 Mixing up the puzzle

```
private void randomize(Graphics g){

    int i,iter=GridSize.height*GridSize.width*GridSize.width;
    Point from;

    for (i=0; i<iter;i++) {
        if ( Math.random() > 0.5 )
            move(new Point(blank.x,(int)(Math.random() *⇐
GridSize.height)));
        else
            move(new Point((int)(Math.random() *⇐
GridSize.width),blank.y));
        drawGrid(g);
    }
}
```

The randomize() method first decides whether to do a horizontal or vertical movement. It then randomly picks a block in that row or column and calls the move() method to shift this block, or blocks. The drawGrid() method is executed between each random movement so that this scrambling process becomes an animated sequence. The number of moves is determined by the size of the puzzle. For instance, in Figure 19-8, 8x8x8, or 512 moves, are performed to get this huge puzzle well mixed up.

Originally this method simulated a madman on the mouse, clicking away frantically at random locations on the puzzle. The problem with this, however, is that a block selected at random has a less than even chance of not being able to move. It had to be decided whether to simply increase the number of iterations or somehow change the code so that every random move would result in a block, or blocks, moving.

▦ Note

You might be wondering why this method simulates lots of moves rather than just shuffling the blocks in some other way.

The answer is that simply scrambling the blocks could result in an unsolvable configuration! By performing a series of simulated moves, the puzzle is guaranteed to be solvable.

Adding Enhancements

Now that you have created the basic game, you may want to add some enhancements to make it more enjoyable and challenging. Most of the ideas included here for enhancing this program come from Joseph Carlson's original Amiga program.

FIGURE 19-8

◎ ◎ ◎ ◎ ◎ ◎

*The 8x8
puzzle!*

Adding a Solve Button

Add a Solve button to the panel and the necessary code to the action() method to *catch* this event when the button is clicked. The applet then works out the shortest path to the solved puzzle, and animates the movement of the blocks to show the applet solving the puzzle.

This can be accomplished by performing a game tree traversal. Your program allocates a score to the current puzzle configuration, based on the number of pieces already in the correct place. Then, it evaluates all the possible moves from this configuration in order, from the highest scoring downward. Since this algorithm is recursive, when the solution is found, all the moves from the current position to the final goal configuration may be obtained by falling back up the tree and recording the moves taken at each depth.

Keep in mind that this process can take quite a while, and consume quite a lot of memory, especially if attempting to solve the 8x8 puzzle!

Using Pictures Instead of Numbers

Instead of numbers, each block could contain a piece of an image. To make this very flexible, the applet could be made to load an arbitrary image, then cut it up into smaller images to use as the blocks.

Improving the Sounds

Better sounds would also improve the look and feel of this game. Joe Carlson's Amiga version has very nice "woody" sounds, but no sound converter has been found that can turn them into sounds that Netscape can play.

Done in combination with pictures instead of wood block images, sounds can be located that somehow relate to the image being displayed. You could have a lot of fun with this!

Creating Smoother Animation

Instead of having a block move abruptly from one position to another, you can modify your game so that the blocks move in smaller steps, perhaps as small as a pixel, to make the animation appear more fluid.

This enhancement may need to be benchmarked on slow machines, such as 33MHz 80486-based PCs, at least until the JIT (just-in-time) Java compilers become available, which promise at least a 10 times speed improvement.

Suggestion Box

- Investigate other layout styles instead of BorderLayout. You can experiment with placing the buttons in different positions relative to the puzzle itself.

- You can create a new window to run the applet in, rather than allocating space in the HTML page. This could look very effective. This window could be made to be resizable. The applet could decide whether to rescale the image or redraw the grid with a new number of blocks when resized.

- Investigate one of the many new Java development environments, such as Microsoft's Visual J++. This is a much better way to program in Java.

- Ensure your bicycle wheelnuts are tight before attempting to ride! Failure to do so could result in a rapid meeting with the pavement!

Summary

I hope you have gained some understanding of how to display graphics, perform simple animation, and incorporate sound into a Java applet. I also hope you have gained an insight into some of the inner workings of Java applets, and that you use this knowledge in developing your own. There are many excellent Java books available now, including this one, to help programmers utilize this very powerful new language.

20

The Game of Worm

Roman Mach

20

The Game of Worm

What Is Worm?

In the game of Worm, you control the direction of an abstract worm on a rectangular playing surface. The worm collects treats while avoiding collision with solid objects. The more treats your worm eats, the longer it gets, until it gets so tangled that free motion is impossible and the game ends with a collision.

Implementing the game of Worm has been a kind of "Hello World" game programming initiation since the days of character-mode terminals. Although it is by no means the easiest or most popular game programming exercise, it requires less logical construction than a tic-tac-toe implementation and as such is easier to describe and implement.

Most implementations of Worm are set on a two-dimensional rectangular surface where the motion of the worm is restricted to the directions left, right, up, and down. Figure 20-1 shows a worm on the playing surface with a nearby treat.

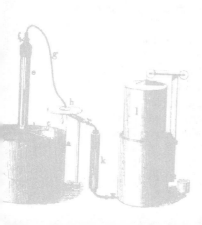

FIGURE 20-1

◎ ◎ ◎ ◎ ◎ ◎

Worm approaching treat on playing surface

A well-designed Worm implementation will let the player learn the ropes by keeping the initial challenge level low and allowing discovery of the game's behavior and underlying strategy. Eventually the player will get hooked and try to devise a plan to position the worm's body to collect the most points. A current and high score table should be an essential element of this game.

In this chapter you will see how to build a basic Worm game that meets these specifications, and then see how the code can be extended to include complex functionality such as self-guiding worms providing the function of a moving barrier.

This implementation of Worm is designed around a square playing surface with an invisible grid to contain the worm segments. The worm is composed of a collection of connected squares moving across the gaming surface. The worm has a head and a tail, and the user is allowed to change the worm's movements in one of two directions perpendicular to the current direction of motion. Upon startup, the worm is headed straight for a wall with which it will collide unless the user changes its direction. Figure 20-2 shows the composition of a worm.

The primary incentive of this game is to collect as many treats as possible before crashing into a wall or other solid object. The treat is a well-identified square placed in a random location on the grid (but not on the worm's body!), and the player tries to intersect the head of the worm with this square. Immediately after the treat is eaten, a new treat is placed somewhere else on the playing surface. The player is given a short break of under a second to collect his or her wits after the worm eats a treat, and can change the worm's direction before it starts moving again. This short delay is crucial if the random location for the treat happens to be right up against a solid object and the worm is heading straight at this object; the player will just have time to switch direction before the collision. Keeping the game fair but challenging is one of Worm's design goals.

As play continues and the worm's body lengthens, the worm will become more constricted in its movements. The player will need to plan ahead, winding the worm's body out of the way of the next treat. Sooner or later the player will have a momentary lapse of concentration or coordination, and the worm's head will collide with some solid object.

FIGURE 20-2

◉ ◉ ◉ ◉ ◉ ◉

Composition of a worm and a treat using square segments

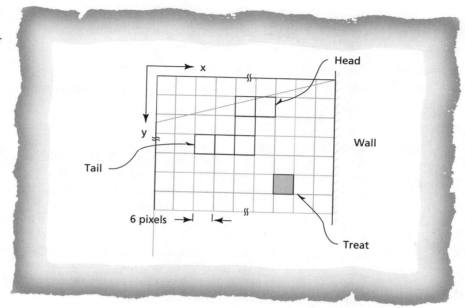

The point of collision is colored red to not only alert the player of the point of contact, but also to confirm that the collision wasn't a fluke or bug in the program.

Additional challenges can be added to the game to make it more exciting for advanced players, such as progressively increasing the worm's speed or adding autonomous worms.

Game Play

Worm is a geometric game based on colored squares, and as such will have different requirements than a game based around scenery. Motion will need to be regular and smooth. Geometry implies logical organization, and thus there will be no fudge factors in the placement or motion of objects. A treat is either eaten or it is not; there are no partially eaten treats.

The most basic design of Worm is simply a playing surface and a single worm. Choosing this as our first goal will confirm that the program provides basic functionality. The final version will include features that provide a very playable interface. Let's outline some of the desired features we would like to see:

- Collision detection with walls and objects

- Random treat placement

- Tail lengthening with play duration

Scoring based on play duration and treat collection

Contrasting coloring of point of collision

Sound when treat is eaten and when collision occurs

Autonomous worms that move to provide additional, moving barriers

The game could be designed with many features that might not be appropriate. Placing many treats at once on the playing surface could distract the player's attention from maneuvering around obstacles, but more important, the player wouldn't have to plan ahead as much for the next treat, taking some strategy away from the game. An illustration of an active screen with only one treat is shown in Figure 20-3.

Many games are designed with a limited number of "lives." Worm will be designed to allow an easy restart after every death. If the player gets hooked, a quick restart will encourage longer game play. The challenge in Worm is simply to score as high as possible and last as long as possible.

Although it may seem like a rigid limitation of the design, playing on a grid with moving square objects can be transformed with minor changes to an entirely different game with similar attributes. For instance, you could create a game called String that provided full 360-degree motion of a pixel-wide string.

Designing Worm

After carefully identifying the features of the game, you will need to consider how best to design the game within a programming framework. If you are writing the game in an older language with fewer operators and constructs, then your approach will very likely be constrained by the language itself. Luckily, Java is a language that includes the

FIGURE 20-3
◉ ◉ ◉ ◉ ◉ ◉
A long worm fills the playing surface, which can make reaching the treat difficult

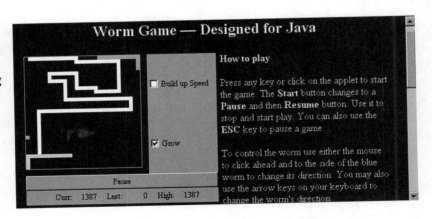

best parts of C++ and object-oriented programming methods to provide many different ways to solve a given problem. Worm will be designed to take full advantage of the language's broad capabilities. Below is a short digression on how not to design a game under Java, followed by a satisfactory solution using object-oriented and event-driven methods.

The Playing Surface–Three Possible Approaches

The playing surface of Worm is based on a Cartesian grid. This means we can denote any location on the surface with an integer x and y coordinate. Each x and y coordinate may occupy a square on the drawing surface as small as one pixel. Figure 20-4 shows the difference between screen and game coordinates. Each square is either occupied or unoccupied. If occupied, it may contain a treat or a portion of the worm's body, which we'll call a *segment*. Because we have full control of what we draw on the display, we are not restricted in how we implement entities on the playing surface.

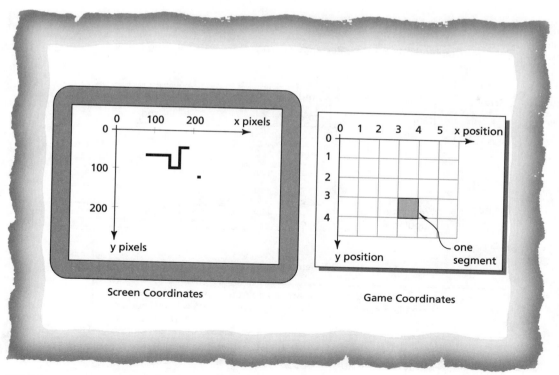

FIGURE 20-4 ◉ *Screen and game coordinates compared*

We will show three approaches that satisfy our requirements, each with its advantages and disadvantages, but show how one is clearly superior. The preferred solution uses a ring buffer to store the worm's segment locations in an ordered fashion. By using the object-oriented framework provided by the Java programming language and hiding the ring buffer implementation, we will show how using an object model benefits the overall design. These three approaches are compared in the matrix in Figure 20-5.

The Graphical Attribute Approach

In this method, each pixel on the playing surface has an associated graphical attribute, such as "red" or "blinking". Keeping track of objects on the playing surface by storing and retrieving a pixel's value can be beneficial, since additional data structures do not need to be designed into the game.

This approach has the disadvantage of being limited to a small class of games, mainly because you cannot directly store complex state information for any given pixel. Attempting to overlap objects and then restoring the playing surface becomes almost impossible with this approach. Worm does not have overlapping objects, and so a pixel-based state method may be feasible.

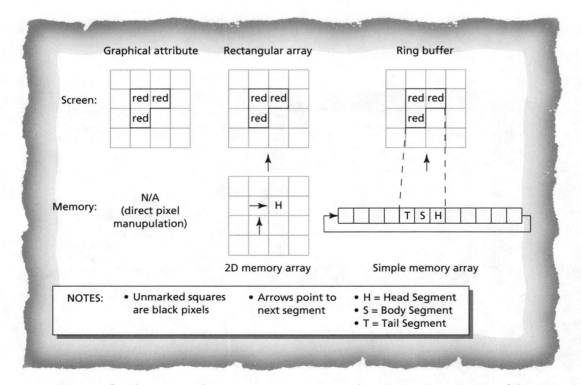

FIGURE 20-5 ◉ *Three Worm designs comparing screen and memory representations of the game*

If we set the color of a worm segment to "blue" and a treat to "green", we can call the appropriate graphics function to get the type of object for any pixel. Calling these graphics functions has the disadvantage of being slightly slower than referencing equivalent data structures in memory. This is because the system may have to perform pixel-to-memory translations and then go to possibly slower graphics memory to retrieve the desired data.

The Rectangular Array Approach

Taking the idea behind the graphical attribute approach and improving on it by building the equivalent data structure in memory affords us better control over state information. It may also be faster, since we don't need to make as many calls to API functions. We can build a rectangular array in memory where each element represents a square on the playing surface. Do not confuse this method with double-buffering, which holds a duplicate pixel-based image of the desired screen contents. During normal use this rectangular array would be processed and pixels would then be set appropriately in a double-buffer.

Each element in our array would be an integer that represents a square on the playing surface. We could mark the state of this square with a 0 if unoccupied, 1 if it is a worm segment, or 2 if a treat. As the game progresses, we could easily calculate which element would be occupied by the worm's head and check its value. If it is 1, then the worm collided with itself, if 2, the worm ate a treat. This solution is exactly what we want; however, we also have to erase our tail.

A simple but incorrect implementation of erasing the tail would be to check the segments in the immediate vicinity of the current tail segment and choose a segment with a value of 1 as the new tail. Since the scanning order is fixed, there will be certain configurations that will cause an incorrect choice of a new tail segment, leading to a portion of the worm's body being left behind on the playing surface!

One solution is to number the position of the next worm segment; for instance, 5 might represent "up". If we were to add additional worms (or other obstacles) to the playing surface, we would need to keep a list of each worm's head and tail.

The Ring Buffer Approach

The preceding rectangular array approach is good and fairly intuitive, but fails on one important point: it's not object oriented. This becomes apparent when we see that our worm encompasses two entities: the data structure that contains our worm's head and tail coordinates, and the playing surface that describes the location of each segment, each with a direction to the next tail segment. The entire implementation, including collision detection algorithms, is completely out in the open. If we were to add new functionality, such as overlapping worms, we would have a greater chance of impacting other, unrelated, code. If we designed the worms to be entities that were responsible for keeping track of their segments' location and ordering, overlapping segments could be easily implemented by adding z-order functionality to the worm object without impacting the drawing code.

An object has methods and attributes; a method for our worm object could be a function that sets a new head position based on the current direction of travel. An attribute could be a linked list of worm segment positions. When we used a worm object, we would never see that the worm uses a linked list to keep track of its segments. We could choose to add a new head segment at a given location and optionally remove a tail segment. We could never remove or alter a segment in the middle of the worm, because Java allows us to hide specific object attributes if there is no reason to make those attributes visible. Our cost of using such an approach is overhead—we need to add functions to access data that we would have accessed directly in the other suggested implementations. These functions may clutter the code, but they serve a hidden benefit: Changing an underlying implementation to accept z-ordering for overlapping worms is never visible to the user of the object except at the interfaces, thus requiring fewer rewrites of the code and potentially fewer bugs.

Worm will use this method of data hiding by implementing the worm as an object under Java. Creating multiple worms is simply a matter of constructing multiple instances of worm objects and integrating their interfaces into the game. The worm class will need, at minimum, to keep track of the segment coordinates in an ordered fashion. A queue providing this functionality and a ring buffer or linked-list implementation is all that is required to establish this relationship. From a practical standpoint, a ring buffer is implemented as a linear array with head and tail pointers. Figure 20-6 shows how we can "unwrap" a ring buffer into a linear array and retain the same functionality.

A linked list is a data structure that is frequently seen in programs. Each *link* is an object that "knows" only about the next link in the list. Linked lists can be extended to allow for knowledge about previous links, as in the case of a *double-linked list,* and can be grown as the need arises. Manipulating such a structure is straightforward, but can be confusing for programmers with experience in BASIC, since it typically relies on pointers, which are usually only seen in C programs. Worm will use the simpler, but less elegant, ring buffer to provide the same basic functionality as a linked list. The ring buffer will consist of a fixed array of Dimension objects, a Java class, and two indices that mark the start and end elements in the buffer.

Interfacing to the Worm

A worm has two goals in life: eat and move without colliding. The worm should be designed to be moved either by the player or by some automaton. We will design a class called SessionManager that will be responsible for moving the worm along the playing surface under the control of the player and checking for collisions with objects, treats, and walls. The SessionManager will not directly interface with the Java graphics API, but it will provide a consolidated interface to the abstract playing grid.

Placing the worm object in a class seems obvious: What is not obvious is how that object should be manipulated. This is purely a design choice left up to the programmer,

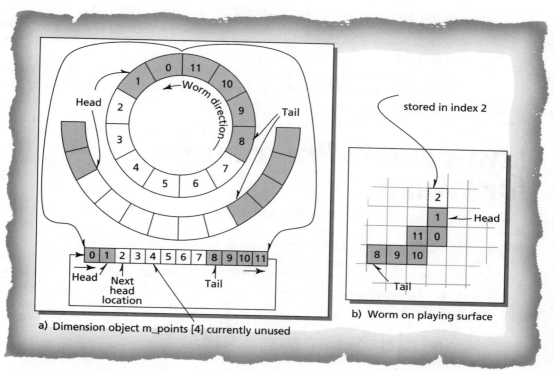

a) Dimension object m_points [4] currently unused

b) Worm on playing surface

FIGURE 20-6 ◉ *A ring buffer unwrapped*

but there are two obvious methods that could be used: leave control of worm motion to the worm object itself, or let the SessionManager dictate the worm's motion and size. In the first case, the worm object would need to manage growth and place collision requests though a collision query class; the SessionManager would just glue the components together through an outside "kicker" function. The latter case would consolidate action, player interface, and collision in one class at the cost of less optimal data hiding. The design of Worm will use the latter approach to show how responsibilities can be distributed among classes for illustrative purposes: Any attempt at optimizing object-oriented design is left up to the reader.

Breathing Life into the Game

Once an abstract gaming surface is complete, we are still missing two important elements: input/output interfacing and real-time activation of the playing surface's objects, both of which are part of the event-driven operating systems that host the Java Applet class. We will accept both mouse and keyboard control input and provide a colorful display with user-controls. We will launch a thread that calls the SessionManager at short, even intervals to make objects move on the playing surface. Each "kick" to the SessionManager corresponds to the head of the player's worm moving one square in the desired direction. Even timing is important for smooth operation. These components will be placed in a class called WormBin.

Once the game provides these fundamental functions, we can start adding features that improve game play, including double-buffering for smooth display changes, scoring, object coloring for visual cues, and sound.

Java-centric Programming for Worm

Java is typically found running under modern operating systems, but could just as easily run an air conditioner or other appliance. The key to this versatility comes at a price: it lacks many useful but potentially dangerous programming shortcuts that C++ provides. With Java you can take advantage of its relatively easy-to-use multithreading and networking capabilities that can be very difficult to program or require custom libraries in other languages. Just keep an eye out for some of the following gotchas when programming.

Multithreading Issues

Since Java code can be event-driven while supporting multiple threads of execution, we must be careful to design with functions that return data that is valid over the scope of the query. This usually means not storing state information that is dependent on event triggers, such as direction changes. The consequence could be lost segments and unexpected behavior.

Java Programming Gotchas

Java is an object-oriented language based on C++. As any C++ programmer discovers when programming Java, pointers are not supported, and returning values from functions has limitations. Objects cannot be used without being created using the *new* operator. Since C++ also has a *new* operator for pointers, the programmer has to remember that these are not pointer manipulations, but object manipulations that can extend across object boundaries.

Returning Values

Values can only be returned by either changing a passed-in object's attributes or by a return value. Passing in an object by reference and assigning it a new object will not change the original object.

Object Instance Assignments

Be careful how you return objects from functions. If your return value is a global object (it will not go out of scope) and it is assigned to another object, and that object is assigned to a third object, the original object is deleted and now points to the third object. Assigning objects in Java is common, but care should be exercised to prevent unexpected game behavior.

Optimizing Performance Under Java

Worm will be implemented with a minimum of allocations during game play to minimize garbage collection effects impacting the performance of the game. Each allocation requires a call to allocate storage and another later to free the storage by Java's garbage collection subsystem. If we can do this once at game startup, then these hidden effects are minimized.

Worm Game Class Components

The game of Worm is comprised of three classes: Worm, SessionManager, and WormBin. The Worm class keeps track of attributes, segment locations, and head direction. We call its functions to change direction and let it update its current position. We can query it to get its current length or get the coordinates to all of its points. SessionManager keeps track of the contents of the playing surface. It interfaces with the player, the worm, and the treat and delivers information to be displayed. WormBin interfaces to the Java APIs for player input and display output and implements the worker thread for real-time gaming. WormBin does not interface directly with the Worm class but goes through the SessionManager class if it needs to do a repaint on all worm segments. WormBin is a class derived from Java's Applet class. This relationship is diagrammed in Figure 20-7.

FIGURE 20-7
◉ ◉ ◉ ◉ ◉ ◉
*Worm class
relationships*

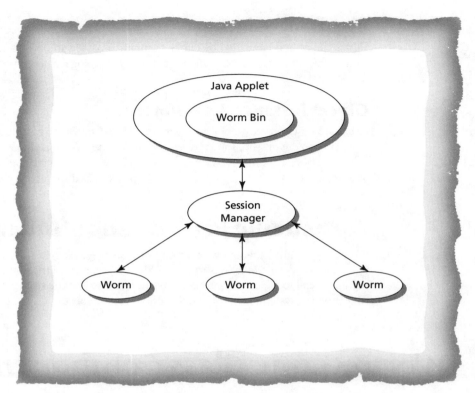

Constructing a Worm

The worm is defined by the variables passed into the constructor for the class Worm. Listing 20-1 shows the constructor for the class Worm; the parameters are defined in Table 20-1.

Variable	NameMeaning
startx	X position to place tail of worm
starty	Y position to place tail of worm
wormlen	Initial length of worm in number of segments
wclr	Color of worm
wormsize	Maximum growth of worm in number of segments
initx	Initial x direction that worm is pointing
inity	Initial Y direction that worm is pointing

TABLE 20-1 ◈ *Worm constructor parameters*

Adding a Queue

The worm's queue, or ring buffer, represents an ordered set of body segment coordinate locations. We can set the maximum size of the worm to any value we wish during construction; however, creating a large buffer may needlessly allocate memory if the final worm size is significantly less. The Java class Dimension, although intended as a size object, can also be used as a position object providing x and y coordinates using the width and height member variables, respectively. Referring again to Listing 20-1, you will see a variable for an array of Dimension objects declared as *Dimension m_points[]*. This variable must first be initialized with a call to *new Dimension[m_wormsize]* indicating we want to create an empty array of size *m_wormsize*. Next, each element of this new array must be initialized by calling *new* again for the desired number of Dimension objects. This is done in the *for* loop.

 # A Note About Variable Names

The Worm code uses a common convention of prefacing member variables with an *m_* to help distinguish them from local variables. You might also see Java code with member variables prefaced with only an underscore. Whichever method you choose is up to you.

Listing 20-1 *Worm class construction*

```
public class Worm {
    Dimension m_points[];
    int m_startidx, m_endidx;
    int m_curridx;
    int m_startx, m_starty;
    int m_wormsize = 4;
    int m_wormlen = 5;
    int m_startxdir, m_startydir;
    int m_regrow = 0;
    boolean m_nextstop = false, m_lastdropped = false;
    boolean m_nextadded = false;
    Dimension dDir;
    Dimension dCurr;
    Dimension dNext;
    Dimension dNewpoint;
    Dimension dOldpoint;
    Color wormcolor;

    // first time initialization
    //
```

continued on next page

continued from previous page

```
public Worm (        int startx,
                     int starty,
                     int wormlen,
                     Color wclr,
                     int wormsize,
                     int initx,
                     int inity)
{
    wormcolor = wclr;
    m_wormsize = wormsize;
    m_wormlen = wormlen;
    m_startxdir = initx;
    m_startydir = inity;

    // set up storage array for worm's description

    m_points = new Dimension[m_wormsize];
    for (int i = 0; i < m_points.length; i++)
        m_points[i] = new Dimension();

    // save start location for worm
    m_startx = startx;
    m_starty = starty;

    // helper dimensions
    dDir = new Dimension();
    dCurr = new Dimension();
    dNext = new Dimension();
    dNewpoint = new Dimension();
    dOldpoint = new Dimension();
}
```

Reinitializing After Each Game

The construction of the queue is done once for the life of the game. Each time the player restarts the game, the worm's queue is refilled with the correct x and y segment positions in tail-to-head order in the *for* loop in Listing 20-2. In this example we always set the worm moving from left to right. Two variables, *m_startidx* and *m_endidx*, point to the head and tail of the worm, respectively. Each time we restart the game, we need only reset these variables to their original values and the game can begin again. This is a handy way of avoiding needless reallocation of the worm objects. Note that we also reset the starting direction of the worm in the *dDir* object.

Listing 20-2 *Reinitializing a worm after each game using the function ReviveWorm()*

```
public void ReviveWorm()
{
    int count, i;

    for (i = 0, count = 0; i < m_wormlen; i++, count++) {
        m_points[count].width = i + m_startx;
        m_points[count].height = m_starty;
    }
    // set the buffer's start and end points
    // which are the head and tail of the worm

    m_startidx = count - 1;
    m_endidx = 0;
    m_regrow = 0;

    // set the current traveling direction

    dDir.width = m_startxdir;
    dDir.height = m_startydir;
}
```

Adding Worker Functions

Since the worm cannot show its implementation to the SessionManager, several useful worker functions are added to the worm object.

The DoYouHaveSegmentAt() Function

The function DoYouHaveSegmentAt(), shown in Listing 20-3, is passed an x and y location on the playing surface. It must reply *true* or *false* if it has a segment at those coordinates. This function demonstrates some interesting aspects of the ring buffer implementation.

First, we assume a worm is never less than one segment in size for the entire worm object. Here we check the worm segments beginning with the tail. You will notice that we don't compare the objects to each other, such as *newpoint == m_points[curridx]*. Some C++ class libraries would override the == operator to allow implicit comparison of the coordinates; under Java this behavior is different and we must compare the variables explicitly. Once we have reached the head, we are done, and no match was found. Notice the comparison *curridx >= m_wormsize*; this comparison correctly wraps around our index when we reach the end of the array to simulate an abstract ring buffer.

Listing 20-3 *The ability to ask if a worm has a segment at a given point*

```java
public boolean DoYouHaveSegmentAt(Dimension newpoint)
{
    int curridx = m_endidx;

    while (true) {
        // if matches, return true
        if (newpoint.width == m_points[curridx].width &&
            newpoint.height == m_points[curridx].height)
            return true;
        if (curridx == m_startidx)
            break;
        curridx++;
        if (curridx >= m_wormsize)
            curridx = 0;
    }
    // no match return false
    return false;
}
```

The GetNextPoint() and SetNextPoint() Functions

The worm is always moving in a direction specified by the *dDir* object that it maintains. This direction changes under the player's control. The SessionManager needs to call GetNextPoint() to identify which point would be the next head location for the worm. This function does not change the worm's head position, because the SessionManager must decide from this information if a collision is imminent. If no collision is detected, the SessionManager will call SetNextPoint() to set this worm's new head position.

The DropLastPoint() Function

The last two functions discussed above are not adequate to control the worm's motion. A means to drop the tail of the worm is also required for each head addition; otherwise, the worm will grow continuously! Code to drop the point could be placed in SetNextPoint(), but we will put it in a function called DropLastPoint() to allow occasional retention of the tail point, allowing for a slower growth of the worm. Thus, DropLastPoint() is selectively called by the SessionManager depending on various factors. The three head and tail manipulation functions are given in Listing 20-4.

To prevent overflow of the *m_points* array and contain the size of the worm to the maximum array size, SetNextPoint() returns *true* if the maximum worm size has been reached, which will force SessionManager to drop the tail segment regardless of other circumstances. In a similar manner, under special circumstances which will be clarified in a later section, an autonomous worm can shrink to zero length. DropLastPoint() will not drop the tail segment if that would cause the worm size to fall to zero. You will notice a variable called *m_regrow* in this function. This variable is used to slowly restore the size of shrunken autonomous worms to their original length.

The variables *m_nextadded* and *m_lastdropped* are used as placeholders for a subsequent call about the worm's growth status from the SessionManager.

Listing 20-4 Three helper functions that control the head and tail segments of the worm

```
public Dimension GetNextPoint()
{
    dNext.width = m_points[m_startidx].width;
    dNext.height = m_points[m_startidx].height;

    dNext.width += dDir.width;
    dNext.height += dDir.height;

    m_nextadded = false;

    return dNext;
}

public boolean SetNextPoint(Dimension newpoint)
{
    int tempidx;

    m_startidx++;
    if (m_startidx >= m_wormsize)
        m_startidx = 0;

    m_points[m_startidx].width = dNewpoint.width
                    = newpoint.width;
    m_points[m_startidx].height = dNewpoint.height
                    = newpoint.height;

    // don't grown beyond max, force a drop by calling
    // routine
    tempidx = m_startidx + 1;
    if (tempidx >= m_wormsize)
        tempidx = 0;

    m_nextadded = true;

    return tempidx == m_endidx;
}

public boolean DropLastPoint()
{
    dOldpoint.width = m_points[m_endidx].width;
    dOldpoint.height = m_points[m_endidx].height;

    if (m_regrow == 0)
```

continued on next page

continued from previous page

```
                    if (CountSegments() <= m_wormlen / 2)
                        m_regrow = 150;

            if (m_endidx == m_startidx) {
                m_lastdropped = false;
                return m_lastdropped;
            }

            m_endidx++;
            if (m_endidx >= m_wormsize)
                m_endidx = 0;

            m_lastdropped = true;
            return m_lastdropped;
        }
```

Returning Worm Segments Through Iterators

When coding for a modern graphical user interface (GUI), you will need to handle the redraw case: When another window covers the game, uncovering the game will require redrawing the playing surface to its complete and current state. The Worm class provides functions that iterate over all worm segments, returning the coordinates of a new point for each call until the head of the worm is reached.

Since we stated earlier that we will hide the internal worm implementation, returning the array of worm segment locations is unacceptable. Consider the following: Adding z-ordering to each point could be accomplished by deriving a new class from the Dimension class, extending it to also contain a value representing the stacking order of the segment. Since most of the time the SessionManager is only interested in the x and y coordinates of a segment, we would expose data that is not relevant to the SessionManager. By providing iterators that deliver coordinate data, we could change our Worm class to only deliver the coordinate portion of the data without changing any of the functions the SessionManager calls. These interactions are described in simplified form in Figure 20-8.

The SessionManager will call IsWormFirst() to find out if the worm has any segments. This should always return *true*, since a zero worm size is not allowed. Next, the SessionManager can call any function associated with that segment. Currently there are only two functions that return the attributes of the current segment: GetCurrentWormSegment(), which returns the coordinates of the worm segment, and GetCurrentWormColor(), which currently always returns the initial color of the worm. A striped worm implementation could be derived from the Worm class without changing any code in the SessionManager. Finally, IsWormNext() is called to check if there are any more segments to process. If no more, then this function returns *false*. IsWormFirst() is only called once, while IsWormNext() is called repeatedly until no more segments remain. These functions are shown in Listing 20-5.

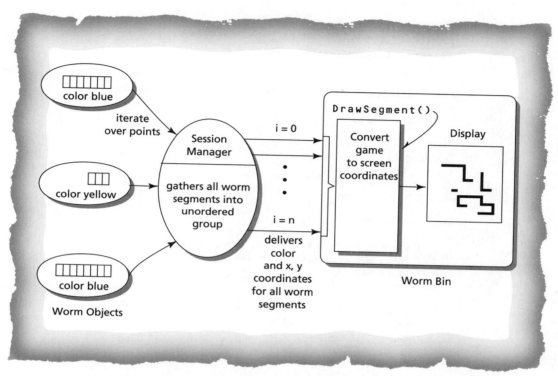

FIGURE 20-8 ◉ *SessionManager providing data hiding for worm segment iterators*

The private function GetWormElement() is called by both IsWormFirst() and IsWormNext() to iterate over the worm segment queue. The *m_nextstop* variable is required since we must return *true* even though we may have reached the last segment. This variable is set so that the next call returns *false* and the calling routine in SessionManager can exit the loop after processing all entries. We set the position *dCurr* to the current index *m_points[curridx]* and return it in GetCurrentWormSegment(). The caller must not reassign this returned value, since it propagates back to the segment array object.

Listing 20-5 *Worm segment iterators*

```
public boolean IsWormFirst()
{
    m_curridx = m_endidx;
    m_nextstop = false;
    dCurr = m_points[m_curridx];
    return GetWormElement();
}
```

continued on next page

continued from previous page

```
public boolean IsWormNext()
{
    return GetWormElement();
}

public Dimension GetCurrentWormSegment()
{
    return dCurr;
}

public Color GetCurrentWormColor()
{
    return wormcolor;
}

private boolean GetWormElement()
{
    // since m_curridx is a valid index, we have to return
    // false one call after we reach the head index
    if (m_nextstop)
        return false;

    // if at head index, the next call says we are done
    if (m_curridx == m_startidx)
        m_nextstop = true;

    // get current index
    dCurr = m_points[m_curridx++];
    if (m_curridx >= m_wormsize)
        m_curridx = 0;

    return true;
}
```

Setting Direction from Player Input

The worm keeps track of its current direction of travel. The SessionManager passes keyboard or mouse input from the WormBin to the worm either into the SetNewDirectionFromMouse() or SetNewDirectionFromKeyboard() function. Each function must take the provided input and appropriately set the new direction of travel. The challenge is to provide the best control for the given input device. Listing 20-6 shows the two input processing functions.

⊞ How to Find a Key Code Without a Manual

A Java keyboard reference never seems to be available when you need it. Use this trick: Put the following code in your keyboard event function: *String s = new String(); s = "Key Value: " + key; System.out.println(s);.* To enable the System.out feature to compile your Java code with debugging enabled and start your applet from a command prompt window, enter *C:\>appletviewer WormBin.html.* Each time you press a key, the key value will be displayed in the command prompt window.

Controlling Input from the Keyboard

Control from the keyboard is fairly straightforward: Choose a direction that corresponds to which arrow key was pressed. The code in Listing 20-6 includes a check for letter keys grouped together for keyboards that do not have arrow keys. This choice of keys is purely based on what seems to be the most ergonomic. A check is made to see if the key pressed was a directional key; if such a key was pressed, then the direction is altered only if the new direction is perpendicular to the current direction. The direction value must be one of -1, 0, or 1. Any other value will result in an incorrect depiction of the worm.

One thing to watch out for: Because the keyboard events can arrive one right after the other, it is possible to rotate the head completely around between a change in the head's position by the SessionManager. The result of this grouping is to cause the head to collide with the body but without turning. The player will see this as a collision indication directly behind the head segment.

Listing 20-6 Player input handling routines

```
public void SetNewDirectionFromKeyboard(int key)
{
    // 1004=up 1005=down 1006=left 1007=right
    // use arrow keys or normal keys (keeps everyone happy)

    if (key == 1004 || key =='u') {
        if (dDir.height == 0) {
            dDir.width = 0;
            dDir.height = -1;
        }
    }
    else if (key == 1005 || key =='j') {
        if (dDir.height == 0) {
            dDir.width = 0;
            dDir.height = 1;
```

continued on next page

continued from previous page

```
            }
        }
        else if (key == 1006 || key =='h') {
            if (dDir.width == 0) {
                dDir.width = -1;
                dDir.height = 0;
            }
        }
        else if (key == 1007 || key =='k') {
            if (dDir.width == 0) {
                dDir.width = 1;
                dDir.height = 0;
            }
        }
    }

    public void SetNewDirectionFromMouse(int wormscale,
                                         int x,
                                         int y)
    {
        // width is 0 if we are moving up or down
        if (dDir.width == 0) {
            if (x > m_points[m_startidx].width * wormscale)
                dDir.width = 1;// move right
            else
                dDir.width = -1;// move left
            dDir.height = 0;
        }
        else {
            if (y > m_points[m_startidx].height * wormscale)
                dDir.height = 1;// move down
            else
                dDir.height = -1;// move up
            dDir.width = 0;
        }
    }
```

Controlling Input with the Mouse

The direction is set differently if the player uses a mouse. The player can click anywhere on the playing surface in a location that does not correspond directly to the current direction of travel. A change in direction is made based on whether the player clicks to the right or left of an imaginary line parallel and through the current direction of motion of the worm's head. This can be determined by getting the position of the head segment and the current direction of travel and calculating the true position of the worm's head in the playing surface. This is the only code in the class Worm that does not strictly adhere to the separation of the display surface from the abstract playing surface. Eventually both functions could be moved to the SessionManager if this separation were desired.

Starting the SessionManager

The SessionManager class's constructor has easier duties than the Worm class's constructor. It must create the player's worm and any additional worms. The constructor in Listing 20-7 shows an array of Worm objects created to support the player's worm and two additional autonomous worms. The player's worm must be assigned to the first element in the array for this implementation of Worm. The array of four Dimension objects is used for guiding the autonomous worms.

The playing surface is 30x30 units across. The maximum player worm size is these two numbers multiplied together and divided by two. This effectively means the player's worm can never occupy more than half the physical space of the playing surface (which already is quite a lot, due to the limited maneuverability available). Refer to Table 20-1 for information on the parameters passed to the worm constructor.

The Restart() function as shown in Listing 20-7 is called to initialize per-game variables. This function is declared public and is called by the class WormBin to restart a game and initialize variables. Restart() iterates through each worm and calls the worm's ReviveWorm() member function to reinitialize each worm's variables. Restart() also clears the collision variables, resets the current score to zero, and calls NewTreat() to randomly place a new treat on the playing surface.

Listing 20-7 SessionManager initialization and the game Restart() function

```java
public class SessionManager {
    static int SIZEX = 30;
    static int SIZEY = 30;
    static int WORMCOUNT = 3;

    boolean m_newtr = false;
    boolean m_showscore = false, m_dontdrop = false;
    boolean m_speedup = false;

    Dimension wMax = new Dimension(SIZEX,SIZEY);
    Dimension dTemp = new Dimension();
    Dimension treatpoint = new Dimension();
    Dimension collisionpoint = new Dimension();
    Dimension newpoint = new Dimension();
    Dimension autopoint = new Dimension();
    Dimension dpoint[] = new Dimension[4];

    Worm worm[];
    int currscore;
    int highscore;
    int lastscore;
    int treatcount;
    int forcedelay;
    int currautoworm;
```

continued on next page

continued from previous page

```
        int adddropidx;
        int grow;
        long age;
        int m_getallidx;
        int dirchange;

        public SessionManager()
        {
            currscore = lastscore = highscore = 0;

            for (int i = 0; i < 4; i++)
                dpoint[i] = new Dimension();

            worm = new Worm[WORMCOUNT];

            worm[0] = new Worm(2, 5, 10, Color.blue,
                                        SIZEX * SIZEY / 2, 1, 0);
            worm[1] = new Worm(2, 15, 20, Color.yellow,
                                        22, 0, -1);
            worm[2] = new Worm(2, 1, 20, Color.cyan,
                                        22, 0, 1);
            Restart();
        }

        public void Restart()
        {
            collisionpoint.width = -1;
            collisionpoint.height = -1;

            lastscore = currscore;
            currscore = 0;
            treatcount = 0;
            currautoworm = 1;
            grow = 0;
            age = 0;
            forcedelay = 0;
            dirchange = 0;

            for (int i = 0; i < WORMCOUNT; i++)
                worm[i].ReviveWorm();

            NewTreat(true);
        }
```

Using the Next() Function

The SessionManager is entirely event-driven. Nothing happens unless the class WormBin
calls it to perform some action or request some data. During game play, WormBin calls
SessionManager once every 100 milliseconds to increment the player's worm position.
No calculations take place between calls to the SessionManager, because WormBin calls

the Java API Thread.sleep() in order to give the illusion of smooth, constant motion. This means the SessionManager must perform calculations quickly and return so the thread can go back to sleep. If the SessionManager were to spend long and different time periods calculating results, the appearance of smooth motion would be lost, because a greater percentage of time would be spent calculating than sleeping. Refer to Figure 20-9 for an illustration of the following sections on the Next() function as used by the SessionManager and the WormBin class.

FIGURE 20-9

The Next() function as it interacts across classes to make the worm appear to move

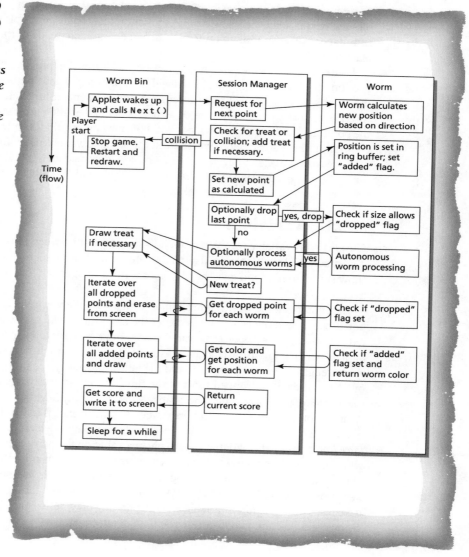

How Next() Works

The SessionManager is called through the Next() function each 100 milliseconds. This function always generates a new head location for the player's worm and may also drop the tail of the worm. The illusion of worm motion is achieved by simply adding a new head segment and optionally dropping the tail segment with each call to Next(); no additional segments need to be modified. Next() is also responsible for collision or treat collection detection. If Next() returns *true*, then the worm collided with an object, informing WormBin to stop the game and display the final score. Additionally, if autonomous worms are enabled, Next() increments their position. The effect resembles the results achieved using simple animation techniques: multiple objects moving simultaneously even though only incremental changes are made to the objects on the playing surface.

Listing 20-8 shows the entire Next() function. This function provides the greatest influence on the play of Worm and as such will be explored in detail. We begin by obtaining the worm's anticipated next point through the worm member function GetNextPoint(). Also notice that we refer to *worm[0]*, which is defined as the player's worm. Based on the point returned, a check is made to see if the new point collides with a treat or another object. If the worm collides with a treat, the *m_newtr* variable is set to add a new treat to the playing surface. A new treat cannot be added immediately, because the worm has not had a new head assigned just yet—the new treat could possibly be randomly placed right under the new head location!

Next() Variables

The *forcedelay* variable tells WormBin how long to wait between calls to Next(), which is normally 100 milliseconds. If a treat is eaten, this delay is set to 300 milliseconds to allow sound to play and give the player a short break to check the location of the new treat.

Assuming that the worm didn't collide with a wall, the worm's SetNextPoint() function is called, and the new point becomes the new worm head segment. SetNextPoint() returns *true* and sets the *forcedrop* variable if we must drop the tail segment, which would happen when the worm reaches maximum length. In a basic game of Worm, the worm length would stay constant and the tail would always be dropped. In this game of Worm, the tail is dropped most of the time, but occasionally it is retained to allow the worm to grow over time. The strange-looking code *if ((age++ % 32) != 0)* is an efficient way of checking for an event once every 32 times Next() is called. The upper portion of the *if* statement is called 31 out of every 32 times Next() executes and normally sets *forcedrop* to *true*. The variable *grow* is given a value only when a treat is consumed, in which case the worm grows for a few segments right after a treat is eaten. The other half of the *if* statement recalculates the score occasionally and tells WormBin to display the new score once every 32 times Next() is called to avoid screen flicker due to rapid score updates. The *m_dontdrop* variable is set depending on whether the player checked the Grow checkbox and may override the state of *forcedrop*.

The final steps are to call DropLastPoint() as needed to drop the player's worm tail. The NewTreat() function is called if a new treat was added and the DoAutoWorms() function is called if autonomous worms are enabled.

Listing 20-8 *The Next() function provides important game state stepping every 100 milliseconds*

```
public boolean Next()
{
    boolean forcedrop;

    m_newtr = false;
    m_showscore = false;

    // do main worm first
    newpoint = worm[0].GetNextPoint();

    if (!SearchForTreat(newpoint)) {
        if (SearchForCollision(newpoint))
            return true;
    }
    else {
        forcedelay = 300;
        m_newtr = true;
    }

    forcedrop = worm[0].SetNextPoint(newpoint);

    if ((age++ % 32) != 0) {
        if (!forcedrop) {
            if (grow==0)
                forcedrop = true;
            else
                grow--;
        }
    }
    else {
        // don't give them any points until they
        // get a treat
        if (treatcount!=0)
            currscore = treatcount * (int)(age/10);
        else
            currscore = 0;

        // increment high score if it is less than
        // the current score
        if (currscore > highscore)
            highscore = currscore;

        m_showscore = true;
```

continued on next page

continued from previous page

```
        }

        if (m_dontdrop == false)
            forcedrop = true;

        if (forcedrop)
            worm[0].DropLastPoint();

        if (m_newtr)
            NewTreat(false);

        // let all other worms move now
        // do only one at a time

        if (currautoworm != 0)
            DoAutoWorms();

        return false;
    }
```

Checking Collisions and Treats

The SearchForTreat() function simply checks if the given points coordinates match the coordinates of the treat. If the coordinates match, the worm is forced to grow, and *true* is returned.

The SearchForCollision() function checks if the worm hit another worm by calling HaveSeg() or if it went outside of the playing surface by calling HitWall(). You can see in Listing 20-9 that HaveSeg() iterates over all worms and calls their DoYouHaveSegmentAt() function, returning *true* as soon as a collision is detected.

Listing 20-9 *Collision and treat detection*

```
private boolean SearchForTreat(Dimension newpoint)
{
    if (newpoint.width != treatpoint.width ||
        newpoint.height != treatpoint.height)
        return false;

    // increase their score faster the longer they
    // have been playing
    treatcount++;
    grow = (int)(age / 100) + 2;

    return true ;
}

private boolean SearchForCollision(Dimension newpoint)
{
    if (HaveSeg(newpoint)) {
```

```
        collisionpoint.width = newpoint.width;
        collisionpoint.height = newpoint.height;
        return true;
    }
    if (HitWall(newpoint)) {
        collisionpoint.width = -1;
        collisionpoint.height = -1;
        return true;
    }
    return false;
}

private boolean HaveSeg(Dimension segpoint)
{
    for (int i = 0; i < WORMCOUNT; i++)
        if (worm[i].DoYouHaveSegmentAt(segpoint))
            return true;

    return false;
}

private boolean HitWall(Dimension segpoint)
{
    if (segpoint.width < 0 || segpoint.height < 0 ||
        segpoint.width >= wMax.width ||
        segpoint.height >= wMax.height)
        return true;
    return false;
}
```

Putting It All Together in the WormBin

The WormBin class is derived from Java's Applet class and implements Runnable, which allows easier control of real-time gaming action. The Next() function is called often and at regular intervals to move objects on the playing surface. Between calls to Next(), the thread is paused for a short period of time to give the illusion of smooth motion. WormBin's Next() function calls SessionManager's Next() function but also handles drawing new head segments and erasing tail segments. Listing 20-10 shows that the SessionManager's Next() function is called first, and *true* is returned on collision. SessionManager remembers if a treat was eaten, and IsNewTreat() is called to allow drawing of the new treat. Because only the class WormBin is allowed to draw to the playing surface, additional code must be added to query the SessionManager for points to draw, and so on.

The iterators IsFirstDropped() and IsNextDropped() iterate over all worms with tail segments that have been dropped for this call of Next(). The tails must be erased before the new heads are drawn; otherwise, holes can appear in worm bodies under special circumstances. Notice that the color black is used to erase the worm segments. Drawing head segments are handled by equivalent IsFirstAdded() and IsNextAdded() functions. Finally, the SessionManager is queried if it is appropriate to draw a new score.

Listing 20-10 *WormBin's Next() function, which handles segment drawing and clearing*

```
private boolean Next(Graphics g)
{
    // call the session manager to get the next
    // worm location. if true returned, we had a collision
    if (smgr.Next()) {
        if(hitsoundData != null)
            hitsoundData.play();
        return true;
    }

    // check if we just ate a treat and created a new
    // one, if yes, we need to draw the new treat
    if (smgr.IsNewTreat()) {
        if(atesoundData != null)
            atesoundData.play();
        try {
            Thread.sleep(100);
        } catch (InterruptedException e)
        {
        }
        DrawTreat(g);
    }

    // erase the tail segment(s)
    if (smgr.IsFirstDropped()) {
        do {
            g.setColor(Color.black);
            DrawSegment(g, smgr.CurrDroppedPoint());
        } while (smgr.IsNextDropped());
    }

    // draw the head segment(s)
    if (smgr.IsFirstAdded()) {
        do {
            g.setColor(smgr.CurrAddedColor());
            DrawSegment(g, smgr.CurrAddedPoint());
        } while (smgr.IsNextAdded());
    }

    // write out score only once in a while to avoid
    // too much flicker
    if (smgr.IsDisplayScore())
        WriteScore();

    return false;
}
```

The run() function is overridden in WormBin from the Applet class and has control of game play. Listing 20-11 shows the entire run() function. A double-buffer is created for drawing. The playing surface is cleared and a static worm and a treat are drawn and then displayed using the PaintWorm() function. The thread is paused until the user starts the game, at which point the game enters an infinite loop until the game ends. The normal sequence includes calling the Next() function to move the worms, calling the repaint() function to copy the hidden drawing buffer to the screen, and finally calling Thread.sleep() to stop the game for about 100 milliseconds. This sequence is repeated until the player's worm collides with an object, then the Next() function repaints any new collision information and pauses the game until the player starts up a new game.

Listing 20-11 *The applet thread run() function*

```
public void run()
{
    int delay;

    if (kicker != null) {
        // create a hidden buffer and clear it
        wormimage = createImage(
                        smgr.GetPixelWidth(WORMSCALE) +
                            BORDERPAD,
                        smgr.GetPixelHeight(WORMSCALE) +
                            BORDERPAD);
        // get context
        wormgraphics = wormimage.getGraphics();
        wormgraphics.setFont(getFont());
        wormgraphics.setColor(Color.black);
        wormgraphics.fillRect(0, 0,
                        smgr.GetPixelWidth(WORMSCALE) +
                            BORDERPAD,
                        smgr.GetPixelHeight(WORMSCALE) +
                            BORDERPAD);

        // reset all variables to beginning,
        // create new worm
        Reset();

        // draw current game status and paint to applet
        // client area
        PaintWorm(wormgraphics,false);
        repaint();

        ThreadPause("Start");

        // loop until system terminates us
        while (kicker != null) {

            // loop while not minimized and have valid
```

continued on next page

continued from previous page

```
                              // worker thread
                              while ( size().width > 0 &&
                                      size().height > 0 &&
                                      kicker != null) {
                                  // get next worm position
                                  if (Next(wormgraphics)) {
                                      // worm collided,
                                      // redraw all new entities
                                      PaintWorm(wormgraphics,true);
                                      repaint();

                                      // stop game until user presses
                                      // mouse button or hits a key
                                      ThreadPause("Start");

                                      // reset all variables to beginning,
                                      // create new worm
                                      Reset();

                                      // draw current game status and paint
                                      // to applet client area
                                      PaintWorm(wormgraphics,false);
                                      repaint();

                                      break;
                                  }
                                  // repaint from hidden area to visible area
                                  repaint();
                                  // sleep for a very short time to make the
                                  // game playable on fast computers
                                  delay = smgr.GetDelay();
                                  if (delay > 0)
                                      try {
                                          Thread.sleep(delay);
                                      } catch (InterruptedException e)
                                      {
                                      }
                              }
                          }
                      }
                  }
```

Adding Autonomous Worms

A true test of Worm's object-oriented design is to see if the Worm object can be easily adapted to support multiple instances and accept autonomous control. This simply means that additional worms should move around the playing surface under their own control. The term *autonomous* means self-guiding and independent of user control and implies the worm will avoid collisions.

Modifying SessionManager

What code needs to be modified and added in order to create one or more worms that guide themselves? Based on the current Worm design, the primary code that needs to change is the SessionManager object. The Worm object needs fewer revisions, because it does not directly participate in the control of the playing surface.

When a player controls the worm through the keyboard, the SetNewDirectionFromKeyboard() function is called. An equivalent function, SetDirection(), will be added, which directly sets the worm direction. A complementary function, GetDirection(), will be added for use during object detection. These functions are given in Listing 20-12.

Listing 20-12 Setting the worm direction from System Manager using helper functions

```java
public void SetDirection(int x, int y)
{
    dDir.width = x;
    dDir.height = y;
}

public Dimension GetDirection()
{
    return dDir;
}
```

The DoAutoWorms() Function

In much the same way as the player's worm is advanced one segment for every call of the Next() function, each autonomous worm advances one segment each time DoAutoWorms() is called. DoAutoWorms() is called at the end of the Next() function by the SessionManager. Essentially all autonomous control is handled by DoAutoWorms(), which is given in Listing 20-13. Since DoAutoWorms() is called once for each call of Next(), two implementations suggest themselves: either increment the position of every autonomous worm for each call, or increment the position of one worm per call. DoAutoWorms() takes the latter approach, which results in progressively slower autonomous worm movement for every autonomous worm added.

Calculating Increments

The variable *currautoworm* increments over the number of autonomous worms for each call of DoAutoWorms() and provides an index into SessionManager's array of worms. The array *dpoint[]* provides four direction variables that correspond to the four available directions of motion. This array is dynamically filled with directions in decreasing order of desirability.

The function GetNextPoint() is called to retrieve the calculated x and y locations of the next head position into the variable *autopoint*, and GetDirection() returns the current head travel direction into *dpoint[0]*. The variable *dirchange* is set at a random value around 10 and decremented for each call to DoAutoWorms(). Once it reaches 0, it is reset to a new random value. When it reaches a value of 1, the current autonomous worm's direction is changed irrespective of whether it touched an object. This feature adds some dynamics to the game, partly randomizing the motion of the autonomous worms.

Evaluating the Calculations

After the above steps have completed, three conditions given below are evaluated, and *dpoint[1]* is set to the newly calculated value using the GetNewDirection() function given in Listing 20-14. The three conditions are

🗡 Is it time to change direction due to dirchange, or has a wall been reached? This is illustrated in Figure 20-10.

🗡 Has the worm reached one of its segments or that of another worm? This is illustrated in Figures 20-11(a) and 20-11(b).

🗡 Is the new head location empty? This is illustrated in Figure 20-12.

The segments are denoted with the symbols S, H, and T, which stand for (body) segment, head, and tail, respectively. Each segment has a subscript of either 1 or 2, where 1 is the target worm and 2 is the colliding worm.

FIGURE 20-10

◎ ◎ ◎ ◎ ◎ ◎

Worm selecting new direction dpoint[1] or dpoint[2] upon reaching a wall

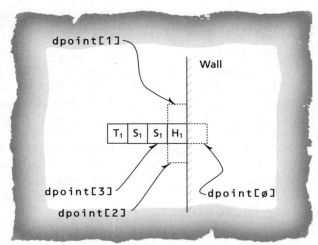

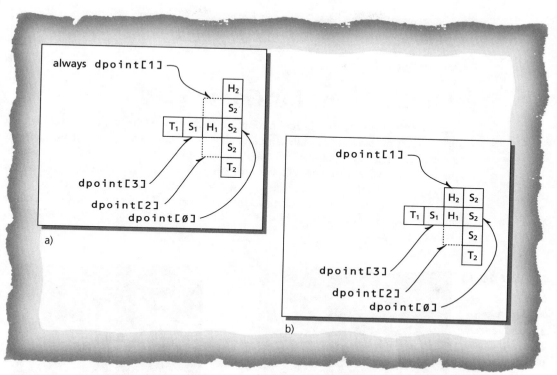

FIGURE 20-11 ◉ *Worm selecting new direction dpoint[1] in illustration (a) and dpoint[2] in illustration (b) due to all preferred paths blocked upon reaching another worm*

FIGURE 20-12

◉ ◉ ◉ ◉ ◉ ◉

Worm direction dpoint[0] is selected as first choice and is free

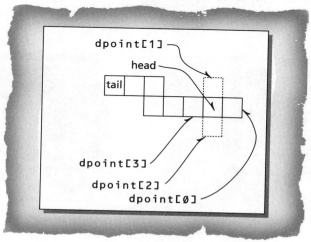

If the worm has reached a wall or *dirchange* has expired, then a new direction, *dpoint[1]*, is chosen at random to the left or to the right of the current head direction. If the worm reaches a worm segment, then the worm is forced to always turn left, and *dpoint[1]* is set appropriately.

Implications for Game Play

This seemingly innocuous programming decision of always having the worm turn left has interesting game play ramifications. A player can block a partly coiled autonomous worm in such a way that the worm coils inward until it can no longer move. If this happens, then it will shrink one segment for each call to Next() until either it finds a new way out or it shrinks to the size of a single segment. If the next head location is free, then the head is set to the new position and the tail is dropped, which keeps the size of the autonomous worm constant. This effect is shown in the sequence of Figures 20-13(a) through 20-13(f).

FIGURE 20-13 (a-f)

◉ ◉ ◉ ◉ ◉ ◉

The sequence shows how a player can trap an autonomous worm and have it coil in on itself

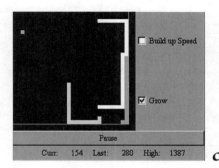

A

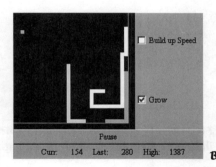

B

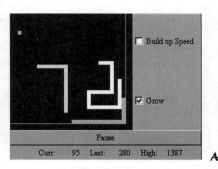

C

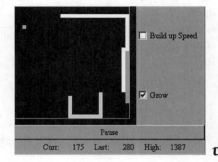

D

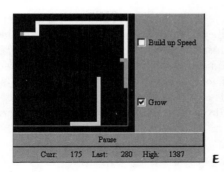

E

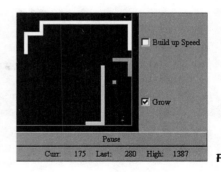

F

The call to the current autonomous worm's NotRegrowing() function, given in Listing 20-15, checks if the worm had recently shrunk due to a self-coiling condition and forces the worm to slowly regrow to its original size, which increases the challenge of the game.

Figure 20-14 shows three stages of motion when worm 1 collides with worm 2. Illustration (a) shows that the worm head can go either right or left. Rather than turning right, the worm will always turn left, as shown in illustration (b), even though only one free space remains in that direction. Illustration (c) shows the worm's head segment stopped because no free space remains, and worm 1 shrinks by one segment.

⧉ Coding Strategies Using *if-else* Statements

Filling out of the *dpoint[]* array in the DoAutoWorms() function is done using eight *if-else* statements. The same result could be arrived at using a more elegant algorithmic solution at the expense of more time and debugging effort. If you feel more comfortable using such simple constructs, don't worry about using them. They may not look pretty, but if the constants are set up correctly from the start, this kind of code can be very robust and easy to decode. Use the algorithmic approach if a pattern appears that will allow use of looping constructs and if the *if-else* statements grow large in number.

If the worm's motion is blocked, additional processing must be performed to find a new direction of motion. The remaining two *dpoint[]* elements are filled out with the last two available directions. Two large *if-else* statements are used to calculate the missing directions. The *dpoint[]* array is evaluated in order by the *for* loop at the end of the DoAutoWorms() function so that the first new direction, *dpoint[1]*, is the direction of highest preference and *dpoint[3]* is the direction of least preference. If the preferred directions lead to a collision, then the other directions are evaluated in-order until a free direction is found. Figure 20-14, illustration (b), shows selection of the secondary choice *dpoint[2]* as the new direction because all other directions are blocked. *dpoint[0]* is by definition a collision, so it is not evaluated in the *for* loop but is used by the *if-else* statement only. If a collision is detected in all directions, then SetNextPoint() is not called and the tail of the worm is dropped, provided the worm will not shrink to a size less than one segment.

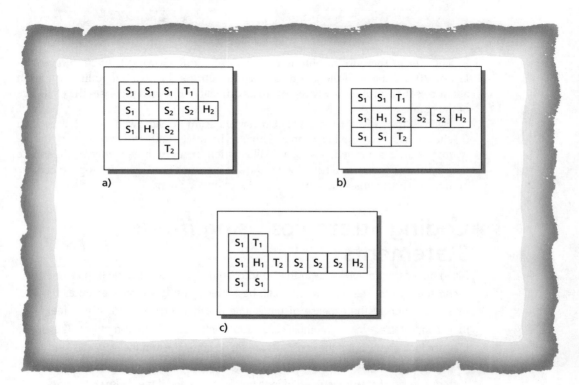

a)   b)   c)

FIGURE 20-14 ◉ *Worm following predefined behavior and reaching a dead end*

Listing 20-13 Controlling the autonomous worms with the SessionManager's DoAutoWorms() function

```
private void DoAutoWorms()
{
    int direction, dx, dy;

    currautoworm++;
    if (currautoworm >= WORMCOUNT)
        currautoworm = 1;

    // save current direction of motion
    dpoint[0] = worm[currautoworm].GetDirection();

    autopoint = worm[currautoworm].GetNextPoint();

    if (dirchange > 0)
        dirchange--;

    // do different things depending on what we hit
    // if hit a wall, go randomly right or left
    if (HitWall(autopoint) == true || dirchange == 1) {

        dirchange = (int)((Math.random() + 1) * 5 + 10);

        // pick a direction at random
        if (Math.random() < 0)
            direction = -1;
        else
            direction = 1;

        dpoint[1] = GetNewDirection(dpoint[0], direction);
    }
    else if (HaveSeg(autopoint) == true ||
            HitTreat(autopoint) == true) {

        // always try to go left if hit an object
        dpoint[1] = GetNewDirection(dpoint[0], -1);
    }
    else {
        // no collision, all done
        worm[currautoworm].SetNextPoint(autopoint);
        // extend worm if it shrunk
        if (worm[currautoworm].NotRegrowing())
            worm[currautoworm].DropLastPoint();
        return;
    }
```

continued on next page

continued from previous page

```
                    // create remaining directions
                    if (dpoint[0].width == 1) {
                        dpoint[2].width = -1;
                        dpoint[2].height = 0;
                    }
                    else if (dpoint[0].width == -1) {
                        dpoint[2].width = 1;
                        dpoint[2].height = 0;
                    }
                    else if (dpoint[0].height == 1) {
                        dpoint[2].width = 0;
                        dpoint[2].height = -1;
                    }
                    else {
                        dpoint[2].width = 0;
                        dpoint[2].height = 1;
                    }

                    if (dpoint[1].width == 1) {
                        dpoint[3].width = -1;
                        dpoint[3].height = 0;
                    }
                    else if (dpoint[1].width == -1) {
                        dpoint[3].width = 1;
                        dpoint[3].height = 0;
                    }
                    else if (dpoint[1].height == 1) {
                        dpoint[3].width = 0;
                        dpoint[3].height = -1;
                    }
                    else {
                        dpoint[3].width = 0;
                        dpoint[3].height = 1;
                    }

                    // skip this first since it is a known collision
                    for (int i = 1; i < 4; i++) {

                        worm[currautoworm].SetDirection(dpoint[i].width,
                                                        dpoint[i].height);
                        autopoint = worm[currautoworm].GetNextPoint();

                        if (HitWall(autopoint) == false &&
                            HaveSeg(autopoint) == false &&
                            HitTreat(autopoint) == false) {

                            // no collision, all done
                            worm[currautoworm].SetNextPoint(autopoint);
```

```
                        // extend worm if it shrunk
                        if (worm[currautoworm].NotRegrowing())
                            worm[currautoworm].DropLastPoint();
                        return;
                    }
                }
                // no places left to go!

                if (worm[currautoworm].NotRegrowing())
                    worm[currautoworm].DropLastPoint();
            }
```

Listing 20-14 *Based on the old direction of motion, a new direction is returned by GetNewDirection() that is perpendicular to the current direction*

```
        private Dimension GetNewDirection(Dimension olddir,
                                          int motion)
        {
            if (olddir.width == 1 || olddir.width == -1) {
                dTemp.width = 0;
                dTemp.height = motion;
            }
            else {
                dTemp.width = motion;
                dTemp.height = 0;
            }
            return dTemp;
        }
```

Listing 20-15 *A counter in the Worm object NotRegrowing() function keeps track of autonomous worm regrowth after a self-coiling shrinking condition*

```
        public boolean NotRegrowing()
        {
            if (m_regrow > 0) {
                m_regrow--;
                if ((m_regrow < 100) && ((m_regrow & 7) == 0))
                    return false;
            }
            return true;
        }
```

Integrating the Game into the Web Page

Using Sun's bundled appletviewer for initial design is recommended, because it is closely tied into the Java standard, allows console debugging, and does not incur browser overhead penalties. Once the design nears completion, the applet should be placed in a Web page and tested using a browser, such as Sun's HotJava or Netscape Navigator 2.0.

Here are some recommended steps to take when designing a Web page for your Java game applet:

- Always provide an overview of the game somewhere close to the applet itself so the player has something to read while waiting for the applet to load.

- Indicate using some appropriate technique that the given Web page will load an applet if the browser supports Java.

- Presize the applet to prevent secondary text flow from distracting the player when the applet completes loading.

- If possible, test the applet using browsers on different platforms for small differences in screen formatting.

Placement and Applet Size

It's a good idea to put your game applet toward the top of the page and any extra text either on another linked page or at the bottom of the main page. The game applet should be small enough to be fully viewable at lower resolutions, such as 640x480. You can adjust the applet size by setting the WIDTH/HEIGHT attributes in the <APPLET> tag as shown in Listing 20-16. Listing 20-17 shows how to read the attributes into the game and adjust the screen size. This code is usually placed in the applet's init() function. Validation of values is not shown but should be performed in your code.

Listing 20-16 HTML Java applet tag with width and height attributes

```
<APPLET code=WormBin.class width=300 height=240></APPLET>
```

Listing 20-17 *Using getParameter() to retrieve width and height parameters from the Web page and calling resize() to change applet's size appropriately*

```
width = Integer.valueOf(
                  getParameter("width")).intValue();
height = Integer.valueOf(
                  getParameter("height")).intValue();

resize(width, height);
```

Instructions

The game design doesn't stop after the applet is complete. You should place some basic instructions somewhere easily accessible to the player. One way to make the instructions flashier is by placing them on a separate Web page and providing a Help button in the applet that calls the instructions' URL.

The instructions should include basic game information such as how to play and the object of the game. Tips should be provided so players can quickly familiarize themselves with game nuances.

Getting Feedback on Your Game

Your Java game is accessed by players over the Internet; why not take advantage of other Internet features to provide feedback from your players by using the "mailto:" feature of Web pages? Put the following link next to your game so players can instantly alert you to play problems or compliment you on your cool game: *<A HREF="mailto:me@myprovider.com">Send Me Mail at me@myprovider.com</A>*

Browser Compatibility

Java is designed to be cross-platform compatible. Due to small differences in the way different operating systems map and align fonts, your applet may look great under Windows 95, but text may be chopped on a Mac. Since most game designers will only have access to one platform, testing may inadvertently be left up to the players themselves.

Don't cramp the text assigned to checkboxes or other controls. The default fonts may not scale correctly on different platforms, leading to chopped or misaligned text. Keep lots of space around checkboxes to prevent alignment problems. Another approach is to use icons for controls and displays. This avoids text formatting problems, but be sure to explain the meaning of the icons somewhere in the Web page!

Keep to the standard 16-color palette unless the game demands more colors. Keeping the color choice generic maximizes the chances the game will appear the same on all platforms.

Although they are not strictly a browser compatibility issue, you should be aware of applet focus problems, particularly if your game relies on keyboard input. Normally, when the applet is started, focus is on the Web page, not the applet; keyboard input goes nowhere until you click on the applet. To set the initial focus on the applet, call requestFocus() in the applet's init() function; this can also help ensure that initial repaint happens correctly.

Future Directions for Worm

The features you have seen implemented into this game of Worm are just a start. There are various features that can be added or tweaked to create a more advanced game. What follows are some suggested improvements that you could add to make the game more interesting. Probably the most challenging but most rewarding enhancement is the integration of network play into Worm. You will find some guidelines for network programming in this section.

Demo Mode

Many commercial games provide a demo mode that simulates play action. You could set a timer that starts the demo after a certain number of seconds have elapsed. Sophisticated demos require simulated player input and knowledge of the playing surface to intelligently adjust play behavior. A less sophisticated approach is to guarantee predictable game response and record a player's actions during game play. The recorded sequence is played back during demo mode.

Worm can be adapted to provide a higher level of demo capability by using the code that runs the autonomous worms. Code would have to be added to direct motion toward the treat, while the autonomous worms' object avoidance routine could be employed for general motion.

Saving the Score

The ability to save your best scores for future reference is an important part of many games. Java's File class can be employed to save the player's score on his or her local machine. A more sophisticated approach is to provide a centralized clearinghouse for scorekeeping. The applet could display the top scores of every user that accesses the game. A CGI-based program could be written that accepts the player's score either automatically while online or with a combination of offline file scoring and online file score uploading. Using the latter technique, the player could play the game offline and later upload the scores to the central server. For information on these subjects, please refer to appropriate texts.

Network Play

Many games provide network play, be it over a modem connection, a local area network, or the Internet. Worm could be adapted to provide TCP/IP socket connections between two or more players, with the playing surface populated by more than one worm. To prevent network latency effects from breaking the timing of two worms chasing the same treat, only the local worm's treat should be visible to the user; alternatively, multiple treats could be placed on the playing surface.

The simplest way of providing network play is by having a central server manage multiple network game requests and assign a player to a given game surface. This capability should be dynamic in that new playing surfaces should be created as more players join the game, limiting the maximum number of players per playing surface. An applet could be designed that shows the current games in progress and allows the player to join any game. Player names should be assigned to their worms so players can challenge each other directly. "Wormholes" could be created that would allow the player to move from one playing surface to another.

Suggestion Box

If you'd like to enhance the game of Worm, here are some suggested improvements:

- Add mines or other objects to avoid.
- Add levels with different-sized playing surfaces or nonrectangular playing surfaces.
- Create "warp holes" that open and close and send you to other levels if you hit them at just the right time.
- Show a replay of the last 10 seconds before collision.
- Add two-player capability (control one from the mouse and the other from the keyboard).
- Modify the worm size to one pixel for a "stringy worm," and allow motion in eight, not just four, directions.
- Add score-saving capability.
- Add network play capability.

Summary

As you have seen, Worm becomes a fairly sophisticated programming exercise once additional worms are introduced; however, this complexity appears mainly in the avoidance and shrink/grow handlers, not in the Worm object itself. Rewriting the code to accept two-player operation would not be very difficult for this reason. Rewriting the code for network play would be relatively easy except for unrelated problems introduced by network latency.

Some object-oriented methods were not used, such as inheritance, but the Worm class could be modified slightly to make it easier to build into a library for future derived worm objects. The worm design could be improved by hiding more of the interfaces: Currently the SessionManager requires that much of the worm's attributes be exposed and under its direct control, which reduces the usefulness of the class for general purpose applications.

Perhaps the best part about Worm is its deceivingly simple interface and game play. Only when the player sees for the first time an autonomous worm coiling into near-oblivion does the underlying complexity of the game surface. Keeping the focus on simplicity and clean design allows you to gradually extend your game's capabilities without losing control of the programming interfaces.

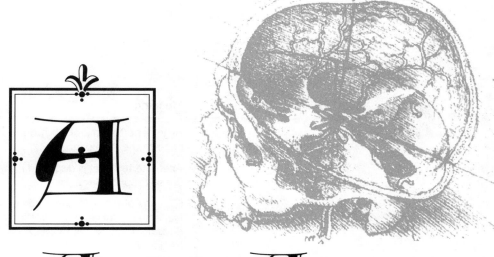

Appendix A:
Java Reference Tables

Applet Tags

The attributes given in Table A-1 can be used within the APPLET tag in an HTML file. These fields allow you to specify the alignment of the applet within the browser, the location of the applet class files, and applet parameters. There are three required attributes in the APPLET tag: CODE, HEIGHT, and WIDTH.

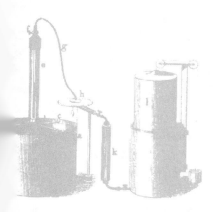

Attribute/Tag Name	Meaning
ALIGN	Alignment (top, middle, bottom) of the applet panel in the Web page.
ALT	Alternate text that is displayed if the browser doesn't support Java.
CODE	Filename of the Java class to be executed. The filename is relative to the location of the HTML document, unless the CODEBASE is specified (*required*).
CODEBASE	URL of the directory that contains the applet class files.
HEIGHT	Height of the applet panel in pixels (*required*).
HSPACE	Size of the left and right margins surrounding the applet panel, in pixels.
NAME	Name of this applet. This attribute is used by the method *java.applet.AppletContext.getApplet()*.
PARAM	This tag is used to provide additional parameters to the applet. The PARAM tag is covered in Chapter 7, Creating Customizable Games with the AWT.
VSPACE	Size of the top and bottom margins surrounding the applet panel, in pixels.
WIDTH	The width of the applet panel, in pixels (*required*).

TABLE A-1 ◈ *Java applet tags*

Comments

Java supports the following types of comments:

```
/*  This is a comment */
//  This is a comment
/** This comment is used by the JDK tool javadoc to generate HTML
    HTML documentation. */
```

Literals

Table A-2 lists literals that can be assigned to variables of the given types. *[floatnum]* represents a sequence of digits with an optional decimal point and an optional exponent, such as 17.13E2. *[intnum]* represents a sequence of digits with an optional octal prefix (0) or hexadecimal prefix (0x or 0X).

Type	Literal	Meaning
boolean	true	
false	True	
False		
char	\b	
\f		
\n		
\r		
\t		
\'		
\"		
\\		
\ddd	Backspace	
Form feed		
Newline		
Carriage return		
Tab		
Single quote		
Double quote		
Backslash		
The char denoted by octal value ddd		
double	*[floatnum]*d, *[floatnum]*D	Double constant
float	*[floatnum]*f, *[floatnum]*F	Float constant

continued on next page

continued from previous page

Type	Literal	Meaning
int, byte, long	0ddd	
0xdd, 0Xdd		
*[intnum]*l, *[intnum]*L	Octal constant	
Hexadecimal constant		
Long constant		
Object	null	Reference to unallocated or invalid object
String	"xxx"	String object with the contents between double quotes

TABLE A-2 ◈ *Literals*

Operators

Table A-3 lists the Java operators in decreasing order of precedence. All operators within the same row of the table have equivalent precedence. *E* denotes an expression.

Operators	Associativity	Meaning
[] .		
E++ *E*-- ++*E* --*E*	Left	
Right	Array/object member access	
Pre/post increment, pre/post decrement (unary)		
+*E* -*E*		
~ !	Right	
Unary plus or unary minus		
Bitwise or logical complement (unary)		
new (*type*)	Right	Creation or cast
* / %	Left	Multiplication, division, modulus

Operators	Associativity	Meaning
+ -	Left	Addition or subtraction
<< >> >>>	Left	Left shift, arithmetic right shift, logical right shift
< <= > >= instanceof	Left	Arithmetic comparison
Type comparison		
== !=	Left	Equal or not equal
&	Left	Bitwise AND
^	Left	Bitwise XOR (exclusive or)
|	Left	Bitwise OR (inclusive or)
&&	Left	Logical AND
||	Left	Logical OR
= += -= *= /= %= >>= <<= >>>= &= ^= |=	Right	
Operation followed by assignment		

TABLE A-3 ◈ *Java operators*

Reserved Words

Table A-4 gives the reserved words in Java, which should not be used as names of identifiers.

abstract	boolean	break	byte	byvalue
case	cast	catch	char	class
const	continue	default	do	double

continued on next page

continued from previous page

else	extends	false	final	finally
float	for	future	generic	goto
if	implements	import	inner	instanceof
int	interface	long	native	new
null	operator	outer	package	private
protected	public	rest	return	short
static	super	switch	synchronized	this
throw	throws	transient	true	try
varvoid	volatile	while		

TABLE A-4 ◈ *Java reserved words*

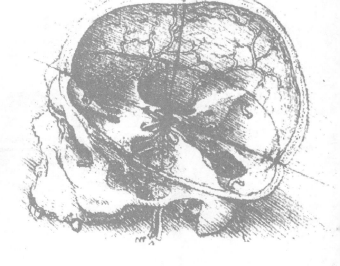

Appendix B:
Java API Reference

Graphical Overview of API Packages

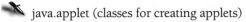

Figures B-1 through B-7 show the class hierarchy diagrams for the following packages of the Java API:

- java.applet (classes for creating applets)
- java.awt (classes of the Abstract Windowing Toolkit)
- java.awt.image (classes for image processing)
- java.io (classes for performing I/O)
- java.lang (fundamental classes of the Java language)
- java.net. (classes for networking)
- java.util. (classes of data structures)

FIGURE B-1

◎ ◎ ◎ ◎ ◎ ◎

java.applet

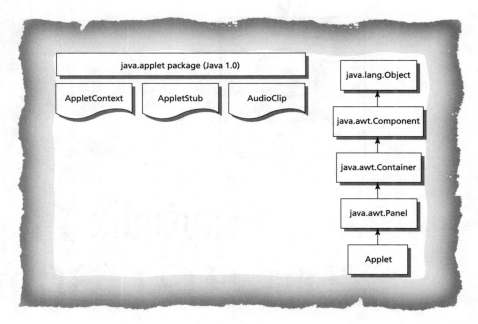

Summary of Selected Packages

Here are classes and interfaces selected from the java.applet, java.awt, and java.lang packages. You'll find these classes to be essential in creating Java game applets and applications. Each class summary follows this format.

Classname

Brief comments about the class.

```
// SELECTED variables and methods in the class
```

The following is *not* intended to be a comprehensive guide to the Java API. Check out Appendix C for further sources of information.

The java.applet Package

The classes in java.applet allow you to create applets and use sound.

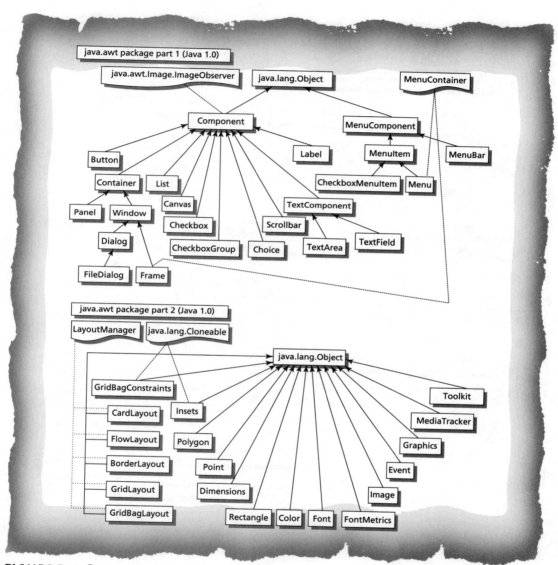

FIGURE B-2 ☉ *java.awt*

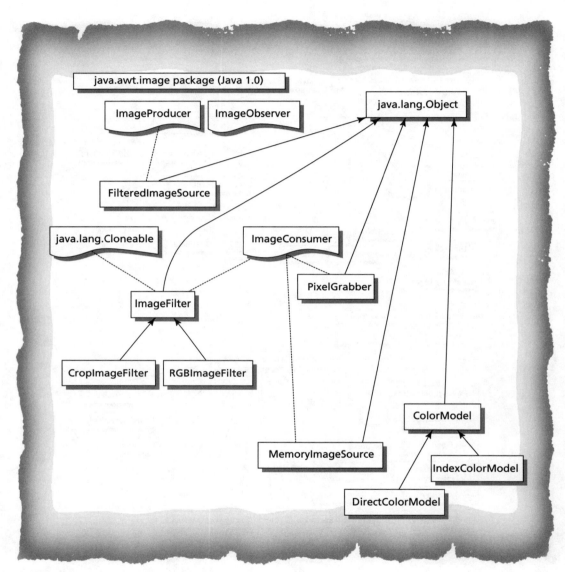

FIGURE B-3 ◉ *java.awt.image*

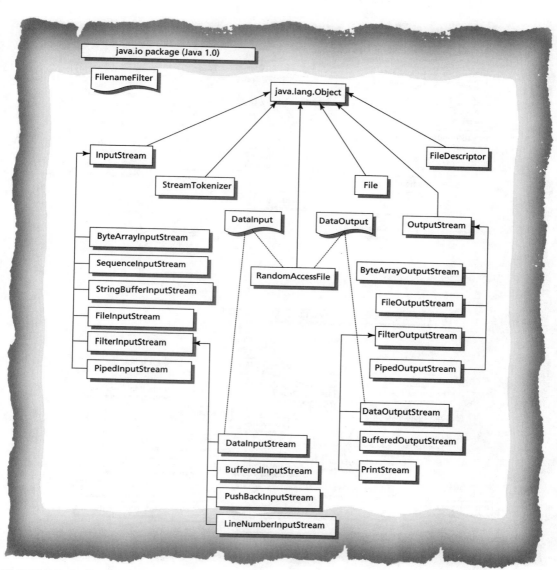

FIGURE B-4 ◉ *java.io*

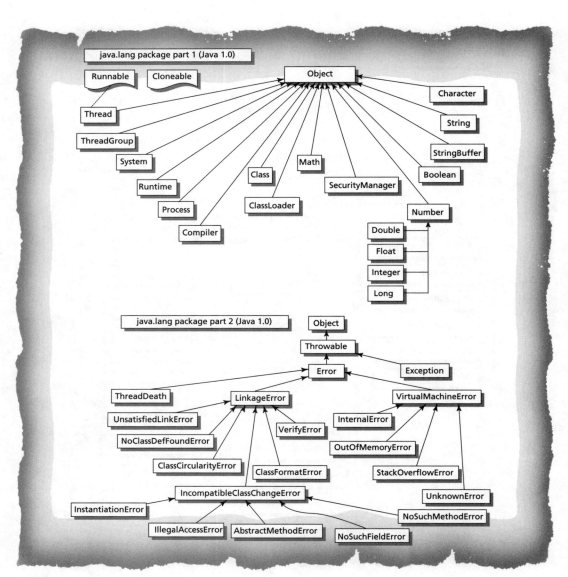

FIGURE B-5 ⊚ *java.lang*

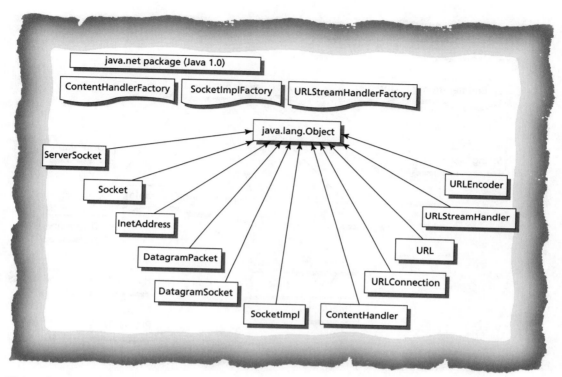

FIGURE B-6 ⊚ *java.net*

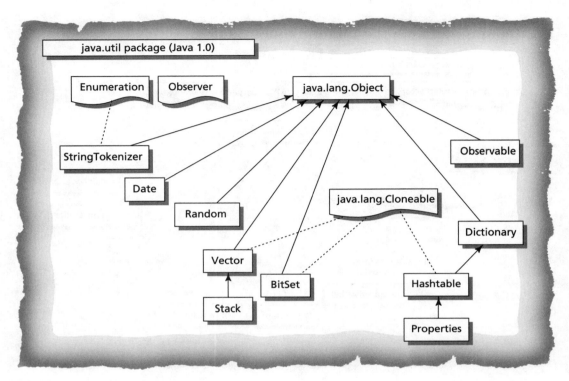

FIGURE B-7 ◉ *java.util*

java.applet.Applet

To create an applet, extend the Applet class, and override the init(), start(), stop(), and destroy() methods. The methods defined in java.awt.Component and java.awt.Container are inherited by the Applet class, and they can be used or overridden.

```
// public instance methods
public void destroy()
public AppletContext getAppletContext()
public String getAppletInfo()
public AudioClip getAudioClip(URL url)
public AudioClip getAudioClip(URL url,String name)
public URL getCodeBase()
public URL getDocumentBase()
public Image getImage(URL url)
public Image getImage(URL url,String name)
public String getParameter(String name)
public String[][] getParameterInfo()
public void init()
public boolean isActive()
public void play(URL url)
```

```
public void play(URL url,String name)
public void resize(int width,int height)
public void resize(Dimension d)
public final void setStub(AppletStub stub)
public void showStatus(String msg)
public void start()
public void stop()
```

java.applet.AppletContext (Interface)

This interface allows an applet to retrieve information about its environment (e.g., the browser or viewer running it). Use the Applet method getAppletContext() to obtain an AppletContext object.

```
public abstract   Applet getApplet(String name)
public abstract   Enumeration getApplets()
public abstract   AudioClip getAudioClip(URL url)
public abstract   Image getImage(URL url)
public abstract   void showDocument(URL url)
public abstract void showDocument(URL url, String target)
public abstract   void showStatus(String message)
```

java.applet.AudioClip Interface

This interface provides a high-level abstraction of audio.

```
public abstract void loop()
public abstract void play()
public abstract void stop()
```

The java.awt Package

The java.awt package contains the classes of the Abstract Windowing Toolkit.

java.awt.Color

This class allows you to create and manipulate RGB colors.

```
// constructors
Color(int red, int green, int blue)
Color(float red, float green, float blue)
Color(int rgb)

// public constants

public final static Color black, blue, cyan, darkGray, gray, green,
lightGray, magenta, orange, pink, red, white, yellow

// public static methods
public static int HSBtoRGB(float hue, float saturation, float brightness)
```

continued on next page

continued from previous page

```
public static float[] RGBtoHSB(int red, int green, int blue, float[] hsb)
public static Color getColor(String nm)
public static Color getColor(String nm, Color v)
public static Color getColor(String nm, int v)
public static Color getHSBColor(float hue, float saturation, float ⇐
brightness)

// public instance methods
public Color brighter()
public Color darker()
public boolean equals(Object obj)
public int getBlue()
public int getGreen()
public int getRGB()
public int getRed()
public int hashCode()
public int toString()
```

java.awt.Component

Component is an ancestor class for many of the GUI components of the AWT, such as
Button, Checkbox, and Frame. The following methods are inherited by subclasses of
Component.

```
public boolean action(Event evt, Object what)
public Rectangle bounds()
public int checkImage(Image image, ImageObserver observer)
public int checkImage(Image image, int width, int height, ImageObserver ⇐
observer)
public Image createImage(ImageProducer producer)
public Image createImage(int width, int height)
public synchronized void disable()
public synchronized void enable()
public Color getBackground()
public Font getFont()
public FontMetrics getFontMetrics(Font font)
public Graphics getGraphics()
public Container getParent()
public Toolkit getToolkit()
public boolean gotFocus(Event evt, Object what)
public boolean handleEvent(Event e)
public synchronized void hide()
public boolean imageUpdate(Image img,int flags,int x,int y,int w,int h)
public boolean isEnabled()
public boolean isShowing()
public boolean isValid()
public boolean isVisible()
public boolean keyDown(Event evt,int key)
public boolean keyUp(Event evt,int key)
public boolean lostFocus(Event evt, Object what)
public boolean mouseDown(Event evt,int x,int y)
public boolean mouseDrag(Event evt,int x,int y)
```

```
public boolean mouseEnter(Event evt,int x,int y)
public boolean mouseExit(Event evt,int x,int y)
public boolean mouseMove(Event evt,int x,int y)
public boolean mouseUp(Event evt,int x,int y)
public void paint(Graphics g)
public void repaint()
public void resize(int width,int height)
public setBackground(Color c)
public setFont(Font f)
public setForeground(Color c)
public synchronized void show()
public void update(Graphics g)
public void validate()
```

java.awt.Container

Subclasses of the abstract class Container, such as Applet, Frame, Dialog, and Panel, inherit the following methods.

```
public Component add(Component comp)
public Component add(String name,Component comp)
public Insets insets()
public Component locate(int x,int y)
public void setLayout(LayoutManager m)
public synchronized void remove(Component c)
public synchronized void removeAll()
```

java.awt.Event

The Event class encapsulates variables, constants, and methods to interpret GUI events.

```
// public instance variables
public Object arg
public int clickCount
public Event evt
public int id
public int key
public int modifiers
public Object target
public long when
public int x,y
// public constants for function keys
public final static int  UP, DOWN, LEFT, RIGHT,
F1,F2,F3,F4,F5,F6,F7,F8,F9,F10,F11,F12,
HOME,END,PGUP,PGDN
// public constants for modifier keys
public final static int ALT_MASK, CTRL_MASK, META_MASK, SHIFT_MASK
// public constants for event types
public final static int ACTION_EVENT,
  GOT_FOCUS, LOST_FOCUS,
  KEY_ACTION, KEY_ACTION_RELEASE,
  KEY_PRESS, KEY_RELEASE,
```

continued on next page

continued from previous page

```
                LIST_SELECT, LIST_DESELECT,
                LOAD_FILE, SAVE_FILE,
                MOUSE_DOWN, MOUSE_UP, MOUSE_DRAG,
                MOUSE_MOVE, MOUSE_ENTER, MOUSE_EXIT,
                SCROLL_ABSOLUTE,
                SCROLL_LINE_UP, SCROLL_LINE_DOWN ,
                SCROLL_PAGE_UP, SCROLL_PAGE_DOWN,
                WINDOW_DESTROY, WINDOW_EXPOSE,
                WINDOW_DEICONIFY, WINDOW_ICONIFY,
                WINDOW_MOVED


        // methods
        public boolean controlDown()
        public boolean metaDown()
        public boolean shiftDown()
```

java.awt.Frame

A Frame provides a separate, resizable, iconifiable window with a title and menu bar.

```
        // constructors
        public Frame()
        public Frame(String title)
        // public constants for cursor types
        public final static int CROSSHAIR_CURSOR,
          DEFAULT_CURSOR,
          E_RESIZE_CURSOR,
          HAND_CURSOR ,
          MOVE_CURSOR ,
          NE_RESIZE_CURSOR ,
          NW_RESIZE_CURSOR ,
          N_RESIZE_CURSOR ,
          SE_RESIZE_CURSOR ,
          SW_RESIZE_CURSOR ,
          S_RESIZE_CURSOR,
          TEXT_CURSOR,
          WAIT_CURSOR ,
          W_RESIZE_CURSOR
        // methods
        public synchronized void dispose()
        public int getCursorType()
        public Image getIconImage()
        public MenuBar getMenuBar()
        public String getTitle()
        public boolean isResizable()
        public synchronized void pack() // inherited from Window
        public void setCursor(int cursorType)
        public void setIconImage(Image image)
        public synchronized void setMenuBar(MenuBar mb)
        public void setResizable(boolean b)
        public void setTitle(String title)
```

java.awt.Graphics

This abstract class declares many of the methods you'll use in creating graphics for games. You can obtain a Graphics object with the Component method getGraphics(); alternatively, override the Component method paint(Graphics g).

```
public abstract void clearRect(int x, int y, int width, int height)
public abstract void clipRect(int x, int y, int width, int height)
public abstract void copyArea(int x, int y, int width, int height, ⇐
int dx, int dy)
public abstract Graphics create()
Graphics create(int x, int y, int width, int height)
public abstract void dispose()
public void draw3DRect(int x, int y, int width, int height, boolean
raised)
public abstract void drawArc(int x, int y, int width, int height, int
startAngle, int arcAngle)
public void drawBytes(byte data[], int offset, int length, int x, int y)
public void drawChars(char data[], int offset, int length, int x, int y)
public abstract boolean drawImage(Image img, int x, int y, int width, ⇐
int height, ImageObserver obs)
public abstract boolean drawImage(Image img, int x, int y, int width, ⇐
int height, Color bkgColor, ImageObserver observer)
public abstract void drawLine(int x1, int y1, int x2, int y2)
public abstract void drawOval(int x, int y, int width, int height)
public abstract void drawPolygon(int xPoints[], int yPoints[], int
nPoints)
public void drawPolygon(Polygon polygon)
public void drawRect(int x, int y, int width, int height)
public abstract void drawRoundRect(int x, int y, int width, int height, ⇐
int arcWidth, int arcHeight)
public abstract void drawString(String str, int x, int y)
public void fill3DRect(int x, int y, int width, int height, boolean
raised)
public abstract void fillArc(int x, int y, int width, int height, int
startAngle, int arcAngle)
public abstract void fillOval(int x, int y, int width, int height)
public abstract void fillPolygon(int xPoints[], int yPoints[], int
nPoints)
public void fillPolygon(Polygon polygon)
public abstract void fillRect(int x, int y, int width, int height)
public abstract void fillRoundRect(int x, int y, int width, int height, ⇐
int arcWidth, int arcHeight)
public void finalize()
public abstract Rectangle getClipRect()
public abstract Color getColor()
public abstract Font getFont()
public FontMetrics getFontMetrics()
public abstract FontMetrics getFontMetrics(Font font)
public abstract void setColor(Color color)
public abstract void setFont(Font font)
public abstract void setPaintMode()
```

continued on next page

continued from previous page

```
public abstract void setXORMode(Color color)
public String toString()
public abstract void translate(int x, int y)
```

java.awt.Image

Image is an abstract class that encapsulates a bitmap image.

```
public abstract void flush()
public abstract Graphics getGraphics()
public abstract int getHeight(ImageObserver observer)
public abstract Object getProperty(String name, ImageObserver observer)
public abstract ImageProducer getSource()
public abstract int getWidth(ImageObserver observer)
```

java.awt.MediaTracker

A MediaTracker object loads and tracks images. Use it to load bitmaps into game applets.

```
// constructor
public MediaTracker(Component comp)

// public constants
public final static int ABORTED, COMPLETE, ERRORED, LOADING

// public instance methods
public void addImage(Image image,int id)
public void addImage(Image image,int id,int w,int h)
public boolean checkAll()
public boolean checkId(int id)
public synchronized Object[] getErrorsAny()
public synchronized Object[] getErrorsID(int id)
public synchronized boolean isErrorAny()
public synchronized boolean isErrorID(int id)
public int statusAll(boolean load)
public int statusID(int id,boolean load)
public void waitForAll() throws InterruptedException
public void waitForId(int id) throws InterruptedException
```

The java.lang Package

The java.lang package contains the fundamental classes of the Java language.

java.lang.Boolean

This is a wrapper class for the boolean primitive type.

```
// constructors
public Boolean(boolean state)
public Boolean(String state)
// public constants
```

```
public final static Boolean TRUE, FALSE
// public static methods
public static boolean getBoolean(String propName)
public static Boolean valueOf(String str)
// public instance methods
public boolean booleanValue()
public boolean equals(Object obj)
public int hashCode()
public String toString()
```

java.lang.Character

This is a wrapper class for the char primitive type.

```
// constructor
public Character(char value)
// public constants
public final static int MIN_RADIX, MAX_RADIX
// public static methods
public static int digit(char ch, int radix)
public static char forDigit(int digit, int radix)
public static boolean isDigit(char ch)
public static boolean isLowerCase(char ch)
public static boolean isSpace(char ch)
public static boolean isUpperCase(char ch)
public static char toLowerCase(char ch)
public static char toUpperCase(char ch)
// public instance methods
public char charValue()
public boolean equals(Object obj)
public int hashCode()
public String toString()
```

java.lang.Class

The Class class defines methods that return information about a class, such as its name (getName()), its superclass (getSuperClass()), and the interfaces that the class implements (getInterfaces()). In addition, you can dynamically create an object of the class, using the newInstance() method. The forName() method returns a Class object from the fully qualified name of a class or object.

```
// public static methods
public static Class forName(String className) throws ⇐
ClassNotFoundException
// public instance methods
public ClassLoader getClassLoader()
public Class[] getInterfaces()
public String getName()
public Class getSuperClass()
public boolean isInterface()
```

continued on next page

continued from previous page

```
public Object newInstance() throws InstantiationException,
ClassNotFoundException
public String toString()
```

java.lang.Cloneable (Interface)

If a class implements the Cloneable interface, instances of the class may be cloned using the Object method clone(). No variables or methods are declared by this interface.

java.lang.Double

This is a wrapper class for the double primitive type.

```
// constructors
public Double(double value)
public Double(String s) throws NumberFormatException
// public constants
public final static double MIN_VALUE
public final static double MAX_VALUE
public final static double NEGATIVE_INFINITY
public final static double NaN
public final static double POSITIVE_INFINITY
// public static methods
public static long doubleToLongBits(double valToConvert)
public static boolean isInfinite(double valToTest)
public static boolean isNaN(double valToTest)
public static double longBitsToDouble(long bitsToConvert)
public static String toString(double d)
public static Double valueOf(String str) throws NumberFormatException
// public instance methods
public double doubleValue()
public boolean equals(Object obj)
public float floatValue()
public int hashCode()
public int intValue()
public boolean isInfinite()
public boolean isNaN()
public long longValue()
public String toString()
```

java.lang.Float

This is a wrapper class for the float primitive type.

```
// constructors
public Float(float value)
public Float(double value)
public Float(String s) throws NumberFormatException
// public constants
public final static float MIN_VALUE
public final static float MAX_VALUE
public final static float NEGATIVE_INFINITY
```

```
public final static float NaN
public final static float POSITIVE_INFINITY
// public static methods
public static long floatToIntBits(float valToConvert)
public static float intBitsToFloat(int bitsToConvert)
public static boolean isInfinite(double valToTest)
public static boolean isNaN(double valToTest)
public static String toString(float f)
public static String toString(float val)
public static Float valueOf(String str) throws NumberFormatException
// public instance methods
public double doubleValue()
public boolean equals(Object obj)
public float floatValue()
public int hashCode()
public int intValue()
public boolean isInfinite()
public boolean isNaN()
public long longValue()
public String toString()
```

java.lang.Integer

This is a wrapper class for the int primitive type.

```
// constructors
public Integer(int value)
public Integer(String s) throws NumberFormatException
// public constants
public final static int MIN_VALUE
public final static int MAX_VALUE
// public static methods
public static Integer getInteger(String propName)
public static Integer getInteger(String propName, int val)
public static Integer getInteger(String propName, Integer val)
public static int parseInt(String str) throws NumberFormatException
public static int parseInt(String str,int radix) throws
NumberFormatException
public static Integer valueOf(String str, int radix) throws
NumberFormatException
public static Integer valueOf(String str) throws NumberFormatException

// public instance methods
public double doubleValue()
public boolean equals(Object obj)
public float floatValue()
public int hashCode()
public int intValue()
public long longValue()
public String toString()
public String toString(int I)
public String toString(int i, int radix)
```

java.lang.Long

This is a wrapper class for the long primitive type.

```
// constructors
public Long(long value)
public Long(String str)
// public constants
public final static long MIN_VALUE
public final static long MAX_VALUE
// public static methods
public static Long getLong(String propName)
public static Long getLong(String propName, long val)
public static Long getLong(String propName, Long val)
public static long parseLong(String str) throws ⇐
NumberFormatException
public static long parseLong(String str,int radix) throws
NumberFormatException
public static String toString(int i)
public static String toString(int i, int radix)
public static Long valueOf(String str, int radix) throws
NumberFormatException
public static Long valueOf(String str) throws NumberFormatException
// public instance methods
public double doubleValue()
public boolean equals(Object obj)
public float floatValue()
public int hashcode()
public int intValue()
public long longValue()
public String toString()
```

java.lang.Math

This class defines static methods that compute mathematical functions, as well as constants for E and PI.

```
// public constants
public final static double E = 2.7182818284590452354;
public final static double PI = 3.1415926535897932846;
// public static methods
public static int abs(int a)
public static long abs(long a)
public static float abs(float a)
public static double abs(double a)
public static double acos(double a)
public static double asin(double a)
public static double atan(double a)
public static double atan2(double a, double b)
public static double ceil(double a)
public static double cos(double a)
public static double exp(double a)
```

```
public static double floor(double a)
public static double log(double a) throws ArithmeticException
public static int max(int a, int b)
public static long max(long a, long b)
public static float max(float a, float b)
public static double max(double a, double b)
public static int min(int a, int b)
public static long min(long a, long b)
public static float min(float a, float b)
public static double pow(double a, double b) throws ArithmeticException
public static double random()
public static double rint(double a)
public static int round(float a)
public static long round(double a)
public static double sin(double a)
public static double sqrt(double a) throws ArithmeticException
public static double tan(double a)
```

java.lang.Object

Object is the root class of Java's class hierarchy, and as a result, all other classes inherit Object's methods. The getClass() method returns the Class object associated with an object.

```
// constructor
public Object()
// public and protected instance methods
protected Object clone()
public boolean equals(Object obj)
protected void finalize()
public final Class getClass()
public int hashCode()
public final void notify() throws IllegalMonitorStateException
public final void notifyAll()throws IllegalMonitorStateException
public String toString()
public final void wait(long timeout) throws InterruptedException,
IllegalMonitorStateException
public final void wait(long timeout, int nanoseconds) throws
InterruptedException, IllegalMonitorStateException
public final void wait()throws InterruptedException,
IllegalMonitorStateException
```

java.lang.Runnable (Interface)

The Runnable interface allows an object to pass itself as the target when instantiating a Thread instance. This interface comes in handy in creating animations.

```
// public methods
public abstract void run()
```

java.lang.String

The String class encapsulates an immutable string of characters (i.e., the characters can't be changed). The StringBuffer class encapsulates character string data that can be altered.

```
// constructors
public String()
public String(String str)
public String(StringBuffer strBuf)
public String(char ch[])
public String(char ch[], int startIndex, int numChars ) throws
StringIndexOutOfBoundsException
public String(byte ascii[], int hiByte, int startIndex, int numBytes)
throws StringIndexOutOfBoundsException
public String(byte ascii[], int hiByte)
// public static methods
public static String copyValueOf(char ch[] [, int index, int count])
// public static methods
public static String valueOf(boolean b)
public static String valueOf(char ch)
public static String valueOf(int i)
public static String valueOf(long l)
public static String valueOf(float f)
public static String valueOf(double d)
public static String valueOf(Object obj)
public static String valueOf(char ch[], int index, int count])
// public instance methods
public char charAt(int index) throws StringIndexOutOfBoundsException
public int compareTo(Sting str2)
public String concat(String str)
public boolean endsWith(String suffix)
public boolean equals(Object obj2)
public boolean equalsIgnoreCase(Object obj2)
public void getBytes(int srcStartIndex, int srcEndIndex, char dest[], int
destIndex)
public void getChars(int srcStartIndex, int srcEndIndex, char dest[], int
destIndex)
public int hashCode()
public int indexOf(int ch, int index)
public int indexOf(String str, int index)
public String intern()
public int lastIndexOf(int ch, int index)
public int lastIndexOf(String substr, int index)
public int length()
public boolean regionMatches(boolean ignoreCase, int thisIndex, ⇐
Sting str2, int str2Index, int numChars)
public String replace(char oldChar, char newChar)
public boolean startsWith(String prefix, int startingChar)
public String subString(int startIndex, int endIndex) throws
StringIndexOutOfBoundsException
char[] toCharArray()
```

```
public String toLowerCase()
public String toString()
public String toUpperCase()
public String trim()
```

java.lang.StringBuffer

This class encapsulates a growable string of characters.

```
// constructors
public StringBuffer()
public StringBuffer(int length)
public StringBuffer(String str)
// public instance methods
public synchronized StringBuffer append(boolean b)
public synchronized StringBuffer append(char ch)
public synchronized StringBuffer append(int i)
public synchronized StringBuffer append(long l)
public synchronized StringBuffer append(float f)
public synchronized StringBuffer append(double d)
public synchronized StringBuffer append(String str)
public synchronized StringBuffer append(Object obj)
public synchronized StringBuffer append(char ch[][, int index, int count])
public int capacity()
public synchronized char charAt(int index) throws
StringIndexOutOfBoundsException
void copyWhenShared()
public synchronized void ensureCapacity(int minCapacity)
void getChars(int srcStartIndex, int srcEndIndex, char dest[], int ⇐
destIndex) throws StringIndexOutOfBoundsException
public synchronized StringBuffer insert(int index, boolean b) throws
ArrayIndexOutOfBoundsException
public synchronized StringBuffer insert(int index, char ch[])throws
ArrayIndexOutOfBoundsException
public synchronized StringBuffer insertChar(int index, int ch) throws
ArrayIndexOutOfBoundsException
public synchronized StringBuffer insert(int index, int i) throws
ArrayIndexOutOfBoundsException
public synchronized StringBuffer insert(int index, long l) throws
ArrayIndexOutOfBoundsException
public synchronized StringBuffer insert(int index, float f) throws
ArrayIndexOutOfBoundsException
public synchronized StringBuffer insert(int index, double d) throws
ArrayIndexOutOfBoundsException
public synchronized StringBuffer insert(int index, String str) throws
ArrayIndexOutOfBoundsException
public synchronized StringBuffer insert(int index, Object obj) throws
ArrayIndexOutOfBoundsException
public int length()
public synchronized void charAt(int index, char newCh) throws
ArrayIndexOutOfBoundsException
```

continued on next page

continued from previous page

```
public synchronized void setLength(int newLength) throws
StringIndexOutOfBoundsException
public synchronized String toString()
```

java.lang.System

This final class defines static variables and methods to access system functions in a platform-independent way. Methods such as arraycopy() (copy an array) and currentTimeMillis() (return the current time in milliseconds) are particularly useful.

```
// public static variables
public static PrintStream err
public static InputStream in
public static PrintStream out
// public static methods
public static void arraycopy(Object src, int srcIndex, Object dest, int
destIndex, int length) throws ArrayIndexOutOfBoundsException,
ArrayStoreException
public static long currentTimeMillis()
public static void exit(int status)
public void gc()
public static String getProperties()
public static String getProperty(String key)
public static String getProperty(String key, String def)
public static SecurityManager getSecurityManager()
public static void load(String pathName) throws UnsatisfiedLinkError
public static void loadLibrary(String libraryName) throws
UnsatisfiedLinkError
public static void runFinalization()
public static void setProperties(Properties props)
public static void setSecurityManager(SecurityManager sec) throws
SecurityException
```

java.lang.Thread

This class encapsulates a separate thread of execution. Threads are covered in Chapter 8, Implementing a High Score Server on a Network, and Chapter 10, Advanced Techniques.

```
// constructors
public Thread()
public Thread(Runnable target)
public Thread(Runnable target, String name)
public Thread(String name)
public Thread(ThreadGroup group, Runnable target)
public Thread(ThreadGroup group, String name)
public Thread(ThreadGroup group, String name, Runnable target)
// public constants
public static int MIN_PRIORITY
public static int NORM_PRIORITY
public static int MAX_PRIORITY
```

```
// public static methods
public static int activeCount()
public static Thread currentThread()
public static void dumpStack()
public static int enumerate(Thread threadArray[])
public static boolean interrupted()
public static boolean isInterrupted()
public static void sleep(long milliseconds) throws InterruptedException
public static void sleep(long milliseconds, int nanoseconds) throws
InterruptedException
public static void yield()


// public instance methods
public void checkAccess() throws SecurityException
public int countStackFrames() throws IllegalThreadStateException
public void destroy()
public final String getName()
public final int getPriority()
public final ThreadGroup getThreadGroup()
public void interrupt()
public final boolean isAlive()
public final boolean isDaemon()
public synchronized void join() throws InterruptedException
public synchronized void join(long milliseconds) throws ⇐
InterruptedException
public synchronized void join(long milliseconds, int nanoseconds]) throws
InterruptedException
public final void resume()
public void run()
public final void setDaemon(boolean state) throws ⇐
IllegalThreadStateException
public final void setName(String newName)
public final void setPriority(int newPriority) throws ⇐
IllegalArgumentException
public synchronized void start() throws IllegalThreadStateException
public final void stop()
public final void suspend()
```

java.lang.ThreadGroup

A ThreadGroup object consists of a set of threads and/or other ThreadGroup objects.
Every thread is a member of some thread group; the thread group provides limits on
the threads it contains.

```
// constructors
ThreadGroup(String grpName)
ThreadGroup(ThreadGroup parent, String grpName) throws
NullPointerException

// public instance methods
```

continued on next page

continued from previous page

```
            public synchronized int activeCount()
            public synchronized int activeGroupCount()
            public final void checkAccess() throws SecurityException
            public final synchronized void destroy() throws ⇐
            IllegalThreadStateException
            public int enumerate(Thread list[], boolean recurse)
            public int enumerate(ThreadGroup list[], boolean recurse)
            public final int getMaxPriority()
            public final String getName()
            public final ThreadGroup getParent()
            public final boolean isDaemon()
            public synchronized void list()
            public final boolean parentOf(ThreadGroup grp)
            public final synchronized void resume()
            public final void setDaemon(boolean daemon)
            public final void setMaxPriority(int priority)
            public final synchronized void stop()
            public final void suspend()
            public String toString()
            public void uncaughtException(Thread thread, Throwable exception)
```

java.lang.Throwable

All errors and exceptions are subclasses of the Throwable class. The methods defined in Throwable provide diagnostics when an error or exception occurs.

```
            // constructors
            public Throwable()
            public Throwable(String message)
            // public instance methods
            public Throwable fillInStackTrace()
            public String getMessage()
            public void printStackTrace(PrintStream prt)
            public String toString()
```

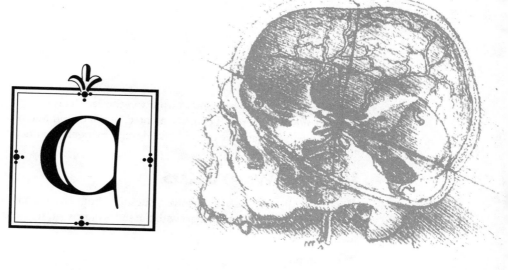

Appendix C: Sources of Java Information

The Internet

The Internet, of course, is an unequaled fount of information about Java. Check out the Web sites and newsgroups that specialize in Java.

Java Web Sites

There are an incredible number of Web sites with information about Java. Here are just a few Web sites to get you started:

- http://java.sun.com/. This site has the latest, definitive Java news and documentation.

- http://www.javaworld.com/. This is the site of a popular Java magazine.

- http://www.gamelan.com/. This site is a searchable directory of Java applets from around the Web.

- http://www.io.org/~mentor/. This site maintains a newsletter devoted to Java issues.

http://cafe.symantec.com/ , http://www.borland.com/, http://www.microsoft.com/. Symantec, Borland, and Microsoft are three companies that have created Java development environments.

Java Newsgroups

Sometimes, the fastest way to resolve a question about Java (or anything else) is to post the question to a newsgroup. Start with the series of newsgroups under comp.lang.java, such as

 comp.lang.java

 comp.lang.java.api

 comp.lang.java.programmer

 comp.lang.java.security

 comp.lang.java.tech

Sound and Image Resources

There are numerous archives of public-domain sounds and images on the Internet that you can use in your games. As of this writing, Java supports .au files (U-LAW audio format) recorded at 8 bits with an 8KHz sampling rate. Attempts to use other audio file formats, or even .au files with different sampling rates, can cause your program to crash! Similarly, images should be in the GIF format to ensure maximum portability of your games.

Here are some sites with sound and image resources:

 To convert between sound file formats, use a utility such as SoX (Sound Exchange). SoX can be obtained at http://www.spies.com/Sox/. SoX works on UNIX and PC platforms.

 The Net has many shareware image editors that allow you to convert between all kinds of image file formats. One of the best is Lview, available at http://world.std.com/%7Emmedia/lviewp.html/. Lview lets you save images in the GIF89a format, which allows you to specify a transparent color for your bitmap. Lview is available for PCs.

 A good place to get public domain sound and image files is http://sunsite.unc.edu/pub/multimedia/. Again, remember to convert what you download to the appropriate Java-compatible format.

 Another interesting multimedia site is somewhere in Poland, http://info.fuw.edu.pl/multimedia.html.

Of course, this list is just a microscopic sample of what's out there. Search the Net and you'll find many more resources!

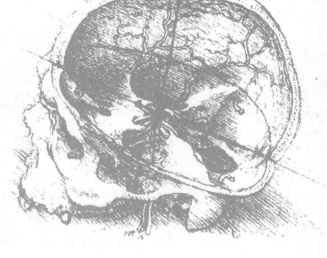

Appendix D: Basic JDK Tools

The Java Developer's Kit (JDK) consists of the following programs:

- javac. This program is the Java compiler that compiles source files written in the Java language to bytecodes.

- java. This program is the Java interpreter that runs Java programs.

- jdb. This tool is the Java debugger that helps you track down bugs in Java programs.

- javah. This tool allows you to interface Java code with programs written in other languages.

- javap. This tool disassembles compiled Java bytecodes.

- javadoc. This program creates HTML documentation for Java source code.

- appletviewer. This program allows you to execute applets without using a Web browser.

The following sections cover selected details of the *javac, java,* and *appletviewer* commands. You will find the complete JDK documentation at the URL http://java.sun.com/.

javac - The Java Compiler

javac compiles Java source code.

Synopsis

```
javac [options] filename.java ...
```

Description

The *javac* command compiles Java source code into bytecodes that can be executed by the Java interpreter. The source files must have the .java extension, and each compiled class is stored in a corresponding .class file. For example, the bytecodes for a class called Murder are stored in the file Murder.class.

If a referenced class is not defined within the source files passed to javac, then javac searches the classpath for this class. The classpath is specified by the CLASSPATH environment variable, or the -classpath option.

Options

Following are some options you can place on the command line when invoking javac.

-classpath `path`

This option specifies the path that javac uses to find classes. Specifying the classpath with this option overrides the CLASSPATH environment variable. For UNIX machines, directories in the path are delimited by colons, as in the following:

```
/escape/users/fan/classes:/usr/local/java/classes:.
```

For Windows machines, directories in the path are delimited by semicolons:

```
C:\ira\programs\java\classes;C:\tools\java\classes;.
```

-d directory

This option specifies the root directory where the .class files are saved. By default, javac saves .class files in the current directory.

-O

This option optimizes the compiled code by inlining static, final, and private methods. You should use this option when compiling your games; however, keep in mind that the resulting .class files may be larger in size. In addition, versions of some browsers may not work correctly with optimized code.

-verbose

With this option, the compiler prints the files being compiled and the class files that are loaded.

Environment Variables

The CLASSPATH environment variable specifies the path that javac uses to find user-defined classes. Directories are separated by colons (UNIX) or semicolons (Windows). See the -classpath option above for examples of paths.

java - The Java Interpreter

java executes Java programs.

Synopsis

```
java [options] classname <args>
```

Description

The *java* command executes the Java bytecodes found in classname.class. The source file for classname.class must include a main() method, from which execution starts (see Chapter 1/Three Sample Applications for further details).

The CLASSPATH environment variable, or the -classpath option, specifies the location of user-defined classes.

Options

Following are some options you can place on the command line when invoking java.

-cs, -checksource

This option tells java to compare the modification time of the compiled class file to that of the source file. If the source file is more recent, it is recompiled, and the resulting class file is loaded and executed.

-classpath `path`

This option specifies the path that javac uses to find classes. Specifying the classpath with this option overrides the CLASSPATH environment variable. For UNIX machines, directories in the path are delimited by colons, as in the following:

```
.:/escape/users/fan/classes:/usr/local/java/classes
```

For Windows machines, directories in the path are delimited by semicolons:

```
.;C:\ira\programs\java\classes;C:\tools\java\classes
```

-noasyngc

This option turns off asynchronous garbage collection. Thus, the garbage collector executes only when it is called explicitly or the program runs out of memory. Normally, it runs concurrently with the program as a separate thread.

-noverify

This option turns off the bytecode verifier.

-v, -verbose

This option tells java to print a message to *standard output* each time a class file is loaded.

-verify

This option tells the bytecode verifier to check all classes that are loaded.

Environment Variables

The CLASSPATH environment variable specifies the path that java uses to find user-defined classes. Directories are separated by colons (UNIX) or semicolons (Windows). See the -classpath option above for examples of paths.

appletviewer - The Java Applet Viewer

appletviewer executes Java applets.

Synopsis

```
appletviewer urls
```

Description

The appletviewer loads, displays, and executes each applet referenced by the documents found at the specified URLs. The applets are referenced using the APPLET tag (see the Applet Tags section in Appendix A for more information). Each applet is displayed in its own window.

Environment Variables

The CLASSPATH environment variable specifies the path that appletviewer uses to find user-defined classes. Directories are separated by colons (UNIX) or semicolons (Windows), as with the *java* and *javac* commands. If CLASSPATH is not set, the appletviewer searches for classes in the current directory and the system classes. appletviewer does not support the -classpath option found in java and javac.

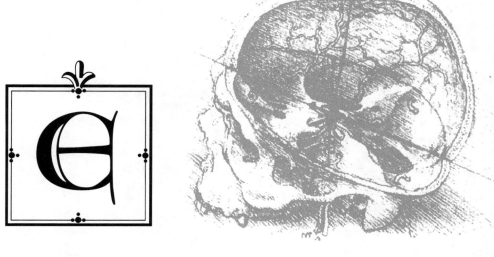

Appendix E: 3D Transforms

This chapter provides supplemental information to augment your understanding of the math and 3D concepts introduced in Chapter 11, Into the Third Dimension, and Chapter 12, Building 3D Applets with App3Dcore.

We will kick-start the process of understanding 3D by making 3D rotations with an informal discussion of rotating points from 2D to 3D.

Rotating Points in 3D

The step from rotating a two-dimensional point in a plane to rotating a three-dimensional point in a volume is not as painful as it first might seem. When working in two dimensions, we use a coordinate system that is made of two axes, x and y. These two axes make a plane that can be compared to a piece of paper. This plane is called the "x-y plane", since it is defined by the two principal axes, as shown in Figure E-1.

A point can be placed anywhere within the bounds of the plane by simply specifying x and y and then rotated by "turning" the whole plane. Imagine putting your hand on the paper and then turning it. What you should see is that the axes remain in the same position while the point follows the paper. Listing E-1 gives the formula for rotating a point in the x-y plane.

FIGURE E-1
◉ ◉ ◉ ◉ ◉ ◉

A two-dimensional coordinate system

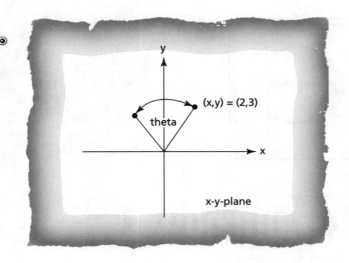

Listing E-1 Rotating a point by theta radians counterclockwise in an x-y plane

```
Xnew = X*Math.cos(theta)-Y*Math.sin(theta)
Ynew = X*Math.sin(theta)+Y*Math.cos(theta)
```

Moving to the third dimension is done by adding the z-axis. This new axis turns the two-dimensional plane into a volume, and points can be placed anywhere within it by specifying the x, y, and z coordinates. The difference between 2D and 3D is that the z-axis introduces two new principal planes: the y-z and z-x planes.

The point shown in Figure E-2 can be rotated by turning any of the three principal planes. A full 3D rotation is done by rotating one plane at a time by a specified angle.

Another way of looking at rotation in 3D is to imagine that you grab one of the axes with your thumb and index finger and turn it. You should "see" that the points rotate about the axis that you are turning while the other axes stand still. Looking at Figure E-1 again, you could also imagine that there is a z-axis pointing out from the paper and that a rotation in two dimensions is done by turning it. Therefore, you could think of a two-dimensional rotation as rotation about an imaginary z-axis.

A 3D Rotation Step by Step

Let's go through the three steps that will rotate a point about all three axes.

Step 1. Rotating About the Z-Axis

This rotation is done in the x-y plane, and it is exactly the same as in the two-dimensional case. The source coordinates X and Y are transformed to Xa and Ya while Z remains the same. This is shown in Figure E-3.

FIGURE E-2
◎ ◎ ◎ ◎ ◎ ◎
*A 3D coordi-
nate system*

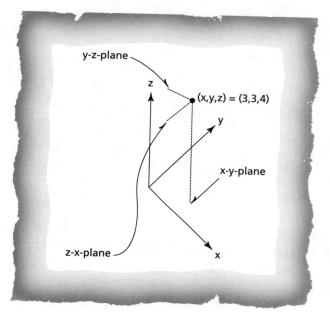

FIGURE E-3
◎ ◎ ◎ ◎ ◎ ◎
*Rotating about
the z-axis or in
the x-y plane*

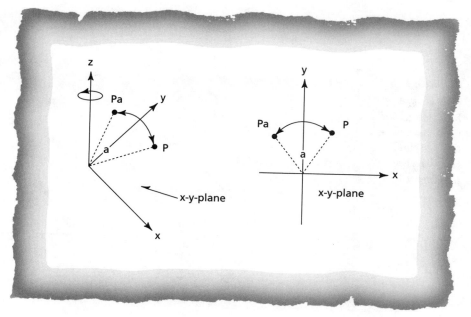

$$x_a = x \cdot \cos a - y \cdot \sin a$$
$$y_a = x \cdot \sin a + y \cdot \cos a$$
$$z_a = z$$

The resulting point Xa, Ya, Za will be used as the source point for the next rotation.

Step 2. Rotating About the X-Axis

The next rotation would be about the x-axis. What we actually do is rotate the point in the y-z plane. Another way of looking at it is as a two-dimensional rotation, but with Y and Z as principal axes (see Figure E-4).

$$x_b = x_a$$
$$y_b = y_a \cdot \cos b - z_a \cdot \sin b$$
$$z_b = y_a \cdot \sin b + z_a \cdot \cos b$$

Step 3. Rotating About the Y-Axis

Using the resulting point from the last operation, the final transformation is made in the same way as described above, and the full 3D rotation is complete, as shown in Figure E-5 and Listing E-2.

$$x_c = x_b \cdot \cos c + z_b \cdot \sin c$$
$$y_c = y_b$$
$$z_c = -x_b \cdot \sin c + z_b \cdot \cos c$$

FIGURE E-4

◉ ◉ ◉ ◉ ◉ ◉ ◉

Rotation about the x-axis or in the y-z plane (two ways of looking at it)

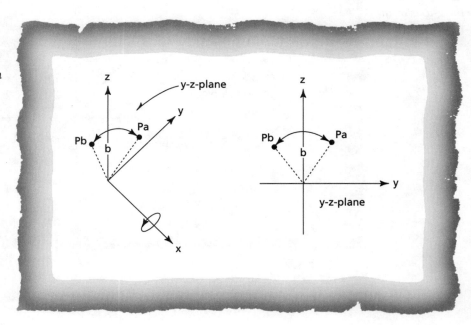

FIGURE E-5

◎ ◎ ◎ ◎ ◎ ◎

Rotation in the
z-x plane

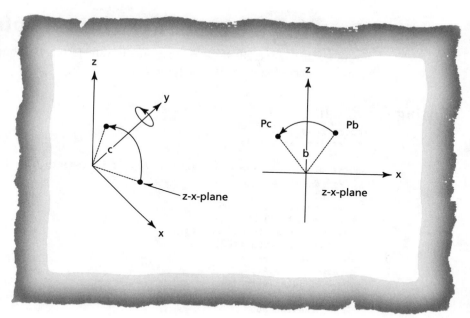

Listing E-2 *Rotating a point in 3D*

```
//-- X,Y,Z will be rotated by a,b,c radians about all principal
//-- axis. The result will be stored in Xnew, Ynew, Znew.

//-- rotate the point in x-y-plane and store the result in
//-- Xa,ya,Za.
Xa = X*Math.cos(a)-Y*Math.sin(a);
Ya = X*Math.sin(a)+Y*Math.cos(a);
Za = Z; //-- z coordinate is not affected by this rotation

//-- rotate the resulting point in the y-z-plane
Xb = X; //-- x coordinate is not affected by this rotation
Yb = Y*Math.cos(b)-Z*Math.sin(b);
Zb = Y*Math.sin(b)+Z*Math.cos(b);

//-- rotate the resulting point in the z-x-plane
Xc = X*Math.cos(c)+Z*Math.sin(c);
Yc = Y; //-- z coordinate is not affected by this rotation
Zc = -X*Math.sin(c)+Z*Math.cos(c);

Xnew = Xc;
Ynew = Yc;
Znew = Zc;
```

Creating a Rotating Points Applet

Just to see that this is actually working, Figure E-6 and Listing E-3 show an applet that spins a number of random 3D points around.

Listing E-3 *Rotating points*

```java
import java.awt.*;
import java.applet.*;

public class RotatingPoints extends Applet implements Runnable{
    //-- # points
    int pts;
    //-- the source points
    double x[],y[],z[];
    //-- the transformed points
    double xt[],yt[],zt[];
    //-- the angles
    double Ax,Ay,Az;
    //-- angular velocity
    double da;
    //-- the thread
    Thread myThread;

    public void init(){
        pts=10;
        x =new double[pts]; y =new double[pts]; z =new double[pts];
        xt=new double[pts]; yt=new double[pts]; zt=new double[pts];
        //-- create some random 3d points
        for(int n=0;n<pts;n++){
            x[n]=Math.random()*100-50;
            y[n]=Math.random()*100-50;
            z[n]=Math.random()*100-50;
        }
```

FIGURE E-6

◎ ◎ ◎ ◎ ◎ ◎

The Rotating Points applet

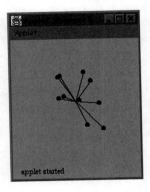

```
      //-- set the angular velocity
      da=Math.PI/10;
      //-- start the thread
      myThread=new Thread(this);
      myThread.start();
   }

   public void run(){
      while(myThread!=null){
         try { myThread.sleep(100);
         } catch ( InterruptedException e) {}
         rotatePoints(x,y,z,xt,yt,zt,pts,Ax,Ay,Az);
         Az+=da;
         repaint();
      }
   }

   public void start(){
      if(myThread==null){
         myThread=new Thread(this);myThread.start();
      }
   }

   public void stop(){
      if(myThread!=null){
         myThread.stop(); myThread=null;
      }
   }

   public void paint(Graphics g){
      int Xo=size().width>>1,Yo=size().height>>1;
      //-- paint all the points
      for(int n=0;n<pts;n++){
         int x=(int)xt[n],y=(int)yt[n];
         //-- set the different colors
         g.setColor(new Color(n<<3,0,0));
         //-- draw a line from origot to center
         g.drawLine(Xo,Yo,Xo+x,Yo+y);
         //-- draw a little circle
         g.fillOval(Xo+x-4,Yo+y-4,8,8);
         }
      }
      private void rotatePoints(double xs[],double ys[],double zs[],
                                double xd[],double yd[],double zd[],
                                int pts,double a,double b,double c){
         for(int n=0;n<pts;n++){
            double Xa,Ya,Za,Xb,Yb,Zb;

            //-- rotate the dource in x-y-plane
            Xa = xs[n]*Math.cos(a)-ys[n]*Math.sin(a);
            Ya = xs[n]*Math.sin(a)+ys[n]*Math.cos(a);
```

continued on next page

continued from previous page

```
            Za = zs[n];

            //-- rotate the resulting point in the y-z-plane
            Xb = Xa;
            Yb = Ya*Math.cos(b)-Za*Math.sin(b);
            Zb = Ya*Math.sin(b)+Za*Math.cos(b);

            //-- rotate the resulting point in the z-x-plane
            xd[n] = Xb*Math.cos(c)+Zb*Math.sin(c);
            yd[n] = Yb;
            zd[n] = -Xb*Math.sin(c)+Zb*Math.cos(c);
        }
    }
}
```

Linear Algebra Basics

Computer graphics algorithms make use of many mathematical concepts and techniques. This section will provide a description of some of the basic notions of linear algebra. Since almost all 3D transformations are done using linear algebra, it is essential to at least understand the basic definitions in this field. If you have worked with matrixes and vectors before but have not used them in 3D graphics, you should browse this section to acquaint yourself with their use in this context.

Orthogonal Normalized Coordinate System

We are all used to the simple and intuitive coordinate system consisting of an x-, y-, and possibly z-axis in which points are placed by specifying coordinates; for example, (x,y)=(2,3). But what do those numbers mean? It's fairly obvious that 2 means the number of scale units on the x-axis and 3 means the number of scale units on the y-axis. Figure E-7 demonstrates.

But what do they stand for? Is it 2 inches to the right and 3 meters upward? Or possibly miles? If nothing is specified on the axis, the numbers stand for units. In 3D graphics we will use the right-handed orthogonal normalized (O.N.) coordinate system, which is mathematically correct (see Figure E-8).

This is not as complicated as it sounds. It simply means that all axes are at a right angle to each other (orthogonal) and have the same length. This length equals one (normalized). In linear algebra you can use any sort of coordinate system, even weird ones, like that shown in Figure E-9. But the O.N. system in Figure E-5 simplifies a lot of linear algebra operations, and since this is the system that we will use when dealing with 3D math, we simply give thanks and move on.

FIGURE E-7

◎ ◎ ◎ ◎ ◎ ◎

Orthogonal normalized coordinate system with two axes

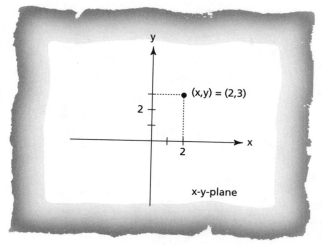

x-y-plane

FIGURE E-8

◎ ◎ ◎ ◎ ◎ ◎

Right- and left-handed O.N. system with three axes

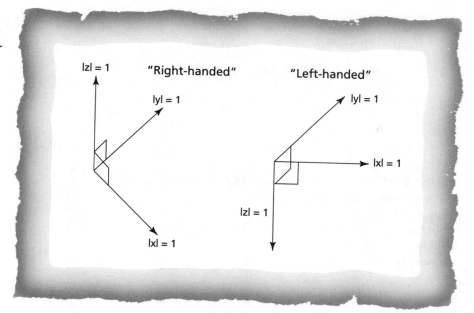

Vectors

There is a fundamental difference between a 3D point and a vector, although these bounds get a little bit fuzzy when dealing with 3D graphics. A point is merely a position in a

FIGURE E-9

◎ ◎ ◎ ◎ ◎ ◎

Weird left-handed, unorthogonal, unnormalized coordinate system with three axes

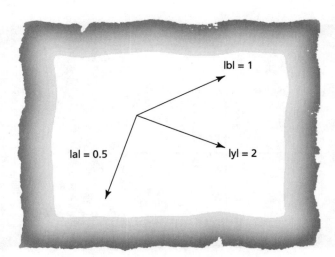

three-dimensional space, while a vector is the difference between two points. This is shown in Figure E-10.

A vector can be described as a directed line segment that has two properties: magnitude and direction.

Magnitude is the length of the vector, and it is calculated as

$$|V| = \sqrt{V_x^2 + V_y^2}$$ in 2D and $$|V| = \sqrt{V_x^2 + V_y^2 + V_z^2}$$ in 3D.

FIGURE E-10

◎ ◎ ◎ ◎ ◎ ◎

A vector is defined as the difference between two points

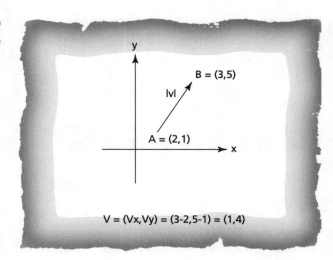

As you can see, there is consistency between the 2D and 3D cases. This is typical when it comes to vector and matrix operations.

The direction of a vector is defined indirectly by its components. In Figure E-10, the components are Vx and Vy. In the 3D case there would also be Vz.

Addition and Subtraction with Vectors

Addition (shown in Figure E-11) is done by simply adding the vectors' components as follows:

$\vec{a} = (4,2)$

$\vec{b} = (-1,2)$

$\vec{v} = \vec{a} + \vec{b} = (4 - 1, 2 + 2) = (3,4)$

Subtraction (shown in Figure E-12) is done by making b a negative number. The expression will barely change, but the graphical representation is totally different, as you might expect.

$\vec{a} = (4,2)$

$\vec{b} = -(-1,2) = (1,-2)$

$\vec{v} = \vec{a} + \vec{b} = (4 + 1, 2 - 2) = (5,0)$

What we do here is turn the vector b so that it points in the "opposite" direction.

FIGURE E-11

◉ ◉ ◉ ◉ ◉ ◉

Addition between two-dimensional vectors

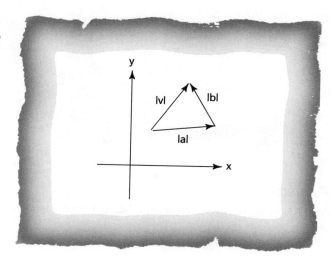

FIGURE E-12

◎ ◎ ◎ ◎ ◎ ◎

Subtraction between two-dimensional vectors

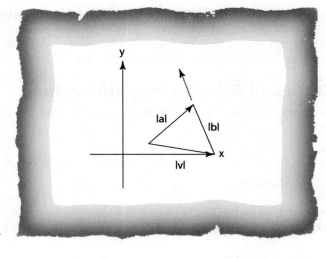

a

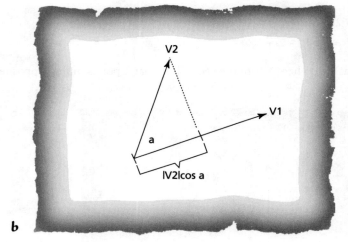

b

Dot Product

Dot product is very powerful and is the foundation for many linear algebra operations.

❖ Dot Product, the Definition

$$V_1 \cdot V_2 = |V_1| \cdot |V_2| \cdot \cos a \qquad\qquad 0 \le a \le \pi$$

Another way of calculating the dot product is by multiplying the components of the vectors as follows:

$$V_1 \cdot V_2 = V_{1x}V_{2x} + V_{1y}V_{2y} + V_{1z}V_{2z}$$

This only works in an O.N. system. The result of this operation will be a scalar (a number) that can be interpreted as the product of the parallel components of the two vectors. This interpretation is very abstract, not very intuitive. Let's look at the behavior of dot product to get a better idea of what it does.

Characteristics of Dot Product

 The result gets smaller as the angle comes closer to 90 degrees and larger as the angle gets closer to zero. The largest value is obtained when the two vectors are parallel or "on top" of each other, because the angle is 0 and cos 0=1. This is shown in Figure E-13.

FIGURE E-13

◉ ◉ ◉ ◉ ◉ ◉

The result of dot product depends on the angle between the vectors

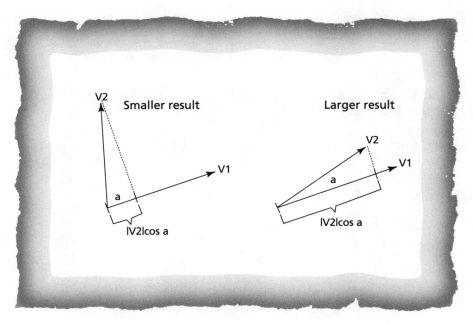

🗡 The dot product can be used to determine if a vector is at a right angle to another vector. At this angle the result will be zero, because $cos\frac{\pi}{2}=0$, as shown in Figure E-14.

🗡 The result will be negative when the angle is larger than 90 degrees (see Figure E-15). This can be used to decide if the vectors point in "opposite" directions.

🗡 When both vectors have magnitude (length) 1, the result of a dot product will be between -1 and 1. This result is actually the cosine value of the angle between the vectors. Figure E-16 shows this. In other words, we could say

FIGURE E-14

◎ ◎ ◎ ◎ ◎ ◎

If the vectors are at a right angle to each other, the result of the dot product will be 0

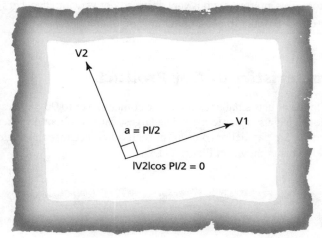

FIGURE E-15

◎ ◎ ◎ ◎ ◎ ◎

If the angle is larger than 90 degrees, the result will be negative

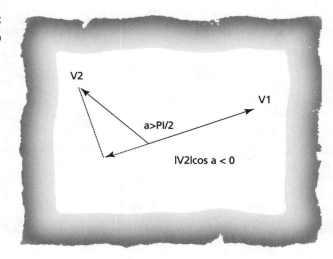

that $\cos a = V_{1x} \times V_{2x} \times V_{1y} V_{2y} + V_{1x} \times V_{2z}$ as long as both V1 and V2 are normalized (length=1).

The Value of Dot Product

Dot product is a powerful operation that can be used in many ways. As will be shown later, a variation of the dot product between two 2D vectors can tell the orientation of a polygon. In 3D the dot product will be heavily used to determine if a point is in front of or behind a plane. The definition of the dot product in combination with other calculations will be used to determine the distance from a point to a line or a plane. It is also used to determine the shading of a polygon, depending on the normal of the polygon and the light vector.

FIGURE E-16

◉ ◉ ◉ ◉ ◉ ◉

Calculating the angle between the vectors

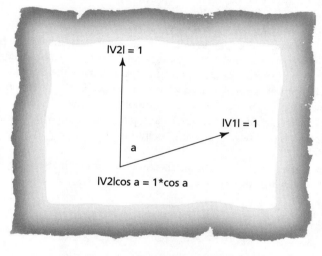

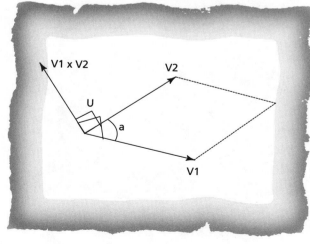

Cross Product

The cross product between two vectors is related to the dot product but produces completely different results. It is linear algebra's way of multiplying two vectors. The result will be another vector that is at a right angle to both of the operands. Let's look at the definition:

Cross Product, the Definition

$V_1 x V_2 = u|V_1||V_2|\sin a$

Another way of calculating the vector product in an O.N. system is using the components of the operands as follows:

$V_1 x V_2 = (V_{1y} \cdot V_{2z} - V_{1z} \cdot V_{2y}, V_{1z} \cdot V_{2x} - V_{1x} \cdot V_{2z}, V_{1x} \cdot V_{2y} - V_{1y} \cdot V_{2x})$

The magnitude of the resulting vector is the same as the area of the parallelogram that the two vectors make. This can be used to calculate the area of a triangle, for example.

The resulting vector is either pointing upward, as in the definition, or downward. U in the definition is a normalized vector that specifies the direction of the result. The direction is decided by how V1 and V2 are placed in relation to each other.

If the smallest rotation that takes V1 and places it "on top" of V2 is counterclockwise, then the result is positive, or "upward," pointing out from the paper toward you, as shown in Figure E-17.

If this is not the case and the smallest rotation is clockwise, then the result is negative, or "downward" into the paper, as Figure E-18 shows.

FIGURE E-17

Vectors with positive orientation

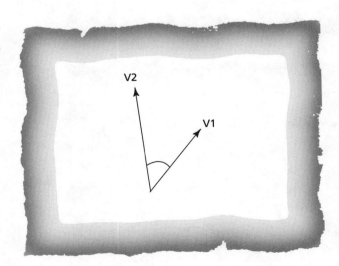

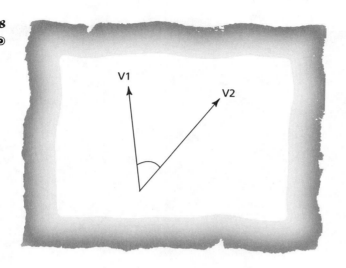

Characteristics of Cross Product

 The cross product is not commutative. What this means is that $V1xV2$ does not produce the same result as $V2xV1$. Looking at Figure E-19, it can be deduced that $V1xV2=-V2xV1$. This "feature" can be used to determine the orientation of a polygon, for example.

 If both $V1$ and $V2$ are normalized, then the result will be a normalized vector also. The resulting vector is the normal to the plane that $V1$ and $V2$ make, as seen in Figure E-20. This "feature" will be used to calculate the normal of a polygon.

The Value of Cross Product

Cross product is in fact very related to dot product. It can be used to calculate the normal of a polygon, determine the orientation of a polygon, compose transformation matrixes, and so on.

Matrixes

A matrix is a rectangular array of numbers or expressions called the elements of the matrix. Matrixes are used as a means of expressing mathematical operations in a compact way. The matrix below, for example, is a 4x3 matrix, which means that there are four rows and three columns.

$$M = \begin{pmatrix} 2 & 1 & 6 \\ 5 & 9 & 3 \\ 0 & 3 & 4 \\ 5 & 8 & 3 \end{pmatrix}$$

FIGURE E-19
◉ ◉ ◉ ◉ ◉ ◉
Cross product is not commutative

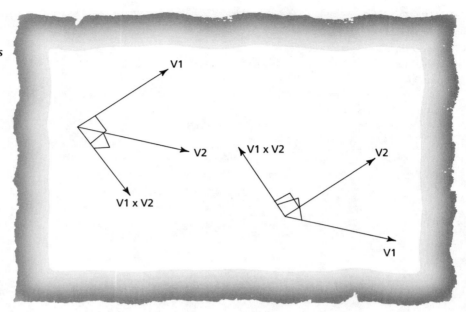

FIGURE E-20
◉ ◉ ◉ ◉ ◉ ◉
Calculating the normal of a plane

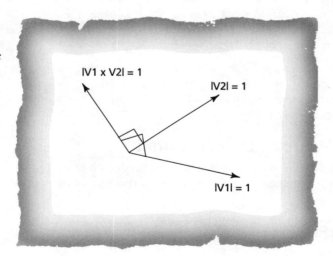

Most of the arithmetic operations that can be applied on "normal" numbers (scalars) are also defined for matrixes. But with matrixes, the operations tend to get very nasty, very fast.

Addition and Subtraction of Matrixes

The simplest operations between two matrixes are probably addition and subtraction. Matrix addition can only be done between matrixes of the same size; otherwise, it is not even defined.

$$M_1 + M_2 = \begin{pmatrix} a_{11} & a_{12} & a_{13} \\ a_{21} & a_{22} & a_{23} \\ a_{31} & a_{32} & a_{33} \end{pmatrix} + \begin{pmatrix} b_{11} & b_{12} & b_{13} \\ b_{21} & b_{22} & b_{23} \\ b_{31} & b_{32} & b_{33} \end{pmatrix} = \begin{pmatrix} a_{11} + b_{11} & a_{12} + b_{12} & a_{13} + b_{13} \\ a_{21} + b_{21} & a_{22} + b_{22} & a_{23} + b_{23} \\ a_{31} + b_{31} & a_{32} + b_{32} & a_{33} + b_{33} \end{pmatrix}$$

Elements with the same index, or the same position, are added, making a resulting matrix that has the same size as the operands.

Multiplication of a Matrix with a Vector

This is one of the most important operations involving matrixes and 3D math and will be heavily used throughout this appendix. It is done in the following way:

$$v' = M \cdot v = \begin{pmatrix} a_{11} & a_{12} & a_{13} \\ a_{21} & a_{22} & a_{23} \\ a_{31} & a_{32} & a_{33} \end{pmatrix} \cdot \begin{pmatrix} x \\ y \\ z \end{pmatrix} = \begin{pmatrix} a_{11} \cdot x + a_{12} \cdot y + a_{13} \cdot z \\ a_{21} \cdot x + a_{22} \cdot y + a_{23} \cdot z \\ a_{31} \cdot x + a_{32} \cdot y + a_{33} \cdot z \end{pmatrix}$$

The result of this operation is a vector of the same size as the operand. There is another way of looking at this operation, though. Suppose that the rows in the matrix are seen as individual vectors. Then we could express the multiplication as three individual dot products. Looking at the first element in the resulting vector, you should observe that it is the dot product of $(a_{11}, a_{12}, a_{13}) x (x, y, z)$. The second element is the dot product of $(a_{21}, a_{22}, a_{23}) x (x, y, z)$. The third element is calculated in the same manner.

Matrix Multiplication with a Vector

Those of you who simply don't want to know how matrixes work internally and simply want to use them for the math-magic that they produce could think of a matrix as a "black box" that contains a certain transform, as Figure E-21 demonstrates.

Multiplication of Two Matrixes

This operation is extremely time-consuming. It is only defined when the number of columns in the left operand matrix equals the number of rows in the right operand.

$$M_1 \cdot M_2 = \begin{pmatrix} a_{11} & a_{12} \\ a_{21} & a_{22} \end{pmatrix} \cdot \begin{pmatrix} b_{11} & b_{12} \\ b_{21} & b_{22} \end{pmatrix} = \begin{pmatrix} a_{11}b_{11} + a_{12}b_{21} & a_{11}b_{12} + a_{12}b_{22} \\ a_{21}b_{11} + a_{22}b_{21} & a_{21}b_{11} + a_{22}b_{21} \end{pmatrix}$$

Even if this operation seems to be complicated, it is very similar to multiplying a matrix with a vector. In fact, multiplying a matrix with a vector is a special case of matrix multiplication in which the second operand (the vector) is a matrix with one column.

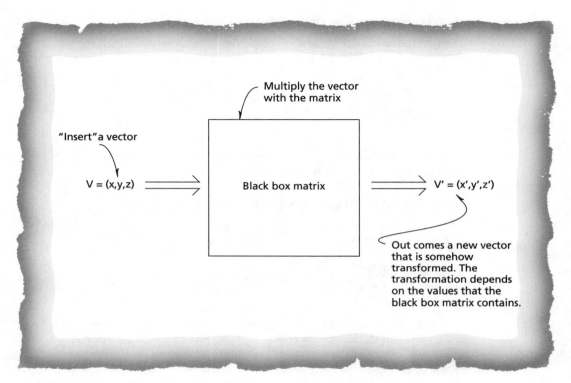

FIGURE E-21 ◉ *Math-magic with a black box*

🔲 Warning!

Multiplication between matrixes is not commutative. This means that M1·M2 will not produce the same result as M2·M1.

Matrixes in 3D Transformations

All basic 3D operations can be expressed as a multiplication between a matrix and a vector. The resulting vector would be some sort of transformation of the operand vector. What the transformation would be depends on the content of the matrix, as in the black box example in Figure E-21. It will be shown that all rotations, scaling, translation, shearing, and so on can be expressed in a conveniently compact way by using a matrix. In the first section of this appendix you saw how to rotate a 3D point in an informal way without using matrixes. You are now about see how to do it formally.

Identifying the Basic Rotation Matrixes

Let's look at part of a listing from the previous section that rotated a point in the x-y plane (or about the z-axis, if you wish).

```
//-- rotate the point in x-y-plane and store the result in
//-- Xa,ya,Za.
Xa = X*Math.cos(a)-Y*Math.sin(a);
Ya = X*Math.sin(a)+Y*Math.cos(a);
Za = Z; //-- z coordinate is not affected by this rotation
```

If all the Java-specific notations are removed and rewritten in a mathematically "clean" way, the calculations above would be represented in this form:

$$x' = \cos a \cdot x - \sin a \cdot y$$
$$y' = \sin a \cdot x + \cos a \cdot y$$
$$z' = z$$

How could these operations be expressed in a matrix? Let's look at the definition of multiplication between a matrix and a vector again.

$$v' = M \cdot v = \begin{pmatrix} a_{11} & a_{12} & a_{13} \\ a_{21} & a_{22} & a_{23} \\ a_{31} & a_{32} & a_{33} \end{pmatrix} \cdot \begin{pmatrix} x \\ y \\ z \end{pmatrix} = \begin{pmatrix} a_{11} \cdot x + a_{12} \cdot y + a_{13} \cdot z \\ a_{21} \cdot x + a_{22} \cdot y + a_{23} \cdot z \\ a_{31} \cdot x + a_{32} \cdot y + a_{33} \cdot z \end{pmatrix}$$

The goal is to substitute the elements in the matrix in such a way that v' would be a rotation of the v. Let's look at the first component in the resulting vector and try to get x' right.

$$x' = \cos a \cdot x - \sin a \cdot y$$
$$V_x' = a_{11} \cdot x + a_{12} \cdot y + a_{13} \cdot z$$

Let's make the following substitutions for the first row in the matrix and see what happens:

$$\begin{aligned} a_{11} &= \cos a \\ a_{12} &= -\sin a \\ a_{13} &= 0 \end{aligned} \quad => \quad v' = M \cdot v = \begin{pmatrix} \cos a & -\sin a & 0 \\ a_{21} & a_{22} & a_{23} \\ a_{31} & a_{32} & a_{33} \end{pmatrix} \cdot \begin{pmatrix} x \\ y \\ z \end{pmatrix} = \begin{pmatrix} \cos a \cdot x - \sin a \cdot y + 0 \cdot z \\ a_{21} \cdot x + a_{22} \cdot y + a_{23} \cdot z \\ a_{31} \cdot x + a_{32} \cdot y + a_{33} \cdot z \end{pmatrix}$$

The x component in v' is exactly the same as x' in the mathematical expression. This means that the first row in the matrix is correct. Let's look at the second.

$$y' = \sin a \cdot x + \cos a \cdot y$$
$$V_y' = a_{21} \cdot x + a_{22} \cdot y + a_{23} \cdot z$$

Let's make the following substitutions for the second row in the matrix and see what happens:

$$a_{21} = \sin a$$
$$a_{22} = \cos a \quad => \quad v' = M \cdot v = \begin{pmatrix} \cos a & -\sin a & 0 \\ \sin a & \cos a & a_{23} \\ a_{31} & a_{32} & a_{33} \end{pmatrix} \cdot \begin{pmatrix} x \\ y \\ z \end{pmatrix} = \begin{pmatrix} \cos a \cdot x - \sin a \cdot y + 0 \cdot z \\ \sin a \cdot x + \cos a \cdot y + 0 \cdot z \\ a_{31} \cdot x + a_{32} \cdot y + a_{33} \cdot z \end{pmatrix}$$
$$a_{23} = 0$$

Making the similar substitutions to the remaining row, we find out that the 3x3 matrix for rotating a point about the z-axis is

$$R_z = \begin{pmatrix} \cos a & -\sin a & 0 \\ \sin a & \cos a & 0 \\ 0 & 0 & 1 \end{pmatrix}$$

Using Matrixes to Rotate Vectors

How can this matrix be used? First of all, any vector multiplied with this matrix will be rotated by *a* degrees about the z-axis. The black box example illustrates this in an intuitive way in Figure E-22.

The other rotations can be deduced in the exact same way by identifying the elements in the matrix with the informal expressions.

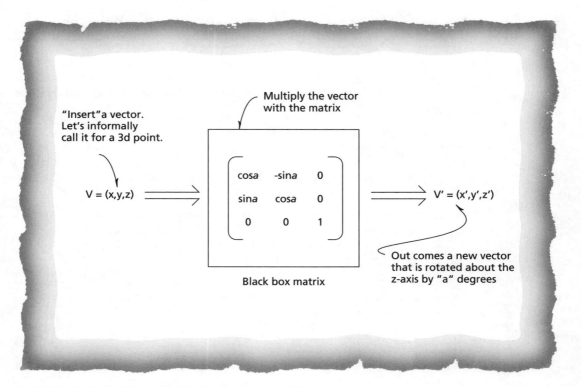

FIGURE E-22 ◉ *Using the black box to rotate 3D points*

Scaling

Another important transform that can be expressed in a 3x3 matrix is scaling. Scaling (see Figure E-23) is the same as multiplying the components of a vector by a factor. Expressed in the form of a matrix multiplication with a vector, it would be

$$v' = M \cdot v = \begin{pmatrix} S_x & 0 & 0 \\ 0 & S_y & 0 \\ 0 & 0 & S_z \end{pmatrix} \cdot \begin{pmatrix} x \\ y \\ z \end{pmatrix} = \begin{pmatrix} S_x \cdot x \\ S_y \cdot y \\ S_z \cdot z \end{pmatrix}$$

FIGURE E-23

◎ ◎ ◎ ◎ ◎ ◎

Scaling four points

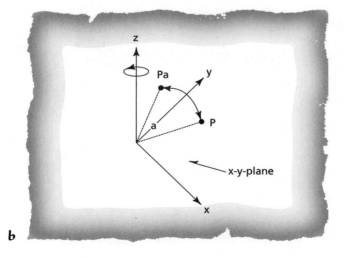

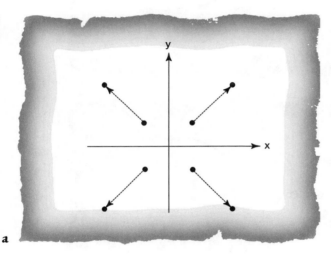

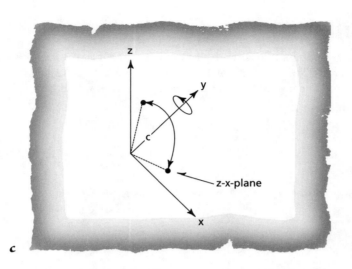

c

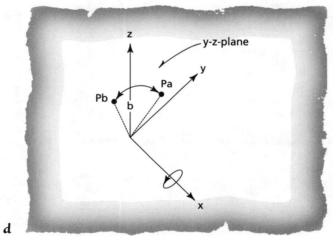

d

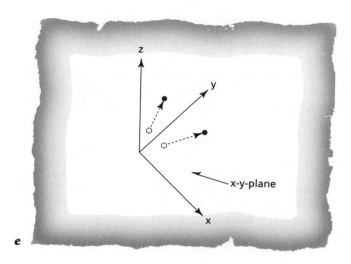

Before we move on, we should acquaint ourselves with the four rotation matrixes given in Table E-1.

Matrix

$$R_z(a) = \begin{pmatrix} \cos a & -\sin a & 0 \\ \sin a & \cos a & 0 \\ 0 & 0 & 1 \end{pmatrix}$$

$$R_y(a) = \begin{pmatrix} \cos a & 0 & \sin a \\ 0 & 1 & 0 \\ -\sin a & 0 & \cos a \end{pmatrix}$$

$$R_x(a) = \begin{pmatrix} 1 & 0 & 0 \\ 0 & \cos a & -\sin a \\ 0 & \sin a & \cos a \end{pmatrix}$$

$$S(x,y,z) = \begin{pmatrix} S_x & 0 & 0 \\ 0 & S_y & 0 \\ 0 & 0 & S_< \end{pmatrix}$$

TABLE E-1 ◈ *Rotation matrixes*

Packing Several Rotations into a Single Matrix

As you have seen in the previous section, rotations can be expressed in a formal way by using matrixes and vectors. The real power of a matrix is that it can contain several transforms. Until now we have only looked at matrixes containing a single rotation. To understand how we could make several rotations by simply multiplying a matrix with a vector, we need to do a little math.

Let's say that we have a vector v that we would like to rotate about the z-, y-, and x-axes, in that order. Doing one transformation at a time with the matrixes in previous section, we could express this operation mathematically in the following way:

$$v_z = R_z \cdot v$$
$$v_y = R_y \cdot v_z \qquad => \qquad v' = R_x \cdot R_y \cdot R_z \cdot v$$
$$v' = R_x \cdot v_y$$

What does this tell us? First of all, the matrixes Rx, Ry, and Rz can be multiplied into a single matrix that we can call R. The expression is now simplified to a multiplication between a matrix and a vector.

$$v' = R \cdot v$$

In Figure E-24, you can look at the black box example again and view this operation in an informal way.

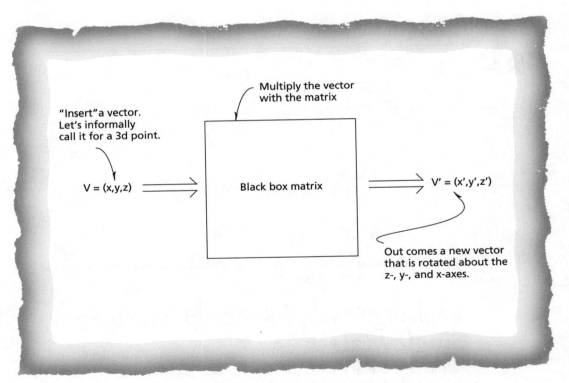

FIGURE E-24 ◉ *Using the black box to rotate a 3D point about all axes*

What about the three-matrix multiplication? As we saw earlier, that kind of an adventure would take a massive amount of calculations. Using symbolic math, the matrix containing all three rotations can be precalculated and then built in one shot without doing any matrix operations. The result will be the same, though. Without going into the details, here is the matrix that will rotate a vector about all three axes. The previously calculated matrix does the following transforms:

$$R_{zyx}(\gamma,\o,\theta) = R_z(\theta) \cdot R_y(\o) \cdot R_z(\gamma)$$

$$R_{zyx}(\gamma,\o,\theta) = \begin{pmatrix} \cos\o \cdot \cos\gamma & -\cos\o \cdot \sin\gamma & \sin\o \\ \sin\o \cdot \sin\theta \cdot \cos\gamma + \cos\theta \cdot \sin\gamma & -\sin\theta \cdot \sin\o \cdot \sin\gamma + \cos\theta \cdot \cos\gamma & -\sin\theta \cdot \cos\o \\ -\cos\theta \cdot \sin\o \cdot \cos\gamma + \sin\theta \cdot \sin\gamma & \cos\theta \cdot \sin\o \cdot \sin\gamma + \sin\theta \cdot \cos\gamma & \cos\theta \cdot \cos\o \end{pmatrix}$$

▦ WARNING!

Since matrix multiplication is not commutative the order in which the rotations are made is important. A matrix that is composed of $R_x \cdot R_y \cdot R_z$ will not perform the same rotation as a matrix that is composed from $R_z \cdot R_y \cdot R_x$.

Moving to 4x4 Matrixes

The 3x3 matrixes that we have used so far can obviously rotate 3D vectors, but there is a major transform that has been overlooked up until now. That is translation, which simply means displacement. Figure E-25 demonstrates this.

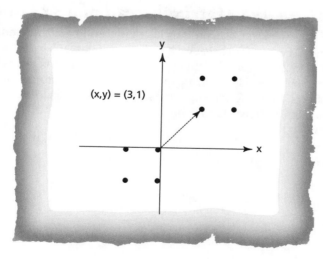

This transform cannot be expressed in a 3x3 matrix and would have to be implemented as a special "feature," which would not be consistent with the math that we have looked at this far. What we would like at this point is to be able to express all transforms using matrixes, whether we are doing rotation or translation. Expanding the 3x3 matrixes to 4x4 offers some new possibilities. What we are doing is actually moving to the fourth dimension, but all calculations will be done in a single plane. Each plane in the 4D space is a 3D space. Think of a plane in 4D space as a 3D space where time stands still. Since all calculations are done in a single plane, we would still be in the third dimension. That was just some mathematical mumbo jumbo and is of no practical use to us at this point. What is important, though, is how this can be done practically and what the implications are.

The implications are far less then one might expect, and the impact from moving to a 4x4 matrix is close to none. Let's begin by looking at how translation can be expressed in a 4x4 matrix.

$$v' = T \cdot v = \begin{pmatrix} 1 & 0 & 0 & T_x \\ 0 & 1 & 0 & T_y \\ 0 & 0 & 1 & T_z \\ 0 & 0 & 0 & 1 \end{pmatrix} \cdot \begin{pmatrix} x \\ y \\ z \\ 1 \end{pmatrix} = \begin{pmatrix} 1 \cdot x + 0 \cdot y + 0 \cdot z + 1 \cdot T_x \\ 0 \cdot x + 1 \cdot y + 0 \cdot z + 1 \cdot T_y \\ 0 \cdot x + 0 \cdot y + 1 \cdot z + 1 \cdot T_z \\ 0 \cdot x + 0 \cdot y + 0 \cdot z + 1 \cdot 1 \end{pmatrix} = \begin{pmatrix} x + T_x \\ y + T_y \\ z + T_z \\ 1 \end{pmatrix}$$

What are the changes from the 3x3 matrix? First of all, the vector has one more element, which should always be 1. This has no implication, since in the implementation we will informally call a vector for a 3D point, ignoring the fact that there should be a 1 as the last element. Second, a row has been added to the matrix that should always be (0 0 0 1). Third, there is another column. It is the new column that offers the possibility to store more information in the matrix. Remember the black box? You could say that we are now using a smarter black box.

Why Use a 4x4 Matrix Instead of a 3x3 Matrix?

Having a consistent way of expressing all transforms in a single matrix is in itself reason enough. The transforms that we have looked at this far have all been fairly simple. The most complicated one was probably the composed matrix that did three rotations in one shot, but in real life (and as you will see later on) a matrix can contain quite a few transforms, including translation and scaling. Table E-2 prepares us for the next step by showing basic 3D transform matrixes.

Function		Matrix
Rotation about z-axis	$R_z(\alpha) =$	$\begin{pmatrix} \cos\alpha & -\sin\alpha & 0 & 0 \\ \sin\alpha & \cos\alpha & 0 & 0 \\ 0 & 0 & 1 & 0 \\ 0 & 0 & 0 & 1 \end{pmatrix}$
Rotation about y-axis	$R_y(\beta) =$	$\begin{pmatrix} \cos\beta & 0 & \sin\beta & 0 \\ 0 & 1 & 0 & 0 \\ -\sin\beta & 0 & \cos\beta & 0 \\ 0 & 0 & 0 & 1 \end{pmatrix}$
Rotation about x-axis	$R_x(\gamma) =$	$\begin{pmatrix} 1 & 0 & 0 & 0 \\ 0 & \cos\gamma & -\sin\gamma & 0 \\ 0 & \sin\gamma & \cos\gamma & 0 \\ 0 & 0 & 0 & 1 \end{pmatrix}$
Translation	$T(x,y,z) =$	$\begin{pmatrix} 1 & 0 & 0 & T_x \\ 0 & 1 & 0 & T_y \\ 0 & 0 & 1 & T_z \\ 0 & 0 & 0 & 1 \end{pmatrix}$
Scaling	$S(x,y,z) =$	$\begin{pmatrix} S_x & 0 & 0 & 0 \\ 0 & S_y & 0 & 0 \\ 0 & 0 & S_z & 0 \\ 0 & 0 & 0 & 1 \end{pmatrix}$

TABLE E-2 ◈ *The basic 3D transform matrixes*

Using 4x4 Matrixes

In order to show that a 4x4 matrix is not harder to work with than a 3x3 matrix, Figure E-26 shows an example of a set of transforms expressed in one matrix.

As you can see, this transformation contains translation, scaling, and rotation. The order in which these transformations are made is important, though. Figure E-27 shows the procedure step by step. (All matrixes are referred to by their name in Table E-2.) The mathematical expression for this transform would be

$$v' = T(4,4,0) \cdot R_z(\tfrac{\pi}{2}) \cdot S(2,2,2) \cdot v$$

Don't be fooled by the order in which the matrixes are written. It is not the leftmost matrix that is the first transform, but the one closest to the vector.

FIGURE E-26
◉ ◉ ◉ ◉ ◉ ◉
*Source and
destination*

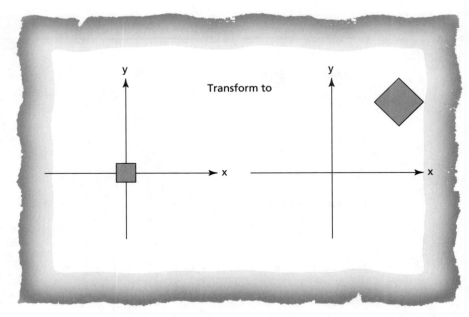

FIGURE E-27 ◉ *A set of transformations*

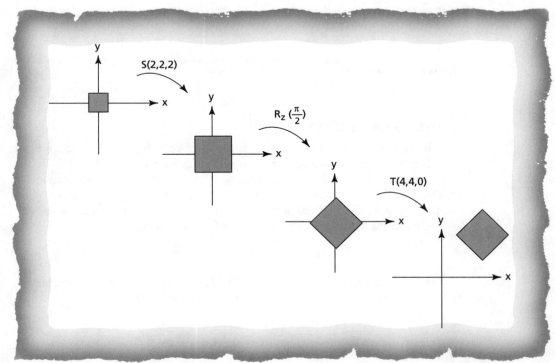

Creating a Matrix Class

Now that we have put some of the math behind us, we can start looking at how all this can be implemented. Using a matrix class seems appropriate. The goal is to hide the calculations from the user and make it work like a black box. All matrix compositions should be made transparent. For starters we could use the class in Listing E-4, which contains the bare essentials. The complete fMatrix3d class can be found on the CD-ROM.

Listing E-4 *A simple matrix class*

```
/**
 * A generic 3d matrix class that implements the rotation
 * about the principal axis, translation and scaling.
 */
class fGeneric3dMatrix extends Object {
    double xx, xy, xz, xo;
    double yx, yy, yz, yo;
    double zx, zy, zz, zo;

    /**
     * Constructs the identity matrix.
     */
    public fGeneric3dMatrix(){
        makeIdentity();
    }
    /**
     * Resets the matrix.
     */
    public void makeIdentity(){
        xx = 1; xy = 0; xz = 0; xo = 0;
        yx = 0; yy = 1; yz = 0; yo = 0;
        zx = 0; zy = 0; zz = 1; zo = 0;
    }
    /**
     * "Smart" multiplies a rotation about Z-axis
     */
    public void concatRz(double az){
        double ct = Math.cos(az);
        double st = Math.sin(az);

        double Nyx = (yx * ct + xx * st);
        double Nyy = (yy * ct + xy * st);
        double Nyz = (yz * ct + xz * st);
        double Nyo = (yo * ct + xo * st);

        double Nxx = (xx * ct - yx * st);
        double Nxy = (xy * ct - yy * st);
        double Nxz = (xz * ct - yz * st);
        double Nxo = (xo * ct - yo * st);
```

continued on next page

continued from previous page

```
      xx = Nxx; xy = Nxy; xz = Nxz; xo = Nxo;
      yx = Nyx; yy = Nyy; yz = Nyz; yo = Nyo;
   }
   /**
    * "Smart" multiplies a rotation about Y-axis
    */
   public void concatRy(double ay){
      double ct = Math.cos(ay);
      double st = Math.sin(ay);

      double Nxx = (xx * ct + zx * st);
      double Nxy = (xy * ct + zy * st);
      double Nxz = (xz * ct + zz * st);
      double Nxo = (xo * ct + zo * st);

      double Nzx = (zx * ct - xx * st);
      double Nzy = (zy * ct - xy * st);
      double Nzz = (zz * ct - xz * st);
      double Nzo = (zo * ct - xo * st);

      xx = Nxx; xy = Nxy; xz = Nxz; xo = Nxo;
      zx = Nzx; zy = Nzy; zz = Nzz; zo = Nzo;
   }
   /**
    * "Smart" multiplies a rotation about X-axis
    */
   public void concatRx(double ax){
      double ct = Math.cos(ax);
      double st = Math.sin(ax);

      double Nyx = (yx * ct + zx * st);
      double Nyy = (yy * ct + zy * st);
      double Nyz = (yz * ct + zz * st);
      double Nyo = (yo * ct + zo * st);

      double Nzx = (zx * ct - yx * st);
      double Nzy = (zy * ct - yy * st);
      double Nzz = (zz * ct - yz * st);
      double Nzo = (zo * ct - yo * st);

      yx = Nyx; yy = Nyy; yz = Nyz; yo = Nyo;
      zx = Nzx; zy = Nzy; zz = Nzz; zo = Nzo;
   }
   /**
    * "Smart" multiplies a translation
    */
   public void concatT(double x,double y,double z){
            xo+=x; yo+=y; zo+=z;
   }
   /**
    * "Smart" multiplies scaling
    */
```

```
    public void concatS(double sx,double sy,double sz){
       xx *= sx; xy *= sx; xz *= sx; xo *= sx;
       yx *= sy; yy *= sy; yz *= sy; yo *= sy;
       zx *= sz; zy *= sz; zz *= sz; zo *= sz;
    }
    /**
     * Multiplies the vector "ps" of 3d points and stores the result
     * in "pd".
     */
    public void transform(fArrayOf3dPoints ps,fArrayOf3dPoints pd){
      for (int i=0; i<ps.npoints; i++) {
        double x=ps.x[i]; double y=ps.y[i]; double z=ps.z[i];
        pd.x[i] = x*xx + y*xy + z*xz + xo;
        pd.y[i] = x*yx + y*yy + z*yz + yo;
        pd.z[i] = x*zx + y*zy + z*zz + zo;
      }
    }
}
```

Using the matrix class from Listing E-4, the code for making the transformations seen in Figure E-27 would be

```
fGeneric3dMatrix M;
M.makeIdentity();          //-- make identity matrix
M.concatS(2,2,2);          //-- scale the points
M.concatRz(Math.PI/2);     //-- rotate about z-axis
M.concatT(4,4,0);          //-- translate by 4,4,0 units
M.transformPoints(xf,yf,zf,xt,yt,zt,pts); //-- transform the points
```

In the matrix class, all methods starting with "concat" are actually selective matrix multiplications. What this means is that only the elements that are affected are recalculated, saving lots of time.

```
/**
 * A 3d matrix that hides the making of the different
 * transforms
 */
class fMatrix3d extends fGeneric3dMatrix {
   /**
    * construct the matrix
    */
   public fMatrix3d(){
      super();
   }
   /**
    * let matrix contain the MCS to WCS transform
    */
   public void makeMCStoWCStransform(fPoint3d pos,fAngle3d agl,fPoint3d
scale){
      makeIdentity();
      concatS(scale.x,scale.y,scale.z);
      concatRx(agl.x);
      concatRy(agl.y);
```

```
        concatRz(agl.z);
        concatT(pos.x,pos.y,pos.z);
    }
    /**
     * let matrix contain the WCS to MCS transform
     */
    public void makeWCStoVCStransform(fPoint3d pos,fAngle3d agl){
        makeIdentity();
        concatT(-pos.x,-pos.y,-pos.z);
        concatRz(-agl.z);
        concatRy(-agl.y);
        concatRx(-agl.x);
    }
    /**
 * A transform used in camera classes.
 */
    public void makeLookAtPointTransform(fPoint3d p0,fPoint3d p1){
        fPoint3d vecZaxis=new fPoint3d(p1,p0);
        vecZaxis.normalize(1);
        fPoint3d vecXaxis=new fPoint3d();
        vecXaxis.vectorProduct(new fPoint3d(0,1,0), vecZaxis);
        vecXaxis.normalize(1);

        fPoint3d vecYaxis=new fPoint3d();
        vecYaxis.vectorProduct(vecZaxis,vecXaxis);

        xx=vecXaxis.x; xy=vecXaxis.y; xz=vecXaxis.z;
        yx=vecYaxis.x; yy=vecYaxis.y; yz=vecYaxis.z;
        zx=vecZaxis.x; zy=vecZaxis.y; zz=vecZaxis.z;
        xo = yo = zo = 0;
        xo = xx*(-p0.x) + xy*(-p0.y) + xz*(-p0.z) + xo;
        yo = yx*(-p0.x) + yy*(-p0.y) + yz*(-p0.z) + yo;
        zo = zx*(-p0.x) + zy*(-p0.y) + zz*(-p0.z) + zo;

    }

}
```

Summary

Armed with the math and the classes supplied in this chapter you have all the basic tools to make 3D transforms. In Chapter 11 you learned how to use these classes to create some real 3D graphics. If you wonder where the classes fPoint3d and fAngle3d came from, don't worry. You can find them on the CD just like all other classes. The fPoint3d and fAngle3d classes contain all the basic and not so basic operations that can be performed with vectors. The most important operations are described in this appendix and the implementation is very straightforward.

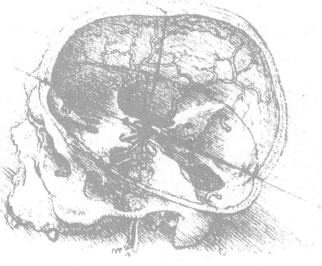

Index

h

I

M

O

P

Books have a substantial influence on the destruction of the forests of the Earth. For example, it takes 17 trees to produce one ton of paper. A first printing of 30,000 copies of a typical 480-page book consumes 108,000 pounds of paper, which will require 918 trees!

Waite Group Press™ is against the clear-cutting of forests and supports reforestation of the Pacific Northwest of the United States and Canada, where most of this paper comes from. As a publisher with several hundred thousand books sold each year, we feel an obligation to give back to the planet. We will therefore support organizations that seek to preserve the forests of planet Earth.

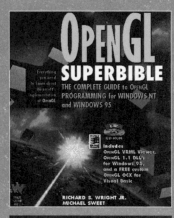

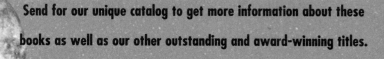

This is a legal agreement between you, the end user and purchaser, and The Waite Group®, Inc., and the authors of the programs contained in the disk. By opening the sealed disk package, you are agreeing to be bound by the terms of this Agreement. If you do not agree with the terms of this Agreement, promptly return the unopened disk package and the accompanying items (including the related book and other written material) to the place you obtained them for a refund.

SOFTWARE LICENSE

1. The Waite Group, Inc. grants you the right to use one copy of the enclosed software programs (the programs) on a single computer system (whether a single CPU, part of a licensed network, or a terminal connected to a single CPU). Each concurrent user of the program must have exclusive use of the related Waite Group, Inc. written materials.

2. The program, including the copyrights in each program, is owned by the respective author and the copyright in the entire work is owned by The Waite Group, Inc. and they are therefore protected under the copyright laws of the United States and other nations, under international treaties. You may make only one copy of the disk containing the programs exclusively for backup or archival purposes, or you may transfer the programs to one hard disk drive, using the original for backup or archival purposes. You may make no other copies of the programs, and you may make no copies of all or any part of the related Waite Group, Inc. written materials.

3. You may not rent or lease the programs, but you may transfer ownership of the programs and related written materials (including any and all updates and earlier versions) if you keep no copies of either, and if you make sure the transferee agrees to the terms of this license.

4. You may not decompile, reverse engineer, disassemble, copy, create a derivative work, or otherwise use the programs except as stated in this Agreement.

GOVERNING LAW

This Agreement is governed by the laws of the State of California.

LIMITED WARRANTY

The following warranties shall be effective for 90 days from the date of purchase: (i) The Waite Group, Inc. warrants the enclosed disk to be free of defects in materials and workmanship under normal use; and (ii) The Waite Group, Inc. warrants that the programs, unless modified by the purchaser, will substantially perform the functions described in the documentation provided by The Waite Group, Inc. when operated on the designated hardware and operating system. The Waite Group, Inc. does not warrant that the programs will meet purchaser's requirements or that operation of a program will be uninterrupted or error-free. The program warranty does not cover any program that has been altered or changed in any way by anyone other than The Waite Group, Inc. The Waite Group, Inc. is not responsible for problems caused by changes in the operating characteristics of computer hardware or computer operating systems that are made after the release of the programs, nor for problems in the interaction of the programs with each other or other software.

THESE WARRANTIES ARE EXCLUSIVE AND IN LIEU OF ALL OTHER WARRANTIES OF MERCHANTABILITY OR FITNESS FOR A PARTICULAR PURPOSE OR OF ANY OTHER WARRANTY, WHETHER EXPRESS OR IMPLIED.

EXCLUSIVE REMEDY

The Waite Group, Inc. will replace any defective disk without charge if the defective disk is returned to The Waite Group, Inc. within 90 days from date of purchase.

This is Purchaser's sole and exclusive remedy for any breach of warranty or claim for contract, tort, or damages.

LIMITATION OF LIABILITY

THE WAITE GROUP, INC. AND THE AUTHORS OF THE PROGRAMS SHALL NOT IN ANY CASE BE LIABLE FOR SPECIAL, INCIDENTAL, CONSEQUENTIAL, INDIRECT, OR OTHER SIMILAR DAMAGES ARISING FROM ANY BREACH OF THESE WARRANTIES EVEN IF THE WAITE GROUP, INC. OR ITS AGENT HAS BEEN ADVISED OF THE POSSIBILITY OF SUCH DAMAGES.

THE LIABILITY FOR DAMAGES OF THE WAITE GROUP, INC. AND THE AUTHORS OF THE PROGRAMS UNDER THIS AGREEMENT SHALL IN NO EVENT EXCEED THE PURCHASE PRICE PAID.

COMPLETE AGREEMENT

This Agreement constitutes the complete agreement between The Waite Group, Inc. and the authors of the programs, and you, the purchaser.

Some states do not allow the exclusion or limitation of implied warranties or liability for incidental or consequential damages, so the above exclusions or limitations may not apply to you. This limited warranty gives you specific legal rights; you may have others, which vary from state to state.

D I G I T A L
CONNECTION™

About Digital Connection™

Digital Connection is a premier developer of information technologies. It has been integral in the development of major U.S. commercial online services and the Internet for more than a decade. Digital Connection is a leader in graphical user interfaces, networking, object-oriented development, and database technologies, and is recognized as a pioneer in Java development.

Its accomplishments range from multimedia games and complex financial transaction systems to interactive videodisc kiosks and million-plus user online services.

The Digital Connection team possesses a unique combination of expertise in technology, usability, and business strategy that translates into well-integrated, high-impact solutions for its corporate clients.

Digital Connection is proud to have been technical consultant on *Java How-To* for Waite Group Press™.

We can be reached at:
http://www.pangaea.net/digital/
Digital Connection
372 Central Park West
New York, NY 10025
212.866.7000 (voice)
212.662.9560 (fax)
digital@pangaea.net

Partial Client List:

Avis, CBS Technology, Chemical Bank, Children's Television Workshop, Citicorp, Continental Grain, IBM Corporation, Meca Software, Merck, Montage Picture Processor, NY Philharmonic, Philips Electronics, Prodigy Services Company, Simon & Schuster, Tishman Spear, US West, WGBH:Nova

SATISFACTION REPORT CARD

Please fill out this card if you wish to know of future updates to
Black Art of Java Game Programming, **or to receive our catalog.**

First Name: _____ **Last Name:** _____

Street Address: _____

City: _____ **State:** _____ **Zip:** _____

E-mail Address _____

Daytime Telephone: (   ) _____

Date product was acquired: Month _____ **Day** _____ **Year** _____ **Your Occupation:** _____

Overall, how would you rate *Black Art of Java Game Programming*?

☐ Excellent ☐ Very Good ☐ Good
☐ Fair ☐ Below Average ☐ Poor

What did you like MOST about this book? _____

_____

_____

What did you like LEAST about this book? _____

_____

_____

Please describe any problems you may have encountered with installing or using the disk: _____

_____

How did you use this book (problem-solver, tutorial, reference...)?

_____

What is your level of computer expertise?

☐ New ☐ Dabbler ☐ Hacker
☐ Power User ☐ Programmer ☐ Experienced Professional

What computer languages are you familiar with? _____

_____

Please describe your computer hardware:

Computer _____ Hard disk _____

5.25" disk drives _____ 3.5" disk drives _____

Video card _____ Monitor _____

Printer _____ Peripherals _____

Sound Board _____ CD ROM _____

Where did you buy this book?

☐ Bookstore (name): _____
☐ Discount store (name): _____
☐ Computer store (name): _____
☐ Catalog (name): _____
☐ Direct from WGP ☐ Other _____

What price did you pay for this book? _____

What influenced your purchase of this book?

☐ Recommendation ☐ Advertisement
☐ Magazine review ☐ Store display
☐ Mailing ☐ Book's format
☐ Reputation of Waite Group Press ☐ Other

How many computer books do you buy each year? _____

How many other Waite Group books do you own? _____

What is your favorite Waite Group book? _____

_____

Is there any program or subject you would like to see Waite Group Press cover in a similar approach? _____

_____

_____

Additional comments? _____

_____

_____

Please send to: **Waite Group Press**
200 Tamal Plaza
Corte Madera, CA 94925

☐ **Check here for a free Waite Group catalog**

STOP!

BEFORE YOU OPEN THE DISK OR CD-ROM PACKAGE ON THE FACING PAGE, CAREFULLY READ THE LICENSE AGREEMENT.

Opening this package indicates that you agree to abide by the license agreement found in the back of this book. If you do not agree with it, promptly return the unopened disk package (including the related book) to the place you obtained them for a refund.